PENGUIN BOOKS

THE SALON.COM READER'S GUIDE TO CONTEMPORARY AUTHORS

Laura Miller helped found Salon.com in San Francisco in 1995. Her criticism and book reviews have appeared in *The New York Times Book Review*, *The Washington Post Book World*, *The Village Voice*, the *San Francisco Examiner*, and *The New York Observer*. She is now New York Editorial Director for Salon.com and lives in Manhattan.

Adam Begley is the books editor of *The New York Observer*. He lives in Northamptonshire, England.

The
salon.com

Reader's Guide

to Contemporary

Authors

EDITED BY **Laura Miller**

WITH **Adam Begley**

PENGUIN BOOKS

PENGUIN BOOKS

Published by the Penguin Group
Penguin Putnam Inc., 375 Hudson Street,
New York, New York 10014, U.S.A.
Penguin Books Ltd, 27 Wrights Lane,
London W8 5TZ, England
Penguin Books Australia Ltd, Ringwood,
Victoria, Australia
Penguin Books Canada Ltd, 10 Alcorn Avenue,
Toronto, Ontario, Canada M4V 3B2
Penguin Books (N.Z.) Ltd, 182–190 Wairau Road,
Auckland 10, New Zealand

Penguin Books Ltd, Registered Offices:
Harmondsworth, Middlesex, England

First published in Penguin Books 2000

10   9   8   7   6   5   4   3   2   1

Illustrations by Zach Trenholm

Some of the selections in this book first appeared on Salon.com's Web site.

LIBRARY OF CONGRESS CATALOGING IN PUBLICATION DATA
The Salon.com reader's guide to contemporary authors / edited by Laura Miller, with
Adam Begley.
        p.   cm.
    Includes bibliographical references and index.
    ISBN 0 14 02.8088 X
    1. American fiction—20th century—Bio-bibliography.   2. English fiction—20th
century—Bio-bibliography.   3. Reading interests.   I. Title: Reader's guide to contemporary
authors.   II. Miller, Laura.   III. Begley, Adam.
PS379.S225   2000
813′.509 a B—dc21   99–089012

Printed in the United States of America
Set in Sabon
Designed by Mia Risberg

PREFACE

BY Laura Miller

The title *The Salon.com Reader's Guide to Contemporary Authors* is no mere matter of form, although to make our point perfectly clear perhaps the word "reader" ought to be italicized and underlined. From the beginning, Dwight Garner (who conceived of the project) and I (who edited it) intended this book for those remarkable and slightly mysterious individuals who read contemporary fiction for pleasure. We didn't imagine an audience of researchers or scholars or critics or prize committees or members of the publishing industry, even if some of those people still do occasionally read a book in the hope of enjoying it. It seemed to us that, although you can find a complete bibliography of an author's work and a survey of critical responses to that work in several excellent, comprehensive references, none of these resources really answer the question that matters most to someone holding a novel in his or her hands: Why should I read this?

And, if you suspect that you might like, say, Margaret Atwood's writing, a newspaper or magazine review of her latest novel isn't likely to tell you if the new book is one of her best, how it fits in with the rest of her fiction, or how it compares to books by other, similar writers. In fact, it's quite possible that the review will stick to a plot summary and the mildest expressions of opinion, that it will seem cautious and uninspired, and that by the time you finish it you won't have any clearer sense of whether Atwood is for you or not.

For, while most of us read fiction to be moved, captivated, delighted, and provoked, most of today's writing about reading doesn't reflect the intensity of our best (and worst) reading experiences. It's easy to find passionate writing about film and music by critics who know their field and care about it deeply. Mainstream literary criticism is anemic by

v

comparison, and academic literary criticism usually isn't about literature at all. We hope this book helps to change that. In a world packed with easier, flashier opportunities for diversion, many people still do make the choice to read because it satisfies a hunger that only a good book can sate. This volume is our attempt to speak to that craving.

The Salon.com Reader's Guide is for you if: you love a book and want to find out more about the author; you love all of an author's books and want to track down similar ones by other writers; you belong to a reading group and are looking for new books for the group to explore; you're wondering what critics think of an author you admire (or despise); your college roommate or brother-in-law insists that you'd love so-and-so's novels but you'd like to know a bit more before you take the plunge; you work in a bookstore or library and want to learn more about contemporary fiction in order to better serve your customers or patrons; you walk into a bookstore or a library and have no idea where to start; you've been choosing the new books you read by their covers or reviews in the local newspaper and are thinking there's got to be a better way; you usually read only nineteenth-century classics and you'd like to expand your horizons—or if you've got a free evening, a weekend, a long flight, or a vacation ahead of you, and you're just looking for a book that won't waste five or six irreplaceable hours of your life.

Above and beyond our hope that this book will lead you to other books, we've also designed it to be a good read in and of itself. We selected contributors whose criticism for our Web site, Salon.com, and for other publications struck us as exceptionally engaged, lively, perceptive, and smart. They made us think, laugh, and question our preconceptions. They made us want to argue with them all night, and they made us want to head for the local bookstore with a shopping list. We don't expect you'll always agree with them because we certainly don't. Like every review you read in a newspaper or magazine, the entries in this guide are opinions, and opinions come in many varieties—all varieties, in fact, except "right" and "wrong." Other publications and critics opt for a lofty, detached, authoritative approach to literature, an approach that makes literary fiction seem like a dead and dusty monument. Whether a novel or short story is good, great, or mediocre, whether an author is writing for the ages or for the dustbin of history, whether a literary trend represents a daring advance or a dismaying sidetrack—all of these questions are and should be up for debate because debate, like enthusiasm, keeps the literary world interesting and alive.

Who's In and Who's Not

Neither time nor money were available to us in infinite quantities, so we had to set some parameters for the list of writers to be included in this book. We decided to limit it to authors who write or wrote fiction in English, whose major works were published since 1960, and who had published more than one book. We wanted to focus on writers whose literary reputations did not yet seem firmly set, either because they were still alive and working or because they hadn't been studied extensively. Norman Mailer's literary legacy, for example, still struck us as up for grabs, while we felt we'd already read everything we needed (or wanted) to read about the individual Beats. Authors who are better known for their nonfiction writings we decided to save for a second volume.

Most of the authors covered in this book write literary fiction, but we've included a few writers of bestselling commercial fiction as well. Some, like Jacqueline Susann, are here because they significantly shaped the way publishers and authors relate to the reading public. Others, like John Grisham, are included because we'd never read their books and wanted to know what the fuss was about, but most, like Stephen King, were chosen because we've read their books and enjoyed them and thought it was high time to stop pretending otherwise. We've also included a few authors who wrote and published their major works before the 1960s, but whose popular impact (massive in the case of J.R.R. Tolkien) wasn't felt until later.

You'll find entries in this book for authors you've never heard of and, conversely, no entries for authors you might consider more significant. Since we knew from the start that this guide couldn't be comprehensive, we decided to let our contributors' enthusiasm and curiosity be our guides. We requested their feedback on our initial list of about five hundred authors. If a critic we trusted made a convincing case on behalf of a seemingly obscure novelist, we added that author to our final list. With a few exceptions (see Alice Walker), if no one voiced any interest in an author's work, that name was cut. We reasoned that if we let received opinions regarding literary importance direct too many of our choices, we'd wind up with a guide as dutiful and lifeless as the stuff we were trying to counteract.

As a result, the book you're holding in your hands could be called willful and irresponsible. Some sacred cows take a hit or two. Allegedly minor voices are exalted. Designated titans are treated with insufficient reverence. The favorite writer of somebody somewhere has been omitted; somebody else's bête noire gets too much credit. The list is probably insufficiently balanced in some way. These sorts of offenses are inevitable when you're compiling a book based on personal preferences (and we warmly encourage anyone who's convinced it should have been done differently to put together their own book).

Once we'd divvied up the entries, we encouraged our contributors to think of you, the reader, as an intelligent, interested friend or relative who'd just asked, "So tell me about John Updike. What are his books like?" With some authors, a bit of biographical background was called for, while others seemed to cry out to be defended from charges ranging from arrogance to impenetrability to frivolity, and still others needed to be rescued from oblivion. We asked each contributor to recommend a handful of the author's books (these titles are set in boldface in the entry's bibliography) and to single out the book to select if you only read one of those (you'll find an * by that title in each bibliography). Finally, we requested that each entry suggest other writers you might want to seek out if you like the work of the author in question. You'll find those recommendations in the "See Also" section at the end of each entry.

You'll also find, scattered throughout the *Salon.com Reader's Guide*, lists of recommended books gathered from well-known authors and brief essays on assorted literary topics. The lists (appearing under the rubric "Book Bag") are a popular weekly feature on our Web site, *Salon.com Books* (www.salon.com/books/). The essays take on intriguing issues that don't fit within the format of an author entry.

Most of the contributors to this book spent many hours reading and writing in exchange for monetary compensation that was, we must confess, pretty close to negligible. We think the thoughtfulness, commitment and passion for reading they brought to the task shines in these pages, and it's our fondest wish that this book will inspire similar feelings in you, too.

A note on bibliographies: Each author entry features a bibliography that includes a complete listing of the author's prose fiction published in book form and, in many cases, listings of selected books of nonfiction and poetry as well. Plays, screenplays, and other dramatic works intended for performance are not listed. The publication date indicated for each title is the date of its earliest publication, although many British, Australian, and African titles were not published in the United States until later. Readers seeking a more comprehensive bibliography of an author's work will want to check The Gale Group's Contemporary Authors, *a multivolume reference available in most research libraries. Many of the books listed in this guide are, alas, currently out of print; however, the boom in online bookselling makes these books easier to find than ever.*

ACKNOWLEDGMENTS

Many people played important roles in the creation of this book. First among them are Dwight Garner, who came up with the idea and who participated in the early editing, and David Talbot, the founder of Salon.com, whose infectious enthusiasm and support for new ideas and good writing have made so many wonderful things happen (many of them seemingly impossible). The staff of Salon.com generously committed their time and energy to this project in countless ways when both were in great demand elsewhere. Craig Seligman, Brian Blanchfield, and Paul Lesniak provided invaluable help with a thousand essential matters. Laurie Walsh, Kathryn Court, and the rest of Penguin Books were marvels of encouragement and patience, and Ellen Levine was always a sagacious advocate. Zach Trenholm's extraordinary caricatures were part of our plan for this book from the very beginning, and it is a great pleasure to see that dream realized.

Others who went out of their way to offer advice and moral support include the best of best friends, Andrew O'Hehir, David Gates, Michael Pietsch, Sarah Vowell, Carter Scholz, and, especially, the formidably well-read and thoughtful Jonathan Lethem.

Finally, the contributors to *The Salon.com Reader's Guide to Contemporary Authors* never failed to delight and impress me with their intelligence, cheerfulness, and diligence in researching and writing their entries. Although they were motivated by their love of books and reading rather than by any desire for my thanks, they have my abundant gratitude.

C O N T E N T S

INTRODUCTION

BY **Laura Miller**

It's one thing to say the literary landscape has been radically transformed in the past four decades, and something else again to revisit the territory of 1963 by leafing through *Esquire* magazine's special literary issue published in July of that year. The society it depicts seems startlingly remote. There's a charming naivete to the magazine's confidence in its ability to suss out the scene, from the seven full pages it gives Norman Mailer to evaluate nine books from his chief competitors (yes, they're all men) to the photo essays about the swingin' lives of a beatnik poet and a young Hollywood screenwriter, to the cover story about Allen Ginsberg's jaunt to India, a piece which manages to deftly skirt the small matter of the poet's homosexuality. But most endearing of all is a "chart of power" assembled by L. Rust Hills and stoutly entitled "The Structure of the American Literary Establishment," complete with biomorphic shapes indicating "The Red-Hot Center," "Squaresville" (*The New York Times*, naturally), and "The Cool World." Twenty-four years later, Hills rather sheepishly reprised his guide to "the literary universe" for *Esquire*, noting that, in the years between 1963 and 1987, "everything began to come apart and change more or less entirely."

That sense of protean fragmentation prevails today. The world of established literary giants, each one solemnly tapping out his version of the Great American Novel on a manual typewriter, has since dissolved into a fluid, unpredictable marketplace where the next critically-acclaimed, hit-first novel might be written by a fifty-seven-year-old horse-breeder from North Carolina or by a thirty-six-year-old former aerobics instructor from India. The teapot of the literary world has weathered several tempests—controversies over trends, styles, and personalities—in the past forty years, but the sense of a monolithic shared culture seems to be gone for good.

Before I go into how and why that happened, it's important to note that if people in the book business often have shapely wrists, it's because they've elevated hand-wringing to the level of an Olympic sport. Decrying the precipitous decay of literary culture has been a popular activity for as long as writers have lamented their fates, in other words, for as long as there have been writers. In his 1891 novel, *New Grub Street*, George Gissing complained that "more likely than not," a really good book "will be swamped in the flood of literature that pours forth week after week and won't have attention fixed long enough upon it to establish its repute . . . The simple, sober truth has no chance whatever of being listened to, and it's only by volume of shouting that the ear of the public is held." Protesting the decline of bookselling is a venerable tradition as well, as an 1887 letter to *Publishers Weekly*, written by the publisher Henry Holt, attests. Long before the advent of television—in fact, even before radio or movies—Holt grieved the passing of the days when "many a substantial citizen" would "drop into the book-store of an evening . . . Now most of those book-stores no longer exist, at least as book-stores. They are toy-shops and ice-cream salons with files of Seaside Libraries in one corner." Those insidious "files of Seaside Libraries" were contributing to "a real diminution . . . in the reading habit" long before the Internet threatened to destroy civilization as we know it.

Nevertheless, things have decidedly changed. The literary establishment *Esquire* mapped in 1963 stood on the verge of the counterculture-led upheavals of the late '60s, the anti-novel metafictional experiments of the '70s, the identity politics-inspired attacks on the canonization of "dead white men" in the '80s, and a whole cavalcade of much-reviled crazes and trends, not to mention the ascension of such formerly lowbrow media as TV and popular music to the role of defining the spirit of the times. The writers surveyed in this book published their fiction against this tumultuous backdrop.

At the beginning of the 1960s, most American novelists took the greats of previous generations—particularly Ernest Hemingway and F. Scott Fitzgerald—as their models. Writers pursuing more idiosyncratic paths in the manner of William Faulkner, writers like Vladimir Nabokov and Flannery O'Connor, were active and even celebrated, but at the center stood the ideal of a big, bestselling, realist novel of social reportage, a form whose obsolescence the young novelist Jonathan Franzen bemoaned in an essay he wrote for *Harper's* magazine in 1996. Franzen maintains that the last "challenging" novel to find a mass audience and to "infiltrate" the national imagination was Joseph Heller's *Catch-22*, published in 1961. *Catch-22* is a satirical war novel about the yawning gap between officially sanctioned reality and the experiences of its characters, and its success indicated that American culture had begun to entertain doubts about all authoritative pronouncements, including, perhaps, the Great American Novel.

As the decade closed, authors like Kurt Vonnegut, Jr., Richard Brautigan, and Ken

Kesey were sharing young readers' shelf space with such icons as J.R.R. Tolkien, Robert Heinlein, and Carlos Castaneda, whose writings were more likely to blow the mind than define the age. Books by literary lions like John Updike, Saul Bellow, and William Styron still made it to the number one spot on *The New York Times* bestseller list, but women and blacks were already protesting the way they had been portrayed by such writers. The audience for literary fiction had begun to splinter, and the very notion that one novelist could speak for an entire nation or generation seemed worse than improbable; it was outright and inexcusable hubris. By the 1980s, the bestseller lists belonged to authors of fat volumes of commercial fiction, books whose visceral, rather than social or psychological, concerns could be counted on to appeal to the largest number of readers: thrillers, sagas, horror stories, and the women's genre sometimes known as "shopping and fucking" novels.

In the 1970s, members of various groups who had once compliantly read the designated Big Book of the moment by authors like Mailer and his designated "Talent in the Room," increasingly demanded fiction by and about people like themselves. Women, in particular, defected, leading to a boomlet in novels of middle-class female discontent, a trend that helped launch the career of Margaret Atwood, among many other women writers. Because women continue to buy and read more fiction than men, this development profoundly changed not only the publishing market but the way authors see their place in the world. Franzen wrote, "Writers like Jane Smiley and Amy Tan today seem conscious and confident of an attentive audience. Whereas all the male novelists I know, including myself, are clueless as to who could possibly be buying our books."

This interest in fresh perspectives also fostered a literary blossoming among racial and sexual minorities. Although multicultural idealism would eventually become problematic, it provided early support for major talents—Toni Morrison and John Edgar Wideman in the United States, Salman Rushdie and Ben Okri in England—who otherwise might never have been read, or perhaps even published. At its best, multiculturalism expanded the horizons of the literary audience and immeasurably enriched the variety of fiction available in the average bookstore. Later, at its worst, it led to the glorification of second-rate writers, the establishment of a subtle climate of bad faith, and the exasperation of successful authors of color who chafed at multiculturalist demands that they properly represent their races.

In the meantime, during the 1970s, a coterie of white male novelists retreated to American universities to pursue a variety of experimental writing sometimes called metafiction (because it was often about the nature of fiction itself) or, more generally, postmodernism. Writers like John Barth, Robert Coover, Stanley Elkin, Donald Barthelme, and William Gass were still enshrined in the reading lists of college-level English classes in the late 1970s and early 1980s, but they increasingly fell by the wayside as fiction writers and editors outside the academy embraced realism. In a sometimes bafflingly abstract 1977 diatribe entitled *On Moral Fiction*, the novelist John Gardner attacked the postmodernists for what he considered a solipsistic obsession with form over the concerns of "true art," which "seeks to improve life, not debase it." (This salvo, notorious for its disdainful naming of names, further confused readers who had thought that Gardner was himself a postmodernist.) *On Moral Fiction*, like the feminist and multicultural critiques of its time, is a classic example of the American penchant for denouncing perceived schools of writing on grounds that fuse aesthetics and ideology—in other words, bad writing isn't just bad, it's evil. (British writers prefer simply to attack one another's character, a tactic that makes their quarrels much more entertaining.)

The 1980s gave critics much to complain about, beginning with a literary trend often called minimalism, but also, less sympathetically, "K-Mart realism." Was minimalism indeed the prevailing American literary form of the 1980s? It certainly seemed to be, what with *The New Yorker* and *Esquire*, two of the foremost American showcases for literary fiction, firmly in its thrall and so many emerging writers naming Raymond Carver as their model. Carver wrote spare, stoic prose about working-class people whose lives hover at the brink of despair. In his style, if not his subject matter, he was an heir to Hemingway, and after his death in 1988 he was held in particularly great reverence. The teacher and editor Gordon Lish (whose own experimental novels would suggest a greater affinity with the metafictionists) was a tireless advocate for minimalism and is known to have stripped Carver's early stories down to their very bones.

Carver wrote mostly short stories, a form that had come to seem marginal in the 1960s and 1970s as fewer and fewer magazines published fiction. The short story, however, proved to be ideally suited to the needs of the writing workshops and MFA programs in creative writing that were sprouting up in many universities during the 1980s. Critics who disliked minimalism often blamed the trend on these programs—particularly the creative writing program at the University of Iowa—and accused universities of graduating indistinguishable writers of "cookie cutter" fiction. It's true that the clean, declarative sentences that are a signal trait of minimalist fiction are the easiest kind of competent writing to teach, and that minimalism's restrained, quirk-free, almost documentary approach is the least likely to offend or irritate a classroom of ten fellow writers. However, it should be noted that university-level creative writing programs also trained such original voices as David Foster Wallace and Denis Johnson (not to mention Flannery O'Connor).

There did seem to be an overwhelming number of young minimalist writers coming up in the mid-1980s, and they did tend to sound an awful lot alike, a situation that, more than anything else, may have stoked the irritation of critics. That irritation, however, paled in comparison with the seething wrath inspired by the rise of the Brat Pack, a trio of mediagenic young writers who emerged at about the same time. The actual books written by Jay McInerney, Brett Easton Ellis, and Tama Janowitz don't have much in common, but the three became permanently linked in the minds of the public. They stood for an attempt to transplant the devices of celebrity culture into the literary world, and despite the handsome sales figures the Brat Pack enjoyed at first, in the end the operation was not a success.

The Brat Pack were young, they photographed well, and they seemed to lead exciting, glamorous lives. McInerney and Ellis hung out at nightclubs with pop stars and models, and Janowitz even made a video that was aired on MTV. The press treated them as the voices of a generation, and people who didn't read a lot of novels bought and read the Brat Pack's books. But the core audience for literary fiction has always regarded them with suspicion. Ten years later, it's remarkable how much outright animosity still greets mention of their names, considering that, since the 1980s, they've had lackluster careers and have exerted no noticeable influence on American fiction. For those idealists who cherish the literary world as the last refuge of the genuine and profound in a larger culture driven by artifice and hype, the Brat Pack interlude is a past trauma whose psychic bruises have yet to heal. Publicity certainly does sell books, but many readers remain leery of any new writer introduced to the public with an excessive amount of fanfare; the writer's second book, justly or not, is quite likely to tank.

In Britain, an influx of fiction from writers dubbed "post-colonial" paralleled the multicultural movement in the United States during the 1970s and 1980s, after the Angry Young Men of the 1950s and 1960s (a loose grouping of writers, including Kingsley Amis and John Braine, who offered an often scabrous alternative to the genteel upper-middle-class literature of the preceeding generation) had for the most part devolved into unvarnished misanthropy and neo-conservatism. At the same time, the creative writing program at the University at East Anglia founded by Malcolm Bradbury and Angus Wilson fostered an impressive roster of graduates, including Rose Tremain, Kazuo Ishiguro, and Ian McEwan—a decidedly eclectic crew. McEwan became associated with Julian Barnes and Martin Amis as part of a cadre of stylish, sometimes controversial younger writers, championed by Bill Buford, an American who had taken over the editing of the literary journal *Granta*. In 1983 *Granta* put out a list of "The 20 Best British Novelists Under 40" that proved remarkably prophetic and furthered the impression among minimalism-weary American readers that most of the really exciting new books were being written on the other side of the Atlantic or in Latin America, which was exporting such magic realists as the Nobel Prize-winning Gabriel García Márquez to a worldwide readership starved for epic, imaginative fiction.

Of course, the version of history that I've just presented—of a unified literary establishment that fractured into a array of niche interests—is only one way to interpret the changes in English language fiction in the past forty years. Some observers see the various permutations of the novel and short story as a response to the movies. Film can use straightforward storytelling to reflect the way we live now as well as or better than the traditional realist novel. As a result, writers increasingly turned to techniques that can't be accomplished on-screen, or at least not easily, such as formal experimentation, fabulism, and, above all, the artful deployment of voice. Few, in 1960, would have predicted that Nabokov's 1955 novel *Lolita* would, by the end of the century, be cited more frequently and more fervently by young American writers naming their influences than books by Hemingway or Fitzgerald. The quintessential novel of unreliable narration, written by a novelist who prized an elegant, imagistic style and an elusive authorial stance while despising philosophy and moralizing in fiction, *Lolita* didn't conform to mid-century notions of an era-defining work. The wizardry of Nabokov's masterpiece, however, was irrevocably literary: no movie could convey such a shimmering suspension of multiple realities.

Narrative nonfiction has also become a competitor for readers' attention. Truman Capote's *In Cold Blood* (1966), which he described as a "nonfiction novel," and Mailer's *The Executioner's Song* (1979) are among those writers' finest books and have the advantage of applying the artistry of the novelist to stories made all the more compelling for being true. Tom Wolfe, a founder of the New Journalism of the '60s, wrote a much-discussed essay, "Stalking the Billion-Footed Beast: A Literary Manifesto for the New Social Novel," for *Harper's* magazine in 1989 in which he reviled minimalism and called on novelists to bring the research skills of journalists to bear on their work and to paint panoramic portraits of our times. Wolfe had the wild success of his own 1987 novel, *The Bonfire of the Vanities*, to back up his claim that the public craved this kind of social novel, but his call-to-notepads inspired more critical debates than fiction. In 1996, as autobiographies like Mary Karr's *The Liars' Club* extravagantly outsold literary fiction, James Atlas heralded the "Age of the Literary Memoir" in *The New York Times* magazine. "Fiction isn't delivering the news," he wrote. "Memoir is."

The critic Sven Birkerts, on the other hand, blames the evaporation of "the Great American Novel, that elusive, totalizing entity that would register like a faithful mirror the hopes, energies, contradictions, and failings of postwar America," on the triumph of a culture of ceaseless, vapid electronic babble in which literature just isn't taken seriously anymore. Although Birkerts belongs firmly in the tradition of those cultural Cassandras and doomsday scenarists who have been depicting society's imminent slide into darkness since the age of Aristotle, he has a point. Authors often seem to be returning the slight by excluding pop culture and the media from their fictional worlds; such ephemera are often thought to trivialize or date the work.

However, a handful of literary novelists have been intent on conveying the media-saturated texture of contemporary life, most notably Thomas Pynchon and Don DeLillo, perhaps the most critically revered writers of fiction working today. These authors depict a world of disorienting complexity and outlandish, even absurd events often directed by unseen, sinister forces. They pack their hefty novels with science, history, philosophical ruminations, and dozens of characters, techniques that earned them the epithet "encyclopedic." The encyclopedic novelists borrowed material and themes from all corners of high and popular culture, but particularly from the intellectual vein of science fiction, a genre with a tradition of speculation about the nature of humanity and about the more monstrous aspects of complex technologies and the societies that create them. (Pynchon's *Gravity's Rainbow* was nominated for a Nebula, science fiction's most prestigious award, in 1974.) The visions of writers whose work resides solidly within the science fiction genre—William Gibson and Philip K. Dick in particular—gained wider audiences as readers found startlingly prophetic reflections of contemporary life in their fantastic and often outright paranoid scenarios.

The question of how contemporary fiction should deal with mass culture was explicitly taken up by an heir to the encyclopedic tradition, the young novelist David Foster Wallace, in "E Unibus Pluram: Television and U.S. Fiction," as essay published in the *Review of Contemporary Fiction* in 1993. Wallace describes a new generation of "Image-Fiction" writers so acclimated to the mass media that they "use the transient received myths of popular culture as a world in which to imagine fictions about 'real,' albeit pop-mediated characters." (Mark Leyner, one of these writers, produces fiction that incorporates influences ranging from ad copy to scientific treatises, in what Wallace describes as "witty, erudite, extremely high-quality prose television.") Wallace then questions the "irony and ridicule" deployed by these writers because, he claims, television is already ironic about itself, and thus the medium has deftly co-opted its would-be satirists. "Television . . . has become able to capture and neutralize any attempt to change or even protest the attitudes of passive unease and cynicism that television requires," Wallace maintains. He ends by calling for sincerity and for novelists who "treat of plain old untrendy human troubles and emotions in U.S. life with reverence and conviction."

Most (if not quite all) of the authors covered in this book consider themselves to be aiming for something like that, whether they deal with life in the United States or in Nigeria, whether they write complicated, brainy epics or quiet domestic dramas, whether they take as their subjects urgent political situations or eternal metaphysical quandaries. It's conventional to bemoan the fact that the novelists of 2000 mean less to their society than the novelists of 1960 meant to theirs, but the literary landscape I explored in the process of editing this book also seems much richer and more varied than the one obtained forty years ago. Readers themselves—from Oprah Winfrey to the organizers of the private reading groups that have proliferated across the nation to the participants in Internet discussion groups like Salon.com's Table Talk community—are increasingly determining which are the "important" books from a staggering array of new titles published each year, based on criteria that often defy the literary establishment's. These are tough times for publishers and perhaps for authors as well, but for readers an abundance of voices and stories await at local (and virtual) bookstores. The red-hot center may be impossible to find, but we have the whole world instead.

The

salon.com

Reader's Guide

to Contemporary

Authors

Abbey, Edward
1927–1989
b. Home, Pennsylvania

FICTION: Jonathan Troy (1956), The Brave Cowboy (1956), Fire on the Mountain (1962), Black Sun (1971), *The Monkey Wrench Gang** (1975), Good News (1980), **The Fool's Progress** (1988), Hayduke Lives! (1990)

NONFICTION: Desert Solitaire: A Season in the Wilderness (1968), Appalachian Wilderness: The Great Smoky Mountains (1970), Slickrock: The Canyon Country of Southeast Utah (with Philip Hyde, 1971), Cactus Country (1973), The Journey Home: Some Words in Defense of the American West (1977), Back Roads of Arizona (1978), The Hidden Canyon: A River Journey (1977), Desert Images: An American Landscape (1979), Abbey's Road: Take the Other (1979), Down the River (1982), In Praise of Mountain Lions (with John Nichols, 1984), Beyond the Wall: Essays from the Outside (1984), The Best of Edward Abbey (1988), One Life at a Time, Please (1988), A Voice Crying in the Wilderness: Essays from a Secret Journal (1990), Confessions of a Barbarian: Selections from the Journals of Edward Abbey, 1951–1989 (1994), **The Serpents of Paradise: A Reader** (1995)

Celebrated as a brilliant, sardonic environmental polemicist and chronicler of the Southwestern landscape, Abbey thought of himself primarily as a novelist, and during the final decades of his life he nursed grievances against both critics and admirers who had slighted his achievements as a fiction writer. He spent much of the 1950s studying philosophy at the University of New Mexico, where he wrote a master's thesis on anarchy and violence. Abbey's literary career began with the execrable bildungsroman *Jonathan Troy,* followed by two intermittently successful modern westerns with an existential bent: *The Brave Cowboy* (later made into a Kirk Douglas movie titled *Lonely Are the Brave*), and *Fire on the Mountain.*

In 1968, after supporting himself for several years by working as a seasonal park ranger in Utah, Abbey published the first of his eleven nonfiction books, the angry, elegiac essay *Desert Solitaire*; it remains his most popular title and is justly considered a classic of American writing on the meaning and value of wilderness. His fourth novel, *Black Sun,* tells the story of a man whose lover disappears after they spend an ecstatic period together at a fire-lookout tower in Grand Canyon country; the book includes some of Abbey's finest evocations of the alien beauty of the desert and some of his most bathetic musings on love and solitude. Abbey's best novel by far is *The Monkey Wrench Gang*, a hugely entertaining comic fantasy about a quartet of eco-saboteurs who roam the Southwest destroying roads, billboards, bridges, and bulldozers, and who dream of demolishing the West's greatest symbol of technocratic hubris, Glen Canyon Dam.

So compelling is Abbey's anarchistic vision that it was instrumental in inspiring the formation of Earth First!—an organization whose more zealous and naive members sometimes attempted to emulate the demolition tactics of the novel's protaganists. *The Monkey Wrench Gang* draws its satirical force from both a gleeful countercultural violation of middle-class norms (its Vietnam vet George Washington Hayduke, "a saboteur of much wrath but little brain," could have come straight from the pages of the underground comix) and a Twainian, mock-heroic exuberance. *Good News*, Abbey's next novel, is a scabrous but ultimately slight exposition of a post-apocalyptic Arizona in which Abbey's worst ecological nightmares have come to pass. The author's most ambitious and explicitly autobiographical novel is *The Fool's Progress*; despite some fine passages of reminiscence about Appalachian boyhood on a Depression-era farm, the book is a showcase of many of Abbey's least attractive qualities (among them his willful cantankerousness, xenophobia, and self-pitying machismo). A posthumous sequel to *The Monkey Wrench Gang*, *Hayduke Lives!*, was published in 1990.

See Also: Cormac McCarthy's Border Trilogy, which includes All the Pretty Horses, portrays a Southwest very different from Edward Abbey's, but it is similarly transcendent and haunted by the loss of its pristine perfection. The novels of Carl Hiassen transplant the theme of violent, comic revenge against rapacious development to the wilds of South Florida. Barbara Kingsolver offers a feminized version of Abbey country in her novel Animal Dreams.

—*Hal Espen*

Achebe, Chinua
1930–
b. Albert Chinualumogu Achebe in Ogidi, Nigeria

FICTION: *Things Fall Apart (1958), **No Longer At Ease** (1960), The Sacrificial Egg (stories, 1962), **Arrow of God** (1964), A Man of the People (1966), Girls At War (stories, 1972), **Anthills of the Savannah** (1987)

NONFICTION: Morning Yet on Creation Day (essays, 1975), The Trouble With Nigeria (essays, 1983), **Hopes and Impediments** (essays, 1988), Another Africa (essay and poems with photographs by Robert Lyons, 1998)

POETRY: Beware, Soul Brother (1971), Christmas in Biafra (1973)

Achebe's first novel, *Things Fall Apart*, was a landmark of African fiction and has justly remained a classic for more than forty years. Set in the eastern Nigerian village of Umuofia in the late 1880s, it looks back at the fierce collision of Nigeria's Ibo culture—into which Achebe was born—with encroaching European power. Its tragic hero Okonkwo mounts a doomed resistance to the white man that leaves him exiled and destroyed.

Achebe describes with marvelous clarity—in the essays of *Morning Yet on Creation Day* and *Hopes and Impediments*—how he began to write partly in response to distorted Western views of Africa. Contesting Europe's invention of the "dark continent," Achebe retold the story of colonization from a Nigerian viewpoint, portraying a lost society warmly without overidealizing it. He aimed to restore the humanity of Africans—both in their own eyes and those of Western readers. While early critics overemphasized the novel's anthropological aspects, with *Things Fall Apart* Achebe also pioneered the fusion of Ibo folklore and idioms with the Western novel, arriving at an African aesthetic in which the art of storytelling is central to the tale. As he wrote: "Among the Ibo the art of conversation is regarded very highly and proverbs are the palm-oil with which words are eaten."

Though *Things Fall Apart* has never been bettered by its author, it was the first of a tetralogy spanning Nigerian history from 1880 to 1966. In *Arrow of God*, set during British rule in the 1920s, the priest Ezeulu tests the power of his gods against those of his rivals and the white government, while *No Longer at Ease* and *A Man of the People* target corruption among the Nigerian inheritors of power in the 1960s with scourging and satirical wit.

Achebe stopped writing novels during the Nigerian civil war in the late 1960s as he became involved with the defeated secessionist Ibos. (In 1990, a car accident near Lagos left him paralyzed from the waist down and the lack of adequate healthcare in his homeland has made a return risky.) In this period the poetry of *Beware, Soul Brother* and *Christmas in Biafra*, and the short stories of *Girls at War*, voiced his disillusionment with bloodshed and nationalism. (More recent poems can be found alongside Robert Lyons's photographs in *Another Africa*.) *Anthills of the Savannah*, his first novel in more than twenty years, excitingly pursues ideas he set out in his heartfelt polemic *The Trouble With Nigeria*. Under a military regime in the fictional west African state of Kangan, three boyhood friends—a journalist Ikem, a minister Chris, and the Sandhurst-trained military dictator Sam—clash as Sam maneuvers to become president for life. Highlight-

3

ing corruption, Africa's leadership crises, and popular resistance to tyranny, the novel brings women characters to the fore—partly in response to criticism of their backseat role in earlier works. With several narrators and whole sections in pidgin, it is flawed and sometimes cumbersome, but never dull—testament to Achebe's keen, mischievous independence in probing the changing concerns of his society, and with an undeniable moral punch.

See Also: Other African writers whose fiction touches on colonization and emerging nationhood include the Nigerians Wole Soyinka and Ben Okri (whose short stories also reflect the Nigerian civil war), the Kenyan Ngugi wa Thiong'o, the Ghanaian Ayi Kwei Armah and the Somali Nuruddin Farah. For novels that illuminate the position of African women, see Changes *by the Ghanaian Ama Ata Aidoo,* So Long a Letter *by the Senegalese Mariama Bâ, and Farah's political allegory about a circumcised Somali woman,* From a Crooked Rib.

—Maya Jaggi

Acker, Kathy
1947–1998
b. New York, New York

FICTION: Politics (1972), The Childlike Life of the Black Tarantula (1973), I Dreamt I Was a Nymphomaniac: Imagining (1974), Florida (1978), Kathy Goes to Haiti (1978), **The Adult Life of Toulouse Lautrec by Henri Toulouse Lautrec** (1978), New York City in 1979 (1981), **Great Expectations** (1982), **Blood and Guts in High School** (1984), Algeria: A Series of Invocations Because Nothing Else Works (1985), Don Quixote (1986), *****Empire of the Senseless** (1988), Literal Madness: Three Novels (Florida, Kathy Goes to Haiti, My Death My Life by Pier Pasolini, 1988), In Memoriam to Identity (1990), Hannibal Lecter, My Father (1991), My Mother: Demonology (1993), Pussy, King of the Pirates (1996)

NONFICTION: **Bodies of Work** (essays, 1997)

Rebellious, willful, innovative, in search of her own destiny, Kathy Acker made her struggle to find and exert her own voice the secret center of her writing. Her roots were in the punk movement of the 1970s, and after several experiments, all of her preoccupations came together in *Blood and Guts in High School*, the story of a woman living and breathing for sex. Acker's goal was to smash through the rules of language and gender in order to reclaim herself, foiling time and place in order to propose new rules of her own.

Acker was also the gangsta face of postmodern experimentalism. In *Empire of the Senseless*, the hero's motto is "get rid of meaning" as he joins the female half-robot Abhor in Paris on a quest for freedom, love, and their creator—somebody named Kathy. She appropriated classic works like *Great Expectations* and *Don Quixote*, exploding them into violent, pornographic pastiches. Her last novel, *Pussy, King of the Pirates*, celebrates her career-long history of ransacking and plundering.

Acker died from complications from breast cancer in 1998, an ironic end for an artist known for her tattoos, piercings, weight lifting, and other body manipulations and one who spent so much time finding new ways to take possession of her own body.

See Also: Acker admired Alain Robbe-Grillet and Jean Genet and consorted with new narrative writers like Dennis Cooper and Dodie Bellamy, but her work is part of the long-standing literary tradition of savaging the reader—first conceived by the surrealists and including writers like Isaac Babel, William S. Burroughs, and Hubert Selby, Jr.

—*Brian Bouldrey*

Alexie, Sherman
1966–
b. Spokane, Washington

FICTION: *The Lone Ranger & Tonto Fistfight in Heaven (stories, 1993), Reservation Blues (1995), Indian Killer (1996), Toughest Indian in the World (2000)

SELECTED POETRY: The Business of Fancydancing (1992), First Indian on the Moon (1993), The Summer of Black Widows (1996), The Man Who Loves Salmon (1998)

Sherman Alexie began the 1990s as a poor unknown poet and ended them as a one-man cultural industry. A Spokane-Couer d'Alene Indian raised on a reservation in Washington State, he first attracted attention with *The Business of Fancydancing*, a collection of poems and stories about life on the rez. Alexie's Indians weren't noble red men or New Age visionquesters; they played in all-Indian basketball tournaments, got drunk on Annie Green Springs wine, lived in cheap HUD houses, and sold fireworks to whites driving in from Spokane. Above all they were, like Alexie himself, sharply ironic and damned funny. Still, the book would probably have quietly faded away were it not for the prime-time charisma of its author. At readings Alexie honed a stage persona that combined fiery liberal outrage with a Will Rogers-like wit. By the late 1990s, having written the script for the movie *Smoke Signals*, Alexie was preparing to direct a film adaptation of his bestselling novel *Indian Killer* and doing stand-up comedy.

How's the fiction? Pretty good. In his first three books, Alexie's Indian characters carried the uneasy burden of racism with a resigned form of black humor. By the time he wrote *Indian Killer*, though, the black humor had given way to pure rage. *Indian Killer* is a terribly dark, unrelenting novel about a Native American serial killer and the near-race war he triggers. The characters are thinly drawn and uncharacteristically uncomplicated—everyone seems to be either an angry, revenge-hungry Indian or a naive, ignorant white guy. "A lot of people dismiss the book as angry or didactic," Alexie once replied to his critics. "Well of course! People have this view that literature is somehow supposed to be objective. The book is called *Indian Killer*, not *White People Are Really Cool to Indians*."

See Also: Leslie Marmon Silko also writes about Native Americans, as does Gerald Vizenor, who shares Alexie's tough-eye-edged-with-humor attitude and who writes both fiction and nonfiction about the American Indian experience. Simon Ortiz is another American Indian short story-writer whose work inspired Alexie.

—*Bruce Barcott*

Allison, Dorothy
1949–
b. Greenville, South Carolina

FICTION: *Trash (stories, 1988), **Bastard Out of Carolina** (1992), Cavedweller (1998)

NONFICTION: **Skin: Talking about Sex, Class and Literature** (essays, 1993), Two or Three Things I Know for Sure (1996)

POETRY: The Women Who Hate Me (1983)

Dorothy Allison writes about the kinds of experiences—poverty, child abuse, lesbianism—that usually come swaddled in one set of "correct" conventions or another, but she obeys no laws or manners, and that is precisely why her books reach beyond the boundaries of any specific community. Born illegitimate to a proud, violent, and despised rural clan, she survived beatings and rape at the hands of her stepfather, struggled her way to college, and eventually found an uneasy place for herself among the mostly middle-class lesbian feminist activists of the 1970s and 1980s. The tough, passionate women and dangerous men of her childhood remain her preferred characters, but stories in *Trash* and essays in *Skin* testify to her refusal to renounce her renegade sexuality for the sake of genteel sisterhood—often at a high price. Few American writers have had to fight as hard for themselves and their voices, and few are as free of self-pity or as confident in their warmth.

Her first novel, the autobiographical *Bastard Out of Carolina*, was widely praised and became a bestseller. But *Trash*, a collection of short stories published four years earlier, offers the purest distillation of her sinewy lyricism. Allison's storytelling skills tend to be anecdotal, and *Bastard* has the occasional slack moment as she gathers steam for the next episode. Finally, though, Allison's first novel is knitted firmly together by fierce loyalty and the rage of betrayed love. Bone Boatwright, the eponymous bastard and a "stubborn-faced" little girl, grows up in a notorious family of flinty women and drunken, thieving men. Her adored mother, who marries a man who abuses Bone, never musters the strength to defend her child, and Bone faces choices no child should have to make.

Allison, though, shouldn't be mistaken for an "issue" novelist like the throngs of writers who seized upon incest as a primary topic in the late '80s and early '90s. She aims to be something like the bard of the women of her class, and in her 1998 novel *Cavedweller*, the story of a failed rock singer returning to her Georgia hometown to raise the daughters she abandoned, Allison gave her convenience-store managers and beauty-salon proprietors heroic stature. The book is baggier and less focused than *Bastard* but also less claustrophobic.

Allison belongs to that Bible-tinged, Southern-myth-spinning tradition of which Faulkner is the most prominent bloom; she's probably its earthiest. She no doubt acquired these skills, as Bone did, at her grandmother's knee, listening to the old woman "start reeling out story and memory, making no distinction between what she knew was true and what she had only heard told. The tales she told me in her rough, drawling whisper were lilting songs, ballads of family, love, and disappointment. Everything seemed to come back to grief and blood, and everyone seemed legendary."

See Also: Carolyn Chute strives, like Allison, to capture the lives of working- and underclass families in Maine. Blanche McCrary Boyd is another Southern lesbian with a rich sense of humor and a wild streak.

—Laura Miller

Every Novel Is a Lesbian Novel

By Dorothy Allison

When I think of the books that shaped my lesbian imagination, it is frankly embarrassing. The truth is that my ideas of romance and erotic authority and lesbian life patterns came out of some truly awful books—when there were any books that mentioned lesbians at all. I don't mean embarassing and bad in the sense that they were badly written—though, of course, that is a factor—but embarassing because I believed, truly and completely, in the fatalistic and brutal things that were told to me about who I could be as a grown-up lesbian. I was born to a very poor, violent family where most of my focus was purely on survival, and my sense of self as a lesbian grew along with my sense of myself as a raped child, a poor white Southerner, and an embattled female. I was Violet Leduc's Le Batard much more than I was Le Amazon, that creation of upper-class Natalie Barney. People tell me that class is no longer the defining factor it was when I was a girl, but I find that impossible to fully accept. Class is always a defining factor when you are the child one step down from everyone else.

At the age of thirteen I was always calculating how to not kill myself or how not to let myself be killed. That tends to stringently shape one's imagination. I did not plan to fill up a hope chest and marry some good old boy and make babies. I did not want to be who the world wanted to make me. I was a smart, desperate teenage girl trying to figure out how to not be dismissed out-of-hand for who I was. I wanted to go to college, not become another waitress or factory worker or laundry person or counter help woman like all the other women I knew. Everywhere I looked I saw a world that held people like me in contempt—even without the added detail of me being a lesbian.

The only "lesbian" books I could find then were the porn under my stepfather's bed or those gaudy paperbacks from the drugstore which inevitably ended with one "dyke" going off to marry while the other threw herself under a car. This did not persuade me to be straight, but it did prove to me that fiction should be distrusted. No way I would kill myself for falling in love with my girlfriends. No, I had more deadly reasons to feel hopeless. To find a way out of the world as I saw it, I read science fiction. To sustain my rage and hope, I read poetry and mainstream novels with female heroines. And I read books by Southerners for ammunition to use against Yankees who would treat me mean. Always I read as a lesbian.

Everyone says that their first lesbian book was Radclyffe Hall's wretched *Well of Loneliness*, but that didn't do it for me. I knew from a very early age that I was a femme, and while I might fall in love with Stephen, I did not want to be her. (Well, actually, I couldn't even imagine falling in love with Stephen—that brooding, bossy, ridiculous upper-class creature who would never fall in love with someone like me anyway.) If you limit the list to self-defined lesbian books, then we get down to just one: Rita Mae Brown's *Rubyfruit Jungle*. But looking for self-defined lesbian books was never how I approached the subject. I always reinterpreted books to give me what I needed. All books were lesbian books—if they were believable about women at all, and particularly if they were true to my own experience.

I remember when I first read Barbara Smith's essay on why Toni Morrison's *Sula* was a lesbian novel, how this great grinding noise went through my brain. Of course, I thought, and so was Carson McCuller's *Member of the Wedding* and *My Ántonia* by Willa Cather. I always knew that. In that moment my whole imagination shifted, and I admitted what had always been so: I had spent my adolescence re-interpreting the reality of every book, movie, and television show I had ever experienced—moving everything into lesbian land. Of course, that was how I had kept myself semi-sane and developed an idea of how to love someone, how to be part of a community, and maybe even find happiness.

I read Mary Renault as lesbian—even her novels that featured only men. There was her novel about two women on a houseboat, with the one of them writing westerns to support them both, *The Friendly Young Ladies*, which was definitely about lesbians, but all Renault's work seemed to me to carry forward the same themes. (I discovered that every woman I have ever dated had read not only *The Persian Boy* but *Fire from Heaven*, and recognized them as lesbian texts—as if Alexander the Great was really, truly just another wounded butch underneath it all.) I read books for the queer subtext and because they advocated a world I understood. Books about outsiders, books about inappropriate desire, books where the heroes escaped or fought social expectations, books where boys were girlish or girls were strong and mouthy—all were deeply dykey to me, sources of inspiration or social criticism or life-sustaining poetry.

Flannery O'Connor—that astonishing, brave, visionary who told hard truths in a human voice—was an outsider holding a whole society up to a polished mirror. She was as ruthless as one of her own characters, and I loved her with my whole heart. Surely, she was a lesbian, I told myself and took comfort from her stubborn misfit's life, the fact that she lived with her mama and never married. I did not need her to sleep with a woman to prove her importance to me, though

I would have been grateful to think of her with a great love comforting her as lupus robbed her of all she might have done.

If I set aside Flannery O'Connor, I would have to say that science fiction made me who I am today. I spent my childhood buried in those books. Every science fiction novel I fell into as a child, regardless of the gender or sexual persuasion of the author, widened my imagination about what was possible for me in the world. There were those perfectly horrible/wonderful stories about barbarian swordswomen who were always falling in love with demons, and there were the Telzey stories and the Witch World books and countless brave and wonderful novels told from inside the imaginations of "special" young girls. Mindreading seemed to me to code queer. Alien suggested dyke. On another world, in a strange time and place, all categories were reshuffled and made over.

These days with everyone so matter-of-fact about sexual identity it is hard to explain how embattled I was as a girl, how embattled the whole subject seemed to be. It was entirely different for women ten years younger than me if they grew up in an urban center, and different again a decade later for everyone regardless of where they grew up. I wonder what it must be like for those lesbians younger than me who have never had to make that translation. How do they read books, watch movies and television, and shape their own sense of being queer in the world today? Sometimes I wonder if books are as lifesaving for teenagers today as they were for me when I was a girl. But then I go to speak to some group and there are those young people clutching books to their hearts, asking me what I am reading with the same kind of desperate passion I felt whenever I went to a library or bookstore. No doubt it is different these days, but that passion still seems to be there. Books are still where some of us get our notions of how the world is, and how it might be.

So what "lesbian" books shaped me? *Sula* and *Member of the Wedding* definitely. I reread them now, and for me they remain lesbian books. I think my lifelong struggle not to be as ridiculous, obvious, and oblivious as young Frankie saved me from being quite as blind to my own obsessions. Of course, this didn't help me to foresee all the other ways I would become as ridiculous as Frankie was. You can't get everything from books. And I know my sense of the honor between women and the importance of female friendship was buoyed up by *Sula*.

I would also put in one of the Ann Bannon novels—perhaps *Odd Girl Out* or *Beebo Brinker*, though I find them difficult to reread these days. When I was young, Bannon's books let me imagine myself into her New York City neighborhoods of short-haired, dark-eyed butch women and stubborn, tight-lipped secretaries with hearts ready to be broken. Her books come close to the kind of books that had made me feel fatalistic and damned in my youth, but somehow she just managed to sustain a sense of hope. And of course, there was her romantic portrait of the kind of butch woman I idealized. I would have dated Beebo, no question, although, like a lot of my early girlfriends, she would have grown quickly bored with my political convictions and insistence on activism.

Yes, *Rubyfruit Jungle* would be on my list because it made me laugh out loud and fantasize about moving to New York City and lobbing grapefruits at rich white men while dating actresses and writing my own novels. It was also written with a kind of joyful passion that countered all those deadly suicidal lesbian novels I had grown to hate.

I would want to list *Patience and Sarah* by Isabel Miller because it is a love story I believed and a couple I could imagine walking around in my own little Southern neighborhood. It is hard for me to honor and enjoy romantic fiction and love stories. While I sometimes felt that, by the time I first read it, I was a little too old and untrusting for *Patience and Sarah*, I never doubted the truth of their love. It remains, thankfully, a book I enjoy.

There is one book I would put on any list of my most important and that is *The Female Man* by Joanna Russ, although I loved all her Alyx books. It is as hard and mean and fine as a Flannery O'Connor short story, if you could imagine Flannery stepping into an experimental mode more perverse than the one she managed with *Wise Blood*. It is also a true feminist classic, although I find that when I say that too many people smirk and look away. So, let me also say that it is almost as romantic as *Patience and Sarah*, with equally believable lovers and madwomen.

I wish that everyone would read Joanna Russ's books. I remember with pleasure *Picnic on Paradise*, the first novel where the character Alyx appears. At the time, I was about as doctrinaire as any lesbian-feminist in history, but I remember realizing that it made no difference to me that Alyx was not the lesbian I had first thought her to be. She was screwing a teenage boy with Walkman headphones plugged into his ears every chance she got, and still seemed completely a dyke to me. Russ gave me the idea that there were lots of different ways to be queer, and that even running off to another planet might not fix my life. She made me think that I better pay a bit more attention to life on this planet, and of course she also had a sense of humor. I require a sense of humor in all things.

Oh, what a relief it is to live in the world we have made! As cruel and prejudiced as it is, it is not the world in which I was a girl. We do not have to live hidden lives. We do not have to re-imagine ourselves into the bland over-mind. We have books, stacks and stacks of books on every imaginable subject written by lesbians, all kinds of lesbians.

11

Alvarez, Julia
1950–
b. New York, New York

FICTION: How the Garcia Girls Lost Their Accents (1991), **In the Time of the Butterflies** (1994), * ¡Yo! (1997)

NONFICTION: Something to Declare (essays, 1998)

POETRY: The Housekeeping Book (1984), Homecoming (1984), The Other Side/El Otro Lado (1995), Seven Trees (1999)

In her three novels to date, Julia Alvarez has given us an amusing (if at times irritatingly superficial) portrait of the moneyed class in the Dominican Republic of the 1950s. She's drawn to the period just prior to the fall of the dictator Rafael Trujillo, and Alvarez herself spent the first ten years of her life in the Dominican Republic (where her father was involved in the political underground), fleeing with her family to New York in 1960.

In her first novel, the effervescent *How the Garcia Girls Lost Their Accents,* a group of upper-class Dominicans—raised with servants, multiple residences, loud outfits, louder jewelry, and perfect hair and nails (fetishized with scary frequency)—adjust to the rigors and humiliations of the immigrant experience in America. Alvarez missed the opportunity to make good use of the Trujillo regime as back story; the heinous politics of the island could have lent the book some needed heft.

Alvarez based her engaging second novel, *In the Time of the Butterflies*, on the true story of the four martyred Mirabel sisters, three of whom were killed in the struggle against Trujillo. The characters, storyline, and dynamic political and cultural setting are far better integrated in this book, and Alvarez—also a poet and essayist—appears to have matured remarkably as a storyteller. She returned to the characters introduced in *The Garcia Girls* with *¡Yo!* her most enterprising and successful effort so far. While Alvarez's plots are generally entertaining, her writing tends to be conservative, cautious, and at its worst a little corny and dull. But with *¡Yo!* Alvarez uses to great effect a refreshing and playful narrative device: She has everyone who has ever met the protagonist, Yo, tell anecdotes about her; everyone, it seems, has a chance to speak except Yo herself.

See Also: Junot Diaz's celebrated first book, the short-story collection, Drown, *offers a grittier, more masculine depiction of Dominican-American life.*

—Deborah Kirk

Amis, Martin

1949–
b. Oxford, England

FICTION: **The Rachel Papers** (1973), Dead Babies (1975), Success (1978), Other People: A Mystery Story (1981), Money: A Suicide Note (1984), Einstein's Monsters (stories, 1987), **London Fields** (1989), Time's Arrow; or, the Nature of the Offense (1991), *The Information** (1995), Night Train (1997), Heavy Water (stories, 1999)

SELECTED NONFICTION: The Moronic Inferno and Other Visits to America (1986), Visiting Mrs. Nabokov and Other Excursions (1993)

Despite his precocious debut with 1973's *The Rachel Papers*, Amis has always seemed a novelist made-to-order for the 1980s: a sparkling talent yoked to an impoverished soul. His aptitude for energetically bitter social satire found plenty of grist in the era of Thatcher and Reagan, and he populated his books with ruthless elitists and charismatic frauds. His main theme—that a brutal rivalry for dominance defines all human relations—occupied him both before and after that Darwinian decade, and probably has its roots in his relationship with his father, the late, acclaimed, and equally misanthropic novelist Kingsley Amis.

The sum of a Martin Amis novel often feels slight, which is disconcerting because the parts—his sentences, pages, and set pieces—can be so gratifying. These virtuoso performances can make you laugh out loud at his ingenuity, his eye, his extravagant yet surgical disgust. Amis's forte is the descriptive list, the litany of outrages encountered, say, on a street in London or in the course of an American book tour. He's at his best when he casts aside his pedestrian moral sensibility and goes too far, and his characters are most winning when they're least human. It's the howling debauches of the obese filmmaker John Self (*Money*), the troglodytic musings of the petty hoodlum Keith Talent (*London Fields*), the preening

13

adolescent hypocrisies of Charles Highway (*The Rachel Papers*), and the near-epileptic seizures of self-loathing that plague Richard Tull (*The Information*) that you remember afterwards, not Amis's vague gestures in the direction of substance.

"If the prose isn't there, then you're reduced to what are merely secondary interests, like story, plot, characterization, psychological insight and form," the author told the *Paris Review*, and in an Amis novel, plot and character really are "mere," but only because he's not much good at them. At times he takes up a heavy theme—most persistently, the threat of nuclear war—but this tends to feel like borrowed gravitas, a calculated attempt to look "serious." In *Time's Arrow*, which describes the death and life of a Nazi concentration camp doctor in reverse (the doctor grows younger, people sit down at tables to deposit food on their plates, etc.), this is particularly glaring, with the Holocaust introduced to lend import to what's essentially a stunt (and not a particularly amusing one). Even Amis's more substantial books often feel logy in the middle, as if the story were a toy engine, struggling to animate the static prose and keep everything moving along. Frequently a shadowy, manipulative, quasi-authorial character secretly controls the action for fiendish and unexplained ends—ends which one suspects include Amis's need to make sure something happens.

Because it speaks so forthrightly of the author's greatest passion, his ambition, *The Information* is Amis's sharpest and most satisfying book. Like *Success*, it juxtaposes the fortunes of two men: Gwyn Barry, a novelist whose sentimental, politically correct claptrap has brought him fame and fortune, and his failed and poisonously envious friend, Richard Tull, who pens unpublishable experimental fiction so grueling that everyone who reads it gets a migraine. The novel that followed, *Night Train*, feels like a distinct departure, not just because of its middle-aged American female narrator (a cop) or its noirish trappings, but because it ventures into something very like soul-searching. Centering on the suicide of a woman who has it all (which for Amis means beauty, brains, and sex every night—there's something endearingly naive about his belief that good looks should ward off despair), it hints at a long-overdue investigation into what actually makes life worth living. It also has his least stylish prose, which suggests that his dazzle may be fatally linked to shallowness.

Amis got stuck with the grating epithet "bad boy" in part because his work defied the genteel British fiction of the previous generation, but also on account of his reputation for racy, glamorous living, at least compared to the poky lives of most authors. He winds up in the newspapers a lot—in 1995, for example, when, in the course of divorcing his first wife, he jettisoned his longtime agent (alienating her husband, his good friend, the novelist Julian Barnes) in favor of the notorious Andrew "The Jackal" Wylie. This move sparked an angry editorial from A. S. Byatt, who accused Amis of running up the costs of the publishing industry by demanding huge advances in order to pay for his divorce and extensive dental work. (Only in England would such an accusation constitute a flung gauntlet.) For whatever mysterious reasons people become celebrities, he is one—a rare thing in literary circles—and therefore the target of much resentment.

Amis has published two collections of journalism, but without the ferocity of his fiction they're disappointingly polite. Despite its wonderful title, his collection of pieces about America, *The Moronic Inferno*, can't compete for savagery with the gorgeous horrors of New York City as depicted in *Money*.

See Also: Will Self's fiction is often so reminiscent of Amis's that he was once thought to be a pseudonymous persona for the novelist, though Self favors more outlandish scenarios. Geoff Nicholson writes delightful, profane portraits of London life, without Amis's sour edge.

—*Laura Miller*

Antrim, Donald
1959–
b. Sarasota, Florida

FICTION: Elect Mr. Robinson For a Better World (1993), *The Hundred Brothers (1997), The Verificationist (2000)

When critics and journalists sound off about the "next" generation of American fiction, they tend to toss out the following names—Rick Moody, Jeffrey Eugenides, and Donald Antrim. The trio attended Brown University at roughly the same time, they all studied under Angela Carter, they each now live in Brooklyn, and they're friends. Donald Antrim might be the most idiosyncratic (and wackiest) talent of the trio. His slim, fussy, perfectly calibrated novels are full of dark, Pynchonesque absurdities and more than a whiff of apocalyptic dread.

Antrim's first novel, *Elect Mr. Robinson for a Better World*, plunks you into a sleepy suburban town that's gone haywire: Neighbors fire Stinger missiles at one another when they're not embedding their lawns with massive spikes to skewer would-be intruders. (In one scene, the town's mayor is drawn and quartered by citizens driving subcompact cars.) Antrim's black humor is as spiky as those lawn armaments and, sentence by sentence, *Elect Mr. Robinson* is a pleasure to read, if almost too cerebral a performance.

The Hundred Brothers, which is quite literally about one hundred squabbling brothers gathered for an annual meal, is another pitch-black comedy, but with more emotional meat on its bones. It's a surprisingly acute (if outlandish) take on the vicissitudes of sibling relationships. The event turns into a free-for-all of broken furniture and hurled insults, with nearly every brother harboring either a physical or psychic bruise. While *The Hundred Brothers* ends on a strange and falsely abrupt note, the novel remains true to its central subject: "the sorry indignities that pass as currency between us in lieu of gentler tender."

See Also: The absurdities, and the deft wordplay, in Antrim's work call to mind Thomas Pynchon's early novels, Angela Carter, and two young Brits: Will Self and Tibor Fischer.
—*Dwight Garner*

Atwood, Margaret
1939–
b. Ottawa, Ontario

FICTION: The Edible Woman (1969), **Surfacing** (1972), **Lady Oracle** (1976), Dancing Girls and Other Stories (1977), Life Before Man (1979), Bodily Harm (1981), Encounters with the Element Man (1982), Unearthing Suite (1983), Bluebeard's Egg and Other Stories (1983), Murder in the Dark: Short Fictions and Prose Poems (1983), The Handmaid's Tale (1985), *Cat's Eye (1988), Wilderness Tips and Other Stories (1991), **The Robber Bride** (1993), Good Bones and Simple Murders (stories, 1992), Alias Grace (1996), The Labrador Fiasco (1996)

SELECTED NONFICTION: Survival: A Thematic Guide to Canadian Literature (1972), Day of the Rebels, 1815–1840 (1976), Second Words: Selected Critical Prose (1982), Strange Things: The Malevolent North in Canadian Literature (1996)

SELECTED POETRY: Selected Poems, 1965–1975 (1978), Selected Poems II: Poems Selected and New, 1976–1986 (1986), Morning in the Burned House (1995), The Circle Game (1998)

Margaret Atwood's work is often described as Canadian, feminist, and grim. This constellation would not ordinarily suggest a writer of enormous popular appeal, but Atwood is not an ordinary writer.

Atwood has actively participated in defining the characteristics of Canadian literature. "Canada is not an occupied country. It's a dominated country," she has said, arguing that survival is the national obsession, as the frontier has been for the U.S., and the notion of the island in Britain. Her own work represents Americanism by using noise and casual or brutal acquisition. This Americanism is often expressed through Canadian characters. The issue comes together effectively in Atwood's second novel, *Surfacing*, when the protagonist, while in the Canadian wilderness, comes upon a heron that has been mysteriously lynched.

Her feminism is equally incontrovertible. The classic Atwood protagonist is usually a woman involved in a destructive sexual relationship, having survived a destructive childhood. The narrative focus is very tight—no one is better than Atwood at the accumulation of perceptions and personal history that establishes fictional character. Her details are perfectly chosen, intrinsically arresting, and absolutely persuasive. The Atwood protagonist is witty, imaginative, and self-absorbed. She has a job that is interesting, at least to the reader, though rarely high-paying. The men in her life are not her equal. But the women in her life also disappoint and betray her.

Mothers in Atwood's books often eat their young. *The Robber Bride* is unusual in its depiction of friendship among women, though these particular friendships arise entirely as a defense against the super-villainess, Zenia, a woman with the destructive capacity of a car bomb. Among Atwood's young girls, friendships are decidedly unfriendly. They evidence the clubby viciousness at which girls excel—see particularly, *Lady Oracle* and *Cat's Eye*. Atwood's is a feminism of isolation and the individual rather than connection and community. The family is important only as a matter of personal history. And wherever Atwood perceives feminism to be operating a sort of club, she declines to join.

So it does sound grim: murdered herons, abusive childhoods, isolated victims, and bad sex. But Atwood is often a very funny writer, even when her topic is not. Many of her novels are broadly comic. The best of these are *Lady Oracle* and *The Robber Bride*. Even when she is most serious, her protagonists have too much volition, too much energy to depress.

Plus there are the pleasures of her prose. Her second life, as a poet, is always evident. She draws her images from myth and fairy tale. Her narrative strategies are playful. Like many writers, she sometimes seems as interested in the question of how a story can be told as she is in the story itself.

Atwood's plots lean strongly, and not always persuasively, on the fantastical. Events are foretold, fortunes are read, visions are seen, the dead appear or speak. These elements often underpin the emotional climax of the book. Her narration is always so firmly grounded in an individual's limited point of view that alternative psychological explanations for fantastic events can't be ruled out. Still, the reader is not encouraged to settle for psychology.

Cat's Eye is perhaps the novel in which Atwood's usual interests, images, and strategies come together most marvelously. The narrator, Elaine, is a successful artist haunted by a girlhood friendship she cannot entirely recall. The story follows Elaine from forgetfulness to remembrance and is astonishing in its painstaking, painful depiction of childhood. "Little girls are cute and small only to adults," Elaine observes. "To one another they are not cute. They are life-sized."

Atwood's most famous novel is the atypical *The Handmaid's Tale*. In the feminist dystopian tradition of science fiction, this is a book set in the near future, in a society run by Christian fundamentalists. It is indeed a grim book whose protagonist, Offred, while no less sensitive than the usual Atwood heroine, is considerably more trapped and tormented.

The well-received *Alias Grace* represented another departure for Atwood: her first work of historical fiction. Woven of careful and evocative period detail, the novel is an intensely imagined account of the case of Grace Marks, who was convicted of murder in northern Canada in 1843. Atwood constructs Grace's first-person account so that it manages to conceal as much it reveals. Reviewers noted Atwood's cunning in crafting an ending that was happy for those who wished it so and chilling for readers who prefer to be chilled.

Atwood is a prolific and accomplished poet, essayist, and writer of short stories. In her most recent collection, *Good Bones and Simple Murders*, she experiments with a form that falls somewhere between these three. Of particular note are "Unpopular Gals," Atwood's meditation on the fictional role of the villainess and "Happy Endings," her funniest metafictional piece. Her earlier stories are more traditional. Among the most famous of these, "Bluebeard's Egg" and "Rape Fantasies" showcase her gift for writing stories that feel lighthearted but are actually deadly serious.

Atwood is as appealing to scholars as she is to lay readers. Supernaturally prolific as she is, even more has been written about her than by her. *Margaret Atwood: A Biogra-*

phy came out in 1998, authored by Nathalie Cooke, a professor at McGill University and former president of the Margaret Atwood Society. It is the first book-length biography. "I try to stay more or less out of it," Atwood has said, in reference to such scholarly works. "I think of it as a kind of job-creation project."

See Also: Molly Gloss's Dazzle of Day, *Carol Emshwiller's* Ledoyt, *Jane Smiley's* The All True Adventures of Lizzie Newton, *and A. S. Byatt's* Possession.

—*Karen Joy Fowler*

Auster, Paul
1947–
b. Newark, New Jersey

FICTION: *THE NEW YORK TRILOGY:* **City of Glass** (1985), Ghosts (1986), **The Locked Room** (1986), In the Country of Last Things (1987), Moon Palace (1989), **The Music of Chance** (1990), Leviathan (1992), Mr. Vertigo (1994), Timbuktu (1999)

SELECTED NONFICTION: White Spaces (1980), *The Invention of Solitude (1982), **The Art of Hunger** (1991), **Hand to Mouth** (1997)

POETRY: Unearth: Poems, 1970–1972 (1974), Wall Writing: Poems 1971–1975 (1976), Facing the Music (1980), Disappearances (1988)

In his collection of essays, *The Art of Hunger*, Paul Auster wrote the following in praise of the high-wire performer Philippe Petit: "With an ambition and an arrogance fit to the measure of the sky, and placing on himself the stringent internal demand, he wanted, simply, to do what he was capable of doing." Perhaps he was writing about a kindred spirit, for what the New Jersey-born author does on the page is itself a performance of verbal high-wire artistry. Fearlessly symbolic, unapologetically theoretical, Auster's writing is a perilous creation, a combination of intellectual élan and raw nerve.

However, Auster was nearly forty before he was able, "simply, to do what he was capable of doing." Prior to that time, he sustained himself by taking a variety of odd jobs: working as a groundskeeper at a Catskill hotel, designing board games, and shipping out

19

as a merchant seaman in an oil tanker in the Gulf of Mexico. In his 1996 memoir, *Hand to Mouth*, which Auster subtitled "A Chronicle of Early Failure," he described suffering then from "a constant, grinding, almost suffocating lack of money that poisoned my soul and kept me in a state of never-ending panic."

Auster has pointed to 1979 as his watershed year, and to the receipt of a small inheritance, brought by the death of his father, as the liberating factor. As if to make up for his slow start, Auster went on to publish seven novels in the next eight years. The first, *City of Glass*, would be the initial offering in a trilogy of three slender, cerebral meditations on the elements of the detective novel. Together, *City of Glass*, *Ghosts*, and *The Locked Room* would make up what Auster has called The New York Trilogy. In all three books, he constructs his detective stories in such a way that, as one reviewer noted, the physical gives way to the metaphysical, and the pursuit of his quarry becomes a search for answers to "the Big Questions—the implications of authorship, the enigmas of epistemology, the veils and masks of language."

Likewise, Auster's later novels—particularly *The Country of Lost Things*, *The Music of Chance*, and *Leviathan*—reveal a writer more interested in the play of ideas than the imperatives of plot. His novels are structured like riddles, the solutions to which he's either forgotten or never bothered to work out in the first place. Before turning his hand to prose, Auster was known primarily as a poet and translator, with a special affinity for the French. This kinship exhibits itself in novels such as *Moon Palace* and *Mr. Vertigo* as a fondness for experimentation, word games, and an emphasis on the philosophical over the emotional. It shows up, as well, in the way he infuses realism with playfulness and combines existentialism with a haunting, film-noir glamour.

In love with chance and the manifestations of coincidence, Auster never met a digression he didn't like. Tucking essay material into the folds of his storylines, Auster will pause for a lengthy reverie on the Tower of Babel or *Don Quixote*, and even allows himself to step into the book's pages to play detective with the other characters. If the death of his father provided the catalyst for change in his life, it would also provide the subject for his first and, for some, most wholly satisfying work, a memoir. In *The Invention of Solitude* Auster devotes the first half of the book—titled "Portrait of an Invisible Man"—to chronicling the life of a man who remained endlessly elusive, unknown, and

20

FIVE BOOKS I LIKE THAT HAVE SOMETHING TO DO WITH MOVIES *by Pauline Kael*

The Apprenticeship of Duddy Kravitz by Mordecai Richler

It's like a Dickens story told by Philip Roth. Duddy is the teenage runt from the Montreal ghetto who will become a movie mogul. When the unscrupulous kid asks his austere, educated uncle, "Why didn't you ever have time for me?", the uncle answers truthfully, "Because you're a *pusherke*. A little Jew-boy on the make. Guys like you make me sick and ashamed." This exuberant, richly satiric novel might be better known here if it hadn't come out of Canada (reputed to be the land of the earnest). It's vulgar in the best sense of the word.

Margaret in Hollywood by Darcy O'Brien

The late Darcy O'Brien, well-known for such books as *Murder in Little Egypt* and *A Dark and Bloody Ground*, was the son of two early movie stars: the muscular George O'Brien and the cool, beautiful Marguerite Churchill. Renaming Marguerite Margaret and making her his narrator, he tells the lightly fictionalized story of his independent-minded mother—who instinctively, from the age of five, takes pleasure in performing. He tells it in a succinct, levelheaded way. He may be the least fussy of all the writers who have tackled sensational material; he's not inspired, but he's blessed with good sense.

Paradise Fever by Ptolemy Tompkins

The author—the son of Peter Tompkins, who cowrote *The Secret Life of Plants*—writes in the first person; technically, I suppose, it's a memoir, not a novel. But whatever you call it, he's got a gift. The boy Tolly, who has deeply confusing feelings about his pop-guru father, is hooked on the hidden forces in grisly horror movies. Monsters like the Creature from the Black Lagoon and the ghouls in *Night of the Living Dead* are his special infatuation. He's haunted by them. At the end the author seems to pull back from what he has been digging up, but the first two-thirds have an unusual kind of intellectual suspense.

Three Squirt Dog by Rick Ridgway

A rowdy pop novel set in a hot summer in suburban Cleveland. The hero, Bud, has just graduated with a B.A. in English and is at loose ends, working in his uncle's used-record shop. Ridgway gets at the dumb hormonal energy of that time in our lives when sex and rock and movies are all mixed up together. Bud and his friends represent the knowledgeable side of shopping-mall culture—"Debra Winger in *Urban Cowboy*. Oww—if you laid all the boners raised by that actress end to end you'd have a monorail to Mars."

White Hunter, Black Heart by Peter Viertel

Almost a half-century old, it's still the best Hollywood novel I've ever come across—and it isn't even set in Hollywood. (It takes place in London and Africa.) Viertel worked as John Huston's whipping-boy screenwriter on the locations where Huston concentrated on hunting elephants and incidentally directed *The African Queen*. (There's a matching portrait of a sacred-monster director in Richard Rush's free film adaptation of the Paul Brodeur novel *The Stunt Man*, with Peter O'Toole playing an ornery David Lean.) Viertel had the right background for the task he took on. His father, Berthold Viertel, was the model for the director figure in Christopher Isherwood's novel *Prater Violet*, and his mother, Salka Viertel, collaborated on the writing of several Garbo pictures.

ultimately unknowable. In the process, he proves again that truth is stranger than fiction by uncovering the story of his grandfather's 1919 murder at the hands of his wife in Kenosha, Wisconsin.

In recent years, Auster's prose has provided worthy fodder for adaptation into motion pictures. In 1993, *The Music of Chance* was filmed by Philip Haas, and in 1995 Auster's two screenplays, *Smoke* and *Blue in the Face* were directed by Wayne Wang and Auster himself, respectively. Auster again moved behind the camera in 1998 to film his screenplay, *Lulu on the Bridge*.

Auster's work has elicited strong partisan feeling. On the one hand, his sensibility has been attacked as "essentially dry, academic and theoretical—a mechanical engineer impersonating Kafka and Beckett." On the other, Auster was nominated in 1991 for a PEN/Faulkner Award for *The Music of Chance*, and in France he was named Chevalier de l'Ordre des Arts et des Lettres, and awarded the Prix Medicis for foreign literature for *Leviathan* in 1993.

See Also: The novels of Vladimir Nabokov, the novels and plays of Samuel Beckett and the stories of Franz Kafka.

—Hal Hinson

Baker, Nicholson
1957–
b. New York, NY

FICTION: The Mezzanine (1988), Room Temperature (1990), **Vox** (1992), *****The Fermata** (1994), The Everlasting Story of Nory (1998)

NONFICTION: U & I (1991) The Size of Thoughts: Essays and Other Lumber (1996)

"He writes better than I do and he is smarter than I am," Nicholson Baker wrote of John Updike in *U & I*, a pitilessly comic book-length essay on his compulsion to measure himself against that formidable man of letters. "This observation will surprise no one; it came, however, as quite a shock to me." Today most writers feel—or should have the sense to feel—the same dismay when comparing themselves to Baker, who has stocked his agile, capacious mind with enough lumber to create a plausible illusion of omniscience. (His erudite and entertaining 1996 essay collection, *The Size of Thoughts*, concludes with 148 pages on the word "lumber.") From the mechanics of playing the French horn to the esthetics of paper versus plastic coin rolls, from the joys of parenthood to the pleasures of writing on rubber with a ballpoint pen, Baker seeks to give eternal literary life to absolutely everything, in microscopic detail. It's a mad, doomed project, of course. But he presents himself as a sane, funny, good-hearted, self-deprecating Ahab, whose White Whale is his own mind, half-creating the infinitely rich, infinitely engaging world it perceives.

Like the classic modernists Proust, Joyce, Woolf, and Nabokov—and the canonical eccentric Laurence Sterne—Baker cherishes the fantasy of stopping time to examine and inhabit the frozen moment. Arno Strine, the hero of his ingenious 1994 novel *The Fermata*, gets to do this literally; he can halt the universe and turn the human world into a fleshy statue garden in which he's free to undress the women and masturbate, and even to compose pornographic fiction for them to discover when time resumes again. But the same impulse drives *The Everlasting Story of Nory*, a novel of heroically unfashionable sweetness, whose nine-year-old protagonist is modeled closely on Baker's own daughter and whose aim, he has said, is to preserve this magically innocent phase of her girlhood.

Whatever Baker happens to write about, his underlying subject is the imagination's triumph over time. Arno's excursions into what he calls "the Fold" have their formal analogue in the long footnotes that elaborate on this or that point in Baker's first novel, *The Mezzanine*; the premise of a footnote, after all, is that the running text stops and hangs there while the writer discourses on a subtopic, then starts up again. His second novel, *Room Temperature*, manages to stop the flow simply with the narrator's digressions and reminiscences. In his third, *Vox* (the phone-sex novel which had a second life of notoriety when the world learned that Monica Lewinsky had bought a copy for President Clinton), Baker reverts to the Scheharazadian delaying tactic of stories within the story. In these first three novels, not much "actual" time elapses and the plot summaries sound like parodies of fictional experimentalism. *The Mezzanine*: Howie buys a pair of shoelaces at CVS on his lunch hour (135 pages). *Room Temperature*: Mike rocks his baby daughter to sleep (116 pages). *Vox*: Jim and Abby masturbate while talking to each other on a phone chat line (166 pages). But unlike Samuel Beckett's Molloy, who spends six pages transferring his "sucking stones" from pocket to pocket before throwing them away in disgust, Baker's characters seem perfectly happy and endlessly interested. Even Arno Strine, troubling as he is, seems largely untroubled—by his powers, by the use he makes of them, and even by their eventual loss.

This predominance of good cheer distinguishes Baker from most other literary novelists, past or present; it leavens his potentially ponderous intellect and gives his work a feeling of open-eyed, open-minded wonder. Shakespearean-Conradian-Faulknerian-Beckettian "darkness" doesn't exist in Baker's sunny fictional universe, perhaps because of his temperament, perhaps because he's so sophisticated it seems corny, perhaps because he just hasn't gotten around to it yet. Readers who insist that a novel offer tension, conflict, and serious anguishing over morality and mortality won't get far with Baker. And even those willing to go along for the ride may be put off by the baby-makes-three coziness of *Room Temperature* or the kids-say-the-darnedest-things malapropisms of *The Everlasting Story of Nory*, not to mention Nory's own fantastical made-up stories which do seem everlasting. But Baker's strongest fictions—*The Mezzanine*, *Vox*, and, above all, *The Fermata*—make us bracingly nervous, either because we don't know quite what to think about smart, nice, well-spoken (and suspiciously underemployed) people so preoccupied with sex toys and pornography, or simply because we wonder if even a writer this smart can get away with what he's trying to get away with.

In *U & I*—an anatomization of reading, writing, and remembering at least as satisfying as any of his novels to date—Baker claimed that while Updike was his favorite living writer, Iris Murdoch was his favorite living novelist. It's a fair and helpful distinction, and he must have anticipated that it might be applied to his own work. Almost any living novelist is more novelistic than Nicholson Baker, but if there's a smarter, more original writer working today, none of his colleagues want to hear about it.

24

See Also: David Foster Wallace has similarly encyclopedic tendencies—and similarly long footnotes. Steven Millhauser's strange and cozy clockwork universes seem created out of a similar obsessiveness. And Richard Powers, like Baker, elevates the nerdy to the sublime by sheer intellectual wattage.

—*David Gates*

Ballard, J. G.
1930–
b. Shanghai, China

FICTION: The Wind From Nowhere (1962), The Drowned World (1962), The Voices of Time and Other Stories (1963), Billenium and Other Stories (1962), The Four-Dimensional Nightmare (stories, 1963), Passport to Eternity and Other Stories (1963), The Terminal Beach (stories, 1964), The Burning World ([republished in England as The Drought], 1964), **The Crystal World** (1966), The Impossible Man and Other Stories (1966), The Disaster Area (stories, 1967), The Day of Forever (stories, 1967), The Overloaded Man (stories, 1967), The Atrocity Exhibition (stories, 1970), **Vermilion Sands** (stories, 1971), Chronopolis and Other Stories (1971), **Crash** (1972), Concrete Island (1974), High-Rise (1975), Low-Flying Aircraft and Other Stories (1976), The Best of J. G. Ballard ([republished in 1978 as The Best Short Stories of J. G. Ballard], 1977), The Unlimited Dream Company (1979), The Venus Hunters (stories, 1980), Hello America (1981), Myths of the Near Future (stories, 1982), *****Empire of the Sun** (1984), The Day of Creation (1987), Memories of the Space Age (stories, 1988), Running Wild (1988), War Fever (stories, 1990), **The Kindness of Women** (1991), Rushing to Paradise (1994), Cocaine Nights (1996)

NONFICTION: A User's Guide to the Millennium: Essays and Reviews (1996)

Across four decades, fifteen novels, and several dozen short stories, James Graham Ballard has established himself as one of the most singular—and single-minded—visionaries of twentieth-century literature. Pursuing his acknowledged obsessions, Ballard tells essentially the same story over and over again: A lonely, neurotic male protagonist, mesmerized by a threatening environment which he understands as powerful and fertile, gradually slides into a blissful dementia, convinced that union with the hostile landscape will bring psychological or spiritual fulfillment, even (or especially) at the cost of self-obliteration. Ballard's settings vary from the lush forests of equatorial Africa to irradiated atolls in the South Pacific to the barren motorways of suburban London, but all his landscapes are really interiors. The automobile junkyards, drained seas, abandoned resorts and overgrown airfields are projections, emblematic fields of psychic desolation where images of media celebrities and nuclear explosions have replaced human emotion.

Ballard's early short stories, published in the 1950s and early 1960s, placed him squarely in what was then known as the British New Wave of science fiction, a group of young writers more concerned with psychological and sociological critique than with rocket voyages to other planets. As he put it, "the alien planet is Earth." But the distinctive, seductive nature of Ballard's vision emerged in the quartet of apocalyptic novels culminating with *The Crystal World*, in which the entire planet is imagined as metamorphosing into a beautiful but lifeless mineral sculpture. With the stories in *Vermilion Sands*, it remains among the author's most haunting and lyrical depictions of destruction.

In the 1970s, Ballard shifted to savage tales of urban anomie, incorporating a growing fixation with automobile culture, televised violence, and pornography. The collection *The Atrocity Exhibition*—including such infamous stories as "The Assassination of John Fitzgerald Kennedy Considered as a Downhill Motor Race" and "Why I Want to Fuck Ronald Reagan"—written in a collage-style dense with deliberately obscure technical language, may now seem like an arid postmodern gambit. Nonetheless, it engendered *Crash*, undoubtedly Ballard's most notorious and influential novel. This book, in which a protagonist named James Ballard is drawn into a suicidal subculture of car-crash enthusiasts, was understood by many of the author's fans as a paean to technological nihilism. In retrospect, it reads clearly as a satiric cry of protest, a portrait of a man so starved for human contact he will risk his own mutilation or death to achieve it.

As Ballard eventually proved in the heartrending, semi-autobiographical novel *Empire of the Sun*—largely based on his own extraordinary childhood experiences in a Japanese internment camp in occupied China during World War II—he is capable of standing outside his own obsessions and viewing them with a bemused, sympathetic eye. All the lurid, hypnotic strangeness of Ballard's other fiction is present—as is the unmistakable sense that the non-Ballard characters are not quite real—but it becomes clear for the first time that his obsessions with death and desolation are the result of profound personal trauma, not intellectual conceit. If *Empire* is the apotheosis of Ballard's work, *The Kindness of Women* is his ultimate act of transcendence and redemption. Another half-fictional memoir, it follows its narrator's troubled and tragic romantic career from Shanghai through the "craze years" of England in the 1960s, when his beloved wife dies in a freak accident. It leaves him in the end, a widower, a single suburban dad, and a famous writer, grateful to the strong women who have helped him survive his remarkable life and the dreamlike, unforgetabble fictions it has called forth.

See Also: None of the other British New Wave authors of the 1960s achieved anything like Ballard's level of fame, but Brian W. Aldiss, Thomas M. Disch, Michael Moorcock, and Christopher Priest, for example, all share something of his visionary sensibility. Like

Philip K. Dick, another genre-transcending figure, Ballard is an undeniable influence on younger science fiction authors like William Gibson, Neal Stephenson, and Bruce Sterling.

—*Andrew O'Hehir*

Banks, Russell
1940–
b. Newton, Massachusetts

FICTION: Searching for Survivors (1975), Family Life (1975), The New World (stories, 1978), **Hamilton Stark** (1978), The Book of Jamaica (1980), Trailerpark (stories, 1981), The Relation of My Imprisonment (1983), *Continental Drift (1985), Success Stories (1986), **Affliction** (1989), Brushes with Greatness (1989), **The Sweet Hereafter** (1991), Rule of the Bone (1995), Cloudsplitter (1998), Angel on the Roof: The Stories of Russell Banks (2000)

No one has worse luck than the protagonist of a Russell Banks novel. Just as surely as his angry, working-class men will wrong their long-suffering wives and alienated kids, they'll wind up dead or psychically destroyed, both victims and perpetrators of a white capitalist patriarchy run amok. A social realist in the Theodore Dreiser tradition, Banks believes that good novels are inherently political, that they should speak to the times, champion the marginalized, and make you want to be a better person. He even ends his grim, anti-Reaganomics opus, *Continental Drift*, with the exhortation, "Go, my book, and help destroy the world as it is." Yes, he's often didactic, but he's a great storyteller with a sharp eye for character.

In the beginning, though, Banks was more of an experimentalist. His early novel, *Hamilton Stark*, is the blackly witty, metafictional tale of a misanthropic pipefitter, "in many ways a self-centered, immature, cruel, eccentric, and possibly insane man." Not that the eponymous Stark lacks a caustic charm: his daughter, who he abandoned as an infant, is writing a book about him, as is Stark's sole "friend," a bemused but obsessed academic. Both yearn for the grump's approval, and their frustrating attempts to pin their elusive subject to the page are the crux of the book.

Banks's writing grew increasingly dark and serious as he honed in on his eclectic fixation—the sickness of families, race relations, New England life, the Caribbean, and most

27

of all, self-destructive white guys from snowy towns. The premise of *The Book of Jamaica* is juicy enough—an American professor gets mixed up with the legendary Maroon tribe and an old Jamaican murder case—but the uncharacteristically dry prose is pocked by such obvious sermonizing as, "The distance between the world of the wealthy and the world of the poor was so great that he who had wealth was truly a magician."

The impassioned, grandly ambitious *Continental Drift* drives such points home with great improvements in style and narrative, and at a time when social-justice tales were passe for the East Coast literary establishment. Thirty-year-old New Hampshire repairman Bob Dubois, "A common man, a decent man" (albeit an adulterer) is sick of the grind, sick of his shabby home, sick of repeating his father's stunted life, so he drags his family to the greener artificial grass of Florida. Meanwhile, Vanise Dorsinville is desperate to flee the abject poverty and brutality of Haiti. Bob ends up in a trailer, Vanise on a doomed refugee boat—and guess who's the captain? Though the rampant hopelessness is occasionally heavy-handed, this acclaimed novel is always emotionally gripping.

Banks grew up hardscrabble in the woods of New Hampshire, the eldest son of a violent, alcoholic plumber, an experience that gave him an acute understanding of the disturbing undertones in father-son relationships and of tragically flawed but ultimately sympathetic men. Wade Whitehouse, the raging, hard-drinking small town cop of *Affliction*, is haunted by his raging, hard-drinking dad. Wade's daughter is scared of him, his ex-wife married a professional man, and he's feeling so unbearably frustrated and persecuted that he implodes. In an era of white male-bashing, Banks defends his lower-middle-class working men as disenfranchised. But, like John Ford and Tobias Wolff, he also equates masculinity with a horrific, genetic disease passed down from the cavemen.

Evocative of his short stories in its lyrical examination of small town values, *The Sweet Hereafter* details the aftershocks of a fatal schoolbus wreck on a depressed upstate New York hamlet, a community that just might be able to heal itself. The teenage cult favorite, *Rule of the Bone*—about a kid who dumps his abusive, trailer-park life for adventures with bikers, pedophiles, and a Jamaican drifter named I-Man—wants to update Huck and Holden for the modern-day outsider. The allusions seem forced, and Bone's voice is sometimes unconvincing, but there's plenty of savvy commentary on the fetishization of "exotic" black culture.

That race is the "central and inescapable fact of American life and character" is the bedrock of *Cloudsplitter*, a take on the infamous abolitionist John Brown. Painstakingly researched, brimming with ideas about racial activism past and present, but written in a stilted, nineteenth-century-style voice, the tome is both an admirable effort and a grueling read. Though Banks implies that whites have a moral obligation to reject their privileges, Brown is less an idealized hero than a quintessential Banks character—an authoritarian prone to dark nights of the soul who eventually destroys everything around him. Indeed, *Cloudsplitter* is caught between a wrenching fatalism and an unshakeable hope that individuals can make a difference. That's Banks, the optimistic tragedian.

See Also: Banks fans might enjoy the hardluck smalltown life stories of Richard Russo. And though Banks casts his sociological net far wider, Bobbie Ann Mason and Tobias Wolff also write realistic novels about the "forgotten" class.

—Sia Michel

Banville, John
1945–
b. Wexford, Ireland

FICTION: Long Lankin (stories, 1970), Nightspawn (1971), **Birchwood** (1973), Doctor Copernicus (1976), Kepler (1981), The Newton Letter: An Interlude (1982), Mefisto (1986), *****The Book of Evidence** (1989), Ghosts (1993), **Athena** (1993), **The Untouchable** (1997)

Imagine adding healthy dollops of Samuel Beckett's gallows humor and Yeats's myth-mindedness to a Wilkie Collins mystery, then to this already strong cup stir in a learned fascination with science, art, and politics and you will get some idea of the heady brew John Banville cooks up in his novels. Whether delving into the intricacies of Renaissance astrophysics, Flemish painting, or Communist ideology, he never lacks for high-energy thinking. And, although he wears his stylistic allegiances to his canonical Irish predecessors on his sleeve, he can muster the page-turning propulsiveness of an aspiring bestseller. By bringing, for instance, Beckett's lithe doom to mystery/suspense fiction, Banville not only ups the ante for the genre, but he's found a market niche for the old master's lyric despair. It is precisely this rare joining of storytelling verve to an elegant literary sensibility that makes Banville the kind of writer whose books you press upon friends, eager to share your glee at a real find.

Banville's protean gifts as a stylist have permitted successful forays into a number of fictional categories. His three earliest books—*Long Lankin*, a collection of short fiction, and the novels *Nightspawn* and *Birchwood*—are all self-consciously experimental. They tease at the limits of narrative form, sometimes too strenuously so. Their depictions of psychological inwardness and macabre violence were laid aside for the next two novels, *Kepler* and *Doctor Copernicus*, a pair of traditionally plotted historical outings that dazzle the ear with musical prose as well as prod the brain with meticulous recreations of Renaissance scientific debate. When Banville returned to Gothic atmospherics—as he did in his best novel, *The Book of Evidence*—he did so with a newly accomplished grasp of narrative strategy.

Told in pitch-perfect first person, *The Book of Evidence* is the confession of murderer Freddie Montgomery, an all-around screw-up whose obsession with a painting leads to a crime as casually inept as the rest of his life. Banville turns the cagey trick of making Freddie so deliciously despicable—his insufferable arrogance is based on a deft and witty intelligence—that you hang on his every word. Enveloping the reader in his own claustrophobic narcissism, Freddie convinces us that his fate, not that of the poor housekeeper he thoughtlessly brains, deserves our compassion. With a nod to Milton's debonair Satan, Banville burrows into the seductions of evil to produce a novel that implicates his readers as co-conspirators.

In his next two novels, Banville followed Freddie (or a Freddie-like character, never completely shedding his experimental roots, Banville leaves this an open question) in his post-prison excursion to a mysterious island (*Ghosts*) and later into the heart of Ireland's organized crime world (*Athena*). No matter how beautifully the sentences click into place, a bloody mess is never far from the page.

In his most recent novel, *The Untouchable*, a fictionalized account of the English spy and art historian, Sir Anthony Blunt, Banville shows his mastery of yet another genre, the spy novel. In the manner of John le Carré's easily digestible erudition, he serves up an irresistible (and determinedly commercial) account of England's famous Fourth Man espionage scandal. Even in this effort to break out of the confines of purely literary fiction, Banville stills delivers a densely allusive, unabashedly intellectual book. He's the kind of prodigiously gifted writer who could try his hand at a Harlequin Romance and turn in a work of art.

See Also: Banville's eerie lyricism finds echoes in J. G. Ballard and Angela Carter, along with newcomers like Margot Livesey (Criminals), *Iain Sinclair* (Downriver), *and Rupert Thompson* (The Insult *and* Soft!)*.

—*Albert Mobilio*

Barker, Pat
1943–
b. Thornaby-on-Tees, England

FICTION: Union Street (1982), Blow Your House Down (1984), **The Century's Daughter** (1986), The Man Who Wasn't There (1988), *THE REGENERATION TRILOGY: *Regeneration (1991)*, **The Eye in the Door** *(1993)*, **The Ghost Road** *(1995)*, Another World (1998)

Pat Barker is a remarkable, astringent writer, her prose puttied through with hard sympathy for her characters, most of them British working class from the sooty north (she's from industrialized Thornaby-on-Tees). Her first three novels—*Union Street*, *Blow Your House Down*, and *The Century's Daughter*—became something of a rallying cry in U.K. feminist circles. Barker gave voice to the voiceless, to pale wives of hopeless drunks, to women who slog in factories. But she did so unpatronizingly. These protagonists aren't just pitiable prole tokens; they can be complicit, too, in their own oppression. And they are ever-complex.

But in the '90s, fearing she'd become typecast, Barker embarked on a new subject (World War I) and a new gender (men, of the shellshocked variety). She'd begun writing from the male standpoint in 1989's *The Man Who Wasn't There*, inspired by her own absent father. A historical trilogy ensued, pivoting on real-life characters—Dr. W. H. R. Rivers, the distinguished neurologist and anthropologist, and the poets Siegfried Sassoon, Wilfred Owen, and Robert Graves—plus fictional characters, most memorably the bisexual amnesiac Billy Prior. *Regeneration*, the first installment, centers on Rivers's dismaying job, which is to treat soldiers traumatized by trench warfare—in order to get them back to the battlefield.

The Eye in the Door hones in, dolefully, frighteningly, on the homosexual witch-hunts conducted during the war. And *The Ghost Road* shadows Prior as he is sent back to France, while also (less successfully) limning Rivers's fieldwork memories of a cult-of-death South Pacific tribe. This last won the Booker Prize for fiction. It *is* great, though, arguably, *Regeneration* remains Barker's masterpiece. Just listen: "He remembered the day before Arras . . . passing the same corpses time after time, until their twisted and blackened shapes began to seem like old friends. At one point he'd had to pass two hands sticking up out of a heap of pocked and pitted chalk, like the roots of an overturned tree."

31

Barnes, Julian
1946–
b. Leicester, England

FICTION: Metroland (1980), Before She Met Me (1982), Flaubert's Parrot (1984), Question and Answer (1986), Staring at the Sun (1986), *A History of the World in 10½ Chapters** (1989), Talking it Over (1991), The Porcupine (1992), Cross Channel (1996), England, England (1998)

AS DAN KAVANAGH: Duffy (1980), Fiddle City (1981), Putting the Boot in (1985), Going to the Dogs (1987)

NONFICTION: Letters from London (1995)

The versatile Barnes writes charmingly in several modes without seeming particularly committed to any one. His most popular novel, *Flaubert's Parrot*, shrouds the slender story of its elderly narrator's difficult marriage in a mass of appreciative musings on the French novelist. The tone is autumnal, but restless, and the book is packed with interesting, if not always enlightening, historical details. "Perhaps love for a writer is the purest, the steadiest form of love," he writes before launching into a defense of Flaubert against a list of stupid, doctrinaire accusations ostensibly issuing from politically correct critics. This voice—aggrieved, complacently sensible, and nostalgic—runs through all of Barnes's fiction, whether he's dabbling in postmodernism (*Flaubert's Parrot* or *A History of the World in 10½ Chapters*) or following more conventional novelistic forms (*Before She Met Me* or *Staring at the Sun*). For all Barnes's Francophilia, it's a quintessentially postwar British voice, that of someone who feels he's the last person left who understands fair play, yet is nonetheless compelled to protest vainly the outrages of contemporary life.

Barnes's amiable, inventive, and learned ramblings through the attics of history have won him most of his readers. The best of these books, *A History of the World in 10½ Chapters*, reads more like a collection of linked stories, beginning with a woodworm's sardonic account of its sojourn on Noah's Ark and of the failings of its captain. Onboard, bickering, opportunism, and scheming prevail; the unicorn gets casseroled by the envious, petty humans; and the whole enterprise is driven by terror rather than faith: "Noah . . . was a God-fearing man; and given the nature of God, that was probably the safest line to take." This kind of dry, debunking humor is Barnes at his best. He also writes compellingly about the extremities of political compromise and cruelty in parts of *History*, *The Porcupine*, and the short story collection *Cross Channel*—perhaps because these scenarios confirm his dim view of humanity.

In the middle range, though—in his coming-of-age novel *Metroland* and in various early novels of adultery (unfaithful wives are a recurring motif)—Barnes's diffidence makes for pleasant but unmemorable fiction. In these books, he writes as if he could just as easily be doing anything else, and it's hard not to read them with the same lack of conviction. Barnes is an emotionally guarded writer, and when he does choose to rhapsodize (the "half chapter" paean to love in *History*), the results are more sentimental than impassioned.

Besides penning the hard-boiled detective novels in the *Duffy* series under the name Dan Kavanagh, Barnes contributes lucid and highly satisfying "Letters from London" essays to *The New Yorker*, some of which have been collected in a book of the same title.

See Also: Part of a crowd of young British writers taken up in the 1980s by Granta editor Bill Buford (now The New Yorker's fiction editor), Barnes sometimes shows the influence of his onetime friend, Martin Amis; however, he lacks Amis's savage energy. Admirers of Flaubert's Parrot should enjoy Alain de Botton's How Proust Can Save Your Life, and David Lodge writes equally enjoyable, if gentler, British social satire.

—*Laura Miller*

Barth, John
1930–
b. Dorchester County, Maryland

FICTION: The Floating Opera (1956), **The End of the Road** (1958), **The Sot-Weed Factor** (1960), Giles, Goat-Boy; or The Revised New Syllabus (1966), Lost in the Funhouse: Fiction for Print, Tape, Live Voice (stories, 1968), *Chimera (1972), LETTERS (1979), Sabbatical: A Romance (1982), **The Tidewater Tales: A Novel** (1987), The Last Voyage of Somebody the Sailor (1991), Once Upon a Time: A Floating Opera (1994), On with the Story (stories, 1996)

NONFICTION: The Literature of Exhaustion, and the Literature of Replenishment (1982), The Friday Book: Essays and Other Nonfiction (1984), Don't Count on It: A Note on the Number of the 1001 Nights (1984), Further Fridays: Essays, Lectures, and Other Nonfiction 1984–1994 (1995)

As the doyen of "postmodern" novelists in America, John Barth has typically enjoyed two discrete followings. The first are academics, who have found in Barth's playful, wildly-convoluted fictions a permanent gold mine for analysis and criticism. The second are college students, who identify romantically with Barth's existential heroes and his vision of the world as a random, madcap, menacing place, where nothing is what it seems to be and truth is just a construct, a fiction in itself. There are no answers to anything in the Barthian universe, and no solace beyond stories, legends, and narrative invention.

"Intellectual and spiritual disorientation is the family disease of all my main characters," Barth has said. "We tell stories and listen to them because we live stories and live in them. Narrative equals language equals life: to cease to narrate . . . is to die." As a writer, Barth's model and muse is Scheherazade, of the *Thousand and One Arabian Nights*, who spun stories for the sultan every evening to escape execution. Generally, Barth's novels are huge, labyrinthine affairs, shot through with comedy, fantasy, ribaldry, wordplay, allegory, literary allusion, and structural culs-de-sac. Just when you think you've grasped Barth's point, rest assured—you haven't. There is always something else behind the door. Barth undercuts himself at every turn, tells you straight out that he can't be trusted, and begs you only to enjoy the ride—the "funhouse," as he constructs it fresh from book to book.

Barth grew up in the Tidewater region of Maryland, and most if not all of his novels are set there. He was one of a set of fraternal twins, and became a writer in adulthood, he thinks, "in part because I no longer had my twin to be wordless with"—hence his fascination with the mechanics of language. His first three novels, all of them comedies "dealing with the problem of nihilism," were conceived as a piece and written in quick succession. Todd Andrews, the hero of *The Floating Opera*, recognizes that nothing has meaning and decides to commit suicide, only to realize before the deed is done that his vision of reality is neither more nor less significant than anyone else's, and that suicide is just as meaningless as staying alive. The theme is repeated in *The End of the Road*, with the exception that the hero's object lesson is far more terrible and utterly closed to humor. And in *The Sot-Weed Factor*, written in the style of an eighteenth-century hero quest, innocence is lost completely when Ebenezer Cooke, first Poet Laureate of Maryland, is subjected to every indignity the nascent colony and its inhabitants can heap upon him.

Giles, Goat Boy, *Lost in the Funhouse*, and *Chimera*, for which Barth won the National Book Award in 1973, are all difficult, willfully self-conscious fictions that seek to extend the traditional boundaries of the novel, a goal Barth set for himself in his famous 1967 essay, "The Literature of Exhaustion." More recently, Barth has doubled back, spewing out "prefaces," "postscripts," mock treatises, and windy explanations for all his books to date. The unreadable *LETTERS* finds characters from Barth's earlier novels corresponding with him in the hope of justifying themselves. *Sabbatical*, *The Tidewater Tales*, and *The Last Voyage of Somebody the Sailor* are all set in boats on Chesapeake Bay, where fables of life, love, death, sex, fiction, meaning, and the lack of it are traded back and forth among characters old and new. *The Tidewater Tales* is the best in this series, or at least the best contained; readers can be forgiven for tiring of the game by the time they've finished all three. A collection of autobiographical pieces, as illusory and open-ended as any of Barth's fiction, appeared in 1994 as *Once Upon a Time: A Floating Opera*, bringing Barth's work full circle and further blurring whatever "truth" the reader can perceive. As always, Barth is obsessed with narration, myths, and the ultimate futility of words.

For many years, Barth has taught at Johns Hopkins University in Baltimore, where he is currently professor emeritus in the Writing Seminars. He remains the academic's dream novelist, his work arbitrarily challenging in structure and form but redeemed by inventiveness, huge erudition, humor, and an unquenchable sense of adventure.

35

See Also: Barth accepts the postmodernist label while remaining sui generis, *linked at least in flights of fancy to Vladimir Nabokov, Jorge Luis Borges, Saul Bellow, and Thomas Pynchon.*

—*Peter Kurth*

Barthelme, Donald
1931–1989
b. Philadelphia, Pennsylvania

FICTION: Come Back, Dr. Caligari (stories, 1964), **Snow White** (1967), Unspeakable Practices, Unnatural Acts (stories, 1968), City Life (stories, 1970), Sadness (stories, 1972), Guilty Pleasures (satires, 1974), **The Dead Father** (1975), Amateurs (stories, 1976), Great Days (stories, 1979), *Sixty Stories (1981), Overnight to Many Distant Cities (stories, 1983), Paradise (1986), Sam's Bar (1987), **Forty Stories** (1987), The King (1990)

NONFICTION: The Teachings of Don B.: Satires, Parodies, Fables, Illustrated Stories and Plays (1992), Not-Knowing: The Essays and Interviews of Donald Barthelme (1997)

Donald Barthelme's fiction went out of style after such writers as Raymond Carver and Ann Beattie reinvented the classic realist short story, and these days it's hard to believe that work so downright bent appeared regularly in *The New Yorker*. If you cross-bred Kafka and Ronald Firbank, or Borges and S. J. Perelman, you'd get something like Barthelme, but you'd still miss that sexiness, that scattershot omniscience—a Barthelme piece might allude to Goethe or ZZ Top, Piaget, or Sergeant Preston of the Yukon—and those glimpses of a sad, kind heart behind all the high-spirited virtuosity.

Barthelme was at least as smart about his own work as any critic, and a lot lighter on his feet. Here and there in his fiction he posted notices about its esthetic, such as his *Bartlett's*-ready formulation "Fragments are the only form I trust." But these remarks never smell of capital-T Theory, arty mystification or coldly "metafictional" self-involvement. Rather, they're winks and nods to readers he obviously considers as smart as he is; much of the pleasure of reading Barthelme is how welcome he makes you feel while subjecting you to a vertiginously high level of entertainment. Here's an exchange from his story "The Genius": "Q: What do you consider the most important tool of genius today? A: Rubber cement." It takes a scratch of the head, but then you get it. Rubber cement: collage. Collage: the twentieth century's defining artistic procedure, from such high-modernist cut-and-paste jobs as "The Waste Land" (to which Barthelme alluded repeatedly) to loop-and-sample-based hip-hop music.

Barthelme began publishing actual collages—of nineteenth-century engravings accompanied by enigmatic texts—in his third short story collection, *City Life*, but he also created much of his fiction by an analogous process of appropriation and juxtaposition.

His 1964 story "The Joker's Greatest Triumph" grafts a passage from Mark Schorer's biography of Sinclair Lewis onto a deliciously moronic plot from a Batman comic book. His 1967 novel *Snow White* transplants the Perrault/Disney fairy tale to the East Village and retells it as a menage à huit. In his posthumously published novella, *The King*, characters from Arthurian legend fight World War II. Such juxtapositions and transpositions suggest a culture and a collective consciousness where, as a character says in "The Piano Player," "everything is in flitters." This prospect gave old-time modernists the willies, but for Barthelme a decentered cosmos occasioned esthetic exhilaration, not spiritual exhaustion. The language of his fictional fever dreams features headsnapping shifts of diction and a word hoard brimful of slang, jargon, technical terms—and such linguistic oddments and discards as "flitters."

Barthelme's density (and his inability to take seriously the convention of plot) make his novels feel pathless, yet page by page each is a delight. The best may be *The Dead Father*, in which a talking statue-carcass (part Jehovah, part Lear, part Donald Barthelme) is hauled, protesting, across the countryside to its grave. *Snow White* is a grab bag of small wonders, and the relatively conventional *Paradise*, an almost-realist account of a Manhattan menage à quatre, has its funny (and tender, and sexy, and sad) moments. His *New Yorker* "casuals" and "Talk of the Town" pieces were the best such work since White and Thurber; many have been posthumously collected in *The Teachings of Don B.* Still, Barthelme's perfectly-pitched, beautifully-shaped stories will last the longest: "Critique de la Vie Quotidienne," "The Sandman," "I Bought a Little City," "The Death of Edward Lear," and a couple of dozen more drop-dead masterworks. Those who can't find the original collections should start with *Sixty Stories*. But *Forty Stories* isn't just leftovers: "Some of Us Had Been Threatening Our Friend Colby" is worth the price by itself.

See Also: Barthelme's often lumped with John Barth and Robert Coover, but he's really not much like either of them or anybody else. Fans of Gen-X word-jocks like Mark Leyner might enjoy Barthelme, but so might readers who appreciate pared-down, exquisitely-shaped stories like those of Amy Hempel or the early Raymond Carver.

—*David Gates*   37

Bass, Rick

1958–
b. Fort Worth, Texas

FICTION: **The Watch* (stories, 1989), **Platte River** (novellas, 1994), **In the Loyal Mountains** (stories, 1995), The Sky, the Stars, the Wilderness: Novellas (1997), **Where the Sea Used to Be** (1998), Fiber (1998)

NONFICTION: The Deer Pasture (1985), Wild to the Heart (1987), Oil Notes (1989), Winter: Notes from Montana (1991), The Ninemile Wolves: An Essay (1992), The Lost Grizzlies: A Search for Survivors (1995), The Book of Yaak (1996), Brown Dog of the Yaak: Essays on Art and Activism (1999)

Rick Bass's dispatches arrive every year or so from the Yaak Valley, a remote Montana wilderness. Whether fiction or literary eco-journalism, they're imbued with a transcendent love of the earth and the belief that its miraculous flora and fauna are endangered by human rapaciousness.

Although Bass is a respected nature writer whose articles often appear in *Sierra* and *Audubon*, his reputation rests primarily on his fiction. Ostensibly set in the American South or West, these books actually transpire in a mysterious netherworld just beyond the reach of language, where natural science fuses with legend. The result is just short of magic realism. Still, rock-solid nature remains the primal, ineffable core of Bass's moral universe. His characters reveal what they're made of in relation to the land and its creatures.

The stories of *The Watch*, Bass's fiction debut, often pit outdoorsmen against nature or each other in elemental confrontations. This may seem superficially akin to the machismo of Thomas McGuane, Barry Hannah, and Jim Harrison, who write of wild boys not eager to grow up, but closer inspection of this book and *In the Loyal Mountains* reveals a fascination with ritualistic combat as the path to maturation, not a flight from it. Two of the novellas in *Platte River* feel mythological, as though the gods of ancient Greece were playing out their destinies in contemporary America. One character is a giant able to tote a Volkswagen on his back. Others swim wintry, ice-choked rivers with the abandon of sea creatures.

In *Where the Sea Used to Be*, Bass's first novel, a manipulative oil billionaire dares a young geologist to find oil where he couldn't. Old Dudley is a force of nature himself—

the nasty, brutish side. In Bass's version of a love story, the voluptuous Montana hills are as much a love object as the boss's eco-conscious daughter. Unaccustomed to the novel's long stretch, Bass nonetheless proves himself, and his one-of-a-kind prose retains its extraordinary beauty.

See Also: Probably the only trained petroleum geologist among American fiction writers, Bass has said he was first inspired to write fiction after reading Jim Harrison's Legends of the Fall. *That novella collection and later Harrison novels like* Dalva *and its sequel,* The Road Home, *speak in a language similar to Bass's—grounded in the outdoors and aspiring to neo-Hemingwayesque eloquence.*

—Dan Cryer

Bausch, Richard
1945–
b. Fort Benning, Georgia

FICTION: Real Presence (1980), Take Me Back (1981), The Last Good Time (1984), **Spirits, and Other Stories** (1987), Mr. Field's Daughter (1989), The Fireman's Wife and Other Stories (1990), Violence (1992), *****Rebel Powers** (1993), Rare and Endangered Species (stories, 1994), Good Evening Mr. and Mrs. America and All the Ships at Sea (1996), The Selected Stories of Richard Baush (1996), **In the Night Season** (1998), **Someone to Watch Over Me** (1999)

A devoted author of domestic fiction, Richard Bausch writes with all the lonely nostalgia and the closed-circuit inevitability of a midnight walk around a suburban block, suggesting a crisis evaded and the need for a breath of fresh air. Bausch's are broken homes full of housebroken characters. Doting single parents and mannered youths find they have overcompensated for their missing spouses and underprepared for the perverse world outside. The homes themselves are regularly broken and entered; the families' thresholds are crossed. A survey of Bausch's work finds a litany of imposters ruining the established yet fragile intimacies indoors: older, objectionable fiances and in-laws, criminal acquaintances, needy neighbors, repressed abuse, and runaway alcoholism.

Bausch's forte is for the frailty of familial intimacies. His disruptive charlatans, on the other hand, are often simplified, overexplained and unbelievable, and their influence predictable. Late in *The Last Good Time*, a distant relative of the protagonist's seductress shows up to report that she is a pathological fraud and our sweet old hero has been had. Such abrupt resolutions are typical of his early novels. Likewise, in *Violence*, the story of a man (out for a walk) mistakenly credited with saving lives in a 7–11 holdup and burdened afterward by destructive tendencies, Bausch sacrifices character development for a hasty resolution (reminiscent of Hitchcock's *Marnie*), in which memories of child abuse are recovered.

As a short story writer, though, Bausch is more a friend of irresolution. In the title story from his recent collection *Somebody to Watch Over Me*, we are forced to decide who is the right (or less wrong) participant in an especially uncomfortable dinner argument, and Bausch is (graciously) no help. One of the combatants is left outside the off-putting four-star restaurant she has fled, sitting in the passenger seat of their car, "assuming the look of someone to whom an apology is due." The work in his first collection *Spirits and Other Stories* (much of which is collected in the Modern Library's *Selected Stories of Richard Bausch*) is stronger still, if less risky. Written with perfect pitch, "Ancient History," depicts an adolescent's insular relationship with his widowed mother, the very shame of which is what's ultimately most suggestive.

Bausch is at his best in his characteristic laments for lost or pride-prohibited parent-child love. It is what fuels *Rebel Powers*, his finest novel. In this coming-of-age story, a journeyed army brat adjusts to yet another hometown—one where his court-martialed father has been imprisoned—and to sharing cramped quarters with his mother's love interest. The family dynamics here have a mathematical elegance; the true Bausch hero is always tempted to solve for X and invariably cannot, so removed are his thoughts from expression, so stern and clipped is the author's dialogue. Rarely in literature can the exchange "Are you listening, son? Yes, sir," carry such freight.

See Also: It has been observed that Bausch shares a regional terrain (the mid-Atlantic states) with Anne Tyler, and an emotional terrain with Tobias Wolff. But, for quiet, contemporary short fiction about men and women, or parents and children, in their mutual abyss, try Charles Baxter.

—Brian Blanchfield

Beattie, Ann
1947–
b. Washington, DC

FICTION: Distortions (stories, 1976), Chilly Scenes of Winter (1976), Secrets and Surprises (stories, 1978), Falling in Place (1980), **The Burning House** (stories, 1982), Love Always (1985), **Where You'll Find Me, and Other Stories** (1986), Picturing Will (1989), What Was Mine (1991), **Another You** (1995), **My Life, Starring Dara Falcon** (1997), *Park City: New and Selected Stories** (1998)

In the mid-1970s, while still in her twenties, Ann Beattie became an unlikely successor to the Three Johns (first O'Hara, then Cheever, then Updike) as the quintessential *New Yorker* short-story writer. A piece of snarky 1970s apocrypha held that *The New Yorker* edited its short fiction by cutting the last page of the manuscript. Beattie's elliptical stories flummoxed some readers, but she was famously cited as a herald of What It's Like Out There—"there" being among the disillusioned men and women of the American upper-middle class, struggling with lost dreams of youth and residing in the magazine's geographical subscriber base.

Beattie's characters look back with bewilderment on the unfulfilled promise of the 1960s (as O'Hara's characters did with the 1920s, as Cheever's did with the late 1930s, and as Updike's did with the 1950s). The alcohol in the work of the Johns was often supplanted in Beattie's stories by marijuana. Infidelities were as rampant, but divorce—once a dark possibility, then, in Updike, a grudging last resort—was everywhere. As Lorrie Moore has astutely said, Beattie was the first writer for whom divorce and remarriage were a given, deployed without explanation. Beattie may also have been the first mainstream straight writer for whom gay characters were a similar given.

She made her hardcover debut with the simultaneous publication in 1976 of a collection of stories, *Distortions*, and a novel, *Chilly Scenes of Winter*. The novel is the story of a twenty-seven-year-old man heartbroken to the point of stasis because his girlfriend went back to her husband. Pop culture references abound (not knowing who Janis Joplin is defines one character; being aghast at that lack of knowledge defines an-

41

NAVEL-GAZING RAISED TO AN ART *by Ann Beattie*

Reader's Block by David Markson
The character Reader contemplates writing a novel out of the flotsam and jetsam (provided) of civilization's so-called progress, to which Reader's own life seems to have moved in counterpoint. No one but Beckett can be quite as sad and funny at the same time as Markson can. It's nearly an allegory, yet the shifting sands of time have left no clear model for its point of departure.

Out of Sheer Rage by Geoff Dyer
Dyer's tongue-in-cheek, heart-on-sleeve, disingenuously ingenuous account of trying and failing to write a biography of D. H. Lawrence really hit—for this procrastinator—where it hurt, persuading me that the unexamined life might well be the best thing one could hope for. This takes self-consciousness to a new level. A brilliant tour-de-force of life as a fishbowl.

The Magician's Wife by Brian Moore
In the spirit of *Rosencrantz and Guildenstern Are Dead*—which has influenced far more contemporary American fiction than critics seem to realize—Moore presents the dawning consciousness of a young woman imagining she might be set free in conjunction with the story of her resolute magician husband, who has been pressed into the service of a cause he barely understands. The characters strain to understand, but the undertow of history is too great. The book raises interesting questions about how far one does, or does not, get in the process of self-reflection.

All Around Atlantis by Deborah Eisenberg
Among the most brilliant (and sneaky) of American short-story writers, Eisenberg creates characters who yearn to reach another level of consciousness, but who seem to doomed to implode. The story "Mermaids," and what it says about childhood, and what it says even about television screens, is particularly amazing. She gets the claustrophobia, and the self-consciousness, of adolescence all too perfectly.

Midair by Frank Conroy
The (forgive me) recovered memory of the title story is a true dazzler. But Conroy lets the reader in on the secret from the beginning, so the tension in the story has to do with our perspective on what the character himself does not have a perspective on. It's sad and funny and a great illustration of what Flannery O'Connor said was necessary: having something function on a literal, then a symbolic level. This elevator does.

other). Everywhere, characters face how much happier they'd be if they hadn't had their consciousness raised in the '60s—a sentiment Beattie manages both to share and mock.

It's on Beattie's stories, though, that her reputation rests—apparently slice-of-life stories whose tight structure slowly reveals itself. There's really no such thing as a slice-of-life story, of course, because, in presenting it, a writer is presenting this slice of this life. The randomness is merely ostensible, a methodology at the heart of such brilliant Beattie stories as "The Cinderella Waltz," "The Weekend," "Greenwich Time," or (her masterpiece) "The Burning House."

In the 1980s, Beattie fell slightly out of fashion—ultimately a blessing. She seemed to concentrate more on her novels than her stories, yet her stories in that period got stranger and richer. No longer marketed as an oracle, Beattie took the kind of chances necessary for an artist to evolve. Chances like that won't always succeed, but having taken them, Beattie developed as a writer toward her excellent recent novels, *Another You* and *My Life, Starring Dara Falcon*.

In 1998, Beattie published *Park City: New and Selected Stories*. Though only fifty, she'd been publishing stories for a quarter-century. Reading the earliest ones now is to receive dispatches from the '70s, as perfectly of their time and as timeless as Joni Mitchell's *Blue* or the mid-career films of Jill Clayburgh.

See Also: Naturally, the Three Johns give you a sense of the tradition into which Beattie arrived, and which, in some ways, she toppled. If there's any such thing as "a New Yorker *writer" today, she's probably a woman. While Alice Munro and Annie Proulx could hardly have a more different aesthetic than Beattie, the* New Yorker-*ist of them all, Lorrie Moore, writes like Beattie's brainy, funnier little sister.*

—*Mark Winegardner*

Begley, Louis
1933–
b. Stryj, Poland

FICTION: Wartime Lies (1991), **The Man Who Was Late** (1992), As Max Saw It (1994), ***About Schmidt** (1996), Mistler's Exit (1998)

Because Louis Begley is a lawyer and writes novels about old men and old money, reviewers lump him with Louis Auchincloss. In fact, if Auchincloss is our diminished Edith Wharton, Begley is in certain ways our James: a psychological (not a sociological) novelist, the outlines of whose novels are irregular, his plots full of uncanny coincidence and symbols, unreliable points of view, and ornate, almost epistolary dialogue. Unlike

James, Begley has a genius for sex. He is perhaps the only writer who can still make a sexual encounter the tragic climax of a novel; his sex scenes reveal more character, need, and loneliness and (for that reason) are sexier and more troubling than anybody else's I know.

Wartime Lies, Begley's autobiographical first novel, published when he was fifty-seven, is the story of a little Polish-Jewish boy who hides from the Nazis, pretending to be a gentile. He never recovers his integrity. As an old man, the refugee finds himself drawn to a bitter poem by Catullus: "The man with the sad eyes believes he has been changed inside forever," Begley writes, "like a beaten dog . . . He has no good deeds to look back upon. Still, it is better to say the poem over and over. He will not howl over his own despair."

Clammed-up despair and duplicity haunt Begley's protagonists, but his subsequent novels are set among jet-setters and captains of industry. All but one of Begley's anti-heroes are born into the WASP establishment. The greatest of them, Albert Schmidt, is an anti-Semite horrified by his daughter's impending marriage to a Jew, Schmidt's own protégé and a junior partner in his law firm. The dangerously, beautifully intimate portrait of a self-deluded man, *About Schmidt* may be Begley's most perfect novel, but each of the five will have readers who love it best. My personal favorite is *The Man Who Was Late*, which harnesses Begley's sensuality and (half-absurd, and always self-suspecting) snobbery to a mechanical, sternly romantic plot, which is unfolded with semi-comic stiffness through old letters and diary entries: A businessman kills himself after throwing away the love of his life. But I also love *Mistler's Exit*, a sort of *Death in Venice* parody, for the very opposite reason: The book meanders toward its hero's death with the glamorous, erotically charged randomness of an Antonioni film.

See Also: Jerzy Kosinski (a closer cousin than Louis Auchincloss). Great precursors include Vladimir Nabokov, Ford Madox Ford, and the recently translated novels of Pierre-Jean Jouve (naturally, Begley characters read Jouve in the original).

—Lorin Stein

44

Bell, Madison Smartt
1957–
b. Nashville, Tennessee

FICTION: The Washington Square Ensemble (1983), **Waiting for the End of the World** (1985), Straight Cut (1986), *****The Year of Silence** (1987), Zero db (stories, 1987), **Sol-**

dier's Joy (1989), Barking Man and Other Stories (1990), Doctor Sleep (1991), Save Me, Joe Louis (1993), All Souls' Rising (1995), Ten Indians (1996)

NONFICTION: Narrative Design: A Writer's Guide to Structure (1997)

If there's a literary award for sticking your neck out, here's a nomination. Madison Smartt Bell has always tried to do the difficult—not to say crazy—thing. Without being cultish or remotely cynical, he makes novels out of racial conflicts that edge into chaos and even extreme violence. More to the point, Bell insists on making up characters no white guy from Tennessee could possibly have seen from the inside. You've got your choice of mad bombers underneath New York, explosively rebellious Haitian slaves, thugs and drug dealers in an array of ethnic derivations, an ascetic banjo virtuoso, a beloved woman dying from an overdose of pills. These characters embrace delirium with sweet familiarity, which makes for some sparkling moments of reading. If delirium's the link, it's definitely a link this writer knows something about.

The Washington Square Ensemble, about a quartet of slap-happy drug dealers, is shot through with levity that even grim death can't destroy. Subsequently, *Waiting for the End of the World* contains outlandish subplots and a surprise ending that doesn't quite work but is positively uplifting in its audacity. After that, *The Year of Silence* is full of descriptive tenderness. One character practices for his debut at Carnegie Hall on a piano made from a board with the black notes painted on with shoe polish. He has a roommate in love with Marian, the central figure in the book, whose death from a cocktail of drugs and self-imposed exile is powerfully rendered and genuinely sad.

Odd, then, that the pure pleasure of his earliest novels seems to have been an element Bell felt he needed to contain. He is sharp enough to recognize that such free-floating elements of pity and surprise can be harnessed, but a lamentable part of his artistic-development seems to have been that in tying these down he's made his struggle between good and evil a dutiful undertaking and consequently a pain. *All Souls' Rising*, which made Bell a finalist for a National Book Award, is a fantastically detailed account of the slave revolt that overthrew French planters in eighteenth-century Haiti. Despite the grue-some vignettes nestled within its accurate and informative picture of strife, you may have to flog yourself to make it to the end. Bell's latest, *Ten Indians*, about a white guy who starts a Tae Kwon Do studio in Baltimore and winds up teaching members of opposing gangs how to fight, is even more sparsely sprinkled with rewards.

What this long chain of work has come down to, for the time being, is that a highly intelligent novelist is grappling vigorously with racism. This is good, but it's too reduc-tive to pass for fiction and for art. Bell's portrayal of black/white tensions is beginning to serve the reality of the conflict—the shape and solidity of the wall—better than it does

45

the agenda of either side. At forty-two, he's got a huge future. The big connection, the one he knows is there, waits to be made.

See Also: Jujitsu for Christ, *a little-known gem by science fiction writer Jack Butler, that combines acute social conscience with an elastic narrative style. Rafi Zabor's* The Bear Comes Home *treats music as if it were a living entity, a character. While bluegrass frees the hero in Bell's* Soldier's Joy, *however, Zabor's protagonist is liberated by jazz.*

—Sally Eckhoff

Bellow, Saul
1915–
b. Montreal, Quebec

FICTION: Dangling Man (1944), **The Victim** (1947), The Adventures of Augie March (1953), **Seize the Day* (novella, stories and a play, 1956), Henderson the Rain King (1959), Herzog (1964), Mosby's Memoirs (stories, 1968), **Mr. Sammler's Planet** (1970), **Humboldt's Gift** (1975), The Dean's December (1982), Him With His Foot in His Mouth and Other Stories (1984), More Die of Heartbreak (1987), A Theft (novella, 1989), The Bellarosa Connection (novella, 1989), Something to Remember Me By (novellas, 1991), The Actual (1997), Ravelstein (2000)

NONFICTION: To Jerusalem and Back: A Personal Account (memoir, 1976), It All Adds Up (essays, 1994)

Born in a Jewish slum in Montreal, raised from the age of nine in Chicago, Saul Bellow is widely considered the greatest post-War American novelist, and he has won the biggest prizes, including the Nobel. Asked recently what part of his life he regretted, he told an interviewer "I gave a lot of time to women and if I had my time again I don't think I would do it that way . . . I married several times with my ends in view and I didn't reckon on the ends of the wives. Then I found myself being carried out of my depth."

I quote this because it is so Bellow, it could have come out of a Bellow novel. (In fact it did—Bellow is quoting almost verbatim from *More Die of Heartbreak.*) That combination of self-knowledge and fake innocence is the hallmark of his heroes, all recognizable versions of himself: overeducated bulls stumbling through the china shops of love,

marriage, fatherhood, celebrity, bohemia, and academe. On the way they ruminate thickly on the eternal verities and the crimes of the twentieth century, following each erection like a signal from some transcendental daemon. They are boring, infuriating monsters of self-absorption and have flattered several generations of like-minded introspective men (including the members of the Nobel Committee), but they have nothing to do with Bellow's greatness.

Bellow's chief glory—the glory of most great novelists—is that his characters have wandered off the page and into the world, in Bellow's case, *en masse*. People who like Bellow like to compare him to Dickens, but Dickens left us a few epitomized individuals (Skimpole, Micawber, Fagin and company), while Bellow has left us an army of loosely assembled parts: eyes like this, nape like that, insteps reminiscent of something else, a nose "originally fine but distorted by restless movement." Even Bellow's best-dressed characters give an impression of skewed wigs and ill-fitting suits. They run around generating plots, on the slenderest of motives, with impersonal, centrifugal intensity. Think of the Beastie Boys in the "Sabotage" video; think of early Almodovar or John Waters, or even late Warhol: These are Bellow's cinematic equivalents. Bellow's women, short or tall, are marvelous, larger-than-life wet dreams: earthy, intelligent, put together or falling apart, in either case spilling out of their clothes, at the mercy of their own sexuality. The men (all but the heroes) are full of scams. That's what exports: this WPA-mural panorama of appetites not quite in check.

Bellow's major novels fall into several categories. There's the apprentice work: *Dangling Man*, a *Notes from Underground* rewritten for wartime bohemians (with the memorably bad last line "Long live regimentation"), and *The Victim*, Bellow's first lasting work, the uncanny tale of a struggling, upwardly mobile Jew hounded by a ruined member of the Establishment.

Then come the three longer novels on which Bellow's reputation rests. A picaresque overlaid with pseudo-Emersonian solemnity, *The Adventures of Augie March* follows its hero's rise from Chicago urchin, during the Depression, to footloose European playboy after the War. Here Bellow busts out that weird prose of his, not yet under control ("There's the burning of an atom. Wild northern forests can go like so many punk sticks. Where's the competitor fire kindling, and what will its strength be? And another thing is that while for the sake of another vigor is lacking, for the sake of the taste of egg in one's mouth there's all-out effort, and that's how love is lavished," etc.). He refines this slangy translationese in *Henderson the Rain King*—a strong, botched, modern-day *Rasselas* set in an MGM-style Africa—and *Herzog*, which follows the romantic entanglements of a cuckolded Romantic scholar at work on his magnum opus. None of these novels has aged gracefully, and although Bellow's later two Big Novels, *Humboldt's Gift* (a wonderfully screwy fictionalization of Bellow's troubled friendship with the poet Delmore Schwartz) and *More Die of Heartbreak* (about the romantic travails of a hapless botanist) are funnier books, none approaches the passion of *The Victim* or Bellow's masterpieces: *Seize the Day* and *Mr. Sammler's Planet*.

You can't read *Seize the Day* without awe and regret; Bellow has never stretched half so far as he did in this tiny slice of life. Having failed as a movie actor, salesman, and husband, Tommy Wilhelm—the only vulnerable (or inarticulate) hero Bellow has ever managed to write—finds himself, in his mid-forties, living in the same hotel as his father on the Upper West Side, broke, popping sedatives, confiding in a shady old neighbor who persuades him to invest his last few hundred dollars in the stock market. Alone among Bellow heroes, who spend most of their time dodging love, Tommy yearns for connection—with his dead mother, with his father, with a new wife, with his kids in Connecticut. Tommy makes Bellow's existential questers look like a bunch of jerks.

So, in his own way, does Arthur Sammler, hero of Bellow's most perverse, sophisticated novel, *Mr. Sammler's Planet*. An elderly, widowed survivor of the Nazis—and, before the war, a member of the Bloomsbury circle—Sammler is (as everyone in the book keeps pointing out) a remnant of sanity and culture in a world gone mad: again the Upper West Side, this time the late 1960s. Bellow subjects Sammler to various barbarities: invited to lecture at Columbia on "the British Scene in the Thirties," he's jeered off the stage (" 'Why do you listen to this effete old shit? What has he got to tell you? His balls are dry. He's dead. He can't come' "); his younger relatives burden him with their empty sexual intrigues and shrink-sponsored brattiness; in the novel's greatest scene, a handsome black pickpocket corners Sammler and reveals his big dick.

Here, as in *The Victim*, Bellow's precursor is Kafka: every minor character acts out the desires and terrors of the guilty hero, who keeps insisting that these specters have nothing to do with him. Some readers have charged the book with racism, which is understandable (Sammler dismisses the sexual revolution as a quest for "niggerhood") but misses the point. *Mr. Sammler's Planet* is about blackness as fantasy, whiteness as the badge of the solipsist. Solipsism, of course, is the general condition and limitation of Bellow's novels. And while we suffer that limitation less gladly than readers did at mid-century, Bellow bodies forth our lunacy and lack of connection as nobody else has done.

See Also: Bellow's nearest rival in style and subject, Bernard Malamud, in his later short stories devotes an even greater prose genius to grasping the artistic dilemmas of modernity. Two notable (very different) younger writers have claimed Bellow for their master: Martin Amis, whose doppelgängers owe a clear debt to The Victim, *and John Clayton, whose little-known masterpiece,* Radiance, *adapts Bellow's rhythms and non-naturalistic dialogue to a more skeptical quest for* menschlichkeit.

—*Lorin Stein*

Berger, John
1926–
b. London, England

FICTION: A Painter of Our Time (1958), The Foot of Clive (1962), Corker's Freedom (1964), G. (1972), **Pig Earth** (1979), *Once in Europa (1987), **Lilac and Flag: An Old Wives' Tale of a City** (1990), **To the Wedding** (1995), King (1999)

NONFICTION: Permanent Red: Essays in Seeing (in US, Toward Reality, 1962), The Success and Failure of Picasso (1965), A Fortunate Man: The Story of a Country Doctor (with photographer Jean Mohr, 1967), Art and Revolution: Ernst Neizvestny and the Role of the Artist in the U.S.S.R. (1969), The Moment of Cubism, and Other Essays (1969), The Look of Things (essays, 1972), Ways of Seeing (1972), A Seventh Man: A Book of Images and Words about the Experience of Migrant Workers in Europe (with photographs by Mohr, 1975), About Looking (essays, 1980), Another Way of Telling (with photographs by Mohr and F. Maspero, 1982), And Our Faces, My Heart, Brief as Photos (1984), The Sense of Sight: Writings (essays, 1985), Keeping a Rendezvous (essays, 1991), **Photocopies** (1996), Pages of the Wound: Poems, Drawings, Photographs, 1956–96 (1996)

49

"I work by the light of my senses," John Berger once explained. Like his muse, the German critic Walter Benjamin, he's a dazzling intellectual guided by a humane Marxist politics that never loses sight of the concrete, sensuous world. Benjamin believed that the material world could be brought to speech directly, bypassing the mediation of abstract language.

In his art criticism, screenplays, (*Jonah Who Will Be 25 in the Year 2000*, 1976), poetry, documentary nonfiction, and most expressively in his essays and fiction, Berger has

The **Salon.com** Reader's Guide to Contemporary Authors

taken up Benjamin's challenge. He writes like a Cubist, scrutinizing his subjects from different angles. All his writing is an intense act of seeing that tries to capture gestures, moments, objects, bodies, lives, without assuming any coherence of events or consistency of meaning. Sounds bristlingly postmodern, but Berger is not difficult. He's a generous writer; encircling his characters with thoughtfulness, empathy, and respect: the Cubist multi-perspective as a loose embrace.

Berger's fiction does not explain; he bears witness and describes as precisely as he can the "enigma" of lived experience. In his early novels, that sensuous precision works in fascinating tension with Brechtian "estrangement" techniques. The narrator, or "storyteller" as Berger prefers, frequently interrupts to prevent readers from succumbing to the illusion that they are looking through words at a coherent reality. As you might guess, these novels aren't fast reads. But Berger's passionate intelligence keeps them from ever sounding preciously "lit'ry."

His first novel, *A Painter of Our Time*, about a Hungarian artist and Communist exiled in London, is his most overtly political fiction. *Corker's Freedom*, about a middle-aged businessman's tragically foiled bid for freedom, focuses on evanescent sensations and thoughts. In *G.*, the 1972 Booker Prize-winning novel, Berger creates a twentieth-century Don Juan, whose single-minded devotion to the liberating power of sexual passion plays out against the gathering darkness of the first World War.

A collage of juxtaposed fragments, *G.* is brilliant but a bit fussily and self-consciously a "big book." The best place to begin reading Berger is with the *Into Their Labours* trilogy: *Pig Earth*, *Once in Europa*, and *Lilac and Flag*. He pares his language to limpid simplicity, and the storyteller/narrator who interrupts the stories is a more approachable, but also more mythically ancient, character. In these heartbreaking, beautiful vignettes and stories of peasant life giving way to capitalist economies and migrations from farms to factories, the narrating "witness" is an amalgam of old-woman village-gossip, Aesop, and Greek chorus. To prepare for them, Berger moved to a village in the French Alps in the early 1970s, where he has lived since.

To the Wedding is plainer-spoken yet. The "witness" is a blind Athenian street peddler who "hears" and mourns the story of Ninon, who contracts AIDS in a lovely, careless moment with a stranger; Gino, the man who wishes to marry her anyway; and the separate journeys of her father and his mother to the wedding.

Berger said the following in an essay called "The Hour of Poetry" (*Sense of Sight*): "the boon of language is not tenderness. All that it holds, it holds with exactitude and without pity . . . it has the potentiality of holding with words the totality of human experience . . . it is potentially the only human home, the only dwelling place that cannot be hostile." Berger the storyteller shows how that's done, with a simplicity that's the distilled essence of a sophisticated mind and imagination.

See Also: Bertolt Brecht's essays and plays; Walter Benjamin's Illuminations *and* Reflections, *essays and aphorisms on politics, books, history, fashion, photography, the "work of art"; W. G. Sebald's* The Emigrants, *a grave, beautiful novel-documentary of European emigrants, Bergeresque in its elegiac storytelling and the seamless slippage between realism and myth or fairy tale; and lastly, Don DeLillo—the foil, the complement, the yin to Berger's yang. DeLillo's fiction also concentrates on perception and also abjures theory, explanation, and moralism. But where Berger attempts "authentic," honest vision, DeLillo displays and dissects the inauthentic, fraudulent, media-driven depictions of modern, urban, global life as spin and image.*

—Brigitte Frase

Berger, Thomas
1924–
b. Cincinnati, Ohio

FICTION: Crazy in Berlin (1958), Reinhart in Love (1962), **Little Big Man** (1964), **Killing Time** (1967), **Vital Parts** (1970), Regiment of Women (1973), **Sneaky People** (1975), **Who Is Teddy Villanova?** (1977), Arthur Rex (1978), *Neighbors (1980), Reinhart's Women (1981), **The Feud** (1983), Granted Wishes (stories, 1984), Nowhere (1985), Being Invisible (1987), **The Houseguest** (1988), Changing the Past (1989), Orrie's Story (1990), **Meeting Evil** (1992), Robert Crews (1994), Suspects (1996), The Return of Little Big Man (1999)

What if there were a great American novelist with a vision so diverse, timeless and hilarious that literary culture mistook him for an irrelevant virtuoso? That's the fate of Thomas Berger, apparently. Though his popular and critical heyday was the '70s, when he was meaninglessly grouped with the "black humorists," Berger's focus expanded through the '80s. But by the end of that decade he'd mostly lost his audience and been taken for granted by critics, his image blurred by two film adaptations, one good (*Little Big Man*, faithfully Bergeresque but credited to the director and star), and one awful (*Neighbors*).

No summary can do justice to the extraordinarily various assignments Berger has given himself: to visit each genre in turn (Western: *Little Big Man*, Detective: *Who Is Teddy Villanova?*, Dystopia: *Regiment of Women*, Arthurian legend: *Arthur Rex*, etc); to span his career with an anti-Updikean series of novels featuring a lumpen protagonist at different life stages (the four Reinhart novels); to understand and demolish existentialist justifications for murder (*Killing Time, Meeting Evil*); and, whatever else, always to advance his lifelong exercise in deadpan eloquence. The fact that Berger is often painfully funny isn't incidental, but central to his accomplishment. Scenes in Berger's fiction never unfold logically, but instead are warped this way and that by the fleeting and paradoxical responses of his main characters who, though tormented by guilt and experience, remain yearning and gullible and oddly angelic.

Three of Berger's first five novels featured his hopeless alter ego, Reinhart. The books are brilliant, each encompassing a new aspect of American life, but typical of Berger, Reinhart seemed a different character each time out. The two non-Reinharts were *Little Big Man*, the encylopedic Western most usually acclaimed by readers unfamiliar with the author, and *Killing Time*, which was poorly received but now seems Berger's early masterpiece—Jim Thompson noir as done by an American Flaubert.

Neighbors, in 1980, was a watershed book (as well as a comic summit). There, Berger refined a theme of malice, guilt, and victimization that had been emergent in his work. This exploration produced dark masterworks in *The Houseguest* and *Meeting Evil*. *Houseguest* refracts the hostility of *Neighbors* through multiple viewpoints, culminating in that of a female character. Berger had too often previously denied his women the misanthropic, contradictory depths of his men.

Special mention should also be given to Berger's "small town" books—*Sneaky People* and *The Feud*. Without abandoning his trademark mordancy, these are perhaps Berger's tenderest books, and covertly autobiographical of his Cincinnati childhood. Elsewhere in his late career Berger is slight, and riskily droll—*Nowhere, Changing the Past, Robert Crews, Being Invisible*, and *Reinhart's Women* are best savored by initiates.

Berger's giddy program of writing a different book every time out, coupled with the curlicues of his style and his obsessional approach to character make him a sort of auteur within the space of his own career: No matter what genre or mode or scale the "studio" of his vast imagination dictates, the sensibility of the "director"—Berger's uniquely sweet-bitter vision of life—is unmistakable.

52

See Also: Two "lost" novelists, Mark Smith (The Death of the Detective, Doctor Blues) *and Zulfikar Ghose* (The Incredible Brazilian, Figures of Enchantment), *approach Berger's strange, galactically bemused tone. Nabokov, at his most American and humane—say* Pnin *and* Lolita—*might be another comparison. More recently, Jonathan Franzen's* Twenty-Seventh City, *with its faintly absurd Midwestern skullduggery and rich syntax, could be a point of contact with the great lonely island of Berger's work.*

—*Jonathan Lethem*

Berriault, Gina
1926–1999
b. Long Beach, California

FICTION: The Descent (1960), Conference of Victims (1962, republished as Afterwards, 1998), The Mistress and Other Stories (1965), The Son (1966), The Infinite Passion of Expectation: Twenty-five Stories (1982), **The Lights of Earth** (1984), *****Women in Their Beds: New and Selected Stories** (1996), Afterwards (1998)

When Gina Berriault's *Women in Their Beds* grabbed the 1996 National Book Critics Circle Award and the PEN/Faulkner Award for Short Fiction, no one was more surprised than the author herself. Berriault had been laboring in obscurity for forty years. "I've spent most of my life alone, at my table," she told National Public Radio. "It's something that I have got used to."

Loneliness is something Berriault's characters never get used to, though it's at the cold core of their lives. Read Berriault for her exquisite, distilled use of language and the San Francisco Bay Area settings where an emotional fog prevails. Just don't read her expecting warm dramatic resolutions: These are tales of separated souls, alone in rented rooms, after the failure of hope. So her novel *Conference of Victims* visits a family *after* a suicide—the real victims are those left to carry on. In *The Lights of Earth*, probably Berriault's finest novel, a writer suffers through a lover's departure and a neglected brother's death.

Berriault is at her best, however, in the short stories collected in *Women in Their Beds*. In "The Stone Boy," a farmboy accidentally shoots his brother—then goes pea-picking, an act whose seeming coldness makes him more of a pariah than the killing itself. In "Who Is It Can Tell Me Who I Am?," a cultivated librarian can't answer a homeless man's plea to help him understand a poem—a failure of generosity that denies the humanity in both men. The librarian, shut off from others, walks home at night through San Francisco's Tenderloin district, past sleeping street people, "the bundled and the unbundled to whom he gave a wide berth as he would to the dead, in fear and respect." Gina Berriault is not a cheerful read—the bleakness of her tales can be numbing—but she's an excellent cataloguer of an existence that can seem, in one character's words, "a warehouse of fathomless darkness."

See Also: Alice Munro's stories, warmer than Berriault's, share their closeness of observation and their emphasis on details rather than big dramas.

—Jennifer Howard

Bowman, David
1957–
b. Racine, Wisconsin

FICTION: *Let the Dog Drive (1992), **Bunny Modern** (1998)

David Bowman writes brazenly, without shame—the way a toddler runs in circles through the sprinkler, gleefully naked and free—about subjects that lesser, more timid writers wouldn't even broach on the analyst's couch. Yet he's remarkable specifically for the reason that he's *not* out to shock: It takes a certain kind of gentleheartedness to write a bestiality scene so lovely it could move you to tears, and Bowman's got the goods. His two noir-gone-haywire novels, *Let the Dog Drive* and *Bunny Modern*, are potent cocktails whirled at top speed through his deeply idiosyncratic Waring: Their ingredients include old Hollywood musicals, Chandleresque detective fiction, drugs that render their users fearless and feral, middle-aged housewives obsessed with Emily Dickinson, and a world in which electricity (and with it, humanity's ability to conceive) has disappeared. His books aren't easily categorized: *Let the Dog Drive* is part road novel, part love story, part descent into terror; *Bunny Modern* is a screwball romantic comedy crossed with Saturday-afternoon sci-fi. And while both books fall apart slightly at the climax—Bowman's plots tend to dissolve into hallucinatory slapstick violence—there's so much heart in them that it doesn't really matter. Amidst all the bullets, blood, and sliced tendons, there's also love, beautiful love, pattering down like shimmery acid rain. In *Let the Dog Drive*, he maps out a dog's brain with the precision of Galileo and the heart of Nabokov: "A brain the size of a walnut. If we could fly above it, it would resemble a map of the USA composed of six states: a Texas for eating, a California for fucking, a New York for the olfactory center, a Maine for shitting and pissing, a Rhode Island allowing him to fetch and shake hands, and finally an Alaska of love—love for the master or mistress." Bowman has unlocked the secret of writing fiction that's hard-boiled until, miraculously, it's tender.

See Also: Mark Leyner has a similarly furious, hallucinatory energy, and he's funny, but he hasn't got Bowman's heart. In fact, it's tempting to say "see also: the moons of Jupiter," since there's no writer quite like him.

—Stephanie Zacharek

54

FIVE CONTEMPORARY NOIR CLASSICS *By David Bowman*

You know what noir is. I do too. Noir is a gun and a bottle and a girl racing out of the city at midnight in a stolen sports car driven by a gambler wincing from a bullet hole in his left side, the wound bandaged by a money belt full of guilt, sex, and bad karma.

The Girl in the Plain Brown Wrapper by John D. MacDonald

MacDonald, the last literate and unself-conscious pulp writer, was the first to explore the noir possibilities of Florida. All the titles in his Travis McGee series are precious junk. In this one—part John Updike, part Jane Eyre—the lethal Florida beach bum/sexual healer attempts to rescue a housewife held captive in suburbia by her hubby's mind control drugs.

The Black Dahlia by James Ellroy

Ellroy indulges in every cliche of the genre (the two-fisted loner, the femme fatale, the twisted gunsel), but triumphantly reinvents each because he is convinced he is rebuilding noir from scratch. Hooray for delusion. In his best book, Ellroy fictionalizes the notorious true story of the murder of an L.A. whore (literally sliced in two) using the poor girl as a psychic stand-in for the novelist's own murdered mother.

Tapping the Source by Kem Nunn

Nunn created his own subgenre, surfer noir. His first and best novel concerns a young hayseed from the desert who travels to Huntington Beach to find his lost sister, last seen in the company of a psychotic surfer. Imagine Huck Finn hanging ten with a smoking gat in each fist.

Children of Light by Robert Stone

The most unloved child of all Stone's work (even editor Robert Gottlieb hated it), this novel contains the psychic framework of a good noir while simultaneously being the burn-out death of the genre (despite noble attempts at resurrection by Jonathan Lethem [*Gun With Occasional Music*] and Charlie Smith [*Chimney Rock*]). Stone dispenses with the crime elements offstage, and then wallows in drugs, suicide, madness, Oedipal failures, and Mexico—the traditional dumping ground for noir.

Blood Orchid: An Unnatural History of America by Charles Bowden

Bowden, part reporter/all poet, chronicles noir's transcendence from pulp fiction to real life in— guess where—Mexico. This one is about Mexican drug dealers (of course) and a pair of Sioux drifters and Prozac-influenced sexual despair.

Boyle, T. C.

1948–

b. Thomas John Boyle in Peekskill, New York

FICTION: The Descent of Man (stories, 1979), Water Music (1981), Budding Prospects: A Pastoral (1984), Greasy Lake and Other Stories (1985), **World's End** (1987), If the River Was Whiskey (stories, 1989), East Is East (1990), **The Road to Wellville** (1993), Without a Hero (stories, 1994), The Tortilla Curtain (1995), *****Riven Rock** (1998), The Collected Stories of T. C. Boyle (1998)

T. Coraghessan Boyle, lately known as plain T. C. Boyle, is the one-man Barnum and Bailey of contemporary American fiction, an amazingly kinetic storyteller and lover of words and language who enjoys his celebrity as much as any writer who ever lived. "My idea of fame is to get the books out to the public so they read them," Boyle has said. "I want to be read; even if I didn't make any money from the books, I would want to be read." Indeed, with seven novels and five collections of short stories to his credit, Boyle is one of the most reader-friendly writers in existence, not just on the page, where he has proven himself a master of dark comedy, narrative invention, and a thoroughly antic philosophy, but in the classroom—Boyle is a tenured professor at the University of Southern California in Los Angeles—and on the road, where he travels frequently to read from his work at local bookstores and on college campuses. Now past fifty, Boyle admits that his trademark goatee, earring, spiked hair, and boyish sneakers are "an affectation, of a sort. But what the hell. There are five billion of us on the planet all screaming for attention." Boyle loves writing, and he loves his life as an author. "I think I burn with a high flame," he says.

Boyle was born Thomas John Boyle in Peekskill, New York, the son of parents he prefers not to dwell on in interviews. He took the name Coraghessan (pronounced cor-RAG-a-sen) at the age of seventeen, after an Irish relative of his mother's. The fact that no one could pronounce it was all to the good, Boyle thought. He describes himself as a

56

"pampered punk" without direction, who fell into writing while still in college and later enrolled in the Iowa Writer's Workshop, where his teachers included John Cheever and John Irving. "What I like is funny books," Boyle observes. "Evil, wicked, deliciously black and funny books. I cut my teeth on Evelyn Waugh, Kingsley Amis, Thomas Pynchon, Barth, Barthelme, and Coover." Traces of all these writers can be found in Boyle's work, although he is never as concerned as some of his tutors with the meaning—or lack of it—in his fiction. Lorrie Moore has likened Boyle to "Flannery O'Connor with a television and no church," and Boyle replies, "If you are an ambitious artist, as I am, why wouldn't you want to be messianic? Why wouldn't you want to be Tolstoy?" An overwhelming sense of fun pervades all of Boyle's fiction, laden though it is with pessimism, a distantly Catholic sense of predestination, and the darkest possible view of human—and animal—behavior.

One of the first of Boyle's short stories to make a mark was "Heart of a Champion," in which the faithful Lassie gets the hots for a wild coyote and abandons Timmy to his doom. A more recent offering is "Modern Love," where a yuppie couple negotiates safer sex in the age of AIDS and winds up wiping the seats in movie theatres and wearing "full-body condoms." A collection of all Boyle's stories to date appeared in 1998 to great acclaim, even if critics, generally, have not known quite what to make of him. While acknowledging his prodigious talent, reviewers seem almost obliged to attack him, detecting, as David Ulin writes, "the dichotomy at the heart of Boyle's career, where the substantial and the superficial exist together, and the line between art and artifice often ends up looking like a question mark." None of it matters to Boyle or his readers, whose great enthusiasm for his fiction matches his own in creating it.

Three of Boyle's novels are already classics: *World's End*, the multi-generational saga of a much dumped-upon family in upstate New York; *The Road to Wellville*, about John Harvey Kellogg and the American passion for health fads; and the gorgeous *Riven Rock*, the nearest thing Boyle has produced to a "conventional" novel and proof that he is a master not only of style but of characterization, the depths of human feeling, and the nobility of love.

See Also: While acknowledging his debt to the writers mentioned above, Boyle declares, "I don't fit any molds. I'm free-form; everything is discovered as I go along. A lot of people misinterpret what I say because I say everything with a straight face and half of it is ridiculous. After all, Jesus was my role model."

—Peter Kurth

Brautigan, Richard
1935–1984
b. Spokane, Washington

FICTION: **A Confederate General from Big Sur** (1964), **The Abortion: An Historical Romance, 1966** (1966), *Trout Fishing in America** (1967), In Watermelon Sugar (1968), **Revenge of the Lawn: Stories, 1962–1970** (1971), The Hawkline Monster: A Gothic Western (1974), Willard and His Bowling Trophies: A Perverse Mystery (1975), Sombrero Fallout: A Japanese Novel (1976), Dreaming of Babylon: A Private Eye Novel (1977), The Tokyo–Montana Express (1980), So the Wind Won't Blow it All away (1982)

POETRY: The Return of the Rivers (1957), The Galilee Hitch-Hiker (1958), Lay the Marble Tea: Twenty-four Poems (1959), The Octopus Frontier (1960), All Watched Over by Machines of Loving Grace (1967), The Pill Versus the Springhill Mine Disaster (1968), Rommel Drives on Deep into Egypt (1970), Loading Mercury with a Pitchfork (1976), June 30, June 30 (1978)

"Vida was right when she said that I would be a hero in Berkeley." Richard Brautigan could hardly have known how prophetic that final sentence of his novel *The Abortion* would be when he wrote it in 1966. Brautigan had published the novel *A Confederate General from Big Sur*—a curiously despairing and humorous look at West Coast down-and-outers—to no great acclaim in 1964. But when the Haight-Ashbury scene broke into national prominence three years later, Brautigan was poised with an unpublished stockpile of several wistful, pranksterish novels that would propel him to fleeting fame—with his thick blond mane, droopy mustache and nineteenth-century clothing—as the Mark Twain of the Hippies.

Brautigan's novels and short stories (the latter collected in *Revenge of the Lawn*) were piled-high metaphor salads, ninety-nine percent morality-free, and he became a literary icon to the rebellious across the land. *Trout Fishing in America* remains a loopy, engaging, free-form exploration of the national psyche in a hundred or so pages and still retains far more gravity than its mass would lead one to expect. *The Abortion* contains a gem of a premise for a novel: The protagonist tends a library of unpublished manuscripts and provides solace and understanding to the strange souls who show up at the library door at odd hours to add to the collection.

Through the 1970s and into the 1980s, Brautigan's quality of writing, which always depended heavily on wordplay ("His eyes were like the shoelaces of a harpsichord"), seemed to degenerate into an excessive blend of coyness and whimsy. Reading some of his later mixed-genre novels (and most of his poetry) can leave you feeling like you've spent too much time in the "Humorous" aisle at the greeting card store. Brautigan himself became increasingly mired in alcohol and money problems and died of a self-inflicted gunshot wound in 1984.

See Also: Brautigan was launched into mainstream publishing with the help of Kurt Vonnegut, and readers who are taken with Brautigan's style will find a similar impish humor at work in Vonnegut's novels, along with a deeper, more mature level of craft.

—Edward Neuert

Brodkey, Harold
1930–1996
b. Alton, Illinois

FICTION: First Love and Other Sorrows (1957), Women and Angels (1985), *Sto-**ries in an Almost Classical Mode** (1988), The Runaway Soul (1991), Profane Friendship (1994), **The World Is the Home of Love and Death: Stories** (1997)

NONFICTION: **This Wild Darkness: The Story of My Death** (1996), Sea Battles on Dry Land: Essays (1999)

"The rhythm of illness and shock and the truth of death are the original terms of my life, and they make a faery music," Harold Brodkey wrote in a late story; the statement accurately summarizes Brodkey's harsh early life and his obsessive reworking of it in his art. Brodkey's immigrant mother died when he was seventeen months old, and he lost both his adoptive parents in his youth. In his later writing, Brodkey created a daring, idiosyncratic prose style, a "faery music" that seeks to ward off loss by capturing the elusive rhythms of speech and thought.

A few years out of college, Brodkey published *First Love and Other Sorrows*, a competent, well-mannered story collection focusing on young married life which gave little indication of the infinitely nuanced style he soon developed. In the 1970s he began publishing short stories, mostly in *The New Yorker*, pieces of the mammoth autobiographical novel he would work on for nearly thirty years. (It was finally published, much revised, as 1991's *The Runaway Soul*.) The stories follow Brodkey's alter ego, Wiley Silenowicz, through a childhood and adolescence fraught with erotic and emotional treachery. Wiley's adoptive parents, Lila and S. L., emerge as titanic presences, spewing forth torrents of cajoling, seductive language and offering real affection tinged with menacing sexuality.

Brodkey's boastful manner and endless procrastination in producing the novel exasperated a good portion of New York's literary world, but the originality of his writing remains undeniable. Brodkey's inimitable prose style slows down time to examine the emotional intricacies of the passing moment ("Innocence," a notorious 1973 story, spends thirty pages detailing Wiley's efforts to bring his girlfriend to orgasm). At times the words seem to hover just this side of nonsense, but Brodkey is saved by his extraordinarily versatile, almost melodic sense of the possibilities of language: "I don't want the fixed kind of comprehension, which is so satisfying," he explains in the 1985 story, "The Boys on Their Bikes", "but the other kind, which is a sort of response and loss of everything but the response in the flicker, in the exploding novas of the moments, of the new turns one's history is taking in (pardon me) love for one another." *Stories in an Almost Classical Mode* contains much of the Wiley material as it appeared in periodicals in the 1970s and 1980s. The best introduction to Brodkey's work, it allows readers to approach his formidable fictional project in discrete portions: *The Runaway Soul* itself, at over eight hundred densely poetic pages, is a must-read only for initiates. *Profane Friendship*, a shorter novel about a gay romance set in Venice, is still daunting. Despite its many stunning passages, the abstraction of the prose occasionally tips over into obscurity. *This Wild Darkness: The Story of My Death* is Brodkey's haunting, clear-eyed account of the AIDS-related illness that killed him in 1996.

See Also: In his obsession with time's passage, and in spending most of his life on a single piece of autobiographical fiction, Brodkey resembles Marcel Proust. His efforts to develop a language to represent a moment in time has much in common with the similar projects of James Joyce and Virginia Woolf. Among contemporary writers, Philip Roth (in Portnoy's Complaint) *and Jamaica Kincaid (in* Annie John *and* The Autobiography of My Mother) *have drawn parent-figures of mythic proportions to rival Brodkey's Lila and S. L.*

—David Kurnick

WHAT CHILDREN KNOW *By Wendy Lesser*

Stories in an Almost Classical Mode by Harold Brodkey

People either love Brodkey's work or hate it, depending largely on whether they ever met Harold. I met him, and I still love it, at its best. Its best, in this collection, are the title story, "Ceil," and one or two others, all of which focus obsessively on his own childhood and adoptive family.

The Blue Flower by Penelope Fitzgerald

Almost any Penelope Fitzgerald novel could have served this purpose—there are wonderful children in *The Beginning of Spring*, *Offshore*, and *At Freddie's*—but I select this one not only because it is one of her greatest, but because it contains The Bernhard. This is possibly my favorite character in all of her work and certainly her most amazing child. Fitzgerald may well be the best novelist now writing in English; she is certainly unlike anyone else in her ability to create a time and place that is at once true to itself (eighteenth-century Germany, 1950s Italy, turn-of-the-century Russia) and at the same time utterly of a piece with her own marvelous sensibility.

The Child in Time by Ian McEwan

This is my favorite of McEwan's works, though *Enduring Love* (except for the end) runs a close second. It is the last of his works that features children and childhood—after that, he turns to more adult forms of love and hate—but it follows on the wonderfully creepy *The Cement Garden* and the evocative stories in *First Love, Last Rites*. The main child in *The Child in Time* (other than a lost little girl) is a man who wishes he were still a boy, and pretends to be one.

A Fine Balance by Rohinton Mistry

My favorite novel of the past few years—not to be confused with the *best* novel, but having more of a personal connection, because it is a novel that hits you between the eyes, or in the stomach, or wherever you are most likely to feel emotion. The children here are modified Dickens characters: modified to suit a modern sensibility, to make us able to feel strongly about them rather than merely wanting to escape their pathos.

So Long, See You Tomorrow by William F. Maxwell

Like Brodkey, but in the opposite way (wistful and modest rather than loud and boastful), Maxwell focuses obsessively on his own mid-western childhood. Here, in a perfect little novel, he tells the story of a small-town murder from the point of view of a little boy who knew the child of the people involved.

Brookner, Anita
1928–
b. London, England

FICTION: **The Debut** (published in England as A Start in Life, 1981), **Providence** (1982), **Look at Me** (1983), *__Hotel du Lac__ (1984), Family and Friends (1985), The Misalliance (1986), A Friend from England (1987), Latecomers (1988), Lewis Percy (1989), Brief Lives (1990), A Closed Eye (1991), Fraud (1992), Family Romance (1993), Dolly (1993), A Private View (1994), Incidents in the Rue Laugier (1996), Altered States (1996), Visitors (1997), Falling Slowly (1998), Undue Influence (1999)

SELECTED NONFICTION: The Genius of the Future (essays, 1971), Soundings (essays, 1997)

Brookner is the quintessential maiden aunt of contemporary literature—her elegant prose is studded with penetrating asides and an exotically antiquated vocabulary. Who else casually tosses off nouns like "suzerainty," "ichor," and "counterpane"? Such words suit Brookner's characters and their reined-in passions. Concerned with love and its flip side—loneliness—Brookner has been aptly described as an author of anti-romances. Her characters abandon dreams of adoration and sexual bliss to live as sensible, self-sufficient beings. Blanche Vernon of *The Misalliance* "occupied her time most usefully in keeping feelings at bay," and the hero of *Altered States* fantasizes about a stranger he imagines as possessing "an excellent digestion."

Readers and reviewers inevitably draw comparisons between Brookner's solitary heroines and the author herself, who is unmarried and an only child (as are almost all her characters). In 1986, when she won the Booker Prize for *Hotel du Lac*, Brookner joked about her image problem: "I feel I could get into the Guinness Book of Records as the world's loneliest, most miserable woman." But Brookner is no stereotype. An authority on eighteenth-century painting, she became the first female Slade Professor at Cambridge University in 1968, and began writing and publishing fiction in 1981, when she was already fifty-two. Since then, she's produced a novel a year. Given her aura of repressed British gentility, it's surprising to learn that Brookner is actually Jewish—a fact that sometimes surfaces in her fiction by sleight of hand. Here's how we are told of one heroine's ethnicity: "For the very first time, she ate lobster, forbidden on her father's side." No further mention made.

Although Brookner's subject matter has remained consistent over her nearly twenty-year literary career, her novels have altered dramatically in tone. Brookner's first novel, *The Debut*, is a snappy tale of a Balzac scholar who believes her life has been ruined by literature; her academic colleagues are so uninquisitive that only "the porter, darting forward every morning with his meteorological report, appeared to be in touch with the outside or climatic world." In later novels like *Incidents in the Rue Laugier* and *Altered States*, no one's in touch with anything but her own idiosyncrasies. The books come across as inert, circumscribed, and hard to locate chronologically and emotionally. Gone are the levity and wit; now Brookner is churning out family sagas in which generation after generation is silent and unknowable.

For Brookner at her best, seek out the fizzy early novels like *Hotel du Lac*, *Providence*, and *Look at Me*. In *Hotel du Lac*, Brookner's paean to people-watching, romance novelist Edith Hope travels to a resort hotel in Switzerland and muses on love. When her literary agent suggests that she should write for Cosmo-girl executives with briefcases, Edith riffs brilliantly on why her readers prefer the old myth in which the tortoise (a mousy librarian type) bests the hare (a powerful and sexy siren). "In real life, of course," says Edith, "it is the hare who wins. Every time." She writes for tortoises because "[h]ares have no time to read. They are too busy winning the game." "[I]t is the tortoise," Edith explains on behalf of Brookner heroines everywhere, "who is in need of consolation."

See Also: Barbara Pym (Excellent Women) *and Penelope Fitzgerald* (The Bookshop), *each of whom has, like Brookner, been described as a latter-day Jane Austen.*

—Elizabeth Judd

Bukowski, Charles
1920–1994
b. Andernach, Germany

FICTION: Notes of a Dirty Old Man (stories, 1969), Post Office (1971), **Erections, Ejaculations, Exhibitions, and General Tales of Ordinary Madness** (stories, 1972; republished in two volumes as Tales of Ordinary Madness and The Most Beautiful Woman in Town and Other Stories, 1983), South of No North: Stories of the Buried Life (1973), **Factotum** (1975), **Women** (1978), **Ham on Rye** (1982), Horsemeat (1982), Bring Me Your Love (stories,

1983), ***Hot Water Music** (stories, 1983), There's No Business (stories, 1984), Hollywood (1989), Septuagenarian Stew: Stories and Poems (1990), Pulp (1994), Betting on the Muse: Poems and Stories (1996)

SELECTED POETRY: Poems Written Before Jumping Out of an 8-Story Window (1968), Burning in Water, Drowning in Flame: Selected Poems, 1955–1973 (1974), Love Is a Dog From Hell: Poems, 1974–1977 (1977), War All the Time: Poems 1981–1984 (1984), The Roominghouse Madrigals: Early Selected Poems, 1946–1966 (1988)

SELECTED NONFICTION: A Bukowski Sampler (1969), The Bukowski/Purdy Letters: A Decade of Dialogue, 1964–1974 (with Al Purdy, 1983), Under the Influence: A Charles Bukowski Checklist (1984), Run With the Hunted: A Charles Bukowski Reader (1993), Screams From the Balcony: Selected Letters 1960–1970 (1994)

By the time he died in 1994, Charles Bukowski was Hollywood's hippest literary celebrity: Madonna proclaimed him her favorite writer; U2 repeatedly dropped his name; personal friend Sean Penn vowed to play him for free (in the Barbet Schroeder film *Barfly*), a role that ultimately went to Mickey Rourke, another self-professed acolyte.

Revisiting Bukowski's enormous body of work—more than forty books of poetry, seven novels, six short story collections, innumerable fragments and illustrated special editions—makes his appeal abundantly clear. He created a pure Tinseltown persona: the hard-drinking, heavy-gambling, street-fighting, invariably unemployed, grotesquely pock-marked, abused and abusive, late-blooming autodidactic rebel who published his first book of poetry, *Flower, Fist, and Bestial Wail*, at the age of thirty-nine. In the following decade, Bukowski released a poetry collection every year (the best of which is 1968's *Poems Written Before Jumping Out An 8-Story Window*) and quickly established an easily-parsed, post-Beat voice that is narrative, vulgar, and quintessentially Californian: the pugilist with a heart full of poesy.

Bukowski first began publishing prose (unable to earn a living as a poet, he was a postman for two decades) in his fifties. His immensely entertaining, semi-autobiographical first novel, *Post Office*, chronicles his early days as an L.A. drunk, as well as the mind-numbing life of a civil servant, territory he revisited with slightly less vigor in his second novel, *Factotum*. In 1972, Bukowski released his first (highly recommended) collection of short stories, the memorably titled *Erections, Ejaculations, Exhibitions, and General Tales of Ordinary Madness* (re-released in 1983 as *Tales of Ordinary Madness*). Bukowski's early short stories limn the bruised liver of his own life, but a few selections also revealed the workings of a whimsical imagination and a powerful gift for satire. (In his best work, vulgarity is redeemed by a bracing sense of humor.)

64

In 1978, Bukowski released *Women*, a look at his Dickensian childhood, a squalid white-trash youth with a monstrous father and disfiguring boils; *Ham on Rye* covered his segue into an adolescent love affair with cheap red wine, literature (particularly Céline and Hamsun), playing the ponies, and symphonic music (Mahler, whenever possible). This must have been an especially fertile period for Bukowski: In 1983, he released his best short story collection, *Hot Water Music*, which continued the debauched adventures of his alter ego, Henry Chinaski. Wildly prolific, Bukowski continued to cough up an annual book of poetry, the best of which are collected in the anthologies *Love is a Dog From Hell* and *War All the Time*.

By the time he published *Hollywood*, an excoriating look at the making of the film *Barfly*, Bukowski was more than a cult figure; the tone of his prose shifted from hard-boiled drunk to rich, grumpy septuagenarian alcoholic. His last novel, the inferior *Pulp*, reads like a poor homage to Chandler, but *There's No Business*, his polished final collection of short stories, sustains his reputation as the poet laureate of the liquor store.

See Also: In its relentless misanthropy and dirtbag demimonde, Bukowski's work harkens back to such masters of the genre as Louis-Ferdinand Celine and Knut Hamsun.
—*Andrew Essex*

Burgess, Anthony
1917–1993
b. John Anthony Burgess Wilson in Manchester, England

FICTION: Time for a Tiger (1956), The Enemy in the Blanket (1958), Beds in the East (1959), The Right to an Answer (1960), The Doctor Is Sick (1960), The Worm and the Ring (1961, revised edition published 1970), Devil of a State (1961), One Hand Clapping (written as Joseph Kell, 1961), **A Clockwork Orange** (1962), The Wanting Seed (1962), Honey for the Bears (1963), Inside Mr Enderby (as Joseph Kell, 1963), *****Nothing Like the Sun: A Study of Shakespeare's Love Life** (1964), The Eve of Saint Venus (1964), A Vision of Battlements (1965), The Long Day Wanes: A Malayan Trilogy (includes Time for a Tiger, The Enemy in the Blanket, and Beds in the East, 1965), Tremor of Intent (1966), Enderby Outside (1968), **Enderby** (includes Inside Mr Enderby and Enderby Outside, 1968), MF (1971), **Napoleon Symphony** (1974), The Clockwork Testament, or Enderby's End (1974), Beard's Roman Women (1976), A Long Trip to Tea Time (1976), Moses the Lawgiver (1976), Abba, Abba (1977), Nineteen Eighty-Five (1978), Man of Nazareth (1979), **Earthly Powers** (1980), The End of the World

News: An Entertainment (1983), Enderby's Dark Lady, or No End to Enderby (1984), The King-dom of the Wicked (1985), The Pianoplayers (1986), The Devil's Mode (stories, 1989), Any Old Iron (1989), A Dead Man in Deptford (1993), Byrne (1995)

NONFICTION: Here Comes Everybody (published in the U.S. as ReJoyce, 1965), Urgent Copy: Literary Studies (1968), Shakespeare (1970), **Joysprick: An Introduction to the Language of James Joyce** (1973), Ernest Hemingway and His World (1978), On Going to Bed (1982), Ninety-Nine Novels: The Best in English Since 1939 (1984), D. H. Lawrence in Italy (1985), Flame Into Being: the Life and Work of D. H. Lawrence (1985), But Do Blondes Prefer Gentlemen? Homage to QWERTYUIOP: Selected Journalism, 1978–1985 (1986), Little Wilson and Big God (1987), You've Had Your Time: Being the Second Part of the Confessions of An-thony Burgess (1990), On Mozart: A Paean for Wolfgang (1991), A Mouthful of Air: Languages, Languages—Especially English (1992)

Composer, novelist, poet, journalist, screenwriter, Anthony Burgess did not publish his first book until he was almost forty: *The Long Day Wanes* (1956–1959) is a trilogy of novels based on his experience as a civil servant in Malaya. In 1960 a doctor misdiagnosed him with an inoperable brain tumor, and this false alarm galvanized a career that produced over thirty novels in as many years, and a similar amount of nonfiction. Although his work is mostly out of print in America, he was for over two decades among the best-known of serious British novelists, critically acclaimed and commercially successful.

Burgess had a wicked, unerring eye for squalor. Whether describing an electric fire in a bedsitter or the teeth of a pub denizen, his homely details are both hilarious and un-nerving. His novels about F. X. Enderby, a flatulent and feckless poet, are exemplary in this mode. An apostate Catholic, Burgess is, under his humor, deeply moral, haunted by themes of good and evil, of free will, of ends and means at odds. "Ah, what a bloody Manichean mess life is," says Hillier the spy in *Tremor of Intent*, speaking for nearly all Burgess's heroes. *A Clockwork Orange*, his best-known novel, details the moral "refor-mation" of a young thug by operant conditioning, and asks whether the affront to free will is worse than the violence it cures.

Burgess ranged from contemporary satire to historical and science fiction, often plac-ing language and form in the foreground. He drew a distinction between "class 1" and "class 2" writers, the former typified by "transparent" prose in the manner of best-sellers or Somerset Maugham, the latter more concerned with language itself. Burgess has been both sorts of writer, though his best work belongs more to class 2.

In this category, *Nothing Like the Sun* and *A Dead Man in Deptford* mimic an Eliz-abethan style to biograph, respectively, William Shakespeare and Christopher Marlowe. *Napoleon Symphony* is an ambitious attempt to put Bonaparte's rise and fall into the form of Beethoven's "Eroica" Symphony. *MF* is the unlikely story of Miles Faber, brilliant young polymath and Oedipal epigone, told in logomanic prose. *A Clockwork Orange* uses Russo-English argot to suggest the wrenching political changes behind its dystopian future. (The first American editions of this novel omitted a final chapter which Burgess considered essential, in which Alex becomes a well-adjusted bourgeois.)

Burgess's onomastics owe much to his close reading and admiration of James Joyce. His two books on Joyce, though sometimes derided by Joyce specialists, remain worthwhile as a clear but unsimplified introduction to the writer, and even more as a technical brief for Burgess's own prose.

Beset by financial worries, he squandered time in his later years on forgettable screen projects. His later novels, perhaps because of this influence, are firmly "class 1," the posthumously published *Byrne* and *A Dead Man in Deptford* being exceptions. Or perhaps, in *Earthly Powers*, the best of these late novels, the novelist Toomey speaks for Burgess when he writes: "I was thinking like an author, not like a human, though senile, being. As though conquering language mattered. As if, at the end of it all, there were anything more important than cliches."

See Also: In 99 Novels, *Burgess listed the contemporary novels which he valued most highly; among those authors who are closest to his thematic and stylistic territory are Kingsley Amis, Joyce Cary, Graham Greene, and Evelyn Waugh. At his most logophilic, Burgess is indebted to the Joyce of* Ulysses *and* Finnegans Wake.

—*Carter Scholz*

Butler, Robert Olen
1945–
b. Granite City, Illinois

FICTION: The Alleys of Eden (1981), Sundogs (1982), Countrymen of Bones (1983), On Distant Ground (1985), Wabash (1987), **The Deuce** (1989), *****A Good Scent from a Strange Mountain** (stories, 1992), They Whisper (1994), **Tabloid Dreams** (stories, 1996), The Deep Green Sea (1997), Mr. Spaceman (2000)

Robert Olen Butler, best known for his collection, *A Good Scent from a Strange Mountain*, has devoted a good portion of his fiction to portraying the Vietnam war and its legacy, but unlike Tim O'Brien and other American "Vietnam authors," Butler examines the Vietnamese experience as well. His early novels—*Alleys of Eden* and *On Distant Ground*—investigate cultures in conflict and American men lost in Saigon who show a desire that Butler seems to share to shed their (American) identity. In his first book a Saigon bar girl tells the main character, Cliff, he is losing his American soul and soon will be left with the "Vietnamese who was inside of you waiting to get out."

Butler spent a year in Saigon as a U.S. Army intelligence agent and later as an interpreter. Clearly this experience gave rise to much of his writing. Even when he's not writing about Vietnam, his novels often examine clashing worldviews. *Countrymen of Bones*, for example, pits scientists against each other: an archeologist unearthing a New Mexico burial site and an atomic physicist who will destroy it.

But can a white man write effectively about the Vietnamese experience? In a decision that provoked both praise and controversy, the Pulitzer committee awarded Butler's collection, *A Good Scent from a Strange Mountain*, its 1992 award for fiction. The book's fifteen stories about Vietnamese immigrants living in Louisiana, are told in the voices of the immigrants themselves. This marked a change for Butler, who'd rarely used the first person before, and his early works don't have the same directness and fullness of vision. These stories are small masterpieces, wonderfully authentic glimpses into the Vietnamese community, each narrator rendered with a ventriloquist's precision—from a well-educated businessman to a young woman struggling with English. In "Mr. Green," a girl inherits a family parrot who still mimics her beloved grandfather. In "Fairy Tale," a New Orleans bar girl falls for a Vietnam vet because both of them believe that Saigon was once the most beautiful city in the world. A culmination of loss and hope, somehow these stories add up to more than a traditional novel.

In *Tabloid Dreams*, Butler offers twelve more first-person tales, each derived from actual tab headlines: "Titanic Victim Speaks Through Waterbed," "Boy Born with Tattoo of Elvis," "JFK Secretly Attends Jackie Auction." Like *Good Scent*, these stories capitalize on Butler's ability to create vivid, believable voices, and still manage to avoid many sandtraps inherent in the material. Whimsical and ironic the stories also become platforms from which Butler launches inquiries into the nature of (often failed) love, isolation, desire, and a kind of deep regret that often draws his characters together.

68

See Also: Although Butler's recent work has moved away from the Vietnam War, he is often paired with Tim O'Brien.

—*Todd James Pierce*

Byatt, A. S.
1936–
b. Sheffield, England

FICTION: The Shadow of the Sun (1964), The Game (1967), The Virgin in the Garden (1978), Still Life (1985), Sugar and Other Stories (1987), ***Possession: A Romance** (1990), **Angels and Insects: Two Novellas** (1992), **The Matisse Stories** (1993), The Djinn in the Nightingales's Eye (1994), Babel Tower (1996), Elementals (1999)

NONFICTION: Degrees of Freedom: The Novels of Iris Murdoch (1965), Wordsworth and Coleridge in Their Time (1970), Iris Murdoch (1976), Passions of the Mind (1991)

Antonia Susann Byatt's primary literary models are George Eliot and Iris Murdoch, and in her early novels this influence—and sometimes not much else—shows. Like Eliot, she considers the novel an ideal art form because "you can get the whole world in it"; like Murdoch, she wants to depict human beings as seized by and struggling with ideas. And, like both of them, she has produced dense, talky books that can try the patience of even her brainiest and most devoted readers. Her early work is dominated by *The Virgin in the Garden* and *Still Life*, the first two installments in a series of novels about Frederica Potter, a fiercely intellectual girl from provincial Yorkshire who seeks a life of the mind in Cambridge and, later, London in the 1950s and 1960s. There's much to admire in these works—which give the impression of being created by a formidable intelligence—but they're often burdened with too much descriptive detail, and you don't so much read them as wade through them. After her eleven-year-old son was struck and killed by an automobile in 1971, Byatt wrote no fiction for over a decade.

"Early," when referring to Byatt, means before *Possession*, the 1990 bestseller that brought the obscure (if respected) author the Booker Prize. Suddenly, almost violently, Byatt's distinctive talent blossomed; where her first novels remained stubbornly earthbound, *Possession*

69

lifts off easily. It's the story of a pair of modern academics, a young fuddy-duddy and a reserved feminist, who unearth a previously unimagined cache of love letters exchanged by two Victorian poets (based on Robert Browning and Christina Rossetti—the love affair is pure fiction). Part academic satire, part detective story, and part (as it's subtitled) romance, *Possession* marks the debut of a new Byatt, a gifted storyteller and astonishing literary mimic, who can produce verse uncannily like Browning's and Rossetti's, plausibly "Victorian" letters, and wicked parodies of contemporary academic blathering. Like the Browning figure in *Possession*, she merits the epithet "The Great Ventriloquist."

What makes this aptitude more than a parlor trick and Byatt more than a smirking postmodern jester are her motivating passions and beliefs—in the power of reading and writing to rescue human beings from dull, confining lives and in the transformative capacities of the mind. The Browning figure in *Possession* speaks for her in espousing a creative drive that comes not from "the Lyric Impulse—but from something restless and myriad-minded and partial and observing and analytic and curious." If her earlier novels told us about "too clever" bookish young women like Frederica who took "sensual pleasure in reading anything at all," *Possession* simply delivers that pleasure, in abundance. While a character in *The Virgin in the Garden* is all too likely to interrupt a session of necking with thoughts of T. S. Eliot, the entranced scholars in *Possession* are led by the power of poetry and love letters into each other's arms.

Something about the nineteenth century brings out the magic in Byatt. It flourished again in the 1992 novella *Morpho Eugenia*, a work that compares the Victorian country estate to an anthill and tracks the miraculous escape, via literature and natural science, of two of the anthill's drones. (It appeared with "The Conjugial Angel" in *Angels and Insects*.) The third Frederica novel, *Babel Tower*, uneasily combined the old Byatt with the new (while displaying ever more delightful feats of mimicry). Her later short stories, collected in *The Matisse Stories*, made lushly rewarded forays into the realm of fantasy or biting observations on contemporary academic life. When Byatt's more donnish desires aren't leading her to write serious, "important" novels—when she admits her own playful and sensual instincts into the mix (and these, it seems, increasingly refuse to be denied)—she's capable of wonders.

See Also: *The obvious choices are Murdoch and Eliot, but neither has Byatt's streaks of hedonism or literary cheekiness. The Julian Barnes of* Flaubert's Parrot *and* A History of the World in 10½ Chapters *is almost as book-drunk and chameleon-like, but he lacks Byatt's intensity. Finally, Margaret Atwood shares her passionate concern with—and satirical attention to—women and feminism.*

—Laura Miller

OTHER PASTS, OTHER PLACES:
HISTORICAL NOVELS *by A. S. Byatt*

Beloved by Toni Morrison

A tale of pain and courage and terror in the days of slavery in the States, told from the point of view of Sethe, an escaped slave whose former "owner" comes to reclaim her. It rewrites the great nineteenth-century American novels (with their imagery of white and black, light and darkness), attains real tragedy, and is so well-written and so thoroughly imagined that it leaves the reader feeling triumphant instead of downcast.

The Baron in the Trees by Italo Calvino

This long tale usually comes in a volume with *The Cloven Viscount* and *The Nonexistent Knight*. All three are wonderful stories of fantastic adventures which nevertheless reveal something about the life and ideas of the times in which they are set, as well, as Calvino himself said, as being inevitably blso about our own times. The baron in the trees takes to living in the wooded canopy of his estates as a boy, and uses his ingenuity in order to never come down. Set before and during the Napoleonic Wars, this is a modern philosophical tale derived from the eighteenth-century philosophical tale. It is full of wit and surprises.

Abba Abba by Anthony Burgess

This is a short and perfect novel about the death of Keats in Rome. Burgess invents an encounter between Keats and the scurrilous Roman dialect poet Giuseppe Gioachino Belli, who was also a priest and censor. Burgess's brilliant Lancashire translations of the Belli sonnets are part of the richness of the book. "Abba abba" is both the rhymes of the octet of the sonnet, Christ's cry of despair on the cross, and Burgess's own initials, carved on his tombstone, as Keats had carved "Here lies one whose name was writ in water." Burgess is usually unevenly brilliant and inventive—in this tight, moving book, everything comes off.

Lempriere's Dictionary by Lawrence Norfolk

A huge, ambitious book about plots, cabals, wars, and commerce in eighteenth-century London and France. The hero is John Lempriere, author of the classical dictionary, whose life gets wound up in fantastic versions of his own myths. Norfolk has said that everything that seems farfetched is true, and everything plausible is invented. The book gallops and glitters, and Norfolk writes delectably.

The Blue Flower or possibly *The Beginning of Spring* by Penelope Fitzgerald.

How to choose? I only know that writing about other pasts in other places released Fitzgerald's always precise and philosophically witty imagination into new energy. *The Blue Flower* is brief and funny and dreadfully moving, and condenses the (short) life and (compendious) thought of the poet Novalis into a series of unforgettable tiny scenes and thoughts. The *Beginning of Spring* is set in Moscow in 1911 (before war or revolution) and tells the story of an English printer who lives there. It is Jane Austen crossed with Chekhov and Turgenev; its world is Russian, its plot is surprising and funny and alarming. There is no other writer like her.

Canin, Ethan

1960–
b. Ann Arbor, Michigan

FICTION: Emperor of the Air (stories, 1988), Blue River (1991), *****The Palace Thief** (1994), **For Kings and Planets** (1998)

In the 1980s, when hip, young writers proclaimed themselves avatars of the drug-propelled, angst-ridden, media-savvy moment, Ethan Canin was the old geezer of his generation, and proud of it. His debut story collection, *Emperor of the Air*, won praise for being utterly unlike the work of Jay McInerney, Tama Janowitz, and Bret Easton Ellis. This stuff was mature, for God's sake, and—coming from a twenty-seven-year-old student at Harvard Medical School—far wiser than it had any right to be.

A middle-aged man confronts his dying father's infidelity; a young woman comes to terms with her mother's insecurities; a teenage boy marches bravely, and naively, into adulthood. Canin took the measure of age-old questions with a smooth, weightless eloquence. Though he no longer practices medicine, the experience obviously enlarged his perspective beyond his own class and generation.

Since the 1980s, Canin's stature has continued to rise, although the ascension hasn't been effortless. His next book and first novel, *Blue River*, disappointed some readers because of a perceived lack of passion. His Mississippi-majestic prose seemed better suited to summoning up vivid domestic tableaux than to actually explaining family dynamics. With his second set of stories, *The Palace Thief*, Canin regained his easy stride, and in 1996 the literary quarterly *Granta* anointed him one of America's best writers under forty. *For Kings and Planets*, Canin's second novel, had admiring critics invoking Cheever and Fitzgerald.

"How can any man leave this world with honor?" a retired salesman wonders in *Emperor of the Air*. It's a question Canin's fiction is always asking. How do moral tests mold us, reveal who we truly are? On the surface, *Blue River* contrasts "good" and "bad" Sellers brothers: Edward the hard-working, successful doctor and Lawrence the screw-up who never fulfilled his potential. Like many of Canin's men—women are very much in the background in his fiction—Edward is consumed by feelings of guilt and unworthiness. Likewise, in *The Palace Thief*, a prep-school teacher berates himself for not exposing the cheating by a U.S. senator's son who later becomes a captain of industry. But the teacher mistakes weakness for evil; he is harder on himself than any just God would be.

Canin's gift is for the effortless flow of story, usually narrated in a voice that is gentle and rueful. Nowhere is this better realized than in *For Kings and Planets*. Orno, a wide-eyed Midwestern innocent befriends Marshall, a worldly Manhattan sophisticate in college. Awareness of his limitations doesn't prevent the manipulative Marshall from giving in to his self-destructive urges, while Orno, typical of a Canin protagonist, is a far better person than he believes. The novel moves with more dramatic momentum than Canin has previously mustered.

What initially brought Canin acclaim, his signature prose style, is apparently undergoing revision. He has announced that he intends to simplify and rein in any rhetorical effects. "You write a truer book," he said, "when the style is less apparent." The story should "burn from within." Who knows what glorious fiction will yet emerge from Canin's refining fire?

See Also: To find Canin's peers in technique and theme, skip backward a generation or two: the rueful, elegiac voice of Richard Ford's The Sportswriter *or* Independence Day *and the velvety smooth music of John Cheever and Scott Fitzgerald. Look for similar moral themes in Mary Gordon's* Final Payments *or in Robert Stone, especially* A Flag for Sunrise *and* Damascus Gate.

—*Dan Cryer*

Carey, Peter
1943–
b. Bacchus Marsh, Victoria, Australia

FICTION: The Fat Man in History (stories, 1974), War Crimes (stories, 1979), Bliss (1981), Illywhacker (1985), ***Oscar and Lucinda** (1988), **The Tax Inspector** (1991), Collected Stories (1994), **The Unusual Life of Tristan Smith** (1994), **Jack Maggs** (1997)

73

Novelists as inventive and daring as Peter Carey—whose books range from baggy frontier picaresque to historical epic to speculative political allegory to surreal domestic intrigue to economical suburban gothic—are seldom able to create characters as instantly vivid and convincing as his are. Carey's fiction is something rich and rare, arresting on every level: in its ideas, its prose, its emotional authenticity, and its sheer, entrancing storytelling.

A WALK ON THE WILD SIDE: VERY ORIGINAL NOVELS *by Peter Carey*

"Original" is a worn and worrying word, but I have tried to think of modern works that are one-off models in the same way that, say, *Tristram Shandy* is.

The Third Policeman by Flann O'Brien

A book about a bicycle. Surely one of the great comic novels of the twentieth century. It's by an Irishman, of course.

Riddley Walker by Russel Hoban

It is no simple business to invent a world, a history, a language, and if *Riddley Walker* looks, on first glance, like Chaucer in need of spellcheck, do not despair. By the second page you will speak the language like a native.

The Loser by Thomas Bernhard

Thomas Bernhard, the Austrian who hates Austria, has a reputation for being somehow "difficult" but although *The Loser* deals with such weighty subjects as art, ambition, and the futility of endeavor, and although it is scarred by lung disease and suicide, it made me laugh out loud. Sentence by sentence, the structure of the book is at once a mystery and a marvel. Obsessive, elliptical, loopy, and so perfectly splenetic. It is a jewel.

Flaubert's Parrot by Julian Barnes

Barnes has written many wonderful books, but this one is like no other, of his or anybody else's. *Flaubert's Parrot* is new, and always will be.

Sixty Stories by Donald Barthelme

The truth is, I haven't read all sixty. But "The Balloon" is in here, and it is so fantastically "made-up" and carries such a heavy payload of joy and wonder. It is always with me, something for me to always stretch towards.

Even Carey's most outlandish scenarios (a man suffers a heart attack and is convinced he's awoken in hell because he's finally able to see his family and his work as they truly are; a half-demented clan running a foundering car dealership in the boondocks sucks a pregnant tax inspector into its poisonous orbit) are all grounded in a deep understanding of human desires, from the sweet to the perverse. Brilliant, ambitious women, destined for trouble, stride through his novels, like the eponymous nineteenth-century heiress in the Booker-winning *Oscar and Lucinda*, who convinces a gambling preacher to help her build a glass church in the Australian back country. The rage of these women against a world that stifles and underestimates them parallels one of Carey's abiding concerns: the frustrations of provincial and post-colonial dreamers. The severely deformed hero of *The Unusual Life of Tristan Smith*, growing up in a small, imaginary island nation, longs to become a great actor and eclipse the spectacular, culturally invasive, and often lethal circuses of an equally mythical world power. In *Jack Maggs*, a former convict made good returns to Dickens's London to claim a son who wants nothing to do with his uncouth sire.

For all the wonders Carey concocts and all the intelligence of his themes, it's the people he writes about who linger after you close one of his books, marveling at how the past few hours have simply evaporated. Even the characters you can't quite love are indelibly, often heartbreakingly real.

See Also: Readers taken with Tristan Smith *might also enjoy Katherine Dunn's* Greek Love, *and the British novelist Jim Crace has something like Carey's smart, unshowy versatility.*

—*Laura Miller*

Carr, Caleb
1955–
b. New York, New York

FICTION: Casing the Promised Land (1980), ***The Alienist** (1994), The Angel of Darkness (1997)

NONFICTION: (With James Chace) America Invulnerable: The Quest for Absolute Security, from 1812 to Star Wars (1988), The Devil Soldier: The Story of Frederick Townsend Ward (1992)

Caleb Carr was a military historian with a few obscure books to his name when his second novel, *The Alienist*, became a surprise bestseller in 1994. Publicists dubbed the book "*Ragtime* meets *Silence of the Lambs*," a description that's both apt and ridiculous. Set in New York City in the 1890s, *The Alienist* combines historical figures like Theodore Roosevelt (then New York's police commissioner) and crusading journalist Jacob Riis with fictional characters like psychologist Dr. Lazlo Kreizler (the "alienist" of the title), to tell the story of the search for a serial killer who is preying on young male prostitutes. Carr has done his homework, and there is some pleasure to be had in his evocations of turn-of-the-century New York: dinners at Delmonicos, encounters with figures like J. P. Morgan, and trips through the city's tenements and saloons. Carr's prose, however, is functional at best, and his dialogue can be as wooden as a plank on the Brooklyn Bridge. Carr's most recent novel, *The Angel of Darkness*, offers more of the same. This time out, his posse of sleuths is after a female serial killer who murders infants. Carr's father, Lucien Carr, was a seminal and controversial figure in the early years of the Beats—he introduced Jack Kerouac, Allen Ginsberg, and William S. Burroughs to each other, and was convicted for a murder whose circumstances remain murky. Caleb Carr's studied, straightforward fiction can be seen, fairly or unfairly, as a reaction to Beat-era excess and exuberance.

See Also: Look for E. L. Doctorow's Ragtime *if you want a historical novel with more lyricism or emotional insight.*

—Dwight Garner

Carter, Angela
1940–1992
b. London, England

FICTION: Shadow Dance (1966), The Magic Toyshop (1967), Several Perceptions (1968), Heroes and Villains (1969), Love (1971), The Infernal Desire Machines of Doctor Hoffman (1972), Passion of New Eve (1977), **The Bloody Chamber and Other Stories** (1979), Black Venus' Tale (1980), Fireworks: Nine Profane Pieces (1981), War of Dreams (1983), **Nights at the Circus** (1984), Come Unto These Yellow Sands (1985), Saints and Strangers (1987), Old Wives Fairy Tale Book (1990), **Wise Children** (1991), *****Burning Your Boats: The Complete Short Stories** (1996)

NONFICTION: Nothing Sacred: Selected Journals (1982), Expletives Deleted: Selected Writings (1992), Shaking a Leg: Collected Writings (1998)

Carter enjoyed little renown during her life, but after her death from lung cancer in 1992, the reading public woke from its trance, like a princess in one of the fairy tales she adapted, and commenced to love her. She became a darling of English departments, and when *Burning Your Boats: The Complete Short Stories* was published in 1996, it made the cover of *The New York Times Book Review*, although several of her works still remain out of print.

She was always a tough case: an extravagant fabulist in an age of anorectic naturalism, a feminist who found savagery inherent in eroticism, a literary jeweler who made glittering tales when those around her churned out realistic psychological novels. Her short stories are generally, and correctly, considered her best work, particularly the 1979 collection *The Bloody Chamber*, which mines fairy tales for psychosexual melodrama and heady sensuality. In the hypnotic title story, the virginal narrator marries a sinister wealthy older man whose "strange, heavy almost waxen face" both repels and attracts her. He chooses her for her "promise of debauchery only a connoisseur could detect," and gives her a ring of keys to his seaside mansion, with one prohibited room. This Bluebeard, however, encounters resistance where he least expects it.

An unrepentant child of the sixties ("that ramshackle yet glorious decade"), Carter devoted her first few (mostly realistic, if lushly-written) novels to the sexually tangled relationships of young, bohemian Britons of the time. Later, she opted for unmoored, imaginary settings better suited to what she called her "social realism of the unconscious": mythical nations, brothels, circuses, castles, forests, and actual but symbolically dense places, like Hollywood and London. In *The Infernal Desire Machines of Dr. Hoffman*, for example, a maddeningly indistinct North American someplace is disordered by devices that bring the populace's dreams to life. Although an avowed leftist and feminist, as an artist Carter remained an anti-utopian; Dr. Hoffman's machines wreak bloody havoc.

For if Carter was anything, she was perverse, a feminist whose main characters are often beautiful men. Her fascination with the interplay of chaos and reason, rules and transgression, purity and decadence, betray a sensibility closer to de Sade's than William Morris's. Torture occurs in her fiction almost as frequently as sex, and her books are full of exquisitely cruel counts and doomed maidens as well as such boundary tramplers as hermaphrodites, winged women, unrepentant whores, centaurs, famous murderesses, and incestuous siblings.

Carter's hothouse prose sometimes gets so overgrown it stifles itself, and although she could spin a compelling yarn, her novels tend to read like one interesting thing after another, rather than one continuously engaging thing. In this there was something decidedly eighteenth century about her, as if she had simply decided to skip the modern notion of the novel entirely. It makes her writing seem archaic, but also tremendously sophisticated.

Besides her adult fiction, Carter penned children's books, edited collections of fairy tales, and wrote a great deal of journalism and an influential book of essays championing unrestrained female sexual freedom entitled *The Sadean Woman*.

The Female Gothic

By Elaine Showalter

"We live in Gothic times," Angela Carter wrote about the 1970s in the afterword to her short story collection *Fireworks*. She meant it as a compliment. Growing up in boring postwar South Yorkshire, Carter was fascinated by the emancipatory license of the Gothic tale, and with what she described as its "imagery of the unconscious—mirrors; the externalized self; forsaken castles; haunted forests; forbidden sexual objects." The Gothic tradition, she decided, was the antidote to everyday morality and feminine domestic realism: It "grandly ignores the value systems of our institutions; it deals entirely with the profane."

Indeed, since the 1790s, when Ann Radcliffe's "horrid" novels about haunted castles, sinister but seductive aristocrats, and persecuted but courageous heroines, became international best-sellers, the Gothic tale has been a popular genre for both rebellious women writers and imaginative women readers. In its classic form, the Gothic novel involved a terrifying confrontation between the heroine and a powerful male who represented an oppressive but sexually thrilling patriarchal system. Almost as soon as it appeared, however, women writers began to parody its lurid conventions through gullible heroines who are avid consumers of Gothic fiction, but learn that real life is less exciting. In Jane Austen's *Northanger Abbey* (1813), young Catherine Morland has to grow up and understand that "charming as were all Mrs. Radcliffe's works . . . it was not in them perhaps that human nature, at least in the midland counties of England, was to be found." Today, in mass-market romance paperbacks like Amanda Quick's 1998 best-seller *With This Ring*, the heroine is often a writer of Gothic novels who finds a way to revise the genre. "In most horrid novels," explains

Quick's heroine about the books she writes under the pseudonym "Mrs. Yorke," "the mysterious lord of the haunted abbey or castle turns out to be the villain . . . but in Mrs. Yorke's books, he generally proves to be the hero."

In the 1970s, feminist literary critics began to interpret the Female Gothic as a parable of women's fantasies, desires, and nightmares. In *Literary Women*, Ellen Moers placed Mary Shelley's *Frankenstein* at the center of the tradition, and saw it as a reflection of women's displaced anxiety about birth, expressed in an obsession with monsters and freaks. Other critics saw, behind the struggle with the father-figure, a quest for the dead or absent mother who holds the key to the mysteries of female sexuality. The heroine penetrates the labyrinthean inner spaces of an imprisoning architecture that is also the female body. As Juliann Fleenor explained in *The Female Gothic*, "The mother represents what the woman will become if she heeds her sexual self . . . and if she becomes pregnant . . . To become the mother is to become the passive and perhaps unwilling victim of one's own body." In *The Girl Sleuth*, novelist Bobbie Ann Mason even saw elements of the Female Gothic in the Nancy Drew series; the motherless Nancy is always stumbling upon a Freudian treasure-house of hidden chambers, locked jewelboxes, and secret compartments, scenes which are an unconscious "celebration of masturbation: 'I can feel something with my fingers!' Nancy said in an excited voice . . . 'It's a tiny knob!' "

For Angela Carter, however, the Gothic tale's affinity with fairy tale, pornography, and the surreal made it the ideal form for exploring the feminine creative imagination. Her collection of stories, *The Bloody Chamber*, which rewrites classic fairy tales—including Bluebeard, Beauty and the Beast, and Little Red Riding Hood—alongside material from the Marquis de Sade, is the most revolutionary and intense of all the contemporary Female Gothics. In the title story, the seventeen-year-old heroine marries a fabulously rich libertine marquis, and accompanies him to his remote castle. There she is aroused against her will by his violent and fetishistic sexual initiation. She then disobeys his command and unlocks the door to his secret room, the "bloody chamber" in which she discovers the embalmed bodies of his murdered wives. Horribly different from Virginia Woolf's famous "room of one's own," for Carter, the bloody chamber is nonetheless also an important space for the woman writer to acknowledge and possess. The room/womb is the source of both creation and destruction, the woman writer's equivalent of Yeats's "foul rag-and-bone shop of the heart," from which all poems start.

In her comic novel *Lady Oracle* and her short story collection, *Bluebeard's Egg*, Margaret Atwood too used the Female Gothic tradition to rewrite the dark scripts of women's destiny and to shape them towards activity and survival. In

Lady Oracle, Joan Foster is a secret writer of historical Costume-Gothic fiction, fighting its conventions of virginal heroines running through mazes in tight bodices, loose fichus, and stiff petticoats in order to free herself from suffocating inhibitions and fears. In writing a novel she calls "Stalked By Love," Joan comes to resent her own frightened Gothic heroine: "I wanted her to fall into a mud puddle, have menstrual cramps, sweat, burp, fart. Even her terrors were too pure, her faceless murderers, her corridors, her mazes and forbidden doors." She also realizes that the dashing, monomaniacal Gothic hero has his own exhausting role to live up to, and may want to be "gray and multi-dimensional and complicated" himself: "Was every Heathcliff a Linton in disguise?" She wonders whether it is time to "write a real novel, about someone who worked in an office and had tawdry, unsatisfying affairs."

But while the Female Gothic changes, its thrilling and erotic fantasies do not seem to give way to bleak realism. As Joyce Carol Oates notes in her essay on "The Aesthetics of Fear," "The powerful appeal of the Gothic world is that its inhabitants, who resemble civilized and often attractive men and women, are in reality creatures of primitive instinct." Oates has set many of her stories, novels, and plays in this Gothic world. In contrast to the multigenerational family stories of Anne Tyler or Carole Stone, Oates writes (most notably in *Zombie* and also in her genre fiction under the pseudonym "Rosamond Smith") about murderous sisters, psychopathic sons, and the uneasy collusion of vampire and victim; and even parodies the Gothic in such novels as *A Bloodsmoor Romance* and *Bellefleur*. She has also reviewed the true-crime literature of serial killers, and analyzed the anguished psychology of people like Ted Bundy's friends, Joel Rifkin's mother, and Jeffrey Dahmer's father, as well as the totemic rituals of necrophiliac "art."

Indeed, stalkers and serial killers have replaced Bluebeard as the mythic villains of the millennial Female Gothic, and women novelists of the 1990s immerse themselves in rape, mutilation, and murder, as if an unflinching confrontation with the bloodiest chambers of the body is an initiation rite into the boy's club of contemporary fiction and art. Competing with popular slasher movies about screaming women threatened by psychopathic killers, in which a boyish heroine finally outwits, outruns, or outcuts the villains, Susannah Moore's *In the Cut* and A. M. Homes's *The End of Alice* update the genre in grisly cautionary tales of independent young women living at the edge of urban gender boundaries, who are pursued, punished, and carved up by men with sharp phallic weapons. The heroines of these novels do not always escape alive, but the writers, like the invincible "final girls" of the horror film, seem triumphant. A woman doesn't have to live in Gothic times to write Gothic fiction, but it helps.

Carver, Raymond
1938–1988
b. Clatskanie, Oregon

FICTION: Put Yourself in My Shoes (stories, 1974), **Will You Please Be Quiet, Please?** (stories, 1976), Furious Seasons (stories, 1977), **What We Talk About When We Talk About Love** (stories, 1981), The Pheasant (stories, 1982), Cathedral (stories, 1983), If It Please You (stories, 1984), The Stories of Raymond Carver (1985), Elephant, and Other Stories (1988), *Where I'm Calling From: New and Selected Stories** (1988), Short Cuts: Selected Stories (1993)

SELECTED NONFICTION: Fires: Essays, Poems, Stories, 1966–1982 (1983), Carver Country: The World of Raymond Carver (1990), No Heroics, Please: Uncollected Writings (1992)

SELECTED POETRY: In a Marine Light: Selected Poems (1987), All of Us: The Collected Poems (1997)

Writing in the 1960s was generally a matter of exuberance, insolence, drugs, and experimentation. Raymond Carver, who began publishing his terse short stories in the 1970s, helped bring fiction back to small facts, won with difficulty and painfully expressed. As he became better known, readers grew familiar with "Carver people"—aimless and bewildered blue-collar souls between marriages and between jobs—and "Carver's world"—all stray ends, polluted streams, and rooms rented from widows. He was celebrated as the leader of a school of minimalist fiction, and was often described as America's Chekhov, delivering not the corniness of mere stories but the real stuff itself: what comes between stories. For a few years, talk was abroad of a Carver-led short story renaissance. By the time he died—at the age of fifty, in 1988—he was probably the most influential literary writer in the country.

Though he didn't hide from the press, Carver became as mythical a figure as Salinger or Pynchon. He had worked at dead-end jobs, he was an alcoholic, and he smoked too much, too; lung cancer was what finally killed him. In photos, he didn't look like a writer; he looked like a laborer—so, to some, he was a saint of authenticity, telling us the straight dope about stunted, one-day-at-a-time lives. The fact that he kept to short forms (essays, poems, stories) enhanced the myth: Such brutal honesty about such hard truths

81

could hardly be asked to fill out looser forms. He was so securely canonized that by 1993, when the filmmaker Robert Altman was publicizing *Short Cuts*, his adaptation of a number of Carver stories, he did so in the company of Carver's widow, Tess Gallagher, and spoke often about his feelings of inadequacy in the face of his material.

Some of the stories do have an ugly power. If you're in the mood for a downer, "The Calm" and "So Much Water So Close to Home" should hit the spot. And Carver's touch with humor—particularly of a sad-one-moment, pugnacious-the-next, headed-nowhere-fast kind—is usually skillful. But most of his writing is mannered. The repetitions signifying a stumbling exasperation ("Will you please be quiet, please?"), the sentences that start on a high note only to give way beneath you, the foot-dragging rhythms, those not-an-epiphany epiphanies . . . It gets to seem mighty gimmicky mighty fast.

And since he repeatedly said that he wanted to be thought of as a realist, not a minimalist, maybe we should ask: Who are these "Carver people" who do nothing but brood, drink, and watch their lives fall apart? For his fans, of course, Carver nailed the essence of loser America. But if you strip people from any class of their pride and energy, it's inevitable that you'll be left with little but despair. It's hard not to find his work monotonous and bathetic: all that booze, all those cigarettes and lonely failures to connect, that tenderly-highlighted inarticulateness. Carver flattens out his characters and their lives, then invites us to admire how humane and truthful he's being. Story after story wants to do little, finally, but wipe you out and make you feel desolate—to give you a good, long look at the raw nothingness of it all.

How then to explain his reputation? It may be that, for writing students, Carver's (easily mimicked) approach suggested a quick way to achieve the appearance of heavy truth. A little misery here, a broken family there, an awkward attempt at God knows what before all dissolves into entropy once again—*voila*, Insta-Depth. And for readers? My guess is that, for some of them, "literature" is a kind of faith always in danger of succumbing to evil forces (mammon, vulgarity, indifference). For such readers, Carver's stories—which, if you buy into them, have an aura of misery reluctantly illuminated by shafts of radiance—can be occasions for worship and prayer, religious services for those still hoping for redemption by art.

The Carver myth of course wasn't Carver's fault. He did indeed grow up working-class, and he did know tobacco and alcohol all too intimately. But by his own account he was a bookish, sensitive guy who had wanted to be a fiction writer from his teens. He studied writing at a number of colleges, did a stint at the Iowa Writer's Workshop, and spent much of his life as a teacher of creative writing. He worked closely (as the journalist Dan Max has shown) with the editor Gordon Lish on shaping his early stories for maximum literary impact—better, in other words, to remember him as a writer, not an oppressed hod carrier, and as one who did remarkably well for himself.

The easiest way to sample Carver is to pick up *Where I'm Calling From*, an anthology of the stories he considered his best. If you want to explore further, try the individual collections. His early stories, gathered in *Will You Please Be Quiet, Please?* and *What We Talk About When We Talk About Love* have a menacing, off-balance feel. The later ones, collected mainly in *Cathedral*, are more relaxed, but perhaps less compelling. Skip the poems, which are embarassing, and the essays, which are worse.

See Also: If your tastes run to the minimal, you'll want to sample Ann Beattie, Frederick Barthelme, and Bobbie Anne Mason. If you prefer painful themes churning beneath mundane surfaces, then Richard Ford, Tobias Wolff, and Russell Banks may please. If you're drawn instead to writers who aren't so officially sanctioned, you might try Charles Bukowski and Charles Willeford, gifted lower-depths wallowers who wrote with comic-book gusto yet could also summon up currents of bitterness and melancholy. For sweet and funny visions of stray-ends America free of authorial gloom, you aren't likely to go wrong with the work of Tom Perrotta, William Price Fox, Sarah Gilbert, or James Wilcox.

—Ray Sawhill

Chabon, Michael
1963–
b. Washington, D.C.

FICTION: *The Mysteries of Pittsburgh** (1988), A Model World, and Other Stories (1990), **Wonder Boys** (1995), Werewolves in Their Youth (1999)

Back in the spring of 1988, an impossibly young writer published an impossibly elegant novel about five impossibly charming young people tripping adventurously through the hazards of incipient adulthood. *The Mysteries of Pittsburgh* captured a certain hopeful Fitzgeraldian expectancy in the waning months of the Reagan Administration. But then the 1990s turned out to be more or less a sequel to the 1980s, when adventure meant snowboarding vacations, and so Chabon, after his brief burst of acclaim, was unfairly forgotten by trendspotters.

Chabon often writes like a kind of seventh-grade prodigy, but his ebullience is balanced by the rigor of his writing. His sentences sound, in the best sense, labored over, and his wild allusive riffs—on history, books, architecture, dead jazzmen and ballplay-

83

ers—aren't done for show, but for the sheer joy of it. His second novel, *Wonder Boys*, is darker and stranger than *Mysteries*, but also funnier—following an aging writer as he careens through the detritus of his marriage and career. Chabon's short stories don't, on the whole, have as strong a personality as his novels. While you can tell he admires literary gemcutters like Cheever, he isn't really one of them. Still, his first collection, *A Model World*, has some terrific vignettes. In *Werewolves in Their Youth*, Chabon moves deeper into Fitzgerald territory—that place where young married couples dance separately with strangers, where former football heroes stare down the dwindling time clock of youth, and every party is a disaster waiting to happen.

See Also: Chabon was often misguidedly lumped with Jay McInerney, but Ethan Canin is much closer to him in style and temperament. Donna Tartt, in The Secret History, *gave a pulped-up rehash of* The Mysteries of Pittsburgh.

—*Adam Goodheart*

Cheever, John
1912–1982
b. Quincy, Massachusetts

SELECTED FICTION: The Way Some People Live (stories, 1943), The Enormous Radio and Other Stories (1953), **The Wapshot Chronicle** (1957), The Housebreaker of Shady Hill (stories, 1958), Some People, Places, and Things That Will Not Appear in My Next Novel (stories, 1961), **The Wapshot Scandal** (1964), The Brigadier and the Golf Widow (stories, 1964), Bullet Park (1969), The World of Apples (stories, 1973), **Falconer** (1977), ***The Stories of John Cheever** (1978), Oh, What a Paradise It Seems (1982)

NONFICTION: The Letters of John Cheever (1988), The Journals of John Cheever (1991)

His 1978 magnum opus, *The Stories of John Cheever*, sold half a million copies in hardcover—surely a record for an American short story collection. Cheever owed some of his popularity to purely literary qualities: a cadenced style, a flair for the humor of incongruity, and the lyrical codas that pull a number of his tales back from the abysses toward which they seem to be heading. But for many readers he also performed an almost redemptive function—defending American suburbs against the commonplace charge that they are stagnant sloughs of conformity and ennui.

Reading the evocative last line of Cheever's magnificent 1954 story "The Country Husband"—"it is a night where kings in golden suits ride elephants over the mountains"—a defensive suburban reader could transfer its mythopoeic aura from the writer's imaginary Shady Hill to her own real-life Shaker Heights or Grosse Pointe or Ladue. When *Time* devoted a 1964 cover story to Cheever, the piece's title, "Ovid in Ossining" (Ossining, New York, being Cheever's hometown), emphasized this blend of the fabled and the suburban in his work. Although in other groups of stories he scrutinized the mores of New Englanders in their summer retreats, of social-climbing couples in Manhattan, and of American expatriates in Rome, Cheever was best-known for his depictions of white-collar husbands who take the train to work in the city and the wives and kids they leave behind.

More than one hundred of his stories first appeared in *The New Yorker*, many of whose readers were those very suburbanites with chips on their shoulders. (Late in his career, when *The New Yorker* was still trapped in a prison of gentility and Cheever had entered a bawdy phase, he found a market in *Playboy*.) He was justly proud of his musical style, which owed something to Fitzgerald and even more to *The Book of Common Prayer*. In "The Brigadier and the Golf Widow," a story that gave its title to one of his collections, he posed himself a stylistic challenge—"It all began on an autumn afternoon—and who, after all these centuries, can describe the fineness of an autumn day?"—and met it splendidly: "The clear and searching sweep of sun on the lawns was like a climax of the year's lights. Leaves were burning somewhere and the smoke smelled, for all its ammoniac acidity, of beginnings. The boundless blue air was stretched over the zenith like the skin of a drum."

A phenomenon of twentieth-century American literature is the writer whose gift runs to the short story but who stretches himself to produce novels because that's what wows critics and book clubs—Peter Taylor and Eudora Welty come immediately to mind. But Cheever had started plugging away at a novel early in his career, and though it took him decades to publish one, when it came—*The Wapshot Chronicle*, in 1957—the strain, if any, was not evident. His inventiveness never flagged, but some of his later novels suffer from their whimsical construction. He managed to keep the material in *The Wapshot Chronicle* and *Falconer* under control, and they are the tightest and richest of his long works.

Falconer, which grew out of Cheever's stint as a volunteer writing instructor in Sing Sing prison, is also his most assured exploration of homosexuality. A family man who had extramarital affairs with women, Cheever, as he aged, took up with men as well, and one could put together a fascinating collection of stories and novel-excerpts chronicling his long journey out of the closet.

By the time of his death, Cheever had been heaped with honors and prizes—the

Pulitzer, the Howells Medal, the National Book Critics Circle's award, among others. He was at his best in those brushed-with-magic tales—"The Enormous Radio," "The Swimmer," "The Country Husband," and "Torch Song," among others—in which middle-class American men and women take on the dimensions of sibyls, sorcerers, satyrs, and nymphs even as Fate gives them the pummeling it reserves for humans.

See Also: Scott Donaldson's John Cheever: A Biography *is illuminating and well-proportioned. Cheever admired another master of the short story, Jean Stafford (1915–1979), enough to initiate an anthology in which his work appeared alongside hers and others'* (Stories by Jean Stafford, John Cheever, Daniel Fuchs, William Maxwell, *1956). Like Cheever, Stafford was a brilliant stylist whose stories sometimes hark back to mythology; start with her* Collected Stories *(1969).*

—Dennis Drabelle

Chute, Carolyn
1947–
b. Portland, Maine

FICTION: *The Beans of Egypt, Maine (1985), **Letourneau's Used Auto Parts** (1988), Merry Men (1994), Snow Man (1999)

"Welcome to Maine, Vacationland" read the state's cloying license plates, invoking a Yankee paradise where lobsters simmer in every beachfront homeowner's pot. Carolyn Chute (pronounced *Chewt*) writes with devastating clarity about the other Maine—rural, far inland—where men and women work the graveyard shifts, drink their booze out of jelly glasses, and have sex almost as indiscriminately as they trot out their firearms.

Chute's first and finest novel, *The Beans of Egypt, Maine*, is a primitivist, white trash chunk of sour feeling that provoked (not-quite-valid) comparisons to Faulkner. Chute's portrait of the robust Bean family ("the tackiest people on earth," one character calls them) is pieced together from a series of unsentimental vignettes that expose the family's ignorance, violence, and extreme poverty—leavened only slightly by Chute's frequent good humor and her on-again/off-again affection for the Beans. (Chute has had to defend that affection against critics who found the book voyeuristic and grotesque; in a postscript to a heavily-revised paperback version of the novel, she also denies that incest was implied in the infamous "nap" scene that opens the novel.)

Chute's next two novels, *Letourneau's Used Auto Parts* and *Merry Men*, also set in Egypt, Maine, are lesser works, although both have moments that rival anything in *Beans*. *Letourneau's Used Auto Parts* is about "Big Lucien" Letourneau, a minor character in *Beans*, who runs not only two salvage yards but Miracle City, a plot of shacks where he salvages down-on-their-luck people. *Merry Men*, which clocks in at nearly seven hundred pages, is Chute's most ambitious (and least winsome) attempt to chronicle Egypt's hurdy-gurdy past and present; it teems with characters and spans four decades. Chute's passion for social commentary has grown overly apparent—when not writing, she frequently dabbles in grass-roots, pro-firearm politics—and threatens to drown out her abundant narrative gifts. *Snow Man*, published in 1999, is anything but a return to form—it's an absurd political fantasy about a member of an "ultra-right-wing militia" who murders a U.S. Senator.

See Also: Dorothy Allison's fiction about dirt-poor Southern families is equally earthy, if more lyrical and heroic.

—*Dwight Garner*

Clancy, Tom
1947–
b. Baltimore, Maryland

FICTION: *The Hunt for Red October** (1984), Red Storm Rising (1986), **Patriot Games** (1987), **The Cardinal of the Kremlin** (1988), Clear and Present Danger (1989), The Sum of All Fears (1991), Submarine (1993), Without Remorse (1993), Debt of Honor (1994), Executive Orders (1996), Rainbow Six (1998)

When Tom Clancy took time off from his job in an insurance firm to write his first novel, *The Hunt for Red October*, the military thriller was a moribund genre. Preposterous spy and intrigue novels had their fans, but the audience for books that fetishized military equipment was limited mainly to *Guns & Ammo* subscribers. The only publisher interested in the amateur Navy historian's novel was Naval Institute

Press, which until then only published works of military scholarship. But the novel was a gripping work of suspense, and Clancy's fan base quickly expanded from the military (including then-Commander-in-Chief Ronald Reagan) to critics to, it seems today, everybody. Tightly-plotted and densely-researched, Clancy's tale of a Soviet submarine whose crew scrambles to defect validated the military thriller genre as a writerly pursuit. And, of course, a lucrative one: His novels have inspired movies, spin-off nonfiction books on military units, video games, and millions of dollars in sales.

Clancy, by his own admission, isn't a very good writer. His characters—including his beloved hero, former Marine Jack Ryan—are cookie-cutter sorts, and Clancy's attempts to fill out their more human aspects are usually forced and awkward. His main strength is plot. He has an unparalleled knack for creating military crises that are possible if implausible—terrorists explode a nuclear device at the Super Bowl in *The Sum of All Fears*, and in *Debt of Honor* a 747 crashes into the Capitol building. The respect Clancy commands in military circles has given him a remarkable amount of access for a civilian, and his books reflect a dense knowledge of the latest devices. Still, many of his books suffer from bloated stories, and by 1998's *Rainbow Six*, Clancy seemed to be running on autopilot, the plot threads slowly coming together to point at that inevitable conclusion: War is hell, but the good guys always win.

See Also: While few cover America's anti-terrorist forces with Clancy's rigorous detail, John le Carré, Ken Follett, and Martin Cruz Smith have all written above-potboiler-level novels set in top-secret milieus.

—*Mark Athitakis*

Coe, Jonathan
1961–
b. Birmingham, England

88

FICTION: The Accidental Woman (1987), A Touch of Love (1989), The Dwarves of Death (1990), **The Winshaw Legacy** (published in England as **What a Carve Up!**, 1994), *****The House of Sleep** (1997)

Had Jonathan Coe stuck with the small-scale literary gamesmanship of his first three novels, he might have remained a clever, minor writer. But with *The Winshaw Legacy, or What a Carve Up!*, and *The House of Sleep* he expresses an almost nineteenth-century faith in the ability of a novel to immerse you in a created world that resonates with the actual world at every turn. The modern subject that occasioned that leap of faith is one as worthy of rage and compassion as the workhouses and orphanages of Victorian England: the legacy of Margaret Thatcher and Conservative Party rule in Britain.

The Winshaw Legacy, the chronicle of a family of upper-class monsters and the young novelist who hires on to write their story, springs from Coe's curiosity about what it would be like to make Thatcher and her followers feel a fraction of the fear and powerlessness they inflicted on others. In the appallingly funny climax, Coe takes this fantasy of revenge so far that you may find yourself gasping, unable to laugh. *The House of Sleep*, less overtly political, is perhaps richer—a labyrinthine tale of coincidence, missed connections, and unexpected reunions, in which the characters struggle to find a common language. Coe's aesthetic response to his subject—a world ruled by the ethic of weaken, divide, and conquer—has been to renew the possibilities of the novel as both story and social chronicle, to speak in an uncommon language that is completely accessible.

See Also: The inevitable Martin Amis has covered some of the same ground, but can't match Coe for compassion or imaginative drive. Though very different in many ways, Hanif Kureishi's fiction provides some of the richest writing about contemporary London to be found anywhere.

—*Charles Taylor*

Coetzee, J. M.
1940–
b. Cape Town, South Africa

FICTION: Dusklands (two novellas, 1974), In the Heart of the Country (1977), **Waiting for the Barbarians** (1980), *Life & Times of Michael K (1983), Foe (1986), **Age of Iron** (1990), **The Master of Petersburg** (1994), Disgrace (1999)

NONFICTION: White Writing: On the Culture of Letters in South Africa (1988), Doubling the Point: Essays and Interviews (1992), Giving Offense: Essays on Censorship (1996), Boyhood: Scenes From Provincial Life (1997)

Perhaps any great writer is an amalgam of unlikely elements, but John Michael Coetzee is more unlikely than most. An English speaker of mostly Afrikaner ancestry, Coetzee has from birth been something of an outsider within the isolated and paranoid world of white South Africa, a society he has compared to a prison. His writing often features compelling and intimate descriptions of his country's harsh, spectacular landscapes, to which he feels a passionate, almost visceral attachment. Yet his books also have a more mysterious and universal dimension, a quality of modernist fable and even of absurdist existential exploration. More clearly than any other major living author, Coetzee is heir to the traditions of Franz Kafka and Samuel Beckett. Forces of politics and history are never far away in his fiction, but they tend to descend like cruel, impersonal weather systems, crushing some individuals and sparing others with a capricious lack of clarity or intention.

Only one of Coetzee's books, *Age of Iron*, is explicitly concerned with race and apartheid in contemporary South Africa. Despite its compelling descriptions of township violence, even that novel is strongly allegorical, reflecting the author's enduring preoccupation with the ambiguous nature of dialogue between master and slave. The tense, awkward relationship in *Age of Iron* between a dying white liberal and the homeless man she takes in continually repeats itself in Coetzee's fiction, from the spinster narrator's bewildered coupling with a servant in *In the Heart of the Country* to Fyodor Dostoevsky's charity toward a troublesome beggar who may be a police spy in *The Master of Petersburg*. Despite the comfortless character of Coetzee's moral vision, which offers little hope that the trauma and guilt of human history can ever be ameliorated, he clearly believes that the human struggle to communicate is honorable (although often futile) and that human life, even at its most ignoble, is inexpressibly precious.

Dusklands and *In the Heart of the Country* offer intriguing glimpses of Coetzee's descriptive powers, but both now have the dusty odor of 1970s experimental fiction. With *Waiting for the Barbarians*, a harrowing account of the downfall of a well-meaning administrator in a remote village on the fringes of a decaying empire, Coetzee's writing makes a quantum leap. Like all his books, *Barbarians* can be read in a single evening, but its pungent evocation of a menacing yet beautiful country that both is and is not South Africa, its exploration of what it means to be human in the face of monstrous cruelty, stays with you for a lifetime. *Life & Times of Michael K* is even better. The deeply affecting story of a simple and sheltered Cape Town gardener who becomes a war refugee, this is a brilliantly executed view of history from the bottom. Although understanding almost nothing of the events swirling around him, Michael has a will to live and a genuine love of the country that enables him to outlast the soldiers and bureaucrats who persecute him. The end of the apartheid era has sent Coetzee further afield for material. *Foe*, a parodic reflection of Daniel Defoe's *Robinson Crusoe*, is a bit dry, but *The Master of Petersburg*, a mystical mystery novel whose hero is Dostoevsky, is a cold, witty, and richly imagined meditation on art and love. With *Disgrace*, he won his second

Booker Prize and, in relating the fate of a scholar of Romantic poetry cast out of his job after a misbegotten affair with a student, tells us something we all suspect and fear—that political change can do almost nothing to eliminate human misery.

See Also: Coetzee's cryptic but spellbinding memoir, Boyhood, *is a must-read for fans. Although he is historically and personally connected to Nadine Gordimer, the other great white South African novelist of late apartheid, they are very different writers. Besides Kafka and Beckett, he can be linked to more realistic ironists concerned with the colonial experience, such as V. S. Naipaul and Paul Theroux.*

—Andrew O'Hehir

Colwin, Laurie
1944–1992
b. New York, New York

FICTION: Passion and Affect (stories, 1974), Shine on, Bright and Dangerous Object (1975), Happy All the Time (1978), **The Lone Pilgrim** (stories, 1981), Family Happiness (1982), Another Marvelous Thing (stories, 1986), *****Goodbye without Leaving** (1990), **A Big Storm Knocked It Over** (1993)

NONFICTION: Home Cooking: A Writer in the Kitchen (1988), More Home Cooking: A Writer Returns to the Kitchen (1993)

Laurie Colwin's people eat well. Her novel *Happy All the Time*—perhaps her best-known book—could just as easily have been titled *Hungry All the Time*; its central characters, a pair of young married couples in New York City, are always whipping up delectable picnics and soulfully proper meals out of whatever's lying around. But Colwin tricks you. These people might live in sweetly sloppy Greenwich Village apartments or artfully decorated penthouses, send their children to the best (progressive) private schools, and have offbeat yet respectable jobs as colonial-history professors or concert pianists—but that's far from a guarantee of tranquility. In their hearts, Colwin's characters are in serious turmoil.

For instance, the lovers in *Another Marvelous Thing*, a series of related short stories,

91

seem terrifically contented: They go to campy horror movies, share work stories, and ramble through fields together. They are also in solid marriages to other people. Though the arrangements of the affair are civilized and easy—they often are in Colwin—the feelings aren't. The moral, however, is not that they should have just behaved themselves; simply getting mixed up with other human beings causes trouble, Colwin seems to be saying, but that doesn't mean one shouldn't risk it.

Colwin, who grew up in suburban Philadelphia, once described her characters as "people whose problems are not directly economic. Not because I'm a shill for the upper middle class—believe me, I've spent most of my life not having money . . . Because I want them to have moral problems. Ethical problems. Dilemmas with identity." While a handful of her protagonists can be cloying, the majority are easy for readers to love.

Frequently, the work her characters do leads to spiritual or intellectual progress. In *Shine on, Bright and Dangerous Object*, a portrait of grief, it comes through studying rock 'n' roll piano; in *Goodbye Without Leaving*, the key is overlapping immersions in gospel music and Jewish tradition. Her protagonists are surreptitious outlaws: entirely appropriate at first glance, but they instigate emotional revolution.

Colwin also wrote two cookbooks, both in the no-nonsense, compassionate tone of a older sibling dispensing dinner-party instructions over the phone. Her chapter titles alone are priceless: "Alone in the Kitchen With an Eggplant"; "Desserts That Quiver"; "How to Disguise Vegetables"; "Jam Anxiety." Each recipe is actually an essay of brevity and charm.

Colwin's death from a heart attack at age forty-eight was a blow for the many admirers of her prose. Between her fiction—most of it still in print—and her eminently followable cookbooks, however, Colwin's influence is alive and well.

See Also: Laurie Colwin has been compared to such chroniclers of the urban bourgeoisie as John Updike and John Cheever, and to slyly precise masters of the domestic, like Colette and Jane Austen. Alison Lurie also comes to mind, as do Fay Weldon and—for wit amid devastation—Lorrie Moore.

—Emily Gordon

Cooper, Dennis
1953–
b. Pasadena, California

FICTION: Closer (1989), Frisk (1991), **Wrong** (stories, 1992), Jerk (1993), **Try** (1994), *Guide (1997), Period (2000)

POETRY: Idols (1979), The Tenderness of Wolves (1982), Safe (1984), He Cried (poems and stories, 1984), **The Dream Police: Selected Poems 1969–1993** (1995), All Ears: Criticism, Essays, and Obituaries (1999)

"I say more than I pretend to," says the speaker of Dennis Cooper's 1981 poem "Hustlers"—words that could serve as a *caveat lector* for this daring and disturbing writer's entire body of work. Cooper has established himself as the bard of a scorched emotional landscape, a world populated by kids so dazed that the mere possession of feelings—let alone their expression—seems an unaffordable luxury.

From the poems he began publishing in the mid-1970s to his four full-length novels, virtually all of Cooper's writing focuses on graphically depicted sexual and physical abuse of young men. His strongest books are the novels, *Try* and *Guide*, which manage to effectively balance the terror with a sense of ethical urgency. Although both focus on bloody scenarios, the characters also seek to escape their brutalized lives and form less damaging connections (as Ziggy, the numbed hero of *Try* puts it to his best friend with typical Cooperian eloquence, "You have to believe me, 'cos . . . your being alive is, like, *so important.*") Pulsing quietly through both books is a suspicion that things should be different, that life might become less intolerable.

Although he has provoked outrage in both conservative and liberal readers, it's impossible to mistake Cooper for an advocate of violence. The pained sputterings of his heroes are themselves powerful arguments against their own mistreatment. Cooper's unlikely achievement is to have fashioned a whole poetic language out of his characters' inarticulateness and seeming emotional indifference; in his books, artistry masquerades as nonchalance.

See Also: Aside from the trio of visionary French writers to whom he is often compared (de Sade, Rimbaud, Genet), Cooper's most important forebear is William S. Burroughs. Among his contemporaries, there's Gary Indiana, whose novel Resentment *(1997) skillfully explores a terrain of sex-and-death. Similar stylistic experiments—although with quite different subject matter—include Eileen Myles's brilliant 1994 story collection* Chelsea Girls, *which shares the oblique eloquence of Cooper's work, and Robert Gluck's* Jack the Modernist *(1985).*

—David Kurnick

Coover, Robert
1932–
b. Charles City, Iowa

SELECTED FICTION: The Origin of the Brunists (1966), **The Universal Baseball Association, Inc., J. Henry Waugh, Prop.** (1968), **Pricksongs & Descants** (stories, 1969), The Water Pourer (1972), *****The Public Burning** (1977), A Political Fable (stories, 1980), The Convention (stories, 1982), Spanking the Maid (stories, 1982), In Bed One Night & Other Brief Encounters (stories, 1983), Gerald's Party (1986), Aesop's Forest (stories, 1986), Whatever Happened to Gloomy Gus of the Chicago Bears? (1987), A Night at the Movies; or You Must Remember This (stories, 1987), Pinocchio in Venice (1991), **John's Wife** (1996), Briar Rose (stories, 1997), Ghost Town (1998)

Although his subjects are diverse, Robert Coover is always deconstructing myth, mythmaking, story, and storytelling. He has written about fundamentalism, baseball, movies, the Old West, fairy tales, the Rosenbergs, Richard Nixon, and the Cat in the Hat. He has retold fairy tales in *Hair O' The Chine, Briar Rose, Aesop's Forest,* and *Pinocchio In Venice,* and has reworked pop culture myths in *A Night at the Movies* and *Ghost Town.* He emphasizes the sense of entrapment in the very familiarity of these tales, a feeling that his characters are repeating their actions endlessly and without enlightenment.

Coover's first novel, surprisingly, is realist. *The Origin of the Brunists* relates the formation of an apocalyptic Christian sect and shows few direct links to Coover's later work, apart from its acuity of language and a grim world view. His charming second novel, *The Universal Baseball Association,* tells the story of a lonely man who runs an entire baseball league in his imagination; by novel's end the phantom league has acquired a kind of reality superior to its creator's. Coover's third book and perhaps his most important, *Pricksongs & Descants,* completes this movement to the interior; here he stakes out territory he will later occupy obsessively. Every story in this collection is a metafic-

94

tion, aware of the contingencies of story qua story, employing the devices of naturalism to subvert naturalism. The primacy of narrative both reinforces and undermines the reality of what is narrated, a technique that defines all of Coover's later work.

The results can be brilliant. *The Public Burning* is Coover's great book. Centered on the execution of Julius and Ethel Rosenberg, it draws characters and events from real life, but is less a historical novel than an American fantasia. Uncle Sam, in stovepipe hat and striped trousers, becomes as real as Richard Nixon. The Rosenbergs die, as indeed they did, not for what they might have done, but to legitimate the story America tells to and about itself.

Everything Coover writes is charged with raw eroticism and a barely contained violence which sometimes crosses into misogyny and misanthropy. Though usually under control, at times this demonic energy seems undirected. When he chooses a stage broad enough to accommodate it, and when the mundane holds the imagined in tension—as when he escalates the gossip, fantasies, and dreams of a small Midwestern town into horrific surrealism in *John's Wife*—it can be illuminating, but in the claustrophobic milieu of, say, *Spanking the Maid* or *Gerald's Party*, things can turn tedious or ugly.

Coover's interest in narrative forms has led him to teach courses in hypertext, computer-based fiction which is supposed to supersede the linearity of print, but which is so far more hype than text. He has not yet produced a hyperfiction, probably wisely, since he has long since achieved its promised effects on the page.

See Also: Coover's voice is uniquely his own, but his metafictional concerns are shared by many writers, including John Barth, William Gass, John Hawkes, Harry Mathews, Flann O'Brien, Gilbert Sorrentino, and Rudolf Wurlitzer.

—*Carter Scholz*

Coupland, Douglas
1961–
b. Baden-Soellingen, Germany

FICTION: Generation X: Tales for an Accelerated Culture (1991), Shampoo Planet (1992), Life after God (stories and essays, 1994), **Microserfs** (1995), Girlfriend in a Coma (1998), Miss Wyoming (2000)

NONFICTION: Polaroids from the Dead (essays and stories, 1996)

After coining the moniker *Generation X* with his bestselling 1991 novel of that title, Douglas Coupland has made a career out of lamenting the plights of various middle-class, post–Baby-Boom Americans, from the "global teens" depicted in *Shampoo Planet* to the workaholic computer programmers of *Microserfs*, all of them wistfully disaffected. *Generation X* was his first and its title instantly became the ubiquitous nickname for forty-seven million Americans. It follows three friends, Andy, Claire, and Dag—shiftless post-collegiates all—as they dream and wander through a stark, created-from-nothing Palm Springs landscape. The book was cele-brated for its unusual format, with witty cartoons and definitions ("bleeding ponytail," "McJob," "veal-fattening pen") scattered in its margins. With it, Coupland proved himself a modestly thoughtful and compassionate—if somewhat sentimental—Zeitgeist-gazing journalist with a penchant for the minutia pop culture.

With the world watching, Coupland followed up with *Shampoo Planet*, hardly a convincing argument for growth in the author's scope or talents. His subjects are affluent teenagers at fitful war with their parents and grandparents. Coupland villainizes the older generation, blaming them for frittering away the future, leaving their kids with little more than the stumps in a clearcut redwood forest. The book is competent, but not much more than a hollow retread of the already slight *Generation X*.

With the short fiction and essays in *Life Before God* Coupland set out to map his generation's spiritual evolution without the benefit (or curse) of *Generation X*'s statistics, quotes, and catchphrases. The possibility that Coupland's finger remained firmly pressed to his own personal pulse, that his generational spokesmanship might be largely narcissistic, became harder to ignore.

Finally, though, with *Microserfs*, Coupland found a better use for his talents. Based on the lives of a group of Microsoft employees, *Microserfs* started out as a long story in *Wired* magazine and allowed Coupland to fuse his infatuations with the here-and-now, pop culture, technobabble, and workplace culture. Although the plot is strained, he shrewdly renders the singular, engagingly bizarre culture and psyche of the legendary software company. With *Girlfriend in a Coma*, unfortunately, he returned to loftier aims, titling the novel, aptly, after a song by the whiny rock band, The Smiths. The story of a girl who wakes up from a twenty-year coma, travelling instantly from the 1970s to the 1990s, it follows another gang of chronically mopey friends, this time through a global apocalypse.

Coupland's on-again/off-again knack for capturing the lives of young people in the 1980s and 1990s has it strengths, but they're almost all journalistic. Unable to create plausible—or even varied—characters, he may enjoy a seemingly unending supply of book contracts but the result is fiction that is twice as wide as it is deep.

See Also: Coupland has dozens of would-be imitators, but anyone who savors his breezy, observational philosophizing will find more meat in the author who clearly inspired him, Kurt Vonnegut.

—*David Eggers*

Crews, Harry
1935–
b. Alma, Georgia

FICTION: ***The Gospel Singer** (1968), Naked in Garden Hills (1969), This Thing Don't Lead to Heaven (1970), Karate Is a Thing of the Spirit (1971), **Car** (1972), The Hawk Is Dying (1973), The Gypsy's Curse (1974), A Feast of Snakes (1976), The Enthusiast (stories, 1981), Two (stories, 1984), All We Need of Hell (1987), **The Knockout Artist** (1988), Body (1990), Scar Lover (1992), The Mulching of America (1995), Celebration (1998)

NONFICTION: A Childhood: A Biography of a Place (memoir, 1978), Blood and Grits (essays, 1979), Florida Frenzy (essays and stories, 1982), Madonna at Ringside (1991), Classic Crews: A Harry Crews Reader (fiction, memoir, and essays, 1993)

A tenant farmer's son, Harry Crews grew up dirt-poor in what he has called "the worst hookworm and rickets part of Georgia." He turned to fiction, "out of a fear and loathing for what I was and who I was. It was all out of an effort to pretend otherwise."

The characters in Crews's fiction tend to be similarly mortified by their white trash beginnings; they'll cut almost any bargain that promises physical or moral redemption. Many of them escape the swamplands of Georgia and Florida by becoming freakish performance artists—absurdist one-trick ponies. Herman Mack, the protagonist of 1972's *Car*, eats an entire Ford Maverick; in 1988's *The Knockout Artist*, Eugene Biggs exploits his ability, via his fantastically vulnerable jaw, to knock himself out.

In another writer's hands, these grotesque, implausible allegories might be funneled into ruthless short stories, *a la* Kafka's "The Hunger Artist." Crews, however, is so tickled by the fuss his "artists" kick up that he can't tune it out. He employs expansive supporting casts (lots of midgets, psychopaths, social uglies, and neo-Bubbas), spraying peripheral hoopla through the air like glitter. In his capable hands, Crews's comically-bent sagas become spectacles of antic miracle and wonder; the best of these wacked-out Southern Gothics have a star-spangled earnestness that might remind you of Robert Altman's *Nashville*. (If you can find them; much of Crews's early work has been allowed to drift out of print.)

While *Car* and *The Knockout Artist* are perhaps Crews's most exuberant and entertaining books, his first novel, *The Gospel Singer*, and his memoir, *A Childhood*, are his most lucid and penetrating. In *The Gospel Singer*, a young man manages to flee his small Georgia town by becoming a nationally famous evangelist and singer, only to be dragged back down by violence and simmering racial hatreds. *A Childhood* is a clear-eyed, and surprisingly tender, account of Crews's youth in a place where "there wasn't enough cash money . . . to close up a dead man's eyes."

Crews has written more than his share of clumsy sentences, and many of his books can, at times, feel like bumpy, rudderless rides. (*All We Need of Hell*, the tale of a tough-guy lawyer who's going to seed, sounds like *Heart of Darkness* as line-read by pro wrestlers.) In his most recent novels, Crews has become more of a belter—he's less likely to worry his way through a complex sentence or thought. But by and large, his words have lost none of their flat-footed swat.

Many of Crews's books end violently, and when you tally up all the carnage, it's tempting to write him off as an easy fatalist, a connoisseur of ruin. ("The smell of blood is on them," Crews has said of his books, "the sense of mortality is a little too strong.") What sticks in your mind about his work, though, is the voluminous, hurdy-gurdy sweep of his comic and moral vision. His Southern-fried landscapes teem with heretofore unidentified life.

See Also: In a better world, Harry Crews's cult following would surpass that of another bare-knuckled writer, Charles Bukowski.

98

—*Dwight Garner*

Crichton, Michael
1942–
b. Chicago, Illinois

FICTION: The Andromeda Strain (1969), The Terminal Man (1972), Westworld (1974), The Great Train Robbery (1975), Eaters of the Dead: The Manuscripts of Ibn Fadlan, Relating His Experiences with the Northmen in A.D. 922 (1976), Congo (1980), Sphere (1987), Jurassic Park (1990), Rising Sun (1992), Disclosure (1994), The Lost World (1995), Airframe (1996), Timeline (1999)

NONFICTION: Five Patients: The Hospital Explained (1970), Jasper Johns (1977), Electronic Life: How to Think about Computers (1983), Travels (1988)

Although Michael Crichton has written fourteen novels, four works of nonfiction, seven screenplays, and nine other books under pseudonyms, it is not necessarily clear that he is a writer. He is, without a doubt, perhaps the most successful crafter of popular entertainment in this century. *The Andromeda Strain*, *The Great Train Robbery*, *Jurassic Park*, *The Lost World*, *Disclosure*, *Rising Sun*, *Twister*, and the television show *ER*, among others, all emanated from his pen, quickly moving from print to visual media, usually finding spectacular financial success. Crichton himself was equally adaptable, directing seven of the movies made from his books. In 1995 alone, his earnings were twenty-two million dollars.

Crichton was a medical student working with Jonas Salk when he wrote his first book, *The Andromeda Strain*, in 1969. Telling the story of an extraterrestrial virus with doomsday capabilities, the novel quickly became a bestseller, then a hit movie, and spawned the term "techno-thriller" for its heavy use of medical and scientific fact. With his extraordinarily prescient anticipation of such future threats as AIDS and superbacteria, Crichton invented the genre of biological crisis. In subsequent novels such as *Disclosure*, which dealt with reverse sexual harrassment, and *Rising Sun*, which exploited American fears of Japanese economic power, Crichton proved similarly adept at tapping into latent public fears, fanning them into high-grossing flames. With *Jurassic Park* and its sequel, *The Lost World*, Crichton drew together every American child's obsession— dinosaurs—with the creeping adult terror of new reproductive technologies in his tale of an all-female dinosaur colony cloning itself willy-nilly, with dire long-nailed results.

Avant la lettre, Crichton also invented synergy, that late '90s notion of "properties"—articles, essays, screenplays, or works of fiction—that move fluidly, and profitably, from print to film or television. Crichton's "novels" are so sketchy of character ("It didn't matter who the people were," he said of writing *The Andromeda Strain*), so studded with nonnarrative chunks of technical fact, and so relentlessly cinematic that it is never entirely clear whether one is reading a novel, an article about a pressing social concern, or a screenplay. Nor can one ever be sure whether all the "facts" displayed so aggressively are, in fact, real. *The Andromeda Strain*, for instance, with its fictional virus, concludes with pages of footnotes referencing real texts, but the book also makes use of "unclassified" government documents that are plainly made up, the real and the unreal blending together seamlessly. It's infotainment. More than such French avant-gardists as Alain Robbe-Grillet or Georges Perec, Crichton has taken the novel as we know it apart, rendering it transparent to information, visual media, and advertising. His books are, quite literally, screens, unapologetically machines for making money. Despite their huge popular success, not a single one really features any sort of flesh-and-blood hero. The "hero," instead, is the concept.

Is this art, even popular art? Does it matter? As all print solids dissolve into the electronic ether, the only thing that can said for certain of Crichton's protean work is that it is very, very good business.

See Also: Robin Cook and Tom Clancy write commercial fiction with similarly suspenseful plots and wooden characters—Cook about the medical profession and Clancy about the military. Crichton has written genre crime novels under the pseudonyms John Lange and Jeffrey Hudson.

—*Stacey D'Erasmo*

Cunningham, Michael
1952–
b. Cincinnati, Ohio

FICTION: Golden States (1984), A Home at the End of the World (1990), Flesh and Blood (1995), ***The Hours** (1998)

Michael Cunningham wants to write the Great Gay Novel. There's no such thing, it's pure dumb hubris, yet he has a not-bad chance of pulling it off. To the remarkable extent that he's already staked his claim as a literary voice, he's concentrated on two

BOOKS FROM THE EDGE THAT BELONG
IN THE CENTER *by Michael Cunningham*

Although every book should be more widely read than it is, the following five beauties have been particularly sorely neglected. These are favorites of mine—the list, of course, could have been far, far longer.

Aquamarine by Carol Anshaw

This remarkable first novel traces three different possible futures, all stemming from a single cathartic moment in a woman's life. I found it stunning when I picked it up in 1992; I've still never read anything quite like it.

I Remember by Joe Brainard

This is one of the more peculiar books I've ever read, and I think about it often. Brainard simply accumulates anecdotal memories, one on top of another, deadpan, until they begin to add up to a life, and then to imply, mysteriously, the existence of a soul.

Atlantis: Three Tales by Samuel Delany

If Samuel Delany were writing in the same innovative, intelligent way and his books were not science fiction, he'd be known to every serious reader and not just a relatively small band of us.

The Mirror by Lynn Freed

Freed is certainly well-known enough, but I would like to move to a parallel dimension in which everything is exactly as it is in this dimension with one exception: Lynn Feed is a huge bestseller, and *The Mirror* was among the most-discussed books of 1998.

The Force of Gravity by Robert S. Jones

This brilliant novel, Jones's first, about a man's mental disintergration, was too dark and harrowing for just about everybody and didn't sell despite its strong reviews. It's a pitch-black gem, a terrifying book with the power to harm.

themes: the deep, romantic friendships of gay men with women, and the depredations of AIDS.

Given their lofty aims and their eagerness to achieve big effects, both *A Home at the End of the World*, the novel that established his reputation, and the long family saga *Flesh and Blood* are surprising for their workmanlike prose (you have to go searching to find a metaphor) and their structural blobbiness. But they may have just been apprentice work. *The Hours* really is a literary novel, ostentatiously patterned on Virginia Woolf's *Mrs.*

Dalloway but so confident and yet so genuinely modest (an homage, not an imitation) that it wins you over. The interweaving chapters follow the psychologically fragile Woolf on a day in 1923, while she is writing *Mrs. Dalloway*; a discontented young mother in late '40s Los Angeles, who is reading *Mrs. Dalloway*; and a happily coupled lesbian in late '90s Manhattan, who has been nicknamed Mrs. Dalloway by her closest friend, a poet dying of AIDS. Though *The Hours* is slimmer than Cunningham's earlier novels, it's far more complex. The questions: Can he bring this level of authority to the bulky gay saga he has always wanted to write? Or have his ambitions themselves changed?

See Also: Other novelists who have chronicled late twentieth-century gay life include David Leavitt (who is less concerned with the family), Stephen McCauley (who writes in a lighter vein), and Dale Peck (the artiest—and when he's good, the finest—of the bunch).
—*Craig Seligman*

Danticat, Edwidge
1969–
b. Port-au-Prince, Haiti

FICTION: Breath, Eyes, Memory (1994), Krik? Krak! (stories, 1995), The Farming of Bones (1998)

Edwidge Danticat published three books of fiction while still in her twenties and has been anointed by Oprah and the *New York Times*, chosen for *Granta*'s 1996 list of "20 Best Young American Novelists Under 40" and nominated for the National Book Award. Such accolades suggest that she's a writer of unusual accomplishment, but alas, no. To be fair, Danticat's first three books show occasional flickers of graceful writing, but on the whole her basic fictional mechanics are crude and her authorial vision sophomoric and unbelievable.

How could a writer of such modest abilities become so exalted? It's hard to escape the conclusion that the critics are guilty of race pandering, and that an increasingly cynical and commercially-shrewd publishing industry has designated Danticat—youthful, attractive, educated, Haitian—as the next Alice Walker.

According to an interview with Danticat, she was courted throughout graduate school by an editor at Soho Press who had read a portion of *Breath, Eyes, Memory* in

102

manuscript. Danticat had begun that manuscript in high school, and despite the intervening years, it reads like a high school student wrote it. Among the myriad themes Danticat trots out in this Haitian-American saga of spiritual and generational reconciliation are sexual trauma, eating disorders, abandonment, racial shame, feminism, breast cancer, alcoholism, unrequited love, political upheaval, the plight of the immigrant, the romanticized Haiti versus the "real" Haiti, folklore, filial duty, postpartum adjustments, and the recovery movement. The novel is a shaggy dog story, rife with unintentional false trails and amateurish plotting, often kicked along by wooden dialogue whose expository function Danticat doesn't even try to disguise.

Krik? Krak!, Danticat's second book, follows the same pattern (a number of the stories were written while Danticat was an undergraduate). Despite fits of captivating imagery (a prostitute who works at home sees the shadow of her little boy, cast on the bedsheet curtain dividing the room, stretch to the size of a man), the collection is distractingly self-conscious. *The Farming of Bones*—about the genocidal massacre ordered in 1937 by Haiti's neighbor country, the Dominican Republic—has longer passages of fully realized, confidently crafted writing, but also more of Danticat's customary vagueness and simplistic, knee-jerk themes (the hard-working, caring Haitian sugar cane workers versus the evil Dominican gentry). How many times must one read, say, scenes describing characters as being in two places or wearing incompatible expressions at once, or events that could not have happened in the time period or sequence given, or stilted conversations that reveal plot action that the characters couldn't possibly know or foretell, or action that is predicated on relationships that were never established? Again, the landscape is all that seems real. Danticat's work seems built wholly of atmosphere. As has, apparently, her career.

See Also: If you really like Danticat, Alice Walker will probably ring your chimes as well. Otherwise, a AAA guidebook to the West Indies is probably comparable.

—Kate Moses

Davenport, Guy
1927–
b. Anderson, South Carolina

FICTION: Tatlin! (1974), Da Vinci's Bicycle (stories, 1979), Eclogues (stories, 1981), Trois Caprices (stories, 1982), Apples and Pears and Other Stories (1984), The Jules

Verne Steam Balloon (1987), The Drummer of the Eleventh North Devonshire Fusiliers (1990), *A Table of Green Fields (1993), The Cardiff Team: Ten Stories (1996), Twelve Stories (1997)

SELECTED NONFICTION: The Geography of the Imagination: Forty Essays (1981), Every Force Evolves a Form (1987), A Balthus Notebook (1989), Charles Burchfield's Seasons (1994), The Hunter Gracchus and Other Papers on Literature and Art (1996), Objects On A Table: Harmonious Disarray (1998)

Guy Davenport's ten collections of short stories are all improbable and mostly enjoyable, even when they don't work as "stories." A professor of classics, a Rhodes scholar, winner of a MacArthur grant, essayist, visual artist, and renowned translator, Davenport writes fictions that defy plot—they defy even their subjects—and are instead myths of desire, or of prayer, or of the act of creating art or love. "Tatlin!" from his collection of the same title, borrows an actual, but little-known Russian sculptor and speculates on how he came to be himself. The story reads like a haunting of the place inspiration comes from. "The Concord Sonata," from *A Table of Green Fields*, tries to fathom the riddle of a paragraph Thoreau once wrote. In the same collection is "Gunnar and Nikolai", in which a young teacher models a sculpture of Ariel on a student who's infatuated with him: "Imagine you can walk on the wind just under the speed of light . . . Fatigue is as unknown to you as to a bee," the teacher says to his model. All the stories are cast in this prose style, as elegant as any in use.

"I am not writing for fellow critics, but for people who like to read, to look at pictures, and to know things," Davenport begins in his collection of essays, *The Hunter Gracchus*. Perhaps. The essays are, like his fiction, formidably erudite, but accessible for all of that. *The Geography of the Imagination*, for example, provides insight for the academic and an education to the casual reader, and Davenport's book-length essay on the history of the still life, *Objects on a Table: Harmonious Disarray*, may alter forever your experience of museums and junk shops.

104

See Also: Readers who like Davenport's mix of history, surrealism, myth and erotica should check out Anne Carson, another classicist, and Jeanette Winterson, as well as Felisberto Hernandez, Jean Rhys, Jamaica Kincaid, and Isak Dinesen.

—Alexander Chee

Davies, Robertson
1913–1995
b. Thamesville, Ontario

FICTION: *THE SALTERTON TRILOGY: Tempest-Tost (1951), Leaven of Malice (1954), A Mixture of Frailties (1958), THE DEPTFORD TRILOGY:* **Fifth Business** *(1970),* **The Manticore** *(1972),* **World of Wonders** *(1975), THE CORNISH TRILOGY:* ***The Rebel Angels** *(1981), What's Bred in the Bone (1985), The Lyre of Orpheus (1988),* High Spirits: A Collection of Ghost Stories (1982), Murther & Walking Spirits (1991)

NONFICTION: A Voice from the Attic: Essays on the Art of Reading (1960), The Heart of a Merry Christmas (1970), Stephen Leacock (1970), One Half of Robertson Davies: Provocative Pronouncements on a Wide Range of Topics (1977), The Enthusiasms of Robertson Davies (1979), Robertson Davies, The Well-Tempered Critic: One Man's View of Theatre and Letters in Canada (1981), The Mirror of Nature (lectures, 1983), Reading and Writing (lectures, 1993), The Merry Heart: Reflections on Reading, Writing, and the World of Books (1997)

AS SAMUEL MARCHBANKS: The Diary of Samuel Marchbanks (1947), The Table Talk of Samuel Marchbanks (1949), Samuel Marchbanks' Almanac (1967), The Papers of Samuel Marchbanks (excerpts from three titles above, 1985)

The late Canadian professor with the thespian beard and Macassar-oil vocabulary is the one truly entertaining writer of the past twenty years who can make you feel smarter than you really are—for a while. Most fiction in recent memory takes place in a laboratory of sensation. Davies relocates the proving ground for psychological truth to a university library—he was Master of Massey College in Toronto for almost twenty years—where the shelves are collapsing under the weight of exotic reference materials nobody would ever have heard of if it weren't for him. The role of horse manure in restoring violins, the erotic duties of certain saints, art forgery techniques every scholar should know: His erudition would choke you if he didn't feed it to you delicately, like a trayful of cerebral eclairs.

There's cool obscure information and there's obscure obscure information, however, and the difference is what makes some of Davies's novels irresistibly complex and others—*What's Bred in the Bone*, for one—chatty and dry. *Fifth Business* is his nonpareil, centering on one brilliant device, a rock that got packed into a snowball and pegged at the wrong person. The wildly unrelated elements he works in bring unexpected dimen-

105

sions to his parsing of human nature. A small-time magician turns tyrannical virtuoso, an opportunistic marriage implodes, and the hero goes on a one-legged campaign to canonize the crazy lady who was accidentally beaned by the leitmotif. This beginning novel of The Deptford Trilogy has a near-demonic energy that peters out before the end of the series, but not before the reader is catapulted most of the way into a brand-new appreciation of what history can do for poor slobs like us.

Davies careens all over the place in The Cornish Trilogy, too. Again the charm and intrigue that enliven the first book may propel you energetically into the second one, only this time, you won't get as far before it hits you that the characters don't matter enough. *The Rebel Angels*, the first volume of the three, is probably Davies's most lovable work, and the only one with a female protagonist. Passionately devoted to education, the author never quite figured out women's intellectual stake in higher learning, and peopled his work with helpless drudges and eat-'em-alive gals who spell certain death to thinking men. But when he does get around to drawing a thoroughly self-possessed female, she can be a lulu, and there are two of them here. Maria Theotoky, heart-stopping beauty and student of New Testament Greek, makes a dandy catalyst for the liberation of a precious manuscript. Even better is Maria's mother, a simon-pure gypsy with a whole fortune in solid gold coins in her basement and a million tricks up her sleeve.

It's strange indeed that Davies admired the thinking of "the duke of dark corners," Carl Jung, and yet had such a hard time with the vagaries of art and artists, not to mention sex. The last two books in The Cornish Trilogy deal with painting and opera, respectively, but can't seem to encompass these two creative pursuits unless they're rolled out thin and flat. Though Davies revered creativity and was nourished by it, he seemed to think artists themselves were a pesky and unrealized element—like a lot of women, maybe?—and needed to be vigorously managed. Davies started out as an actor and was a prolific playwright as well, but if he had any tenderness for the foot soldiers in the creative arts, it's hard to tell. Furthermore, erotic pleasure in his novels seems to exist for people who are too crude or too freaked out to master anything else.

This and other awkward aspects of Davies's characters suggest an author distancing himself a bit from humanity, just as the odd and deliberately stagey names Davies gives to some of his bit players—Liesl Vitzliputzli, Milo Papple, Dr. Gunilla Dahl-Soot—mark them as grotesques. There but for the grace of God, with a capital G, dear reader, go you. The creeping feeling of inadequacy that Davies eventually imparts can be a little draining, but his images of human ingenuity and perversity are great can-openers for the imagination. Look for the gypsy lady and the snowball, and you'll come out way ahead.

See Also: Siegfried Sassoon's Memoirs of a Fox-hunting Man *is set in the same time frame—World War I—as* Fifth Business. *The writing is similarly matter-of-fact and coolly sexless, which means the hero's passion for riding to hounds can assume an airless, archival beauty that's Davies all the way.*

—Sally Eckoff

Davis, Lydia
1947–
b. Northampton, Massachusetts

FICTION: The Thirteenth Woman and Other Stories (1976), Sketches for a Life of Wassily (stories, 1981), Story and Other Stories (1983), **Break It Down** (stories, 1986), *****The End of the Story** (1995), **Almost No Memory** (stories, 1997)

Lydia Davis has three distinct fan clubs. Most of her admirers know her as a French-translator; she is to her generation what Francis Steegmuller was, and Richard Howard is, to theirs: an intellectual stylist able to handle gracefully the most diverse, sophisticated French texts, from Blanchot to *Swann's Way*. A smaller coterie knows Davis for her own short stories—though to call these "short stories" is somewhat misleading: some are fables, some epigrams, some pensées, some stripped-down pastiches. Many are black-comic vignettes of marital horror (as if Louise Glück had written *Meadowlands* in prose); most are very short.

The third, perhaps the smallest, club is devoted to Davis's novel, her masterpiece, *The End of the Story*. The story is purely metafictional: a novelist-narrator sits down to reconstruct the end of an affair, years before, with a younger man.

On its surface, *The End* shares with Davis's short fiction a certain Gallic austerity. There are no place names, no brand names, no sex scenes, and there is next to no dialogue. Davis names neither of her main characters. Her diction is circumspect, self-conscious, uptight. Her account of the lies we tell in love, to ourselves and each other, can make a reader skim (like covering your eyes in a movie). Her narrator's account of the writing process amounts to a defense of the art. This is not a novel to take on a trip for two. It is, however, very funny, mordant, original, and (despite its relative obscurity) influential: certainly one of the great short novels of the 1990s.

See Also: *Although she has sometimes been compared to Paul Auster, another French translator addicted to spare sentences and pared down vocabularies, Davis is closer—in* *her subtlety and humor—to Glück and—in the immediacy of her prose—to the Jamaica Kincaid of* My Brother.

—*Lorin Stein*

de Bernieres, Louis
1954–
b. London, England

FICTION: **The War of Don Emmanuel's Nether Parts** (1990), **Senor Vivo and the Coca Lord** (1991), **The Troublesome Offspring of Cardinal Guzman** (1992), *****Captain Corelli's Mandolin** (1994)

The novels of Louis de Bernieres exhibit a great fondness for women and children, for goats, jaguars, sorcerers, heretical levitating priests—and for the two policemen and four military men (out of a large cast of bullies, hypocrites, and torturers) who try to remain decent in the midst of brutal nationalisms, terrorisms, arms-smuggling rings, drug cartels, a latter-day Catholic Inquisition, and World War II. De Bernieres's first three novels are set in a mythical South American country that combines the most interesting features of Chile under Pinochet, Argentina under the generals, and Columbia under its druglord shadow government.

The trilogy covers ten exceptionally busy years. Guerrilla groups fight with the army and with each other; a very ordinary colonel learns how to "disappear" people; the Indian Aurelio becomes a brujo; and Dona Constanza discovers the joys of sex with her Communist abductor and is permanently won over to the people's cause. Then the entire village of Chiriguana goes into exile with their band of pet jaguars and, on the ruins of an Incan city, builds a utopian town devoted to lovemaking and festivals. And that's just the first book.

In the second, a philosophy lecturer named Dionisio Vivo undertakes a one-man letter-writing campaign against the coca gangs and becomes a national hero and a great brujo. In the last, the enchanting and improbable characters we've come to love, all of them now residents of the legendary town Cochadebajo de los Gatos, fight off Monsignor Aquilar's goon squad of crusaders. The novels are funny and bawdy, with characters so full of juicy eccentricities you want to bite into them. But de Bernieres also uses his sensory language to show us brutish physical realities like rape, torture, and mutilation.

Captain Corelli's Mandolin, de Bernieres's best novel to date, is a quieter, more tempered work, bathed in the classical light of epic and tragedy. On a Greek island during WWII, Dr. Iannis and his daughter are forced to billet Captain Antonio Corelli, one of the occupying Italian soldiers. Antonio is a playful, humanely civilized man who woos the resisting Pelagia with his mandolin. De Bernieres joins comedy and tragedy in seamless virtuosity to feed the starved senses and heal some of the wounds of our damaged reality.

See Also: Gabriel García Márquez, Peter Høeg, Salman Rushdie, and Carlos Castenada are four other authors who combine real, regional history with fable and surrealism.

—*Brigitte Frase*

Delany, Samuel R.
1942–
b. New York, New York

FICTION: The Jewels of Aptor (1962), *THE FALL OF THE TOWERS TRILOGY:* Captives of the Flame ([republished in 1968 as Out of the Dead City], 1963), The Towers of Toron (1964), City of a Thousand Suns (1965), The Ballad of Beta-2 (1965), Empire Star (1966), Babel-17 (1966), The Einstein Intersection (1966), Nova (1968), Driftglass: Ten Tales of Speculative Fiction (1971), Equinox (1973), *Dhalgren** (1975), **Trouble on Triton** (1976), **Tales of Nevèrÿon** (Return to Nevèrÿon series, 1979), **Neveryóna** (Return to Nevèrÿon series, 1983), **Flight from Nevèrÿon** (Return to Nevèrÿon series, 1985), **Return to Nevèrÿon** (Return to Nevèrÿon series, 1986), Stars in My Pocket Like Grains of Sand (1984), Driftglass/Starshards (collected short fiction; 1993), They Fly at Ciron ([written in 1962], 1992), Hogg ([written in 1973], 1994), The Mad Man (1994), Atlantis: Three Tales (1995)

NONFICTION: The Jewel-Hinged Jaw: Notes on the Language of Science Fiction (1977), The American Shore: Meditations on a Tale of Science Fiction by Thomas M. Disch (1978), Heavenly Breakfast: An Essay on the Winter of Love (1978), Starboard Wine: More Notes on the Language of Science Fiction (1984), **The Motion of Light in Water: Sex and Science Fiction in the East Village** (1988, 1990), The Straits of Messina (1989), Silent Interviews:

On Language, Race, Sex, Science Fiction, and Some Comics (1994), Longer Views (1995), Times Square Red, Times Square Blue (1999)

An ambitious autodidact in the grand tradition, Samuel Ray Delany, Jr. has been called the "most individual of America's individualist writers." For four decades and in a half-dozen genres, Delany has outraged and comforted readers with formally innovative, determinedly eclectic, and uniquely heartfelt work.

Kathy Acker described his fiction as "a conversation between you and Samuel Delany about the possibilities of being human." Delany seems driven by the desire to honestly communicate previously unspoken (or previously unspeakable) aspects of the human experience—even his grungiest material is surprisingly warm in tone. As William Gibson put it, "I remember being simply and frequently grateful to Delany for so powerfully confirming that certain states had ever been experienced at all, by anyone."

Delany's early work exuberantly crossbred an astonishing array of elements: space opera conventions, linguistic theory, bisexual triads, mythic archetypes, and the emotional complexities of sadomasochism. This phase ended in 1968 with the publication of the award-winning *Nova*, an attempt to do for the outer space swashbuckler what *Moby-Dick* did for sea stories, and the writing of his first pornographic novel, the Grand Guignol fantasy *Equinox*.

After a long silence, Delany re-emerged in the mid-1970s with three startling novels: *Hogg* (unpublished until 1995), a clear-eyed depiction of rape and sexual abuse, and perhaps the most effectively offensive work in American literature; *Dhalgren*, the portrait of a bisexual drifter in a late 1960s city and a massive centrifuge of era-summarizing ambition, hyper-naturalist technique, science fictional motifs, poetics, urban gangs, and structuralist theory; and *Trouble on Triton*, an "ambiguous heterotopia" which seamlessly blends interplanetary warfare, Jamesian character-determined prose, and feminist satire to describe its blond hetero hero's imagined victories and true defeats.

An early devotee of poststructuralist and feminist theory, Delany began *Return to Nevèrÿon*, an archeological fantasy series that was to occupy him on and off through the 1980s. Often described as "A Child's Garden of Semiotics," the series encompasses slave revolts, women warriors, dragons, Lacanian analysis, bondage-and-discipline, an alternative Genesis, and the invention of writing. Its disarmingly straightforward prose contrasted with 1984's rococo *Stars in My Pocket Like Grains of Sand*, a tragedy of intercultural-interspecies communication and sexuality which remains to date Delany's last science fiction novel.

In the 1980s and 1990s, Delany has devoted himself to criticism, autobiography, and studies of interracial and interclass urban relations. Often the strains have been intertwined, as in *The Motion of Light in Water: Sex and Science Fiction in the East Village*, a beautiful and moving account of his life in the early 1960s. The effect of AIDS on the sexual cultures and industries of Manhattan became a focal point in Delany's writing, starting with "The Tale of Plagues and Carnivals" from *Return to Nevèrÿon* and continuing through his pornographic scholarly mystery-romance *The Mad Man* (in which a young African-American scholar finds true love with a homeless redneck and true satisfaction with a considerably wider range of partners) and a nonfiction book on Times Square.

See Also: *During the first two decades of his career, Delany was closely associated with science fiction writers Joanna Russ and Thomas M. Disch, and with pornographer Michael Perkins.*

—Ray Davis

DeLillo, Don
1936–
b. New York, New York

FICTION: Americana (1971), End Zone (1972), Great Jones Street (1973), Ratner's Star (1976), Players (1977), Running Dog (1978), **The Names** (1982), **White Noise** (1985), **Libra** (1988), **Mao II** (1991), *****Underworld** (1997)

Just for the fun of it, try to imagine Don DeLillo's career back-to-front, with his eleventh novel—the massive, dazzling *Underworld*—as his debut. It would make sense, in a way, because a large chunk of *Underworld* takes place in the Arthur Avenue section of the Bronx, the Italian-American neighborhood where DeLillo grew up. These sepia-tinted evocations of childhood haunts are as close as he has come to autobiographical writing, the starting point for so many of today's novelists.

Had he begun with *Underworld*'s bang—no, bang is too tinny for a book about the bomb—had he begun with the megaton detonation of *Under-*

111

world, DeLillo would now be the literary equivalent of a household name. His great theme—personal, political, commercial, and technological conspiracy, and all the conspiracies that language seems to echo—would be familiar to every literature-loving American. We would all be just a little more paranoid and a little more in love with the play of words, the mesmerizing connectedness.

Enough fantasy. DeLillo began in 1971 with a novel, brilliant in spurts, called *Americana* (how's that for staking out territory?). The first-person account of a television executive who drops out, hits the road, and makes a home movie about himself, *Americana* is a melting pot bubbling with a mishmash of ingredients; with hindsight we can identify all the tasty jumbled bits as very DeLillo. He published five more novels in the '70s, four of them slim, hard-edged, comic, and despairing. *End Zone* fuses football and nuclear war; *Great Jones Street* tells a rock star's story of drug deals and political repression; *Players* brings in assassination, terrorism, and capitalism's most brazen conspiracy, the New York Stock Exchange; *Running Dog* tracks the violent chase after another home movie, this one supposedly a Nazi sex revel shot in Hitler's bunker. The other novel of the '70s was *Ratner's Star*, the anomaly in DeLillo's collected work, a long, crowded puzzle of a novel that blends science fiction and higher mathematics (not for beginners).

"The less I think about my earlier work," DeLillo once said, "the happier I am." A bit harsh. The pre-1980 novels suffer only in comparison with the astounding successes that came after, a winning streak kicked off by *The Names*. Set in Greece, the seventh novel shimmers, bright sun casting sharp-edged shadows; the landscape radiates terrorist menace. A spooky cult murder heaves the loose-jointed plot into motion. At the heart of the cult's mystery? The alphabet, building block of language.

Ah, *White Noise*—the popular favorite, locus classicus for fans of postmodern irony. Easily DeLillo's funniest, it's a meandering tale told by Jack Gladney, professor of Hitler Studies at the College-on-the-Hill. Jack and his fourth wife Babette share an all-consuming fear of death—not good if "an airborne toxic event" (a chemical spill, that is) drifts into your neighborhood. *White Noise* features the best supermarket scenes in American literature.

112

Compared with the bright, flat surface of *White Noise*, *Libra* is a dark plunge—into conspiracy, into the mind of Lee Harvey Oswald. On its own, the Dealey Plaza assassination sequence, a wrenching fourteen-page prose approximation of the Zapruder film, is solid proof that DeLillo is a modern master. It's not too much to say that in this novel he makes history. The only question is whether we should be most amazed at the impeccable research, the load of fact revealed about what he calls "the seven seconds that broke the back of the American century"—or should we instead pay homage to his power of invention, the second sight that delivers, say, Oswald's dying thoughts?

Between *Libra* and *Underworld*, two looming monuments, there's the perfect gem, DeLillo's most exquisite book, *Mao II*, the story of Bill Gray, a reclusive novelist who believes that terrorists have displaced writers as shapers of contemporary consciousness. But the photograph, the replicated image—especially the broadcast image—turns out to be more powerful than the car bomb. In *Mao II*, DeLillo brings to life a post-literate waif named Karen Janey, a "thin-boundaried" girl who has a talent for fusing with televised phenomena; Bill Gray says Karen "carries the virus of the future." This gets to the heart of DeLillo, who is always keenly aware of the extra-literary. He charges his novels with the energy of other media—television, radio, photography, film, the World Wide Web.

Underworld, in fact, resembles DeLillo's idea of the Web: "There are only connections . . . All human knowledge gathered and linked, hyperlinked." A kaleidoscopic Cold War chronicle, 827 pages long, the novel takes as its twin themes waste and the bomb (or shit and death). Behind every character—whether it's Nick Shay, DeLillo's male lead, an executive with a waste management company, or Lenny Bruce rattled by the Cuban missile crisis, or a suburban mom in 1957 spurning her space-age vacuum cleaner because it reminds her of Sputnik—everywhere DeLillo rigs up his network of obsessive concerns. It's a conspiracy of connections proliferating with every paragraph.

And it begins with the best stretch of writing DeLillo has yet produced, a fifty-page re-creation of the famous baseball game between the Brooklyn Dodgers and the New York Giants—a game played on October 3, 1951, the same day the Soviet Union tested its second atomic bomb. The writing is slap-me convincing and lyrical, too, as though DeLillo had arranged sentences for the sheer beauty of mingled sounds and by accident told immutable truth. Required reading.

DeLillo is the author of three plays; the most recent, *Valparaiso*, premiered in Cambridge, Massachusetts, in January 1999. And there is also *Amazons* (1980), a novel he wrote under the pseudonym Cleo Birdwell, a comic romp that purports to be, as the subtitle has it, "An Intimate Memoir by the First Woman Ever to Play in the National Hockey League."

See Also: The usual brainy suspects, especially Thomas Pynchon and William Gaddis. DeLillo has professed admiration for Norman Mailer and Joan Didion; his male action heroes seem to me clearly related to their counterparts in the novels of Robert Stone; and he has had a powerful influence on David Foster Wallace and Richard Powers.

—Adam Begley

Dexter, Pete

1945–
b. Pontiac, Michigan

FICTION: God's Pocket (1983), **Deadwood** (1986), *Paris Trout (1988), Brotherly Love (1991), The Paperboy (1995)

Pete Dexter's five novels radiate a sense of place so strong it could melt the paint off your car. Yet you can't pin Dexter down as a regional writer—his repertoire embraces too much. Born in Michigan and reared in Georgia, Illinois, and eastern South Dakota, he drove a beer truck and sold baby pictures door-to-door. He worked for newspapers in Philadelphia, Sacramento, and north Florida. Maybe this explains how he developed a native's fluency with place and a musician's ear for dialect. In *God's Pocket* and *Brotherly Love*, Dexter uses the rough slang of South Philadelphia; in *Paris Trout* and *The Paperboy*, it's the slippery drawl of the rural Southeast. In *Deadwood*, it's an Old West argot of Dexter's own brilliant invention.

Dexter says he started writing fiction after he was nearly beaten to death in a bar fight in South Philadelphia in 1982, when the patrons objected to a newspaper column he had written about the neighborhood. The scene is fictionalized in Dexter's first novel, *God's Pocket*, about the aftermath of the killing of a young, mob-connected construction worker.

In Dexter's moral universe, each act of violence spawns a chain of repercussions. Few writers can render savagery with Dexter's skill. He captures the unreal detachment of the dying and transforms the banality of violence into a form of poetry. In *God's Pocket*, here is the boy getting his skull crushed with a pipe: "But there was a cracking noise and he couldn't remember what it was, and somehow they couldn't hear him anyway. And for a long second he looked up into the sun and went blind in the light." In Dexter's tour de force, *Paris Trout*, for which he won the National Book Award in 1988, a young girl is shot by the evil Trout in a scene choreographed like a ballet.

If all of this makes Dexter's books sound unbearably grim, take heart. He also has a wicked sense of humor. His Western masterpiece, *Deadwood*, is knee-slapping funny at times, even though the novel is constructed around the murder of Wild Bill Hickok.

See Also: For Dexter's literary companions, try Richard Price and Flannery O'Connor.
—*Maryanne Vollers*

114

Dick, Philip K.
1928–1982
b. Chicago, Illinois

FICTION: Solar Lottery (published in England as World of Chance, 1955), A Handful of Darkness (stories, 1955), The World Jones Made (1956), The Man Who Japed (1956), Eye in the Sky (1957), The Cosmic Puppets (1957), The Variable Man and Other Stories (1957), Time Out of Joint (1959), Dr. Futurity (1960), Vulcan's Hammer (1960), ***The Man in the High Castle** (1962), The Game-Players of Titan (1963), **Martian Time-Slip** (1964), The Penultimate Truth (1964), The Simulacra (1964), Clans of the Alphane Moon (1964), **Dr. Bloodmoney; or, How We Got Along after the Bomb** (1965), **The Three Stigmata of Palmer Eldritch** (1965), **Now Wait for Last Year** (1966), The Crack in Space (1966), The Unteleported Man (1966), The Ganymede Takeover (with Ray Nelson, 1967), Counter-Clock World (1967), **Do Androids Dream of Electric Sheep?** (1968), **Ubik** (1969), Galactic Pot-Healer (1969), The Preserving Machine and Other Stories (1969), A Maze of Death  (1970), Our Friends from Frolix 8 (1970), We Can Build You (1972), The Book of Philip K. Dick (stories, published in England as The Turning Wheel, 1973), **Flow My Tears, the Policeman Said** (1974), **Confessions of a Crap Artist** (1975), Deus Irae (with Roger Zelazny, 1976), A Scanner Darkly (1977), The Best of Philip K. Dick (stories, 1977), The Golden Man (stories, 1980), **VALIS** (1981), The Divine Invasion (1981), **The Transmigration of Timothy Archer** (1982), The Man Whose Teeth Were All Exactly Alike (1984), Robots, Androids, and Mechanical Oddities (stories, 1984), Lies, Inc. (stories, 1984), In Milton Lumky Territory (1984), I Hope I Shall Arrive Soon (stories, 1985), Ubik: The Screenplay (1985), Puttering about in a Small Land (1985), Radio Free Albemuth (1987), The Collected Stories (five vols., 1987), Mary and the Giant (1987), Nick and the Glimmung (1988), The Broken Bubble (1988), The Little Black Box (1990), Gather Yourselves Together (1994)

NONFICTION: The Shifting Realities of Philip K. Dick: Selected Literary and Philosophical Writings (1995)

Dick has become a totemic figure, exemplary of the possibility of art arising from rapidly written genre fiction yet also seemingly exceptional, a bohemian autodidact who stumbled through genius and madness, a genre all his own. He wrote forty novels which engage with science fiction but satisfy few of the conventional requirements of that audience, as well as eight "mainstream" novels set mostly in suburbia and prefiguring the defeated milieu of Raymond Carver and Fredrick Barthelme. A devoted cult has dragged into posthumous publication extensive letters and ephemera, as well as a five-volume *Collected Stories*. His work has been colonized by academics and Hollywood, with results both good and awful. And the last few of his books are shrouded in an off-putting aura of religious obsession. Where to seek in this wild fecundity for proof of his supporters' claim that he is among the century's most important writers?

If the novel is an imperfect form Dick stands a chance, for he is the most imperfect of writers. His tales concern paradox, paranoia, and illusion, and they are riddled with lapses of taste, coherence, and writerly rigor—reading Dick is foremost a disorienting experience. Yet it can also be deeply restorative, for here is a writer who has turned unflinchingly, even somewhat merrily, to the task of confronting the mad incoherence of being human.

Dick began in the 1950s as a writer split. His serious aspirations resulted in a series of novels of middle-class life which move steadily from ponderousness to a quiet authority. Too quiet—they only appeared posthumously. Meanwhile, Dick's instinctive satires of everyday reality were being uncorked in the science fiction tales he'd been writing, for money and perhaps also because his unconscious demanded it. The cartoonish iconography of science fiction—and the way it allowed formally disjunctive games at a time when these were uncommon in American writing—gave Dick his true opportunity.

In the 1960s Dick abandoned realism and united the two strands of his work: the scrupulous observation and psychology of the "serious" novels with the antic inventions and morbid disruptions of his SF. He then reached the level of emotional and moral commitment to absurdist motifs that marks his greatness.

First came *The Man in the High Castle*, an elegant alternate history of World War II where the Japanese rule over California; it remains an ideal entrance into his work. *Martian Time-Slip*, the somber tale of interplanetary emigration that followed, is even finer. In *Dr. Bloodmoney* (his only pastoral utopia, albeit made possible by nuclear war), *The Three Stigmata of Palmer Eldritch*, and *Now Wait for Last Year* (both chaotic and funny accounts of multiple realities which never resolve), the quality of the writing declines. But these five books, written between 1960 and 1965, remain one of the great hot streaks in the history of novel-writing, and a testament which would stand if Dick hadn't written another word.

He wrote millions. Always on the edge of poverty and psychic disrepair, between 1965 and 1976 Dick batted out thirteen mediocre novels and three flawed masterpieces:

Do Androids Dream Of Electric Sheep?, a noirish meditation on the marginal difference between alienated humans and humanized androids (it inspired the film *Blade Runner*); *Ubik*, set in a world where an over-the-counter remedy is required to keep human beings from aging into dust in minutes; and *Flow My Tears, the Policeman Said*, where a television star wakes up one morning in a world where he is no longer famous, and a fascist cop discovers love.

At the end Dick's philosophical questing gave way to theological arcana, though not before one bitter, clear-eyed pause: *A Scanner Darkly*, his repudiation of the drug use that had sometimes stoked his visions and a summit of Burroughsian paranoia. Last came three novels that are beautiful and tragic in their questing in mysticism for the personal solace Dick was unable to find elsewhere. *VALIS*, *The Divine Invasion*, and *The Transmigration of Timothy Archer* are unlike on the surface: The first is an autobiographical metafiction about enlightenment, the second a recapitulation of SF in religious terms, the third the "realist" masterpiece which had eluded him in the 1950s, and a fitting place to finish.

The conundrum of Dick's place in literature will be argued for some time; what's certain is the quality he shares with the greatest of writers: His books inspire love.

See Also: *A taste for Philip K. Dick is often found in common with a liking for Thomas Pynchon—they have absurdity and conspiracy in common, but little else. William S. Burroughs, early Kurt Vonnegut, and J. G. Ballard are often associated tastes as well, but none of these comparisons quite do justice to Dick's homely, yearning humanity. Steve Erickson is in some ways closer. Stanislaw Lem also sometimes evokes Dick's reality games. Readers questing in eccentric backwaters of the SF genre for "another Philip K. Dick" have located, at different times, Barrington Bayley, D. G. Compton, and Barry Malzberg—all unusual and undervalued writers, but not of Dick's stature.*

—Jonathan Lethem

Of This World: Why Science Fiction Can't Be Dismissed

By John Clute

Once upon a time—about a century ago—something happened in the world of books that, for a while, boded no ill. H. G. Wells, Arthur Conan Doyle, P. G. Wodehouse, and Edgar Rice Burroughs consciously invented (along with a lot of other writers like Robert Louis Stevenson or Bram Stoker who didn't have a clue) the kind of story we now think of when we think of popular genres: detective stories, science fiction, horror, superman adventures, etc. These writers, responding to insatiable demands for copy from the sharp editors who ran up-and-coming new magazines, created stories that could be repeated: Sherlock Holmes and Tarzan are nothing if they don't happen again and again. They created *markets*, and they created, only half-unwittingly, the monster of the Demand for the Same.

In doing so, Wells and Doyle and their colleagues laid the foundations for the world of literature we live in now. In 1999, most of what most of us read is genre. Sometimes this is obvious—science fiction, which is what I'm most concerned about, has for many decades now been stigmatized as a genre literature that adults needn't bother with. Sometimes the formula is not so obvious. Novels written by university professors and set in the groves of academe are far more rigidly predictable than anything but the most routine SF novel, but they have escaped the stigma of being labeled as genre. They can be read in public by adults, not because they are particularly *worth* being read in public by adults, but because they carry no mark of Cain.

Other genres include the bestseller genre, the disaster genre, the *roman à clef* that fails to conceal the identity of a very recent American president genre, the shopping and fucking genre, the sexually obsessed Christian male in New England midlife crisis genre, the Hollywood satire genre, the European experimental novel with unusual sex on page seventy-four genre, and so on.

What these genres all share is that they exist and also that they do not exist. The reason for this ontological ambivalence is pretty simple: The main beneficiaries of generification in 1999 are not the writers who are forced to pretend to write within some cookie-cutter restraint or the readers who devour the stale because they do not know how to identify the new. The ones who benefit are publishers and retailers, who find it *easier* to market books like widgets than to play the heartrendingly difficult game of coping with something that has not been done before. Their enthusiasm for the new is therefore limited.

So genres exist—constant users of any large bookstore can instantly tell what any piece of fiction is *supposed* to be about by its title, by its cover, by its location in the shop—and genres also do not exist. Those same constant shoppers, if they are wise, know that miracles lurk beneath the contemptible covers retailers demand. They even, occasionally, buy a book simply because it looks interesting.

But why (and here I come to my own main concern) is this sly salutary worldly knowledge about the difference between a book and its cover so rarely applied to science fiction? It's certainly not the case with some other genres. A detective writer like P. D. James or Patricia Cornwell, a writer of thrillers like Carl Hiaasen, a Cold War spy novelist like John Le Carré—all of these can slide upmarket with ease and, without losing the allure of their genre underpinning, appeal to an audience that does not believe it dabbles in kid's stuff.

A writer like P. D. James may even stumble into the composition of an SF novel. But when James did publish hers—it is called *The Children of Men*—she made it very clear in various public statements that she had *not* written a science fiction novel at all. No, her tale was not full of futuristic gadgets; her tale was about real men and women in the real world. That her setting is thirty years hence, and that her story involves the highly science-fictional discovery that the human race has become sterile, these facts count for nothing against her horror (and presumably her publisher's horror) that her work might be crippled by identification with a genre that cannot be worth writing in.

Any reader of SF knows that this is nonsense, that SF, as a mode of exploratory writing, has provided a broad platform and a rich vocabulary and network of thoroughly tested icons for hundreds of innovative writers for many decades now. (And any SF reader who looks at *The Children of Men* recognizes that the book is indeed SF, but also that it is very *bad* SF.)

There are at least three reasons for dismissing science fiction as trash. The obvious reason is that, alas, most of it *is* trash. But all SF, good or bad, is marketed in the same way, so that the trash is indistinguishable from the good stuff. *Star Trek* novelizations march side by side with writers who, if they didn't have the SF label gummed to their foreheads, would rightly be understood as major creative figures of the last half-century. I mean writers like Philip K. Dick, Avram Davidson, Samuel R. Delany, Ursula K. Le Guin, Thomas M. Disch, Octavia Butler, Lucius Shepard, James Tiptree, Jr., Gene Wolfe, Michael Swanwick, William Gibson, Bruce Sterling, Brian Aldiss, and a dozen more.

A second reason is that the most significant writers of American SF have been creators of "thought experiments," stories whose primary purpose is to dramatize ideas about the world and the tools we invent, or might invent, in order to transform it. Since such tools and ideas have traditionally come from the hard sciences, science fiction can be terribly simpleminded about genuinely complex issues (like human nature). And SF is often subjected to the fearful, self-defensive disparagement that "humanists" heap on scientists.

The third reason for writing off SF as trash is that, until about 1975, American science fiction told a central story that has now become embarrassing to many of us. It was the story of the technology-led triumph of the American Way in the star-lanes of the big tomorrow. It is embarrassing nowadays because it is racist, technophilic, provincial, arrogant; and because it is *wrong*. The SF story was originally the story of how America made it all work; and things haven't exactly turned out that way.

But so what? Just because hick triumphalists hijacked SF for a few decades does not mean that the very notion of speculative fiction is inherently bogus. Throughout the twentieth century the best of the kind of writing that Americans ghettoize as science fiction has, in other countries, hardly been treated as a genre at all. Unlike any other category of contemporary literature, SF is a mode of looking at the world and its potential. Science fiction offers writers an intensely bracing angle of view, especially in a time of constant innovation and crisis, and it is a scandal that in 1999 so many writers of such considerable talent have pursued this and continue to do so in obscurity.

But this is a world of book covers, and of retailers; all of whom seem to operate in a state of perpetual panic about *labels*. When Karen Joy Fowler releases a very great SF novel called *Sarah Canary*—in which the males who run the nineteenth century fail to identify an alien trapped on Earth because she resembles a human female and is therefore invisible to them—her publisher has conniptions at the thought that somebody might call it by its honorable and proper name. When a revered non-SF writer such as Doris Lessing publishes a series of books—the Canopus in Argos sequence—which she is perfectly happy to call SF, reviewers on both sides of the Atlantic rush to her "defense" insisting that it's anything but.

Gene Wolfe, in a sequence of novels called Book of the New Sun, published a profound meditation on history, God, time, and power; and his SF publisher gave it dust jackets that evoke Brak the Barbarian. Gore Vidal, in *The Smithsonian Institution*, publishes a hilarious (and intermittently profound) SF satire on American governance and mores; but SF readers would never know what they were missing because of the queasy "dignity" of Random House's marketing campaign for the book.

The losers are us.

We are the ones who live here, in this world, on the verge of the next century. We cannot afford to exclude any vision—any way of looking at the world—that human beings have invented for ourselves. As the futures we are heir to fall like rain upon our heads, we're going to need all the help we can get to see our way through.

Didion, Joan
1935–
b. Sacramento, California

FICTION: Run River (1963), Play It as It Lays (1970), A Book of Common Prayer (1977), **Democracy** (1984), The Last Thing He Wanted (1996)

NONFICTION: *Slouching towards Bethlehem** (1968), **The White Album** (1979), Salvador (1983), Miami (1987), After Henry (1992)

Reading Joan Didion's fiction is a little like looking at Le Corbusier furniture: It's pristine, beautiful, downright perfect, and yet not particularly inviting to live with—a little cold, a little cruel, a little too angular to accommodate human curves. Phrase by phrase, Didion's prose style is impeccable. There's nary a word out of place. But one does not usually read novels for phrase-by-phrase perfection; that is why one reads haiku.

A native of California, Didion's work is an aesthetic Death Valley. It doesn't so much suck the reader in as suck him dry. After finishing her

121

first novel, *Run River*, I felt parched, thirsty for the merest drop of humor. The action, such as it is, takes place on a ranch outside Sacramento between 1938 and 1959. The protagonist, Lily Knight, is Manifest Destiny's daughter, not to mention daddy's little girl. "I'm not myself if my father's dead," she thinks, though she's hardly a paragon of self-possession while he's alive. Lily anticipates Didion's other characters in that she doesn't so much live her life as stumble through it, oblivious to choice, personifying the notion that history, according to Didion, is "a history of accidents."

While the author's own illustrious career epitomizes the accelerating accomplishments, drive, and will of women in the 1960s and 1970s, her characters seldom do. Witness Didion's most infamous main character, Maria ("pronounced Mar-*eye*-ah") Wyeth from 1970's *Play It as It Lays*. Nihilistic enough to make Bret Easton Ellis weep, Maria chooses her gynecologist because his office is near Saks (where she has her hair done), caps off her abortion by going to buy a "silver vinyl dress," marvels that two friends "still believe in cause effect," and concludes, on the book's last page, that she "knows what 'nothing' means." This, more than any of Didion's novels, is a love-it-or-hate-it affair. I found its portrait of passivity maddening, though a trustworthy friend adores the novel for "its disaffection," because "generally you only get to read about such destructive behavior in terms of guys," and because "there's almost no girly sentimentality."

Didion is of course also celebrated for her nonfiction, especially her essay collections *Slouching Towards Bethlehem* and *The White Album*, which offer portraits of the social anarchy of the 1960s and 1970s from the Haight-Ashbury hippie scene to her own mental breakdown. Just as the concerns of these books (encapsulated by *Slouching*'s Yeats epigraph that "the center cannot hold") informed the malaise of the first two novels, so does Didion's later reporting affect her later novels. Her nonfiction books *Salvador*, *Miami*, and *After Henry* explore Latin American politics, the Iran-Contra scandal, and other Reagan-era conspiracy theories.

Didion's 1977 novel *A Book of Common Prayer* takes place in the fictional Latin American country Boca Grande. Narrated by an American expatriate, it tells the story of Charlotte, an American mother, "immaculate of history," accidentally thrown in history's path when her daughter is accused of terrorist activities. Charlotte is another typical Didion dodo (to whom "revolution" equals the Boston Tea Party). This book is infinitely skippable. More compelling is Didion's next political novel, *Democracy*. The plot begins in Honolulu among a family "in which the colonial impulse marked every member" and ends with a member of that family, Inez Christian, in self-imposed exile in Kuala Lampur after reaching its boiling point at the 1975 American evacuation of Saigon. Still, it's not political intrigue that gives the book its seductive momentum, but rather Didion's touching portrait of Inez's lifelong love affair with covert wheeler-dealer Jack Lovett; the couple, their yearning for each other stretching across years and national borders, are rare characters for Didion—real, fleshy, engagingly passionate.

122

The casual reader probably won't enjoy *The Last Thing He Wanted* much, but the novel is a useful summation of Didion's career and concerns. It is all her books all at once: visiting California, Miami, Latin America; commenting on love and marriage in the context of politics and history (its destiny couple, Treat and Elena, annoyingly duplicate *Democracy*'s Jack and Inez); and, in the form of a character called "the not quite omniscient author," including reporter's memoir outside of the main plot. Here Didion (in the guise of "I") admits, "I realized that I was increasingly interested only in the technical, in how to lay down the AM-2 aluminum matting for the runway, in whether or not parallel taxiways and high-speed turnoffs must be provided . . . " Therein lies the answer as to why Didion's nonfiction reportage stands up better than her novels. She is a creature of fact, not fiction.

See Also: Bret Easton Ellis, another novelist who's lived in the void, not to mention Los Angeles.

—*Sarah Vowell*

Doctorow, E. L.
1931–
b. New York, New York

FICTION: Welcome to Hard Times (1960), Big as Life (1966), *****The Book of Daniel** (1971), **Ragtime** (1975), Loon Lake (1980), Lives of the Poets (stories, 1984), **World's Fair** (1985), Billy Bathgate (1989), The Waterworks (1994), City of God (2000)

NONFICTON: Jack London, Hemingway, and the Constitution: Selected Essays, 1977–1992 (1993)

123

Although Edgar Laurence Doctorow's two best novels—*The Book of Daniel* and *Ragtime*—are as strong as anything in postwar American fiction, his career has been inconsistent. His 1960 debut, *Welcome to Hard Times*, is a fine first effort, a modernist Western that appropriates the conventions of the genre to frame a meditation on good and evil in a small frontier town. *Big as Life* (1966), on the other hand, is less successful, a science fiction novel kept out of print, at the author's insistence, for more than twenty years.

Nothing in his early work, however, hints at the stunning breakthrough of *The Book of Daniel*, an angry, raw, discursive work absolutely blistering in its power. Narrated by the adult son of a Julius and Ethel Rosenberg-like couple—American Communists executed for treason—the novel encompasses, in strikingly personal terms, the political and social turmoil of the 1950s and 1960s and the private consequences of public deeds. Four years later, Doctorow brought a still broader perspective to *Ragtime*, a panoramic portrayal of turn-of-the-century America, that, like John Dos Passos's *U.S.A.* trilogy, mixes fictional characters and historical figures. A monumental act of the imagination, *Ragtime* strikes at the essence of American mythology, gracefully detailing the contradictions of that supposedly halcyon time.

Particularly impressive is *Ragtime*'s seamless structure, the novel as elaborate tapestry, where the various narrative threads are subtly interwoven for maximum effect. Yet a looseness of construction marks Doctorow's subsequent fiction, an almost accidental quality that undermines the authority of his voice. *Loon Lake*, for instance, shifts point of view constantly among its 1930s-era characters and the author, whose explication of the writing process in a series of stream-of-consciousness passages gives the book a jagged, disconnected edge. Likewise, *Lives of the Poets*, although here the disconnection arises from Doctorow's overwrought language, which swirls through the pages like an obscuring wind. Even *World's Fair*, his most autobiographical work and the best of his post-*Ragtime* efforts, suffers from an air of incompletion, as Doctorow vividly renders the life of an eight-year-old boy during the Depression, only to end inconclusively. It's as if, in recreating the peculiar, floating quality of childhood, Doctorow has internalized its open-endedness and then embedded it within the very marrow of the book.

Doctorow's two most recent novels, *Bill Bathgate* and *The Waterworks*, represent a return to the structural elegance of *Ragtime*. Yet these later books come with their own sets of problems and don't reach the level of Doctorow's finest work. *Billy Bathgate* revisits the territory of 1930s boyhood, but the novel's dense, dreamy style of writing—reminiscent in many ways of *Lives of the Poets*—clashes with the capacities of its fifteen-year-old narrator, a Bronx street urchin whose drab life turns Technicolor when he falls under the sway of legendary gangster Dutch Schultz. *The Waterworks* does a better job of matching language and content, spinning its tale of 1870s New York in a faux-gothic style that evokes both the formality and the seediness of the era. But all its surface beauty ultimately cannot disguise an unsettling slightness.

Is Doctorow a great, if flawed, novelist, or simply a good one who's produced some great books? Even his least substantial fiction has much to recommend it, from the deftly evoked historical textures to the uniformity of vision—a gentle strain of liberal humanism, of old-fashioned social justice—that flows throughout Doctorow's writing like a subterranean stream. Then, there's the matter of his political activism (reflected in his 1993 essay collection *Jack London, Hemingway, and the Constitution*) which has given

Doctorow a certain stature as that most endangered of species, the public man of letters for whom literature is a force of conscience in the world. Yet if these are the components of an exemplary literary *vita*, one can't help feeling that, on some more essential level, Doctorow's career remains oddly unfulfilled.

See Also: Doctorow's work belongs with much twentieth-century American political fiction, beginning with John Dos Passos's U.S.A. Billy Bathgate *is reminiscent of James T. Farrell's* Studs Lonigan *(although its sweeping serpentines of language bring to mind William Faulkner, if Faulkner had been born and raised in the Bronx), while* Welcome to Hard Times *has a lot in common with Thomas Berger's* Little Big Man, *which uses similar material to analogous effect.* The Waterworks *covers similar territory, in its re-creation of nineteenth-century New York, as Caleb Carr's* The Alienist.

—*David L. Ulin*

BACK TO THE '50S *by E. L. Doctorow*

The Moviegoer by Walker Percy
   A novel whose action is oblique, slantwise, Southern existential. What has remained with me is its almost French quietness.

The Adventures of Augie March by Saul Bellow
   As an aspiring young writer I felt liberated by this rousing, freewheeling Jewish picaresque assault on narrative correctness. I imagine it set many of my generation free.

The Invisible Man by Ralph Ellison
   A monumental, hammered-out novel of perfected technical mistakes. I cannot conceive of post-war American literature without it.

Wise Blood by Flannery O'Connor
   Poetically imagined and religiously inspired, its sentences gleam like chrome. As the first great workshopped novel (and, some would say, the last), it can be read also as a series of stand-alone chapters.

On the Road by Jack Kerouac
   Considered as the boisterous self-assertion of a carful of derelicts, it becomes a spiritual gloss on the 1930s proletarian novel. Should be read in a rush, as it seems to have been written. All writers coddle the fantasy of automatic writing and I am critically indulgent of one who was foolish enough to think it a practical possibility.

Dorris, Michael
1945–1997
b. Louisville, Kentucky

FICTION: **Yellow Raft in Blue Water** (1987), The Crown of Columbus (with Louise Erdrich, 1991), **Working Men** (stories, 1993), Sees Behind Trees (1996), Cloud Chamber (1997)

NONFICTION: Native Americans: Five Hundred Years After (1975), *The Broken Cord: A Family's Ongoing Struggle with Fetal Alcohol Syndrome** (1989), Rooms in the House of Stone (1993), Paper Trail (essays, 1994)

It's hard to think of Michael Dorris without his wife, novelist Louise Erdrich: The two burst onto the literary scene in the 1980s with stories of Native American life that felt like new information, opening the way for writers like Sherman Alexie and Greg Sarris. They dedicated their books to each other and edited each other's work, seemingly living out the ideal writerly marriage. They separated shortly before Dorris's suicide in 1997 under painful and murky circumstances.

Dorris wrote fiction of wildly uneven quality. His collection of short stories, *Working Men*, contains a few gems, and his first novel, *Yellow Raft on Blue Water*, is a vivid story of reservation life, told through the voices of three generations of Native American women. The youngest of these, fifteen-year-old Rayona—a bronco-riding, tough-minded girl—has a voice that sticks in your mind. But in his later works of fiction, Dorris's lyric impulses get out of hand. *Cloud Chamber*, his second novel, tries for epic grandeur—the story spans several generations of Irish-American immigrants—and strikes a desperately inflated tone. *Crown of Columbus*, a novel co-written with Erdrich, based on a search to find the Spanish explorer's lost diary, is hardly worth mentioning, a get-rich-quick scheme timed to coincide with the five-hundredth anniversary of Columbus's expedition. Dorris will be best remembered for his nonfiction book, *The Broken Cord* (winner of the National Book Critics Circle Award), about his adoption of a three-year-old Sioux boy, who suffered from then-little-known Fetal Alcohol Syndrome. The trials of his life as a single father, blundering into one of the tragedies of contemporary Native American life, put his storytelling gifts to their finest service.

See Also: Readers who liked Yellow Raft on Blue Water *should try Erdrich's novels, especially* Love Medicine *and* The Beet Queen. *Sherman Alexie provides a more wry, bare-boned take on contemporary Native American life.*

—Lisa Michaels

Doyle, Roddy
1958–
b. Dublin, Ireland

FICTION: *THE BARRYTOWN TRILOGY:* **The Commitments** *(1987),* **The Snapper** *(1990),* ***The Van** *(1991),* **Paddy Clarke Ha Ha Ha** (1993), **The Woman Who Walked Into Doors** (1996), A Star Called Henry (1999)

anguage in Roddy Doyle's Barrytown Trilogy (named for a fictional working-class neighborhood of Dublin strongly resembling Kilbarrack, where Doyle taught school for many years) sounds like a great, ongoing, cacophonous squabble. Whether it's the rock band nursing dreams of glory in *The Commitments*, the Rabbitte family coping with their eldest daughter's out-of-wedlock pregnancy in *The Snapper*, or the head of that clan, Jimmy Rabbitte, Sr., having it out with his mate Bimbo in *The Van*, nearly every insult expresses more familiar (and often familial) warmth than homilies or endearments ever could. Displaying an astounding ear for the comic and musical potential of plain talk, Doyle layers his characters' voices as if they were instruments, each fighting to be heard yet somehow making one harmonious noise. The Barrytown Trilogy achieves a sort of rude lyricism. Even at its most profane (especially at its most profane), the lilt of the language lifts right off the page.

Doyle was already venturing into less comic territory by the end of the trilogy; at its heart, *The Van* is the story of a traditional and big-hearted man dealing with the question of who he is when he's no longer the family breadwinner. But *The Van* didn't prepare Doyle's readers for the rich interior language of *Paddy Clarke Ha Ha Ha*, winner of Britain's Booker Prize in 1993. Doyle seems to be telling us the story of ten-year-old Paddy from right inside the boy's head. That's the only place where Paddy, fearful of disturbing the precarious balance of his parents' crumbling marriage, can acknowledge what he hopes for, and what he fears. An amazing feat of sensual recall, the book is alive to the sights and sounds of childhood—the smell of your mother after she's been doing laundry, the texture of a favorite food, or the way, at bedtime, your cold bed gradually takes on the welcoming warmth of your own body. But language is also a key to the book's tragedy. Coming from a writer whose characters up to that point had run roughshod over each other to throw in their two cents, the idea of a bright kid holding himself in check to smooth out his world is the saddest thing.

Significantly, the book that followed, *The Woman Who Walked Into Doors*, is Doyle's first novel written in the first person: Paula Spencer, an alcoholic, thirty-nine-

127

year-old raising her four kids alone after kicking out her abusive husband. Some Irish readers and critics felt Doyle had betrayed the family atmosphere of the Trilogy to take on the issue of domestic abuse, but the power of *The Woman Who Walked Into Doors* comes from the way he marries the loving bluntness of his early books to a heightened sense of observation and a wounding emotional power. Paula details her abuse with a brutal, unapologetic matter-of-factness. The book's harsh, utterly clear-eyed view of Catholic culture puts it within yelling distance of the fiction of Edna O'Brien and Brian Moore, largely because of Doyle's willingness to portray the abuse as the logical outcome of a religion that orders the unlucky to suffer and serve.

See Also: The criticism of Irish culture that rears its head in The Woman Who Walked Into Doors *is somewhat reminiscent of Brian Moore's first novel* The Lonely Passion of Judith Hearne *and the fiction of Edna O'Brien. Frank McCourt's hugely popular memoir,* Angela's Ashes, *offers a much darker version of Irish family life but, as in Doyle, one where language sings.*

—*Charles Taylor*

Drabble, Margaret
1939–
b. Sheffield, England

FICTION: A Summer Birdcage (1963), The Garrick Year (1964), **The Millstone** ([republished in 1973 as Thank You All Very Much], 1965), Jerusalem the Golden (1967), The Waterfall (1969), The Needle's Eye (1972), **The Realms of Gold** (1975), The Ice Age (1977), ***The Middle Ground** (1980), **The Radiant Way** (1987), A Natural Curiosity (1989), The Gates of Ivory (1991), The Witch of Exmoor (1996)

SELECTED NONFICTION: Wordsworth (1966), Arnold Bennet (biography, 1974), For Queen and Country: Britain in the Victorian Age (1978), A Writer's Britain: Landscape and Literature (1979), Angus Wilson (biography, 1995)

In her native Britain, Margaret Drabble is known as the quintessential "Hampstead novelist." Yes, she lives in that rich, leafy London neighborhood peopled by liberals and artistic types, but her roots are in the industrial North. The characters in her novels, no matter how well-heeled they become, frequently hail from dour, claustrophobic families, and though they travel the world, they tend to be tied to a crazy mother in a damp house in the hinterlands.

Drabble worries over her characters and wants them to be happy, and she narrates her later novels like an omniscient, nineteenth-century author who isn't afraid to speak directly to the reader. In *The Witch of Exmoor*, she asks us to guess the protagonists' professions just by looking at them (well, just by her description of them) and then she evaluates our answers: "You have not guessed quite right about Nathan. He is not an academic, though that, with those . . . untidy stained baggy weekend trousers, is what he ought to be. He ought to be a professor of immunology or anthropology but in fact he is in advertising, and on a weekday, in his business suiting, he is more convincing in the role." If you don't find this sort of thing irritatingly arch, then reading Drabble's books can be like spending time with a smart and interesting friend; she's absolutely sure you're her type of person.

Drabble writes primarily about the profound issues affecting women—how to find a place in the world, how to combine satisfying work with family—and the nitty-gritty details of their everyday lives—putting on makeup, washing the dishes, cleaning up after friends who've puked on the floor. In her early books, which are written in the first person, Drabble delves deeply into the psychology of a single protagonist. In *A Summer Bird-Cage*, Sarah tries to figure out what to do with her "lovely, shiny, useless new degree" while also wondering why her beautiful sister, Louise, married a semi-famous playwright she doesn't seem to love. In *The Millstone*, Rosamund Stacey has her first sexual experience in her early twenties, gets pregnant, and decides to keep the baby.

As Drabble and her protagonists got older, she switched to the third person, and her books grew longer and more ambitious. In *The Middle Ground*, Kate Armstrong, a newspaper columnist, confronts middle age with her children grown, her relationship ended, and her career grown stale. In *The Realms of Gold*, renowned archaeologist Frances Wingate ends a long relationship with a married man she hasn't stopped loving. In Drabble's later novels—especially the trilogy comprising *The Radiant Way*, *A Natural Curiosity*, and *The Gates of Ivory*—Drabble explores not only one woman's psyche but the state of British society as a whole. The news may not be good (these were the Thatcher/Major years, after all), but Drabble doesn't lose hope. Maybe she *is* the quintessential Hampstead novelist, after all.

See Also: If you like Margaret Drabble's intense psychological explorations, try Iris Murdoch. For more witty gossip about the upper-middle classes, try Alice Adams.

—*Laurie Muchnick*

Dubus, Andre
1936–1999
b. Lake Charles, Lousiana

FICTION: The Lieutenant (1967), Separate Flights (stories, 1975), **Adultery and Other Choices** (stories, 1977), Finding a Girl in America (stories, 1980), **The Times Are Never So Bad** (stories, 1983), **Voices from the Moon** (1984), The Last Worthless Evening (stories, 1986), *Selected Stories (1988), **Dancing After Hours** (stories, 1996)

NONFICTION: Broken Vessels (1991), Meditations from a Movable Chair: Essays (1998)

Dubus (pronounced du-BUSE) is one of the few contemporary American writers to have built a substantial reputation on the short story alone. (He has chosen not to reprint his early novel, *The Lieutenant*. *Voices from the Moon*, though published as a novel, is novella-length.) In an era when the short story has become a kind of lifestyle accessory among the advertisements in *The New Yorker*, a bed-and-breakfast for the soul, Dubus has kept faith with its difficulties and discomforts.

His constant theme is the relations between men and women or—what is a weaker version of the same thing—between men and the world of men. Like Hemingway, he is better writing about wounded souls than about the mythos of manhood. Unlike Hemingway, he often writes from a female point of view; his strongest characters are women. His distanced, elegiac tone recalls Joan Didion. At his best he is as matter-of-fact and penetrating as Chekhov, though sometimes a self-conscious earnestness betrays him into floridity or moralizing.

But you don't read Dubus for his philosophy. You read him for his quicksilver perceptions, for the deceptively simple sentence that reveals the truth of a situation or a person—revelations that break briefly like light, or grace, unexpected and unearned, through the gray overcast of his characters' lives.

He feels a kind of tough dismay, never quite nostalgia, for lost romantic ideals of marriage, womanhood, manhood, and is pitch-perfect when recording the tension between dreams and reality, essence and circumstance, hope and truth. His lapsed or troubled Catholics (the majority of his characters) are emblems of the moral negotiation required by a world too uncertain for catechistical answers.

Selected Stories is a true best-of collection, and an excellent introduction to his work. The novella *Adultery* is a masterpiece, an unflinching look at faith and fidelity, mortality and morality. Dubus seems to have a special affinity for the novella-length, which permits him to develop character at novelistic depth, but does not require the novel's density of incident.

A collection of essays, *Broken Vessels*, appeared after a 1986 accident that cost him a leg; in that book, and the more recent *Meditations from a Movable Chair*, his macho side is more gratingly on display than in his fiction, where it is effaced by the extraordinary sympathy his characters compel him to.

See Also: Some other writers who visit similar territory are Raymond Carver, Richard Yates, James Salter, and Frederick Exley.

—*Carter Scholz*

Dunne, Dominick
1925–
b. Hartford, Connecticut

FICTION: The Winners: Part II of Joyce Haber's "The Users" (1982), **The Two Mrs. Grenvilles** (1985), People Like Us (1988), *An Inconvenient Woman (1990), The Mansions of Limbo (1991), A Season in Purgatory (1993), **Another City, Not My Own: A Novel in the Form of a Memoir** (1997)

NONFICTION: Fatal Charms and Other Tales of Today (1987), The Mansions of Limbo (essays, 1991), The Way We Lived Then: Recollections of a Well-Known Name-Dropper (1999)

Best-selling novelist, crime reporter, chronicler of the lives of the rich and famous, Dominick Dunne is a writer by accident, a former Hollywood film producer and society maven whose personal triumphs, failures, and tragedies are both the subtext and the motor of his work. Dunne has been called "the K-Mart version of Truman Capote," "Judith Krantz in pants," and (by Tina Brown, who launched his magazine-writing career at *Vanity Fair*) "a magic little fellow," whose far-flung connections in the American *haut monde* have made him the undoubted king of celebrity journalism, both courted and feared by the people whose lives and dark secrets he recounts.

"People tell me things," Dunne has said. "They always have." Dunne was born in

131

Hartford, Connecticut, to a large and prosperous Irish-Catholic family—one of his brothers, permanently estranged, is the novelist John Gregory Dunne—and from earliest childhood had a yen to be accepted by the more wealthy, proud, and bigoted Protestant mainline clans who constituted society's old guard. "I made up my mind then that I was going to move in the upper circles of society and lead an exciting life," says Dunne. "And being an outsider to it made me a better writer about that life." His initial career as a Hollywood producer ended in 1980, when the effects of alcohol and drug abuse left him broke, divorced, unemployed, and in despair. Sobered up, he became a writer, and had just published his first novel, *The Winners*, when a new calamity struck—the murder of his only daughter, Dominique, at the hands of her stalker boyfriend. The killer was eventually convicted only of manslaughter and served less than three years of jail time. Dunne was beside himself, and a new career was born.

"The rage I felt for that man knew no bounds," Dunne explains. "Ever since, I have sought out themes about rich people who go unpunished or underpunished in the justice system. I got into exposing cover-ups of crimes by the rich and famous. And I got good at it." With a lifetime contract at *Vanity Fair*, Dunne has covered most of the sensational trials and scandals of the last fifteen years—Claus von Bülow, the Menendez Brothers, O. J. Simpson, William Kennedy Smith—and has spun most of them into novels, barely disguised fictions in which he appears as himself in a variety of alter egos. At the same time, he has produced profile after profile of diamond-drenched divas and celebrities, many of whom are his personal friends (Elizabeth Taylor, Nancy Reagan, Queen Noor of Jordan, etc.).

Dunne's novels tend to be naughtier and more gossipy versions of his magazine work, whether he's writing about current scandals (O. J. Simpson in *Another City, Not My Own*, the Kennedy clan in *A Season in Purgatory*) or older ones (*The Two Mrs. Grenvilles*, *An Inconvenient Woman*, *People Like Us*). Dismissed and frequently belittled by critics, he remains the society scribe par excellence, vastly popular among readers with an insatiable appetite for celebrity dish.

See Also: No one, really. With the imminent passing of Dunne's own generation, "society" as it used to be understood will no longer exist. There are simply too many celebrities to account for.

—*Peter Kurth*

Eisenberg, Deborah

1945–
b. Chicago, Illinois

FICTION: Transactions in a Foreign Currency (stories, 1986), Under the 82nd Airborne (stories, 1992), **The Stories (So Far) of Deborah Eisenberg** (1997), *****All Around Atlantis** (stories, 1997)

Deborah Eisenberg is a masterly practitioner of the kind of short story that briefly dips into the life of someone—in Eisenberg's case, usually a woman—at a moment when an understanding reaches fruition. The character feels her life shift and then solidify, and then at last she sees: She has been living in bad faith; or she must leave her lover; or she has decided to cast her lot with the world's winners or losers; or she has grasped at last that a friendship has been wasting her time; or she determines to reach out to the other flawed sufferers around her. The author fastidiously avoids overt statements of feeling or evaluation. All is intuited through gestures, glances, and brief, unexplained flarings of anger. This is a perfectly fine type of fiction, but an awful lot of people write it, and its indirection can make it feel attenuated or, worse, cagey. Perhaps it's really saying something, or perhaps it's merely conjuring an aura of significance.

Eisenberg's favored characters are often either young, naive, awkward women negotiating the social rapids of New York City for the first time or American visitors to Latin American nations in political turmoil, self-absorbed tourists about to sink in over their heads. The Indians and their troubles, glimpsed from a distance, stand for the authenticity Eisenberg's characters flinch from; the region's secret wars parallel the infidelities her child heroines barely intuit in the baffling adult world.

In her most recent collection, *All Around Atlantis*, however, Eisenberg's stories have become meatier and her heroines less passive and hapless. The Latin American stories still retain a vaguely moralistic quality, but the wonderful dry humor that has always distinguished her fiction has both leavened and deepened the stories set in the States. With them, her work transcends genre and becomes marvellously unique. Some of them—like the tale of a scholarship girl at a boarding school facing life after her defensive mother's death—feel as eventful and fleshed out as short novels.

See Also: Lorrie Moore is like a suburban Eisenberg with an even sharper wit. If you substract the humor from Eisenberg and add an oceanic sense of how time and emotion interpenetrate each other, you've got Alice Munro.

—Laura Miller

"Under the 82nd Airborne" by Deborah Eisenberg (The Stories (So Far) of Deborah Eisenberg)

A deluded Blanche Dubois-esque woman travels to a war zone to visit her daughter, thinking she's about to have a vacation on a beach. Reading the story, I was reminded of an interesting definition of sin I once heard—that it is first an abandonment of yourself. The heroine, who has abandoned herself before we meet her, is both contemptible and heart-rending, and Eisenberg moves her through a failing, chaotic world described with delicacy and a rare sense of intelligent wonder. The end is a knockout.

"Vandals" by Alice Munro (Open Secrets)

This is an extraordinarily deep and complex story. It is also subtle—I had to read it several times before I understood it. Told through an older woman, Bea, who has loved a hard, cruel man, and a young girl, Liza, who was close to them both, the story is broadly about territory, nature, control, sex, and rage. Most profoundly, it is about motherhood—or the abdication of it—and the girl's rage at the older woman for refusing to behave like a mother when the girl needs her to. "Vandals" is one of the most powerful, artistically beautiful things I've ever read.

"Helping" by Robert Stone (Bear and His Daughter)

The Dirty Harry of short stories, except nobody gets killed. A cranky Vietnam vet sick of his job as a counselor falls off the wagon while his lawyer wife is being hassled by child-abusing bikers. His

Ellis, Bret Easton
1964–
b. Los Angeles, California

134

FICTION: *Less Than Zero (1985), The Rules of Attraction (1987), **American Psycho** (1991), The Informers (1994), **Glamorama** (1999)

So, you hate Bret Easton Ellis as much as the next guy. You find him "misogynistic" (as has the National Organization of Women), and his fiction "the literary equivalent of a snuff flick" (as has Jonathan Yardley of *The Washington Post*). Maybe you even wife says to hell with it and pours herself a stiff one. The writing is beautiful and masterful. The dialogue is full of ugly charm, and moral boundaries expand and contract with heartbroken, drunken senselessness. When the hero wades out into the snow with a loaded gun, we're on his side, even though, technically, he's acting like an asshole.

"Separating" by John Updike (Too Far to Go)

As he meanders through chores and family functions, a father lets his children know that he and their mother are separating. What is remarkable about this story is the intense sensitivity with which it's told: The story opens in dozens of petal-like details and moments of feeling. In a very small setting, Updike creates a whole world that is by turns heartless, trivial, abundant, empty, tender, funny, and deep. His acknowledgment of every character's complexity and mystery, and his ability to make us feel it gives the story great energy and movement even at its most quiet and somber moments.

"The Lower Garden District Free Gravity Mule Blight or Rhoda, A Fable" by Ellen Gilchrist (Victory over Japan)

The story of a materialistic, indiscriminately sexy woman who dreams she's crushing the skulls of her husband's sheepdogs while her mother's sad little face peeps down the stairs. She's getting divorced, and she needs money so she's trying to pawn her wedding ring and then collect insurance money on it. She's also trying to screw the insurance man. She's irrational and she thinks awful, anti-Semitic thoughts. She's an absurd jerk and she's hilarious and she enjoys the physical world to the hilt. She's human appetite, lovingly regarded in all its buffoonery. I once compared this story to *The Lucy Show* for a disapproving undergraduate class. One of them grandly responded that he didn't read literature for *The Lucy Show*. How unfortunate for him.

felt a secret thrill when death threats forced him to cancel his book tour following the publication of *American Psycho*.

You know the basic facts (perhaps even better than you do the fiction): At age twenty, a preppy Bennington undergraduate from L.A. transformed a series of homework assignments—with a little salesmanship by literary über-agent Binky Urban—into a bestseller called *Less Than Zero*. *Less Than Zero* is the deadpan tale of a New England college student's return to Los Angeles for Christmas vacation, a binge that encompasses everything from mid-morning suntanning to midnight gangbanging, told in MTV bursts that read like adolescent hearsay but linger like great poetry.

The novel made Ellis rich and famous, and so of course he moved to Manhattan and wrote a second novel that bombed. *The Rules of Attraction* wasn't as awful as most critics claimed for the simple reason that so awful a novel is linguistically impossible. In truth, the book—written in a series of (un)dramatic monologues by a bunch of drugged students at a college that, were libel not an issue, might as well have been called Bennington—is innocuous enough.

Whereas society may never forget *American Psycho*—or forgive Bret Easton Ellis for writing it. Even before publication, the book had its enemies—most notably Paramount Communications chairman Martin Davis, who allegedly forced subdivision Simon & Schuster to cancel Ellis's contract. Enter Random House Kingpin Sonny Mehta with an offer to publish Ellis's epic—the guilt-free confession of a New York investment banker who prefers "murders and executions" to "mergers and acquisitions."

Within days, the American journalism community was asking the same question it always does when it puts a popular villain on trial: Did the accused act out of ignorance or out of arrogance? In other words, did Ellis write about "skinning Torri a little, making incisions with a steak knife and ripping bits of flesh from her legs and stomach while she screams in pain" the same way he did about Whitney Houston's discography (1985–1987) because he couldn't tell the difference between the two, or because he believed we couldn't? Ellis claimed at the time that he was a moralist, but he also claimed that he had no idea that the public would react to his book so violently—so he wound up guilty of both charges and once again we could all sleep at night confident that we lived in a great society, sullied only by the likes of Bret Easton Ellis. In the eight years following *American Psycho*, he published only one book, *The Informers*, a collection of short stories (written before *American Psycho*) set in the Los Angeles of *Less Than Zero*. For all its vampiristic pretenses, *The Informers* failed to shock or appall anybody.

Ellis has described *Glamorama*, his fifth novel, as being about "my feelings about being famous," and also as about "this generation's preoccupation with bullshit." In a sense, the models who populate it and the terrorist organization that drives its plot are irrelevant: *Glamorama* is as autobiographical as anything Ellis has ever penned. Ellis lives in the world we have all created together, and just as *Glamorama* is a portrait of the author as seen through the funhouse mirror of popular disdain, *Less Than Zero*, *American Psycho*, and the rest most deeply belong to our collective autobiography. So, you hate Bret Easton Ellis as much as the next guy. Are you sure you hate Bret Easton Ellis as much as you hate yourself?

See Also: Bret Easton Ellis has an unfortunate reputation for belonging to the Brat Pack's holy trinity. But his most avid readers are unlikely to enjoy anything but the downtown settings of novels by Jay McInerney (a hopeless sentimentalist) and Tama Janowitz (a helpless humorist). A. M. Homes is also sometimes mentioned in conjunction with Ellis for the slice-and-dice plot of The End of Alice, *but, as is so often the case with prose generated on college campuses, the violence is precious and unfelt. In fact, Ellis is so unique in his abilities that the only novelists this writer can recommend in the same vein are Martin Amis (c.f.,* The Information*) and Thomas Pynchon (c.f.,* V.*), both of them gritty satirists who steadfastly refuse critical classification.*

—Jonathan Keats

Ellis, Trey
1962–
b. Washington, D.C.

FICTION: **Platitudes** (1988), Home Repairs (1993), Right Here, Right Now (1999)

In a 1989 essay called "The New Black Aesthetic," Trey Ellis identified himself as a member of the "postliberated generation" of black artists, a group whose credo involves "shamelessly borrowing and reassembling across both race and class lines." Ellis paid tribute to Ishmael Reed, Clarence Major, Toni Morrison, John Edgar Wideman, George Clinton, David Hammons, and Richard Pryor as icons of this emergent group. Then just twenty-seven, Ellis had already published *Platitudes*, a modernist novel that successfully incorporates his ideas about aesthetics and "blackness" while echoing the structural playfulness found in such white writers as Flann O'Brien and Gilbert Sorrentino.

Aiming to acknowledge the influences of cultural nationalism and feminism without being restricted by them, Ellis unfolds *Platitudes* via ideological, sexually charged exchanges between aspiring novelist DeWayne Wellington and successful black feminist writer Isshee Ayam. His outrageous send-ups of black feminism do resemble Reed's fearless satires (Ayam's "books" include *Chillun o' de Lawd*, and *My Big Ol' Feets Gon' Stomp Dat Evil Down*). Like Reed, he's a natural wit whose work always includes at least one gem that will make readers laugh out loud.

Lately Ellis has turned from the screeds and creeds that often dominate discussions of black literature. *Home Repairs*, while funny and intelligent, focuses on one man's sexual maturity (or lack of it), more *Portnoy's Complaint* than, say, *The Terrible Twos*. The satire of modern religion and the American obsession with self-improvement in *Right Here, Right Now* is less pointed than *Platitudes*. Ironically, Ellis's attempts to escape the black literature ghetto imposed by mainstream critics have been largely unsuccessful. While white peers such as Jay McInerney and Brett Easton Ellis hog the spotlight with less ambitious and less accomplished work, Ellis continues to scribble away in relative obscurity.

See Also: Ellis is the spiritual heir of bold satirists such as George Schuyler (Black No More), *Ishmael Reed, and Steve Cannon* (Groove, Bang and Jive Around). *Contemporaries with similar approaches include Paul Beatty* (White Boy Shuffle), *Christopher John Farley* (My Favorite War), *and Darius James* (Negrophobia).

—*Jabari Asim*

Erdrich, Louise
1954–
b. Little Falls, Minnesota

FICTION: **Love Medicine** (1984), *****The Beet Queen** (1986), Tracks (1988), The Crown of Columbus (with Michael Dorris, 1991), **The Bingo Palace** (1994), Tales of Burning Love (1996), The Antelope Wife (1998)

NONFICTION: The Falcon: A Narrative of Captivity and Adventures of John Tanner (1994), The Blue Jay's Dance: A Birth Year (1995)

POETRY: Jacklight (1984), Baptism of Desire (1989)

We know a lot of intimate details about Louise Erdrich: her Native American heritage (she's half-Chippewa), which has informed her remarkable output of poetry, fiction, and nonfiction; her striking good looks; her intense collaborations with her late husband, Michael Dorris; the five children they raised together; and his suicide in 1997. It's compelling stuff, no question, and it's made her a favorite among reviewers and magazine editors. But Erdrich's achievements as a novelist, as both a luminous prose stylist and a first-class storyteller, should be considered first. She brought long-overdue attention to Native American fiction, and then brilliantly transcended it, bypassing the rootsy marginalizing that so often beleaguers writers associated with an "ethnic" (forgive me, but what else do you call it?) subgenre.

In her bestselling first novel, 1984's *Love Medicine*, Erdrich introduced a cast of characters that she would return to again. Lulu Lamartine, Marie Lazarre, Lipsha Morrissey, and Nector Kashpaw take turns narrating the story, which unfolds elliptically over a period of fifty years. It's a tale of love, friendship, and faith among several Native American families in North Dakota, with the sharply drawn characters moving the plot forward while undercurrents of magic, religion, tribal customs, and the politics of reservation life give the book a densely layered quality. Erdrich revisits these themes and characters in book after book.

Erdrich's astonishingly original imagery and flawless dialogue were a revelation when *Love Medicine* (which earned the National Book Critics Circle Award for fiction) first appeared, but her second book, *The Beet Queen*, remains her best to date. She uses the same multi-voiced narrative style, but with an even more satisfying story—a multigenerational, magic realist saga with vibrant characters and a marvelous sense of humor—not something Erdrich always brings to the party, but a deftly handled delight when she does.

In addition to several works of nonfiction, among them *The Blue Jay's Dance*, a lovely chronicle of the birth of a child and the first year after, four more novels followed in which Erdrich returned to the landscape charted in *Love Medicine*, with uneven results. *Tracks* had Erdrich's gorgeous, lyrical prose and featured vividly imagined characters, but the storyline lacked the brilliant architecture of her earlier work. *The Bingo Palace* and *Tales of Burning Love*, however, proved Erdrich was still at the top of her game, especially the latter—an affecting, unrestrained look at a man's life by his five ex-wives. In *The Antelope Wife*, Erdrich plunged deep into Native American myths, writing an interesting, if quirky, collection of episodes that doesn't fully cohere. Her exploration of the same small but expanding universe of people is often likened to Faulkner's excursions to Yoknapatawpha County. *The Crown of Columbus*, which she co-wrote with Dorris, isn't part of this saga or up to the standards that both she and her husband had previously set for themselves.

Erdrich and Dorris were separated when the news of his suicide rocked the literary world. Rumors that he had been accused of abusing his children circulated, and what had once looked like a phenomenally stable and loving literary family fast became an awful tragedy. Erdrich's admirers await her next book with the hope that she'll be able to continue writing as prodigiously as before.

See Also: Michael Dorris's novel A Yellow Raft in Blue Water *and memoir* The Broken Cord. *Barbara Kingsolver and Leslie Marmon Silko also write about Western and Native-American life.*

—Deborah Kirk

Erickson, Steve
1950–
b. Santa Monica, California

FICTION: Days between Stations (1985), **Rubicon Beach** (1986), **Tours of the Black Clock** (1989), Leap Year (1989), *****Arc d'X** (1993), Amnesiascope (1996), The Sea Came in at Midnight (1999)

NONFICTION: American Nomad (1997)

For all his time-travelling, his dream logic, his cinematic jump cuts, his erotic interludes, his postapocalyptic future worlds, Los Angeles novelist Steve Erickson is an old-fashioned guy. No matter how dystopian his settings or how bitter his characters or how open-ended his conclusions, his narrative voice never quite sheds its fundamental idealism. He (that is to say, his characters) have two central quests, the personal and the political—looking for love and looking for America. Which is to say that he writes very restless books. Every one of them is a road trip of sorts through time and space, pitting his characters' memories against the republic's history.

Perhaps the best place to start is either 1989's *Tours of the Black Clock*, a gripping tale of Hitler's private pornographer that doubles as a perceptive analysis of twentieth-century evil, or *Arc d'X*, which skips from the age of Jefferson as seen through the eyes of his slave and lover Sally Hemings to Berlin on the cusp of the millennium. Erickson's earlier novels, *Days Between Stations* and *Rubicon Beach*, feature protagonists obsessed with the past and are written in a hard-boiled West Coast version of magical realism. *Leap Year* centers on the 1988 presidential election, though a better bet is his beautiful, gut-wrenching nonfiction narrative about following the campaign trail in 1996, *Ameri-*

L.A. NOVELS *by Steve Erickson*

Death of Speedy by Jaime Hernandez

Life among las locas, east of a Los Angeles River where no water flows: Amid the urban punk rubble she never quite fits into, running with grrrls tough enough to get by with one r, Maggie is distinguished as much by her enduring spirit as by her endless remorse at not somehow being better than she is, even as she's better than everyone around her. Funny, violent, sexy, tender and devastating, rejecting sensationalism as forcefully as sociological cant, disdaining cheap emotion as determinedly as glib resolutions, like a classic nineteenth-century novel this barrio masterpiece even has pictures. Quite a few of them.

Flow My Tears, the Policeman Said by Philip K. Dick

Possessed by a vision his erratic voice could barely keep up with, Dick confronted the meaning of reality before moving on to the bigger question: the meaning of humanity. In the L.A. of the future—1988—Police General Felix Buckman flies over a city that awaits his judgment, where he lives in a depraved marriage with a woman whose appetite for sex and drugs is limitless; she also happens to be his sister. Her life disgusts him only slightly less than her death shatters him, and as night chases him across town he slowly comes apart, the inherent meaningless of reality overtaking whatever meaning humanity still holds.

Black Dahlia by James Ellroy

All the dreams of postwar paradise distilled into one hallucinatory horror show from Hollywood Boulevard to the Tijuana Border, compared to which the debauchery at the heart of *Chinatown* is about as shocking as a convent whisper. In the only city where murder is interchangeable with lust, where the unspeakable is confused with ecstasy, its final pages barely withstanding the heat of its own fever, this is a black epic of all L.A.'s obsessions—what they buy and what they cost.

The Zoo Where You're Fed to God by Michael Ventura

A middle-aged medical surgeon, living in the moors of Echo Park, feels madness blow across him one night in the Santa Anas, and emerges on the other side of the wind as a surgeon of the soul. In a city that disenfranchises people from their identities, he dreams of operating on himself in a desperate, exploratory search for a nervous system, until one night he finds the head of a gerenuk inside his own heart, the paw for a tiger inside his lungs, and the foot of a chimpanzee inside his stomach. How strange that his body had become an Ark. Too passionate to be merely ruminative, too anarchic to be merely spiritual, finally this brilliant *tour de force* is too physically unsettled to be merely metaphysical, its conclusions lying far beyond the axis where man meets beast and bliss meets madness.

141

Weetzie Bat by Francesca Lia Block

Life among the crazees, west of the L.A. River: With the baby she's had by three fathers, and her gay pals Dirk and Duck, and her lover-man My Secret Agent Lover Man, Weetzie is distinguished as much by her eternally good heart as her wild-child ways. Always hip without ever losing her bracing naivete, way cool without a cynical bone in her body, she careens across a shimmering '80s Wonderland of futuristic diners and retro-martini lounges and exotic hot dog stands that's half Hell-A and half Shangri-L.A., where love is the most dangerous angel in a city full of them.

can *Nomad*. *Amnesiascope* is Erickson at his most Erickson: a synthesis of memory and guilt, history, and the lack of it (i.e., Los Angeles), patriotism and eroticism. Finally, *The Sea Came in at Midnight* is a philosophical-doomsday kinky-sex road-trip novel about a teenage girl who survives a mass suicide at the turn of the millennium to become the sex slave of an "apocalyptologist" known only as The Occupant.

See Also: Three other authors who understand that the trick of making surrealism believable is a straight face are: Philip K. Dick, Thomas Pynchon, and Jonathan Lethem.

—*Sarah Vowell*

Fitzgerald, Penelope
1916–
b. Lincoln, England

FICTION: The Golden Child (1977), **The Bookshop** (1978), Offshore (1979), Human Voices (1980), At Freddie's (1982), Charlotte Mew and Her Friends (1984), Innocence (1986), *__The Beginning of Spring__ (1988), The Gate of Angels (1990), **The Blue Flower** (1995)

NONFICTION: Edward Burne-Jones (1975), The Knox Brothers (1977)

Penelope Fitzgerald's is an art that sneaks up on its readers, surprising them with its quiet ingenuities and hidden erudition. Before you know it, you've gathered all manner of information from her novels—how to compose lines of type, the effects of the Thames's tidal rhythms on its resident river barges, the laundry habits of the eighteenth-century German bourgeoisie—while being amused and provoked by her sly wit.

Considered by many critics to be among the finest British writers alive, Fitzgerald was over sixty when her first novel, a deft museum mystery written to entertain her terminally ill husband, was published. Before that she led a full and varied life, often chronicled in her early fictions. Her work in a Suffolk bookshop led to *The Bookshop*, in which a beleaguered bookseller faces parochial resistance to her prominent window displays of *Lolita*; her war years at the BBC shaped the short comic novel *Human Voices*; and raising her children on a houseboat in Chelsea provided the material for her vivid, elegiac tale of river life, the Booker Prize-winning *Offshore*.

Thereafter, her focus shifted. Since the mid-1980s Fitzgerald has marshalled her

"THIS IS IT" *by Penelope Fitzgerald*

With each one of these novels I thought, as soon as I'd read the first page, "*this is it*." It's difficult to argue about this, although I've sometimes had to, but in reading many hundreds of novels, some of them very good, I've only had the sensation quite rarely.

A Pale View of Hills by Kazuo Ishiguro
A novel unlike any other, set in the wasteland of Nagasaki after the war, where a seemingly quiet story of mothers and their small daughters takes an undefinably sinister turn.

Kruger's Alp by Christopher Hope
The first novelist I read who treated South African politics not as a tragedy but as a black farce (which, of course, is tragedy the other way up).

Hôtel du Lac by Anita Brookner
Exquisitely, meticulously written but still—there isn't any other word for it—romantic.

The Snapper by Roddy Doyle
You have to laugh, you can't help it, and you feel picked up and shaken by its energy, but I hope Roddy Doyle won't mind my saying that the great virtue of this book is tenderness.

The Restraint of Beasts by Magnus Mills
The jacket picture of this brilliantly original first novel is, in my view, a mistake. The displaced Scottish fence-wirers don't kill anyone . . . There are just a few unfortunate accidents.

---

broad intellectual and artistic resources to create evocative fictions of other times and places. While her early novels are entertaining comedies of manners, it is in the later work that her gifts really shine. Perhaps most uncanny is her ability to inhabit other cultures—postwar Italy in *Innocence*, pre-revolutionary Moscow in *The Beginning of Spring*, and most famously, life among eighteenth-century German romantics in her fictionalized account of the life of Novalis, the much-acclaimed 1995 novel *The Blue Flower*, which won the National Book Critics Circle Award in 1997.

All of these works are remarkable for their subtle economy. Fitzgerald wears her extensive research lightly, and the spare elegance of her prose helps offset the richness of the material. She has a keen taste for culinary detail (not surprising in someone who once worked in the Ministry of Food): It is hard to forget *The Blue Flower*'s pig snout boiled in peppermint schnapps, or the cow heel broth in her novel of Edwardian Cambridge, *The Gate of Angels*. A notable weakness, however, is plot: Her novels have a dreamy languor; though they are physically slight, they often read slowly. This is a pleasure for readers who will savor her careful observations of human vanity and pride—caught in such acute phrases as "the ruthlessness of the timid" or "the terrible aim-lessness of the benevolent"—but may frustrate those who seek a more defined story or resolution.

Fitzgerald's first book, a biography of the pre-Raphaelite artist Burne-Jones (she also wrote a biography of her literary father, Edmund Knox, and his brothers), describes the artist possessing "a modest irony peculiarly his own"; it's a phrase that might equally apply to its author.

See Also: Fitzgerald's earlier work was compared with that of the wry and observant Barbara Pym, and to trace that lineage further back, Jane Austen. She is more overtly intellectual than either, so a more apt peer might be A. S. Byatt.

—*Sylvia Brownrigg*

Fleming, Ian
1908–1964
b. London, England

FICTION: Casino Royale (1953), Live and Let Die (1954), *****Moonraker** (1955), Diamonds Are Forever (1956), From Russia, With Love (1957), Doctor No (1958), **Goldfinger** (1959), For Your Eyes Only (1960), Thunderball (1961), The Spy Who Loved Me (1962), **On Her Majesty's Secret Service** (1963), You Only Live Twice (1964), Chitty Chitty Bang Bang (1964), The Man with the Golden Gun (1965), Octopussy (1966)

144

The name was Bond, James Bond, and he was the first British pop superstar, one whose shaken-not-stirred mystique refuses to die. Equal parts killing machine, superstud, and sommelier, Bond would dispatch a villain with a commando chop to the neck, then reflect on the meaning of death over a glass of wine—which Fleming would be sure to describe as "a superb '48 Medoc."

Basted in the womb in some pheromone-rich broth that made him preternaturally attractive to all women, Bond was not only a master of all dudely activities—skiing, golfing, card-playing, knowing the 13:40 back-axle ratio of the Continental Bentley, stopping an endless procession of weird Dick Tracy-ish villains from destroying the world, etc.—but an egregious connoisseur whose brand-name savoir-faire outdoes the ravings of the most over-the-top shopping-and-fucking novel. In the middle of a dangerous pursuit of Goldfinger across Europe, Fleming will stop everything to note that "Bond would have liked to stay outside the town and sleep on the banks of the Loire in the excellent Auberge de la Montespan, his belly full of *quenelles de brochet*." That "excellent"—so gratuitous, so smug, so idiotically satisfying—is pure Fleming.

Fleming's skillfully written, fast-paced tales are great fun, but despite hints of darkness they're too formulaic to rank with Hammett, Chandler, or Simenon. Still, they're a major cut above the run of genre thrillers. Fleming's high-dilettantish aperçus on anything and everything, his utter lack of irony, his genius for the grotesque, and his oddly affection-inspiring hero, make these books true originals.

See Also: If you could cross Cigar Aficionado *and* Dick Tracy *with* Town and Country *and graft it onto a Raymond Chandler novel, you might get close to Fleming.*

—*Gary Kamiya*

Ford, Richard
1944–
b. Jackson, Massachussetts

FICTION: A Piece of My Heart (1976), The Ultimate Good Luck (1981), **The Sportswriter** (1986), **Rock Springs: Stories** (1987), Wildlife (1990), *Independence Day (1995), Women with Men (1997)

Winning the 1996 Pulitzer Prize has become the keystone of Richard Ford's reputation, but the book he won it for, *Independence Day*, is hardly a definitive representation. Frank Bascombe, who narrates both that novel and 1986's *The Sportswriter*, is garrulous, urbane, charming—negotiating the comforts and travails of married-and-divorced middle-class life in the Northeast Corridor. It would have been hard to guess from the hard-boiled man's world of Ford's first two novels, *A Piece of My Heart* and *The Ultimate Good Luck*—with their pressed-to-the-wall mood of existential crisis and omnipresent threat of violence—that Ford would find his way to Frank's easy equanimity. But Ford is deceptive in that way. He's been pegged as a "Southern writer" in the mold of both William Faulkner and Walker Percy, and lumped with the 1980s strain of Hemingway-esque minimalism most often associated with his friend Raymond Carver, all the while producing his two most famous books as a kind of loquacious Percy-in-Cheever-

145

country. Which merely underlines the expansive reach of Ford's agile narrative voice.

Some would say that voice is all Ford has. It's true that tense plotting is not what drives his novels. *A Piece of My Heart* is less noteworthy for the central parallel stories of an ennui-paralyzed law student and an Arkansas drifter who find their separate ways to an uncharted island in the Mississippi delta, than for the supporting cast of characters and the sometimes comic details of backwoods life. Old coots dine on braised squirrel, fish for crappies, and warn their visitors about the giant gar that lurk in deep water and can pull a grown deer to the bottom in a flash. And every once in a while, his characters philosophize in their reduced language about the exigencies of luck, fate, and personal choice: "One day you think you never even made a choice and then you have to make one, even a wrong one, just so you're sure you're still able."

As the title implies, Ford refined these notions in *The Ultimate Good Luck*, where yet another drifter, a Vietnam veteran, tries to win back his ex-girlfriend by traveling to Mexico to bribe her drug-dealing brother out of prison. The tone is hard-boiled, the language and narrative more spare than in the first novel. Self-knowledge seems linked more than ever to the landscape itself—the "patterned feel" of a "known locale" paralleling a kind of internal landscape.

Since *The Sportswriter* (written, he says, as a challenge from his wife to create a "happy character"), Ford has alternated between the hard- and the soft-boiled: the merciless wide-open vistas of Montana with its mining towns and guns and small-time convicts; or the "civilized" middle-class world of Frank Bascombe and his like. Start with *The Sportswriter* and you get one kind of Ford; start with *Rock Springs* (the story collection that followed *The Sportswriter*) and you get another. But life's hairpin turns of luck and choice are always his greatest concern.

Although Ford is not primarily a short story writer, *Rock Springs* is one of his most satisfying books, full of firearms, bad marriages, and whiskey-fueled behavior. In "Communist," that most tired of Hemingway rite-of-passage devices, the hunting trip, serves as a rite of passage for yet another of literature's adolescent boys waiting to grow up. But Ford's grasp of the particulars of his story—the countryside, a lake full of snow geese, the mother's strange boyfriend (the "Communist" of the title), the play of light and weather—and his modulation of voice between adult narrator and adolescent memory, give this story a mythic power.

Here and in other Ford tales, when we get a scene of domestic mayhem witnessed through the eyes of an adolescent narrator, the effect is nearly hallucinatory, like one long, sustained Primal Scene. That's how we get the novel *Wildlife* (in typical Ford fashion, it's the 1960 summer of rampant Montana forest fires when the narrator's homelife goes up in flames) and "Jealous," the central of the three longish stories that make up *Women with Men*. The other two stories in that book are about middle-class American men (a writer and a businessman) behaving badly in France. These guys are Bascombe without the charm, and the stories are nearly sunk by our inability to sympathize.

That leaves Bascombe as the emblematic Ford narrator: worldly-wise, charming, an exurban New Jersey armchair philosopher treading water. By the time of *Independence Day*, he's living in what he calls "the Existence Period" of his life, trying to avoid unnecessary emotional risk without amputating life's passion. Again, nothing much happens in *Independence Day*. But as the sportswriter-turned-realtor tries to sell a piece of property to a retired Vermont couple, collect rent from a man in the "colored" section of town, check in on his birch beer stand, and connect with his troubled teenage son by taking him on a road trip to the basketball and baseball Halls of Fame, the texture of his life becomes palpable, as real as our own, and expands to take in every corner of American life itself.

See Also: Ford has cited his friend Raymond Carver as an important influence; Tobias Wolff is another member of their circle.

—*Jon Garelick*

Fowler, Karen Joy
1950–
b. Bloomington, Indiana

FICTION: Artificial Things (1986), Peripheral Vision (1990), *__Sarah Canary__ (1991), __The Sweetheart Season__ (1996), __Black Glass__ (stories, 1998)

There's almost always something strange about to happen in the stories and novels of Karen Joy Fowler, which mostly explore why and how people want strange things to happen. Ghosts and Venusians and DEA agents traipse through her books, just as they probably do through our lives—both conspicuous and incognito. But try to categorize Fowler's fiction as fantasy (in light of her 1987 Hugo Award) and you'll be in trouble, for literary sophistication abounds, as do magical realism and postmodern schizophrenia. And don't forget the feminism that underscores everything.

Categorizing Fowler, then, is mostly a job for future grad students, but reading Fowler, thankfully, is more gratifying than confusing. In *Sarah Canary*, a Chinese immigrant finds himself beholden to a female specter in the Pacific Northwest of the nineteenth century: Is she a godly emissary? Or insane? Fowler's protagonists often see themselves as standing outside important events, like the all-women softball team who entertain World War II–era America in *The Sweetheart Season*, and yet when the story is done, those events could not have happened without their presence. This is how Fowler understands and reconsiders history, which is why her writing both suffers and prospers from a lack of linear logic.

But history has been mostly a story told by boys to other boys. Fowler knows this, and her characters learn it, too. So her stories and novels are more than genre-benders, and her elegant prose and sad worldview are more than window dressing. Prepare to be surprised, and you'll still be surprised.

See Also: Fowler's powerful feminism resembles that of Margaret Atwood, and the two writers share an abiding interest in history, but the conflicts in Fowler's work tend to be more situational and less explicitly ideological. In Sarah Canary, *Fowler explores Asian emigrant experience in the Pacific Northwest, in a way that's reminiscent of Robert Olen Butler's fiction about the Vietnamese in Louisiana.*

—**Alan Michael Parker**

Fowles, John
1926–
b. Leigh-on-Sea, Essex, England

FICTION: The Collector (1963), The Aristos: A Self-Portrait in Ideas (1964), **The Magus** (1966; rev. 1978), *****The French Lieutenant's Woman** (1969), The Ebony Tower (1974), **Daniel Martin** (1977), Mantissa (1982), A Maggot (1985)

NONFICTION: Wormholes (1998)

POETRY: Poems (1973)

John Fowles is a rarity in the world of letters, a novelist with both a mass audience and the reputation of a literary giant among critics in the university and the press. A writer of profound erudition and lush, romantic tastes, Fowles despises the attention his work has received from anyone but his readers. His contempt for academics is as famous as his concept of himself as "an outsider" who writes books that are hymns to freedom. Fowles is obsessed with freedom, as he is also obsessed with power, choice, the mystery of nature, the English countryside, and the memory of some idealized "lost domain," an Eden, or Arden, where human beings once roamed unafraid, in full awareness and defiance of their fate—death.

"All my books are about that," Fowles says flatly. "The question is, is there really free will? Can we choose freely? Can we act freely? Can we choose? How do we do it?" His first novel, *The Collector*, was overtly the story of a young woman's kidnapping and confinement at the hands of a psychopath, but more deeply a commentary on the difference between people who realize their true natures and others—the majority—who have abdicated their lives under the pressure to conform. *The Collector* sold as a thriller, just as *The Magus*, Fowles's indescribable mixture of stray philosophy, Bildungsroman, nature-writing, and mumbo-jumbo, appealed to its vast audience as a fantasy, an epic adventure with supernatural overtones that managed to leave every question it raised maddeningly unanswered.

Fowles's gifts are for epic storytelling and stormy, wild atmospherics; his weaknesses are verbosity and a chronic reluctance to provide endings to his books. In *The French Lieutenant's Woman*, his most famous and commercially successful work, Fowles introduces himself as the twentieth-century narrator of a nineteenth-century novel, thus giving rein to his stupendous narrative style while undercutting the genre at every turn. Narrators are no longer omniscient, says Fowles, declaring outright that he has no idea of what's really going on in his novel and providing two equally ambivalent endings to the story. As with Fowles's characters, so with his legion of fans: They must choose for themselves.

In 1978, Fowles produced a revised edition of *The Magus*, hoping to rectify what he considered to be serious problems in the text. But nothing he has done in *The Magus* or elsewhere has succeeded in bridging the gap between those who simply adore Fowles's fiction and those who think it's mostly hot air—flowery, overwrought, discursive and willfully enigmatic. With *Daniel Martin*, Fowles consciously abandoned "literary gymnastics" and produced what he calls "a long journey of a book" in a more naturalistic style. *Daniel Martin* does have an ending, but it takes forever to get to it, and a passion for Fowles is required to stay the course.

Fowles's two subsequent novels, *Mantissa* and *A Maggot*, must be rated as self-indulgent failures, but he proved himself a master of short fiction in his 1974 collection, *The Ebony Tower*, and a compendium of his nonfiction writing—essays, treatises, and criticism—was published to great acclaim in 1998 as *Wormholes*.

149

See Also: Fowles has been compared to Dickens, Tolstoy, Thomas Mann, and Thomas Hardy, his own chosen hero. For sheer breadth of narrative and earnestness of delivery, he is equalled in our time only, perhaps, by John Irving.

—*Peter Kurth*

Franzen, Jonathan
1959–
b. Western Springs, Illinois

FICTION: *The Twenty-Seventh City (1988), Strong Motion (1992)

"When I got out of college in 1981, I hadn't heard the news about the death of the social novel," wrote Jonathan Franzen in "Perchance to Dream," a 1996 essay published in *Harper's* magazine bemoaning the cultural irrelevance of literary fiction. An author who likes to write about cities (so far, St. Louis and Boston), and who favors vast, complex plots that pull in everything from family power struggles and real estate speculation to gender relations and the dumping of toxic waste, Franzen looks like the likeliest candidate to revive the form. And unlike most other practitioners of wide-screen fiction, he writes straightforward prose with engrossing, if conventional, storylines and a minimum of postmodern high jinks.

In *The Twenty-Seventh City*, Franzen takes an improbable (and troublingly paranoid) scenario about a cabal of Indians led by the female former police chief of Bombay trying to seize covert control of St. Louis and unfolds it with rigorous, involving realism. *Strong Motion* gives a pair of prickly lovers the task of unearthing a chemical company's role in a rash of Massachusetts earthquakes. These books may sound like thrillers, but they're filled with compelling characters, moral insight, and daringly imagined passages, such as an interlude in *Strong Motion* describing the alienated existence of an urban raccoon. Even if Franzen were the only one writing "the social novel," it would still have a pulse.

See Also: Thomas Pynchon, Don DeLillo, and Franzen's friend David Foster Wallace all write big books in which conspiracies often drive the action, but they're more experimental and therefore less accessible.

—Laura Miller

Gaddis, William
1922–1998
b. New York, New York

FICTION: The Recognitions (1955), *****JR** (1975), **Carpenter's Gothic** (1985), **A Frolic of His Own** (1994)

Deeply concerned with the values by which people live, Gaddis filled his work with fierce anger and bitter humor at how people fail themselves and others, at all forms of laziness and greed and stupidity. It overflows with bleak sorrow, outrage, and a desperate laughter that, while it doesn't heal, provides the only refuge in a world where most people spend their best efforts on tasks not worth doing.

For Gaddis, what *is* worth doing often goes unappreciated. The disappointed and neglected artists, writers, and composers who inhabit his books can be read, to some degree, as surrogates for Gaddis himself, whose monumental 956-page first novel met with critical and commercial indifference.

The Recognitions is a comic inferno that already displays Gaddis's powers at their full: his extraordinary ear for speech, his intricate plotting, and a supple style that bridges the lyrical, the elegiac, and the gothic, while keeping up a counterpoint of irony, wit, and pratfall. The book centers on Wyatt Gwyon, a failed seminarian and aspiring painter who works as a restorer—and, finally, a forger—of Flemish masterpieces. Brilliant and erudite, the novel has an exaggerated reputation for difficulty that ignores its nonstop humor. Reviews were either distantly respectful or openly disdainful of its ambition, but uniformly ignorant of its accomplishments (Jack Green's *Fire The Bastards!* is an indignant and very funny indictment of the reviewers), and the book sold poorly, although it gained a devoted underground following.

Twenty years passed before the publication of *JR*. At 726 pages, it is Gaddis's most challenging and essential novel, a scabrous, hilarious condemnation of American business and its genius for degrading everything it touches, informed by Gaddis's experience as a corporate copywriter. Eleven-year-old J. R. Vansant, as touching as he is appalling, builds a paper empire of penny stock and junk bonds from an elementary school phone booth, drawing dozens of hapless adults into his disastrous orbit. Prophetic of 1980s Wall Street, *JR* is told in relentless overlapping dialogue, without chapters or breaks, that, like its New York setting, is at once exhilirating and draining.

Unity of setting, relative shortness (262 pages), and Gaddis's knowledgeable reworking of familiar, almost trite, romantic elements make *Carpenter's Gothic* the most approachable of his books, though the plot is perhaps his darkest. Its interlocking intrigues lead, as usual, to disasters both local and global.

In *A Frolic of His Own*, Oscar Crease is a middle-aged college instructor who sues a Hollywood producer for plagiarizing his unpublished play. The novel is not merely a satire on lawyers. Oscar's high-minded principles are undercut by his ceaseless petulance, self-absorption, and greed. The lawyers and jurists, while equally venal or biased, recognize as Oscar does not that justice and the law are entirely separate things; and Gaddis's lengthy pastiches of legal opinions show more than a grudging respect for the intellectual rigor of the law, imperfect as it is. Despite the characteristic multiple, frantic threads racing one another toward chaos, *Frolic* ends on a note of, if not hope, at least respite.

See Also: Though Gaddis is routinely compared to other "encyclopedic" novelists such as Joyce, Pynchon, and Barth, his work is unique and dissimilar. In interviews he cited the influence of Evelyn Waugh, Samuel Butler, and Ronald Firbank. Of his contemporaries, William H. Gass, with whom he is sometimes confused, shares with him an outrage at contemporary America ("a country of decent people who do terrible things") and a finely wrought style, but they are very different writers. Other writers as diverse as Joseph McElroy, Don DeLillo, David Markson, and John Sladek have acknowledged influence or admiration.

—Carter Scholz

Gaines, Ernest J.
1933–
b. Oscar, Louisiana

FICTION: Catherine Carmier (1964), **Of Love and Dust** (1967), Bloodline (stories, 1968), *The Autobiography of Miss Jane Pittman** (1971), In My Father's House (1978), **A Gathering of Old Men** (1983), **A Lesson Before Dying** (1993)

Born on a Louisiana plantation and left in the care of a remarkable aunt, Ernest James Gaines went to work at the age of eight, chopping sugar cane for fifty cents a day. Although he escaped his harsh environment at age fifteen when he joined his parents in California, he's always felt a strong connection to his Southern origins—a bond he's maintained in the intervening years by returning often to Pointe Coupee Parish.

All of Gaines's fiction is set in the South, and as might be expected, he counts William Faulkner among his main influences, along with Turgenev, Gogol, and Tolstoy. Gaines places his characters in a world of his own creation, rural St. Raphael Parish, the equivalent of Faulkner's Yoknapatawpha County. Echoing his predecessor's emphasis on dialogue enriched by colorful Southern dialects, Gaines masterfully invokes the rhythms and patterns of everyday speech. Through deceptively simple exchanges and surprisingly spare physical descriptions, he offers homages to ordinary black individuals who risk danger and even death in pursuit of the dignity and respect often denied them in the South. These individuals are often men, like Marcus Payne, the young ex-con in *Of Love and Dust*, who challenges the prohibition against interracial love; Charlie Biggs in *A Gathering of Old Men*, who provokes deadly consequences when he finally asserts himself after fifty years of acquiescence; and Jefferson in *A Lesson Before Dying*, a doomed death-row denizen whose sense of himself emerges once he is taught to read and write.

However, until recently (before Oprah's Book Club made *Lesson* a best-seller) Gaines's best-known hero was a heroine. The eponymous star of *The Autobiography of Miss Jane Pittman* was based in part on the beloved aunt who raised Gaines. Miss Jane's "memoir" is the tale of a one hundred-ten-year-old black woman who was born in slavery and lived into the civil rights struggle of the early '60s. Most impressive about Gaines's panoramic novel is his ability to create and sustain a convincing voice for his centenarian protagonist. He told an interviewer that after compiling his research he said, "I must in some way . . . give her all this information and let her tell this thing the way she would tell it, as an illiterate black woman a hundred years old talking about these things . . . I cannot just give her hunks of history and throw them to her."

History looms large throughout Gaine's books, which have occasionally come under fire for lacking a "protest" aspect. Such criticism is inaccurate, however, because it fails to recognize how cleverly—and subtly—Gaines indicts American society for its failure to own up to its own glorious aims. Already a best-selling novelist before Oprah's anointment, Gaines challenges the notion that black male novelists cannot attract the attention of white readers: More than one million copies of *A Lesson Before Dying* are in print.

See Also: In addition to William Faulkner, admirers of Gaines's work should check out Flannery O'Connor, Ralph Ellison, and James Alan McPherson.

—*Jabari Asim*

Gaitskill, Mary

1954–
b. Lexington, Kentucky

FICTION: **Bad Behavior** (1988), *Two Girls, Fat and Thin (1991), **Because They Wanted To** (1997)

The casual precision with which Mary Gaitskill writes about the social and sexual mores of the post-sixties generation is so shocking and so funny that it shows just how far a lot of us still are from fully assimilating them. All of her books have episodes of sadomasochistic sex, but her fiction is no more graphic than that of most of her contemporaries (and many of her predecessors). Her bad-girl reputation comes mainly from the frankness with which she writes about the emotions connected with sex. For Gaitskill, sex is a lens that brings personalities into focus. Her characters are generally young and bohemian, often struggling artists—characters much like the writer and her friends.

In 1988 she published her first book, *Bad Behavior*, a collection of stories that are comically inflated yet psychologically meticulous, like Road Runner cartoons written by Stendhal. One of her protagonists is a Dexedrine freak. Two others are prostitutes. "A Romantic Weekend" chronicles an S&M tryst that flops. But this list is misleading: You can't pigeonhole her by her subject matter. Voyeurism is barely a factor in these fanatically analytical stories, and they certainly aren't arousing. A couple of them, hard-edged but sad, explore broken friendships (female friendship is a recurring theme), and the collection concludes with a quiet study of family relationships in a surprisingly wistful register.

In 1991 Gaitskill published *Two Girls, Fat and Thin*, a wonderful novel with a more down-to-earth tone. The thin girl of the title, Justine Shade, is a typical Gaitskill creation: a writer, a budding masochist, a lost little girl in a grown-up's body. The fat girl, Dorothy Never, is a real original: lonely, un-

154

MEN AT EXTREMES   *by Mary Gaitskill*

The Confessions of Nat Turner by William Styron

A fictionalized account of Nat Turner's slave rebellion. I have read that many African-Americans did not like this story told by a white man, and I can understand that on principle. However, having known nothing of Turner when I began the book, I finished it feeling awed and moved by his life. I've never read anything that so clearly revealed the concept of benevolent slavery as an impossible lie; Turner's owner is portrayed as a genuinely kind person, but in spite of his intentions, his kindness becomes a more deeply destructive cruelty in the end. Styron makes us understand how Turner, portrayed as a profoundly moral man with a sensitive nature, could become a killer. Even though he killed civilians, including an innocent young girl who had been friendly to him, I saw him as a hero. I don't know if the book tells the literal truth about Nat Turner, but for me that's beside the point. It is an extraordinary story of a fight for justice, of how honor and mercy destroyed can come to life again.

Continental Drift by Russell Banks

The intersecting stories of a struggling blue-collar worker desperate for a better life and a poor Haitian woman desperate to come to America. This is about powerless people chewed up by social forces. It is also about something deeper and more difficult to put into words. Banks writes about tragedy in a way that is uplifting and strangely calming. He evokes primal mystery, the forces which we, in our lives and deaths, embody without knowing how or why. The senseless deaths depicted here are unjust, but Banks's acceptance of the *fact* of death gives his characters great dignity. This book, in its profound acknowledgment of suffering, is an instrument of healing as well as a work of art.

The Ordinary Seaman by Francisco Goldman

A handful of South American men in need of work are tricked into traveling to a harbor in New York City where they become virtual slaves, trapped on a worthless ship, working for an unscrupulous American dilettante. This book is also about powerless people who are victimized by social forces, and it brilliantly depicts the various ways they cope with it, in their actions and their inner lives. This becomes a depiction of the ingenious complexity and resilience of human nature in its most essential form. It is rendered with tremendous vitality, intelligence, and sweetness. That combination alone makes it rare in modern American letters.

China Men by Maxine Hong Kingston

155

Interwoven stories about the men of an immigrant Chinese family and what they experienced in America. I was surprised to realize, after I'd finished it, that *China Men* is a nonfiction account drawn from Kingston's own family history. I thought it was a novel employing the first-person narrative, not only because it uses storytelling methods common in fiction, but because the world it creates is observed with such extraordinary perception and feeling that it seems magical. What it describes is not always beautiful; Kingston's ancestors experienced much cruelty and hardship. But her telling of it is beautiful because she goes to the inmost depth of experience, a place she could have only reached with her imagination. She uses nonfiction to do what I have previously only seen done in the best fiction: Through words she expresses a truth that is beyond words.

appealing, and a little cracked, but also strong, purposeful, and self-made. After being repeatedly molested by her father in her adolescence, Dorothy has rescued herself, partly through her involvement with the cult of the Ayn Rand-like novelist Anna Granite—an episode in which Gaitskill shows a penchant for a highly idiosyncratic brand of literary satire. Although Justine's adolescence is much more conventional, Gaitskill nails the horror that high school is for teenage girls so painfully that somehow it seems nearly as awful. The book entwines the two girls' mostly unrelated stories, building to an ugly episode that suggests a growing disenchantment with kinky sex (a disenchantment that becomes something of a theme in her next book), and it ends on a note of unforced and unguarded beauty as the two unlikely friends fall asleep in each other's arms. Exquisite moments like this crop up in each of Gaitskill's books, and their rarity is a mark of her assurance: She doesn't pursue them, she doesn't push them, she lets them happen when they will.

The stories in Gaitskill's most recent collection, *Because They Wanted To* (1997), are less outré on the surface but fuller and more complex underneath. In "The Dentist," a former stripper develops an impossible crush on the man who has extracted one of her teeth; seated at a table of jaded friends bantering about sex, she longs for him, "at home with his entertainment center," and it's hard not to hear some of that longing as the author's. In "The Blanket," she uses a couple's rape fantasy as an occasion to examine the simultaneous beauty and repulsiveness of male physical power; she's interested in the line where it mutates from turn-on into threat. The final four stories, linked in a furiously ambitious novella called "The Wrong Thing," take the scrutiny of consciousness to microscopic extremes: Gaitskill presses her metaphorical prose to a pitch of figurativeness and analysis so weirdly artificial that it's mesmerizing.

"People put such a premium on being happy," Gaitskill once said in an interview, "and while I have nothing against being happy, I think deeper life experience isn't necessarily being more happy, it means allowing yourself to have more of whatever experience you are having." Whether her stories are about sex or not—and often they deal with sex only glancingly—their richness is in their language and their characters' perceptions, and those perceptions, of course, are Gaitskill's own.

See Also: Vladimir Nabokov has been a primary influence on Gaitskill in his humor, his attention to language, and his delight in perverse sexuality. Both Valerie Martin's A Recent Martyr *and Mary McCarthy's early stories in* Cast a Cold Eye *are as dry-eyed and intricate in their exploration of sexual and emotional behavior.*

—*Craig Seligman*

Gardner, John
1933–1982
b. Batavia, New York

FICTION: The Resurrection (1966), The Wreckage of Agathon (1970), Grendel (1971), ***The Sunlight Dialogues** (1972), Jason and Medeia (1973), Nickel Mountain: A Pastoral Novel (1973), The King's Indian (stories, 1974), October Light (1976), In the Suicide Mountains (1977), Freddy's Book (1980), The Art of Living and Other Stories (1981), **Mickelsson's Ghost** (1982), Stillness and Shadows (1986)

SELECTED NONFICTION: The Life and Times of Chaucer (1977), On Moral Fiction (1978), On Becoming a Novelist (1983), The Art of Fiction: Note on Craft for Young Writers (1984), On Writers and Writing (1994)

After John Gardner's death in a motorcycle accident in 1982, his name was ringed with a critical hush. Yet he seemed to be everywhere in the 1970s. When he wasn't tossing out novels as thick as bricks, or publishing an epic poem, or a short story collection, or a biography of Chaucer, he was stirring up controversy with *On Moral Fiction.* This work exhorted writers to create art that "clarifies life, establishes models of human action, casts nets toward the future, carefully judges our right and wrong direction," and didn't hesitate to drub those didn't. Gardner practically invented that tone of voice, the den mother's scold, with which, nowadays, William Bennett holds forth on values.

Gardner's specialty was the philosophical novel, which has always been rather an outcast in America. The nasty things Nabokov said about Dostoevsky and Thomas Mann set the tone for the fiction of the 1960s, at least for American writers, and it is

157

against that cool, somewhat amoral joy in the meshing of perception and language that Gardner wrote his novels. His success (not only critical—Gardner's novels were actually best-sellers) was, perhaps, a gauge of how much readers had come to miss overt "thinking" in fiction. In Gardner's view, the novel was philosophy by other means. Which is the kind of thing that makes the Nabokovian wince with aristocratic disdain.

Gardner's best novel, *The Sunlight Dialogues*, is a vast web of plots and counterplots revolving around Taggert Hodge, The Sunlight Man, and his pursuit by the police chief of Bavaria, New York, Clumley. The book is dense and overlong, but in the end Clumley and Taggert Hodge don't just represent positions—the dreary fate of so many of Gardner's characters—but project real human needs and tensions. *Mickelsson's Ghosts*, received the worst critical reception (probably payback by the literati for *On Moral Fiction*), but also works. Mickelsson, like Gardner, is a philosophy professor, recently divorced, in debt to the IRS, and suffering spiritually from his dyspeptic opposition to the liberal imagination. It is a violent, passionate book, but Gardner finds in it a real place for his asides and positions.

Grendel, Gardners third and best-known novel, tells the story of Beowulf from the monster's point of view. It has become a part of the high school curriculum, which favors tendentious allegories (*Lord of the Flies*, *Animal Farm*), especially if they work against the Pelagian heresy that people are born good. All the characters in the book, who are either muppet-like monsters of unqualified evil or Renaissance Faire jesters, minstrels and knights, rehearse, for no apparent reasons, the arguments of the great philosophic schools. In *October Light*, Gardner lets loose all his vices, although this was his most acclaimed novel while he was alive. James Page is an old coot, representing the rock-ribbed Republican side of things, living in Vermont with his sister Sally Abbot, an amalgam of demonic liberal beliefs. One day James shoots out the television and chases Sally upstairs, where he locks her in. Sally, in her room, finds a novel, *The Smugglers of Lost Souls Rock*. This is the kind of novel Gardner believed people like Robert Coover and Thomas Pynchon were doing—a nihilistic thing, encouraged by the likes of Sally Abbot.

See Also: Gardner either taught, befriended, or pissed off half of contemporary American literature. In his "camp" he saw such writers as Joyce Carol Oates, English novelist John Fowles, and Toni Morrison.

—Roger Gathman

Gass, William H.
1924–
b. Fargo, North Dakota

FICTION: *Omensetter's Luck (1966), **In the Heart of the Heart of the Country** (stories, 1968), Willie Masters' Lonesome Wife (1971), **The Tunnel** (1995), Cartesian Sonatas (novellas, 1998)

NON-FICTION: Fiction and the Figures of Life (1970), **On Being Blue** (1975), The World within the Word (1978), The Habitations of the Word (1985), Finding a Form (1996), Reading Rilke: Reflections on the Problems of Translation (1999)

When William Howard Gass published his first novel, *Omensetter's Luck*, in 1966 critics responded with great cheers—the book was hailed as a stylistic bellwether and the author instantly vaulted into the literary pantheon. His follow-up collection of short stories, *In the Heart of the Heart of the Country*, appeared two years later to similar kudos. Thereafter Gass reigned as part of blurbdom's holy trinity of postmodern masters—"like Pynchon, Barth, and Gass"—yet, except for one novella, he published no fiction for twenty-seven years. During this long hiatus he worked on his magnum opus, *The Tunnel,* wrote three volumes of deftly challenging essays about fiction (and one brilliant *tour de force* about the color blue), and became the high priest of metafiction. The long wait heightened expectations—as it had with Pynchon who didn't publish for seventeen years after *Gravity's Rainbow*—and lent a mythic glow to Gass's already heady reputation. But, when *The Tunnel* finally appeared in 1994 to mixed reviews, there was some sense of a letdown—the curtain had been pulled back to reveal the wizard was merely a pretty damn good novelist.

That fact was plainly evident in *Omensetter's Luck*, an intricately designed meditation on the lives of three men in a small Ohio river town. With Gass, there's generally very little plot to summarize; the action takes place within each sentence, its balance, rhythm, and intellectual aerodynamics. (It's no surprise he's a big fan of Gertrude Stein). As you might expect from a philosophy professor, Gass can't get past the sheer fact of human consciousness—that we actually think so wows him, that he never bothers to generate much in the way of plot momentum. Instead, there's dexterous wit, brainy but plainspoken lyricism, and a microscopic look at the mind, as if it were a mass of words instead of cells. The Midwest (Gass was born in Fargo, North Dakota, and has taught for decades at Washington University in St. Louis) is again the setting for *In the Heart of the Heart of the Country*, in which Gass deepened his modernist-inspired experiment to

159

pin the deep grammar of cogitation to the page. His characters exist almost solely as linguistic figments, shorn of psychological and emotional particulars; the people are not as memorable as the prose. A Mid-western austerity governs these spare tales—for instance the famous novella, "The Pedersen Kid," is confined simply to a boy's journey to tell a family he's found their half-frozen son—but they still pulse with an unmistakable bloodbeat, the sound of English sentences giving birth to themselves.

The Tunnel is less a novel than a 651-page rant. This bitter screed in the manner of Dostoevsky's *Notes from Underground* is delivered by a history professor who has written a book about guilt and innocence in the Third Reich. He packs a lifetime's worth of bile and recrimination into his train-length sentences. This stream-of-consciousness rancor is certainly no picnic, a fact Gass acknowledges. Early on, he notes, "There are Muses for several sorts of writing, but none for any kind of reading. Wouldn't one need divine aid to get through *The Making of Americans, Ivanhoe, Moll Flanders,* or *Grace Abounding*?" You may not need angelic hands to turn Gass's pages for you, but you will want to read him with your deep-think receptors set on high.

See Also: Any of the '60s metafiction gang: Barth's Sot Weed Factor, *Coover's* The Origin of the Brunists, *Gaddis's* JR, *Joseph McElroy's* Lookout Cartridge, *and, of course, Pynchon. Try some of the early novels of Paul West, such as* Alley Jaggers *or* Bela Lugosi's White Christmas.

—*Albert Mobilio*

Gates, David
1947–
b. Middletown, Connecticut

160   **FICTION: Jernigan** (1991), *****Preston Falls** (1998), Wonders of the Invisible World (stories, 1999)

Once you meet Peter Jernigan or Doug Willis, the rascally protagonists of David Gates's *Jernigan* and *Preston Falls,* they can be hard to shake—not that they're particularly appealing guys. As fumbling, literary-minded fathers in their late thirties, Jernigan and Willis are primarily suburban drunks, always angling to get in the car, slam a tape in the deck, and get out of their own lives.

Breaking Up with the Beats

By David Gates

In 1958, decades before his conversion to neoconservatism, the young leftist intellectual Norman Podhoretz ended his essay "The Know-Nothing Bohemians" with what we now recognize as his characteristic either/or pugnacity: to oppose or support the Beat generation, he argued, "has to do . . . with being for or against intelligence itself." William Burroughs and Allen Ginsberg, probably even Jack Kerouac, were surely better-wired and immeasurably lighter on their feet than an earnest A-minus student like Podhoretz. Nevertheless, Podhoretz was smart to recognize the Beats early on as anti-canonical writers whose work demanded, both implicitly and explicitly, that we stand with them or against them. I was only eleven when Podhoretz's piece came out, but when I discovered the Beats a few years later, I felt the pressure too. So did my friends. So has every generation since.

The Beats believed that literary formalism reflects and perpetuates political, social, racial, sexual, psychic, and spiritual oppression; their writing was in part an altar call on behalf of a freer, more passionate, more intuitive life and letters. In Kerouac's *On the Road*, the open highway and the writer's life seem like metaphors for each other. Directly or indirectly, the Beat sensibility transformed much of American culture. As Burroughs wrote, "Kerouac opened a million coffee bars and sold a million pairs of Levis to both sexes. Woodstock rises from his pages." Yet this essentially literary movement failed to transform American literature.

Two of the Beats' Big Three were novelists, but they have few significant followers. Conventional mimetic fiction still prevails as it did in the '50s: The diorama-like illusion of real-seeming people in real-seeming settings and situations, with incidents selected and contrived to give the work a distinct and dramatic shape. Such work interested the Beats only as reading matter. (Burroughs liked to kick back with Frederick Forsyth.) Their own narratives turn away from the world of getting and spending in favor of fictionalized memoirs of themselves and their fellow outsiders or nightmare fantasias in which scraps of the social and political world bob like rotten meats in a foul stew of language.

Thematically, Beat fiction isn't far from the literary mainstream. John Cheever's Francis Weed, in the 1954 story "The Country Husband"—published a year before Ginsberg wrote "Howl"—looks to a freer, less artificial life as yearningly as any Beat, though he ultimately can't get up the nerve to live it. But the Beats think differently about what fiction is. Cheever, half-anthropologist and half-fabulist, peoples an imaginary suburbia with plausible (if sometimes ostentatiously loony) imaginary suburbanites. The Beats crank up the rhetoric— and when they hit the right cadence, there's not a split-level left standing. In *Naked Lunch*, Burroughs evokes "a vast subdivision, antennae of television to the meaningless sky. In lifeproof houses they hover over the young, sop up a little of what they shut out. Only the young bring anything in, and they are not young very long." On the one hand, there is the Beats' truth and prophetic intensity; on the other, Cheever's verisimilitude and negative capability.

Readers don't have to choose sides, even if Norman Podhoretz says they do. Writers, though, can't afford to keep an open mind. The Beats' ethic of spontaneity and subjectivity, their suspicion of form and their openness to aleatory techniques are strong temptations to beginners. Kerouac's "Essentials of Spontaneous Prose," for instance, recommends "no pause to think of proper word but the infantile pileup of scatological buildup words till satisfaction is gained"— and no revisions after the fact. In a list entitled "Belief & Technique for Modern Prose," he reminds writers that "You're a Genius all the time." This sounds like a lot more fun than Flaubert sweating bullets all day to grind out two sentences. More fun for the writer, at least.

Mainstream writers, of course, do something like what Kerouac recommends: spewing out thoughts, images, snatches of dialogue. (Even so mandarin a personage as Nabokov once obliged an interviewer by reading out a few of such random, incomprehensible notebook jottings.) And the Beats did, in fact, revise their work. In a 1955 letter, Burroughs tells Ginsberg of sorting through a hundred pages of letters and journal fragments "to concoct 1 page" of his pre-*Naked Lunch* novel *Interzone*. Still, the Beats have no legends of hunger artistry like Pound cutting "The Waste Land" or Gordon Lish cutting Raymond Carver; fairly or unfairly, the popular image of the Beat writer is Kerouac speeding his brains out, a mile-long roll of paper chugging through his chattering typewriter. And the Beats have no achievements like Carver's "Fat," that short, exquisitely shaped, devastatingly powerful piece in which every word pulls its weight.

In *Interzone*, Burroughs made wicked sport with just this sort of talk: " 'Not bad, young man, not bad. But . . . you will observe in my production every word got some kinda awful function fit into mosaic on the shithouse wall of the world.' " This is a masterstroke of contempt. For Burroughs, literary formalism is collaboration with the cosmic status quo, the doctored "reality film," the prison-house of time, space, and language. "What scared you all into time?" he wrote in *Nova Express*. "Into body? Into shit? I will tell you: 'the word.' " The conviction that both words and phenomena are unreal doesn't dispose a novelist either to fuss over *le mot juste* or to get lost in the passions and conflicts of mere deluded worldlings.

Podhoretz was right that our attitude toward the Beats has something to do with our attitude toward intelligence. But it didn't occur to him that the Beats might have been smart to be skeptical of intelligence. And if the Beats trusted too much that their subjectivities would somehow mesh with their readers' subjectivities—at least they trusted. Kerouac didn't tweak his sub-picaresque plots or shape his scenes for dramatic effect, but he somehow got readers to experience a mood and a moment so strongly that they tried to re-create it in their own lives. Dean Moriarty, *On the Road*'s pseudonymized Neal Cassady, is one of American literature's great characters; so is Kerouac's ongoing, unprettified self-portrait under such names as Sal Paradise and Jack Duluoz: a needy, self-doubting depressive prone to both spiritual panic attacks and arias of ecstasy.

Still, sooner or later, every would-be writer who takes the Beats to heart has to make Podhoretz's Choice, and I had to go the other way. For one thing, some of this stuff just wasn't readable—though I'd still rather slog through *Minutes to Go* or Kerounac's onomatopoeic sea poem at the end of *Big Sur* than *Finnegans Wake*. For another, I didn't believe in magic: The Burroughs/Brion Gysin notion of exposing hidden truths by cutting up and folding in texts seemed as silly as Yeats or James Merrill summoning up spooks at the Ouija board. But mostly it became obvious to me that I wasn't a genius all the time, and that I could only make my work better by working on it. The Beats reverenced the work in part for the process of its creation. ("The usual novel," Burroughs wrote to Ginsberg during the writing of *Naked Lunch*, "has happened. This novel is happening.") This is a smart way of "reading" a Charlie Parker solo, in which the kick is to witness its coming into being; but it began to seem to me a dubious approach to a text, in which the words count for everything and what's in the writer's mind, heart, and soul count for nothing.

In the end, Beat dogmatism and messianism wore me out. Burroughs, particularly, loved to hand out free advice in his books—"cut lines of control," "storm the reality studio"—and I began to think that my relations with reality were none of his damn business. Anyway, I'd begun to wallow in what the Buddhist Catholic Kerouac would have dismissed as the world of Maya—that is, the world as imagined by Dickens and Austen, Tolstoy and George Eliot. (I could always do penance with Beckett's elegant deprivations.) But my choice was simply a matter of taste and temperament; it wasn't about intelligence (as Podhoretz would have said) or about collaborating with literary Nova criminals (as true believers might think). And I don't offer this account of my backings and forthings as covert advice. The Beats were my first vicarious mentors, and they have my gratitude, my admiration—my love, is what I'm avoiding saying. It's just that they can't have me.

Gates writes transfixing character studies; the plots are somewhat negligible, constructed of perfectly pitched scenes of heartbreak and emotional brinksmanship. *Jernigan* begins on the first anniversary of Peter's wife's death in a car crash and watches him struggle toward normalcy and rehab. "It looked like the scene out of an old *Twilight Zone*," Jernigan muses about his wife's accident. "Pretty inappropriate thing to be thinking, but." That's precisely the allure of Jernigan's self-aware and self-defeating intelligence—nothing's too inappropriate to mention.

Preston Falls is more ambitious and gripping. Willis flees the city for his family's summer house and eventually vanishes. The novel then switches to his wife's point of view, and her wait for his return is as harrowing and intense as any thriller. The short stories collected in *Wonders of the Invisible World* prove Gates's range even further. He's a master at inhabiting his characters—unstable housewives, a drug-addled grandfather, even an older gay man feuding with his young, ex-porn-star lover.

Critics often call Gates's books "depressing," which is not entirely fair. They're full of puns, buoyancy, and scholarly playfulness: When Willis's wife goes out for grub, he quips "a la recherché de Frank Perdue." Gates, a book and music critic for *Newsweek*, stuffs his work with popular culture, from *Star Trek* to *Straight Outta Compton*. If he could be faulted for anything, it's that this giddy surface sometimes gets the better of him, but it plays off an unspoken tragedy. If you let them, Gates's high-res, domestic dissolutions will take you much, much deeper.

See Also: *Those eager to steep themselves in middle-aged, middle-class angst might turn to Richard Yates's* Disturbing the Peace *or Richard Ford's* The Sportswriter *and* Independence Day. *Seek more alcoholic haze in Frederick Exley's* A Fan's Notes.

—*Austin Bunn*

Gibson, William
1948–
b. Conway, South Carolina

FICTION: *Neuromancer (1984), **Count Zero** (1986), Burning Chrome (stories, with John Shirley, Bruce Sterling, and Michael Swanwick, 1986), **Mona Lisa Overdrive** (1988), The Difference Engine (with Bruce Sterling, 1991), Agrippa: A Book of the Dead (with Dennis Ashbaugh and Kevin Begos Jr., 1992), Virtual Light (1993), **Idoru** (1996), All Tomorrow's Parties (1999)

William Gibson invented the word "cyberspace," and that coinage marked him as a prophet of the Internet age. But his most influential act of alchemy was more cultural than linguistic: Before Gibson, computers were for nerds; after *Neuromancer*, computers were cool. It wasn't simply a matter of dressing up the nerds in leather and mirrorshades and calling them "keyboard cowboys"—cliches of the Gibson-inspired "cyberpunk" movement that would age fast. What keeps the hipness of *Neuromancer* and its sequels ever-green is the power of Gibson's insight into how computer technology catalyzes exhilarating and scary social change. Not punk style but visionary substance gives these books their perennial *frisson*: they're science fiction for the long haul.

Gibson's future is a networked chaos, teeming with street life, beyond government control, squalid and fecund, fertilized by fast-mutating technology and animated by the constants of human fear and desire. The literary vehicle Gibson chooses to ride into this future is the Chandler/Hammett noir whodunit: Transplanting into the future the staples of this genre—like hired-gun protagonists, a world-weary atmosphere, and a sense that vast plots and conspiracies are unfolding just out of view—Gibson adopts the detective-style narrative as a slender thread to lure the reader through the disorienting maze of his writing.

Dense, sharp, and hypnotic, *Neuromancer* remains Gibson's most arresting work. From its celebrated

165

opening ("The sky above the port was the color of television, tuned to a dead channel"), it plunges you into its violent, sad world just as thoroughly as the "decks" its characters use immerse them in the Matrix—an "information space" filled with polygons representing nexuses of corporate, governmental, and military power.

Count Zero and *Mona Lisa Overdrive* are the two sequels to *Neuromancer* in what's known as the Sprawl trilogy (Gibson's name for the future urban agglomeration of the U.S.'s eastern seaboard). Amid infestations of voodoo spirits and premonitions of apocalyptic unions, these books carry forward the first novel's tale of the birth of a new kind of artificial intelligence in the Matrix. The jagged short stories in *Burning Chrome* were the seedbed for the Sprawl tales, especially "Johnny Mnemonic," "Burning Chrome," and the astonishing "Gernsback Continuum"—a deconstruction of the history of science fiction, and Gibson's place in it, disguised as a bit of futuristic architecture criticism.

Gibson hopscotched back to a less distant future in his most recent novels, *Virtual Light*—set in a San Francisco whose decommissioned Bay Bridge has become home to a squatter community—and *Idoru*, in which an aging rock star marries a Japanese pop idol who exists only as a media creation. *Idoru* is Gibson's best work since *Neuromancer*: The gentler perspective of its savvy teenybopper protagonist, who learns the limits of fandom and the ambivalence of celebrity, shifts his writing away from hardboiled noir toward a richer emotional palette. More than Gibson's earlier work, his newer books give us a lyrical refraction of the entropy of our own world—they're like stop-motion studies of the present decaying into the future.

See Also: Gibson's fans are also likely to enjoy the science fiction novels of Philip K. Dick, the dark visions of William S. Burroughs, and the polymathic opuses of Thomas Pynchon. They will also want to explore the work of his successor to the cyberpunk crown, Neal Stephenson.

—*Scott Rosenberg*

166

Goodman, Allegra
1968–
b. Honolulu, Hawaii

FICTION: **Total Immersion** (1989), *****The Family Markowitz** (1996), Kaaterskill Falls (1998)

Allegra Goodman writes circles around most other young writers by not writing circles around them. Her confident, unfussy style borrows from Grace Paley and Philip Roth, but Goodman sounds like nobody else. She's a wise-beyond-her-years observer of the clashes between orthodoxy (religious, academic, you name it) and modern liberalizing impulses, and at its best, her fiction is as funny as it is shrewd and moving.

Goodman is something of a prodigy. She published her first book, the story collection *Total Immersion*, while still a student at Harvard. (Goodman, who lives in Cambridge, Massachusetts, wrote her next two books while raising two children and finishing her Ph.D. dissertation.) Her youth has never seemed to show through; she sees the world more clearly than many novelists who are twice her age.

Goodman's first novel, *Kaaterskill Falls*, was nominated for a National Book Award, but some readers are likely to be more charmed by her two earlier, and somewhat zanier, collections of short fiction. *Total Immersion* and *The Family Markowitz* are notable not only for their multilayered assessments of what it means to be a Jew in the final quarter of the twentieth century, but for their grouchy good humor. The story "Onionskin," from *Total Immersion*, takes the form of a student's anguished letter to her professor, in which she attempts to explain why she stood up in class one day and shouted, "Fuck Augustine!" In one of the linked stories in *The Family Markowitz*—the better of these two collections, if only because the stories reverberate so expertly off of one another—one character complains that his brother has spent endless years in therapy only to develop "the most complicated persona possible—the expatriate Brooklyn Jew in Oxford." Goodman never settles for easy riffs or cheap ironies, however; her prose has a steady, silent reserve that always indicates she has bigger things on her mind.

Set during the 1970s, *Kaaterskill Falls* takes its title from the upstate New York town where a tight-knit Orthodox Jewish community spends its summers. Goodman casts her net widely; the novel is told from the perspectives of nearly a dozen characters, ranging from staunch traditionalists to worldly nonconformists. The most memorable of these characters is the British-born Elizabeth Schulman, the devout mother of five who covers her black hair with an auburn wig yet "spent her pregnancies with Austen and Tolstoy" and longs for more freedom. You finish *Kaaterskill Falls* wishing that its author had spent more time with the conflicted-yet-sensible Elizabeth instead of attempting to probe so many different psyches, and there isn't much of the deft comedy that salted Goodman's previous two books. But even if it lacks a certain measure of juice, *Kaaterskill Falls*, like almost everything Allegra Goodman has written, will not make you feel as if you've wasted a moment of your time.

See Also: Grace Paley, Philip Roth, and Cynthia Ozick are writers from earlier generations who have tackled the perplexities of contemporary Jewish life.

—*Dwight Garner*

TOO SOON TO TELL *by Laura Miller*

The entries in the *Salon.com Reader's Guide* cover authors who have published more than one novel or short story collection, but sometimes just one book can generate a lot of interest in a writer. Here is a partial list of authors to watch in the twenty-first century.

Aimee Bender: Some say there's a new literary trend afoot called American Magic Realism. If so, Bender, author of the 1998 short story collection *The Girl in the Flammable Skirt*, is at its forefront. Her inventive fables of modern life—a pair of "mutant" girls, one with a hand of fire and the other with a hand of ice, a veteran who returns home without lips—are related in the simplest of language, and they blend fairy-tale scenarios with the more surreal aspects of daily life in contemporary America.

Lan Samantha Chang: In a little over one hundred pages, the austere, heartbreaking title novella in Chang's 1998 collection *Hunger* plumbs the agonies of an unbalanced immigrant marriage and the repercussions of artistic frustration on parent-child love. Not a word is wasted, and Chang looks very much like the Asian-American heir to the best of the domestic realists of the 1980s.

Junot Diaz: The fact that Diaz's first short story collection, *Drown* (1996), didn't attain the kind of popular success promised by his six-figure advance shouldn't detract from the accomplishment of his work. His tough, stark tales of young men's lives in the barrios of the Dominican Republic and the slums of New Jersey are written in a streetwise Spanglish that captures the uneasy borderlands his characters inhabit.

Jeffrey Eugenides: The mixture of mythic elegy and mordant humor in Eugenides's celebrated 1993 novel *The Virgin Suicides* marked him as a writer pursuing the mysterious spiritual undercurrents in seemingly prosaic suburban lives. His next book, portions of which have appeared in *The New Yorker*, looks to be a further investigation into Eugenides's entwined interests in myth and obsession: It's set at least partly in Greece and concerns an incestuous brother and sister.

Charles Frazier: *Cold Mountain* was a surprise bestseller in 1997 and also won the National Book Award, a remarkable achievement for a novel so deeply rooted in the pre-Industrial rhythms of Blue Ridge Mountain life that its readers must simply succumb to its otherworldly cadences if they want to enter it at all. The elemental story of a Civil War deserter travelling miles by foot to reunite with his lost love (a preacher's daughter learning to run a farm for the first time), *Cold Mountain* is a work of passionate commemoration honoring a lost way of life.

Ken Kalfus: Anyone inspired enough to propose the literary crossbreeding of John Updike with Italo Calvino would probably also think to add a dash of sassy pop sensibility as well, so perhaps Kalfus's 1998 short story collection, *Thirst*, shouldn't have seemed so very startlingly and exhilaratingly versatile. Early samplings from *PU-*, a collection of fiction based on his sojourn in post-Soviet Russia, suggest that he has plenty more surprises and delights to pull out of his hat.

Arundahti Roy: With a jill-of-all-trades resume that would put Jack London to shame, Roy decided in her mid-thirties to turn novelist, and produced a tale of family intrigue, set in India, full of polycultural wordplay and non-chronological storytelling that took the literary world by storm: *The God of Small Things* (1997). She's said she won't write another novel, but hundreds of thousands of readers are hoping she'll change her mind about that.

George Saunders: Saunders's first collection, 1996's *CivilWarLand in Bad Decline*, envisioned a future of dilapidated, totalitarian theme parks powered by unfettered capital and riven with violence. His is a world of unlikely, possibly fraudulent products and businessmen who spout hilarious jargon to the luckless underling protagonists. In short, Saunders is a brilliant satirist of postmodern life, the type whose most outlandish work has the unsettling tendency (shudder) to come true.

Donna Tartt: Sensation greeted news of the hefty advance paid for this twenty-eight-year-old author's first novel, *The Secret History* (1992), a semi-plausible but nevertheless compelling variation on *Crime and Punishment* set in a small New England college with a group of precocious friends as the culprits. The fans she acquired with that book are still eagerly awaiting Tartt's follow-up.

Colson Whitehead: A former TV critic and music journalist, Whitehead represents a new, culturally omnivorous generation of African-American novelists with an ironic take on race relations. His first novel, *The Intuitionist*, published in 1998, is an alternate-history noir about a female elevator inspector taking on an old-boys union, the mob, and her mentor's mysterious past: part Ralph Ellison, part Haruki Murakami.

Gordimer, Nadine
1923–
b. Springs, South Africa

FICTION: Face to Face (stories, 1949), The Soft Voice of the Serpent and Other Stories (1952), The Lying Days (1953), Six Feet of the Country (stories, 1956), A World of Strangers (1958), Friday's Footprint and Other Stories (1960), Occasion for Loving (1963), Not for Publication and Other Stories (1965), The Late Bourgeois World (1966), A Guest of Honor (1970), Livingstone's Companions (stories, 1971), Selected Stories ([published in England as

No Place Like: Selected Stories], 1975), **The Conservationist** (1974), **Some Monday for Sure** (stories, 1976), *Burger's Daughter** (1979), A Soldier's Embrace (stories, 1980), Town and Country Lovers (stories, 1980), **July's People** (1981), Something Out There (stories, 1984), A Sport of Nature (1987), My Son's Story (1990), Crimes of Conscience: Selected Short Stories (1991), Jump and Other Stories (1991), Why Haven't You Written?: Selected Stories 1950–1972 (1993), None to Accompany Me (1994), The House Gun (1998)

SELECTED NONFICTION: The Essential Gesture: Writing, Politics and Places (1988), Three in a Bed: Fiction, Morals, and Politics (1991), Writing and Being (1995), Living in Hope and History (1999)

Less than ten years have passed since apartheid was officially dismantled in South Africa, but it's hard to remember now how different things once were—how, for four decades, black majority rule seemed inevitable and yet also impossible. Now that the dream has finally been realized it's difficult to appreciate the risks Gordimer once took with mere words, and the courage she exhibited in performing what is one of literature's most important functions: to imagine possibilities when it appears there are none. Taken together, Gordimer's novels and short story collections complete a portrait, more than fifty years in the making, of South Africa's total social paralysis under apartheid and its subsequent slow recovery.

Gordimer's own sense of otherness was instilled at an early age—she was an English speaker in an Afrikaner mining town, the daughter of Jewish immigrants in a Catholic school, a white woman surrounded by the black men who worked in the mines—yet she was one of few colonial writers to refuse exile, and she never left the country until she was thirty. By that time, she had already published her first novel, *The Lying Days*, about a young white woman witnessing the effects of apartheid, as well as two collections of short stories, many dealing with the master/servant dynamic—often the only personal relationship between blacks and whites that apartheid afforded. In 1958, she published *A World of Strangers*, about a British writer's struggle to befriend black intellectuals in segregated Johannesburg. In both works there's a righteous

indignation, as well as a naive idealism, about the imminence of a multiracial South Africa.

In the 1970s, as the possibility emerged that revolutionary ideals might be lost in the revolution itself, disillusionment replaced much of the hopefulness in Gordimer's writing. In *A Guest of Honor*, a British colonial administrator and supporter of the freedom movement returns from exile once the movement has triumphed, only to find that victory has driven people further apart. *The Conservationist*, which won the Booker Prize in 1974, examines the tensions between a white landowner and the black squatters who have settled on his land.

Burger's Daughter signalled a shift in focus for Gordimer. She became increasingly preoccupied with—and completely unforgiving of—the way the self-deceit of a nation infects the lives of individuals. One of several of her novels originally banned in South Africa, *Burger's Daughter* is the story of Rosa Burger, the daughter of an anti-apartheid activist who has died in prison. Expected to take up the struggle where her father left off, Rosa feels suffocated and seeks refuge and an independent life abroad. "I don't know at what point to intercede makes sense, for me," she concludes before leaving. "Every week the woman who comes to clean my flat and wash my clothes brings a child whose make-believe is polishing floors and doing washing . . . I went without saying goodbye."

This message that there is no room for self-definition in a politically repressive environment, and that context determines character resonates throughout Gordimer's work. In the short story "A Correspondence Course," a white liberal divorcée's world is so carefully, pathetically preserved that when her daughter begins a correspondence with a well-known political prisoner, she both relishes and resents the danger introduced into their quiet suburban home.

In *July's People*, her most important work, Gordimer imagines the days immediately following the revolution and asks what happens to lives that have been defined in opposition to something once that something has been removed. A white family, forced out of their home by black rioters, are taken in by their servant July and must now live as he lives, trusting their lives to him. In that book, as in *A Sport of Nature*, about a white woman who marries a powerful black politician, and *My Son's Story*, about a colored activist whose son discovers he's having an affair with a white woman, Gordimer exposes the impossibility of true intimacy within a climate of fear. With cold frankness, she describes sex as a liberating form of self-exile.

Although she had been considered for the Nobel Prize for years, it wasn't until she won it in 1990 that Gordimer's critics made their complaints heard outside South Africa (there had always been quiet grumblings among Africans about her political affiliations): she's too much of an idealogue, not enough of an activist; her marriage to an art dealer carries with it the whiff of bourgeois complacency; her devotion to free speech (she is a founding member of the predominantly black Congress of South Africa Writers) allegedly faltered when it came to works by those with opposing political views. Others found Gordimer's prose turgid and didactic. (It is true that her staccato rhythms can be unsettling; the "em-dash" has never known a bigger fan.) The literary establishment wondered where she would turn her attentions, now that the great struggle was over. Indeed, many were quick to jump on her 1998 novel *The House Gun*—about a white family in the new South Africa forced to confront a legacy of violence when their son is charged with murder—as a lightweight effort.

But such accusations seem petty in the context of Gordimer's sixty-year career—as if anyone writing so doggedly and passionately about a single subject for so long might be doing so based on false convictions. There is an African adage which says that "people are people through other people," and Gordimer's work has always been driven by the desire to find her own humanity through the people around her—the fifteen million formerly on the other side of the color bar. A few years after Gordimer accepted the Nobel Prize, a reporter asked her how she felt about some critics' suggestions that there might not be literary life in South Africa after apartheid. "Their interest was in something called apartheid . . . we can't offer them that anymore," she bristled. "But the whole rest of life is what we are living."

See Also: Other white African writers who have covered similar territory are Doris Lessing, Andre Brink, and J. M. Coetzee. Several exiled colonial writers—V. S. Naipaul and Ariel Dorfman most notably—have also explored themes of personal and political alienation, and of the impossibility of forgetting a violent past.

—*Cynthia Joyce*

Gordon, Mary
1949–
b. Far Rockaway, New York

FICTION: Final Payments (1978), ***The Company of Women** (1980), **Men and Angels** (1985), Temporary Shelter (stories, 1987), The Other Side (1989), **The Rest of Life: Three Novellas** (1993), Spending: A Utopian Divertimento (1998)

NONFICTION: Good Boys and Dead Girls (essays, 1991), **The Shadow Man** (memoir, 1996), Seeing Through Places (essays, 1999)

In a crucial essay in her astringent collection *Good Boys and Dead Girls*, lapsed Catholic Mary Gordon finds herself attending a Latin Mass on Long Island. She listens approvingly to the priest talk of the austerity of the Lenten fast. Then she looks around her at the working-class congregation: "I suspect that their Lenten meals will be largely made up of fish sticks and Velveeta; not *omelettes aux fines herbes* but deviled eggs."

This is Gordon in a nutshell, perhaps revealing more than she wants to: The discriminating, highly personal intelligence, with its framework of aesthetic taste planted as firmly as a medieval cathedral; a penchant for high moral seriousness and more than a touch of snobbery. Perhaps Gordon has earned it—she was a Catholic girl from lower-middle suburbia who turned her religious passion toward literature and aesthetics. A preference for *omelettes aux fines herbes* over deviled eggs is virtually her central doctrine.

If Gordon is a brilliant and severe critic, in her bestselling fiction she explores an often agonized and profoundly self-conscious female subjectivity. Her signature work, *The Company of Women*, is a highly original female *bildungsroman*, telling the story of Felicitas Taylor, an extraordinary young girl raised by a de facto community of single Catholic women clustered around an aging, charismatic priest. It's her warmest and most sympathetic novel, and far more compelling in its portrait of the alternate universe of religious American Catholics than Gordon's overpraised debut, *Final Payments*.

The rest of Gordon's fiction is patchy and problematic. Her sense of the larger social and economic world is relentlessly vague, and her heterosexual male characters are no better than wild guesses. But all her books (except the embarrassing "erotic" novel *Spending*) have marvelous moments. Few novels have treated the passions and torments of motherhood as seriously as *Men and Angels*, although its lurid Stephen King plot seems ill-suited to Gordon's talents. *The Other Side* is a noble effort at an Irish-American family epic, but too often devolves into dull plotlessness. The three novellas about the dangers of love in *The Rest of Life*, however, build to a contemplative tour de force of Jamesian power and beauty—perhaps Gordon's best writing.

Gordon is also the author of a memoir, *The Shadow Man*, a wrenching exploration into the murky life history of her beloved father, who was born a Lithuanian Jew and morphed into a right-wing and even anti-Semitic Catholic, a character so fictitious and self-invented he makes Jay Gatsby look like an amateur. If Gordon's piercing prose and hypersensitive narrative consciousness sometimes slide her into a morass of hysterical self-regard, that's the risk her writing always runs; *The Shadow Man* is nonetheless a remarkable father-daughter legend told with inimitable passion.

See Also: Gordon is arguably the most accomplished and serious of a group of female novelists that includes Alice Adams, Alison Lurie, and Anne Tyler. As an Irish-American writer, she is connected to William Kennedy and Alice McDermott, as well as to her spiritual foremother, the underappreciated Mary McCarthy.

—Andrew O'Hehir

Gowdy, Barbara

1950–
b. Windsor, Ontario

FICTION: Through the Green Valley (1988), **Falling Angels** (1989), **We So Seldom Look on Love** (1992), *__Mister Sandman__ (1995), The White Bone (1998)

Barbara Gowdy is a quiet subversive. While some writers crank out books that seem calculated to cause a scandal, to be labelled "transgressive," Gowdy shatters taboos so blithely that she doesn't even seem to know they exist. Necrophiles, transsexuals, exhibitionists—her characters break the rules; neither their bodies nor their desires conform to expectations. In "Sylvie," a story from the collection *We So Seldom Look on Love*, the title character has an incomplete Siamese twin—just a pair of legs—growing out of her abdomen. She runs off with a traveling sideshow and blithely refers to herself and her new friends as "freaks," but in Gowdy's world, there's nothing wrong with being a freak.

Gowdy's best novel is *Mister Sandman*, an astonishingly funny tale of a family with a lot of secrets. The remarkable thing about the Canarys is that even though they sound totally dysfunctional—both parents are gay; the children could be labelled a compulsive eater, a slut, and an idiot savant—they are supremely functional. They all love each other and bring each other happiness. Imagine that. *The White Bone*, Gowdy's most recent novel, continues her project of empathizing with characters outside the bounds of most fiction; only in this case, her characters are a herd of African elephants. I wish she had stuck to humans.

See Also: Susan Swan is another delightfully twisted Canadian writer. Try her novel, The Wives of Bath.

—Laurie Muchnick

Grisham, John
1955–
b. Jonesboro, Arkansas

FICTION: A Time to Kill (1989), The Firm (1991), The Pelican Brief (1992), **The Client** (1993), The Chamber (1994), The Rainmaker (1995), **The Runaway Jury** (1996), The Partner (1997), *****The Street Lawyer** (1998), The Testament (1999), The Brethren (2000)

John Grisham writes beach novels, and not just because it's easier to squint past his clunky prose and cartoon characters if you're wearing sunglasses when you read them, or because his fast plots and fascinating premises go down umbrella-drink smooth. Grisham writes beach novels because that's where most of his protagonists end up: on the sand and out of work. Supposedly, his thrillers are about lawyers and the law, but ultimately, most of his books are about quitting.

He didn't start out that way. Grisham was still practicing law when he wrote his first novel, *A Time to Kill*. Its hero, Jake Brigance, is a small-time, small-town Mississippi lawyer defending a black man who murders the redneck rapists of his nine-year-old daughter. Since Grisham's home state is arguably the most racially volatile in the union, he's at his most gripping when painting the big picture in black and white. But it's this black-and-white hue that flattens out the characters, who are either good guys or bad guys morally, and either movie stars or character actors physically. (It's a no-brainer that Hollywood came calling.)

Grisham's second novel, *The Firm*, is the mold for most of the books that follow: the golden-boy hero (Mitch McDeere is pretty boring but has a *very* busy schedule); the paranoid plot; the Southern setting; and the happy, tropical ending. His next one, *The Pelican Brief*, finds golden-girl law student Darby Shaw playing Bionic Woman to Mitch McDeere's Six Million Dollar Man: It has a paranoid plot, a Southern setting, and a happy, tropical ending.

175

Because of Grisham's contempt for American jurisprudence, these two books are really just the two longest lawyer jokesin history. His idealistic legal protagonists get jaded over the course of the book, become too good for the law, and begin to feel above it. Which is at first glance rather charming, but on further reflection, reprehensible. Shaw, en route to the beach at the end of her admittedly horrific ordeal, says, "I'm going to a place where subpoenas are frowned upon." (And free speech. And democratic elections. And Miranda Rights, etc.)

The next two novels are less glamorous, but more satisfying in terms of characterization and subject matter. Unlike the "perfect little cheerleader" Darby Shaw, the female lead of *The Client* is a middle-aged recovering alcoholic named Reggie Love. Her rapport with her precocious trailer-park-child client is probably the most endearing relationship of the author's oeuvre. *The Chamber* throws the same Grisham cookie-cutter lawyer hero into uncharacteristically complex and grisly circumstances: namely, defending his racist grandfather from the death penalty.

In *The Rainmaker*, Grisham's back to his old treasonous tricks: the same-old-same-old young Memphis attorney fights the good fight (and wins) and *still* lets his law license expire at the end, vowing to never register to vote again just so His Purity never has to stink himself up with jury duty. That Grisham lives in *Mississippi*, where people have died for the right to vote, makes this train of thought especially sickening.

Late-breaking Grisham holds more promise. *The Runaway Jury* and *The Street Lawyer* have two of his most intellectually intriguing premises since *A Time to Kill*. The former contemplates what would happen if a jurist set out to sabotage a landmark tobacco case. The latter depicts a D.C. corporate drone who stumbles into working for the homeless and discovers all kinds of things Grisham's previous beach bums never experienced, like winter and holding onto a job.

See Also: Jonathan Harr's A Civil Action *(1995), a nonfiction bestseller about an idealistic, talented lawyer who gets caught up in a big case, quits the law, and hits the beach.*
                                                                                    —*Sarah Vowell*

Gurganus, Allan
1947–
b. Rocky Mount, North Carolina

FICTION: *Oldest Living Confederate Widow Tells All (1989), Blessed Assurance: A Moral Tale (1990), **White People** (1991), Plays Well with Others (1997)

Allan Gurganus has an altogether unparalleled knack for not only imagining other people—the most basic skill for any fiction writer—but for wholly *inhabiting* them, inside and out, with all their ignoble tics and scabs. It's not realism that makes his characters so tactile (there are, after all, uncircumcised angels flitting about Gurganus's fanciful world) but instead a virtuosic flair for dynamic, old-timey storytelling—this, and his dazzling and dexterous command of voice. He seems to have nothing less than a choir at his fingertips. Even at his most fallible, the voices in his repetoire, and the stories they relate, are fiercely riveting.

Gurganus's celebrated first book, *Oldest Living Confederate Widow Tells All*, is the sprawling and exuberant life story of ninety-nine-year-old Lucy Marsden, the garrulous widow of the title. It's a grand, velvety soup of a novel—comedy, tragedy, and banality strewn willy-nilly throughout, all of it rendered in the stubborn, ungrammatical (and beautifully sustained) old-lady-speak of its half-blind protagonist. His follow-up, the short story collection *White People*, was just as smashing a critical success, due in no small part to the dense sublimity of the novella *Blessed Assurance*, which recounts a nineteen-year-old's struggles to collect weekly funeral insurance payments from an elderly black woman in the part of a Southern town known as "Baby Africa."

Shortly after the publication of *Oldest Living Confederate Widow Tells All*, Gurganus told an interviewer that his intent had been to write "a funny book about the worst possible situation." By the mid-1990s, the worst possible situation seemed to have settled upon Gurganus himself: He'd lost more than thirty of his Manhattanite pals to AIDS, finding himself a widow of sorts. The result was the novel *Plays Well with Others*, a jumbled, sometimes weepy, sometimes ridiculous valentine to the heady, prelapsarian days of disco and bathhouse sex that took Gurganus only five mournful months to write. His publisher billed it as the pandemic's "long-awaited great novel," but it didn't live up to its hype. Written with Humbertian gusto ("Now I know she loved me, Trudy. Truly."), *Plays Well with Others* chronicles the lives of three artists in New York City, one of whom, a gorgeous if wantonly oversexed male composer, succumbs to the virus in the early 1980s. While sincerely poignant, it failed to reach the heights set by such AIDS-inspired fiction as Paul Cameron's *The Weekend* or Edmund White's *The Farewell Symphony*. Despite its flaws, however, *Plays Well with Others* should be considered little more than a quiet, shaky misstep in what appears to be one of the most promising careers in American literature.

See Also: You can't help but hear the melodious, whispery voice of Tennessee Williams— with its slightly shabby elegance and damp, otherworldly yearning—echoing through the best of Gurganus's prose. Fans of Oldest Living Confederate Widow Tells All *would likely enjoy Lee Smith's* Fair and Tender Ladies *or any of Eudora Welty's winsome Southern fictions.*

—Jonathan Miles

Hannah, Barry

1942–
b. Meridian, Mississippi

FICTION: **Geronimo Rex** (1972), Nightwatchmen (1973), *****Airships** (stories, 1978), **Ray** (1980), Black Butterfly (stories, 1982), Power and Light (1983), The Tennis Handsome (1983), Captain Maximus (stories, 1985), Hey Jack! (1987), Boomerang (1989), Never Die (1991), **Bats Out of Hell** (stories, 1993), **High Lonesome** (1996), Men Without Ties (stories, 1997)

Barry Hannah has been called "the Jimi Hendrix of American short fiction," "the best young fiction writer to appear in the South since Flannery O'Connor," and "the maddest writer in the U.S.A." (by Truman Capote, no less). But no comparison can really do justice to this wildly idiosyncratic author. Hannah has written eight novels, five collections of short stories, and one novella in prose that virtually defies categorization, using his nearly magical inventiveness with words to create a madcap melange of sex, violence, and loopy individualism in which almost anything can (and usually does) happen.

Hannah's predilection for extremes has led him to flamboyantly break with the conventional rules of character and plot. In *Ray*, the protagonist serves in both the Civil War and in Vietnam, in addition to practicing medicine in Alabama. In *The Tennis Handsome*, a woman is raped by a walrus. Refusing to repeat himself, Hannah tries to reinvent whichever genre he's working in every time he sits down. Lately, however, Hannah has become more interested in grounding his work in the real world of historical facts. Such books as *Bats Out of Hell* and *Men Without Ties*—both written after he stopped drinking—display a growing interest in autobiography and spirituality. Hannah currently lives in Oxford, Mississippi, and teaches at the University of Mississippi.

See Also: The short stories of Flannery O'Connor and the novels of Walker Percy, although each bears only a passing resemblance to the supremely original Hannah.

—*Hal Hinson*

Harrison, Jim

1937–
b. Grayling, Michigan

FICTION: Wolf: A False Memoir (1971), A Good Day to Die (1973), **Farmer** (1976), *****Legends of the Fall** (novellas, 1979), Warlock (1981), Sundog: The Story of an American Foreman (1984), **Dalva** (1988), The Woman Lit by Fireflies (novellas, 1990), Julip (novellas, 1994), The Road Home (1998)

NONFICTION: Just Before Dark: Collected Nonfiction (1991)

POETRY: Selected and New Poems, 1961–1981 (1982), The Shape of the Journey: New and Collected Poems (1998)

Jim Harrison knows appetites; he is their poet laureate. In his eleven books of poetry, three novella collections, seven novels, and innumerable essays, he has probed and charted the breadth of human appetites—for food, for drink, for art, for sex, for violence, and most significantly, for the great twin engines of love and death. His characters hunger for a wild and sinewy abundance: in his words, for "mental heat, experience, (and) jubilance," for a life squeezed to the pips. In this, Harrison is somewhat a throwback—not to the Pleistocene era, as some critics have suggested, charging him with all manner of machismo—but to early nineteenth-century Romanticism. In his most recent novel, *The Road Home*, a character is described as having been born in the wrong century; Harrison might have been writing about himself.

Nowhere is this more evident than in *Legends of the Fall*, a novella that many consider his finest fictional accomplishment to date. (It's also his best-known, primarily due to Edward Zwick's 1994 film adaptation, which—thanks to Brad Pitt's lusty performance as Tristan Ludlow—has become a sorority house classic.) Both epic and saga, *Legends of the Fall* chronicles the travails and torments of a Montana clan in language and imagery so tightly compressed that it verges on a sort of High Plains fable. Tristan Ludlow—hunter, soldier, sailor, wrangler, Byronic rakehell—is the epitome of Harrison's masculine ideal: elemental, antisocial, inordinately passionate, supremely self-sufficient. As the critic Robert Burkholder wrote, "Tristan is what so many of the other characters yearn to be but cannot—at least not in an age that defines romance as the rape of the land in the name of progress." Indeed, *Legends of the Fall* is partly an elegy for an endangered (if not wholly extinct) species of man.

Like most of Harrison's works, *Legends of the Fall* is also an elegy for an equally endangered landscape. His descriptions of the natural world are some of the most lyrical in contemporary literature, but they are also tinged with fear and anger at the frailty of it. In recent years, his work has become increasingly concerned with the loss of wildlife and wildness—what he terms "the narrowing point of the present"—and with the more lamentable aspects of Native American history, displayed in the novels *Dalva* and *The Road Home*. Nevertheless, he has not allowed polemics to intrude upon his work. Didacticism inspires in him a gruesome shiver. "I can't stand art that is preachy," he once said. "Life is more interesting than ideas."

"I like grit, I like love and death, I'm tired of irony," he told an interviewer in 1990. "As we know from the Russians, a lot of good fiction is sentimental . . . The novelist who refuses sentiment refuses the full spectrum of human behavior, and then he just dries up. Irony is always scratching your tired ass, whatever way you look at it. I would rather give full vent to all human loves and disappointments, and take a chance on being corny, than die a smartass."

See Also: No writer is more closely allied—personally and aesthetically—to Harrison than longtime pal Thomas McGuane. They sometimes get lumped with tough-but-tender guy authors like Andre Dubus, James Dickey, Richard Ford, and Raymond Carver. Harrison's crotchety, iconoclastic environmentalism—and his occasional swipes at melodrama—is kindred to that of the late Edward Abbey. Rick Bass is a Harrison devotee, and his writing displays a firm discipleship.

—*Jonathan Miles*

Hawkes, John
1925–1998
b. Stamford, Connecticut

FICTION: **The Cannibal** (1949), **The Beetle Leg** (1951), The Goose on the Grave: Two Short Novels (1954), *****The Lime Twig** (1961), Second Skin (1964), Lunar Landscapes: Stories and Short Novels, 1949–1963 (1969), The Blood Oranges (1971), Death, Sleep, and the Traveler (1974), **Travesty** (1976), **The Owl** (1977), The Passion Artist (1979), Virginie: Her Two Lives (1982), Adventures in the Alaskan Skin Trade (1985), Innocence in Extremis (1985), Whistlejacket (1988), Sweet William: A Memoir of an Old Horse (1993), The Frog (1996), An Irish Eye (1997)

N O N F I C T I O N : Humors of Blood and Skin: A John Hawkes Reader (autobiographical notes, 1984)

He loved the colors of corrosion; he loved innocence and loved to pit it against brutality. He loved horses (especially when they crush their riders or would-be abductors), and he loved the stench of manure. An aesthetic sensualist of the rotting and the perverse, John Hawkes announced that plot and character are the enemies of fiction. His novels tried to make fiction out of pure voice and imagination.

He'd begin with the grotesque, the mutilated, the insane, and he'd give it a voice. In his early novels a broken landscape mirrors the characters' dementia. Detail after detail shines in complex paratactic sentences. Syntax itself threatens to collapse as a mountain of precisely observed decay is carefully itemized and smashed into indecipherability, with humans characterized by goiters, hooks, bizarre prosthetic devices.

Hawkes's masterpieces, three nightmarish novels, rise from this impasto of landscape, character, and plot: *The Cannibal, The Beetle Leg,* and *The Lime Twig.* I reread them with grisly pleasure and astonishment. The work that follows, though, becomes ridiculously mannered. Beginning with *Second Skin,* Hawkes developed his "lyric" voice. In the four novels that followed an artificial inseminator of cows on a floating tropic island recalls the history of suicide and violence that led him to flee to his pastoral bliss; obese and deformed narrators sing of sensual pleasures; the erotic becomes hallucinatory and/or ludicrous; tiny fetuses appear in clusters of grapes; a father watches his daughter pissed on by a horse; horses talk; enema tubes, chastity belts, and phallic carrots proliferate ominously.

"I have written increasingly about the imagination itself," Hawkes said of his later work. What he means by "the imagination" seems to be some substrate where incest fantasies and pornographic projections are encouraged to articulate themselves in a purple rhetoric that is profusely lyrical and vaguely comic, but mostly fustian horseshit.

Travesty, "a comic novel about the fatal importance of the imagination," is the last sighting in prose of a lucid and brilliant Hawkes. He began to vacation in France, where his later work continues to be admired, and he started reading the "pornosophers," a group of writers (Bataille, Klossowski, Leiris) who, under the influence of de Sade and perhaps Diderot, created a combination of philosophy and pornography that is laconic and frightening. It led Hawkes to abandon the distance and rational handbrakes that had kept his earlier work vibrating resonantly between beauty and meaning.

Eventually Hawkes's perversions became affectations, and the affectations became his style. Though, as he said, he remained a "pure" artist, his purity became more and more lordly. (His late works tend to take place in chateaux, among seignoral roues and their accomplices, students, and victims.) He ended up writing pornosophic contrivances, while still displaying a truly majestic ear for the poetry of prose.

See Also: Hawkes's acknowledged influences include Nathanael West (particularly, I think, the collage of debris that decorates Miss Lonelyhearts' dream landscape), Djuna Barnes (the mesmerized, glacial, sleepwalking sentences), and Flannery O'Connor (the suspicion that random evil is part of a moral design). American transgressive postmodernists influenced by pornosophy include Kathy Acker and Dennis Cooper.
—*Michael Silverblatt*

Heller, Joseph
1923–1999
b. Brooklyn, New York

FICTION: **Catch-22* (1961), **Something Happened** (1974), Good as Gold (1979), God Knows (1984), Picture This (1988), Closing Time (1994)

NONFICTION: No Laughing Matter (with Speed Vogal, 1986), Now and Then (1998)

Psychologists call it the Double Bind. Joseph Heller, perhaps drawing on his experience as an ad copywriter, gave it a far, well, *catchier* name. "There was only one catch and that was Catch-22," Heller wrote in his best-known work and also his best. The soldiers in Heller's novel, WWII Air Force pilots stationed on an island off the coast of Italy, were trapped within a logical paradox even Kafka would have found disconcerting: In order to get out of combat duty, they had to prove they were crazy—but anyone who actually wanted out of the war was considered automatically sane.

Catch-22, published in 1961, is less a novel than a collection of wonderfully pointed comic set pieces about a strange band of characters caught in the twisted logic of the war machine. Piling absurdity upon absurdity, Heller builds to an apocalyptic conclusion, the humor of the earlier chapters giving way at last to an existential horror show. *Catch-22* is today considered such a classic—it has even been assigned as a required text at the

U.S. Air Force Academy in Colorado Springs—that it's often forgotten that initially some critics found it disconcertingly flip; others simply thought it was badly written.

Heller waited more than a decade before unleashing his next novel—*Something Happened*, a nearly six-hundred-page-long chronicle of gray flannel ennui in which practically nothing ever does happen. Deliberately repetitious, it details the desiccated existence of Bob Slocum, a sad, amoral lump of a man living the epitome of quiet desperation—and trying to figure out just when his life started going wrong. Lacking the antic energy (and, for the most part, the humor) of his earlier work, *Something Happened* is nonetheless a powerful and disquieting read.

Nothing Heller wrote afterwards was affecting was his first two books. The post-Watergate political satire *Good as Gold*, allowed him to draw on his own Coney Island boyhood and to embark upon extended riffs on the evils of "fake Jew" Henry Kissinger. In *God Knows*, a 350-page theological stand-up routine, King David himself reflects on the absurdities of the world from a vantage point outside the normal confines of time and space. It's an oddly cheery book, particularly considering that the writing of it was interrupted by Heller's debilitating bout with Guillain-Barré syndrome, a potentially deadly nervous system disorder; Heller wrote about the experience in another oddly cheery book, 1986's *No Laughing Matter*, written with his friend Speed Vogal.

The deeply eccentric and generally unsatisfying *Picture This* (1988) is a sprawling reflection on (among other things), the paintings of Rembrandt, the death of Socrates and the evils of global imperialism. More recently, Heller returned to his roots with the 1994 novel *Closing Time*, a sort of minor-key sequel to *Catch-22*. If Heller never wrote another *Catch-22*, well, neither has anyone else, as the supremely self-confident author himself was fond of pointing out. Nothing Heller wrote is utterly without charm, and even his most scattered works have their moments of savage genius. There's just one catch: You'll find most of these moments in the very first book he wrote.

See Also: Catch-22 *is close in spirit to Kurt Vonnegut's* Slaughterhouse Five. *The irreverent humor of much of Heller's work resembles Philip Roth's, though the dark paranoia of* Catch-22 *is more reminiscent of Thomas Pynchon (Heller is much easier to read).* Something Happened *recalls Saul Bellow's* Herzog, *another brooding monologue depicting a life gone quietly astray.*

—*David Futrelle*

BOOKS THAT MADE ME LAUGH *By Calvin Trillin*

Catch-22 by Joseph Heller
  I read this when it was first published, and, like just about everybody else, I was struck by the freshness of Heller's humor. The title and the characters and the comic viewpoint are now all part of the culture.

Reuben, Reuben by Peter De Vries
  This isn't as compact as some of De Vries's earlier books, but I find it hilarious—particularly the first section. All of De Vries's books are full of throwaway lines that other writers would try to build a novel around.

St. Urbain's Horseman by Mordecai Richler
  This is my favorite Richler book, although his latest, *Barney's Version*, comes close. The chapter about the hero going to dinner at the home of his English lawyer is something I still can't read without laughing out loud.

The Dog of the South by Charles Portis
  Fans of Charles Portis are divided between this book and *Norwood*. A few of them even risk the disdain of the cognoscenti by publicly favoring *True Grit*, the one Portis book that had a large popular following.

Lucky Jim by Kingsley Amis
  I think of this as the prototype of any number of comic novels about academics (mostly hapless) at English universities (mostly red brick). I happened to have to enjoyed many of the ones that came later, written by people like David Lodge and Tom Sharpe.

184

Helprin, Mark
1947–
b. New York, New York

FICTION: A Dove of the East and Other Stories (1975), Refiner's Fire: The Life and Adventures of Marshall Pearl, a Foundling (1977), **Ellis Island and Other Stories** (1981), Winter's Tale (1983), **A Soldier of the Great War** (1991), *Memoir from Antproof Case (1995)

The **Salon.com** Reader's Guide to Contemporary Authors

Many people can't stand Mark Helprin. Some abhor his hard-line *Wall Street Journal* editorials and his adoration of the free market. Others find him a ludicrous over-writer, in love with lush archaisms that fall short of real substance—three of his novels bulge to over five hundred pages, but the reader never feels that the narrative circle has closed. Further, he lies to interviewers—saying that his mother was "sold into slavery" (she wasn't) and that as a child he had to tell stories, Scheherazade-like, to earn his supper from his father (he didn't).

True, at times Helprin's fiction tips into whimsy overload, making you wish for simple normality, and it's irritating to stumble, seemingly at random, upon yet another lecture about the grievous error Marxists make in underrating the human spirit. Though reviewers liken him to heavyweights like Rushdie and García Márquez, as yet he can't carry that weight. He's too idiosyncratic to connect much to the outside world, much less to serve as the voice of anyone beside himself.

On the other hand, those harangues last only a paragraph, and though Helprin is an episodic plotter (he would have been entirely at home devising predicaments for Pearl White), at its best his prose is spellbinding and ecstatic. Each of his books ponders the same core themes: the necessity of dreaming in a prosaic world; the redemptive power of love; the beauty and horror of war; the triumph of the human spirit in the face of the sheerest adversity. But despite many spurts of pretty writing, neither *A Dove of the East*, his first short story collection, nor the picaresque *Refiner's Fire* quite gets its act together. In later, and more successful, works like *Ellis Island*, *A Soldier of the Great War*, and *Memoir from Antproof Case*, he learned to make prose serve his lunatic narratives rather than undercut them.

Ellis Island's title novella is a wonder-filled vision of Jewish New York as an immigrant's magic castle (its hero is blown to Brooklyn and dances back to Manhattan with thousands of Hasidim), but it stops dead with a heartrending conclusion that embraces both the pain and the possibility of America. *Winter's Tale* is entertaining in spots even if its panoramic canvas doesn't cohere in any meaningful way, while *Soldier*, which follows the adventures of a young Italian gentleman through World War I, almost does, and is well worth reading for its gorgeous descriptions. The book to read is *Memoir from Antproof Case*. From the opening parody of *Moby-Dick* through Helprin's endlessly inventive plotting (the nameless hero gets shot out of airplanes twice, fights to the death with Walloons, and wages a lifelong battle against coffee, the scourge of humanity), this is a masterpiece of poker-faced comedy. In the funniest passage, the narrator is forced to eat kosher turkey anus at a company dinner. Later, he develops a taste for it.

Certainly, Helprin's not for everyone. Many find him arch, cloying, or plain pretentious. But if his goofiness and sumptuous imagery win you over, it's hard not to let him carry you off: The ride is unmatched, and the scenery intoxicating.

See Also: Salman Rushdie, particularly Midnight's Children *and* Haroun and the Sea of Stories, *as well as García Márquez and Louis de Bernieres's loopy magic-realist pastiches. Or explore Helprin's literary ancestry and read Isaac Bashevis Singer.*

—Jesse Berrett

Hiaasen, Carl
1953–
b. Fort Lauderdale, Florida

FICTION: Powder Burn (with William D. Montalbano, 1981), Trap Line (with William D. Montalbano, 1982), A Death in China (with William D. Montalbano, 1984), Tourist Season (1986), Double Whammy (1987), Skin Tight (1989), Native Tongue (1991), *****Strip Tease** (1993), **Stormy Weather** (1995), **Lucky You** (1997), Sick Puppy (2000)

NONFICTION: Team Rodent: How Disney Devours the World (1998), Kick Ass: Selected Columns of Carl Hiaasen (1999)

Carl Hiaasen began his career as a reporter with the *Miami Herald* covering a wide range of subjects in and around southern Florida. In 1981, he turned from fact to fiction with the publication of *Powder Burn*, a thriller written with fellow journalist William D. Montalbano. Hiaasen went on to write two more novels with Montalbano before publishing his first solo work, *Tourist Season*, in which a terrorist group targets tourists in order to ruin Miami as a vacation hot spot. Since then, Hiaasen has worked his way onto the bestseller lists by setting highly entertaining, down-home social satire within the standard thriller framework. *Double Whammy* centers on Florida's bass-fishing industry, *Skin Tight* on its plastic surgeons, and *Native Tongue* on its theme park developers. The latter so stoked the author's biting wrath, that one reviewer was prompted to describe Hiaasen as a South Florida mixture of "Jonathan Swift, Randy Newman and Elmore Leonard." Since 1993, Hiaasen has produced four more novels, with his home-brew blend of politics and violence becoming increasingly surrealistic in each one. As Hiaasen's writing has grown sharper and more expressive, however, the plots of his books have also become increasingly predictable and formulaic.

Hijuelos, Oscar
1951–
b. New York, New York

FICTION: Our House in the Last World (1983), *****The Mambo Kings Sing Songs of Love** (1989), The Fourteen Sisters of Emilio Montez O'Brien (1993), **Mr. Ives' Christmas** (1995), Empress of the Splendid Season (1999)

Author of four novels, almost all equally meaty and epic in scope, Oscar Hijuelos is a writer drawn not only to intricacies of voice and character but to sweeping appraisals of community (the Cuban immigrant's), place (Manhattan's Upper West Side), and time (the 1950s and 1960s). His works seem singed by nostalgia for Cuba, his parent's native land, and he laces them with reflections on the strong (sometimes too strong) ties of family and a near-encyclopedic knowledge of photography, jazz, comics, and Hollywood B-films. Although Hijuelos is undoubtedly a superlative prose stylist, there's a thrust to his voice that, at its best, is raw and lustful, and at its worst, becomes a gush of clichés desperately in need of a firm red pencil.

His 1990 Pulitzer Prize-winning *The Mambo Kings Sing Songs of Love* is Hijuelos's best-known book, but his first was *Our House in the Last World*, a thinly veiled and often harsh portrait of his childhood. Its elegant warmth and accessible style garnered impressive reviews, but it was *Mambo Kings* that really hit the mark. Told from the perspective of a has-been mambo star wallowing in booze-soaked memories during his final days, *Mambo Kings* is a book so libidinous and colorful that it might make you blush. Teeming with the dreams and fantasies of its narrator's delirium, it recounts the story of two brothers, Nestor and Cesar Castillo, who insinuate themselves into New York's Latin music scene and, with their one hit, "Beautiful Maria of My Soul," make it as far as a guest appearance on the television show *I Love Lucy*.

Hijuelos followed this success with *The Fourteen Sisters of Emilio Montez O'Brien*, a century-spanning book about a hyperbolic Irish-Cuban family in rural Pennsylvania. Many critics compared it to a family album. Others, observing an almost uncomfortable similarity, called it a homage to the maestro of magic realism, Gabriel García Márquez. But for all its generous, feminine tone, too often the book slips into sentimentality—and never lives up to its title. Emilio doesn't appear until halfway through the novel, which, despite Hijuelos's masterful exposition, leaves you waiting too long for the story to commence.

Hijuelos's characters are often dreamers: men (and women) whose romances are hard-fought but rarely realized. Accordingly, grief and death play decisive roles in his fiction, no more evidently than in *Mr. Ives' Christmas*. The tale of a Manhattan advertising executive whose life is defined by his only son's untimely death, *Mr. Ives' Christmas* is drenched in a melancholy both bitter and transcendent. It's a small book, attempting neither to preach nor preen, but also admirably stark and unapologetic in its pursuit of faith.

In the end, it's Hijuelos's inconsistency that's most frustrating. Despite his intriguing details and exhilarating prose, reading his books sometimes feels like a long search for the spine—i.e., plot—holding all that dazzling backstory together.

See Also: Similar preeminent Latin voices include Julia Alvarez, Francisco Goldman, and the Puerto Rican author Rosario Ferré. Closer to Hijuelos's territory, however, are the raucous streets of old New York described in the nonfiction works of chronicler Luc Sante.

—*Jenifer Berman*

Hoban, Russell
1925–
b. Lansdale, Pennsylvania

188

FICTION: The Lion of Boaz-Jachin and Jachin-Boaz (1973), Kleinzeit (1974), **Turtle Diary** (1975), *Riddley Walker (1980), Pilgermann (1983), **The Medusa Frequency** (1987), Fremder (1996), Mr. Rinyo-Clacton's Offer (1998), Angelica's Grotto (1999)

NONFICTION: The Moment Under the Moment (1992), The Russell Hoban Omnibus (1999)

POETRY: The Last of the Wallendas and Other Poems (1997)

Loss lies at the root of Russell Hoban's adult fiction, now mystifyingly unread beyond a slowly expanding circle of devotees. He's better known for his children's books, particularly a series about Frances, an anthropomorphic badger, which was illustrated by his late wife Lillian. Frances is quite cuddly, but one critic described Hoban's bestselling kid's novel *The Mouse and His Child* as "Beckett for children."

Hoban's other hit was *Riddley Walker*, a novel set in England many years after a nuclear holocaust and written in a dialect that's as rough-hewn and fumbling as the society it depicts. In these second dark ages, the story of our fall from grace is preserved in travelling puppet shows, and the measure of how much humanity has lost is betrayed in small, piercing touches; for example, dogs no longer want our company.

But Hoban also writes with a poet's ear about everyday life, teasing out its sweet sadness. "It was novembering hard outside; the dark air sang with the dwindle of the year, the sharpening of it to goneness that was drawing nearer," he writes in *The Medusa Frequency*, describing a London evening as experienced by a man pining, like most of his heroes, for an absent woman. This fellow, a blocked writer, undergoes a treatment that has him chatting philosophically with the severed head of Orpheus and communicating with the legendary sea monster the Kraken via his Apple II computer—for the other side of Hoban's wild and moony melancholy is an absurdist penchant for finding the archetypal in the mundane. One of Hoban's finest books, *Turtle Diary*, has no fantastic elements at all, just two ordinary, middle-aged people springing a pair of sea turtles from an aquarium. Yes, it sounds sappy and "inspirational" but it's actually astringent, masterfully observed and ruefully worldly-wise.

An American expatriate living in London, Hoban has lately written books so metaphysical, mythological, and quirkily coy that he can't get them published in his homeland.

See Also: *The work of both Kurt Vonnegut and Barbara Pym contains some ingredients of the Hoban cocktail, as do the writings of the turn-of-the-century American allegorist James Branch Cabell.*

—*Laura Miller*

Hollinghurst, Alan
1954–
b. Stroud, England

FICTION: *The Swimming Pool Library** (1988), **The Folding Star** (1994), **The Spell** (1998)

POETRY: Confidential Chats with Boys (1982)

Alan Hollinghurst is Britain's bard of the phallus, its poet of the prick. "Short, stocky, ruthlessly circumcised, and incredibly resilient and characterful," crows a gay man about a new trick's willy in Hollinghurst's first novel, *The Swimming Pool Library*. Or take this, from *The Spell*, his third: "He was very proud of his broad-backed dick, which reared off at an angle as if long since tugged askew by the obsessive attentions of his right hand."

The priapic aspect of what Hollywood writer-director Preston Sturges called "Topic A" dominates Hollinghurst's work: Some of his characters live for sex, a few die for it, and nearly all of them get prodigious amounts of it with minimal effort.

The Swimming Pool Library remains Hollinghurst's most rewarding book. It not only chronicles the mostly amorous adventures of Will Beckwith, a preening twenty-five-year-old with a yen for "sporty-looking boys"; the novel also conjures up a whole century of gay London life, with cameo appearances by the great tenor Peter Pears (at a performance of *Billy Budd*, an opera by his lover, Benjamin Britten, in which Pears originally sang the title role) and, thanks to an ancient film clip, the fey novelist Ronald Firbank. The novel's rich world of personally and artistically interlocking gay relationships undermines the old chestnut that because homosexuals don't, as a rule, procreate they must lead superficial lives.

Set mostly in an old Flemish city, *The Folding Star* is a story of obsessive love—that of an older tutor for his teenaged pupil—which effortlessly deals out its plot and contains some of the author's most brilliant writing. The novel was short-listed for the Booker, Britain's most prestigious literary prize, but lost apparently because some judges were rattled by its raw sexual passages (the book did win the James Tait Black Memorial Prize). In *The Spell* Hollinghurst has made England the site of a sexual rondelay involving four gay characters: a father and his son, the father's new lover, and the new lover's ex (a civil servant whose affair with that son thrusts him into London's Ecstasy-taking, house-music-grooving gay milieu).

Hollinghurst's work has nearly every quality a novelist can aspire to: vivid characterization, seamless construction, wit and style. My only misgiving is the tendency of his gay guys to be of a type—irresistible beauties for whom hunks fall out of trees. At times these conquerors seem like the sexual counterparts of those oil or press tycoons who populate the wish-fulfillment novels of writers like Harold Robbins. It will be interesting to see how Hollinghurst's own aging (he is in his mid-forties) affects his *dramatis personae*.

See Also: Before Hollinghurst, Angus Wilson (1913–1991) was England's finest openly gay novelist. His flair for multilayered social comedy is especially evident in Hemlock and After *(1952) and* Anglo-Saxon Attitudes *(1956).*

—Dennis Drabelle

Homes, A. M.
1952–
b. Washington, D.C.

FICTION: Jack (1989), **The Safety of Objects** (1990), *In a Country of Mothers (1993), The End of Alice (1996), Music for Torching (1999)

Thumbing through the work of novelist and short story writer Amy M. Homes, a reader might come across a young man making love to his sister's Barbie doll. Or a twelve-year-old boy carefully peeling off his scabs and meticulously preserving them, like precious art objects, in a box. Or a salesman who makes a daily ritual of urinating in his boss's potted plant. In an age so tolerant (or indifferent) that it has become nearly shock-proof, Homes constantly puts that tolerance to the test.

Homes has looked into the darkest corners of the American soul and discovered dysfunction, perversion, and the slaughter of innocence. In her first novel, *Jack*, she examines the aftershocks suffered by a teenage boy when his father comes out of the closet. In 1990, Homes followed up her debut with *The Safety of Objects*, a collection of disturbing, artful stories that further enhanced her standing as the David Lynch of fiction writers. In 1993, Homes again ventured into the realm of cultural taboos with her second novel, *In a Country of Mothers*, which explored a psychiatrist's maternal obsession with her patient.

But nothing in Homes's past work prepared readers for the septic intensity of her

191

next novel. Grouped with the likes of Bret Easton Ellis's *American Psycho*, *The End of Alice* was tagged a work of transgressive fiction. Told from the point of view of an incarcerated child molester corresponding with a young woman obsessed with a twelve-year-old boy, it featured a parade of depravity ranging from pedophilia and rape to murder. Throughout her career, Homes has demonstrated a perverse sensitivity in the exploration of her themes that borders on grace and often elevates her work above sensationalism and exploitation. Still, it may be that in the end, she'll rank higher up on the gross-out scale than on the one that measures literary merit.

See Also: The territory Homes explores is remote, so few have gone before her or followed in her footsteps. However, because of its shock value, reviewers have linked her work to that of Brett Easton Ellis and punk novelist Kathy Acker.

—Hal Hinson

Hornby, Nick
1957–
b. London, England

FICTION: *High Fidelity (1995), About a Boy (1998)

NONFICTION: Contemporary American Fiction (essays, 1992), Fever Pitch (1993)

In two novels, Nick Hornby has pulled off a pretty amazing trick: transforming the ugly cliche of the aging male hipster into a persona that's funny, complex, and most impressive of all, deeply human. Of course, Hornby has a vested interest in doing this since his own life mirrors the fears and preoccupations of his thirtysomething protagonists. He began his career chasing down next big things as a book and pop music critic, then found success with his first salvo on the subject of manliness, *Fever Pitch*. A memoir of his life as a fan of the soccer team London Arsenal, it doesn't always translate for American readers, but it adeptly catalogues the anxieties of anybody whose hobby turns into a sort of madness.

The book became a bestseller in England, but even Hornby himself couldn't have been prepared for what happened next. His first novel, *High Fidelity*, swiftly achieved the status of a minor classic, particularly among music fans who found their record-geek passions mirrored in the character of Rob Fleming. Using a wry, caustic style that bor-

TALES OF CONTEMPORARY BOHEMIA *by Ann Powers*

High Fidelity by Nick Hornby

The best rock and roll novel I've read is, naturally, about a fan, since fans are the true agents of rock's erotic imagination (and every rock musician is first a fan). Hornby's "hero" is a perpetual adolescent schlumping toward middle age; his rock dreams get in the way of his real life, but the music leads him toward the difficult epiphany he deserves.

Tales of Beatnik Glory by Ed Sanders

This fat, jolly volume by a spirited counterculture raconteur follows the quixotic adventures of Sanders's alter ego, Sam Thomas, on the hippie frontier. Sanders animates the many freaks Thomas encounters in red-blooded Technicolor; he loves them all without falling for their bullshit.

Sleepless Nights by Elizabeth Hardwick

Approaching reminiscence as a philosophical practice, this impressionistic *roman à clef* wanders through the bohemian haunts that shaped the sensibility of an American woman of letters—jazz clubs, expatriate cafes, the lonely nests of socialists. The portrait of Billie Holiday that comes early in the book is a cruelly insightful masterstroke.

Macho Sluts by Pat Califia

Post-Stonewall queer radicalism remains an elemental force within contemporary bohemia, and Pat Califia is one of its fierce founding mothers. This gloriously nasty collection of stories about sadomasochism as a sexual persuasion and a source of identity helped bring a venerable lifestyle into public view, with all its complexities intact.

The Story of Junk by Linda Yablonsky

Its stern, arid depiction of junkie life isn't what makes this book valuable. It's the attentiveness and respect Yablonsky grants ordinary bohemia, as it survives in restaurant kitchens and rented flats, with some of its denizens scoring success, and others succumbing to vice and accident. She evokes a place where real people live as well as die.

rows heavily from both American TV humor and minimalist fiction writers, Hornby puts Fleming through his paces. The owner of a failing record shop, Rob loses his longtime girlfriend and begins to question his once adamant belief that you can't really be a serious person with fewer than five hundred records. It's a lightweight, speedy read, but underneath the R&B references is a hilarious yet revealing study of the male psyche. Easily one of the best novels ever to tackle pop music as its theme, it's also a fine book about the nature of obsession, and how sensitivity and humanity often get strangled in its clutches.

Having found a comfortable world to write about, Hornby cut his second novel *About a Boy*, from similar cloth. Framed by the suicide of Nirvana frontman Kurt Cobain, the novel revolves around Will Freeman, an idle mid-thirties Londoner who finds himself attracted to single mothers; he even pretends he's a single father himself to meet more of them. But Will gets more than he bargained for—the book *does* read like a film treatment—when he meets Marcus, an ungainly, painfully unhip twelve-year-old. Revelations about finding true happiness beyond hipsterdom ensue, but Hornby's already mined this territory. While funny and balanced, much of *About a Boy* feels like a retread—a sophomore slump, as they say in the music biz. If Hornby wants to avoid becoming the sort of one-hit wonder filed away in Rob Fleming's racks, he'll need to expand beyond this narrow milieu. Hipsterdom's a nice place to visit, but you wouldn't want to live there.

See Also: In theme and style, Hornby's work recalls Jay McInerney, whose Bright Lights, Big City *enjoyed a similar meteoric success amongst young urbanites. And those who loved* High Fidelity *for its spot-on thinking about pop music would do well to track down Don DeLillo's excellent novel on the perils of rock stardom,* Great Jones Street.

—*Mark Athitakis*

Irving, John
1942–
b. Exeter, New Hampshire

FICTION: Setting Free the Bears (1969), **The Water-Method Man** (1972), The 158-Pound Marriage (1974), **The World According to Garp** (1978), The Hotel New Hampshire (1981), ***The Cider House Rules** (1985), A Prayer for Owen Meany (1989), A Son of the Circus (1994), Trying to Save Piggy Sneed (stories and essays, 1996), **A Widow for One Year** (1998)

John Irving is the modern-day inheritor to the great nineteenth-century storytelling tradition of Charles Dickens, Thomas Hardy, William Makepeace Thackeray, and Anthony Trollope. In a career spanning thirty years, he has delivered large, sprawling novels, both skeptical and sentimental, in which existence is a complicated balancing act, and even the most fulfilled lives are touched by searing loss. As Irving sees it, the most important element of his work is the way he follows his characters across generations, allowing a succession of old hurts, fixations, and relationships to come into play again and again. "So much of what is emotionally felt about a novel is felt as the effect of the passage of time," he told the *Los Angeles Times*. "The passage of time has always been important in my novels, as it was for the novels of the nineteenth century."

It's odd, then, how little Irving's first three novels follow that form. His debut, *Setting Free the Bears*, is a 1960s-style black comedy, mixing a pinch of Kurt Vonnegut, a dash of Terry Southern, and Irving's own keen sense of absurdity to tell the story of two drifters who decide to release all the animals from the Vienna Zoo. Likewise *The Water-Method Man*, which revolves around a graduate student with a urinary tract infection (the title refers to his unorthodox treatment) and may be Irving's funniest book. *The 158-Pound Marriage* is, by its author's standards, barely more than a short story, a spare, modern novel about marital infidelity on a New England college campus. Only with *The World According to Garp* did Irving finally break through, both creatively and commercially. At six hundred-plus pages, featuring a wide range of characters and taking on everything from the writer's life, feminism and single parenthood, to the psychology of the family, *Garp* was Irving's first book with the broad social canvas and sweeping chronology of his literary role models, and its success allowed him to quit his day job as a high school English teacher.

To this day, *The World According to Garp* remains Irving's best-known novel, but it's hardly his best. That distinction is shared by *The Water-Method Man* and *The Cider House Rules*, in which all the threads of Irving's aesthetic come together with the most authority and grace. The story of a foundling in early twentieth-century Maine raised at a combination orphanage/abortion clinic before setting out on his own, *The Cider House Rules* is the most overtly Dickensian of Irving's novels, populated by a cast of slightly exaggerated characters, and vividly evoking and commenting on the social fabric of its times. On the heels of *The Hotel New Hampshire*—Irving's weakest effort—it also marked a remarkable turnaround, from superficiality to profundity, launching the "mature" phase of his career, which includes *A Prayer for Owen Meany*, *A Son of the Circus*, and *A Widow for One Year*. These books aren't uniformly accomplished; *A Prayer for Owen Meany* can be gimmicky in places—with its (literally) miniature protagonist whose every line of dialogue is rendered in capital letters to indicate his high-pitched shout—while *A Son of the Circus* seems forced. Still, they share a fully articulated, consistent sense of purpose, a moral vision. At its heart is the notion that, as Irving himself has suggested, "I don't see comedy and tragedy as contradictions . . . I don't see that unhappy endings undermine rich and energetic lives."

This idea drives virtually all of Irving's work, but as he's grown older, he's managed to weave it more subtly into the fabric of his fiction. That's not to say the theme has grown understated; *A Widow for One Year*, for instance, kicks in with the accidental death of two teenage brothers, whose younger sister grows up to be a novelist in part to seek a filter for her loss, while the main action of *A Prayer for Owen Meany* begins when the narrator's mother dies after being struck in the head by a foul ball. Yet if there's something random about these tragedies, it's quieter than in *The World According to Garp*, where bad things happen to good people with savage regularity, or *The Hotel New Hampshire*, so casually brutal to its protagonists that it's nearly impossible to read. Instead, Irving has gained a fuller understanding of how such moments impact his characters' humanity, which in turn gives the best of his recent novels the complexity of his nineteenth-century progenitors, as well as the gravity to which he's always aspired.

See Also: Irving's most obvious analogues are the Victorian masters after whom he has consciously patterned his works. Contemporary writers who share his sense of the absurd and the way humor and sadness are often inextricably linked include Kurt Vonnegut (who was his instructor at the Iowa Writers Workshop), and T. Coraghessan Boyle. Still, when it comes to the sheer scope of Irving's storytelling, few twentieth-century authors compare.

—David L. Ulin

Ishiguro, Kazuo
1954–
b. Nagasaki, Japan

FICTION: A Pale View of Hills (1982), An Artist of the Floating World (1986), ***The Remains of the Day** (1989), **The Unconsoled** (1995)

*T*he Remains of the Day, the story of an English butler in painstaking denial of both his employer's Nazi collusion during World War II and his own lost hopes for emotional fulfillment, is a stately and melancholic diagnosis of tragic reserve, and a book now taken for granted as a masterpiece by a writer still just in his mid-forties. The plot of Kazuo Ishiguro's third novel is neglible: the butler Stevens drives his master Lord Darlington's car across England and ruminates on the past glories of Darlington Hall, on the death of his father, himself a great butler, and on Miss Kenton, the housekeeper whom he might have once dared to love. The voice of Ishiguro's butler is arduously deferential—perhaps as a Japanese emigré raised in British schools the author was uniquely placed to know how servility infiltrates self, culture, and history. *Remains* is an essay in the use of unreliable narration—not in this case to show a gross comic disparity between the narrator's observations and the reader's perceptions, but instead to scrupulously detail the workings of self-abnegation.

Ishiguro's first two novels, each of which concern postwar Japan, were dry runs for *The Remains of the Day*. *A Pale View of Hills* and *An Artist of the Floating World* are each brief, elliptical, and precise. *Pale View* is told by a Japanese housewife now living in England, *Artist* by a retired painter and patriarch, but their voices, as they recount lives pierced by hesitation and regret, are similarly mournful, digressive, and finally, unreliable. *Pale View* is the more striking of the two for its barely glimpsed images of horror— but both books disappear beneath the shadow of Ishiguro's third.

Perhaps *Remains* was not only a consummation, but a dead end. Perhaps Ishiguro felt misunderstood as a historical realist, or was sick of awards—he'd won one for each of his first three books, climaxing in the Booker for *Remains*. Whatever the reason, he defied expectation and acclaim with the sprawling, brilliant, and exasperating fabulation *The Unconsoled*. The dreamlike epic of Ryder, a celebrated composer/pianist struggling to pull off a concert tour stop in a surreal European city, *Unconsoled* insists on comparison to Kafka. The amnesiac Ryder meets with every possible frustration: accusatory relatives, manipulative journalists, and drunken rivalrous musicians. Several dozen minor characters are given five- or ten-page speeches, in set pieces alternately hilarious, harrowing, and stultifying. *The Unconsoled* seems at once a great psychological dystopia and the most hilariously distended entry yet in the booktours-are-hell genre. It's also a riveting instance of a highly controlled writer challenging his own methods at every level of his narrative. I'm tempted, finally, to call *The Unconsoled* promising, for it shows its author pushing towards another, completely different kind of masterpiece.

See Also: Pale View of Hills *and* The Remains of The Day *recall the Henry James of* "The Turn of the Screw" *and* What Maisie Knew, *respectively.* The Unconsoled *evokes Kafka, and Kafka's inheritors: Stanislaw Lem in* Memoirs Found in a Bathtub, *Ian Banks in* The Bridge, *and, especially, several of the works of the great and confounding German novelist Thomas Bernhard.*

—*Jonathan Lethem*

James, P. D.

1920–

b. Phyllis Dorothy James White in Oxford, England

FICTION: Cover Her Face (1962), A Mind to Murder (1963), Unnatural Causes (1967), Shroud for a Nightingale (1971), The Maul and the Pear Tree: The Ratcliffe Highway Murders, 1811 (with Thomas A. Critchley, 1971), **An Unsuitable Job for a Woman** (1972), **The Black Tower** (1975), Death of an Expert Witness (1977), **Innocent Blood** (1980), The Skull Beneath the Skin (1982), A Taste for Death (1986), Devices and Desires (1989), The Children of Men (1992), *Original Sin (1994), A Certain Justice (1997)

FICTION: Time to Be in Earnest (2000)

For almost four decades, Phyllis Dorothy James has been pushing the boundaries of the genteel English whodunit. Her 1962 debut, *Cover Her Face*, established her as heir to the 1930s' puzzle-making tradition of Agatha Christie and Dorothy Sayers. In that tradition, policemen are poets (like James's Adam Dalgliesh) or peers; gardening is a full-time vocation; and every stately home conceals a gathering of blackmailers, seducers, and murderers. A hospital administrator for nineteen years, James set many of her early novels in medical institutions: particularly memorable is the claustrophobic nursing home in *The Black Tower*. Recently, she's broadened the range of milieus: *Original Sin*, for example, takes place within a family-owned publishing firm. Such settings allow James to create the convincingly detailed characters and communities that readers cherish. In *Original Sin*, the precise descriptions of Peverel Press's Thameside quarters, as well as the red herrings provided by professional rivalries among family members, make the novel one of James's most engrossing.

James's genius lies in preserving a traditional form—in which the order disrupted by the murderer is reassuringly restored by the detective—while modernizing it with emotionally darker characters and a skepticism about the likelihood of even poetic justice. In her most recent mystery, *A Certain Justice*, the relatively simple murder plot is less interesting than the widening circles of damage caused by the inability of the victim, Venetia Aldridge, to love her daughter or accept the love of others. James frequently sounds this theme of damage caused by maternal neglect, perhaps to greatest effect in *Innocent Blood*. Her one non-mystery novel, *The Children of Men*, a gloomy science fiction parable á la Aldous Huxley's *Brave New World*, conversely suggests maternal—and romantic—love as the means to renew a barren society.

Also unsettling in *A Certain Justice* is the virtual absence of the glamorous Scotland Yard Commander Dalgliesh, who has appeared in ten of James's thirteen novels. His functions are taken over by Detective Inspector Kate Mishkin (introduced in *Original Sin*), whose working-class background, gender, and youth make her a symbol of contemporary striving rather than traditional order. Like Dalgliesh himself and private detective Cordelia Gray, who appears in *An Unsuitable Job for a Woman* and *The Skull Beneath the Skin*, Mishkin is fiercely independent of both familial ties and organized social supports. James's emphasis on personal agency and individual effort as means for overcoming the obstacles of early poverty or neglect reflect a Tory nostalgia for an England innocent of multiculturalism and the welfare state; appropriately enough, James was created Baroness James by Margaret Thatcher in 1991.

See Also: Readers who have exhausted James turn to Ruth Rendell for a similarly gentlemanly detective (Inspector Wexford), multilayered plots, and an appreciation of the evil lurking in contemporary culture, or to Elizabeth George, although the quivering sensibilities of her aristocratic Inspector (Viscount) Lynley and his love interest, Lady Helen Clyde, could send anyone running to Raymond Chandler for a dose of pulp vulgarity.

—*Laura Morgan Green*

Janowitz, Tama
1957–
b. San Francisco, California

FICTION: American Dad (1981), *Slaves of New York (1986), A Cannibal in Manhattan (1987), The Male Cross-Dresser Support Group (1992), By the Shores of Gitchee Gumee (1996), A Certain Age (1999)

Tama Janowitz was a friend of Andy Warhol, and she endured the same sort of media snipes he did. During the height of her fame in the late 1970s and 1980s, critics carped that her success—like Warhol's—was less the result of talent than shameless self-promotion. Perhaps this was because Janowitz was a precocious (her first novel, *American Dad*, was published when she was twenty three), flamboyant Manhattan scene-maker whose personal style ran to leopard-print gowns, ivory makeup, and blood-red lipstick and who was, well, prone to shameless self-promotion.

In her heyday, Janowitz left no talk-show couch unturned. In 1986 Janowitz and a group of friends stormed Manhattan's Four Seasons restaurant, the lunchtime oasis for media and business executives, to hand out advance chapters from *Slaves of New York*, her breakthrough collection of short stories. (They were evicted before they could commit publicity.) For the debut of *The Male Cross-Dresser Support Group* she appeared at Elaine's, the literary bar, with a conga line of drag queens. Warhol had reportedly counseled Janowitz: "Don't pay attention to what they write about you. Just measure it in inches." Before long, the writer needed a yardstick.

Often, she was lumped with other youthful and highly visible writers like Jay McInerney and Bret Easton Ellis. But all the hoopla obscured the serious writer within: Janowitz is, in fact, a highly original satirist whose farcical narratives will survive as accurate impressions of New York's demented social landscape. Her best work can be found in *Slaves of New York*, a collection of short stories, many of which were first published in *The New Yorker*.

See Also: Other satirists who zero in on urban life include Evelyn Waugh, David Sedaris, and Fran Leibowitz.

—*Maryanne Vollers*

Johnson, Charles
1948–
b. Evanston, Illinois

FICTION: Faith and the Good Thing (1974), Oxherding Tale (1982), The Sorcerer's Apprentice (1986), *****Middle Passage** (1990), **Dreamer** (1998)

NONFICTION: Being and Race: Black Writing Since 1970 (1988)

Charles Johnson rose to national prominence in 1990 when he became only the second black American to win the National Book Award, for his novel *Middle Passage*. The symbolism of the award couldn't have been richer; the previous African-American winner was Ralph Ellison (for *Invisible Man*, thirty-seven years earlier), whose work and ideas profoundly shaped Johnson's own. He used his acceptance speech to reclaim Ellison from American literary critics who, he later complained, "believed in the 1960s that a black American writer should have only one subject—race—and one theme—victimization."

Although Johnson's best-known novels deal with major events in African-American history (the slave-ship voyage from Africa to America in *Middle Passage*, the inner life of Martin Luther King, Jr., in *Dreamer*), his work is as much about the aesthetics of fiction and the interplay of Eastern and Western philosophy as it is about white and black America. Johnson earned his Ph.D. in philosophy, apprenticed under John Gardner (*On Moral Fiction*), and has been a lifelong skeptic of simplistic notions about America's racial dynamics.

All those influences came to the fore in his early works. *Faith and the Good Thing* follows a young woman from Georgia as she makes a physical and metaphysical journey north to Chicago. In the story collection *The Sorcerer's Apprentice*, Johnson plays with fictional forms and philosophical ideas. One story recasts the Frankenstein tale in the Old South; another imagines a black doctor treating a crash-landed alien (whose ailment, it turns out, is more existential than physical). In *Oxherding Tale* Johnson created a modern slave narrative about a mulatto in the antebellum South, and he returned to this approach in *Middle Passage*. In that book, Johnson draws a portrait of the freed slave Rutherford Calhoun, a cook's helper on a slave ship who, among other issues, wrestles with his own identity. "[I]n myself I found nothing I could rightly call Rutherford Calhoun," narrates the main character, "only pieces and fragments of all the people who had touched me, all the places I had seen, all the homes I had broken into. The 'I' that I was, was a mosaic of many countries, a patchwork of others and objects stretching backward to perhaps the beginning of time."

Johnson continued to probe issues of identity in his 1998 novel, *Dreamer*, about a man whose physical resemblance to Martin Luther King, Jr., is so great that he's hired to act as the civil rights leader's security decoy. *Dreamer* received a decidedly quieter reception than *Middle Passage*, which was much undeserved. The novel reveals Johnson at the height of his literary and philosophical powers; the author takes us into the private life of King and lets us feel the complex psychological weight of the minister's final two years.

See Also: For more on Johnson's ideas about black American writing, see his 1988 collection, Being and Race. *His essay about growing up in Evanston, Illinois, and his beginnings as a writer are the highlight of the 1997 anthology,* Black Men Speaking.

—*Bruce Barcott*

Johnson, Denis

1949–
b. Munich, West Germany

FICTION: *Angels (1983), **Fiskadoro** (1985), The Stars at Noon (1986), **The Resuscitation of a Hanged Man** (1991), **Jesus' Son** (stories, 1992), Already Dead: A California Gothic (1997), The Name of the Word (2000)

POETRY: The Man Among the Seals (1969), Inner Weather (1976), The Incognito Lounge (1982), The Veil (1987), The Throne of the Third Heaven of the Nations Millennium General Assembly: Poems, Collected and New (1995)

In *The Stars at Noon*, the narrator says she came to Nicaragua because "I wanted to know the exact dimensions of hell." The words could apply to the brilliantly daring novels of Denis Johnson. Johnson is contemporary literature's preeminent chronicler of extremity. A master of devastation and redemption, he writes about madness and drugs like no one else, fusing a shockingly original poetic language that still radiates with the wild heat of some nameless high and the no-bullshit sensibility of a survivor.

Like Jimi Hendrix, whose guitar solos he has said influenced him, Johnson is a scary virtuoso. In the middle of one of his paragraphs, everything going along like it should in the safe novel-world—things happening, people talking, verbs and nouns tick-tocking along—you'll suddenly look down and notice this huge void under your feet. Johnson (who, not surprisingly, is also a major poet) seems to write out of two places at once—the one where we put in our time, and that other one, where our losses and visions wait. He strings sentences between them and the words crackle and smoke.

Take this passage from "Car Crash While Hitchhiking" from the collection *Jesus' Son*, in which the narrator observes, looking at a dying man, "His blood bubbled out of his mouth with every breath. He wouldn't be taking many more. I knew that, but he didn't, and therefore I looked down into the great pity of a person's life on this earth. I don't mean that we all end up dead, that's not the great pity. I mean that he couldn't tell me what he was dreaming, and I couldn't tell him what was real."

Johnson's first novel, *Angels*, concerns the desperate destinies of a young woman and a criminal drifter. Johnson's other works are more experimental than *Angels*, but it has the truest, most tragic line. At once a dead-on depiction of the American underbelly, a feverishly exact phenomenology of drug experience (Johnson, who almost skidded off the druggy rails himself, writes with authority on this subject) and a heartbreaking, Dostoevskyan tale of spiritual renewal in the shadow of death, *Angels* is a classic.

Johnson changed pace astonishingly with *Fiskadoro*, a hypnotically imagined account of life after a nuclear war. It is a dizzying performance: If in *Angels* the characters hallucinate, in *Fiskadoro* the world itself is the hallucination. Endlessly allusive and yet frighteningly concrete, *Fiskadoro* is an utterly original work.

The Stars at Noon is a novel about moral numbness and betrayal, narrated by a shady American semi-prostitute in revolutionary Nicaragua. (Johnson has covered war zones all over the world for various magazines.) Seamy elements of Graham Greene and Joseph Conrad float around in a murky broth, the whole sweating with terror and written in a hazy, ellipsis-riddled style.

Johnson's next novel, *The Resuscitation of a Hanged Man*, set in Cape Cod, concerns an intense, God-obsessed young man's weird descent into a sad madness. Johnson's most explicit meditation on theological themes, its exploration of tortured faith recalls Simone Weil and Kierkegaard.

All of these books are extraordinary, but *Jesus' Son*, a collection of linked stories, is a masterpiece. It returns to the party-in-hell terrain of *Angels*, but brings to it a truly avant-garde willingness to break the narrative illusion. At the end of "Car Crash," for example, after a nightmarish account of his experience in detox, the narrator simply says to the reader, "And you, you ridiculous people, you expect me to help you." Here Johnson is risking more, showing more, than ever before.

Johnson's longest and most ambitious novel, *Already Dead: A California Gothic*, takes Johnsonian demons that had hitherto been merely phantasmagorical and makes them real. With its wild mix of genres and narrative techniques—not to mention an actual demon—*Already Dead* is both consummately weird and genuinely moving. But it is ultimately too agnostic, too lacking in a single authorial perspective, to be completely successful.

Johnson has written two perfect books, but perfection isn't what he's about. His voice is so strong it sometimes obscures his characters'. His plots can dissolve into space. He's too intense, too risk-taking, to make the rabbit jump out of the hat every time. It doesn't matter. He's touched by the fire.

203

See Also: Robert Stone's Dog Soldiers *covers the same drugged-out apocalyptic terrain that Johnson's fiction does. Herman Melville's* Pierre *is as flat-out weird as* Fiskadoro, *while Rimbaud's vertiginous* A Season in Hell *echoes the precise ravings that reverberate through the heads of Johnson's antiheroes. Graham Greene's* The End of the Affair *shares Johnson's obsession with redemption and an absent God, and Leonard Gardner's* Fat City—*a work that Johnson has paid homage to—echoes his sad empathy with life's losers.*

—*Gary Kamiya*

Johnson, Diane

1934–
b. Moline, Illinois

FICTION: Fair Game (1965), Loving Hands at Home (1968), Burning (1971), **The Shadow Knows** (1974), Lying Low (1978), Persian Nights (1987), **Health and Happiness** (1990), *Le Divorce (1997), Le Marriage (2000)

NONFICTION: Lesser Lives: The True History of the First Mrs. Meredith (1972), Terrorists and Novelists (essays, 1982), Dashiell Hammett: A Life (1983), Natural Opium: Some Travelers' Tales (1992)

Whatever Diane Johnson has most recently published—biography, essays, fiction, travel writing—tends to be the genre of hers that her readers profess to admire most. Her elegant and astute literary criticism and her innovative, collage-like biographies had overshadowed her fiction during most of the 1980s, but when Johnson published *Le Divorce* in 1997 and the novel became a bestseller, everyone suddenly recalled that she'd been refining her particular talent as a writer of fiction for decades.

Johnson's early novels invariably center on well-meaning but complacent middle-class women of vaguely liberal political inclinations who are jolted out of their comfortable worldviews by disruptive events. Of her early, more comic books, *Burning* is the best, although it lies unimaginatively within the genre of social satires about wacky Californians: The sheltered wife of a Bel Air orthopedic surgeon loses her backyard hedge to L.A. County fire regulations and gets entangled in the chaotic life of her neighbor, a guru-like shrink who doses his patients with ample amounts of sex and drugs. After *Burning*, Johnson's novels grew darker, with violence and racial and class tensions fissuring the smooth lives her characters try to erect. *The Shadow Knows* depicts the spooked existence of a recently divorced Sacramento woman whom financial peril, a faithless lover, and a mysterious tormentor menace from all corners. In *Lying Low*, a vain, aging ballet dancer gets mixed up with counterculture militants, and in *Persian Nights*, the spoiled, adulterous wife of a San Francisco surgeon finds herself alone in a community of foreign doctors in Iran on the brink of the revolution. None of these books quite gels into a truly captivating novel (they are all too long by a third), although each contains many gems of social observation.

With *Health and Happiness*, though, Johnson hit her stride by jettisoning the more somber elements of her earlier fiction. The novel is a shrewd, witty ensemble piece set in a San Francisco hospital and full of ironic plot twists. A gentler version of Evelyn Waugh, Johnson dispenses an array of smart and highly amusing sketches—nurses gossiping about doctors, surgeons behaving with reckless pomposity, a brother-and-sister pair of Chinese immigrants squabbling. *Le Divorce* does the same for American expatriates in France, from dodgy art experts and retired CIA operatives to the narrator's sister, a Californian almost perfectly Francofied but for the fatal mistake of using granulated sugar instead of cubes. Like all of Johnson's heroines, Isabel Walker (whose sister has been left by her French husband) is well-intentioned but naive and all too easily misled by her robust sexual appetite. "I know we are supposed to mind that," Isabel says of the idealized simulacrum of America presented by EuroDisney, "but it's hard not to appreciate, while you're there, the absence of gum wrappers and assault weapons." You could almost say the same of Johnson's novels—that the less they reach for seriousness, the more they please. Her later work offers the rare pleasures of light fiction that is never less than supremely intelligent.

See Also: Those who like the unsettling qualities of Johnson's early fiction should try the recently republished novels of Paula Fox. For confectionary (but not necessarily non-nutritious) satires like Le Divorce, *seek out the work of David Lodge.*

—*Laura Miller*

Jones, Thom
1945–
b. Aurora, Illinois

FICTION: *The Pugilist at Rest (1993), Cold Snap: Stories (1995), Sonny Liston Was a Friend of Mine: Stories (1999)

Thom Jones may be the only male writer to successfully plumb the topic of late-twentieth-century sensitive machismo without putting down his gun, figuratively at least. After turns as a Marine, a boxer, and an ad copywriter, Jones was catapulted to literary stardom when, in 1992, his story, "The Pugilist at Rest," was plucked from *The New Yorker* slush pile and published to much acclaim. It's his best story so far and tells you much about Jones and his work. This controlled rant takes up, among other things, Marines in Vietnam, Schopenhauer, the beauty of a recruit's cobalt blue eyes, charity, fear, Theognis, combat, temporal lobe epilepsy, and dogs specially trained to keep seizure victims from suffocating. In other words, life and survival.

In his first collection, *The Pugilist at Rest*, Jones focused on characters in extreme situations: boxers, soldiers, deep-sea divers, alcoholic surgeons, cancer patients—all written in a locomotive style that backs up the subject matter. Jones himself is famously fucked up: he has temporal lobe epilepsy, takes antidepressants, and enjoys owning up to these facts. He loves playing dumb in his fiction, but can't quite hide his idiosyncratic smarts. To wit, a character mulls over the repercussions of having just slept with his best friend's wife: "I knew that either Clendon would become so pissed he would leave that nasty-ass bitch or he would weasel under and suffer worse than that alienated hero in the Russian novel *Crime and Punishment*, Clendon's favorite character of all time. I believe the dude's name is Raskolnikov." This juxtaposition of ballsyness and brainyness is signature Jones.

Jones examines the great weakness and vulnerability behind his characters' defensive posturing more closely in his second collection. If *Pugilist* is a book of jerks, then *Cold Snap* is its corrective. Instead of soldiers and boxers we get an Aboriginal model, a diabetic, an invalid. He brings us from the Vietnam of *Pugilist* (where a character strips his M-16 as the NVA approaches) to the home front, where a guy worries about the antifreeze level in his car and his sister, who's lobotomized herself with a .22 squirrel pistol. Jones tempers the smoke and explosions of *Pugilist*, but the literal and figurative gun—a way to destroy and be destroyed—remains. Jones eliminates this tentativeness from his next collection, *Sonny Liston is a Friend of Mine*, and returns to the unabashed exuberance and freshness of *Pugilist*. He's in his comfort zone again, letting his concussive narratives pour forth, seemingly unmediated, from his fevered mind. Here's a writer for whom a kind of madness is an inexhaustible muse.

See Also: Though not so macho, another alternative to predictable suburban domestic fiction is George Saunders's story collection CivilWarLand in Bad Decline, *equally serious and absurdly entertaining meditations on life. Denis Johnson's novel* Already Dead *and Robert Stone's* Dog Soldiers *similarly conjure the lives of men discovering the fragility and limitations of the warrior mentality.*

—*Hugh Garvey*

206

Jong, Erica
1942–
b. New York, New York

FICTION: *****Fear of Flying** (1973), How to Save Your Own Life (1977), Fanny: Being the True History of the Adventures of Fanny Hackabout-Jones (1980), **Parachutes and Kisses** (1984), Serenissima: A Novel of Venice ([reissued in 1995 as Shylock's Daughter], 1987), Any Woman's Blues (1990), Inventing Memory (1997)

SELECTED POETRY: Fruits & Vegetables (1971), Becoming Light: New and Selected Poems (1991)

NONFICTION: Witches (1981), The Devil at Large: Erica Jong on Henry Miller (1993), Fear of Fifty: A Midlife Memoir (1994), What Do Women Want?: Bread, Roses, Sex, Power (1998)

Erica Jong has perhaps been too successful at what market researchers call "branding": her name will forever be linked with that famous catchphrase she introduced to the world (and of which she herself seems thoroughly sick): the Zipless Fuck. In 1973's *Fear of Flying*, Jong's legendary "mock-memoir" of the sexual revolution, Jong describes the Zipless Fuck as a "platonic ideal"—a breathless, perfect encounter in which "zippers fell away like rose petals, underwear blew off in one breath like dandelion fluff."

Jong's spunky heroine, Isadora Wing, never, of course, comes close to achieving that ideal—hopping from bed to bed (and continent to continent) with a succession of unlikely, unsuitable partners who are limp pricks in more ways than one. Despite her reputation, Jong is less a pornographer than a comedian—and her most famous novel, while only intermittently erotic, is thoroughly and deliciously funny.

Jong followed her auspicious debut with three more "mock memoirs"—*How to Save Your Own Life*, *Parachutes and Kisses*, and *Any Woman's Blues*—the last of the bunch

SMART AND SEXY *by Erica Jong*

Nothing Like the Sun: A Story of Shakespeare's Love Life
by Anthony Burgess

The best contemporary novel ever written about Shakespeare and an erotic novel to boot. It takes its imagery straight out of the sonnets, imagines a dark lady who is the incarnation of the muse all poets must worship (though they die anyway), gives the necessary weight to the few known facts of Shakespeare's life, yet takes off into the realm of myth and Eros on kaleidoscopic wings of words. Faithful to Shakespeare's creed that without language, Eros is dumb.

Life Force by Fay Weldon

Women may reassure their lovers that size doesn't matter, but here is a witty story about the way a well-hung man, the proud possessor of "a magnificent dong," changes the lives of four female friends.

The Golden Notebook by Doris Lessing

What intelligent women really feel about sex, politics, men, children, war, and love. The greatness of the sexual musings here is that they are intermingled with intellectual and political musings, as in life. Menstruation, orgasm, obsession with unsuitable men—it's all here, told in the voice of an artist heroine on whom nothing is lost. Do women hate the smell of their menstrual blood? Are they unable to reach orgasm with men they don't love? Doris Lessing wrote about these things first. And best. The intelligence of this book is inspiring.

Portnoy's Complaint by Philip Roth

The novel that made it possible to write about the scuzzy side of sexual fantasy. A raucous epic of masturbation that is really a tribute to impossible oedipal obsessions. It inspired me when I was writing *Fear of Flying*.

In Praise of the Stepmother, The Notebooks of Don Rigoberto
by Mario Vargas Llosa

Two loosely interconnected novels about Eros in marriage (is there such a thing?). Vargas-Llosa proves there is—though it is oedipal Eros in the first novel and fantasy Eros in the second.

purporting to be an original manuscript about an Isadora-Wing–like character named Leila Sand, written by Wing herself. While all of the novels have their moments, only *Parachutes and Kisses* comes close to matching the original's energy and inventiveness. *Fear of Flying*, its humor tinged with real bitterness, was quite obviously the work of a young writer. Jong's later works are surprisingly placid and sentimental, written from the point of view of a generally self-satisfied (if not always sexually satisfied) celebrity author who seems forever stuck in the 1970s.

Beside her Isadora Wing quartet, Jong has also written several curious "historical" novels. The title and the language of *Fanny* is intended to recall John Cleland's legendarily smutty *Fanny Hill: A Memoir of a Woman of Pleasure*—a Novel of Pleasure only for the Reader who hast a stomach for such lit'rary tomfoolery. In 1987's *Serenissima: A Novel of Venice* (later reissued as *Shylock's Daughter*), an aging actress stranded at a film festival in Venice finds herself back in the sixteenth century, transformed into Shylock's daughter and (this is Erica Jong, after all) Shakespeare's lover. Jong's nostalgic Jewish "roots novel" *Inventing Memory: A Novel of Mothers and Daughters*, masquerades as a work of family history.

It's perhaps not surprising that an author whose novels frequently veer off into polemical asides should also be drawn to nonfiction. Almost instinctively contrarian, Jong has a special affinity for those who are (she feels) unfairly maligned: witches, Henry Miller, and Hillary Clinton among them. She also writes confessional poetry in a style that recalls Sylvia Plath, Ann Sexton—and the novels of Erica Jong.

Like many writers whose first novel scores big, Jong has had trouble with her follow-through. It's not entirely her fault: *Fear of Flying* was a success (*de scandale*) in part because of its fortuitous timing. But it was a success also because it was funny, and pointed, and very smart in its dissection of the sexual revolution and its discontents. If her writing today sometimes feels not-so-fresh—well, Henry Miller repeated himself as well.

See Also: Fear of Flying *was initially compared to Philip Roth's* Portnoy's Complaint *and even to J. D. Salinger's* Catcher in the Rye—*though Alix Kates Shulman's funny (if not quite as uninhibited)* Memoirs of an Ex-Prom Queen *is most like it. Jong prefers to compare her work to Henry Miller—his manic, misanthropic (if not misogynistic) rants bear only a vague resemblance to her writings—and Colette.*

—David Futrelle

Kaysen, Susanna

1948–
b. Cambridge, Massachusetts

FICTION: Asa, As I Knew Him (1987), *Far Afield (1990)

NONFICTION: Girl, Interrupted (1993)

Susanna Kaysen is best known for *Girl, Interrupted*, her spectacularly sane memoir of two years spent in a mental institution when she was a teenager, but she's also written two wonderful novels. In her first, *Asa, As I Knew Him*, a woman mythologizes her former lover, demonstrating once again the link between passion and fiction. Her second, *Far Afield*, is a departure, literally: It takes place in a world so strange that I had to check an atlas to be sure it really exists. Kaysen's hero is Jonathan Brand, an anthropology grad student who decides to do his fieldwork in the Faroe Islands, an archipelago located southeast of Iceland. His suitcase is lost *en route*, and so he arrives like a traveler in a fairy tale: carrying nothing but his inner resources and some compensatory money from the airline that he can occasionally scatter like magic seeds to ease his way. While he's there to study the locals, it is they, of course, who teach him how to survive; his neighbor even does him the honor of slaughtering a lamb in his kitchen to give him something to eat during the winter.

See Also: Fans of Girl, Interrupted *would like Lauren Slater's books about her own depression and her work as a psychologist.*

—*Laurie Muchnick*

Kennedy, William
1928–
b. Albany, New York

FICTION: The Ink Truck (1969) **THE ALBANY CYCLE:** *Legs* (1975), *Billy Phelan's Greatest Game* (1978), **Ironweed* (1983), *Quinn's Book* (1988), *Very Old Bones* (1992), *The Flaming Corsage* (1996)

NONFICTION: O Albany! Improbable City of Political Wizards, Fearless Ethnics, Spectacular Aristocrats, Splendid Nobodies, and Underrated Scoundrels (1983), Riding the Yellow Trolley Car: Selected Nonfiction (1993)

William Kennedy has spent most of his literary career chronicling the interlinked histories of two fictional Irish-American families, and through them his grimy hometown on the Hudson River, which, in all its provinciality and corruption, he writes, is "as various as the American psyche itself, of which it was truly a crucible." If

Kennedy's focus might seem narrow, his vision, voice, and imagination are almost Whitmanesque in scope—he is less the author of several books than of one large one, rife with philosophical-cum-metaphysical detours, whose point is that ordinary lives spent in obscure corners of an obscure city contain elements of myth and inexplicable moments of communion with the sacred.

Kennedy is no longer the literary celebrity he was in the mid-1980s, when he emerged from near-total obscurity with the Pulitzer Prize-winning *Ironweed*. His tremendously compassionate novel of death and life among the destitute of the Great Depression suggested to some critics the arrival of a visionary American regional writer on the order of Faulkner. But if Kennedy has not produced another single book with *Ironweed*'s impact, that should not detract from the distinctive achievement of his work as a whole.

Often the plots of Kennedy's Albany novels don't amount to much—*Quinn's Book*, for example, masterfully evokes the teeming, tumultuous landscape of nineteenth-century America, then tells a disappointingly small portion of the grand, Dickensian narrative such a setting demands. Their appeal lies in Kennedy's marvelously realized casts of loners, showboats, eccentrics, and gamblers and in his lyrical yet ruthlessly detailed anecdotal histories of the pool rooms, churches, taverns, and middle-class strivers' houses of Irish Albany. Kennedy's universe ranges from the hustlers "sitting among unswept papers, dust, and cigar butts, bathing in the raw incandescence of naked bulbs, surrounded by spittoons" to "the hypocritical handshakers, the priest suckups, the nigger-hating cops, the lace-curtain Grundys and the cut-glass banker-thieves who marked his city lousy," as the embittered newspaperman Martin Daugherty reflects in *Billy Phelan's Greatest Game*.

Beyond Kennedy's remarkable command of details and scene-setting (undoubtedly honed in his own lengthy journalistic career in Albany, Miami, and Puerto Rico—he did not publish his first novel until he was forty-one), no other North American writer has so cannily and successfully integrated the methods of Latin American magic realism into his work. This goes beyond the half-bird/half-man figure Jack (Legs) Diamond meets while crossing the Atlantic in the biographical novel *Legs*, or Martin Daugherty's unerring psychic visions, or even the remarkable scene at the opening of *Ironweed* in which the dead in St. Agnes Cemetery watch the alcoholic hobo Francis Phelan return to the grave of the infant son who slipped out of his hands twenty-two years earlier.

The deeper Kennedy's readers enter his world, the more the books resonate mysteriously against each other. Francis, the self-exiled drunken Odysseus and psychic center of Kennedy's entire cycle, appears as a key figure in four novels. He is not just father to the legendary bowler and pool shark Billy Phelan and brother to the bohemian painter Peter Phelan (of *Very Old Bones*) but one-time lover of the ill-starred Katrina Taylor Daugherty, mother of Billy Phelan's Martin, who herself emerges as the cycle's best-realized female character in *The Flaming Corsage*. Defeated, agonized, and in the end almost

211

heroic, Francis is Kennedy's version of Huck Finn, grown old and wise in the ways of despair. He will stand as one of American literature's most unforgettable characters.

See Also: Any fan of the Kennedy universe will of course have to read O Albany!, *his labor-of-love history. In it can be found the true stories of many of the Albany scandals and calamities that appear as crucial events in the novels. Kennedy's literary influences range from such aficionados of the American night as F. Scott Fitzgerald, John O'Hara, and Damon Runyon to "magic realists" like Gabriel García Márquez and Mario Vargas Llosa. As the leading figure in a modest Irish-American literary renaissance, Kennedy is also linked to such younger authors as Mary Gordon and Alice McDermott.*

—Andrew O'Hehir

Kesey, Ken
1935–
b. La Junta, Colorado

FICTION: *One Flew Over the Cuckoo's Nest (1962), **Sometimes a Great Notion** (1964), Caverns (as "O.U. Levon," a joint pseudonym for Kesey and students in his graduate writing seminar at the University of Oregon, 1990), Sailor Song (1992), Last Go Round (with Ken Babbs, 1994)

NONFICTION: Kesey's Garage Sale (miscellany, 1973), **Demon Box** (miscellany, 1986)

Kesey's career raises fascinating, vexing questions about second acts in American literary lives and about the contradictions between observing social change and becoming an actor in those changes. As an author, Kesey has really had two careers: the brilliant and immensely promising first act represented by *One Flew Over the Cuckoo's Nest* and *Sometimes a Great Notion*, and the decades of producing scatter-shot, miscellaneous, and generally minor work that follow the events described in Tom Wolfe's essential chronicle of the psychedelic movement, *The Electric Kool-Aid Acid Test.*

Kesey grew up in Oregon and began studying writing at Stanford with fellow graduate students Larry McMurtry and Robert Stone in the late 1950s. His participation as a volunteer in government experiments with LSD and a brief stint as an aide in a mental hospital proved fateful. These experiences strongly influenced the composition of *Cuckoo's Nest*, which is set in a psychiatric ward in Oregon and narrated by a giant, schizophrenic Indian named Chief Bromden. The plot concerns the epic battle between Randle Patrick McMurphy, a free-spirited and very sane patient, and Big Nurse, a repressive, emasculating female villain who enforces the dictates of "the Combine"—the Chief's name for the all-powerful machine of convention in his paranoid vision of social reality. The novel is "dreamed or hallucinated rather than merely written," as Leslie A. Fiedler observed, and its Manichean intensity made it a counterculture classic.

A comic strip come to dense, vivid life, Sometimes a Great Notion is a family saga about an almost absurdly vitalistic clan of Oregon loggers resisting a union takeover. Despite many psychedelic tinges, the novel—which features an effete, feminized East Coast anti-hero trying to come to terms with his virile Western kinfolk—eventually bogs down in conventional melodrama, although the book offers a memorable evocation of the Oregon landscape.

While writing his second novel, Kesey (with a cohort of friends dubbed the Merry Pranksters) was already playing a leading role as master of ceremonies of the Acid Tests, a party-cum-revolution celebrated under the influence of LSD. Becoming a hipster king interrupted and in some respects marked the end of Kesey's life as a serious novelist. The sole exception to this is *Sailor Song*, marketed by its publisher as "the triumphant return of a great American writer." A postmodern ecological fable set in twenty-first-century Alaska, this long novel is a relentlessly rollicking failure whose unrelieved jokiness almost eclipses some sharp satirical touches in the cyberpunk mode. *Last Go Round*, co-written with Ken Babbs, takes place at a rodeo in 1911 and is a pleasant exercise in nostalgia.

See Also: Tom Wolfe's The Electric Kool-Aid Acid Test *is a landmark achievement in the so-called "nonfiction novel." It has become an indispensable part of Kesey's oeuvre, even though he didn't write it. A darker, fictionalized perspective on the period that coincided with Kesey's early career can be found in Larry McMurtry's* All My Friends Are Going to Be Strangers. *Thomas Pynchon's* Vineland *is the kind of book that Kesey might have gone on to write if he had been a more dedicated steward of his novelistic talents.*

—*Hal Espen*

Kincaid, Jamaica
1949–
b. St. John's, Antigua

FICTION: At the Bottom of the River (stories, 1983), *Annie John* (1985), Lucy (1990), The Autobiography of My Mother (1996)

NONFICTION: A Small Place (essays, 1988), **My Brother** (memoir, 1997), My Garden (1999)

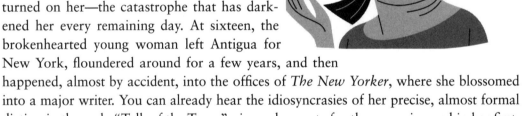

Jamaica Kincaid has, essentially, one story to tell: about a happy Antiguan child who basked in her mother's approval until, at about the time she reached puberty, her mother turned on her—the catastrophe that has darkened her every remaining day. At sixteen, the brokenhearted young woman left Antigua for New York, floundered around for a few years, and then happened, almost by accident, into the offices of *The New Yorker*, where she blossomed into a major writer. You can already hear the idiosyncrasies of her precise, almost formal diction in the early "Talk of the Town" pieces she wrote for the magazine and in her first, voluptuously experimental short stories, collected in *At the Bottom of the River*.

Though the eponymous protagonist-narrators of the novels *Annie John* and *Lucy* have different names, the books are virtual sequels: the former (her sunniest) takes its heroine from childhood to her departure from Antigua; the latter covers her first year in New York, when she worked as an au pair for a well-to-do but unhappily married couple. *The Autobiography of My Mother*, the most clearly made-up of her novels, tells the story of a Dominican woman who spends her sad life searching for clues to her dead mother's past; the prose is gorgeous, the tone solemn, even grim, in its emphasis on isolation and endurance.

Kincaid's nonfiction is splendid. The slim volume (really a long essay) entitled *A Small Place* attacks, with choking rage, the white governors who humbled Antigua before the island became independent and the black politicians who have pillaged it since. *My Brother*, a painfully exposed remembrance of the death of one of her brothers from

AIDS, contains her most magisterial writing. Over the years, she had dealt more and more obliquely with her fierce, intolerant mother; the power of *My Brother* comes from the hair-raising directness with which she makes the case against her.

What most sets Kincaid apart as a writer is her bluntness, wide-eyed and breathtakingly oblivious to the pain it can give. She goes straight for where it hurts most, with a ruthlessness that comes from what she sees (and what probably every writer of merit sees) as her real project, which is to make sense of the senseless. "I am not at all—absolutely not at all—interested in the pursuit of happiness," she has said. "I am interested in pursuing a truth, and the truth often seems to be not happiness but its opposite." She is no easier on herself than she is on any of her targets, but the point of her psychic self-ransacking is not self-laceration. "To condemn yourself is to forgive yourself," she has written, and that statement could stand as the epigraph to her collected works.

See Also: Kincaid's close friend George W. S. Trow, who brought her into The New Yorker, *exerted a major influence on her style. One might point to Maxine Hong Kingston and Toni Morrison as other examples of minority women who write with the power of rage, but really, Kincaid is sui generis.*

—*Craig Seligman*

King, Stephen
1947–
b. Portland, Maine

FICTION: Carrie (1974), Salem's Lot (1975), The Dark Tower: The Gunslinger (1976), Rage (written as Richard Bachman, 1977), **The Shining** (1977), Night Shift (stories, 1978), **The Stand** (1978, republished in 1990 as The Stand: The Complete and Uncut Edition), The Dead Zone (1979), The Long Walk (as Richard Bachman, 1979), Firestarter (1980), Cujo (1981), Roadwork: A Novel of the First Energy Crisis (as Richard Bachman, 1981), Different Seasons (novellas, 1982), The Running Man (as Richard Bachman, 1982), **Pet Sematary** (1983), Christine (1983), The Talisman (with Peter Straub, 1984), The Eyes of the Dragon (1984), Thinner (as Richard Bachman, 1984), Silver Bullet (stories, 1985), Skeleton Crew (stories, 1985), *It (1986), Misery (1987), The Tommyknockers (1987), The Dark Half (1989), The Dark Tower II: The Drawing of the Three (1989), My Pretty Pony (1989), Four Past Midnight (novellas, 1990), Needful Things (1991), The Dark Tower III: The Waste Lands (1991), Gerald's Game (1992), Dolores Claiborne (1993), Nightmares & Dreamscapes (stories, 1993), Insomnia (1994),

Rose Madder (1995), **The Green Mile** (six installments, 1996), Desperation (1996), The Regulators (as Richard Bachman, 1996), The Dark Tower IV: Wizard and Glass (1997), Bag of Bones (1998), The Girl Who Loved Tom Gordon (1999), Hearts in Atlantis (novellas, 1999), The Long Walk (as Richard Bachman, 1999)

He may not embody anyone's ideal of sophisticated literary craftsmanship, but Stephen King's work will probably be read more avidly and widely than that of any other writer in this book. His principal accomplishment has been the revival and modernization of the moribund tradition of horror literature, which had declined into a dusty subgenre confined to booksellers' rear shelves. A master of plot mechanics, King sets his best books in the recognizable, quotidian world of late twentieth-century America; he is uniquely able to evoke terror from such ordinary objects as storm drains, vintage automobiles, and refrigerator magnets as well as from classic Gothic settings like the empty yet malevolent Overlook Hotel of *The Shining*. Like any good horror writer, he plays shamelessly on our fear of death, and on our half-delighted suspicion that all the rational Enlightenment thinking of the last three hundred years has utterly failed to comprehend the true chaos of the universe.

The monsters, ghosts, and insanities that lurk beneath the bucolic landscape of King's territory in rural Maine are often diabolical, extraterrestrial, or ancient in origin. But King's central themes are strikingly serious and contemporary. His greatest concern is with the survival, vindication, and ultimate triumph of the weak and vulnerable. The tangible results of evil in King's universe include bullying, racism, wife-beating, rape, and, above all else, the abuse and murder of children. Few authors in any genre have ever captured the fragility and terror of childhood with such precision, and King's instinctive sympathy for the plight of the nerd, the fat kid, the scapegoat, the queer, is a great source of his appeal.

But there is of course a darker side: King's fixation on manhood. As the ominous, oft-repeated mantra of *Pet Sematary* puts it, "A man's heart is stony ground. He grows what he can, and tends it." In that novel, perhaps King's most terrifying and most profoundly resonant, the things that grow in Dr. Louis Creed's heart (and in the haunted Native American burying ground whose power he cannot resist) hardly bear talking

216

about—a dead child and dead wife are really the least of it. Throughout his work, King repeatedly suggests that every man is a potential vector for evil, that with the wrong stars overhead and the wrong demon at his ankles, he will channel a primordial bloodlust and become a wife-killer, a child-killer, a monster. Whatever this may say about the psychology of Stephen King (who has been married to the writer Tabitha King since 1971 and has three grown children), the truly frightening thing is just how difficult—on the evidence of the society around us—this proposition is to disprove.

King's first successful book, *Carrie*, helped to establish the 1970s market for commercial horror fiction (along with William Peter Blatty's *The Exorcist* and Thomas Tryon's *The Other*). One of his shortest and least sentimental novels, with a female central character combatting a history of abuse, it prefigures the streak of earnest feminism that would surface two decades later in *Gerald's Game*, *Dolores Claiborne*, and *Rose Madder*. The finest achievement of his early career is probably *The Shining*, an unforgettable tale of a haunted, empty hotel, an overly sensitive child, and a riven American family. *The Stand* and *It* are King's two sprawling, multi-character epics in which children (and adults true to their childhood ideals) must battle incalculable evil, and for all their messiness and cloying sentimentality, their scope and narrative drive are irresistible.

When King turned to exploring the plight of women and the popular novelist's relationship with his readership (in *The Dark Half* and *Misery*, one of his wittiest, most acrid books), he no longer dominated the bestseller lists as completely as before. Perhaps sensing that some of the fun had drained out of his work, King responded with the tremendously popular *The Green Mile*, an artless, headlong death-row thriller published in six monthly installments that has something of the tone and emotional force of *To Kill a Mockingbird*. After leaving his longtime publisher, Viking, in 1997 (following a much-publicized dispute over the size of his advance), King published the long-awaited *Bag of Bones*, an attempt to write a literary ghost story in the vein of Daphne du Maurier. While only partly successful, this effort reinforces what we should have known all along: Whether you like him or not, the world's bestselling novelist is no hack, but an honest and committed craftsman. If someone has to be the richest writer in history, we could do a lot worse.

See Also: Much as King is indebted to Mary Shelley and Bram Stoker (neither of whom is nearly as bad as your college professors told you), as well as to Edgar Allan Poe and the original New England horrormeister, H. P. Lovecraft, this critic has long believed that his true literary ancestor is Charles Dickens. King and Dickens share a capacity for shamelessly sentimental yarn-spinning and a love of the grotesque; both use their literary gifts to illuminate the ills of contemporary society. It's impossible to know whether King will share Dickens's literary respectability a century from now, but it's not inconceivable.
—*Andrew O'Hehir*

Kingsolver, Barbara

1955–
b. Annapolis, Maryland

FICTION: **The Bean Trees** (1988), Homeland and Other Stories (1989), *__Animal Dreams__ (1990), Pigs in Heaven (1993), **The Poisonwood Bible** (1998)

NONFICTION: Holding the Line: Women in the Great Arizona Mine Strike of 1983 (1989), High Tide in Tucson: Essays from Now or Never (1995)

POETRY: Another America/Otra America (1992)

The most common gripe about Barbara Kingsolver is a charge she doesn't deny. "I'm a pinko, and I want to change the world," she once told the *Progressive*. All four of her novels have roots in the swath of American countryside stretching from Arizona to the redneck South, and all four deal with politics. She's a biologist by training who writes about the environment, motherhood without men, labor agitation, and Native Americans. Her first novel, *The Bean Trees*, is narrated by an almost apolitical, sassy Southern woman called Taylor Greer, who gets handed an abused Cherokee girl in Oklahoma, names the girl "Turtle," and settles in Arizona. *The Bean Trees* has a squishy end, but Taylor's voice is quirkly and strong, and her squint-eyed take on American culture makes her a kind of girl Huck Finn.

Homeland and Other Stories is an uneven collection dealing with families in various stages of breakdown. It's full of sharp dialogue and meandering, sentimental plots. The best are "Rose-Johnny," about a short-haired woman in a Southern town whose citizens think she's "Lebanese" (lesbian); and "Why I Am a Danger to the Public," about a mine strike in Arizona. They both have the life and spark of *The Bean Trees*. Kingsolver uses her slower, meandering style to good effect in her second novel, *Animal Dreams*, about two sisters disaffected by America during the 1980s. One moves to *contra*-plagued Nicaragua to help the peasants; the other finds a sense of belonging in Arizona by organizing a protest and falling in love with an Apache. All the bleeding-heart postures that make Kingsolver's critics apoplectic are here, but the story doesn't seem willed: It's fleshed out and supported with sharp details of desert landscape, Apache culture, cockfighting, and the Nicaraguan war.

The sequel to *The Bean Trees*, *Pigs in Heaven*, deals with a Native American lawyer who sees Taylor's daughter on *Oprah Winfrey*, recognizes her as a Cherokee, and tries to win her back to the tribe. It's written in a shrill third person with a string of thin characters and unlikely coincidences, and without the vinegar of Taylor's voice. A defensiveness crept into Kingsolver's writing with *Pigs* that she hasn't learned to control. *The Poisonwood Bible*, about a Southern preacher who in 1959 moves his family to the Belgian Congo, is her first shot at a Great Book, but it also feels shrill. Some scenes are harrowing, others are funny—especially the local chief's offer to marry one of the daughters—but *Poisonwood* doesn't match the achievement of *Animal Dreams* in lush detail or control, and the story loses steam about one hundred fifty pages too soon.

What *Poisonwood* does have is information you'll never learn on TV. Kingsolver's healthiest habit is writing about problems ignored or forgotten by mainstream society. But so far she suffers from a self-conscious reflex that plagues all but the best *engagé* writers: a fiery itch to condemn, rather than understand, evil.

See Also: Louise Erdrich also writes about Native Americans. John Nichols's, New Mexico Trilogy, especially The Milagro Beanfield War, *treats political trouble in the rural Southwest with large doses of local color and myth.*

—*Michael Scott Moore*

Kosinski, Jerzy
1933–1991
b. Lodz, Poland

FICTION: *__The Painted Bird__ (1965), __Steps__ (1968), __Being There__ (1971), The Devil Tree (1973), Cockpit (1975), Blind Date (1977), Passion Play (1979), __Pinball__ (1982), The Hermit of 69th Street: The Working Papers of Norbert Kosky (1988)

SELECTED NONFICTION: The Art of the Self: Essays a propos *Steps* (1968), Passing By: Selected Essays, 1962–1991 (1992)

N ot many serious writers would pose bare-chested for *The New York Times Magazine*, but Jerzy Kosinski did, complete with suggestively brandished riding crop. One of the most controversial examples of art imitating an already fictionalized life, the Polish expatriate left behind no greater invention than his own theatrical, troublesome, cracking-at-the-seams persona—by the time he killed himself in 1991, he'd been accused of everything from plagiarism to working for the CIA. While his most popular character—blank-slate Chauncey Gardiner of *Being There*—haplessly stumbled from his garden into the glitzy political elite, Kosinski made an artfully calculated leap from Holocaust survivor to gadfly intellectual. He was contrarian to the core: a deeply pessimistic outsider to whom basic societal rules stank of totalitarian oppression, but also an inveterate ladder-climber hopelessly transfixed by the American fantasy of the self-made man.

His protagonists generally run a gauntlet of evil, conspiratorial forces, just as Kosinski's Jewish family did in Nazi-occupied Poland. His classic first novel, *The Painted Bird*, a haunting, deceptively simple parable of a mute child wandering alone through a strife-ridden Eastern European country, presents nature as inherently depraved, people as stupidly cruel. The ruling metaphor is a peasant artist who captures birds and adorns them in beautiful colors, only to watch them be pecked to death in the sky. The conceit would one day apply to Kosinski: by disingenuously claiming that the work was totally autobiographical, he set himself up for the authenticity scandals of his later career. His second novel, *Steps*, is equally existentialist, following a hollow man who flees through the Iron Curtain to the West and floats through a series of violent and sexually perverse tableaux. Kosinski opted for a more conventional narrative with the satirical novella *Being There*, which eventually became a hit movie starring Peter Sellers.

Kosinski's life sparkled, but his literary formula—alienated eccentric flits between the upper-crust and the demimonde, defies danger, and lives life to the decadent fullest in a series of disjointed episodes—grew tiresome. The Big Emotions seemed forced, the prose clunky, the dialogue bizarrely artificial. Although he tried to spin it as commentary on the artistic process, his increasing reliance on thinly veiled autobiography underscored a certain lack of imagination. In an embarrassing 1975 prank, a journalist submitted twenty pages of *Steps* to several publishers, and all of them rejected it. Even more devastating was a 1982 *Village Voice* hit piece alleging that his novels were partially composed by private editors due to his poor written English. (It also claimed that his pseudonymous 1960 anti-Communist tract *The Future Is Ours, Comrade* was somehow connected to the CIA.)

With the neo-thriller *Pinball* and his final novel, the conceptually provocative but almost unreadable *The Hermit of 69th Street*, Kosinski took a final look at how personal history shapes a work of art, suggesting that a writer's life can and should be his most "original and exciting" production of all. But the author's surprise suicide at the age of fifty-eight suggests he may have thought he'd gotten it all wrong—that no adventure could ever surpass his beautifully doomed birds.

See Also: Given its charismatic, duplicitous subject, James Park Sloan's immaculately researched and insightful Jerzy Kosinski: A Biography *is as gripping as any novel; Kosin-*

ski's idiosyncratic oeuvre bears only vague similarities to such Eastern European writers as Milan Kundera and Ivan Klima, but anyone interested in such post-Holocaust literature as The Painted Bird *might also enjoy Elie Wiesel's* Night, *Cynthia Ozick's* The Shawl, *Isaac Bashevis Singer's* Enemies, A Love Story, *and Art Spiegelman's* Maus.

—*Sia Michel*

Kureishi, Hanif
1954–
b. Bromley, England

FICTION: *The Buddha of Suburbia (1990), **The Black Album** (1995), Love in a Blue Time (1997), Intimacy (1998)

Hanif Kureishi's remarkable screenplays for the films *My Beautiful Laundrette* (1985) and *Sammy and Rose Get Laid* (1987; both films were directed by Stephen Frears) thrum with vibrant conversation. Likewise, in his early fiction, men and women, blacks and whites, straights and gays, capitalists and Marxists, the young and the old, the rich and the poor—all argue passionately about politics, race, religion and sex, making modern Britain look like a shabby but endlessly fascinating cocktail party.

Relishing the kind of cultural chaos that alarms many writers, the half-Pakistani Kureshi is polymorphously perverse—with ideology as well as sex. "I wanted to live always this intensely: mysticism, alcohol, sexual promise, clever people and drugs" thinks Karim Amir, the dazzled, bisexual teenage narrator of Kureishi's first novel *The Buddha of Suburbia*, after his initial encounter with mid-1970s bohemian life. Like Shahid Hasan, the hero of the author's 1995 novel *The Black Album*, he's too green to see that you can't always mix and match. Shahid embarks on an affair with an Ecstasy-popping, miniskirted feminist professor and dabbles in fundamentalism with a Muslim group without forseeing that the two pursuits must inevitably clash.

Initially, the postmodern supermarket of identities didn't daunt Kureishi, who's always believed that love—both familial and erotic—can hold everything together. But with his 1997 short story collection *Love in a Blue Time* and the short 1998 novel *Intimacy*, love suddenly runs aground. Responsibilities and identities have inexorably crusted around the fortyish men in these books: If Kureishi's early novels are coming-of-age yarns, then these are coming-of-middle-age yarns, and the passage is far less sunny. One man mourns "the delinquent dream of his adolescence—the idea that vigour and spirit existed in excess, authenticity and the romantic unleashed self," while another observes that "most of the people he knows are on the move from wife to wife, husband to husband, lover to lover. A city of love vampires, turning from person to person, hunting the one who will make the difference." Does Kureishi grasp yet that the first attitude usually leads to the second?

Kureishi's fiction still opens up, though, when he's writing about family and ethnicity, the maddening perplexities facing immigrants and their children. His refusal to romanticize race makes him one of those rare artists who can explore the subject without disingenuous piety. Alas, the patently autobiographical *Intimacy* (about a man leaving his partner of seven years and their children to chase after a club girl) suggests that the mopey navel-gazing rife in *Love in a Blue Time* has entirely preoccupied the author. Let's hope it's only a phase.

See Also: Armistead Maupin's Tales of the City *captures a bewitching city in one of its finest moments with a brio that resembles Kureishi's, though with a lighter, more pop tone.*

—*Laura Miller*

Le Carré, John
1931–
b. David Cornwell in Poole, Dorsetshire, England

FICTION: Call for the Dead (1961), A Murder of Quality (1962), *The Spy Who Came in from the Cold (1963), The Looking Glass War (1965), A Small Town in Germany (1968), The Naïve and Sentimental Lover (1971), Tinker, Tailor, Soldier, Spy (1974), The Honourable Schoolboy (1977), **Smiley's People** (1980), The Little Drummer Girl (1983), A Perfect Spy (1986), The Russia House (1989), The Secret Pilgrim (1990), The Night Manager (1993), Our Game (1995), The Tailor of Panama (1996), Single and Single (1999)

Everyone knows John le Carré writes superlative spy novels, sleeted in plot twists and betrayals, ever-sad in tone, aching and Dostoyevskian in their protagonists. But what most overlook is how he anoints us with religious novels, as well. Not like Graham Greene, although Greene admired the undercurrents in le Carré's books greatly and called *The Spy Who Came in from the Cold* "the best spy novel I have ever read."

No, le Carré's religiosity isn't a quest for God, as with Greene; it's more a longing for something to believe in. Anything: one's country, one's ideology, one's friends or family. Whither trust, in other words, in a world of Judases. "You teach [agents] to cheat, to cover their tracks, and then they cheat you as well," says the bitter Alec Leamas in *The Spy Who Came in from the Cold*.

Three biographical facts seem to fuel this desolate outlook. First, le Carré's father was a con artist whose misbehavior drove le Carré's mother away. "I think that all my great villains have always had something of my father in them," the author told *Time* in 1993. The extremely supple *A Perfect Spy* and *The Night Manager*, set in the Gulf War universe of arms smugglers, particularly bear this out.

Second, in his youth, le Carré considered joining a monastery. And third, in the 1950s he was a spy himself (a fact he denied until 1993). Bereft child, monk, spy; they have much in common, especially a craving for the "secret hush" as le Carré writes in *Our Game*, adding that a spy's "longing for the inner life is at times unendurable, whether of the religious or clandestine kind."

The Spy Who Came in from the Cold (which has sold over twenty million copies) soldered le Carré's reputation. It is a taut masterpiece, beginning and ending at the Berlin Wall, the best distillation of le Carré's primary theme; that "Cold War horses" on both sides were equally debased because both believed that individuals were expendable—ever-expendable—for the cause.

Granted, the master has stumbled. Most critics contend he's lost his way since the Cold War ended, but this is only half-true. It's more that we aren't as confident of him outside the European milieu he knows so intimately. His rendering of the Middle East in *The Little Drummer Girl* is overheated and unsure. Same goes for Panama in *The Tailor of Panama*.

Mostly, though, he is superb. *The Spy Who Came in from the Cold* remains his highest achievement, closely shadowed by *The Looking Glass War* and each of the George Smiley novels: *Tinker, Tailor, Soldier, Spy*; *The Honourable Schoolboy*; and *Smiley's Peo-*

ple. These last play off Britain's real-life espionage debacle, which unfolded when Kim Philby was exposed as a Soviet mole. Smiley is le Carré's most astonishingly nuanced creation, a plump, conflicted, unassumingly brilliant spy who is undone by a Kim Philby stand-in and his Russian doppelganger, code-named Karla. As the author writes in *The Honourable Schoolboy*: Karla "had set out to destroy the temples of [Smiley's] private faith, whatever remained of them." Belief is ever le Carré's obsession; he is our best mourner, really, in this most agnostic of centuries.

See Also: In tone and import, Graham Greene is spiritual kin to le Carré. None of today's spy novelists come close to le Carré's talent, though Ken Follett approaches the author's skill in plot, if not prose.

—*Katharine Whittemore*

Le Guin, Ursula K.
1929–
b. Berkeley, California

FICTION: Rocannon's World (1966), Planet of Exile (1966), City of Illusions (1967), **A Wizard of Earthsea** (Earthsea series, 1968), **The Left Hand of Darkness** (1969), **The Tombs of Atuan** (Earthsea series, 1971), **The Lathe of Heaven** (1971), **The Farthest Shore** (Earthsea series, 1972), The Word for World is Forest (1972), The Wind's Twelve Quarters: Short Stories (1975), **The Dispossessed** (1974), Very Far Away from Anywhere Else (1976), Orsinian Tales (stories, 1976), Malafrena (1979), The Beginning Place (1980), **The Compass Rose** (stories, 1982), The Eye of the Heron (1983), *****Always Coming Home** (1985), Buffalo Gals and Other Animal Presences (stories and poems, 1987), **Tehanu** (Earthsea series, 1990), Searoad: Chronicles of Klatsand (stories, 1991), A Fisherman of the Inland Sea: Science Fiction Stories (1994), Four Ways to Forgiveness (stories, 1995), Unlocking the Air (stories, 1996)

SELECTED NONFICTION: Dreams Must Explain Themselves (essays, 1975), The Language of the Night (essays, 1979), Dancing at the Edge of the World (essays, 1989), Steering the Craft: Exercises and Discussions on Story Writing for the Lone Navigator or the Mutinous Crew (1998)

SELECTED POETRY: Wild Angels (1975), Hard Words, and Other Poems (1981), Wild Oats and Fireweed (1988), Going Out with Peacocks and Other Poems (1994) rsula Kroeber Le Guin is the science fiction writer read by people who don't read science fiction. Her polished prose, nuanced characterization, and political intelligence distinguish her in a genre where those qualities often come second, or not at all. Although some of her books (*Orsinian Tales*, *Malafrena*, *Searoad*, and *Unlocking the Air*) are ably realist, her voice is truest when it blends naturalism and fantasy. Her home, as she puts it, is "Outer Space and the Inner Lands," and she uses genre elements to serve larger cultural themes, usually feminist, utopian, or Taoist.

The Left Hand of Darkness first marked her as an important science fiction writer. On the ice planet Gethen live androgynes who take on either male or female sexual characteristics only during estrus. This fluidity of gender shapes all aspects of Gethenian life, from politics to culture, more deeply than the new envoy from Earth appreciates, until he must flee with a political exile across the polar ice. Part medieval political intrigue, part ethnography, part adventure story—and full of reflection on individuality, friendship, and social roles—it sounds all Le Guin's major themes in swift, sure prose as compelling as a dream.

The Dispossessed, widely considered her masterpiece, posits an anarchist colony on a moon orbiting a capitalist home world. Certainly among the best utopian novels of the century, it nevertheless has a slight, perhaps unavoidable, tendency to preach. Le Guin makes the eminently reasonable but far from startling case that neither pure anarchy nor pure capitalism answer all human needs.

Her own favorite work, Earthsea, is a series of four novels relating the moral education of a sorcerer who must come to terms with his shadow self. Magic on the world of Earthsea is a rigorous affair with an almost Newtonian balance of action and reaction, and a Taoist mindfulness of light and darkness coupled. Another work with a distinct Taoist bent is *The Lathe of Heaven*, a dystopian nightmare of trapdoor realities influenced by the work of Philip K. Dick. One of the pleasures of this dark novel is Le Guin's witty deconstruction of many science fiction cliches.

Le Guin is the daughter of anthropologists Alfred and Theodora Kroeber, and her familiarity with this field pervades her work, particularly *Always Coming Home*. Set in a far-future post-technological Napa Valley, it is an ethnography of the Kesh, a people who live much as pre-encounter California coastal tribes lived. Through various narratives interwoven with poems, fables, maps, field reports, and glossaries, Le Guin portrays this near-utopia as shadowed by a catastrophic past and by dark impulses within the culture itself.

Her short fiction at its best is even more cogent than her novels. Her penchant for fable and emblem is sharply focused in stories like "The Ones Who Walk Away from Omelas," "Sur," and "Newton's Sleep." Lately she has written only short fiction, often with common threads.

See Also: Le Guin was among the first of what has become a substantial feminist presence in science fiction and fantasy. Joanna Russ, Carol Emshwiller, James Tiptree, Jr.

(pseudonym for Alice Sheldon), Octavia Butler, Lisa Goldstein, Karen Joy Fowler, and Pat Murphy are just a few others who have used genre elements to serve a distinct personal vision.

—Carter Scholz

Leavitt, David
1961–
b. Pittsburgh, Pennsylvania

FICTION: *Family Dancing (1984), **The Lost Language of Cranes** (1986), Equal Affections (1989), A Place I've Never Been (1990), While England Sleeps (1993), **Arkansas: Three Novellas** (1997), The Page Turner (1998)

Consider David Leavitt's career a cautionary tale of the hazards that come with early literary success. When his first story, "Territory," was published in *The New Yorker* in 1981, Leavitt was a twenty-year-old undergraduate at Yale. The story set tongues wagging, not only because the author was presumed a bit callow for such an honor, but also because it was the first gay-themed fiction in that august publication. By 1983, Leavitt had completed a story collection, *Family Dancing*, that was nominated for both the National Book Critics Circle Award and the PEN/Faulkner Award. Critics marveled at his knowing examinations of middle-class domestic life—in one story, a precocious, withdrawn boy acts out when his parent's marriage falls apart; in another, a housewife with cancer struggles to make sense of life when she has exceeded the six months doctors gave her to live. For all its apparent wisdom, Leavitt later told an interviewer that *Family Dancing* was the work of "a frighteningly articulate child."

It's not easy to follow up this kind of debut. Leavitt published three more books in short order. His first novel, *The Lost Language of Cranes*, is about a young gay man whose coming out compels his father to accept his own homosexuality; the next novel, *Equal Affections*, charts a family's painful course as the mother dies of cancer (Leavitt's own mother died of the disease); and another story collection, *A Place I've Never Been*, introduces AIDS into Leavitt's fictional world. None of the books enjoyed the kind of unanimous critical approval that *Family Dancing* had, but each further established Leavitt as an able, intelligent observer of the American family under pressure.

226

Then came a literary scandal. Leavitt's next book, *While England Sleeps*, was a departure—a historical novel set in 1930s England that chronicles the love affair between an upper-class writer and a lower-class Communist. The British poet Sir Stephen Spender took legal action, claiming that the plot had been lifted from his 1948 memoir, *World Within World*. The English edition was pulped, and eventually a revised version was published in the U.S. The book is not Leavitt's finest—unconvincing and contrived, it lacks the emotional truths that anchored his earlier work.

Leavitt returned with a collection of three novellas, *Arkansas*. If anything, these pieces were sharper and more ironic than his earlier work, especially "The Term Paper Artist," a clever story about a writer—named David Leavitt—who, struggling with writer's block after a debilitating lawsuit by an elderly British poet, takes to writing term papers for cute, straight UCLA undergrads in exchange for sex. However, *The Page Turner*, the tale of a young aspiring concert pianist and his affair with a middle-aged onetime piano prodigy, doesn't live up to its title; it's a solid but strangely unaffecting read.

*See Also: Peter Cameron (*Leap Year, The Weekend*) has, like Leavitt, written observant and insightful fiction about the intersections of middle-class gay and straight lives. Michael Cunningham (*A Home at the End of the World, Flesh and Blood*) has also written sensitively about the American family as it is altered by homosexuality.*

—*Tom Beer*

Lefcourt, Peter
1941–
b. New York, New York

FICTION: **The Deal** (1991), **The Dreyfus Affair** (1992), *Di and I (1994), **Abbreviating Ernie** (1997), The Woody (1998)

Sweet-tempered and wised-up, the comic novels of Peter Lefcourt are proof that square can be beautiful. Paradise, as his books define it, is middle-class and reassuringly familiar. Comfy hotel rooms, barcaloungers, good take-out, and sex with someone who makes your heart go pitty-pat is his characters' idea of nirvana. Lefcourt is a wonderful combination for an American pop novelist: a romantic smartass with one ear cocked for the strains of swoony violins.

Lefcourt's specialty is wish-fulfillment. In *The Deal* a stone-out-of-luck Hollywood producer manages to hit critical and commercial paydirt with a biopic about Disraeli. *The Dreyfus Affair* is the story of baseball's leading shortstop who finds bliss (and public acceptance) when he fall in love with his black second baseman. And in *Di and I* a screenwriter sent to London to research a mini-series on the royal family (Lefcourt was a TV writer) falls in love with Princess Diana and spirits her way to a suburban California where the two find happiness opening a McDonald's franchise. (It's a pity that this, Lefcourt's best book, now seems destined go unread because of Diana's death.)

Lefcourt moves into more topical—and cynical—territory in *Abbreviating Ernie*, a fantasia on the circuses surrounding the O. J. Simpson and Lorena Bobbitt trials. Even here, he continues to seem an oddity among comic writers—he's got no patience for phonies or bullies or boors, and he still doesn't seem to have a mean impulse in him.

See Also: It's no slight to Lefcourt to say that his writing most often suggests stuff that was too smart and too wild for the wittiest sitcom. The competing and intersecting subplots of Abbreviating Ernie *suggest something of Carl Hiassen's juggling acts.*

—*Charles Taylor*

Leonard, Elmore
1925–
b. New Orleans, Louisiana

FICTION: The Bounty Hunters (1953), The Law at Randado (1954), Escape From Five Shadows (1956), Last Stand at Saber River (1959), **Hombre** (1961), The Big Bounce (1969), The Moonshine War (1969), Valdez Is Coming (1970), Forty Lashes Less One (1972), Mr. Majestyk (1974), Fifty-Two Pickup (1974), Swag (1976), Unknown Man No. 89 (1977), The Hunted (1977), The Switch (1978), Gunsights (1979), City Primeval: High Noon in Detroit (1980), Split Images (1981), Cat Chaser (1982), **Stick** (1983), **LaBrava** (1983), *Glitz (1985), Bandits (1987), Touch (1987), Freaky Deaky (1988), Killshot (1989), **Get Shorty** (1990), Maximum Bob (1991), Rum Punch (1992), Pronto (1993), Riding the Rap (1995), Out of Sight (1996), Cuba Libre (1998), Be Cool (1999)

ass-market crime fans and language aficionados alike can find joy in Elmore

MLeonard's novels. In addition to presenting a vastly diverting vision of America's criminal underbelly, his work displays a masterful understanding of the rhythms of speech and dialogue, the natural flow of internal monologue, the poetry of place names.

Set on the fringes of Detroit, Miami, New Orleans, L.A., and Puerto Rico, Leonard's novels could lazily be called gritty. While the locales and subject matter are bleak, the books are anything but. Though it's often sudden and wince-inducing, there's no horror in Leonard's violence. Instead of palpable evil, there's moral ignorance; instead of sadism, anger; instead of despair, humor. His is a crime world on Prozac, which is why, at thirty-two books and counting, he's daily gaining more fans—from sneakers-and-stockings-wearing commuters to a gushing Martin Amis. What ties his protagonists—ex-cons trying to go straight, tired U.S. marshals, bored bomb squad technicians—together is the desire to live a simple life despite being caught up in something large and insidious. What ties his antagonists together is stupidity and greed.

Leonard started out writing westerns and industrial films, then really hit his stride in the 1980s with crime fiction. His novels are impossible to synopsize, with their crazy plots veering all over the place (he satisfies Raymond Chandler's maxim that a good mystery must still be good, even with the final page torn out). Among the best are *Glitz*, then the poignant *LaBrava*, his 1965 western *Hombre*, the comic *Get Shorty*, and *Stick*.

Like few writers in any genre, Leonard has a talent for receding and letting his characters' thoughts and dialogue tell the story, without calling attention to the writing. It slips in sneakily like a mosquito stinger. Take this example from *LaBrava*:

"The Dade-Metro squad-car cop, drinking Pepsi out of a paper cup, said 'He pulls the trigger, click. He pulls the trigger, click. He pulls the fucking trigger and I come around like this, with the elbow, hard as I can. The piece goes off—no click this time—the fucking piece goes off and smokes the guy standing at the bar next to me with his hands up. We get him for attempted, we get him for second degree, both.' The Dade-Metro squad-car cop said, 'Did you know you rub a plastic-coated paper cup like this on the inside of the windshield it sounds just like a cricket? Listen.' "

Exactly.

See Also: Carl Hiaasen's Florida-based, comic, environmental thrillers possess some of the same madcap glee, but are much more cheery and fantastic than Leonard.

—*Hugh Garvey*

Lessing, Doris
1919–
b. Kermanshah, Persia (now Iran)

FICTION: The Grass Is Singing (1950), This Was the Old Chief's Country (stories, 1952), Martha Quest (Children of Violence series, 1952), **A Proper Marriage** (Children of Violence series, 1954), Five: Short Novels (1955), Retreat to Innocence (1956), The Habit of Loving (stories, 1958), A Ripple From the Storm (Children of Violence series, 1958), *****The Golden Notebook** (1962), A Man and Two Women (stories, 1963), African Stories (1964), Landlocked (Children of Violence series, 1966), The Four-Gated City (Children of Violence series, 1969), Briefing for a Descent Into Hell (1971), **The Temptation of Jack Orkney and Other Stories** ([republished as Volume 1 of Collected Stories, 1978] 1972), The Summer Before the Dark (1973), **The Memoirs of a Survivor** (1975), **To Room Nineteen** (Volume 2 of Collected Stories, 1978), The Diaries of Jane Somers ([including The Diary of a Good Neighbor (1983) and If the Old Could . . . (1984), originally published under the pseudonym Jane Somers], 1984), The Good Terrorist (1985), The Fifth Child (1988), The Real Thing: Stories and Sketches (1992), Canopus in Argos: Archives ([contains Colonized Planet V, Shikasta (1979), The Marriage Between Zones Three, Four, and Five (1980), The Sirian Experiments: The Report of Ambien II, of the Five (1981), The Making of the Representative for Planet 8 (1982), Documents Relating to the Sentimental Agents in the Volyen Empire (1983)], 1992), Playing the Game: Graphic Novel (1993), Winter in July (stories, 1993), Love, Again (1996), Mara and Dann (1999)

NONFICTION: Going Home (1957), In Pursuit of the English (1961), Particularly Cats (1967), A Small Personal Voice: Essays, Reviews, Interviews (1975), Prisons We Choose to Live Inside (1987), The Wind Blows Away Our Words (1987), African Laughter: Four Visits to Zimbabwe (1992), **Under My Skin** (Volume 1 of My Autobiography, 1949–1962, 1994), Walking in the Shade (Volume 3 of My Autobiography, 1949–1962, 1997)

For over half a decade, Doris Lessing has turned her prolific pen to just about every prose form—fiction, autobiography, essays, drama. Yet all of her writing stems from the impulse to lay bare the grid of class, race, and gender relations that governs her middle-class characters' lives. Lessing brings the microscopic intensity of George Eliot and the combative sexual consciousness of D. H. Lawrence to bear on English culture, whether the context is the provincially hierarchical "settler" society of Southern Rhodesia in *A Proper Marriage* or the beleaguered bohemia of "free women" in *The Golden Notebook*. Lessing's reputation as one of the most important novelists of the post–World War II period rests firmly on her contribution to the grand tradition of English social realism. Yet Lessing herself once dismissed George Eliot, to whom she is so often compared, as "good as far as she goes"; she prefers to claim the more cosmopolitan influence of Tolstoy and Balzac.

Indeed, this apparently most British of writers was thirty years old before she set foot in England or published her first novel. Her upbringing on a farm in Southern Rhodesia (now Zimbabwe) acquainted her more thoroughly with the isolation and racial exploitation of white colonial culture than with an imperial literary heritage. Her formal schooling ended at age fourteen, and in *Under My Skin*, the first volume of her autobiography, Lessing notes with pride the real accomplishments of her youth: the ability to "set a hen, look after chickens and rabbits, worm dogs and cats, pan for gold, take samples from reefs, cook, sew, use the milk separator and churn butter, go down a mine shaft in a bucket, make cream cheese and ginger beer . . . drive the car, shoot pigeons and guineafowl for the pot, [and] preserve eggs." By the time she left for London in 1949, she had augmented these accomplishments with two divorces, three children, the obloquy of Communist party membership and anti-apartheid agitation, and the unpublished draft of her first novel.

Colonial race relations, political activism, and the burdens of women have remained her central concerns. Her first novel, *The Grass Is Singing*, about a farmer's wife drawn into a doomed affair with an African worker, approaches its material from a distance. Lessing infuses a simple plot with the intensity of a Greek tragedy: She portrays the wife's murder by the African, Moses, as the inevitable outcome of male violence and female passivity fostered by white settler culture. Lessing depicts the white experience of colonial Africa more urgently and directly in her five-novel Children of Violence sequence (1953–1969), in which she embeds the sexual, political, and intellectual development of her protagonist, Martha Quest, in a detailed evocation of the communist and progressive political and intellectual life of Rhodesia and London in the 1950s and 1960s.

Anna Wulf, the novelist heroine of Lessing's most celebrated work, *The Golden Notebook*, continues Martha's quest: political activism, sexual experimentation, maternity, female friendship, and authorship all feed into her struggle for authentic, integrated selfhood. The declarative simplicity of the novel's opening line—"The two women were alone in the London flat"—belies its explosive effect on several generations of women intellectuals struggling to reconcile the life of the mind, the imperatives of the body, and the gender roles they inherited from the 1950s. But as Lessing herself insists, *The Golden*

Notebook achieved innovations beyond its contribution to what she dismissively terms "the sex war." The novel combines omniscient observation, Anna's own musings in four different journals, and sections from Anna's novel manuscript. These interwoven narratives capture both an individual consciousness and a particular cultural moment with something of the multilayered depth of James Joyce's *Ulysses*.

Public events shape private histories in Lessing's novels, often violently. In *The Good Terrorist*, for example, middle-class Alice Mellings keeps house for a pseudo-communist cadre until a too-successful bombing destroys her illusion of control. In the chilling *The Fifth Child*, terror emerges from the bosom of the family, when Harriet Lovatt gives birth to the sociopathic Ben, the embodiment of a disaffected savagery that, Lessing suggests, will inherit the urban future. Lessing anatomizes a less dramatic, but perhaps more pervasive, anguish in *The Diary of a Good Neighbor, If the Old Could . . .* , and *Love, Again*, in which women whose familial and productive relationships have passed away confront the isolation of aging.

Lessing's scary genius lies in her ability to bring her readers face-to-face with an unadorned reflection of some of our more depressing, but all too human, features. At the same time, her realism has always coexisted with a tendency toward mysticism. Her novels of the 1970s compellingly combine a surface of social and geographic detail with journeys into an inner space that Lessing has described, in *The Real Thing*, as "so much more intelligent than the slow, lumbering, daylike self." In the haunting *Memoirs of a Survivor*, for example, worlds separated by time and space interpenetrate through the vision of the unnamed female narrator, enabling her to save herself and her companions from extinction. But when Lessing leaves humanity entirely behind, as she does in the science fiction sequence Canopus in Argos: Archives (1979–1983), her depictions of warring galactic empires lack the individuality and emotional insight she brings to earthly society. In Lessing's most recent novel, *Mara and Dann*, she returns once again to the theme of earthly apocalypse, with human, if visionary, protagonists.

In *Under My Skin*, Lessing describes her long-ago attempts to explain to her young children her departure from their lives: "[I told them] I was going to change this ugly world, they would live in a beautiful world where there would be no race hatred, injustice, and so forth . . . One day they would thank me for [leaving] . . . I was absolutely sincere. There isn't much to be said for sincerity, in itself."

It is typical of Lessing to emphasize the limits of good intentions, even her own. Yet in doing so, she paradoxically underlines her dedication to a more rigorous sincerity, a vision as stripped of illusion as her art can make it.

See Also: *Writers who share Lessing's unsentimental vision of contemporary mores include Margaret Atwood, Diane Johnson, and Alison Lurie.*

—*Laura Morgan Green*

Lethem, Jonathan

1964–
b. New York, New York

FICTION: Gun, with Occasional Music (1994), Amnesia Moon (1995), The Wall of the Sky, The Wall of the Eye: Stories (1996), **As She Climbed Across the Table** (1997), *****Girl in Landscape** (1998), Motherless Brooklyn (1999)

Jonathan Lethem is the quintessential young novelist who's seduced by a range of influences but unwilling to marry just one. The common thread in his work is his clear, bright prose, marked by an easy, unaffected elegance. But thematically, and in terms of the characters he invents, each of his books stands on its own. His first novel, *Gun, with Occasional Music,* is a futuristic noir thriller—more than one critic described it as a cross between Philip K. Dick and Raymond Chandler—set in a world where the government doles out drugs with names like Acceptol and Forgettol; where the heavies from the Inquisitor's Office have the power to add to or subtract from an individual's "karma card"; and where genetically altered animals like a tough-talking kangaroo walk among humans. Lethem's second book, *Amnesia Moon,* is a road trip across the ravaged America of tomorrow, a nightmare *Wizard of Oz* odyssey.

But even if you were to take the lazy way out and consider *Gun, with Occasional Music* and *Amnesia Moon* straight science fiction, Lethem's characters, even the oddest ones, are hardly generic. Perhaps his most touching creation is *Amnesia Moon*'s Melinda, an adolescent girl covered completely with fur and an awkward mix of preteen uncertainty, unself-conscious loveliness, and youthful brashness. (When we first meet her, she's siphoning gas from a car's tank.) Melinda is moving precisely because her feelings are still so raw—they haven't been civilized out of her yet.

Lethem's books keep getting harder to categorize. *As She Climbed Across the Table* is partly an academic farce, but it's also a love story of sorts: The third party in the love triangle between a brilliant, beautiful physicist and her anthropologist-academic boyfriend is, literally, a black hole in space. For all its sly good humor, *As She Climbed Across the Table* also has a softly beating heart: It captures the capriciousness and unpredictability of love and desire, and the misery of being the unwanted third party, standing off to the side, confused and helpless. *Girl in Landscape* is the most mature, and most sensitive, of Lethem's books yet. Loosely modeled on John Ford's film *The Searchers,* it tells the story of the recently motherless fourteen-year-old Pella Marsh, whose family leaves the apocalyptic wasteland of Brooklyn for a better life on a far-off

SCREENED OUT *by Jonathan Lethem*

Four wonderful novels (and one whole career) obscured by film adaptations, good, bad, and indifferent.

True Grit by Charles Portis

The difference between the novel and the film is that the novel, which like Mark Twain's *Huckleberry Finn* and Thomas Berger's *Little Big Man* perfectly captures the naive elegance of the American voice, is about the inner life of the narrator, a fourteen-year-old girl. The film is, of course, about John Wayne, who in portraying Rooster Cogburn turned his screen image gently on its ear, and won an Oscar. That was nice, but the book should be better remembered.

Endless Love by Scott Spencer

Behind that titter-provoking Brooke Shields movie is one of the best candidates for Great American Novel—a story of teenage romantic obsession told in a voice as rich, intelligent, and full of emotional nuance as the best of Philip Roth or Richard Yates—*The Great Gatsby* meets Terrence Malick's *Badlands*.

They Shoot Horses, Don't They? by Horace McCoy

This brilliantly compressed and gritty tale of a nightmarish dance marathon becomes by implication a expose of Hollywood and Depression America. Let this one stand in for *Nightmare Alley* by William Lindsey Gresham, *Night and the City*, by Gerald Kersh, *Miami Blues* by Charles Willeford, and even the recent *A Simple Plan* by Scott Smith—all excellent noirs. In each of these source novels a surprising amount of what we admire in the films was already present, and in clean, efficient prose.

The Manchurian Candidate by Richard Condon

An abundance of weaker work has blotted out Condon's few best novels, which have a prescient paranoiac verve that holds up nicely—he's sort of a pop DeLillo. *Winter Kills*, another splendid novel, was also made into a lesser-known, but excellent film. Oddly, in the 1950s and 1960s, Frank Sinatra made a habit of starring in films made from underrated novels: both James Jones's *Some Came Running* and Roderick Thorp's *The Detective* are worth a closer look.

Walter Tevis

That the same obscure novelist should hide behind good films as utterly different as *The Hustler* and *The Man Who Fell to Earth* seems impossible. On top of that, his sequel to *The Hustler*, *The Color of Money*, was filmed by another good director—too bad all they took from that book was the title. Stranger still, Tevis wrote two later novels just as good or better, one each in the vein of the earlier gems: *Queen's Gambit* is a grimly realistic story of a female alcoholic chess prodigy that captures the flavor of tournament competition as well or better than *The Hustler*, and *Mockingbird* is a brilliant and generous dystopian moral fable. Each would make a nice film project—not that filming the books would guarantee Tevis the readership this unique American writer deserves.

234

planet. The metaphor of adolescence as foreign territory may be obvious, but Lethem's treatment of the subject isn't. His Pella is sulky, confused, and unabashedly determined all at once. Lethem is unflinching about probing the dark side of Pella's segue into woman-hood, exploring both the awe of female adolescent sexual awakening and the treachery of it. But he's also almost painfully sympathetic to her, capturing perfectly the awkwardness a young woman feels when she's getting ready to fold up her girl self forever.

After the new territory opened up by *Girl in Landscape*, the road ahead could have led Lethem anywhere, but there's no way anyone could have foreseen Lionel Essrog, the hero of *Motherless Brooklyn*. Lionel, a fledgling detective with Tourette's syndrome, is one of Lethem's most memorable characters. His "infirmity"—a compulsive disorder that causes him to shout out strange words and to touch people and things uncontrol-lably—sets him apart, often rather mournfully, from the rest of the world. It's also some-times an excuse for vaudeville: At one point Lionel entertains his dying boss by trying to get to the punchline of a joke without getting tangled up in his tics. Lethem never treats Lionel's syndrome as a novelty, but he recognizes that it gives Lionel a kind of royal dis-tinction, not just among his peers (other aspiring Brooklyn tough guys) but also among the boring, normal mortals we encounter every day. When Lionel compulsively turns a sentence like "Are you excusing Tony?" into "Accusatony! Excusebaloney! Funny-monopoly!", each made-up seemingly nonsensical word is a world of explanation unto itself, as compact as haiku. *Motherless Brooklyn*, Lethem's most confident and most ac-complished book, isn't science fiction at all, and yet it marches right up to the edge of the planet—even as it barely leaves the borough.

See Also: Philip K. Dick has clearly inspired the often treacherous realities in Lethem's fiction, while his startlingly perceptive portraits of adolescent girls recall Shirley Jackson and Carson McCullers.

—*Stephanie Zacharek*

Leyner, Mark
1956–
b. Jersey City, New Jersey

FICTION: I Smell Esther Williams and Other Stories (1983), **My Cousin, My Gas-troenterologist** (1990), ***Et Tu, Babe** (1992), Tooth Imprints on a Corn Dog (stories, 1995), **The Tetherballs of Bougainville** (1997)

The rampant success of Mark Leyner's 1990 book *My Cousin, My Gastroenterologist* on college campuses turned him into that unusual phenomenon, a best-selling experimentalist. Like Kurt Vonnegut before him, Leyner made unconventional prose—in his case, non-narrative, often uncapitalized and strangely punctuated, and hectically imagistic—tremendously appealing to smart young readers by synching it with pop culture and making it very funny. Unlike Vonnegut (who wrote his hits in a more innocent time), Leyner's humor is scaldingly ironic and devoid of pro-social messages. Because his fiction is crueler, it's much funnier, but it also lacks the bemused humanity that makes Vonnegut beloved.

With Leyner, for all his artsy antics, the gag's the thing. Most of his laughs come from the juxtaposition of widely disparate lingos: art criticism with porn, earnest psychological revelation with decor magazine blather, celebrity memoir with pulp thriller, ad copy with scientific exegesis—that later pair a specialty since Leyner once worked as a medical brochure copywriter. ("do you know me," he writes. "my american express card says simply: perishable vertebrate.") A typically grandiose project in one of his stories is "Dino de Laurentiis's production of T.S. Eliot's 'The Love Song of J. Alfred Prufrock,' directed by John Landis who's known for his spectacular special effects, the huge metal robotic women who come and go talking of Michelangelo." Most of his hyperbole, however, is reserved for himself. "I am a terrible god," he announced in *My Cousin, My Gastroenterologist*, and when he turned to parodying his own sudden fame in *Et Tu, Babe*, he described himself as "not your average author. I dress like an off-duty cop: leather blazer, silk turtleneck, tight sharply creased slacks, Italian loafers, pinky ring. I drive a candy-apple red Jaguar with a loaded 9-mm semiautomatic pistol in the glove compartment . . . my life has been one long ultraviolent hyperkinetic nightmare."

Before *Et Tu, Babe*, Leyner's fiction was often so fractured that each sentence had nothing to do with its predecessor; the title of a piece in *My Cousin, My Gastroenterologist*, "Fugitive from a Centrifuge," seems particularly apt. Leyner's voice resembles a radio, with its dial forever turning, picking up random bits of cultural flotsam and jetsam, toying with them for a moment, then moving on. His fans relish his gift for mimicry and knack for capturing the junk-closet aspect of minds raised in a media-saturated world. His later books, in particular, take cheesy, pop-fueled fantasies of masculine mastery to their most ludicrous extremes, making him the satirical Marquis de Sade of the *Playboy* ethos.

Leyner, who originally wanted to be a poet, gave some literary critics a thrill, as well, by promiscuously blending high and low culture and hence embodying the postmodern ideal of pastiche. David Foster Wallace considered him significant enough to single out in his critique of irony and "Image-Fiction" in his essay "E Unibus Pluram: Television and U.S. Fiction" as "hilarious, upsetting, sophisticated and extremely shallow." Leyner's recent books have shown more developed storylines, but he's still a bit like a brilliant, hyperactive child—tremendously entertaining in small doses but exhausting in the long hauls.

See Also: *Leyner's style is quite close to brainy Jewish stand-up comedy, and Woody Allen's fiction seems an obvious cousin. Both Thomas Pynchon and David Foster Wallace weave pop culture and advertising into their also frequently funny novels, with more patently serious intentions and substantial results.*

—Laura Miller

Mailer, Norman
1923–
b. Long Branch, New Jersey

FICTION: The Naked and the Dead (1948), Barbary Shore (1951), The Deer Park (1955), *Advertisements for Myself (stories, essays, etc., 1959), **An American Dream** (1965), Why Are We in Vietnam? (1967), A Transit to Narcissus (1978), **The Executioner's Song** (1979), Ancient Evenings (1983), Tough Guys Don't Dance (1984), Harlot's Ghost (1991), The Gospel According to the Son (1997)

SELECTED NONFICTION: The White Negro: Superficial Reflections on the Hipster (essays, 1957), Deaths for the Ladies and Other Disasters (poems and prose, 1962), The Presidential Papers (1963), Cannibals and Christians (1966), The Pulitzer Prize for Fiction (1967), **The Armies of the Night** (1968), Miami and the Siege of Chicago (1968), Of a Fire on the Moon (1970), King of the Hill: On the Fight of the Century (1970), The Prisoner of Sex (1971), St. George and the Godfather (1972), Marilyn: A Biography (1973), The Faith of Graffiti (1974), The Fight (1975), Some Honorable Men: Political Conventions (1960–1972) (1976), Of Women and Their Elegance

237

(1980), How the Wimp Won the War (1991), Pablo and Fernande: Portrait of Picasso as a Young Man: An Interpretive Biography (1994), Oswald's Tale: An American Mystery (1995), The Time of Our Time (1998)

On an episode of *The Firing Line* broadcast in 1979, William F. Buckley declared Norman Mailer "the most prominent living American novelist," and then "the most notorious American novelist, devoting his time equally to literary production and self-abuse." Or, as Anatole Broyard once put it, "[Mailer's] career seems to be a brawl between his talent and his exhibitionism." For a time, the safe bet would have been exhibitionism by knockout, but now, in the fifteenth round, talent may yet triumph in a split decision.

It has often seemed, in other words, as though Mailer's notoriety would overwhelm his prominence—that the six marriages, the failed campaign for mayor of New York, the fistfights, the wife-stabbing, the disastrous forays into filmmaking, and the political grandstanding would leave a deeper impression than *Why Are We in Vietnam?* or *The Gospel According to the Son*. Mailer's celebrity has been both a burden and a temptation, a distraction from the lonely labor of writing and the source of some of his best work. The luckiest writers ascend gradually to prominence, cultivating their audience as they hone their skills; Mailer was famous at the age of twenty-five, with the publication of *The Naked and the Dead*. Like a child actor, he has since faced the awkward challenge of growing up—or refusing to—in public. Sometimes, therefore, he has confused media attention with historical importance. And sometimes his hubris seems touchingly, charmingly, naive. "If I have one ambition above all others, it is to write a novel which Dostoyevsky and Marx; Joyce and Freud; Stendhal, Tolstoy, Proust and Spengler; Faulkner, and even old moldering Hemingway might come to read, for it would carry what they had to tell another part of the way," Mailer wrote at the end of *Advertisements for Myself*.

Hemingway and the rest, at last report, are moldering still. But if it is easy to ridicule Mailer for failing to realize such an extravagant ambition, it is nonetheless possible to admire him for having had the guts to conceive it and the temerity to confess it. If no other postwar American writer has produced as dazzling and spectacular a series of failures as Norman Mailer, it is because none has dared as much.

Advertisements for Myself begins with a short list of its author's favorite pieces, "for those who care to skim nothing but the cream of each author, and so miss the pleasure of liking him at his worst." The critical consensus is that the cream of Mailer's vast and various oeuvre consists, in chronological order, of *Advertisements for Myself*, *The Armies of the Night*, and *The Executioner's Song*. None of these books is, strictly speaking, a work of fiction: *Advertisements* intersperses stories, magazine articles, and fragments of abandoned novels with extended passages of self-justification; *The Armies of the Night* narrates Mailer's participation in an antiwar demonstration at the Pentagon in October, 1967; *The Executioner's Song* relates, in Balzacian detail, the story of Gary Gilmore, a habitual criminal executed in Utah in 1977. If we define the novel as a hybrid, intermediate form, bounded on one side by journalism and on the other by speculative philosophy, then these books—with their mixture of stubborn empiricism and vertiginous abstraction, their density of detail and complexity of theme—are among the most original and radical novels ever written.

But if we define the novel as a fictional form we encounter a paradox. Mailer is a brilliant journalist and a dogged, if mostly self-taught, philosopher. He is, however, a consistently bad novelist. This is not to say he hasn't produced some good fiction: None of his novels is without pockets of terrific writing, vivid characterization, and narrative dexterity. But Mailer's most successfully executed novels—*The Naked and the Dead*, *Tough Guys Don't Dance*, *Harlot's Ghost*—are curiously unsatisfying. In each, his wilder impulses are checked by the constraints of his chosen genre: the war story, the policier, and the spy novel, respectively. Each one fails to deliver the clean narrative punch these genres demand, and you realize that when he doesn't risk making a fool of himself, Mailer can be something of a bore. And so a second paradox follows from the first: the worse Mailer's novels are, the more pleasure they afford.

By all means, then, skim the cream, but to appreciate Mailer fully you must risk liking him at his worst. His second and third novels, *The Deer Park* and *Barbary Shore*, were widely, and somewhat unfairly, reviled when they first appeared. Neither *The Deer Park*'s attempt to reveal the spiritual corruption of Hollywood nor *Barbary Shore*'s evocation of the political paranoia of the McCarthy era is particularly convincing, but both books have a crude and vivid power that many more polished performances lack. The novel, for Mailer, is less a literary form than an existential gambit, and this is why he is most interesting in triumph or in disaster, and most tired (and tiresome) when playing it safe. So *Tough Guys Don't Dance*, for all its fine evocations of Provincetown and its engaging whodunit structure, is less memorable and less authentic a reflection of Mailer's gifts than the five hundred pages of Pharaonic sodomy that constitute *Ancient Evenings*.

But Mailer's worst novel—the novel whose place in his canon is therefore absolutely central—is *An American Dream*. All of his characteristic preoccupations—Manichean theology, political power, *nostalgie de la boue*, anal sex, and the subterranean connections between them—are on display, knit together in a plot that veers from the incredible to the incomprehensible. Yet the book's chaos seems now to be a vivid and indelible reflection of the disorder of its time and place. It is a work of sublime bravery.

See Also: Because he is Jewish, Mailer is often carelessly grouped with Saul Bellow and Philip Roth. Because he writes about sex, he is sometimes mentioned alongside John Up-

dike. But these writers are much more careful psychological realists than Mailer. Only one of Mailer's contemporaries can legitimately be called his peer: a great novelist who has never written a great novel; a political animal whose politics are an idiosyncratic amalgam of left and right; a writer who has dabbled promiscuously in journalism, movies, and media celebrity; a sexual radical strangely at odds with the sexual revolution. Needless to say, this writer, never one of Mailer's friends, was for a long time his nemesis. Without Norman Mailer and Gore Vidal, American literature in the second half of the twentieth century would not exist; without everyone else in this book, it would.

—A. O. Scott

Malamud, Bernard
1914–1986
b. Brooklyn, New York

FICTION: The Natural (1952), **The Assistant** (1957), The Magic Barrel (stories, 1958), **A New Life** (1961), Idiots First (stories, 1963), **The Fixer** (1966), Pictures of Fidelman: An Exhibition (stories, 1969), The Tenants (1971), Rembrandt's Hat (stories, 1973), Dubin's Lives (1979), God's Grace (1982), **The Stories of Bernard Malamud** (1983), The People and Uncollected Stories (1989), *****The Complete Stories** (1997)

NONFICTION: Talking Horse: Bernard Malamud on Life and Work (1996)

Bernard Malamud's *Complete Stories* is a topological conundrum: an object so much larger on the inside than it appears from without that it should be impossible. The vitality, integrity, and generosity of Malamud's career as one of America's finest story writers isn't an impossibility, though—merely an underappreciated treasure. Explore this marvelous collection to be persuaded of an accomplishment worthy of comparison to the stories of Chekhov, or the great Irishman Frank O'Connor. The best of the seven novels Malamud produced during the same span rival the stories in accomplishment.

Malamud's forms are traditional, his approach scrupulous and self-questioning, his modesty of tone somewhat disguising the glories of his language. His sentences, formed of a deeply American appropriation of Yiddish rhythms and syntax, are magical whatever their subject. Yet Malamud never sacrifices emotional truth for literary effect; his lasting impression on the reader is of a yearning, often tragic, moral presence.

In the 1940s and 1950s Malamud hewed close to his birthright subject as the Brooklyn-born son of immigrant Jews, writing tender tales of poor shopkeepers, tailors, rabbis, and families in mid-century New York. Next, in some of his most acclaimed stories—"The Magic Barrel," "The Jewbird," "Idiots First," and "Angel Levine"—come the fables and fantasies, full of talking animals and angels of redemption or death. In the 1960s Malamud wrote too of teachers and writers and expatriate life in Italy, corresponding to a university career and sabbaticals abroad. Although he presents an endless series of schlemiel-like stand-ins for himself, Malamud's writing isn't baldly autobiographical. His protagonists are regarded with a droll skepticism which averts the painful self-disclosure of, say, Philip Roth.

The Natural, Malamud's first novel and perhaps still his most famous, is an anomaly, his only work devoid of references to Jewish culture. Instead this short, glittering book about a doomed baseball star is crammed with references literary and mythological—particularly Arthurian—and with as much Americana as it can bear. The next is a decisive reverse: The fine and moving novel *The Assistant*, a disarmingly simple tale of a shopkeeper, his daughter, and a hood who becomes shop assistant, is full of Malamud's Brooklyn childhood and centers on his tragic image of the Jew.

Published in 1961, *A New Life*, Malamud's third novel, is an overlooked masterpiece. An academic satire set in a mythical Western American state, *A New Life* includes topical reverberations of McCarthyism, a tenderfoot-goes-West plot evocative of Western movies, and an achingly bittersweet and realistic love story. It may still be undervalued as Malamud's funniest and most embracing novel. The Pulitzer Prize- and National Book Award-winning *The Fixer* is set in Russia, during the revolutionary tumult of the early century, and tells of Jewish handyman—or "fixer"—imprisoned on false charges by an anti-Semitic police state. Despite the heavy historical baggage, the book is personal, searching, even funny—another triumph.

Unfortunately, it was also Malamud's last complete success in the novel form, and oddly, the tendencies which would undermine his remaining attempts are all discernible in *The Fixer*. In that book's prison setting he first displayed his predilection for hopelessly static (or perhaps statically hopeless) situations. These would include: a blocked writer in a condemned building in *The Tenants*, a blocked writer in a failed marriage in *Dubin's Lives*, and the lone survivor of nuclear war in *God's Grace*. Add to this a tendency to unblock that stasis with sudden visionary gestures and a growing weakness for bitter debates with God. But the fables and fantasies which had nicely fed his stories find an uneasy home in these late novels—one detects the sound of a writer trying to persuade himself.

The People and Uncollected Stories, published posthumously, is unnecessary. The lesser stories are better encountered in context in *Complete Stories*, and "The People," a fragment of a novel about a Jewish Indian tribe, is unfinished in every sense, fleshless without the deepening work of revision that was Malamud's method.

If not for this long decline, Malamud would be better recognized as one of America's finest writers. His integrity, dedication to craft (and privacy) are nicely shown in *Talking Horse*, a collection of talks and interviews.

See Also: The forgotten Daniel Fuchs, in his stories of Brooklyn Jews and The Williamsburg Trilogy, *is recommended to admirers of the stories and of* The Assistant *especially. As a classic campus novel of the 1950s,* A New Life *has interesting resemblances to John Barth's* End of the Road. *Otherwise, the expected comparisons to Isaac Babel and Isaac Bashevis Singer are meaningful—but Malamud is so much more American.*

—Jonathan Lethem

Martin, Valerie
1948–
b. Sedalia, Missouri

FICTION: Love (stories, 1977), Set in Motion (1978), Alexandra (1979), A Recent Martyr (1987), The Consolation of Nature and Other Stories (1988), *Mary Reilly (1990), The Great Divorce (1994), Italian Fever (1999)

Valerie Martin is a skeptic who would like to believe, an admirer of commitments whose futility she perceives. The women in her novels—she seldom shows much sympathy for the men—are looking for something to dedicate themselves to; only a couple of the lucky ones have found it.

In *Set in Motion*, a young New Orleans welfare worker who can't feel much of anything looks, unaware that she's doing so, to three men—a drugged-out bartender, a friend's predatory fiancé, and a near lunatic—to break through her shell. (The lunatic finally manages it.) The middle-aged male narrator of *Alexandra* is unmoored, too, until he meets the bohemian beauty of the title and jettisons everything else in his life—it isn't much—to follow her. In both books, a sexual awakening shows the heroine aspects of herself she hadn't seen before.

A Recent Martyr takes the theme farther, contrasting two women, one in the grip of an intense and destructive (and pornographically explicit) affair with a brute of an atheist, the other a novice spending a year outside the convent; the respectful seriousness with which Martin treats this harshly devout young believer no doubt contains a grain of

242

envy. The stories in *The Consolation of Nature* develop these themes while dealing with another fascination of Martin's: animals.

Written in the form of the journal of a loyal young housemaid in the service of Dr. Henry Jekyll, *Mary Reilly* forms a virtuoso pendant to Robert Louis Stevenson's novella. Mary, too, has found salvation through servitude, though hers is a secular devotion. But the more important change the book signals is one of tone. Martin's earlier narrators are cool and somewhat remote; Mary's warm and troubled voice is easy to love.

Ambitious, plotty, and (for all the bleakness of its outlook) good-humored, *The Great Divorce* centers on three women: a veterinarian at the Audubon Park Zoo in New Orleans; a friendless young woman who works as a keeper for the big cats; and a nine-teenth-century murderess. The vet's philandering husband is a cad; the keeper is marginally sane; the murderess's husband (and victim) is a domineering monster. Ellen, the vet, recognizes the futility of trying to save wild creatures from the onslaught of civilization (the title refers to "the breakup of the human species and the rest of nature"), but she struggles along with the frustrated joy of Camus's Sisyphus. Her work sustains her.

Italian Fever chronicles yet another sexual awakening; this time the heroine is an art-loving American divorcée in Italy. Despite the doubts the author expresses here about the ultimate rewards of sex and art, the book has a graceful, lighthearted tone. Martin may be a naysayer, but she's no nihilist; she remains faithful to fiction, after all, and if she has no illusions about what her work, or anyone's, can accomplish, she's still fully aware of its pleasures, and of the world's.

See Also: Those taken with Martin's expertise as a sexual pathologist will also want to check out the fiction of Mary Gaitskill and, in an earlier generation, Mary McCarthy.
—*Craig Seligman*

Matthiessen, Peter
1927–
b. New York, New York

FICTION: Race Rock (1954), Partisans (1955), Raditzer (1961), At Play in the Fields of the Lord (1965), **Far Tortuga** (1975), On the River Styx and Other Stories (1989) *THE WATSON TRILOGY:* **Killing Mister Watson** *(1990), Lost Man's River (1997),* ***Bone by Bone** *(1999)*

SELECTED NONFICTION: Wildlife in America (1959), The Cloud Forest: A Chronicle of the South American Wilderness (1961), Under the Mountain Wall: A Chronicle of Two Seasons in the Stone Age (1962), Sal Si Puedes: Cesar Chavez and the New American Revolution (1969), Blue Meridian: The Search for the Great White Shark (1971), The Tree Where Man Was Born (1972, revised edition 1995), The Snow Leopard (1978), In the Spirit of Crazy Horse (1983), Indian Country (1984), Men's Lives: The Surfmen and Baymen of the South Fork (1986), Nine-Headed Dragon River: Zen Journals 1969–1982 (1986), African Silences (1991), East of Lo Monthang: In the Land of Mustang (1995), Tigers in the Snow (2000)

Before Peter Matthiessen was thirty, he'd served on a ship in WWII, co-founded the *Paris Review*, and abjured literature to captain a charter fishing boat. When that went bankrupt, Matthiessen became a travel writer and naturalist. His work for *The New Yorker* has taken him to the Amazonian hinterlands, turtle-fishing in the Caribbean, and in quest of great white sharks. Matthiessen always gravitates to "endangered ecologies," places hostile to the developed world and the continual pressing in of business and the state.

Matthiessen the significant novelist begins with *At Play in the Fields of the Lord*, a novel famous for the many movie projects that have sprung up around it. In Peru, two mercenaries, Lewis Moon, a half-breed Cheyenne, and Wolfie, his loyal partner, have been hired to attack the Niaruna Indians. Moon's plight is the focus of a sympathy Matthiessen extends to other, more powerfully drawn liminal figures in his later fiction. Reading the novel now, it is hard to overlook its creaky machismo, cartoonish females, and woolly dialogue. Its best parts are set among the Indians, prefiguring the convergence of Matthiessen's interests and artistry in the novels to come.

Far Tortuga, published ten years later, shows an astonishing advance in Matthiessen's art. The author's withdrawal hangs over the novel like a charged atmosphere, creating a tension between what we know of Matthiessen's opinions and his absolute refusal to intervene, to guide us. The novel concerns the last voyage of Captain Raib Avers, an ornery old turtleman who is fishing depleted banks, starts out late with a misbegotten crew, and ends up entangled with some angry Jamaican lowlifes. Each page looks like a poem—five-line paragraphs of abbreviated description, two lines of someone mouthing off, two lines of an answer, another five lines of description, all with the barest of stage directions. What catches the eye or ear is all there is.

Matthiessen's next novel, *Killing Mister Watson*, is based on a true story and told by a dozen Everglade residents at the turn of the century. The enigmatic E. J. Watson—an industrious, bright sugar cane farmer, everybody's friend and at the same time a dangerous man about whom dark rumors swirled—is shot by his neighbors in 1910, ostensibly for murdering his cook and her lover. The book is Matthiessen's crowning work and, like Cormac McCarthy's *Blood Meridian*, taps into brutality as the dark, necessary other of American innocence, the secret sharer of our success.

Killing Mister Watson is the first novel in a trilogy. Unfortunately, neither of the two novels that follow it can match its compulsive, up-close vividness. It was followed by the less focused *Lost Man's River*, in which E. J.'s son, Lucius, at some indeterminate stage of ancientness (the book's sense of when it is placed, exactly, is one of its weak points), tries to find out the truth about his father. The plot creaks with too much to do and too many people to get through. Perhaps disappointment is inevitable. The third novel, *Bone by Bone*, is better. Here E. J. Watson himself is given voice, and one senses how mentally necessary violence is to Watson, how it anchors his identity. However, the trilogy's first book is so perfectly contained that it overshadows its two companions. Writing the sequal to *Killing Mister Watson* is a little like gluing Prospero's wand together again and having a go with a cast of low-rent Calibans in some sequel to *The Tempest*.

See Also: In the first part of Matthiessen's career one can see a similarity of attitude to his friend, William Styron. For the Matthiessen of Far Tortuga *and, particularly,* Killing Mister Watson, Cormac McCarthy *is the author that springs to mind.*

—*Roger Gathman*

Maupin, Armistead
1944–
b. Washington, DC

FICTION: *Tales of the City (1978), **More Tales of the City** (1980), **Further Tales of the City** (1982), Babycakes (1984), Significant Others (1987), Sure of You (1989), Maybe the Moon (1992)

An alchemical confluence of ideal elements—writer, city, and cultural moment—created Armistead Maupin's *Tales of the City*, perhaps the most sublime piece of popular literature America has ever produced. The six books in the *Tales* saga (almost all of which were originally serialized in San Francisco newspapers) are unabashedly frothy; driven by such preposterous plot devices as amnesia, secret identities, providential meetings, and long-lost relatives; and crammed with topical details plucked from San Francisco life in the 1970s and 1980s. Yet they refuse to be simply ephemeral and have the power to soften even the most resolute highbrow or anti-sentimentalist. The devotion of their ever-expanding circle of fans sometimes astonishes even Maupin; he once received a letter from a woman whose brother was buried with a copy of his first book. As with the Beatles, everyone seems to like Maupin's *Tales*—and, really, why would you want to find someone who didn't?

The *Tales* center on a funky apartment house on San Francisco's Russian Hill, presided over by the mysterious, maternal Anna Madrigal, a landlady whose gardening skills (sinsemilla a speciality) are exceeded only by her deftness at intervening in her tenants' muddled lives. The core group includes Mary Ann Singleton, an innocent from Cleveland; Michael "Mouse" Tolliver, a witty, puckish young man searching for Mr. Right; Mona Ramsey, a restless former hippie; and Brian Hawkins, a keen participant in the straight singles scene. Through their adventures, Maupin set out to depict "an elaborate inside joke about the way life worked in San Francisco." The peripheral characters (many based on real San Franciscans) include Valium-addled socialites, closeted movie stars, rock-and-roll widows, and fugitive members of the British aristocracy.

Despite the characters' rueful and frequently baffled quest for romantic fulfillment, there's a giddiness in the very fabric of the *Tales*; it's the rush of liberation, an elixir familiar to any misfit who ever relocated to San Francisco, including Maupin. The author, who remembers himself as an "uptight, archconservative, racist brat" during his Southern youth (he even worked briefly for Senator Jesse Helms), came to San Francisco at the age of twenty-seven and came out of the closet shortly thereafter. His work as a journalist made him privy to all manner of gossip about society high and low, and his participation in the emergence of a new kind of society—a sort of republic of pleasure—fed his desire to write.

The San Francisco depicted in the *Tales* is a place where differences are reveled in rather than just tolerated and where the alienated and the unconventional congregate to form families more loving than the ones into which they were born. At the heart of the early *Tales* are deep friendships between women and gay men, relationships so often unsung or disparaged in real life. Later, as the city staggers under the AIDS crisis (Maupin was one of the first novelists to address the disease), the series portrays the maturing of gay culture in response, and the tone becomes melancholy and nostalgic. In Maupin's only novel outside the *Tales* series, *Maybe the Moon*, another outsider—a dwarf actress—pursues a career in Hollywood. It's a pleasant enough exercise, but it lacks the headlong exhilaration of Maupin's first books.

See Also: Michael Cunningham's A Home at the End of the World *portrays the forging of new families and gay/straight relations in a less pop style than Maupin's. Tom Wolfe similarly combines a shrewd eye for social texture with grabby plotting but, unfortunately, almost no significant characters who aren't straight men.*

—*Laura Miller*

McCarthy, Cormac

1933–
b. Providence, Rhode Island

FICTION: **The Orchard Keeper** (1965), Outer Dark (1968), Child of God (1974), Suttree (1979), *__Blood Meridian, or The Evening Redness in the West__* (1985) **The Border Trilogy:** All the Pretty Horses (1992), **The Crossing** (1994), Cities of the Plains (1998)

Cormac McCarthy, born in Providence, Rhode Island, began his career as a Southern novelist. His first four novels—*The Orchard Keeper*, *Outer Dark*, *Child of God*, and *Suttree*—take place in the hollows and hamlets of eastern Tennessee, where McCarthy made his home until 1974, when he moved to El Paso, Texas. A decade later, with *Blood Meridian*, McCarthy reinvented himself as a Western novelist. An excellent career move: McCarthy, whose earlier work had attracted a devoted but small coterie of readers, became a critical and commercial sensation—the recipient of nearly every major literary award and a staple of the bestseller lists. Reviewers compare him to Melville, Conrad, and Faulkner, and Hollywood studios scramble for the right to bring his episodic, lyrical books to the screen.

The South and the West are regions encrusted with mythology, and McCarthy has been an assiduous student of their literatures. *The Orchard Keeper* and *Child of God* owe an obvious debt to Faulkner, both in the luxuriance of their prose, the occasional obscurity of their narratives, and their brooding, portentous violence. *The Orchard Keeper* is the best of McCarthy's early books because it also picks up Faulkner's most interesting theme: the erosion of a traditional, honor-bound, local way of life by the forces of modernity. But elsewhere, especially in the impenetrable *Outer Dark*, McCarthy jettisons the particularities of history and place in favor of ponderous philosophizing and writing that reads like an unwitting parody of modernism.

At the center of McCarthy's corpus are two enormous, ambitious, and incomparable

247

novels. *Suttree* combines the best and worst of his Southern books with a new element of ribald, folkloric humor. *Blood Meridian*—by any criterion a masterpiece and one of the great American novels of the last quarter century—is an apocalyptic retelling of the Davy Crockett legend. In it, a sociopathic fourteen-year-old called The Kid, sets out from Tennessee sometime in the 1840s and winds up traversing the deserts of northern Mexico with a band of marauding filibusters, killing anything in sight. *Blood Meridian* brings to mind the great Vietnam-era Westerns of Sam Peckinpah. Like *The Wild Bunch* or *Bring Me the Head of Alfredo Garcia*, it lays bare the core of absolute violence that lies beneath the mythology of the West. It offers an indelible portrait of what D. H. Lawrence called "the essential American soul": "Hard, stoic, isolate, and a killer."

John Grady Cole, the hero of *All the Pretty Horses* is, by contrast, hard, stoic, isolate, and a crybaby. *Horses*—which along with *The Crossing* and *Cities of the Plain* comprises The Border Trilogy—brought McCarthy a mass audience. While these books have their share of brutality and difficult language, they are in every way more accessible and less challenging than *Blood Meridian*. That novel unflinchingly stripped away the layers of sentimentality and romance that had adhered to the brutal history of the West; *All the Pretty Horses* reapplied them, turning away from Peckinpah and going back to Howard Hawks and John Ford.

The writing in these books is uneven. Some parts read like bad Hemingway, others like bad Hemingway retranslated from the Spanish. The plots meander and sometimes run aground on shoals of metaphysical mumbo jumbo. But the books are full of arresting passages of description, and unexpectedly moving evocations of the relationships between men and animals. The first section of *The Crossing* in particular, which tells of the doomed, passionate bond between a boy and a wolf, is as good as anything McCarthy has written.

It's hard to blame McCarthy, who labored so long in obscurity, for turning to sentimental, crowd-pleasing cowboy fiction. But the appeal of The Border Trilogy may prove to be ephemeral, just as McCarthy's earlier novels will most likely survive as curious footnotes to a career whose central and enduring achievement continues to be *Blood Meridian*.

See Also: Most recent serious fiction coming out of the South and the West has been committed to a debunking, stripped-down realism, as if to compensate for the sentimentalism of the past. Writers like Wallace Stegner and Larry McMurtry explicitly intended to correct the mythologizing tradition of Zane Grey and Louis L'Amour. McCarthy's work cuts squarely against this realist vein, and so demands to be placed in two traditions at once: The popular Western tradition and the Southern modernist tradition. And yet, if you read far enough back, these traditions converge in the work of James Fenimore Cooper, who is, at his best and worst, McCarthy's true precursor.

—A. O. Scott

McCracken, Elizabeth

1966–
b. Boston, Massachusetts

FICTION: Here's Your Hat What's Your Hurry (1993), *The Giant's House (1996)

Set in 1950s Cape Cod, Elizabeth McCracken's touching and deeply eccentric first novel, *The Giant's House*, is about two loners—a shy, misanthropic young librarian and the tallest boy in the world—and their doomed romance. It's a mature, loopily engaging novel that displays the full range of McCracken's talents: her barbed wit; her knack for aphorisms; and her uncanny ability to tap into the sadness that runs through the center of her character's worlds.

Herself a former librarian, McCracken fills *The Giant's House* with meditations on that orderly, spinsterish profession. (The narrator feels less like a woman "than a piece of civic furniture, like a polling machine at town hall, or a particularly undistinguished WPA mural.") Yet *The Giant's House* doesn't have a mannered or predictable bone in its body. McCracken's almost giddy affinity for these misfits, and for their unlikely passions, illuminates every page. She's written a love story for people who've given up on love.

Here's Your Hat What's Your Hurry, McCracken's first collection of stories, explores many of the same themes. In "It's Bad Luck to Die," for example, a young woman marries a much older tattoo artist who fills up her skin and makes her feel whole for the first time. Other stories are about life's strays who are invited into ostensibly "normal" families. "McCracken is a true romantic, not the sloppy, gushy kind who lie to themselves," the novelist Katherine Dunn has written, "but the robust, ferocious romantic who sees reality with all its chinks, twitches, and zits, and finds it beautiful." Which just about says it all.

See Also: The eccentricity and passion in McCracken's work may put some readers in mind of the short stories and novels of Lorrie Moore.

—Dwight Garner

249

McDermott, Alice

1953–
b. Brooklyn, New York

FICTION: A Bigamist's Daughter (1982), **That Night** (1987), **At Weddings and Wakes** (1992), *Charming Billy (1998)

Like Britain's Penelope Fitzgerald, McDermott is a master of the exquisite miniature. Most of her novels come in at two hundred pages or fewer, and by these less-is-more standards, her National Book Award-winning novel, *Charming Billy*, is a tome. Within such compressed boundaries, McDermott's prose feels chiseled of stone, made to last, extracting great emotion from a mere unexpected turn of phrase or a character's hesitation before speaking. What is not said, of course, speaks volumes. McDermott's narrative strategy is to rearrange time sequence and spiral again and again around several life-defining moments. "That seems to me to be true to our experience," she has said. "You don't look at the past just once. You look at it with the knowledge of the present . . . I like that going over, seeing it again and seeing it in another way."

McDermott's debut in 1982 was auspicious enough. *The Bigamist's Daughter*, a novel about a love affair between a novelist and a cynical editor at a vanity press, was greeted warmly by Anne Tyler and other reviewers. But it was *That Night* that really wowed the critics. Set in suburban Long Island in the early 1960s, the novel tells of teenage love gone wrong. The author's moral vision and innovative story-telling method transform the story from soap opera to mesmerizing meditation on the loss of innocence, social and personal. *At Weddings and Wakes*, also set in the early '60s, observes the ritual visits of the Irish-Catholic Daileys of Long Island to their grandmother and maiden aunts in Brooklyn. Hints of quarrels, misunderstandings and hope destroyed clog the air, giving the novel an atmosphere of cramped, claustrophobic misery. But the tensions are so understated and so elegantly drawn that turning aside is impossible.

Charming Billy may not in fact be a better novel, but it is surely a less devastating lancing of boils. Though Billy Lynch appears only briefly, he is so winning a storyteller, so sweet a sentimentalist, that he provides a warmth that *Wakes* could not afford. But he has drunk himself to death, and family and friends, gathered for his wake, form a chorus both lighthearted and rueful. Set in New York City's outer boroughs and eastern Long Island, the novel examines with devastating clarity the delusions of daydreams, the limits of community, and the self-deception behind the boozy smile.

250

See Also: Besides Penelope Fitzgerald, Mary Gordon, whose Catholics in Final Payments *are more formally religious than McDermott's, but the guilt is similar. Gordon's* The Other Side *is a bitter and beautiful Catholic generational saga.*

—*Dan Cryer*

McElroy, Joseph
1930–
b. Brooklyn, New York

FICTION: **Smuggler's Bible** (1966), Hind's Kidnap: A Paraphrase (1969), Ancient History (1971), **Lookout Cartridge** (1974), **Plus* (1976), **Women and Men** (1987), The Letter Left to Me (1988)

Championed by critics during experimental fiction's heyday in the 1960s and 1970s, Joseph McElroy's self-reflexive novels never quite connected with the audience that made fellow meta-men like John Barth and Robert Coover campus favorites. Perhaps it was his comic touch, which was far drier and less eager to punch up the joke than that of his peers. While others tricked up their narrative self-consciousness with satiric high jinks, McElroy took the meta-enterprise quite seriously—his fiction doesn't wink at you to say, "It's all a game." For him the mechanics of storytelling are a pathway into the heart of human perception.

Plus, a science fiction-inspired novel, features a disembodied human brain orbiting the Earth in a capsule. Although set up only to monitor a photosynthesis experiment, the organ gradually develops a consciousness of its own. McElroy's prose gains in vocabulary and grammar as this brain begins reconnecting to its memories; the result is a bildungsroman of a mind, a "Bringing Up Brainy" in which varieties of language—technical, punning, authoritarian—serve as nutrition.

McElroy jettisoned this linear approach in his massive *Women and Men*, a maximalist tome that hopes to embrace the wild connectivity of life—how everything and everyone seem inextricably webbed—in the late twentieth century. Focusing on two New York apartment dwellers who never quite meet, the novel expands outward even as it deepens its close-quarters look at the fragmented self. Like many of McElroy's novels, its plot (or lack of one) cannot be recounted; these are books best experienced rather than described.

251

See Also: Other members of the metafiction gang such as William Gass, William Gaddis, John Barth, Robert Coover, Thomas Pynchon, and Don DeLillo will all supply the similar kick of serrated smarts and bookish gamesmanship. Gaddis in particular shares McElroy's fascination with the convolutions of human exchange.

—Albert Mobilio

McEwan, Ian
1948–

b. Aldershot, England

FICTION: First Love, Last Rites (1975), In Between the Sheets and Other Stories (1978), **The Cement Garden** (1978), The Comfort of Strangers (1981), *The Child in Time* (1987), The Innocent (1990), Black Dogs (1992), Enduring Love (1998), **Amsterdam** (1999), The Daydreamer (stories, 2000)

From his eerie, early beginnings, Ian McEwan has written fiction that gets under the skin. In novels whose range has broadened and deepened over the years, the English writer has explored the tension between the calm, rational surface on which we generally live, and the dark, underlying furies that threaten to disrupt it.

McEwan's first collections of stories, *First Love, Last Rites* and *In Between the Sheets*, established him as a cool chronicler of the macabre: They included incidents of infanticide and pederasty, and—along with his first novel, *The Cement Garden*, in which an incestuous brother and sister bury their dead mother in the garden—earned him a reputation as a writer out to shock. McEwan unnervingly combined intelligent, almost affectless prose with an uncanny, unexpected, often sexualized violence—also seen in his novella of two dangerously intertwined couples in Venice, *The Comfort of Strangers*.

In 1987 McEwan published *The Child in Time*, which seemed to signal a new, hopeful phase in his work. It centers on a more familiar, domestic horror: the abduction of a couple's three-year-old daughter. Written after McEwan had himself become a parent, the novel is suffused by a warm humanism in contrast to its sinister, futuristic Thatcherite society. There's a poignancy in McEwan's description of the couple's attempt to sustain their love in the face of their loss (a struggle echoed in McEwan's more recent novel *Enduring Love*, in which a loving couple fractures under the pressure exerted by an obsessive male stalker). *The Child in Time* introduced themes and strategies which

NOVELS, NINE TO FIVE: FICTION ABOUT WORK

by Ian McEwan

For obvious reasons, the world of work—so defining in most lives—is rather underrepresented in literary fiction. However, there are some honourable, and even brilliant, excursions.

Rabbit at Rest by John Updike
   The car salesman. The longeurs and the accountancy deceits are beautifully wrought. Rabbit's shafting by Toyota rep, Mr. Shimada, defines a time in the 1980s of American industrial nervousness.

Towards the End of the Morning by Michael Frayn
   The journalist. Frayn is perhaps England's greatest comic writer. Grubby, compromised hacks haven't been done better since Waugh's *Scoop*. (The book was also published with the title *Against Entropy*.)

The Black Cloud by Fred Hoyle
   The astronomer. A huge entity hovering near earth turns out to be a colossal intelligence. It's completely unimpressed by our civilisation; some Beethoven sonatas hold its attention for a while.

Body and Soul by Frank Conroy
   The musician. A wonderful evocation of a young man's mastery of the technique of the classical piano. Conroy is a fine jazz player, with a highly regarded "walking" left hand.

Life Before Man by Margaret Atwood
   The paleontologist. The mind of a scientist neatly inhabited, while the chosen field of the heroine offers some useful, extended metaphors for sexual complication.

would reappear in McEwan's later work: the interweaving of scientific ideas (in this case about time) into the story; and the difference between a rational, masculine approach to problems and a more intuitive, feminine approach. With 1990's cold war thriller *The Innocent*, McEwan returned to butchery: The novel's subtle complexities get lost in the sensational horror of a central scene in which Leonard and his German lover Maria accidentally kill her violent husband and then dismember the body to hide the evidence.

What humanizes even McEwan's most sadistic novels, though, is his surprisingly feminist sensitivity to the ways men and women relate; his acute (if chilling) awareness of the ruthless determinations of masculine desire; and his way of viewing important political events through the eyes of his characters, whether it's the fall of the Berlin Wall in *Black Dogs* or the corruption and hypocrisy of Tory ministers in *Amsterdam*. The latter won Britain's Booker Prize, and has some typically brilliant descriptions, here of composing music and the internecine battles of journalism. It also has a characteristic weakness: an overschematized plot. McEwan's writing is itself a kind of paradox: His novels are compulsively "easy" to read, but invariably leave the reader feeling uneasy.

See Also: McEwan is considered one of the "big three" of English writers—along with Julian Barnes and Martin Amis. He writes far less flamboyant and comical prose than his friend Amis, and as a result, perhaps, creates more recognizable and sympathetic characters. Some of Graham Swift's novels, especially Waterland, *share McEwan's combination of erotic fascination and a peculiarly English melancholy.*

—*Sylvia Brownrigg*

McGrath, Patrick
1950–
b. London, England

FICTION: Blood and Water and Other Tales (1988), The Grotesque (1989), *__Spider__ (1990), **Dr. Haggard's Disease** (1993), **Asylum** (1997)

Although the old-fashioned elements of Gothic fiction—huge, crumbling, remote houses; mysterious deaths; buried secrets; madness; obsession—fill British novelist Patrick Mc-Grath's contemporary forays into the genre, his intentions seem decidedly modern. A master of the unreliable narrator (all his novels are told in the first person), this British novelist wants to play around with our contradictory desires to believe in and yet also get beyond the voice that so insistently relates *his* version of the story. And, at least in McGrath's longer works, it's always a he who tells us the tale, because the author also wants to gnaw away at the roots of traditional authority like one of those rats behind H. P. Lovecraft's walls.

McGrath's first book, a collection of short stories, experimented with some of the more overtly theatrical trappings of the Gothic—dwarves, severed hands, vampires—but in his first novel, *The Grotesque*, he settled into a more psychological formula. The gruff, arrogant, and now utterly paralyzed Lord Coal, of a decrepit manor house called Crook, fulminates helplessly over the devilish doings in his once-serene estate, all of which can be traced back to the scheming butler Fledge . . . or can they? In McGrath's third novel, *Dr. Haggard's Disease*, a limping, morphine-addicted physician grandly mourns the loss of his great love . . . until her grown son materializes and awakens Dr.

254

Haggard's propensity to delusion, calling even his memories into question. In 1997's *Asylum*, a psychiatrist pens the case history of the former wife of a mental hospital superintendent, a woman who ran off with one of her husband's inmates . . . but the psychiatrist's report seems to be concealing his own interest in the affair. Repressed sexuality and guilt roil just beneath the surface in all three.

Putting aside the issue of whether doctors, novelists, and other revered authorities truly deserve our trust, McGrath's novels often read like elegant, gloomy games. There's humor and irony in second-guessing the fellow supposedly in charge (and perhaps something Oedipal as well; McGrath grew up on the grounds of a hospital for the criminally insane where his father was a medical superintendent), despite the grim fates awaiting most of the characters, because they all seem like remote objects of study even when they're whispering in our ears. Only *Spider*, McGrath's second novel, has the tenderness to make doom really hurt. The schizophrenic narrator (just returned from twenty years in "Canada"—more likely an asylum) may have dispatched the tart who seduced his father into murdering his mother, or he may have done something even worse. What's obvious from the beginning, though, is Spider's touching fragility, and his valiant struggle to hold onto a reality that's dissolving all around him. McGrath's own experience working in mental hospitals shows in the meticulously observed crumbling of Spider's mind, and so does a compassion the author restrains in his other books.

See Also: Both Vladimir Nabokov and Edgar Allan Poe specialized in untrustworthy narrators like McGrath's.

—Laura Miller

McGuane, Thomas
1939–
b. Wyandotte, Michigan

FICTION: The Sporting Club (1969), **The Bushwhacked Piano** (1971), *Ninety-Two in the Shade (1973), **Panama** (1977), Nobody's Angel (1982), Something to be Desired (1984), To Skin a Cat (stories, 1986), Keep the Change (1989), **Nothing but Blue Skies** (1992)

NONFICTION: Silent Seasons: Twenty-One Fishing Stories (1988), An Outside Chance: Essays on Sport (1980), Live Water (1996), Some Horses (essays, 1999), The Longest Silence: A Life in Fishing (1999)

Critics tend to peg the novels of Thomas McGuane as warmed-over Hemingway, a dim though understandable reduction. Like Hemingway, McGuane sets much of his fiction in the wilds of Michigan, the Upper Rockies, and the Florida Keys; vigorously masculine, his protagonists fuss, fight, fuck, and fish (occasionally on the very same day); and, too, he shares with Papa a flagrant and tenderhearted passion for dogs, horses, trout, mountains, streams, and tough, almost-but-not-quite-unattainable women. Beyond these, however, there are few likenesses. The world Hemingway invented was an austere one: So long as a man obeyed a strict set of codes, life was more or less a metaphysical no-brainer. In McGuane's world, there are no such codes—or rather, none worth accomodating. Digging out the truth of life means razing the old rules. The difference is played out in every sentence. Hemingway's prose—cool, clean, and ice pick-sharp—reflected his austerity. McGuane's prose glimmers with the opposite.

It glimmers most conspicuously in McGuane's earlier novels—*The Bushwhacked Piano*, *Panama*, and *Ninety-Two in the Shade*—books bursting with the sort of piquant wisecracks, Dadaist dialogue, and madcap linguistic hijinks that prompted Saul Bellow to christen McGuane a "language star." One protagonist describes his grandfather's failed whorehouse/comedy emporium as follows: "He carried things too far. Seltzer bottles. Custard pies. No one goes to a whorehouse for that! They can stay home and watch the Three Stooges. And the girls got tired of it the minute the pies started flying. They always had colds from the Seltzer." In *Panama*, a retired rock star—famous for crawling out the ass of a frozen elephant on stage—nails his hand to the door of his estranged lover as a token act of affection. Barmy episodes like these are commonplace in McGuane's early fiction, when he was dabbling in excess and glitz: hobnobbing with rock stars, ingesting all manner of liquids and powders, and marrying and divorcing—quick as a wink—the actress Margot Kidder. Ultimately, it was slow down or die, and McGuane opted for the longer road.

"I'm trying to remove the tour de force or superficially flashy side of my writing," he admitted to an interviewer while at work on *Nobody's Angel*, his first novel after toestepping on the abyss. Sans the weird, raucous luster, some readers complained that McGuane was just another nifty, aging guy writing about nifty, aging guys. Other readers, however, found a greater depth, a more tenable humanity, in the less acrobatic McGuane. Thematically, he hadn't veered too far: In *Something to be Desired*, *To Skin a Cat*, *Keep the Change*, and *Nothing but Blue Skies* his protagonists are still seeking the true grain of American life, feuding against the "declining snivelization" of modern culture—existential bumblers trying one way or another to wrench themselves free of banality, even if it entails ditching the codes. Like Gogol, he can make you laugh aloud with a sentence, and, with the next, smash your heart into little red pieces.

See Also: Both McGuane and his longtime pal Jim Harrison rail against an America pervaded by greed and chicanery: Harrison with autumnal gravitas, McGuane with a sort of jaundiced cackle reminiscent of J. P. Donleavy, Barry Hannah, and Padgett Powell. Thematically, McGuane has much in common with fellow bird-hunter Richard Ford.

—Jonathan Miles

McInerney, Jay
1955–
b. Hartford, Connecticut

FICTION: Bright Lights, Big City (1984), Ransom (1985), *****Story of My Life** (1988), **Brightness Falls** (1992), The Last of the Savages (1996), Model Behavior (1998)

Jay McInerney's first novel, *Bright Lights, Big City*, was one of those books that, at a certain moment, everybody seemed to be reading. It was funny and deftly written, and it seemed to capture the way its audience—white, moderately sophisticated college students or recent graduates—saw themselves, or wanted to see themselves. The hero, a fact-checker at a starchy New York magazine, has vague literary aspirations and a vocation for substance abuse, and is referred to only as "you." Whether you loved *Bright Lights* or hated it, if you were between eighteen and thirty-five in the middle of the 1980s you could hardly escape it.

In the decade and a half since *Bright Lights*, McInerney has written five more novels which either struggle to transcend his first or settle for rewriting it. The rewrites, while they inevitably fall short of the original, are better on the whole than the attempts to break new ground. *Ransom*, the trivial story of a young American living in Japan, lacks the knockabout comedy and bravura swoops from cynicism to sentimentality that are the signature of McInerney's

257

mature style, and the novel feels portentous and callow. McInerney is never more glaringly superficial than when he tries to be profound.

Luckily, in the underrated *Story of My Life* he returned to the Manhattan demi-monde of dissolute bond traders and debutantes squandering their trust funds on cocaine. Narrated by Alison Poole, a sometime acting student and full-time sexual adventurer, *Story of My Life* may be McInerney's most impressive formal accomplishment: He manages to convey both intelligence and pathos through the voice of a character who is almost willfully inarticulate and devoid of affect.

In *Brightness Falls*, a novel set at the time of the stock market "correction" of October 1987, McInerney tried to broaden his perspective. But his attempt to answer Tom Wolfe's *Bonfire of the Vanities* showed McInerney to be more competent as a novelist of manners than as a large-scale urban realist. *Last of the Savages*, which follows the friendship between an uptight lower-middle-class New Englander and a free-spirited Southern aristocrat from prep school, is at once McInerney's most ambitious novel and his laziest. The narrative is haphazard, the characters flat, and the writing uncharacteristically graceless.

McInerney's most recent book, *Model Behavior*, is either a return to form or a surrender to formula. Its hero has vague highbrow pretensions, a hereditary taste for the sauce, and shares with the protagonist of *Bright Lights* the tragic condition of having been dumped by a fashion model. The seven short stories tacked on to this slim novel are worth the price of the volume. They show McInerney at the top of his form, and offer the strongest evidence yet that he may eventually live up to his early promise.

See Also: Bright Lights, Big City *arrived on the scene alongside Tama Janowitz's* Slaves of New York *and Bret Easton Ellis's* Less Than Zero. *The fact that so much of McInerney's work deals with addiction and recovery makes him one of the unacknowledged godfathers of 1990s confessional nonfiction.* Story of My Life, *for instance, is in its way the forerunner of books like Caroline Knapp's* Drinking: A Love Story *and Elizabeth Wurtzel's* Prozac Nation.

—*A.O. Scott*

McMillan, Terry
1951–
b. Port Huron, Michigan

FICTION: **Mama** (1987), **Disappearing Acts** (1989), ***Waiting to Exhale** (1992), How Stella Got Her Groove Back (1996)

Bookstores had never before been home to anything like Terry McMillan's tour to promote her 1992 novel, *Waiting to Exhale*. Her appearances attracted mobs of ardent female fans. And when she performed passages from her book, the stores turned into call-and-response arenas, with women standing up to testify to their feelings and shout out their likes and dislikes. This was one writer who had hit a nerve. (Inexplicably, the listless 1995 movie adaptation stirred up audiences as effectively as the book had.) A soap opera about four black women in Phoenix—their jobs, their hair, their two-timing, no-good men, etc.—the book is one of those innumerable women's novels in which friends, through all their ups and downs, check in with each other periodically, and together and alone watch life's cycles wheel by. In white hands these days, this is almost always a spent form. With her bawdy humor and unashamed pride in achievement—and with her relish for fleshly and material pleasures—McMillan brought it rousingly back to life. There aren't many middlebrow page-turners that offer anything like her frankness and sass.

Her success retriggered a still-running controversy about whether or not black women writers beat up on black men. (They often do, and sometimes do so entertainingly). It also alerted the publishing industry to the existence of a large group of underserved readers hungry for fiction in which they could see their own lives. The industry responded promptly, and, since then, works from what might be called the "You go, girl!" school of fiction (Bebe Moore Campbell, J. California Cooper) have become a staple in bookstores and on bestseller lists.

McMillan's first two novels—*Mama* and *Disappearing Acts*—are also lively airplane reads. (Avoid her most recent effort, the dizzy *How Stella Got Her Groove Back*, unless your appetite for breathlessly narcissistic gab is really epic.)

See Also: If you're in the market for something similarly female and full-bodied, try the marvelous Lee Smith, who writes lyrically about white mountain folk, or that sturdy entertainer Susan Isaacs, who writes humorous mysteries about Long Island Jews.

—Ray Sawhill

259

McMurtry, Larry

1936–
b. Wichita Falls, Texas

FICTION: **Horseman, Pass By** (1961), Leaving Cheyenne (1963), **The Last Picture Show** (1966), **Moving On** (1970), *****All My Friends Are Going to Be Strangers** (1972), Terms of Endearment (1975), Somebody's Darling (1978), Cadillac Jack (1982), The Desert Rose (1983), Lonesome Dove (1985), Texasville (1987), Anything for Billy (1988), Some Can Whistle (1989), Buffalo Girls (1990), The Evening Star (1992), Streets of Laredo (1993), Pretty Boy Floyd (with Diana Ossana, 1994), Dead Man's Walk (1995), The Late Child (1995), Zeke and Ned (with Diana Ossana, 1997), Comanche Moon (1997), Duane's Depressed (1999)

NONFICTION: In a Narrow Grave: Essays on Texas (1968), It's Always We Rambled: An Essay on Rodeo (1974), Film Flam: Essays on Hollywood (1987), Crazy Horse (biography, 1999), Walter Benjamin at the Dairy Queen: Reflections at Sixty and Beyond (1999)

Once among the most ambitious writers of his generation, Larry McMurtry wrote a series of novels in the 1960s and 1970s that defined the territory where the myths of the Old West collided with the uncertainties of the New. The first, *Horseman, Pass By*, is an unsparing portrait of Texas ranch life; his second, *Leaving Cheyenne*, brings a similar sensibility to a love triangle between a woman and two men. Perhaps the best known of these early works is *The Last Picture Show*, which deftly evokes the faded community of Thalia, Texas, a thinly veiled stand-in for Archer City, McMurtry's hometown. Yet just as impressive are the trio of related novels that followed—*Moving On*, *All My Friends Are Going to Be Strangers*, and *Terms of Endearment*. Here, McMurtry expanded his vision, finding in urban Houston a psychic landscape not unlike Yoknapatawpha County, where recurring characters like Patsy Carpenter and Emma Horton drift from book to book.

McMurtry writes from the perspective of women with a depth and believability that few male authors can approach, and from *The Last Picture Show* to *The Late Child*, it's hard to think of a McMurtry book where a woman doesn't play a central role. It's as if, to reconstruct the landscape of modern Texas, McMurtry chose to write about women in order to look beyond the region's macho stereotypes.

So it's ironic that, for most readers, McMurtry's signature novel is the Pulitzer Prize-winning *Lonesome Dove*, an epic of the Old West and the beginning of a long period of retrenchment for McMurtry. The saga of a nineteenth-century cattle drive, the novel is notable for going back on its author's claim—articulated with savage eloquence in his nonfiction work *In a Narrow Grave: Essays on Texas*—that the classic cowboy story is nothing but a cultural cliche. *Lonesome Dove* became the cusp of McMurtry's career, after which each subsequent title has seemed less and less authentic.

McMurtry appears to recognize this problem; of late, he's devoted much of his attention to a second career as an antiquarian bookseller. "I've written enough fiction," he told *The Texas Monthly* in 1997. "I have one more novel I'd like to write." The novel, most likely, is *Duane's Depressed*, which completes the trilogy begun with *The Last Picture Show* and *Texasville*. That's not to say McMurtry intends to stop writing; he's just published his fourth nonfiction book, *Crazy Horse*, a brief biography that seeks to reimagine another Wild West icon on its author's terms. But whatever direction he may tend towards in the future, it is McMurtry's early work that will stand as his most enduring legacy, a testament to a region in search of itself.

See Also: Readers compelled by the scope of McMurtry's early work would do well to seek out William Faulkner, who, with his linked narratives and interplay of characters, does for the South what McMurtry aspires to do for the American West.

—David L. Ulin

Millhauser, Steven
1943–
b. New York, New York

FICTION: *Edwin Mullhouse: The Life and Death of an American Writer, 1943–1954, by Jeffrey Cartwright** (1972), Portrait of a Romantic (1977), **In the Penny Arcade: Stories** (1986), From the Realm of Morpheus (1986), The Barnum Museum: Stories (1990), Little Kingdoms: Three Novellas (1993), **Martin Dressler: The Tale of an American Dreamer** (1996), The Knife Thrower and Other Stories (1998), Enchanted Night (1999)

There are few American writers writing today who give readers more pleasure page for page than Steven Millhauser—and none who go about it in a stranger way. With his classic American prose style and low-key narrative clarity, he would have made a natural realist (and garnered himself a larger readership), but instead, the writer, who teaches at Skidmore College, chose the path of the anti-realist.

There are two distinct periods in his work. Critics, noting his fondness for games and imaginary worlds, often characterize Millhauser as Borges's American cousin, our own homegrown fabulator, but this simplifies things. Millhauser began as a complex parodist. His first book was *Edwin Mullhouse: The Life and Death of an American Writer, 1943–1954, by Jeffrey Cartwright*. This strange and remarkable work, published in 1972 and still Millhauser's finest, is the story of eleven-year-old Jeffrey's relationship with his classmate, who went with dizzying speed from comic book enthusiast to great novelist, only to commit suicide shortly after. The book has elements of spoof ("Third grade surprised me: I had not anticipated desks"), but goes beyond, showing a lively and malicious wit. By the end we strongly suspect that the genius of the story is the narrator himself, who found, manipulated, and all but executed a hapless Mullhouse in order to accomplish his own literary goals.

One can point to the divide in Millhauser's work with rare exactness. On page eighteen of his third novel, *From the Realm of Morpheus*, the narrator chases a baseball out of the suburbs that had been Millhauser's chosen setting up to that point and into a thicket that leads into the underworld. Millhauser has never come out. Nickelodeons, waxworks, fortune tellers, tiny life-like mechanical figures, and protagonists who run up against the boundary between reality and replication are now his subject. At first this change cost Millhauser his following, but with *Martin Dressler: The Tale of an American Dreamer*, Millhauser's first novel in a decade and the winner of the Pulitzer Prize, he was "rediscovered." Martin Dressler begins as a Horatio Alger–bootstrap tale. The eponymous protagonist displays the necessary energy and unctuousness to work his way up from cigar store helper to hotel bellboy. Now he gains access to capital, buys the hotel he works in, and begins to build new ones, each more ambitious. With success come infinite resources and the revelation of the flinty businessman's artistic side. His *pièce de résistance* is the Grand Cosmo, an entire world in a hotel with elaborate live-action fantasies—the Pleasure Park, the Palace of Dreams, the Moorish Bazaar. The public rejects this—it is too complex for them—and Dressler is left to ask whether genius and commerce can coexist. The reader is left to unpack the metaphor behind this brilliant, tightly wound story.

262   *See Also: If Millhauser appeals to you, there are two ways to go: into the gothic thickets of Jorge Luis Borges and Italo Calvino back through Poe or into the mainstream of suburban American prose realists: John Cheever, John Updike and, more recently, David Leavitt and Ethan Canin.*

—*D. T. Max*

Moody, Rick

1961–
b. New York, New York

FICTION: Garden State (1992), *The Ice Storm (1994), The Ring of Brightest Angels Around Heaven (1995), **Purple America** (1997)

The standard complaints about Rick Moody's fiction—that it's chilly, and that he overwrites—are valid enough. But if you listen closely to his best work, you'll begin to pick up in his prose what Alfred Kazin once described as "the marginal suggestiveness which in a great writer always indicates those unspoken reserves, that silent assessment of life, that can be heard below and beyond the slow marshaling of his thought." Moody's first novel, *Garden State*, is about middle-class kids in New Jersey who seek solace in sex and rock music after almost everything else in life has failed them. It's an awkward book, dotted with nice moments, that nonetheless announced his signal themes—surburban anomie and the difficulties of identifying (and then living up to) the responsibilities that life hands you.

Set in an affluent Connecticut suburb in 1973, Moody's second novel, *The Ice Storm*, is his best, bravest, and most emotionally nuanced book: He strides into Cheever territory and nearly walks away with the deed. *The Ice Storm* plays out over the course of one single, hectic night. As a freak snowstorm bears down on them, the Hood family (Benjamin, the alcoholic father; Elena, his detached wife; Wendy, a fourteen-year-old with raging hormones; and Paul, a stoner) finds itself coming unglued. Moody nails not only the small details—the shag carpets, the bookcases larded with *The Sensuous Woman* and *Jonathan Livingston Seagull*, the Cover Girl Thick Lash mascara—but the larger ones as well. Richard Nixon's bad faith has trickled down; the book's multiple infidelities feel like a subset of a national moral malaise. The book's most famous chapter, about a "key party" that Benjamin and Elena attend—men drop their keys into a bowl, and go home with whichever woman fishes them out—is a masterful set piece.

Moody's two most recent books, the short story collection *The Ring of Brightest Angels Around Heaven* and the novel *Purple America*, are more hit-and-miss. Moody's short fiction is angular and energetic (the subjects include heroin addicts, an engineer who works as an expert witness in personal injury cases, and an actor who survives a car crash), yet it rarely feels fully grounded. The most unexpected and winning piece in *Brightest Angels* might be the final story, "Primary Sources," which is an annotated bibliography of the writer's own life. Like *The Ice Storm*, *Purple America* takes place over

263

the course of one night. It's about what happens when a stammering thirty-eight-year-old man-child gets called home to suburban Connecticut to care for his ailing mother after she is abandoned by his stepfather. In alternating chapters, Moody climbs into each of these character's heads, and he provides a good deal of fine, feeling writing about what he calls "the arrhythmia of desperation." For all of the Updikean brilliance of Moody's prose here, however, the novel lacks Updike's confidence and streaming ease. Moody writes the hell out of *Purple America,* and it contains some of the most gloriously un-buttoned writing to be found in the 1990s. Occasionally, though, the book's title seems all too apt.

See Also: Moody's angular, millennial take on surburban life allows you to return, with fresh eyes, to the work of John Cheever and John Updike.

—*Dwight Garner*

Postmodernism Without Pain

By Rick Moody

As the novelist and critic William Gass has observed, "postmodernism" is not a very efficient term in any discussion of fiction. Who'd want to read anything by such an ungainly name? Who can blame readers for looking for their lead aprons when postmodernism comes to town? Moreover, what seems most postmodern in literature—reflexivity, self-consciousness, playfulness, exhaustion, disenfranchisement—seems to have characterized fictional narrative from its outset, in the wobbling points of view in the New and Old Testaments, in the unusual assembly of narrators in Virgil's *Aeneid,* in the porous relationship between fictional characters and political and religious celebrities in *The Divine Comedy,* in Rabelais and Sterne and Swift and Carroll and Stein and Woolf and Joyce.

So implicit has experiment been to narrative as an enterprise that, in an informed historical continuum, even the most realistic writers—Flaubert, Joyce, Hemingway, later Carver, Frederick Barthelme, Ann Beattie, Mary Robison—are revealed as experimentalists. This is a long way of saying that if what is really important about narrative has been its protean qualities, its shape-shifting, then it is worth lauding and magnifying the names of some of the writers whose experimental motivations or strategies are or have been uppermost in their accomplishments. I'm thinking especially of the experimental writers of the late 1960s and 1970s: John Barth, Donald Barthelme, John Hawkes, Robert Coover, Stanley Elkin, Angela Carter, William Gass, and William Gaddis. None of these writers has achieved the cultural status that he or she deserves, as their fellow travelers Pynchon and DeLillo have managed to do, but they have managed each to turn out astonishing prose works in the decades since the Second World War.

Some examples:

In John Barth's case, we have the excellent early work, an admixture of the conventional novel with some folklorically enriched mythology, *The Floating Opera* and *The End of the Road*, as well as a splendidly multifarious story collection, *Lost in the Funhouse*, and the ambitious later novels much suffused with Scheherazade and the tales of the Arabian nights, *The Sot-Weed Factor*, *Chimera*, and *Giles Goat Boy*.

In John Hawkes's work, there is an early period of astonishingly surreal inventiveness—not really like much else in all of the world of literature (Hawthorne and West might come closest, though Hawkes is without their ameliorating light)—featuring the almost total exclusion of "plot, setting, theme, and character," as the author himself once boasted. I'm thinking especially of his first novel, *The Cannibal*, set in an imaginary postwar Europe that feels more than a little bit like *Mad Max*'s sere postnuclear topographies, as well as the short novels *The Lime Twig*, *The Beetle Leg*, and his finest later work, *Second Skin*.

At the same moment, as Hawkes and Barth began their incantations, Donald Barthelme was taking the short story further than anyone had before (with the exceptions of Kafka and Borges), finding opportunities for renovation, for spontaneity and improvisation that will likely take a generation to surmount or circumnavigate: in which the narrator is suddenly again in elementary school; in which Robert F. Kennedy is saved from drowning; in which a jazz saxophonist competes for the monarchy of his instrument, and so forth. The best spot to begin, for newcomers, is Barthelme's greatest-hits sampling, *Sixty Stories*, but the informed reader might also try *Unspeakable Practices, Unnatural Acts*; *City Life*; or the aptly named *Sadness*; as well as his Dada-esque longer narrative, *Snow White*, which doesn't have too much to do with dwarves.

Robert Coover's work too has featured a preternatural variety of successes, from the awesome anticlerical thunder of his first novel *Origin of the Brunists* (concerning a Southern religious cult that springs up in the wake of a mining disaster), to the exciting and singular narrative experiments of his short fictions in *Pricksongs and Descants*, much of the work concerned with desire and its vicissitudes. The best known of these ditties, "The Babysitter," a compendium of all possible outcomes of a certain night out for a suburban couple, is among the finest American works published in the 1960s. And unlike some of his peers from the period, Coover's work has remained preternaturally inventive right up to the present, especially in *Gerald's Party*, *The Public Burning*, and *Spanking the Maid*.

In Stanley Elkin's oeuvre, the author's initial development was slower, but ultimately a period evolved of such consistency and fertility (*The Dick Gibson Show*, *The Franchiser*, *Searches and Seizures*, *The Living End*, *George Mills*) that Elkin's novels stopped seeming like novels at all, rather like installments, recumbent each against another, of some longer, more sustained comic investigation of voice. Likewise, William Gass, in the oscillation between fiction and essay, between practice and theory, also honed his voice until there was none other like it—an elegant, catalogue-drenched aesthetics-obsessed style that reached its apex in his long, difficult, psychological novel *The Tunnel*, in which an American history professor, in a dazzling multifary of typefaces and diagrams and expostulations, faces down an intellectual crisis.

Hovering over this American movement is, I might mention last but not at all least, William Gaddis, whose arrangement of narrative and dialogue and subliterary forms (the legal briefs in *A Frolic of His Own*, the art historical themes and fraudulences of his first work, *The Recognitions*), serves, in many ways, as the blueprint for the so-called experimental fiction of the 1960s and 1970s. From the first sentence of his published output—"Even Camilla had enjoyed masquerades, of the safe sort where the mask may be dropped at that critical moment it presumes itself as reality"—Gaddis's work was self-evidently at a remove from the work of writers like Roth and Mailer and Bellow and Updike—his coevals—in the way it foregrounded the artifice of the novel.

We should also include Angela Carter, who, on the other side of the Atlantic, brought an acute understanding of folk tales as well as of science fiction and fantasy, into such novels as *The Passion of New Eve*, her collections of stories, *The Bloody Chamber*, with its recurrent werewolves, and *Saints and Strangers*. Likewise her singularly overpowering work of nonfiction, *The Sadeian Woman*.

What connects all of this work, beside the fact of mutual influence (Elkin and Gass were close friends and both taught at Washington University in St. Louis; Hawkes and Coover were close friends and both taught at Brown, where they later hired Angela Carter, etc.), is sheer linguistic prowess, the sense that "more is more," as Elkin once said.

Where much realistic fiction has trafficked in the notion that the narrative voice should be restrained and nonjudgmental, this work is loud, exhibitionistic, partisan, demonstrative, excessive, like the culture from which it mostly derives. These are writers for readers with ears, writers for readers who are used to the predations of franchise restaurants, rock and roll, talk radio, fire-and-brimstone fundamentalism, political assassinations, performing twins, arbitrage.

With the so-called postmodern writers (which might also include any number of Eastern European and Latin American writers, as well as contemporary voices like Susan Sontag, Grace Paley, Ishmael Reed, William S. Burroughs, Jonathan Baumbach, Toby Olson, Alexander Theroux, Joseph McElroy, Ronald Sukenick, Stephen Wright, Pynchon, DeLillo, etc.), fiction crested in its cultural impact, as it also exhausted an epistemological inquiry into what the novel was. Writers of my generation were lucky to have come of age in this moment, when so many people loved to read, loved what literature offered, and loved language-loving language.

What does using "postmodernism," the technical term, do? What mischief does it enact? It blanches out a form that is all about play, all about the excitement and uncertainty of form. It overlooks the possibility that there can be joy in experiment, in language used for its own sake, overlooks the recognition that this joy (and its attendant emotional tonalities) can be just as moving as naturalistic fiction's payoffs. But even my partisan screed clutters up the fiction of the 1960s and 1970s by taxonomy and vivisection. Want to know why I love this work, and why you will too if you read it? Because the world outside becomes gray so quickly, because there's nowhere to go downtown (except to buy jeans), because the movies all have numbers after them. Imagination and language are tireless revolutionaries. They take the base metals of this world and spin them into something else altogether. Find out for yourself.

Moore, Lorrie
1957–
b. Glens Falls, New York

FICTION: **Self-Help** (stories, 1985), Anagrams (1986), **Like Life** (stories, 1990), Who Will Run the Frog Hospital? (1994), *Birds of America** (stories, 1998)

Lorrie Moore's characters confront the erosion of their marriages and relationships, cancer, middle age, and general disillusionment, but Moore's edge, often savage, is always softened by (or at least filtered through) her famous wit, which is not just clever or smirk-worthy. Because she does it when you least expect it, she can make you do that rare thing: laugh out loud.

Moore's protagonists do not have interesting resumes. Quiet, white, middle-class sorts, they teach at community colleges, browse cheese samples at malls, talk to their friends on the phone, have lost or are losing their parents, and eat alone in their apartments. Primarily female, they're attached to distant or dim-witted men who provide them with creature comforts and little else. From *Like Life*'s "Joy": "For a short time she mourned him, believing he anchored her, had kept her from floating off into No Man's Land, that land of midnight cries and pets with many little toys . . . She knew there were only small joys in life—the big ones were too complicated to be joys when you got all through—and once you realized that, it took a lot of the pressure off."

The nine short stories in Moore's first collection, *Self-Help*, are all told in the second

GUIDED TOURS OF DYSTOPIA   *by Lorrie Moore*

The Handmaid's Tale by Margaret Atwood
Although feminine experience is dystopian in most of Atwood's comic novels, here the dystopia is futuristic, unfunny, highly and chillingly designed.

White Noise by Don DeLillo
From Hitler Studies to a poisonous global cloud: Everything in this bleak satire has come true. Which means, I guess, that it was true to begin with. In 1985 its publisher called it "prescient." (How did they know?)

Fiskadoro by Denis Johnson
A beautiful, curious book with a magical, almost incantatory prose style. As with so many futurist visions, human survival involves lonely self-negation.

Paradise by Toni Morrison
Masculine, socioeconomic blight meets feminist sanctuary. The narrative here works from several different (tragic) angles simultaneously. It is a complicated addition to Morrison's ongoing commentary on African-American life.

Galapagos by Kurt Vonnegut, Jr.
The world as we know it is destroyed. But this is an excellent thing. Humans survive by evolving smaller not larger brains. This is the dystopia novel as coolly angry comedy. Its epigraph is Anne Frank's shattering "In spite of everything, I still believe people are really good at heart."

person and in the "how-to" vein, from "How to Be an Other Woman" to "How to Talk Like Your Mother." Its twenty-ish women face the fading of the illusions they've held about their parents and the possibilities of their own lives. The novel *Anagrams* is actually a cycle of stories, each about Benna and Gerard, whose relationship changes slightly in each segment. Constant throughout, though, is Benna's adorable six-year-old daughter: cute, clever, and one slowly realizes, imaginary.

In *Like Life*, another collection—and stronger than her first—Moore taps a similar vein, while refining her skills and perfecting her sensibility. Her second novel, *Who Will Run the Frog Hospital?*, shows Moore at her gentlest, a small, elegiac book about two fifteen-year-old girls growing up in the Adirondacks. Though the writing is as gorgeous as ever, a maybe-too-wistful affection for her young heroines blunts her edge. Coming-of-age delicacy leaves little room for her barbed wit.

With the bestselling *Birds of America*, Moore returned to darkly comic form, working at the very height of her powers, broadening her range, and taking risks both stylistically and personally. In addition to Moore's women, there's a road-tripping gay couple, a middle-aged, much-divorced male, and, for the first time, a story that's clearly autobiographical: "People Like That Are the Only People Here." In it, two parents learn that their toddler has cancer and are tossed headlong into the world of pediatric oncology. The story assembles virtually all of Moore's themes—the perfection of children, the plodding struggle of marriage, the absurd manifestations of human decay, usually in the form of cancer—all leavened by a gallows humor that, here more than anywhere else, is startling given the horrific context.

See Also: Antonya Nelson has a relatively similar grip on doomed relationships and treats the subject with wit; as do Pam Houston, Louise Erdrich, Deborah Eisenberg, and maybe Anne Lamott, who has a heart as big as Moore's, though has perhaps a bit less sophistication.

—*David Eggers*

Morrison, Toni
1931–
b. Chloe Anthony Wofford in Lorain, Ohio

FICTION: The Bluest Eye (1970), *Sula (1973), **Song of Solomon** (1977), Tar Baby (1981), **Beloved** (1987), Jazz (1992), Paradise (1998)

NONFICTION: Playing in the Dark: Whiteness and the Literary Imagination (1992)

Sula—I'm talking about the character here, not the novel—would have winced at the sentimental streak running through *Beloved*, Toni Morrison's best-known book. Sula is bad news, a skeptical fatalist, an idle, amoral artist, an accident so sure to happen it doesn't bother waiting. But she's my favorite; and she lights up Morrison's second novel like a torch. She's a good part of the reason why I insist that *Sula*, the skinny, 174-page novel, is Morrison's masterpiece.

Beloved—I'm talking about the novel here, not the character, who's really just a ringer from *The Exorcist*—is something of an icon, a bit like Morrison herself, the unassailable Nobel laureate, supremely confident in herself as a woman, a black woman, and a black woman writer. *Beloved* is a "contemporary classic," a big book with a colossal subject: slavery. Who wants to knock it? Not me,

because in fact it's beautiful, rich, fierce, harrowing. A damn fine book. But also sentimental. Why should uplift and overripe prose poems clog a novel about a runaway slave willing to slaughter her own children, including her newborn baby, rather than be dragged back to captivity, children in tow?

In *Beloved*, Morrison strains to remind us of goodness and love, as though she feels she has to counter the world's gross tonnage of evil. So we have a white girl busy saving Sethe's life (Sethe the runaway slave, half-dead, hugely pregnant); the white girl chatters all the while about how "Sleeping with the sun in your face is the best old feeling." And we have two of Morrison's specialties, food and sex, served up luscious enough to make us forget all that looming horror. Here, for example, the erotic version of corn-on-the-cob: "How loose the silk. How quick the jailed-up flavor ran free . . . [N]o accounting for how that simple joy could shake you."

I can already hear a grad-school clever argument about how Morrison binds food and sex and the monstrosity of slavery in one tangled life-like whole, but that doesn't change a thing. The music swells, Sula winces.

Morrison began with a bone-dry book, *The Bluest Eye*, about a little black girl raped by her father and driven mad by her yearning for blue eyes, epitome of the white world's ideal of beauty. A sad and bitter story, choked by too many voices, it contains passages as lovely as anything Morrison has written—but it's a minor work in a minor key.

Then comes *Sula*, the story of two little girls, best friends, who grow up very different in "the Bottom," the black neighborhood of a small Ohio city. Sula and Nell are bouncing with life, vividly real but also emblematic. Sula becomes the radical individualist, Nell the pillar of the community, steady, maternal, dutiful. Morrison weaves her tale with just three strands, a place and two families, but she seems magnificently omniscient, as though she had access to the pooled insight of every sociologist, every psychologist, every anthropologist; as though she had solved the riddle of what holds society together, what holds the solitary self together—and what blows it all apart. Though packed with comic scenes and brilliantly inventive, *Sula* ends on a note of rich, full-throated sadness. There's plenty of laughter in the Bottom, but only visiting white folk manage to "hear the laughter and not notice the adult pain that rested somewhere under the eyelids, somewhere under [the] head rags and soft felt hats . . . . [T]he laughter was part of the pain."

Song of Solomon—another marvel, a rambling tale, almost picaresque, freer and more daring than *Sula*, though less precise, less perfect—follows a callow young man's slow steps to redemption. If *Sula* is about self and community, *Song of Solomon* is about self and family. Hints of the fantastic in the first two novels—folklore, and the maybe-magic of myth—blossom here. The ordinary takes wing: Our hero flies.

The weakest of Morrison's novels is *Tar Baby*, a dubious jumble set in the Caribbean, featuring a white candy magnate, his black servants, their beautiful niece, and an ugly cruelty inflicted years ago. Morrison's first extended excursion into the heads of white folk. Only for the loyal fan.

Beloved wiped the slate clean and beckoned, with the same gesture, the august attentions of the Swedish Academy. After which, of course, a disappointment: *Jazz*, a curiously dispassionate, plotless love story set in Harlem in the 1920s. A teenage girl, an older man, and his jealous wife generate some bizarre domestic violence. In the background, the threat of race riots.

Another kind of violence powers *Paradise*: The defensive violence of black people intent on protecting their community. Ruby, Oklahoma, is an all-black settlement founded in 1950, a patriarchy, fortress of righteousness, a prosperous, peaceable community. Persecuted by whites, shunned by lighter-skinned blacks, the people of Ruby have shut out the white world. A few miles from Ruby is the Convent, nun-less since 1970, a shelter of sorts for women, most of them battered and abused, some black, some white. There is no structure to life at the Convent, no rules, no authority. It is an anti-community, a kind of anarchist's paradise. In 1976, the misguided men of Ruby, who think of the Convent as a witches' coven, stage a deadly raid.

The narrative is choppy and needlessly confused, but Morrison's message comes through loud and clear: No haven can be heavenly, no home can smack of paradise, if it begins with exclusion or thrives by triage—some in, some out, some damned, some saved. Morrison is agitating for the abolition of us versus them.

As a storyteller Morrison combines a poet's grace, a radical's fervor, and a great preacher's moral majesty. She writes for and about the African-American community ("If I tried to write a universal novel," she once claimed, "it would be water"). And yet she reaches us all.

See Also: Nobody who "writes like" Morrison is anywhere near as good as she is. If you're after other African-American writers, try James Baldwin or John Edgar Wideman (avoid Alice Walker). If you're after nuanced treatment of racial issues, try Nadine Gordimer. If you just want a novel as good as Sula, *try* The Great Gatsby *or* Billy Budd.

—Adam Begley

Mosley, Walter
1952–
b. Los Angeles, California

FICTION: **Devil in a Blue Dress** (1990), A Red Death (1991), White Butterfly (1992), *Black Betty** (1994), R.L.'s Dream (1995), Gone Fishin' (1997), A Little Yellow Dog (1996), Always Outnumbered, Always Outgunned: The Socrates Fortlow Stories (1998), Blue Light (1998), Walking the Dog (1999)

Walter Mosley has amassed an array of heavy-duty admirers over the course of a comparatively short career; his most famous fan, Bill Clinton, could have read an adulatory review of *A Little Yellow Dog* by Yale literary critic R.W. B. Lewis in *The New York Times*. The most critically lauded mystery writer since Ross Mac-Donald, Mosley has used his renown to expose the conundrums of American racial politics. Escaping the bounds of genre, he's also tried his hand at cultural criticism, allegorical social realism (*Always Outnumbered, Always Outgunned*), and even science fiction (*Blue Light*, a disappointingly hippie-dippy start to a trilogy-long Octavia Butler impression).

Mosley's Easy Rawlins novels form the core of his achievement. Taking snapshots of black and white L.A. every four years or so from 1948 on (*Yellow Dog* takes place in 1963), the series signifies on the detective-fiction canon and discovers crevasses of experience—and new histories altogether—that Philip Marlowe never cared to contemplate. (In fact, Mosley repeatedly rewrites the classics: *The Maltese Falcon*'s famous "Flitcraft parable" in *Devil in a Blue Dress,* or Chandler's "Red Wind" in *Black Betty*.) Mosley's Everyman, Easy Rawlins, does his best to find a rough approximation of justice in a world where black men can never assume that the principle applies to them. A case study in success on the sly, Easy sneakily becomes prosperous, slowly assembles a ramshackle family of his own, and repeatedly gives in to his carnal appetites—all the while fighting for ethical perspective with his old friend, the terrifying Raymond "Mouse" Alexander, an amoral killer who lets loose every desire that Easy keeps pent up.

What makes these novels so appealing to literati is neither their plotting (as clotted as prime Chandler) nor their depiction of action, which did develop from the men's-magazine exclamation points of Mosley's early books to a lyrical and understated narrative flow. Instead, it's Mosley's careful attention to character and setting, his tracing of the slow crumble of a once-vibrant community into a wasteland of addiction and despair. *Devil*, for example, depicts Watts in 1948 not as a burned-out urban core but as a thriving paradise for the black working class. Mosley combines his sense of history with an equally powerful romance of the color line—the real "devil" in his first novel—a cultural barrier continually trespassed by the unmastered forces of the human heart. That ability to fold racial, social, and personal politics inside compelling narrative makes Mosley more a tragedian than a genre writer.

Still, his best work has come within the mystery genre. *R.L.'s Dream* resonates less powerfully than it intends, and *Blue Light* is disappointingly muzzy. The linked short story collection *Always Outnumbered*, on the other hand, makes redemptive poetry of the brute realities of survival. Mosley's speculative fiction is intriguing, but at the moment his work is best approached through the entire Easy Rawlins series.

See Also: Dashiell Hammett and Raymond Chandler are essential to understanding Mosley resonances. Chester Himes's Harlem novels of the 1960s furnish another part of Easy's backbone, as do John Edgar Wideman's Homewood trilogy and the magic-realist questioning of the color line in Charles Johnson and Octavia Butler. James Sallis's underappreciated, laconically poetic Lew Griffin novels take a similar vantage on the world.

—*Jesse Berrett*

Mukherjee, Bharati

1940–
b. Calcutta, India

FICTION: The Tiger's Daughter (1972), **Wife** (1975), Darkness (stories, 1985), **The Middleman and Other Stories** (1988), *Jasmine (1989), The Holder of the World (1993), Leave It To Me (1997)

SELECTED NONFICTION: Days and Nights in Calcutta (with Clark Blaise, 1977), The Sorrow and the Terror: The Haunting Legacy of the Air India Tragedy (with Clark Blaise, 1987), Political Culture and Leadership in India (1991), Regionalism in Indian Perspective (1992)

Few writers cover the collision of Third and First World better than Bharati Mukherjee. Born to a sheltered, Brahmin family, educated in urban Calcutta and grassy Iowa, her life's project seems to be the literary manifestation of culture shock. In Mukherjee's world, characters eat bagels in saris; farmers bring curry to potluck dinners; emmigrants immigrate, immigrants emigrate, and the "the megascale diaspora," as the author has described her characters, discover that not all border crossings deliver them to terra firma.

From the beginning, Mukherjee has maintained a tacit autobiographical presence in her fiction. *Tiger's Daughter*, her first novel, introduces Tara, freshly returned to Calcutta after four semesters at Vassar. (As in most Mukherjee novels, the geo-cultural oscillations—Poughkeepsie/Punjab, Flushing/Formosa, Buffalo/Bengali—are always dazzling.) Tara quickly discovers that India, with its poverty and corruption and her father's plans for an arranged marriage, no longer seems appealing. In her exponentially better second novel, *Wife*, Mukherjee presents Dimple Dasgupta, the faithful village wife who must accompany her husband to the strange world of Queens, where, in her first week, she is drummed out of a Kosher deli for requesting cheesecake. In both books, wives address husbands by their surnames and learn new languages (and about love) by watching American soap operas.

After writing *Wife*, Mukherjee moved from Iowa to Canada (with her husband, the writer Clark Blaise), before returning to New York, where she became an American citizen. During this scattered time, she turned to the short story. Her first collection, *Darkness*, is considerably less interesting than her second, *The Middleman and Other Stories*, winner of the 1988 National Book Critics Circle Award and her first mature work. In *Middleman*, Mukherjee finally distances herself from a tendency toward bathos, and turns to the more unexpected avenues of multiculturalism. "A Wife Story," opens as an Anglo-Indian woman suffers in an audience howling at anti-Indian "Patel" jokes; in the masterpiece "The Management of Grief," a Canadian Air India flight disaster is the backdrop for the rapprochement between a Hindu widow and a Muslim couple who've lost their sons.

Mukherjee then turned "Jasmine," a *Middleman* story, into a novel about a young woman's harrowing journey from rural India to the American Midwest; in its expansive scope and effortless touch, this book remains her finest work. *The Holder of the World*, in which a modern-day "asset-hunter" tells the story of a seventeenth-century Salem woman who becomes a Hindu raja, however, is turgid, under-dramatized, and unconvincing. Her most recent novel, *Leave It to Me*, finds Mukherjee returning to her strengths. It concerns the foul-mouthed Debby DiMartino (formerly Devi Dee), a felonious Indian adoptee from upstate New York who uncovers the dark secret of her heritage. In many respects, Debby/Devi is the perfect metaphor for Mukherjee's mission: an exile fleeing both Old World and New.

See Also: *For a more masculine, less colloquial take on similar subject matter, see the towering epics of V. S. Naipaul and the essays of Ved Metha. Amy Tan deals with similar aspects of Chinese-American culture.*

—*Andrew Essex*

Munro, Alice
1931–
b. Wingham, Ontario, Canada

FICTION: Dance of the Happy Shades (stories, 1968), **Lives of Girls and Women** (stories, 1971), Something I've Been Meaning to Tell You (stories, 1974), Who Do You Think You Are? ([published in the U.S. as The Beggar Maid: Stories of Flo and Rose], stories, 1978), The Moons of Jupiter (stories, 1982), The Progress of Love (stories, 1986), **Friend of My Youth: Stories** (1990), *****Open Secrets** (stories, 1994), Selected Stories (1996), The Love of a Good Woman (stories, 1998)

Recognition came quickly to Alice Munro in her native Canada, where she won prizes for her first two books. But it wasn't until the late 1970s, when her stories started appearing in *The New Yorker*, that she came to be acknowledged in the U.S. as an author of the first rank. (The magazine provided her, she says, with her "first experience with serious editing.")

All along, for those keeping track, she had been proving herself a delectably inventive short story writer. In the past decade, her tales have become evermore ingenious, growing dizzyingly elastic in structure and complex in tone without losing any of their immediacy. It also helps that Munro is the slyest of humorists.

Munro territory is small town Ontario, where she grew up, and urban British Columbia—Vancouver and Victoria—where she spent her young adulthood (she now divides her time between Ontario and Vancouver Island). Her recurrent thematic concerns are generational and class conflict, marital malaise and breakup, youthful alienation from home and subsequent reconnection with the past, and the vulnerability of the flesh to both sexual mayhem and debilitating illness—big subjects, often twined into narratives of extraordinary economy. Munro has shown a keen sense of place, and a still keener psychological acuity, from the start. In the beautiful and often droll linked tales of *Lives of Girls and Women*, she winningly captures every last nuance of small-town experience through the eyes of an adolescent narrator who sees her neighbors' and family's lives as "dull, simple, amazing, unfathomable—deep caves paved with kitchen linoleum."

Munro's other fiction similarly weaves the "unfathomable" into the mundane, while vividly conjuring "the shameful, marvellous, shattering absurdity with which the plots of life, though not of fiction, are improvised" (as a tipsy babysitter, in deep trouble, puts it in "An Ounce of Cure," from *Dance of the Happy Shades*). In cases where extraordinary events—betrayal, murder—take place, the narrative momentum springs less from the events themselves than from the way they resonate over a lifetime. The dream-logic of the mind in reverie is essential to this process. Firm resolutions remain elusive or illusory, and mysteries—such as the disappearance of a teenage girl in the title story from *Open Secrets*—are ambiguously expanded upon, rather than explained away.

Still, Munro never loses sight of the seductive commotion of ordinary human affairs. In 1994's *Open Secrets*, her finest book, her stories become novel-like in their sweep, encompassing whole lifetimes. Each tale plays with chronology and point of view before alighting on an image or phrase that animates the whole picture and lets it shimmer, whether it's of a Canadian woman tracking down her absconded lover to Brisbane, Australia (in "The Jack Randa Hotel"), or the random, ricocheting conquences of a librarian's clandestine correspondence with a World War I soldier (in "Carried Away"). The book's range of settings is eclectic, covering everything from an 1850s Ontario homestead ("A Wilderness Station") to a rural Albania that seems to exist somewhere outside time, but has a most unlikely connection with a 1960s Victoria bookstore ("The Albanian Virgin").

A key pleasure of Munro's stories is the precision with which they evoke changes in social climate, especially when it comes to sexual mores. Counterculture waywardness, or its hangover, wreaks havoc in the early story "Forgiveness in Families," and the more recent "Save the Reaper." Her greatest gift is for showing how glimpsed possibilities—a career ambition, a blinding infatuation—transform themselves into personal histories: ineffable mixtures of gossamer and grit, suffused with the sensation of a life "falling forwards" (as the runaway wife experiences it in "The Children Stay," from *The Love of a Good Woman*). Few writers can catch that headlong motion on the page as Munro does.

If there's any shortcoming in Munro's opus, it is in her working and reworking of autobiographical material to the point where it loses a little of its surprise—although the quality of her writing rarely diminishes. The trick is to take her as she's published, one book at a time, with three or four years between each collection's appearance. And with *Open Secrets* and *Lives of Girls and Women*, this quibble simply doesn't apply. Both are masterpieces, written to last.

See Also: Munro admirers will want to investigate the early Eudora Welty and the linked stories of The Golden Apples. *Two contemporary short story writers working under a Munro influence, and to splendid effect, are David Long and Linda Svendsen.*

—Michael Upchurch

Murdoch, Iris
1919–1999
b. Dublin, Ireland

FICTION: Under the Net (1954), The Flight from the Enchanter (1956), The Sandcastle (1957), **The Bell** (1958), A Severed Head (1961), An Unofficial Rose (1962), **The Unicorn** (1963), The Italian Girl (1964), The Red and the Green (1965), The Time of the Angels (1966), **The Nice and the Good** (1968), Bruno's Dream (1969), **A Fairly Honorable Defeat** (1970), An Accidental Man (1971), The Black Prince (1973), **The Sacred and Profane Love Machine** (1974), A Word Child (1975), Henry and Cato (1976), *****The Sea, the Sea** (1978), Nuns and Soldiers (1980), The Philosopher's Pupil (1983), The Good Apprentice

277

(1985), The Book and the Brotherhood (1987), The Message to the Planet (1989), The Green Knight (1993), Jackson's Dilemma (1995)

SELECTED NONFICTION: Sartre: Romantic Rationalist (1953), The Sovereignty of Good over Other Concepts (essays, 1970), The Fire and the Sun: Why Plato Banished the Artists (1977), Acastos: Two Platonic Dialogues (1986), Metaphysics as a Guide to Morals: Philosophical Reflections (1992), Existentialists and Mystics: Writings on Philosophy and Literature (1997)

Despite the topicality of many of Iris Murdoch's large, extravagantly crowded and ambitious books, she was the last of the great nineteenth-century novelists. When asked to name the writers who had most influenced her, she listed Dickens, Dostoyevsky, and Tolstoy, "wise moralistic writers who portray the complexity and the difficulty of being good." Like them, she was fascinated by how society warps or challenges one's ideas about morality and believed that only those who learned from their suffering, who actively embraced the good, could discover some true, enduring sense of individuality and purpose.

She liked to work on a large canvas. She filled many of her twenty-six novels with a hefty cast of vivid, eccentric, garrulous characters and hectic, melodramatic subplots. Often using a quest (for knowledge, lost love, or the answer to some violent, mysterious event) to set the action in motion, she wrote with a furious energy shared by few of her contemporaries, turning out a novel every two years, as well as plays, essays, and several ambitious philosophical works.

It was her fourth novel, *The Bell*, set in a lay religious community, in which her distinguishing qualities clearly emerged. The book relates how the effort to hang a new bell in an Anglican convent inspires a variety of efforts to pursue—or flee from—spiritual or profane love. There's a good deal of introspection: Murdoch's characters are nothing if not reflective. She was fascinated by groups (religious, occult, artistic) willfully isolated from the larger society, finding that such self-absorbed gatherings threw the dynamics and essentials of human behavior into bold relief. As in many of her novels, a mythical event frames the contemporary action. In this case, it's the history of the convent's original bell, which is said to have flown from its tower many centuries before when a nun was revealed to be having an affair.

The quest for love is at the heart of many of Murdoch's novels, including the somber *The Italian Girl*, the richly allegorical *The Unicorn*, and the farcical *A Severed Head*. In an essay on the nature of fiction she argued that love, along with art, allowed one to escape the isolation of the self, and that love, art, and the practice of a moral life all served

278

to press home the vital idea that "something other than oneself is real." Love is, in fact, "the discovery of reality."

It is never enough, Murdoch suggested, to know what is right if one doesn't act on it. John Ducane, the protagonist of *The Nice and the Good*, is a decent man with a rather simplistic idea of good and evil as two quite separate entities. When he is ordered to investigate the death of a colleague, he discovers a shabby conspiracy involving betrayal, blackmail, and even a version of the occult. His attempt to penetrate these mysteries leads him to realize that a one-dimensional sense of morality is useless, even dangerous. Wisdom, in part, begins with the realization that we are admixtures of good and evil.

There are, however, some figures in Murdoch's universe who are thoroughly evil, displaying an active, motiveless malignity. Foremost in the gallery is Julius King, of *A Fairly Honorable Defeat*. A scientist doing research on biological weapons, King (in part to win a bet about the fragility of relationships) wreaks havoc in the lives of those around him. He lies, forges letters, cruelly manipulates friends and acquaintances, and even has a hand in the destruction of a civil servant writing a (too unreflective) book about the nature of goodness. In the end, some relationships do weather King's efforts, and some fragile sense of good endures. King, unpunished and unrepentant, continues to thrive.

A different kind of evil is at work in *Bruno's Dream*, in which the dying protagonist looks back, with blinding self-pity, over his own life. Even the contemplation of death cannot free him from his self-absorption. Ironically, several of those around him are led to realize the redemptive power of love—and thus lifted out of their isolation—by the harsh example of Bruno's death.

Charles Arrowby, the protagonist of *The Sea, the Sea*, is blinded by a false vision of love and by considerable hubris, bred by his years of success in the British theater. Murdoch, in what is perhaps her best novel, deftly mixes many of her central themes (the redemptive power of art, the liberating effect of true love, the cautionary impact of death on our imaginations) in a rich, swift narrative tracing Arrowby's hard struggle to accept responsibility for his own actions and to differentiate between self-deluding and selfless love.

Critics often complained that Murdoch substituted ideas for characters. In fact, in her later novels (such as *The Book and the Brotherhood* and *The Message to the Planet*) the contemplation of ideas did often take precedence over action or the creation of fully realized characters. But at her best Murdoch, trained as a philosopher, demonstrated a unique ability to pose essential questions about existence within the boundaries of diverse, moving plots, and to create odd, memorable, entirely convincing characters. The importance of ideas in her work, the crucial impact that they can have in intensifying happiness or diluting despair, is bracing. At their best, her characters have a Dickensian vibrancy, and her plots feature an almost joyous embrace of melodrama, of the unforeseen and the unpredictable. She also often demonstrated a sly, ferocious wit, a quality not usually identified with philosophers. Standing defiantly outside the modernist mainstream, she produced a body of work that is powerful, idiosyncratic, deeply meditative, and—like the work of her nineteenth-century models—exuberantly entertaining.

See Also: Part of the tonic appeal of Iris Murdoch's work is that she so often doesn't seem like any other writer. However, John Fowles often displays a Murdochian appetite for stirring a variety of challenging ideas into his narratives. A. N. Wilson shares with Murdoch a fascination with middle-class life, large casts, and broad melodrama, and A. S. Byatt has demonstrated a Murdoch-like love of complex plots, secret passions, and for fashioning startling metaphors for the act of creation.

—Richard E. Nicholls

Naipaul, V. S.
1932–
b. Chaguanas, Trinidad

FICTION: The Mystic Masseur (1957), The Suffrage of Elvira (1958), **Miguel Street** (stories, 1959), *A House for the Mr. Biswas (1961), Mr. Stone and the Knights Companion (1963), The Mimic Men (1967), A Flag on the Island (stories, 1967), In a Free State (1971), Guerrillas (1975), A Bend in the River (1979), **The Enigma of Arrival** (1987), **A Way in the World** (1994)

NONFICTION: The Middle Passage: Impressions of Five Societies (1962), An Area of Darkness (1964), The Loss of El Dorado: A History (1969), The Overcrowded Barracoon and Other Articles (1972), India: A Wounded Civilization (1977), The Return of Eva Perón (1980), A Congo Diary (1980), Among the Believers: An Islamic Journey (1981), **Finding the Center** (1984), A Turn in the South (1989), India: A Million Mutinies Now (1990), Beyond Belief: Islamic Excursions Among the Converted Peoples (1998)

Over a forty-year career, Vidiadhar Surajprasad Naipaul has been feted as one of the finest living writers in the English language, nabbing all the main literary prizes in Britain—where he has lived since the age of eighteen—and attaining knighthood in

1990. His fiction, and the travel writing he increasingly focuses on, have made him perhaps the West's chief literary interpreter of Third World societies. Yet he remains hugely controversial—especially in the countries of Asia, Africa, and the Caribbean about which he writes. While few question the elegance of his fastidious, pellucid prose, many quarrel with the truth of his vision. Among his distinguished detractors have been the Nobel laureates Derek Walcott and Nadine Gordimer, Edward Said, Caryl Phillips, Chinua Achebe, George Lamming and Raja Rao.

Naipaul's early fiction was set in Trinidad, the Caribbean island where he was born into a Hindu family, whose Brahmin ancestors migrated from India in the nineteenth century to work as indentured laborers, losing their high-caste status. These novels satirize Caribbean political life. Like the comic stories of *Miguel Street*, their tone is ironic if genial, distanced from the follies of the islanders they depict.

A House for Mr. Biswas, still widely seen as Naipaul's masterpiece, draws movingly on his father's life as a frustrated journalist and writer (later captured in the memoir *Finding the Center*). The heroic, absurd efforts of the "little" man Mohan Biswas to build his own house in the teeth of his thwarting in-laws, the Tulsis, form a touching allegory for the colonial predicament and a universal metaphor for rootlessness and the quest for belonging.

After *Mr. Stone and the Knights Companion*—his first novel set in Britain, where he attended Oxford University on scholarship—Naipaul's fiction loses its genial edge, hardening into the more acerbic, pessimistic, furrowed-brow tone for which the St. Lucian poet Derek Walcott parodied him as "V. S. Nightfall." Doom, chaos, and brewing political violence touch the colonised who ape their masters in *The Mimic Men*; the displaced exiles of newly independent Africa in *In a Free State*; Jimmy Ahmed, whose life parallels the Trinidadian Black Power leader Michael X, in the scathing *Guerrillas*; and an Indian trader who tries vainly to settle in a central African country in *A Bend in the River*.

This brooding pessimism was reflected in Naipaul's travel writing on the Caribbean and, perhaps most notoriously, his visits to the land of his ancestors, *An Area of Darkness* and *India: A Wounded Civilization*. His contempt for "backward," "half-made societies," which he dismisses as "the bush," re-emerges in his descriptions of the Islamic revival in *Among the Believers* and *Beyond Belief*, although it is arguably tempered in his gaze at the southern United States, *A Turn in the South*. Naipaul then reversed himself on India in the more sanguine *India: A Million Mutinies Now*, repudiating the "neurosis" that had earlier led him to see "only the surface of things."

This apparent change of heart may affect his fiction, which has increasingly journeyed into himself, blurring the novel form in hybrid works of "imagined autobiography." *The Enigma of Arrival*—a slow, minutely observed homecoming to the Wiltshire countryside where Naipaul took up residence with his then-wife Patricia—resonates with a sense of personal loss and mortality. *A Way in the World* reads like a fictional lament for the Trinidad he earlier despised and fled. Probing the wounds of fear and shame that drove him to write, these autumnal novels are among his best.

Naipaul's standing may be subtly diminishing in metropolitan capitals—in 1998, his fellow writer and onetime disciple Paul Theroux wrote an acerbic account of their falling-out in *Sir Vidia's Shadow: A Friendship Across Five Continents*. But his meticulous prose, while often marred by sneering, can also reveal startling truths—not least about himself.

See Also: It is tempting to offer correctives to Naipaul's partial vision, such as Amitav Ghosh's In an Antique Land, *an Indian novelist's delightfully humble travel book on Egypt, or Moyez Vassanji's novel* The Gunnysack, *about the mixed Indian experience of East Africa. For antidotes to his Caribbean gloom, see George Lamming's novel of a colonial childhood,* In the Castle of My Skin, *or Earl Lovelace's warmly panoramic view of Trinidad's people,* Salt. The Lonely Londoners, *the classic novel by fellow East Indian Trinidadian Sam Selvon, views postwar Caribbean migration to Britain as a shared experience rather than the destiny of the loftily isolated artist.*

—Maya Jaggi

Naylor, Gloria
1950–
b. New York, New York

FICTION: **The Women of Brewster Place: A Novel in Seven Stories** (1982), **Linden Hill** (1985), *****Mama Day** (1988), Bailey's Cafe (1992), The Men of Brewster Place (1998)

282

Gloria Naylor worked as a switchboard operator and went door to door as a Jehovah's Witness in New York, North Carolina, and Florida during the 1960s and 1970s. Perhaps that's where she found many of her characters and settings because her books have that sense of understanding that comes from getting around on foot. All five of her novels are about African-American women and men, the communities they make for themselves, and the lives those communities in turn make for them. Naylor's astonishing first novel, *The Women of Brewster Place*, immediately established her as a force in American letters.

The Women of Brewster Place, an interconnected short story collection (or a novel in stories), dramatizes the hardships faced by a group of women living on a dead-end Brooklyn street and won her the National Book Award. *Mama Day*, perhaps Naylor's most accomplished work, is, architecturally, a near-perfect novel, the passionate story of the crisis brought on by the title character's attempts to protect and preserve her family's fortune beyond her death, and the unexpected costs of that fortune. Naylor builds her story by portraying the novel's events from multiple points of view, compressing its history, paradoxically, by this dispersal. *Linden Hill* is occasionally criticized as a mere exercise, due to its being modeled on Dante's *Inferno*, but many critics (rightly) hailed it for its imaginative treatment of class and race. *Bailey's Cafe* and *The Men of Brewster Place* are returns: *Bailey's Cafe* is similar in narrative structure to *Mama Day* (and has characters from that novel as well—a kind of backstory to the earlier book), and *The Men of Brewster Place* is the companion to *The Women of Brewster Place* with its interconnected narratives depicting the same events, now seen through the eyes of the community's men.

Naylor describes her fiction as telling stories that weren't being told, but they still remain firmly within the tradition of the novel. She uses techniques learned, as she has told interviewers, from writers like Faulkner and Austen. Her innovation lies in representing the kind of African-American lives so often left unwritten. Nevertheless, her work has more in common with a writer like Louise Erdrich than with the stylistically adventurous Toni Morrison. Like Erdrich, Naylor returns again and again to the places and characters from her previous novels, while her style is a poetics made from plain talk, prayer, and sharp insults. Each of Naylor's novels does the hard work of combining humor and tragedy, even as it shows how hard it is to live with both.

See Also: Naylor is one of a group of American women novelists—including Louise Erdrich, Carolivia Herron, Toni Morrison, Sandra Cisneros, and Barbara Kingsolver—currently using multiple narrators and points of view to tell stories of the dispossesed.
—Alexander Chee

Nicholson, Geoff
1953–
b. Sheffield, England

FICTION: Street Sleeper (1987), The Knot Garden (1989), What We Did on Our Holidays (1990), **Hunters and Gatherers** (1991), The Food Chain (1992), The Errol Flynn Novel

(1993), *Everything and More** (1994), **Still Life With Volkswagens** (1994), **Footsucker** (1995), Bleeding London (1997), Flesh Guitar (1999)

NONFICTION: Big Noises: Rock Guitar in the 1990s (1991), Day Trips to the Desert (1992)

Geoff Nicholson is the great contemporary chronicler of obsession, a wildly prolific author of erudite and blackly funny shaggy dog tales about smart, wry layabouts who grapple with postmodern paralysis brought on by information and sensory overload. Disastrous at finding human love, Nicholson's heroes turn to shoes, guitars, maps, and Volkswagens. Sometimes this compulsion for control extends to the grandest of scales—in *Everything and More* a department store aficionado builds, then barricades himself inside, the ultimate shopping emporium, and in *Hunters and Gatherers*, a perpetual dilettante tries to create a collection of collectors.

While at first glance Nicholson's plots may seem like shticks, they are not—he delves deeply into the obsessive mind, creating grossly flawed characters that, finally, one can't help but root for. Nicholson's pages flow by with a fluid, breezy intelligence; reading his novels is something like eating a can of Pringles—it's shocking how easily you can go through the whole thing. He is also the author of a whimsical travel book and a homage (yes, very thorough) to the electric guitar. His last three novels, while full of brilliant set pieces, have bordered on the slight and savage, but *Hunters and Gatherers*, *Everything and More*, and *Still Life With Volkswagens* rank among the funniest and smartest deconstructions of modern Western consumer culture.

See Also: Nicholson can be counted among a group of young intellectual British satirists partly inspired by Martin Amis, including Will Self, Nick Hornby, and Rupert Thompson.
—*Rob Spillman*

284

Oates, Joyce Carol
1938–
b. Lockport, New York

FICTION: By the North Gate (stories, 1963), With Shuddering Fall (1964), Upon the Sweeping Flood and Other Stories (1966), A Garden of Earthly Delights (1967), Expensive People (1968), Them (1969), The Wheel of Love and Other Stories (1970), ***Wonderland** (1971), Marriages and Infidelities (stories, 1972), Do With Me What You Will (1973), The Goddess and Other Women (1974), The Hungry Ghosts: Seven Allusive Comedies (1974), The Assassins: A Book of Hours (1975), The Poisoned Kiss and Other Stories from the Portugese (1975), The Seduction and Other Stories (1975), The Triumph of the Spider Monkey (1976), Crossing the Border: Fifteen Tales (1976), Childwold (1976), Night Side: Eighteen Tales (1977), Son of the Morning (1978), All the Good People I've Left Behind (stories, 1978), Unholy Loves (1979), Cybele (1979), Bellefleur (1980), A Sentimental Education (stories, 1981), Angel of Light (1981), A Bloodsmoor Romance (1982), Mysteries of Winterthurn (1984), Last Days: Stories (1984), Solstice (1985), Marya: A Life (1986), Raven's Wing: Stories (1986), You Must Remember This (1987), The Assignation: Stories (1988), American Appetites (1989), Because It Is Bitter, and Because It Is My Heart (1990), I Lock My Door Upon Myself (1990), The Rise of Life on Earth (1991), Black Water (1992), Where Is Here?: Stories (1992), Heat, and Other Stories (1992), Foxfire: Confessions of a Girl Gang (1993), **Where Are You Going, Where Have You Been?: Selected Early Stories** (1993), What I Lived For (1994), Haunted: Tales of the Grotesque (stories, 1994), **Will You Always Love Me?** (stories, 1995), Zombie (1995), First Love: a Gothic Tale (1996), We Were the Mulvaneys (1996), Man Crazy (1997), My Heart Laid Bare (1998), The Collector of Hearts: More Tales of the Grotesque (stories, 1998), Broken Heart Blues (1999)

UNDER THE PSEUDONYM ROSAMOND SMITH: Lives of the Twins (1988), Soul/Mate (1989), Nemesis (1990), Snake Eyes (1992), You Can't Catch Me (1995), Double Delight (1997), Starr Bright Will Be With You Soon (1999)

SELECTED NONFICTION: The Edge of Impossibility: Tragic Forms in Literature (1972), The Hostile Sun: The Poetry of D. H. Lawrence (1973), New Heaven, New Earth: The Visionary Experience in Literature (1974), Contraries: Essays (1981), The Profane Art: Essays and Reviews (1983), On Boxing (1987), (Woman) Writer: Occasions and Opportunities (1988), Where I've Been and Where I'm Going: Essays, Reviews, Prose (1999)

SELECTED POETRY: Invisible Woman: New and Selected Poems, 1970–1982 (1982), The Time Traveler (1986), Tenderness (1996)

The **Salon.com** Reader's Guide to Contemporary Authors

THE DOCU-NOVEL, THICK AND THIN *by Joyce Carol Oates*

The Executioner's Song by Norman Mailer

A massive, one thousand-page documentary novel of numerous voices bearing witness to the troubled life and eventual death (by firing squad, in Utah) of the convicted murderer Gary Gilmore; remarkably for Mailer, a novel in uninflected American vernacular, from which the author himself seems absent.

The World as I Found It by Bruce Duffy

Another massive but intellectually and stylistically rigorous novel of real-life individuals: Ludwig Wittgenstein, the most controversial philosopher of the twentieth century; Bertrand Russell, his elder and, for a time, his mentor; and G. E. Moore, the celebrated Cambridge don. A bold and original work of fiction that imaginatively evokes a vanished world, populated by such men and women as Freud, D. H. Lawrence, Lady Ottoline Morrell, and Karl Krauss. (*The World as I Found It* must be one of the most ambitious first novels ever published.)

Dreamer by Charles Johnson

Succinct, slender, poetic rather than documentary in its language, this bold novel explores the private and public lives of Martin Luther King Jr. Like Johnson's fiction generally, *Dreamer* has a parable-like quality despite its historic/biographical subject.

Cloudsplitter by Russell Banks

Another massive, monumental work, an imaginative evocation of the life of our most controversial abolitionist, John Brown. Visionary martyr? Madman? Figure of destiny? The novel is recounted by Brown's last surviving son, Owen Brown, from a fictitious perspective, in compelling, convincing nineteenth-century-style prose.

The Hours by Michael Cunningham

One of the riskiest, most discussed and successful of recent literary novels, this is a wonderfully imaginative, original blend of biography (the last days of Virginia Woolf, who commits suicide in 1941, in the poetically written prologue) and fiction (the interlocked lives of two contemporary American women linked by their connection with the Woolf novel *Mrs. Dalloway* and by their love for a young man dying of AIDS).

286

Throughout a career spanning almost four decades, Joyce Carol Oates has been one of the most fervently praised and bitterly reviled of American novelists. The author of more than seventy-five books encompassing virtually every literary genre, she has been acclaimed as a social chronicler adept at conveying an American landscape seething with incipient violence; as an acute psychologist of contemporary men and women misshapen by environmental forces and driven by primitive energies; and as a keen observer of historical and cultural phenomena—ranging from John Brown to Chappaquiddick to Jeffrey Dahmer—that have called upon her skills as a master ironist and a Gothic postmodernist.

Yet, as John Updike observed in an influential *New Yorker* review of her 1987 novel, *You Must Remember This*, Oates has received "some of the harshest scoldings ever administered to a major talent." Her reputation remains controversial. Canonized as a major American author and hailed "as the finest American novelist, man or woman, since Faulkner" (by Robert H. Fossum), she also has been damned as a careless "word-machine" in vitriolic attacks by such critics as James Wolcott, whose review of her 1982 novel *A Bloodsmoor Romance* bore the ominous title, "Stop Me Before I Write Again: Six Hundred More Pages by Joyce Carol Oates."

Once dubbed "the dark lady of American letters," Oates has both fascinated and repelled readers with her hugely ambitious yet incisive explorations of the American soul. Her best early novels, such as National Book Award-winning *Them* and *Wonderland*, introduced her unique blend of psychological realism and symbolist architecture, a method impelled, as she told an interviewer, by a "laughably Balzacian ambition to get the whole world into a book." After serving time in obscure academic outposts in the Detroit area, Oates moved in 1978 to Princeton, where she continued not only her prodigious output of fiction but also ventured into new careers as a boxing expert (her book *On Boxing* was widely praised), as a playwright, and as the author of psychological suspense novels published under the name Rosamond Smith. Oates's major novels of the 1980s included the bestselling *Bellefleur*, the finest of her series of postmodernist Gothic tales, and the partly autobiographical *Marya: A Life*, one of several explicitly feminist works and also the first of many novels to "memorialize" Oates's childhood environment of rural upstate New York. Her best work of the 1990s includes the horrific *Zombie*, based loosely on the Jeffrey Dahmer case.

On one issue, there is virtually unanimous agreement among both readers and critics: Oates's hundreds of short stories remain her single finest achievement. From the early "Where Are You Going, Where Have You Been?", a chilling allegorical rendering of a young girl's encounter with a serial killer, to recent O. Henry Award-winning tales such as "Heat" and "Mark of Satan," her short fiction best exploits her instinctive sense of form and her ability to convey psychological states with searing intensity.

For all the vicissitudes of Oates's reputation, her best work assays the contemporary landscape with cutting, ironic force and occasionally, as in the finest passages in *Them*, *Wonderland*, and certain of her short stories, with great emotional power as well. Now entering her sixties, Oates remains one of the most unpredictable and inexhaustible talents in American fiction.

See Also: Those who admire Oates's direct, darkly ironic confrontations with American history might also like Don DeLillo's White Noise, Libra, *and* Underworld. *Readers interested in her depiction of women's issues andintrigued by her allegorical fictional structures should seek out Margaret Atwood's* The Handmaid's Tale *and* Cat's Eye.

—*Greg Johnson*

O'Brien, Edna
1936–
b. Tuamgraney, County Clare, Ireland

FICTION: *THE COUNTRY GIRLS TRILOGY The Country Girls (1960), The Lonely Girl (1962, republished in 1964 as The Girl with Green Eyes), Girls in Their Married Bliss, (1964),* August Is a Wicked Month (1965), Casualties of Peace (1966), The Love Object and Other Stories (1968), **A Pagan Place** (1970), Zee & Co. (1971), **Night** (1972), A Scandalous Woman and Other Stories (1974), Johnny I Hardly Knew You (1977, republished in 1978 as I Hardly Knew You), Mrs. Reinhardt and Other Stories (1978), A Rose in the Heart (stories, 1979), Returning: Tales (1982), *****A Fanatic Heart: Selected Stories of Edna O'Brien** (1984), **The Country Girls Trilogy and Epilogue** (1986), The High Road (1988), **Lantern Slides** (stories, 1990), **Time and Tide** (1992), House of Splendid Isolation (1994), Down by the River (1996)

NONFICTION: Mother Ireland (1976), Arabian Days (1977), James and Nora: A Portrait of Joyce's Marriage (1981), Vanishing Ireland (1986), Tales for the Telling: Irish Folk and Fairy Stories (1986), James Joyce (1999)

POETRY: On the Bone (1989)

Edna O'Brien's fiction holds her readers in a combined state of rapture and dread. The sensuous fullness of her language sharpens your responses so that by the time the inevitable betrayals, heartaches, and sorrows come, you feel them with a piercing clarity. If you could grab hold of one of O'Brien's images and wrestle it up from the page, you'd find long roots sunk deep into the earth. There's blood coursing through her exquisite prose, balancing its seeming delicacy with solidity and weight.

O'Brien is poised between the "interior" novelists of the first part of this century and the great nineteenth-century novelists who made you feel, when you reached the end of their dense, sweeping narratives, that you'd come to the close of a long, extraordinary journey. O'Brien doesn't write epics. Her favored form (at which she may be the greatest living practitioner) is often the short story. She never strays from the boundaries of the heart, the territory she long ago staked out as her own. But the journeys she makes inside those boundaries seem as vast and deep as any expanse of plot carved out by a nineteenth-century novelist, her concerns as large. O'Brien combines a clarity of vision and precision of language with overwhelming emotions, in a way that only the greatest writers have.

The first line of her author's bio on the hardcover of *Night* sums up O'Brien's relations with her native Ireland: "Edna O'Brien, like many Irish writers before her, lives and writes in London." Though she left Ireland shortly after publishing her first novel *The Country Girls*, the voice of the country still courses through her work. Sometimes, that voice is heard in her debt to Joyce: the first-person narrative of *Night*, with its echoes of Molly Bloom, and the title story of her collection *Lantern Slides*, an attempt to write a modern-day version of "The Dead," which, against all odds, succeeds.

O'Brien has extended the tradition of Irish writing by enlarging it to include women's voices. In a country where the church holds such enormous power, *The Country Girls* (followed by two sequels and later published with them in one volume with a newly written epilogue in 1986), a novel in which young girls revealed their sexual and romantic selves, was a radical work. *The Country Girls* was burned by the priest at O'Brien's birthplace, and during her divorce, passages of O'Brien's writing were read aloud in court as proof of her unfitness as a mother. As recently as 1993, Rosemary Mahoney, in her book *Whoredom in Kimmage: Irish Women Coming of Age*, reported a woman who feels that O'Brien brought disgrace upon her town. But O'Brien's writing—which has always shown how emotion makes nonsense of ideology—isn't motivated by a feminist desire for inclusion. That's abundantly clear in the scalding and devastating *Time and Tide*, perhaps her greatest novel. Though she is writing, as she nearly always does, from a woman's point of view—about making a painful, decisive break with your parents; about the breakup of a marriage and the resultant reawakening of desire; about the experience of motherhood; about weathering the death of a child—O'Brien speaks in terms that are too passionate, too large to be confined to one sex.

In her last two novels—*House of Splendid Isolation*, the story of a reclusive, ailing widow whose rambling country house is invaded by an IRA gunman on the lam, and *Down by the River*, a fictionalized account of a rape case that bitterly divided Ireland (a young woman was prevented by the courts from going to England to abort her incest-induced pregnancy)—O'Brien has replaced the fullness of her narratives with shards of her characters' consciousness, a reflection of Ireland's divided psyche, in which each person allows him or herself to see only a bit of the story.

See Also: Joyce has been a profound and enduring influence on O'Brien. And there is no shortage of writers (as disparate as William Trevor and Roddy Doyle) whose topic is Ireland and the Irish state of mind. But to access the territory O'Brien refers to in one of her collections as "a rose in the heart," (meaning the thorns as well as the blossoms), you have to cross the continent to France and read Colette's treatment of the persistence and self-destructive allure of desire in her collected short stories and especially in the connected novellas Cheri *and* The Last of Cheri.

—*Charles Taylor*

O'Brien, Tim
1946–
b. Austin, Minnesota

FICTION: Northern Lights (1975), Going After Cacciato (stories, 1978), The Nuclear Age (1985), ***The Things They Carried: A Work of Fiction** (stories, 1990), **In the Lake of the Woods** (1994), Tomcat in Love (1998)

NONFICTION: If I Die in a Combat Zone, Box Me Up and Ship Me Home (1973)

O'Brien writes into his wounds. Late in the short story collection *The Things They Carried*, he describes his return to Vietnam with his ten-year-old daughter to revisit the paddy-field where his friend and fellow foot soldier Kiowa was killed. With his daughter looking on from a jeep, O'Brien eases himself into water where, twenty years previous, he reclaimed Kiowa's body from the muck. "A lot like yesterday, a lot like never," he writes. "In a way, maybe, I'd gone under with Kiowa, and now after two decades, I'd finally worked my way out." It's a scene of overwhelming power and emotional charge, one of the many shattering crescendoes in the book.

The only catch is O'Brien doesn't have a daughter. Kiowa, the paddy-field, even "O'Brien" himself are all inventions. "My own experience has virtually nothing to do with the content of the book," O'Brien has said. "My goal was to write something utterly convincing but without any rules as to what's real and what's made up." In the hands of a less prodigiously talented writer, toying with facts and the integrity of history would seem reckless and exploitative. But for O'Brien, the power of "story-history" (versus "happening-history") is an obsession that underscores his best work.

O'Brien's three novels about the Vietnam War and its aftermath are considered some of the best writing on the topic, and on war itself. They surge with the electricity of warfare. All of his protagonists are soldiers, some caught in the middle of battle, others only haunted by it.

Of his books about the war itself, *Going After Cacciato* and *If I Die in a Combat Zone . . .* are strong, if less accomplished, preludes to the sublime, heartbreaking *The Things They Carried*. That book's interlocking narratives open with a story that ingeniously lists all the objects that the infantrymen carried (tranquilizers, condoms, photographs, etc.). The collection never looses that wrenching eye for detail. With the Hitchcockian *In the Lake of the Woods*, the entire horror of the war seems to erupt inside a single man. Defamed by a mysterious campaign scandal, Senate-contender John Wade retreats with his wife to their remote cabin where, the reader learns, a terrible crime will later take place. O'Brien has you the entire way, winding to a conclusion as grisly as the best of Stephen King's.

O'Brien's three *other* novels might best stay unmentioned. Like Norman Mailer, O'Brien seems determined to produce an outright dud for every unquestioned accomplishment. Even if you're strong enough to put up with their profoundly dislikeable male protagonists, reading about their tedious obsessions is about as interesting as watching your father build a model airplane—plodding, predictable, and the fun, if there is any, is all his.

See Also: Journalist Michael Herr's Dispatches *provides stunning, less literary accounts of the war. The obvious precursor to O'Brien's fiction is* The Naked and the Dead, *Norman Mailer's debut novel about his experience in World War II.*

291

—Austin Bunn

FICTION: Flowers and Shadows (1980), The Landscapes Within (1981), **Incidents at the Shrine** (stories, 1986), **Stars of the New Curfew** (stories, 1988), *The Famished Road* (1991), Songs of Enchantment (1993), Astonishing the Gods (1995), **Dangerous Love** (1996), Infinite Riches (1998)

NONFICTION: Birds of Heaven (essays, 1995), A Way of Being Free (essays, 1997)

POETRY: An African Elegy (1992)

Ben Okri shot to prominence in Britain, where he has lived since his late teens, when his fifth book of fiction, *The Famished Road*, won the Booker Prize in 1991. Dazzling and original, the novel allegorizes the plight of a perpetually stillborn country—Nigeria—through Azaro, an *abiku* or Yoruba spirit-child destined to die in infancy. The naive yet knowing child-hero is haunted by others' dreams and mirrors the betrayed aspirations of his people.

Set in the run-up to Nigerian independence in 1960, the novel satirizes the corrupt maneuverings of the Party of the Rich and the Party of the Poor while conjuring characters both real and fantastic, from Madame Koto, a chop bar proprietor and witch dispensing palm wine and pepper soup, to the International Photographer recording pre-election bribery and ensuing riots. Okri has the same passionate concern for the continent's predicament as the first generation of post-independence African writers, but his fiction is more formally adventurous and innovative.

A densely figurative, meandering but deeply rewarding epic, rooted in the lives of the poor yet soaring from despair to enchantment, *The Famished Road* is Okri's masterpiece to date, although an easier induction might be the simpler, though marvellously crafted and sometimes bizarrely humorous, short stories of *Incidents at the Shrine* and *Stars of the New Curfew*. Set mainly in Nigeria—often in its chief city Lagos—and in London, they often dwell on stark images of Nigeria's civil war of the late 1960s. Written with staccato clarity, these stories display Okri's minute observation of ghetto life—its scum-filled squalor and transcendant dreams—while charting his movement from naturalism to the fantastical, from mundanity into visions or nightmare. "You cannot talk about reality without also talking about dreams; it is like describing the sea by only writing about the waves and not about what is underneath," Okri has said. His technique, dubbed "spiritual realism" by the critic Kwame Anthony Appiah to distinguish it from Latin American magical realism, is remarkable in seeking to depict African reality from the "inside"—through a local belief system or worldview.

For a more conventional narrative and a revealing portrait of the artist, try *Dangerous Love*, an accessible "reworking" of his second novel, *The Landscapes Within*. In it the painter Omovo learns though life and love in the Lagos ghetto to see with "unbandaged eyes"—a prerequisite both for moral action and for art.

Other works include the poems of *An African Elegy*; the fairytale-like fable *Astonishing the Gods*; the paler sequels to *The Famished Road*: *Songs of Enchantment* and *Infinite Riches*; and the alternately profound and portentous essays of *Birds of Heaven* and *A Way of Being Free*.

See Also: Nigerian writers of an earlier generation include the Nobel prizewinner Wole Soyinka, Chinua Achebe and Amos Tutuola. For innovative fiction that probes national identity in Africa, see the Ghanaian Kojo Laing's Search Sweet Country *and the Somali Nuruddin Farah's* Maps *or* Gifts. *Those with a taste for Okri's fantastical prose might also sample Latin American magical realists, such as the Columbian Gabriel García Márquez and the Brazilian Mario de Andrade.*

—*Maya Jaggi*

Ondaatje, Michael
1943–
b. Colombo, Ceylon (now Sri Lanka)

FICTION: The Collected Works of Billy the Kid: Left Handed Poems (1970), **Coming Through Slaughter** (1976), **In the Skin of a Lion** (1987), *****The English Patient** (1992)

NONFICTION: Leonard Cohen (criticism, 1970), Claude Glass (criticism, 1979), Tin Roof (1982), Running in the Family (memoir, 1982)

SELECTED POETRY: There's a Trick with a Knife I'm Learning To Do: Poems, 1963–1978 (1979), Secular Love (1984), The Cinnamon Peeler: Selected Poems (1989), Handwriting (1999), Anil's Ghost (2000)

Michael Ondaatje's novels fuse poetry and prose into an utterly original and exquisite form. His works explode like great, precise fireworks, illuminating history from the inside, capturing the evanescent and the eternal. He writes poetic operas, time-haunted tales of loss and redemption that also celebrate the color of shadows, the faint smell of false sunflowers, the world's infinite details. Ondaatje is an extravagant and unabashed romantic with a nose for fatality. The combination is potent.

To call someone a "poetic" novelist is to risk conjuring images of an ethereal rhetorician incapable of telling a story. But Ondaatje is an amazing storyteller—in fact, if anything, his plots are excessively dramatic, verging on the lurid. His brilliantly colored imagination probably owes something to his eccentric Dutch-Ceylonese upbringing in Sri Lanka, which he recounts in his wonderful memoir, *Running in the Family*. (One anecdote must suffice: Ondaatje's father, when in his superhuman cups, was given to pulling revolvers on trains and forcing them to run back and forth at his pleasure.)

Ondaatje's early collage (it has been called both a novel and a poem), *The Collected Works of Billy the Kid*, introduces his characteristic search for the poetry hidden in history. Its audacious, genre-bending use of contemporaneous documents, deadpan, colloquial lyricism, and elusive chronology gives the book a fatalistic feel, at once mythical and real.

Ondaatje followed that with *Coming Through Slaughter*, a longer but similarly fragmented, and brilliant novel about the life of the legendary New Orleans cornet player Buddy Bolden, who revolutionized music and went mad at age thirty-one. As in *Billy the Kid*, Ondaatje combines historical documents with jabbing, mesmerizing language, creating a visceral and dreamlike homage to the mad life of New Orleans and its music like "animals fighting in the room."

In the Skin of a Lion is Ondaatje's most conventional and least successful novel, if still a virtuoso performance. Introducing characters who return in *The English Patient*, it is set in 1920s Toronto and concerns the mingled lives of the thief Caravaggio, a runaway millionaire, two women—one a revolutionary, one an actress—and the protagonist Patrick, who loves them both.

Ondaatje's best-known novel is also his finest. *The English Patient*, which won the Booker Prize, is a stunningly beautiful, technically flawless story about four people—three of them damaged, one, the boyish hero Kip, still whole—who come together at the end of World War II in a Tuscan villa. As the three damaged people—the thief Caravaggio, the mysterious "English patient," and the numb, grieving nurse Hana—come to terms with their memories and their losses, Ondaatje explores the nature of wounds, those that can be healed and those that cannot. It is a shockingly ripe book, and it should be too romantic to work. But Ondaatje's gift is to make us remember that what can be imagined is also part of the world. And his imagination—dark, sensual, obsessed with time—strikes sparks of magic everywhere.

See Also: E. Annie Proulx—because they are both completely original stylists.

—*Gary Kamiya*

Ozick, Cynthia
1928–
b. Bronx, New York

FICTION: Trust (1966), The Pagan Rabbi and Other Stories (1971), Bloodshed and Three Novellas (1976), **Levitation: Five Fictions** (stories, 1982), The Cannibal Galaxy (1983), The Messiah of Stockholm (1987), The Shawl (1989), *__The Puttermesser Papers__ (1997)

NONFICTION: Art and Ardor: Essays (1983), Metaphor and Memory: Essays (1989), What Henry James Knew and Other Essays on Writers (1993), Fame and Folly: Essays (1996), Portrait of the Artist as a Bad Character: and Other Essays on Writing (1996)

Even wide-ranging readers are more likely to have encountered Cynthia Ozick's essays (published in virtually every intellectual and literary periodical of note) than her fiction. She has a reputation as a "Jewish writer," that she has often contested, but for an author who describes herself as a Zionist and chooses titles like *The Pagan Rabbi* and *The Messiah of Stockholm* for her books, this objection seems a bit disingenuous. Those titles suggest something homey and folkloric, rather than the philosophically thorny themes and fiercely crafted prose Ozick produces. Nevertheless, her fiction does have the cloistered quality of writing intended for a special audience.

An Ozick story (with the exception of her long, intricate, and now out-of-print first novel, *Trust*, she has favored short fiction) usually begins so handsomely, with such vivid prose and so appealingly authoritative a voice, that starting to read it feels like being swept up by the smartest, funniest, and most charming person at a glittering party. Her characters make an instant and decisive impression, for instance, Ruth Puttermesser, a recurring figure: "though she was no virgin, she lived alone, but idiosyncratically—in the Bronx . . . among other people's decaying parents." Or Lars Ademening, the protagonist of *The Messiah of Stockholm*, an idealistic literary critic who naps "at three in the afternoon—the hour when, all over the world, the literary stewpot boils over, when gossip in the book-reviewing departments of newpapers is the most untamed and swarming."

Too often, though, the reader finishes the tale with Ozick's exquisite, if overheated, sentences wrapped around her throat. Ozick's stories tend to narrow, like the minds of her obsessive and embittered characters, until they end in claustrophobic stalemates. What possesses these people is frequently a furious passion for artistic greatness, for either creating or laying hands on a masterpiece or, more poisonously, for ascending to the firmament of the masters, to be revered. (Judaism, as often as not, serves as rebuke and corrective to this idolatry.) In her 1984 essay "Cyril Connolly and the Groans of Success," Ozick, who suffered uncounted rejections before publishing *Trust* when she was in her late thirties, writes of "the marsh gas writers inhale when they are not getting published . . . when envy's pinch is constant and certain," and she notes, "I have never properly recovered." It shows. Excluded aspirants and the literary frauds who infuriate them haunt her fiction.

Perhaps identifying with the literary brahmins who once cold-shouldered her, Ozick writes of her characters with an Olympian amusement. She grinds their illusions under her heel, but one—the irresistible Ruth Puttermesser—will not be bowed. Ozick grants the bookish lawyer her fondest dreams, of civic, moral and romantic fulfillment, only to make them curdle (hilariously, I admit) in Puttermesser's hands. Yet it's impossible to pity the furiously rationalistic Ruth; like all great characters, she defies condescension. Puttermesser is Ozick's true masterpiece, a creature conceived in love rather than in ambition.

See Also: Ozick gets lumped with Isaac Bashevis Singer a lot, but she doesn't have either his earthiness or his breadth. She admires Louis Begley and Henry James, but there's also something Nabokovian in her merciless treatment of her characters.

—*Laura Miller*

Paley, Grace
1922–
b. New York, New York

FICTION: The Little Disturbances of Man: Stories of Women and Men at Love (stories, 1959), *Enormous Changes at the Last Minute* (stories, 1974), Later the Same Day (stories, 1985), Long Walks and Intimate Talks (stories and poems, 1991), **The Collected Stories** (1994)

NONFICTION: 365 Reasons Not to Have Another War (1989), Just as I Thought (essays, 1998)

SELECTED POETRY: Begin Again: New and Collected Poems ([revised and republished in 1999 in U.S.], 1992)

In Grace Paley's short stories, talk is never cheap; it's priceless. For her characters, conversation is a staple, as essential as food or sex, nourishing them in their passionate engagements with troubled love, leftist politics, and warm and warring families.

You rarely find people who like Grace Paley; mostly, they love her. And though it is difficult to pin down the qualities in her fictions that inspire this fierce and loyal affection, a list might include their wit, immediacy, humanity, and inventiveness, and the fact that the people who inhabit them with such noisy comedy are never less than fully alive.

Paley started by writing poetry, which is apparent in the mobile, seductive rhythms of her prose and in her stubborn care over words. The daughter of Russian immigrants, she chronicled an earlier Jewish immigrant life in her first collection of stories, *The Little Disturbances of Man: Stories of Women and Men at Love.* These vivid New York tales, enlivened by the Yiddish, Russian, and Polish colors in their characters' talk, describe men and women arguing about socialism, Zionism, parenting, and marriage—including amorous Rosie, who works at the Yiddish theater and is mistress to its star, and Faith, the gutsy, lusty, wisecracking mother of two who reappears throughout Paley's fiction and is generally seen as the author's alter ego.

By *Enormous Changes at the Last Minute*, in 1975, Paley was employing a broader ethnic cast, and moving beyond the conventional structure that had shaped her earlier stories. This volume contains the famous autobiographical story, "A Conversation with My Father," which places Paley's aesthetic on the line. In it, an aging father bemoans his daughter's reluctance to write good old-fashioned tales like Chekhov's or de Maupassant's. She explain her moral resistance to plot: "Everyone, real or invented, deserves the open destiny of life." When *Later the Same Day* was published a decade later, some critics shared the father's doubt about the open-endedness of Paley's work; several of these stories are sketchy or fragmented.

Paley has never written a novel because, as she is often quoted as saying, "Art is too long and life is too short." She might have written more, she has also said, if she hadn't poured her energy into activism. Many of her stories feature characters (often mothers) who reflect her own pacifist, feminist, and environmental politics, though in their lively, obstreperous talk, such beliefs never seem dry or didactic. "You're always inventing language," Paley has said of writing, and her aesthetic passion is evident in every line she writes, whether of prose or poetry. Her warm, wry, odd voice is like that of no one else.

See Also: Henry Roth and Isaac Bashevis Singer have written fictions about Jewish immigrant life, as has Philip Roth, who was an early admirer. Deborah Eisenberg or Marianne Wiggins also have a sharp ear for the way people talk. A new generation's Grace Paley, who walks a similar line between laughter and pain and is a virtuoso of the short story, might be Lorrie Moore.

—*Sylvia Brownrigg*

In Defense of Autobiographical Fiction

By Vince Passaro

In the late 1970s, in the middle of a string of sleepless undergraduate nights, I was seated in an auditorium at Columbia University, fading in and out as the poet John Ashbery read from his work. I was young enough for the presence of a major poet, a fashionable major poet in that place and time, to be glamorous; the sleeplessness I found hallucinatory. It was a potent combination. Suddenly, from amid the swirls of color, the buzz of emotion, and the music of verse, a line of Ashbery's in his cultured voice floated down from the stage, almost a physical thing, and burst into my consciousness. It's a line I've never forgotten but have also never been able to find in his books: "There comes a time when no one's actions but your own seem dramatically convincing."

In the flux of a daily life spent thinking about reading and writing, written narrative and voice and image, Ashbery's observation often comes back to me. It seems to me now that he was not merely speaking psychologically, about his own work and life, which was my first impression; rather, he was making an aesthetic judgment about a lot of other people's lives and work as well, a larger and more penetrating observation about the period we live in and about a fundamental change, not often acknowledged, in the way we tell stories.

In other words, Ashbery's elegant line questioned the efficacy of traditional narrative, pointing to the difficulties of plots, of putting together strings of related and dramatically convincing actions performed by characters who are not ourselves, who must defy the usual laws of modern life by gaining control over

298

themselves and their conditions, and yet still must be tangibly believable and real. Even if the reader can be tricked into nostalgic acceptance of such old-fashioned stories, the larger question is why should any serious writer at this late date be expected to create them? What remains now for the writer, assaulted by history and embattled by his own consciousness, that is comprehensible, believable, and worth writing about?

Fiction's sharp turn away from drama and story and action, which frustrates so many of its detractors now, occurred at the same time that photomagazines, movies and radio emerged. After all, in an age of television and film, why should it be the writer's task to provide our culture with its most rudimentary narratives, to tell its heroic stories? "We tell ourselves stories in order to live," as Joan Didion wrote in *The White Album*, a brilliant and fragmentary autobiographical exploration—but what kinds of stories? In the last gasp of the twentieth century, literature does best the one thing only literature can do: capture what it might be like to be inside another person's head. If science keeps working to understand the brain, then in a hundred years it might—and only might—catch up with Didion, with Grace Paley, with Harold Brodkey and Barry Hannah, with writers as far back as Proust and Joyce, with postwar masters like William Burroughs and Max Frisch, with artists as recent as Lorrie Moore, Lydia Davis, and Rick Moody.

In the 1930s the Italian poet and novelist Cesare Pavese efficiently made the modern claim for literature when he wrote, "The style of the twentieth century . . . expresses but does not explain . . . It is a never-ending revelation of inner life in which the subject of the story is the link between reality and imagination . . . The art of the nineteenth century was centered on the development of situations; the art of the twentieth on static essentials. In the first, the hero was not the same at the beginning of the story as he was at the end; now he remains the same."

In other words, the literature of the twentieth century has moved steadily away from narratives of heroic action and myth toward narratives of life as it is lived: quotidian, internalized, and pathological. Autobiography—or seeming autobiography, which is the imaginative adoption of a contemporary persona—is for many writers the most compelling way to make their fiction speak to the confusion and isolation of contemporary life. The most innovative and the most important literature of our time lingers like a shadow figure near the borders of nonfiction and autobiography. This infuriates certain traditionalists and fans of the novel, who don't realize that these works are novels, as validly constructed from the nothing of the blank page and the silence of a room as any long story featuring a multitude of characters and a grand geographical sweep.

In this post-Industrial age, morality stands as the supreme imaginative challenge. We need to know, absolutely must find out, how other people—with their doors closed, windows covered, alarms switched on, voices silenced—live. The individual psyche, cut loose and continuously in danger, makes its mystifying journey; that journey, without clear beginnings or ends, and with no guarantees of change, is the modern story. Our cultural condition of isolation amid electronic impulses requires a voice that can act as the penetrating whale call, the contact channel, within the glut of information, mere exhibitionism, and twenty-four-hour marketing that we call "communications." This is why autobiographical writing matters.

Of course, while autobiographical fiction has thrived in Europe for more than a century, we still regard it with suspicion in the United States. Much has been written, and much of that denunciatory, about the autobiographical inclination of fiction in recent years. The trend is considered base. Part of this reaction is built into the way literature and writing traditionally are taught. Two conflicting rules are crammed early down the craws of apprentices to the art of fiction and those who eventually become their most serious readers: first, that writers should write what they know, and second, that autobiography, memoir, journals, and letters are all lesser artistic forms than the traditional novel. Both are false rules, proved so by many great works of fiction. As it turns out, the real rule is that you must write what you can and read what speaks out loud; and perhaps for that reason, autobiography is the imaginative source for much of the most vibrant and lasting fiction of our century—take a look at *Heart of Darkness*, at *Portrait of the Artist as a Young Man*, at all of Proust. Unlike fiction in any other mode, autobiographical fiction continues to develop, to change and grow. In our lifetimes we have seen Burroughs's brilliant *Queer*, the work of writers like Peter Handke and Thomas Bernhard, the stories of Pavese, and the memoirish fictions of his friend Natalia Ginzberg. For evidence of the here and now, you might look at such recent works as Grace Paley's *Collected Stories*, at Lorrie Moore's story "People Like That Are the Only People Here," at Rick Moody's powerful "Demonology," or at any of Lydia Davis's books.

To read seriously and avidly is to hear a voice and to allow it to continue speaking. Much of what drives us as readers finally is a desire to know the author, to understand his vision, to comprehend his world. If the writing is good, how long before we find ourselves looking at the picture on the flap, reading the brief biographical note? It is not fashionable to admit this, it is considered an impure approach to art, but it is real and it affects most of us and we might as well make a new purity out of its obvious virtues. We are imprisoned and silenced by walls of official sound, starving for actual meaning and real words. The modern novel, focused not on what a character does but what one believably thinks and feels, lies under the loose floorboards, a dark tunnel to the world outside.

Peck, Dale
1967–
b. Bay Shore, New York

FICTION: *Martin and John (1993), **The Law of Enclosures** (1996), Now It's Time to Say Goodbye (1998)

Probably the finest, certainly the most troubling, of younger gay novelists, Dale Peck has produced two exceptional works of fiction and one disaster.

The extravagance typical of older gay writers is missing from the chaste, graceful prose of his celebrated first volume, *Martin and John*. The sentences carry no hint of feverishness, even when the subject matter is cruelty and violence (especially paternal violence), sex and disease. The book consists of eight stories intercut with brief passages that link up to form a ninth one; John is always the narrator, Martin his lover. Eventually the mystery is explained: Martin has died of AIDS, and John is spinning out his grief in stories. This ingenious structure doesn't really turn the book into a convincing novel, though. The Martins are too dissimilar to suggest different aspects of a single personality, and the sentences are more literary (and more brilliant) than anything a bereft lover might write. That's a minor flaw: The stories themselves are moving and wonderfully humane.

Peck's second book, *The Law of Enclosures*, deals with a marriage in its first and final years. In ten chapters, each told partly from the husband's and partly from the wife's point of view, the author shows a couple's love corrode and then, long after they have given up on it, rekindle. The structure is the X of two intersecting vectors, one plunging toward hopelessness, the other ascending toward love and death. But the midsection of the X—by far the greater portion of the marriage—is missing, and in its place Peck has dropped five chapters about his own mother (who died when he was three), his three stepmothers, and his father, a butch plumber whom he writes about with a conflicted mixture of bitterness and love. They're among his finest work, and they fit into the novel's structure with surprising elegance: As autobiographical incidents rhyme with incidents in the surrounding story, the book becomes, on one level, a demonstration of the way a novelist mines life for his fiction.

Now It's Time to Say Goodbye, a lurid and grandiose tale of murder, rape, and abduction, is set in Kansas (where Peck grew up) in twin towns divided by a highway. One side, where virtue resides, is black; the other, a sinkhole of depravity, is white. The somber and agendaless decency of Peck's earlier work gives way here to an obscene yet, at the same time pious jokiness. Most of the characters are cartoons drawn with hostility—the villains are almost uniformly white and straight—and the story unwinds at a hysterical pitch that has nothing to do with the flat beauty of Peck's earlier prose. What in the world could explain this about-face in tone?

Peck's first two books announced an important new voice; his third one strains it with shouting. It's impossible to predict whether he'll wind up as a major novelist or as a footnote in the literary history of his generation.

See Also: The preeminent chronicler of contemporary gay male life is probably Michael Cunningham, but readers who respond to Peck's perverse side may prefer the all-but-deranged work of Dennis Cooper.

—*Craig Seligman*

Percy, Walker
1916–1990
b. Birmingham, Alabama

FICTION: *The Moviegoer (1961), The Last Gentleman (1966), Love in the Ruins: The Adventures of a Bad Catholic at a Time Near the End of the World (1971), Lancelot (1977), The Second Coming (1980), The Thanatos Syndrome (1987)

NONFICTION: The Message in the Bottle: How Queer Man Is, How Queer Language Is, and What One Has to Do with the Other (1975), Lost in the Cosmos: The Last Self-Help Book (1983), State of the Novel: Dying Art or New Science (1988), Signposts in a Strange Land (1991)

For a fiction writer, Walker Percy displayed some rare, even alarming tendencies. "I do not consider myself a novelist," he wrote in 1962, "but a moralist or a propagandist . . . What I really want to do is to tell people what they must do and what they must believe if they want to live." Not exactly the mollycoddling art-for-art's-sake credo to which American readers have grown accustomed, John Gardner's plea for moral fiction notwithstanding. And indeed, if there were times late in his career when Percy appeared determined to become the Pope John Paul of American literature, his polemical streak seems the natural by-product of this Catholic convert's agonizing struggle for faith. (He found it and wanted to share the gift.)

Percy's magnificent first novel, *The Moviegoer*, remains his best, in part because it can't quite discover any solutions to its protagonist's despair, other than an awareness of it. Life makes mincemeat of doctrine. In this case, Percy allowed his congenital doubts on ethical and religious matters to override his equally native wish for certainty. Published in 1961 when the author was a forty-five-year-old, nonpracticing doctor living in Covington, Louisiana, *The Moviegoer* won the National Book Award, much to the astonishment of its disdainful publisher, Alfred A. Knopf. The author Thomas McGuane lauds *The Moviegoer* as the novel that was as influential for writers of the 1960s and 1970s as Hemingway's *The Sun Also Rises* was for the Lost Generation. A rare marriage of lyricism and satire, *The Moviegoer* hums insouciantly along without much of a plot, chronicling the desultory days of the charming Binx Bolling, a young New Orleans stockbroker baffled by his next move in life. Should he marry? Join the church? Live in the movies? He's Saul Bellow's dangling man gone South, his existential angst no less profound for being worn as lightly as a seersucker suit. As was his ambition, Percy grafted the European philosophical novel favored by Camus and Sartre onto a gleefully deadeyed depiction of the new-money boosters and stoic aristocrats uneasily cohabiting in the postwar subdivisions of the South.

The next novel, *The Last Gentleman*, is also quite good as an account of another deracinated, good-hearted Southerner who can't figure out what to do with himself (obviously, the prime Percyean archetype). This time, Percy must have felt that his seeker actually had to find something, which may explain the unconvincing deathbed baptism that closes the book but feels jury-rigged, an act of desperately willed Catholicism. As in Percy's other novels, an old priest eventually turns up and, with palsied, liver-spotted hands, offers grace and dénouement, although less religiously inclined readers will feel this narrative (and the others) have been insufficiently resolved.

And that's the problem with much of Percy's subsequent fiction, despite the generally high quality of the language and sustained moments of comic brilliance. The two best of the remaining lot are the energetic *Love in the Ruins*, a futuristic satire set during an era of racial inversion (blacks on the top, whites on the bottom), and *The Second Coming*, which though saddled with a nearly incoherent presentation of the arrival of God's grace (never an easy job for a novelist), nonetheless succeeds as a romantic fairy tale of language as grace, as a numinous form of intersubjectivity.

In the other two novels, Percy's increasingly strident Catholicism seems to have gotten the better of his craft. What's good for the soul can sometimes be fatal to the art. *Lancelot* is a choleric rant of a monologue, spoken by a murderer to a silent priest (yes, another priest). Poorly structured, this book boils over with spleen at the modern world, as does Percy's last fiction, *The Thanatos Syndrome*, which despite the respectful reviews it received is Percy's weakest effort, barbed as it is with a moral certitude that comes dangerously close to being intolerant of its readers. Those disenchanted by the late novels but still in the mood for Percy's linguistic philosophy and more nimble acts of moralizing may prefer his essays, available in three volumes, the strongest being the heartfelt and amusing *The Message in the Bottle*.

See Also: Percy is such a distinctive voice in American fiction that there's not much like him out there. Still, readers wishing for kindred spirits (with some stylistic overlap) might try Richard Ford's The Sportswriter *and* Independence Day, *as well as Nancy Lemann's novels* Lives of the Saints, Sportsman's Paradise, *and* The Fiery Pantheon, *and in nonfiction,* Ritz on the Bayou, *her account of the trial of Louisiana Governor Edwin Edwards.*

—Will Blythe

Phillips, Jayne Anne
1952–
b. Buckhannon, West Virginia

FICTION: Counting (1978), **Black Tickets** (stories, 1979), *****Machine Dreams** (1984), Fast Lanes (stories, 1987), Shelter (1994), Motherkind (2000)

Great books deserve great titles. So it's fitting that Jayne Anne Phillips's fitful, brooding talent was first unleashed in a story collection titled *Black Tickets*. Phillips's stories *were* one-way tickets to ride. Brimming with criminals and lonelyhearts and terminal misfits, and set in unforgiving Appalachian landscapes (Phillips was born in rural West Virginia), they took you to places you hadn't been before—places you found yourself aching to visit again.

Published when Phillips was only twenty-seven, *Black Tickets* made her an instant critical darling; profiles of the author zeroed in not only on her exacting prose but her long dark hair and "huge, intelligent eyes." (For a few years in the early '80s, Phillips seemed like the closest thing literature had to a rock star.) Two decades later, some of these stories—including the much-anthologized "Lechery," about a troubled fourteen-year-old girl who sexually molests little boys—can seem self-conscious and overwritten.

PRIMAL LOSS *by Jayne Anne Phillips*

These are books focused wholly or partially on childhood in which the child's point of view is obviously or not so obviously that of the writer (her)himself. They are not only studies of a world but of an evolving artist's consciousness in that world: particularly ways of looking, speaking, remembering, inventing, and bearing witness that were forged in childhood and comprise the evolution of an artist. Truth or fiction? It doesn't matter. What matters is literature as a means of survival and descent into mystery, the knitting together of time and loss into meaning and ever-presence—not the denial of death, but death's utter defeat, the triumph of language.

A Death in the Family by James Agee
Agee's masterpiece, in which a father's sudden death becomes a prayerful inquiry into identity itself.

They Came Like Swallows by William Maxwell
Maxwell's brief, beautifully rendered novel in which a boy loses his mother.

An Angel at My Table by Janet Frame
Frame's distilled, harrowing survival of her own life.

During the Reign of the Queen of Persia by Joan Chase
The interwoven, overlapping consciousnesses of girl cousins and sisters in Ohio.

Stop-Time by Frank Conroy
The classic autobiography of a young man in which time, memory, and identity coalesce into improvisational triumph.

Careful, He Might Hear You by Sumner Locke Elliott
Wonderful novel about an Australian boy caught in a custody battle between the working-class aunt who has raised him and the wealthy aunt enamored of his absent father. Inexplicably out of print on three continents, but available in libraries.

But *Black Tickets* remains, as Tillie Olsen put it, the "unmistakable work of early genius trying her range."

Machine Dreams, Phillips's first novel, more than delivered on *Black Tickets*'s promise. A multigenerational saga that plays out against the backdrop of both World War II and Vietnam, *Machine Dreams* extends and amplifies the themes Phillips introduced in her earlier work—how isolated families are forced to adapt to societal change, and how a rootless generation tried (and often failed) to flee the dead-end lives that awaited them in West Virginia's hollers. *Machine Dreams* is related, in alternating chapters, by various members of the Hampson family—mother and daughter, father and son. These chapters occasionally take the form of letters home, first from the father, Mitch, who fought in WWII, and later from Billy, who goes missing in Vietnam. The book's best writing, however, builds from the ordinary details of small-town life: neighborhood parties, fumbling attempts at sex, a wife watching her husband take measurements for an air-raid shelter. Phillips piles up this kind of sensory detail in prose that is determinedly unsentimental, yet the net effect is a work that is unaccountably tender and melancholy, and wise in ways that few American novels are. The book is her finest moment.

Phillips followed *Machine Dreams* with another collection of stories, *Fast Lanes*, and, a full decade later, a second novel, *Shelter*. Set in a West Virginia girls' camp in the summer of 1963, *Shelter* is a fable-like tale about four young girls (Lenny, Alma, Cap, and Delia) and their frequently terrifying encounters with the outside world, as represented by Carmody, a former convict; Parson, a Bible-obsessed drifter; and Buddy, the young son whom Carmody abuses. *Shelter* has its moments—Phillips catches all that's bewildering and oddly powerful about these girls' slowly awakening sexuality—but the novel is overwhelmed by the Faulknerian density of Phillips's language. Whatever narrative drive *Shelter* has is buried beneath a groaning load of overheated and vaguely threatening imagery.

See Also: Jayne Ann Phillips's fiction defies easy comparisons, but another writer who expertly explores West Virginia's coal-mining regions is the late Breece D'J Pancake, whose one work of fiction is a now-classic collection entitled The Stories of Breece D'J Pancake. *Russell Banks has a similarly strong feel for the realities of working-class lives, and some of the spikier, sexier stories in* Black Ticket *may remind some readers of Mary Gaitskill's work.*

—*Dwight Garner*

Piercy, Marge
1936–
b. Detroit, Michigan

FICTION: Going Down Fast (1969), Dance the Eagle to Sleep (1970), **Small Changes** (1973), **Woman on the Edge of Time** (1976), The High Cost of Living (1978), Vida

(1980), *Braided Lives** (1982), Fly Away Home (1984), **Gone to Soldiers** (1987), Summer People (1989), He, She, and It (1991), The Longings of Women (1994), City of Darkness, City of Light: A Novel (1996), Storm Tide (with Ira Wood, 1998), Three Women (1999)

NONFICTION: Parti-Colored Blocks for a Quilt: Poets on Poetry (essays, 1982)

SELECTED POETRY: The Moon is Always Female (1980), Circles on the Water: Selected Poems of Marge Piercy (1982), Stone, Paper, Knife (1983), My Mother's Body (1985), Available Light (1988), Mars and Her Children (1992), What Are Big Girls Made Of?: Poems (1997), Early Grrrl: The Early and Uncollected Poems (1999), The Art of Blessing the Day: Poems with a Jewish Theme (1999)

A Martian reading chronologically through Marge Piercy's thirteen novels would not only learn everything she needed to know about the flowering and senescence of North American antiestablishment politics—particularly the women's movement—she'd also have fun doing it. True, critics who do not share Piercy's political convictions have objected that her male characters are cardboard villains and her women overloaded embodiments of patriarchal oppression; her prose style more functional than elegant. Nevertheless, the Martian reader would probably get hooked on Piercy's heroines— determined, sexy survivors of bad marriages, alienating jobs, and menacing institutions (universities, mental hospitals, government agencies)—and her sharp observations of gender and class warfare.

Piercy's first two novels, *Going Down Fast* and *Dance the Eagle to Sleep* have a period flavor: A former Civil Rights activist and SDS organizer, Piercy writes with grim authority of the battle between "the System" and a ragtag opposition of the disaffected and the disenfranchised. It is with her third novel, *Small Changes*, however, that Piercy finds her characteristic focus—women's awakening to feminist consciousness in the days before legal abortion, affirmative action, and organized day care. *Small Changes* follows the interwined lives of two women. Working-class Beth flees community expectations of early, exhausting marriage for Boston, communal housing, and lesbianism. Middle-class Miriam futilely attempts to square her sexual and intellectual desires with conventional domesticity. Five subsequent novels track similar heroines through the sexual and political conflicts of the 1960s and 1970s. The titular heroine of *Vida* is an antiwar activist still on the run after her participation in a bombing ten years previously. Jill Stuart, the protagonist of *Braided Lives*, like Piercy herself, escapes working-class Detroit for the University of Michigan, suffering or witnessing poverty, rape, illegal abortion, verbal and physical abuse, and the diminishment of female ambition by male demands.

Woman on the Edge of Time illustrates Piercy's recurring interest in fantasy (also an element of *The High Cost of Living*). In this utopian polemic, Piercy imagines a future in which language and desire are gender-neutral, technology is managed for the good of all, and the inhabitants are smugly baffled by such old-fashioned effluvia as gas-guzzling automobiles and racial discrimination.

In more recent novels, Piercy frequently locates her themes of social and sexual struggle in the past. *He, She, and It* interweaves the sixteenth-century Yiddish myth of the Golem with the story of a futuristic Jewish community. In *Gone to Soldiers*, World War II provides a backdrop for the adventures of characters usually ignored by history, including women Resistance fighters, journalists, and pilots. *City of Darkness, City of Light* attempts less successfully to humanize a dizzying selection of historical participants in the French Revolution, including Maximilien Robespierre, who appears as "Max." Meanwhile, in novels such as *Summer People* and *The Longings of Women*, Piercy continues to meld combative social analysis, eventful narrative, and confused but feisty heroines into the almost oxymoronic whole that is her enduring contribution—a good feminist read.

See Also: In short story collections such as Enormous Changes at the Last Minute, *New York writer Grace Paley gives the political ferment of the 1960s a voice as sassy, colloquial, and unabashedly female as Piercy's. English chroniclers of the same decades of change for women, who create scenes as vivid and heroines as engaging as Piercy's, include Margaret Drabble and Fay Weldon.*

—Laura Morgan Green

Powers, Richard
1957–
b. Chicago, Illinois

FICTION: Three Farmers on Their Way to a Dance (1985), **Prisoner's Dilemma** (1988), *The Gold Bug Variations (1991), Operation Wandering Soul (1993), **Galatea 2.2** (1995), **Gain** (1998), Plowing the Dark (2000)

For a long time the standard advice handed out to young novelists has been "Write what you know." What distinguishes Richard Powers from most young novelists (he is in his early forties, which still counts as young) is that he knows everything. Unlike

WORLD ENGLISH *by Richard Powers*

The last forty years have witnessed the apotheosis of World English, a phenomenon in many ways without precedent in the the planet's history. English literature, too, has been brilliantly enlarged by an explosion of novels that derive neither from the British Isles nor from North America. The decolonizing of the globe continues to produce colonial revolts that forever change the shape of the mother tongue. (The linguistic determinists tell only half the story: Place reinvents language every bit as much as language reinvents place.) Englishes proliferate beyond any list's attempt to be representative, but here is a Nigerian, an Indian, an Australian, a South African, and a Trinidadian, sharing little but a linguistic genome more fluid than that of Darwin's finches.

Midnight's Children by Salman Rushdie

Salman Rushdie's sprawling epic of Indian history, politics, and religion conjoins the coming-of-age tale of two boys to the coming-of-age tale of the entire subcontinent. The tale of Saleem and Shiva—born on the stroke of Indian Independence, a Hindu and Muslim swapped at birth—becomes a magic allegory examining all the knobby excrescences of nationhood and identity.

Things Fall Apart by Chinua Achebe

Achebe describes, in harrowing detail, the disintegration of an Igbo village and the dissolution of its leader under the onslaught of Western colonial contact. This work, and its sequels that appeared throughout the 1960s, sparked a literary outburst throughout West Africa, writing that in turn retroactively altered the patrimony of the English novel.

Oscar and Lucinda by Peter Carey

Two damaged innocents who share an incurable passion for gambling fall in love and attempt to transport a glass church across the impassable wilds of the Australian interior. Peter Carey's highly wrought style and intricate, neo-Dickensian plot invoke all the mad British enterprise on that Asian island-continent.

A Bend in the River by V. S. Naipaul

This novel might be called the darker shadow of *Heart of Darkness*. A West Indian of East Indian descent, V. S. Naipaul casts one of the coldest eyes imaginable on the horrors of colonization and decolonization. A Muslim Indian businessman, a witch, a Belgian priest, a white intellectual,and his high-gloss wife are all drawn into the maelstrom of Mr. Kurtz's—and Mr. Mobutu's—Africa.

The Golden Notebook by Doris Lessing

Anna, Doris Lessing's fiercely self-realized heroine, records her life in a series of differently colored notebooks: blue for a personal diary, yellow for fictional transformation, red for her experiences with Communism, black for a memoir of Africa, and golden for her struggle for sanity, where all the other colors come together. Lessing is a novelist of ideas possessed of the greatest passion.

most of his contemporaries, who launch their careers with earnest little coming-of-age stories, Powers, at the age of twenty-eight, made his debut with *Three Farmers on Their Way to a Dance*, a dense, rigorous meditation on causality, the randomness of the universe, the history of photography, and the horrors of World War I. The five novels that followed—*Prisoner's Dilemma*, *The Gold Bug Variations*, *Operation Wandering Soul*, *Galatea 2.2*, and *Gain*—have, for all the prodigious diversity of their subjects, displayed the same tense, epigrammatic style, the same relentless braininess, and the same moral seriousness as the first.

Powers, who majored in physics at the University of Illinois, has forgotten more about science than most novelists (or literary critics) ever bother to learn, and he has an uncanny ability to infuse the architecture of his plots and the rhythms of his prose with the essence of his learning. Thus *Prisoner's Dilemma*, which ingeniously applies the abstractions of game theory to human affairs both grand and intimate, is composed of sentences that, like cells carrying the genetic code of the organism they inhabit, serve as statements and examples of the book's amibitious themes. *Gain*, much of which is devoted to the chemistry of soap-making and the alchemy of capitalist expansion, etches the logic of the market and the dialectic of alkalis and lipids into its very syntax. And *The Gold Bug Variations*—Powers's longest, best, and most intimidating novel yet—is constructed according to the logic either of a Bach fugue or the human genome project, or both at once.

Powers's books are sometimes forbidding, always cerebral, and often easier to admire than to enjoy. But for all the chilly precision of his mind, it is the sentimental fullness of his heart that distinguishes him from many of his contemporaries. He is often grouped with the other young white male followers of Thomas Pynchon and Don DeLillo—David Foster Wallace, Jonathan Franzen, and Jeffrey Eugenides. And though Power's debt to Pynchon and DeLillo is clear and acknowledged, and though he shares with writers like Franzen and Wallace a tendency to wear his brain on his sleeve, his work never feels as chilly or solipsistic as theirs. He is motivated above all by sympathy for his characters, and by a rather traditional concern with the emotional textures of family life, work, and relationships. He is, in many ways, an old-fashioned realist, who cares equally about the fates of individuals and about the larger structures in which they, whether they know it or not, are embedded.

Each of Powers's novels is subject to a kind of mind/body split: On one level a set of intellectual problems unfolds: What are the limits of artificial (or, for that matter, human) intelligence? How does the elegant regularity of genetic recombination coexist with the chaos of the lives it sets in motion? How can knowledge of the past be mobilized to prevent the catastrophes of the future? And in the foreground, shadowed by such abstract questions, are heartbreakingly concrete ones: How do we confront the mortality of our parents? Of other people's children? Our own? Why is love so hard to find, and so much harder to sustain? Why does all the knowledge in the world fail to make us happy, whole, or good?

See Also: The idiosyncracy of Powers's methods makes it hard to match him with other writers. While his connection to DeLillo is often overstated, both Galatea 2.2 *and* The Gold Bug Variations, *in their depictions of the romantic loneliness of scientists and the ethical and aesthetic dimensions of scientific research, recall DeLillo's early novel* Ratner's Star. Three Farmers on Their Way to a Dance *has striking affinities witn Bruce Duffy's* The World As I Found It, *its only serious rival for the title of most overachieving first novel of the mid-1980s. Other writers come to mind—Martin Amis for his fascination with theoretical physics, Rick Moody for his sense of the mysteriousness of ordinary life in late-twentieth century America—but the best way to understand what drives one of Powers's elusive, strangely heartfelt books is to read another one.*

—*A. O. Scott*

Price, Reynolds
1933–
b. Macon, North Carolina

FICTION: **A Long and Happy Life** (1962), The Names and Faces of Heroes (stories, 1963), A Generous Man (1966), Love and Work (1968), Permanent Errors (stories, 1970), The Surface of the Earth (1975), The Source of Light (1981), Mustian: Two Novels and a Story (1983), *****Kate Vaiden** (1986), Good Hearts (1988), The Tongues of Angels (1990), The Foreseeable Future: Three Long Stories (1989), Blue Calhoun (1992), Michael Egerton (1993), The Collected Stories (1993), The Promise of Rest (1995), **Roxanna Slade** (1998)

SELECTED NONFICTION: Things Themselves: Essays and Scenes (1972), A Palpable God: Thirty Stories Translated from the Bible with an Essay on the Origins and Life of Narrative (1978), **A Common Room: New and Selected Essays** (1987), Clear Pictures: First Loves, First Guides (memoir, 1989), A Whole New Life: An Illness and a Healing (1994), Letter to a Man in the Fire (1999)

SELECTED POETRY: The Collected Poems (1997)

"**W**hither the Southern novel?" asks intrinsically Southern novelist, poet, playwright, and Duke English professor Reynolds Price in his 1989 collection of essays, *A Common Room*. For many readers and critics the answer to that question is: right to his North Carolina doorstep. But Price also says wearily (in the same volume), "After a writer is called regional three times, he knows that the word is neither complimentary nor merely descriptive." Nevertheless, and though Price's range may stretch from turn-of-the-century North Carolina to modern-day England, his obsession with Southern family life is where he works out his themes of moral crisis, shifting relationships, and the piercing nature of love.

After he suffered a near-fatal case of spinal cancer in 1984, which has left him confined to a wheelchair ever since, Price also began to explore other topics—such as his relationship to the Bible—but love remains his true religion. His daunting bibliography traverses so many genres that getting a handle on him often feels a little like trying to fill a teacup with a firehose.

Price got off to a walloping start in 1962 with the eloquent *A Long and Happy Life*, the first of a four-book series about the Mustian family. It won the Faulkner Award (and perhaps more impressively, the praise of Dorothy Parker in *Esquire*). The surprise and joy of Price is that his most successful fiction is told from the point of view of female narrators, and he has often been praised for his facility with women's voices. If you read nothing else by Price, make it his 1986 bestseller and National Book Award winner, the hypnotic *Kate Vaiden*, and you will have encountered him at his epic best. *A Long and Happy Life* makes a gratifying follow-up, with the twilight of *Roxanna Slade* rounding out an unofficial troika of novels about atypical Southern women.

Perhaps some of Price's chafing about his status as a regional writer stems from the fact that anyone expecting the visceral Southern gothic of Faulkner, Tennessee Williams, and Flannery O'Conner won't find it here. Certainly there are plenty of unplanned pregnancies, untimely and violent deaths, Baptist hymns, and fried chicken dinners, but instead of club-footed traveling salesmen and bayou strangulations, Price treats us to Christmas pageants, unsullied creeks, and changing light. His dialogue is not embellished and he keeps dialect to a minimum. At times though, Price's poetic regional parlance tends to get tangled in metaphorical missteps and a mannered phrasing that can make for distracting reading: It's possible for a cake to have too much frosting on it. Even so, Price's fiction can never quite be reduced to his proximity to the Mason-Dixon line. Whither the Southern novel? Price's true question is, whither the human heart?

See Also: *Price is often compared to Eudora Welty, and for sheer longevity and richness, they are fit companions. Truman Capote's* Grass Harp *also presents a lyrical Southern*

312

coming of age. A less likely stablemate is Walker Percy, whose version of a modern South is more immediate and makes for a punchier read.

—Alison Powell

Price, Richard
1949–
b. Bronx, New York

FICTION: **The Wanderers** (1974), Bloodbrothers (1976), Ladies Man (1978), The Breaks (1983), *Clockers (1992), **Freedomland** (1998)

Richard Price's career path resembles that of certain movie stars—startlingly early success, followed by druggy dissolution, and finally redemption via critically applauded achievement. Price would recognize the scenario: He's written many high-profile screenplays (*The Color of Money, Sea of Love, Kiss of Death*) and seen most of his novels made into movies (in which he always makes a cameo appearance). Deeply indebted to Hubert Selby's *Last Exit to Brooklyn*, Price's first novel, *The Wanderers*, revs up its readers with tall tales of teenage derring-do on the mean streets of the Bronx, rendered with the author's trademark cinematic flash and male swagger. Only twenty-four, Price garnered national attention for his sometimes shocking (for 1974) coming-of-age story but he then seemed at a loss for a follow-up. His next book, *Bloodbrothers*, returned to the working-class turf he had already successful plowed—with a measurably diminished effect, though it did show his surefire ear for the un-pretty speech of un-pretty people.

313

Ladies Man, his third novel, sprang from his *Penthouse* article about sexual anomie in the 1970s. His midlife crisis sends a salesman through a battery of Catskills single weekends, gay S&M bars, and massage parlors, best thought of as a sociological tour of the Me Decade. Price himself describes *The Breaks*, his next outing, as having been written "in a blind panic . . . All of a sudden I ran out of autobiography and I started spinning my wheels." For a while he turned to screenplays, but it was on city streets he once again found his footing as a novelist—in *Clockers* he dug deep inside the mind of the New Jack crack-dealers of the 1980s and early 1990s. His most revelatory creation in this murder mystery is Strike, a nineteen-year-old African-American coke dealer with a Kiwanis Club business ethos. Strike's got a mental calculator that adds up the implications of every transaction. He always wears shoes, never sneakers, when visiting his parole officer, "to suggest he wasn't the type who ever need to *run* anywhere."

Price makes inner-city African-Americans even more central in *Freedomland*—a gutsy move in the current atmosphere of literary turf wars. In an urban dystopia of housing projects and edgy cops, a single white mother claims her child was stolen by a black carjacker. Using the bare bones of the infamous Susan Smith story, Price turns up the heat on the race factor to dizzy us with the scent of panic and rage. This is a novel about bad blood that doesn't offer reconciliation or uplift—it's a searing downer but an irresistibly readable one. Right now, there's no writer in America with a surer grip on the emotional temperature of our cities.

See Also: Go to the source, Hubert Selby's Last Exit to Brooklyn. *For a more political take on savage city youth, there's Sol Yorick's* The Warriors. *Set in Pittsburgh, John Edgar Wideman's Homewood trilogy—*Damballah, Hiding Place, Sent for You Yesterday—*also successfully pries at the roots of urban desperation.*

—*Albert Mobilio*

Proulx, E. Annie
1935–
b. Portland, Maine

FICTION: Heart Songs and Other Stories (1988), *****Postcards** (1992), **The Shipping News** (1993), Accordion Crimes (1996), Close Range: Wyoming Stories (1999)

For Edna Annie Proulx, composing sentences has never been an indoor sport. "The most fun thing about writing," she told an interviewer in 1993, "is jumping in my pickup truck and taking off—stop along by a graveyard, write some, and then sleep in the truck." Proulx's restlessness rubs off on the men and women in her books. She's interested in what happens to people when the rug is yanked out from under them. In her haunting first novel, *Postcards*, her doomed protagonist careers across the country on a forty-year road trip. In *The Shipping News*, which won the 1993 Pulitzer Prize and became that year's surprise bestseller, Proulx uproots a hack journalist and his family from upper New York State, and drives them northward. In both books, her upcountry rednecks filter the world through bleary eyes and crippling cultural jetlag.

For her readers, too, Proulx can provide hard traveling. Her talent is enormous but ungainly. You bounce along her sentences—which teem with huge inventories of arcane objects, natural phenomena, and words that don't appear in dictionaries—the way you do along rutted, washboard dirt roads. She's among America's most truly idiosyncratic literary voices. Proulx developed her interest in the antiquated and obscure while she was a struggling journalist trying to support her three children. Among her earliest works were *Back to Barter* (1981) and *The Complete Dairy Foods Cookbook: How to Make Everything From Cheese to Custard in Your Own Kitchen* (1982).

Proulx's first fiction book, *Heart Songs and Other Stories*, is a slim collection of nine stories that deftly probe blue-collar life in small-town New England when the dispossessed working class is confronted by a young, Volvo-driving bourgeoisie. Proulx's next two books, the novels *Postcards* and *The Shipping News*, pick up on the idea of territorial curses. Starker and less playful than *The Shipping News*, *Postcards* may be Proulx's most deeply felt book. It's the tale of Loyal Blood, a man who spends his life running from a crime so terrible that it renders him forever incapable of touching a woman. "There's something truly fucked up about you," a near-stranger says to him, out of the blue. "I don't know what it is, but I can smell it. You're accident prone. You suffer losses. You're tilted way far off center." Three years after the runaway success of *The Shipping News*, Proulx published the odd and strangely brittle *Accordion Crimes*, an ambitious series of linked stories, set from 1890 to the present, about lonely, hard-luck immigrants (Italian, Polish, Irish, German) and their deep-seated love of accordion music. It's an easy book to admire, and a difficult one to like. Proulx's prickly talent remains very much in evidence, however, and where she will go next is among the more compelling questions American literature has to offer.

315

See Also: E. Annie Proulx is a relative rarity in American letters—a writer who literally sounds like no one else—but admirers of her rural New England books may want to investigate working-class writers like Caroline Chute and Dorothy Allison.

—Dwight Garner

Puzo, Mario
1920–1999
b. New York, New York

FICTION: The Dark Arena (1955), *__The Fortunate Pilgrim__ (1964), **The Godfather** (1969), Fools Die (1978), **The Sicilian** (1984), The Fourth K (1990), The Last Don (1996), Omerta (2000)

NONFICTION: *The Godfather* Papers and Other Confessions (1972), Inside Las Vegas (1977)

*T*he Godfather. There's no way around it. No matter that Mario Puzo has written a half-dozen other novels, some good, others not. Who cares that his second novel, *The Fortunate Pilgrim*, is perhaps the finest fictional account of the Italian-American immigrant experience? It's *The Godfather*, particularly through its movie adaptations, that we can recite chapter and verse. Its saga of a Mafia family's intergenerational struggle is probably, pace *Huck Finn*, the most familiar story in American culture. The first real "blockbuster" book, Puzo's operatic tale sold 21 million copies worldwide and, many argue, changed the dynamics of the publishing business. So when you talk about Puzo, you talk about *The Godfather*.

Except for a weird, extended digression about Sonny's girlfriend's gynecological problems, Coppola quite faithfully transcribed the book to the screen. Puzo pared down the talky dialogue to pseudo-mythic utterances for the movie—"Luca Brasi sleeps with the fishes"—and thus the book feels less Shakespearean and more like the gritty realist genre effort it was, in fact, meant to be. And the novel's wiseguys don't resemble archetypal forces of nature so much as refugees from a Hemingway novel—ambivalent about the codes by which they've chosen to live. Aside from codifying an American myth and gracing it with memorable language ("I made him an offer he couldn't refuse") Puzo's most notable achievement in *The Godfather* may be bringing up the volume on gangland's social dimension—the chitchat of murderous men—and making possible logomaniacal progeny such as *Pulp Fiction*.

The Fortunate Pilgrim, Puzo's heartfelt and deliciously detailed second novel about Depression-era Italians in New York, is a benchmark book for anyone interested in the vast majority of immigrants who didn't stuff horse heads in people's beds. Centering around an Italian matriarch (she was drawn from his own mother, who also, Puzo has admitted, served as the model for Vito Corleone), the story treads a familiar path—old

ONE-HANDED READING *by Susie Bright*

The Godfather by Mario Puzo

This was the first book I was ever handed by another person and told, "This is dirty." A whole crew of little girls in my eighth-grade class in Edmonton, Alberta, were circulating it, and it wasn't because of their interest in the Mafia—it was because of the book's lurid description of the Godfather's son's huge cock and the woman he meets who has a cunt big enough to accept and enjoy it. It was the first time I had ever been exposed to the "big cock" meme. I was sheltered enough that I had no idea that bigger was supposed to be better, and I found this enormously titillating.

A Garden of Sand by Earl Thompson

Another book placed directly in my lap by a girlfriend who said, "I don't like that prissy erotica stuff—this is something that actually gets you off." While *The Godfather* was violent, it didn't mix violence with sex. *Garden of Sand* had anger, guilt, violence, and sex all mixed in one pot and sometimes in a few brutal paragraphs. Two characters really shocked me—a mother who has an incestuous relationship with her son and a furious dwarf who wreaks revenge on a prostitute, but I couldn't get those scenes out of my head. This time, I didn't like having my friend know that I was turned on by the same things she was . . . I refused to talk to her about the book afterward. I was ashamed of myself for enjoying it and pissed at her for knowing I would.

Notes of a Dirty Old Man by Charles Bukowski

Is this what men really think about women? I found this on my father's bookshelf, at the height of Bukowski's reign as the drunken bard of the LA Free Press. I'd never heard someone be such a bastard in print before, but he was so damn eloquent about it. Made me wonder how the women in his life would tell the same story.

Don Juan in the Village by Jane DeLynn

These were the notes of a dirty old dyke and the first unrepentant one at that. Jane DeLynn wrote about what it's like to love ugly, to love reckless, to be absolutely hateful and sopping wet all at the same time. I cheered because she'd broken the dreadful lesbian romance canon, and then I realized that there weren't any women authors talking about sex hunger like this, and precious few men, either.

world versus new, family versus outsiders—yet still transcends its sociology with tactile evocations of lived life. Puzo describes it as "my most literary book," and upon its publication critics agreed; many thought he was on the track to become another Malamud or Roth.

Of course, the siren call of dollars led Puzo astray. After *The Godfather* his commercially targeted novels—*Fools Die, The Fourth K, The Last Don*—sprung either from Las

Vegas glitz or Mafia blood. A well-researched novel about the Sicilian Cosa Nostra, *The Sicilian*, is the one book worth reading among the lot. As poet laureate of the Mafia, Puzo has never been able to escape telling its highly marketable tales; the solicitations from publishing and the movies are offers, it seems, he can't refuse.

See Also: Pietro di Donato's Christ in Concrete *is another strong candidate for best book in the rather slender category of Italian-American immigrant novel. For Mafiana, Nicholas Pileggi's* Wiseguy *and Sammy "The Bull" Gravano's* Underboss *feature confessional tales from real, live, made men of letters.* Corsican Honor *by William Heffernan is a more than servicable novel about old world gangsters in the stagy, operatic style of* The Godfather.

—*Albert Mobilio*

Pynchon, Thomas
1937–
b. Glen Cove, New York

FICTION: V. (1963), **The Crying of Lot 49** (1966), *Gravity's Rainbow** (1973), Slow Learner (stories, 1984), Vineland (1990), Mason & Dixon (1997)

Like an MIRV missile, the arc of Thomas Pynchon's reputation splits into multiple trajectories. During the seventeen long years after *Gravity's Rainbow* (while *Vineland* was still a fan-club rumor), the legend of the vanished, militantly anonymous author traced a neck-bending arc, his silence echoing louder and louder, the critics' awe welling up as they contemplated his three-book contrail: *V.*, the wildly original debut; *The Crying of Lot 49*, a sassy, pocket-sized gloss on what was already a remarkably coherent worldview; and then the massive, magnificent *Gravity's Rainbow*. Before *Vineland*, Pynchon was all ascent. After *Vineland* (and after the confused reception of *Mason & Dixon*), everything depends on who you ask: Pynchon is either safely among the stars, looped in a wobbly orbit, or has crash-landed.

But back to the launching pad: *V.* is an astonishment, probably the best first novel of our time. Meet Benny Profane, "a schlemihl and human yo-yo," and Herbert Stencil, a man with a mission. They belong at opposite ends of a seesaw; in the middle, the beveled fulcrum is an inverted V-shape. V. may be a woman, an automaton, a sewer rat, or Venus; the vanishing point, history's entropic end, or a local conspiracy tied in with "The Big One, the century's master cabal." Whatever it is, Stencil is dedicated to pursuing it. Chubby, helpless, lovesick, Profane drifts among a loose affiliation of artsy New York City wastrels and keeps the novel on the street, the here-and-now of America in 1956. Stencil, grim, sophisticated, relentless, takes us to Cairo, Southwest Africa, Malta; he is a time-tourist, too, scrolling through the century's calendar, questing after V.

Meaning or no meaning? Conspiracy or entropy? Stencil or Profane? Bit of both. Take a tip from one of the two hundred or so named characters in this picaresque jamboree: Says McClintic Sphere, a jazzman, "Keep cool, but care."

In the 1980s, Pynchon semi-disowned *The Crying of Lot 49*—a "story," he called it, "marketed as a 'novel' . . . in which I seem to have forgotten most of what I thought I'd learned up till then." But at one hundred twenty-seven pages it provides an excellent introduction to the twin monuments on either side. It's a book for beginners and cultists: Our heroine, Oedipa Maas, is a bit of both. She thinks she's discovered a conspiracy—W.A.S.T.E., or the Trystero, a shadow postal system, sort of like the Internet before computers.

The only appropriate response to *Gravity's Rainbow* is humble gratitude. Be thankful for the incredible hard work that went into it—not just the research (my God, the things Pynchon knows!) but the stretching of imagination and the deep focus of the writing, which in places is as beautiful as prose gets.

Only a reader terminally afraid of difficulty and fierce originality will hold out against the brave, goofy charm of the opening scene. "Pirate" Prentice, waking from a dark dream in London in the last days of the Blitz, under the mind-shattering threat of Germany's V-2 rocket, proceeds, with the help of his hungover mates, to create one of his famous Banana Breakfasts: "it is not often Death is told so clearly to fuck off."

No exaggeration to say that *Gravity's Rainbow* is as complex as the V-2 (00000 series), the ballistic missile that Tyrone Slothrop, our disintegrating hero, tracks for 760 packed pages. To know the novel fully you would need to know your physics, your chemistry, your math, your animal behaviorism (how else to appreciate Slothrop tangling with a trained octopus?), your military, diplomatic, and literary history—and virtually everything about pop culture in the first three quarters of the century. But even those of us who won't ever be mistaken for a rocket scientist, who quail before "yaw control" equations, and can't carry a vaudeville tune—we, too, can get sucked up into the whirling extravaganza of *Gravity's Rainbow*. We can be terrified by it, laugh till we cry, then keep on crying.

The silence of the next seventeen years was in fact interrupted by *Slow Learner*, a collection of previously published stories, nothing earthshaking, but no embarrassments either.

Then comes the novel that seems to me a pure embarrassment, a dud to make you

319

wonder where in the world *Gravity's Rainbow* came from. *Vineland* is a comic novel set in northern California in 1984, the year of Ronald Reagan's re-election. Betrayal, both personal and political, sours the comic mood; the narrative rambles as always, but this time around the prose slouches, casual to the point of sloppiness. The usual agglomeration of wacky trivia, cameo characters, songs, and labored puns leads nowhere.

Last and luckily not least, *Mason & Dixon*, written in a hybrid language that yokes postmodern sensibility to eighteenth-century locutions. Some critics loved this old-fangled prose—I hated it, especially in a novel as long as *Gravity's Rainbow* (though nowhere near as dense). Pynchon recreates the epic adventures of Charles Mason and Jeremiah Dixon, the two Englishmen who set out in 1765 to survey the disputed boundary between Maryland and Pennsylvania, a daring westward march into wilderness. The "Visto" cleared by the surveyors' axmen, a livid scar some 240 miles long, is the crux of the novel, its organizing principle, much like V. and the V-2. Pynchon is famous for flattening his characters so that they fit the comic-book high jinks of his plots. Here, he flattens history, with amusing and also deeply troubling results. Dixon asks Mason, "No matter where in it we go, shall we find all the World Tyrants and Slaves?" Pynchon's answer is yes—and that goes for past, present, and future.

Mason & Dixon offers ample proof that Pynchon still has the stuff to dazzle us. Of all our great novelists, Pynchon, who studied engineering, is at once most sympathetic to, and most suspicious of, the scientific mind. In our tech-tyrannized times, we need him.

See Also: In the nineteenth century, Herman Melville (Pynchon, says critic James Wood, is "the clear inheritor of Melville's broken estate"); in the twentieth century, James Joyce and Don DeLillo; in the twenty-first, David Foster Wallace.

—*Adam Begley*

Reed, Ishmael
1938–
b. Emmett Coleman in Chattanooga, Tennessee

FICTION: **The Free-lance Pallbearers** (1967), **Yellow Back Radio Broke-Down** (1969), Mumbo Jumbo (1972), The Last Days of Louisana Red (1974), *****Flight to Canada** (1976), The Terrible Twos (1982), Reckless Eyeballing (1986), The Terrible Threes (1989), Japanese by Spring (1993)

AFRICAN-AMERICAN NOVELS *by Ishmael Reed*

W. E. B. DuBois was right when he said that "outsiders" often choose African-American leaders. This can be said of cultural and artistic leaders as well. Those chosen usually represent what their white patrons demand. In the 1960s, when the patrons were left, you had to be left. In the 1950s, you had to profess uncritical loyalty to a reading list composed entirely of white males. Cold-Warrior Ralph Ellison praised Richard Wright for being "guided" by Marx and Freud, men whose theories are now undergoing a stiff challenge.

In the 1970s and 1980s white middle-class feminist were the patrons, and so you had to bash black men. Bell Hooks said that white women consumers warned her that she could only get over if she wrote for them. The current neo-liberal and right wing sponsors tell their surrogates the same thing. I wish to cite books by five African-American writers, published since 1960, who wrote what they saw as the truth instead of what a patron ordered.

The Man Who Cried I Am by John A. Williams

Like John O'Killens before him, John A. Williams has written novels that challenge American hypocrisy and depict a variety of African-American male characters. *The Man Who Cried I Am* is probably the best novel written about the 1960s and the hostility that black male writers faced during this period of political and cultural upheaval. Malcolm X, Chester Himes, and the late black cartoonist, Ollie Harrington are among the recognizable characters. John A. Williams is probably the best African-American writer of the century, but will never be recognized as such by the white establishment. They consider him to be "impudent."

The Salt Eaters by Toni Cade Bambara

The late Toni Cade Bambara was the true successor to Zora Neale Hurston, whose masterpiece was *Tell My Horse*. *The Salt Eaters* is a sincere critique of patriarchal attitudes of the leaders of the 1960s civil rights movement. So damaged by this oppression is the lead character, Minne Ransom, that she undergoes traditional West African healing. Ms. Bambara knew what she was talking about. While visiting Nigeria, she was initiated into the cult of Oshun, a spirit of the rivers.

Days Without Weather by Cecil Brown

Africans were brought to this hemisphere to be used as equipment. Booker T. Washington said that his mother's enslaver had the same regard for her as he would for a cow. African-Americans are still being used. In *Days Without Weather*, a comic novel, Cecil Brown writes about how the corrupt American film industry markets African-Americans and promotes stereotypes for the entertainment of suburban audiences.

321

Groove, Bang and Jive Around by Steve Cannon

Raunchy, outrageous, hilarious—this political hoodoo thriller has all the sounds of Professor Longhair and Fats Domino. New Orleans-born Steve Cannon, known affectionately as Professor Steve by the hundreds who visit his salon on the Lower East Side of Manhattan, has devised a unique writing style that has influenced a younger generation of avant garde artists.

NONFICTION: Shrovetide in Old New Orleans (essays, 1978), God Made Alaska for the Indians: Selected Essays (1982), Writin' is Fightin': Thirty-Seven Years of Boxing on Paper (1988), Airing Dirty Laundry (1993)

SELECTED POETRY: Conjure: Selected Poems, 1963–1970 (1972), New and Collected Poems (1988)

You don't turn to Ishmael Reed's fiction for fully-rounded characters in whose detailed and textured world you lose yourself only to re-emerge refreshed and renewed. You turn to it for zigzaggy energy, iconoclastic brains, and freaky satire. His novels are less likely to call to mind comparisons with *Middlemarch* than with Krazy Kat, R. Crumb, and *Richard Pryor Live in Concert*. They're like underground comix for the literary audience.

Reed, perhaps the premier trickster figure of current American letters, is a whirlwind of industry and deviltry. He has written plays, as well as volumes of poems and essays, and has founded small magazines and a prize-awarding literary organization, the Before Columbus Foundation. Although generally well-reviewed, and turned to by the media for his reliably corrosive observations and commentary, he has seldom gotten the credit he has earned as a literary innovator. (It's the fate of humorists, even savage ones, not to receive the recognition they deserve for their achievements as technicians, let alone as artists.) In *Mumbo Jumbo*, for instance, Reed mixed up fictional and historical figures, and spliced newsreel and fantasy elements into his story lines, three years before E. L. Doctorow was lauded for doing similar things in the smoother and more polished *Ragtime*.

Usually at his best in short bursts of invention and ridicule, Reed may be more valuable as a provocateur than for any of his individual works, some of which are reminders of how exhausting and antic 1960s-style writing can be. And recently his attitudes have taken a more earnest, and more predictably multicultural, turn than his fans might prefer. (It's a lot more fun watching Reed go nuts than it is learning what he actually believes.)

But when he's on his game, no writer has been better at conveying how crazy, man, crazy our racial jambalaya can render a soul. His most sustained performance, and the best place to start, is *Escape to Canada,* a harlequinade on the traditional slave narrative.

See Also: Similar purveyors of cartoon prankishness include Terry Southern and the early Thomas Pynchon. For naughty little boy glee, it's hard to beat Southern's Candy *and* Blue Movie, *both of them as rude and pleasing as a well-turned dirty joke. Pynchon's* V. *and* The Crying of Lot 49, *written before his ambition overwhelmed his wit, are generous packages of intricacy and nuttiness, sure to tickle paranoid, pot-smoking grad students everywhere.*

—*Ray Sawhill*

Rice, Anne
1941–
b. New Orleans, Louisiana

FICTION: *VAMPIRE CHRONICLES: *Interview with the Vampire (1976),* **The Vampire Lestat** *(1985), The Queen of the Damned (1988), The **Tale of the Body Thief (1992), Memnoch the Devil (1995), The Vampire Armand** (1998),* The Feast of All Saints (1979), **Cry to Heaven** (1982), *LIVES OF THE MAYFAIR WITCHES:* The Witching Hour (1990), Lasher (1993), Taltos (1994), The Mummy (1989) Violin (1997), *NEW TALES OF THE VAMPIRES:* Pandora: New Tales of the Vampires (1998), Vittorio the Vampire (1999)

NOVELS UNDER THE PSEUDONYM A. N. ROQUELAURE: The Claiming of Sleeping Beauty (1983), Beauty's Punishment (1984), Beauty's Release: The Continued Erotic Adventures of Sleeping Beauty (1985)

NOVELS UNDER THE PSEUDONYM ANNE RAMPLING: Exit to Eden (1985), Belinda (1986)

"When I get dismissed as a 'pop' writer," mega-bestselling authoress Anne Rice once complained, "I go crazy." Ah well. The mind-boggling sales of Rice's books—by 1989, a paperback copy of one of her books was selling every twenty-four seconds—undoubtedly affords some compensation for a stubborn critical consensus: That this New Orleans-based novelist, despite increasingly heavy-handed attempts at intellectual and philosophical weightiness, is, in the end, a quite distinctive "pop writer."

Rice skyrocketed to fame with the 1976 publication of *Interview with the Vampire*, still her best-known—and best—work. In this tale of a sensitive New Orleans vampire's melancholic struggles with his own immortality, Rice cannily combined the erotic and the Gothic, returning the vampire story to its steamy, homoerotic nineteenth-century roots. Like *Interview*, *Feast of All Saints*, a tale of half-caste mulattoes in nineteenth-century New Orleans, and *Cry to Heaven*, a saga about the sensual lives of operatic castrati in seventeenth-century Italy, combined a flair for sumptuous period detail with a deeply felt authorial empathy for the plight of outcasts: sexual, racial, and physical. Like most cult novelists, Rice owes her huge and remarkably loyal audience to the neurotic texture of those three early books, with their almost palpable sense of loss. (*Interview*'s child vampire, Claudia, is modeled on the five-year-old daughter Rice lost to leukemia.)

After a triumph with the engrossing 1985 *The Vampire Lestat* (which follows *Interview*'s deuteragonist, a suave French nosferatu who becomes a Bowie-esque 1980s rock star), Rice's subsequent contributions to her Vampire Chronicles started displaying more energy—and bulk—than inspiration. *Queen of the Damned* narrated the six thousand-year career of the Mother of All Vampires, and you feel just about every minute of it. Later works were even more seriously marred by a pseudo-intellectual and -theological grandiosity that tended to crush the hothouse Gothic moodiness that is Rice's real forte. *Memnoch the Devil*—weighing in at a thousand pages and written, all too believably, in five months—features numbingly lengthy chats with, among others, God and the Devil. Equally unwieldy were the evil-Orthodox-Jews-versus-horny-angels-epic *Servant of the Bones*, and the overwrought, Hammer Films-esque Mayfair Witches series.

It's possible that criticism of the pretentious *Memnoch* and its ilk has affected this author, despite her famous disdain for reviewers. The late 1990s have seen Rice return to her strong suit: lifestyles-of-the-sexually-marginal-rich-and-famous travelogues tricked out in supernatural garb. *The Vampire Armand* picks up the story of one of *Interview*'s supporting characters and divertingly follows his homoerotic wanderings from medieval Kiev to the steamy world of Renaissance Venice. In 1998, Rice published the first of a New Tales of the Vampires series featuring an all-new cast of vampires; the, well, fresh blood has had salubrious effects. In *Pandora*, Rice somewhat more successfully than before marries her "philosophical" interests with her novelistic strengths. The book traces the career of a (what else?) steamily beautiful Roman senator's daughter whose journey from Rome to exotic Antioch nicely parallels the book's thematic preoccupation with the conflict between Western, masculine "reason and law" and Eastern, feminine "mystery and emotion." And Rice returns, with evident pleasure, to the Italian Renaissance in the second of the New Tales: *Vittorio the Vampire*, in which a hunky sixteen-year-old Italian becomes vampirized by a beautiful . . . oh, you know.

See Also: Rice fans are bound to enjoy the extensive series of vampire novels by Chelsea Quinn Yarbro, to which Rice is heavily indebted. A thriving subgenre of vampire novels has appeared since Rice's success. Among the best of these are Poppy Z. Brite's violent and adolescent-angst-soaked epics.

—*Daniel Mendelsohn*

Robbins, Tom
1936–
b. Blowing Rock, North Carolina

FICTION: Another Roadside Attraction (1971), *****Even Cowgirls Get the Blues** (1976), Still Life with Woodpecker (1980), Jitterbug Perfume (1984), Skinny Legs and All (1990), Half Asleep in Frog Pajamas (1994)

Tom Robbins has been larking about the universe for nearly seventy years now, writing novels concerned mostly with sex, mysticism, and the value of a groaning pun. Robbins's debut novel, *Another Roadside Attraction*, concerned (nominally) the body of Christ, which had been stolen from the Vatican and smuggled to an abandoned hot dog stand in Washington State. The editor who discovered the manuscript deemed it a work of genius: "It has the potential," he wrote, "to be for the youth of today what *Catcher in the Rye* or *Catch-22* were for their times." Robbins did go on to become a counterculture icon—the groovy Zen dude—but his work hasn't held up as well as his editor hoped. His first two books, *Attraction* and *Even Cowgirls Get the Blues* (for God's sake DO NOT RENT THE MOVIE), are generally considered his best by the Robbins cognoscenti. They can usually count on their man to deliver a novel with wacky characters (*Cowgirls'* big-thumbed girl Sissy Hankshaw, *Attraction's* Plucky Purcell, *Woodpecker's* Pacific island princess Leigh-Cheri Furstenburg-Barcalona); a meandering narrative loaded with digressions about things like the early Christian persecution of dental science; rimshot jokes; and plenty of Robbins's hippie-era sexual philosophy.

From *Half Asleep in Frog Pajamas*: "Q-Jo was excited about a transcendentalist porno film entitled *Deep Thoreau*," Badda-bing! For those still into Terence McKenna-style head trips, Robbins plays the role of cosmic jester. Those of a later generation may find that his style and philosophy remind them a little too much of the creepy old Zen guy hanging around the coffeehouse.

See Also: Robbins's fans will probably also enjoy Kurt Vonnegut's more playful fiction and Robert Pirsig's Zen and the Art of Motorcycle Maintenance.

—*Bruce Barcott*

Roth, Philip
1933–
b. Newark, New Jersey

FICTION: Goodbye, Columbus and Five Short Stories (1959), Letting Go (1962), When She Was Good (1967), **Portnoy's Complaint** (1969), Our Gang (1971), The Breast (1972), The Great American Novel (1973), My Life as a Man (1974), The Professor of Desire (1977), The Ghost Writer (1979), Zuckerman Unbound (1981), The Anatomy Lesson (1983), Zuckerman Bound ([contains The Ghost Writer, Zuckerman Unbound, and The Anatomy Lesson with epilogue "The Prague Orgy"], 1985), *The Counterlife (1986), Deception (1990), **Operation Shylock** (1993), **Sabbath's Theater** (1995), American Pastoral (1997), I Married a Communist (1998), The Human Stain (2000)

NONFICTION: Reading Myself and Others (1975), The Facts: A Novelist's Autobiography (1988), Patrimony: A True Story (1991)

Of the major writers who came to dominate American fiction in the 1950s and 1960s, Philip Roth has been among the most frequently reviled. Generations of hostile readers have arraigned him for his solipsism, misogyny, and self-hatred. They see in his works a leering vulgarity, an unfocused rage, and an almost absurd preoccupation with an ever-narrowing range of subjects: the topography of Newark, New Jersey, in the 1950s; the troubled relationship between demanding Jewish fathers and their wayward Jewish sons; and the tribulations of being someone very much like . . . Philip Roth.

Roth's ongoing investigation of the inner life's contradictions and perversities has proven nonetheless to be a remarkably successful literary project. His characters are "inexplicable" experiences to themselves; their lives are "never to be solved." And yet they strive to balance the turbulence of their emotions with the stringency of their thinking. Caught in their passions, they can never know themselves or others, but the attempt to do so remains "a terribly significant business."

Roth published his first book, *Goodbye, Columbus*, to immediate acclaim and controversy. In retaliation for his satiric depiction of suburban Jewish philistinism, rabbis across the country excoriated his name. When he spoke at Yeshiva University in 1962, the moderator's first question to him was: "Mr. Roth, would you write the same stories you've written if you were living in Nazi Germany?" Today, *Goodbye, Columbus* hardly reads like a willful provocation. The social portraiture may be harsh, but the accounting of first love is tender and wistful. The title story ends with a young man catching his first glimpse of Roth's most persistent concern, the opacity of the self: "What was it inside of me that had turned pursuit and clutching into love, and then turned it inside out again?"

The 1960s were not an especially happy time for Roth. Enduring the bitter fallout of a failed marriage, he produced two large, bleak novels of couples in distress: *Letting Go* and *When She Was Good*. It was only with *Portnoy's Complaint* that Roth did truly let go, inventing for himself what he called a "dynamic, stagey, less page-bound voice." With its publication, Roth became one of America's funniest, as well as one of its most notorious, authors. Here was a novel utterly unlike anything else in the annals of American literature—or in the archives of American lechery. In one long and anguished howl, New York City assistant commissioner Alexander Portnoy relates his erotic misadventures to a silent psychiatrist; in the process, he accomplishes for masturbation all that *Lady Chatterly's Lover* achieved for copulation.

At the time, feminists and traditionalists assailed *Portnoy's Complaint*'s campaign to "put the id back in yid" and for its sexual aggression, failing to recognize that Roth's novel was hardly a liberationist's handbook. Portnoy is an unhappy man, and he is fully aware that his parents are not the repressive, monstrous philistines his imagination helplessly makes them out to be. "Torn by desires that are repugnant to my conscience, and a conscience repugnant to my desires," he is, like the narrator of *Goodbye, Columbus*, a divided self who cannot know why it is that he does what he does.

After the success of *Portnoy's Complaint*, Roth seemed in danger of becoming the prisoner of his own audacity. Known as the "bard of jerking off," he had achieved "not literary fame, but sexual fame," and, as one of his characters would put it, "sexual fame stinks." With *My Life As A Man*, Roth finally established the combination of emotional intensity and self-reflexive experiment that would characterize the rest of his work. In novel after novel, Roth would transform the events of his own life into fiction, even as he dramatized the efforts of an invented writer—Nathan Zuckerman—to do the same.

If the initial efforts at self-invention were sometimes feeble, they would soon become dazzlingly complex and affecting. *The Counterlife* presents a complex set of variations on a simple premise: A middle-aged man undergoes risky heart surgery in order to remain sexually active. In one set of stories, Nathan's brother Henry either dies or survives to lead a new life in Israel. In another set of stories, Nathan himself either dies or survives to lead a new life in England. For all the experimental fireworks, the book hews closely to Roth's abiding concern with the charge that he had betrayed his family and his faith. With an almost geometrical precision, the book balances the madness of Jewish extremism and the bitter reality of anti-Semitism, the temptation to flee domesticity and the hesitant approach toward fatherhood, the airy freedom of the writer's imagination and the brute reality of bodily love: "beneath the blanket, these beautiful undulations that are not syntactical."

Since *The Counterlife*, Roth has continued to create extravagant "mirrors of the self." *The Facts* and *Patrimony* offer themselves as unvarnished autobiography. *Operation Shylock*, by contrast, is a breathtakingly intricate exercise in the counterfeiting of identity: A writer named Philip Roth enters a contest of wills with an impostor who has assumed his name. Roth's most recent novels introduce a new cast of alter egos: In *Sabbath's Theater*, a randy puppeteer whose Celine-like descent into cruelty and madness calls forth some of Roth's most powerful writing; and in *American Pastoral*, a well-tempered hero with a "golden gift for responsibility" whose idyllic suburban life is shattered by the upheavals of the 1960s.

In these later novels, Roth continues to balance emotional extremism and intellectual clarity. The tone, however, has darkened. Embittered by experience, the Nathan Zuckerman of *I Married A Communist* longs to recede from the "agitation of the autobiographical." If Roth's career is any demonstration, however, those agitations are far from over.

328

See Also: Much of Roth's fiction reads like a blend of Henry James's moral sophistication, Franz Kafka's metaphysical wit, and Louis-Ferdinand Celine's diabolical grimace. The combination of self-reflexive plotting and sexual farce brings to mind Milan Kundera. Roth's attentions to the predicament of the Jewish writer are echoed in the work of Saul Bellow and Cynthia Ozick; the wise patriarchal storyteller of The Ghost Writer *bears at least a passing resemblance to Bernard Malamud.*

—Alexander Star

Rush, Norman

1933–
b. San Francisco, California

FICTION: **Whites** (stories, 1986), *Mating (1991)

In 1978, Norman Rush—an American college instructor—left for Botswana where, together with his wife, he would co-direct that country's U.S. Peace Corps program for the next six years. Within eight years of his return to the U.S., he had translated his African experience into two volumes of highly distinctive fiction: *Whites*, a story collection, and *Mating*, a novel that won the National Book Award.

Whites's six stories sketch the fates of Americans, Britons, and one memorably unfortunate Dutchman in Botswana. Rush's acerbic, staccato prose cuts each sentence into a prism through which to glimpse the ever-shifting aspect of cultural collision. The altruistic Western impulse to help Third World unfortunates gets complicated when the unfamiliarity of the new milieu untethers behavioral norms. Freed from their own culture, these do-gooders—medical personnel, diplomats, missionaries—show little sense of restraint or common decency. The results can include murder, illness, a satisfying romp in the sack, or simply an invasive nosiness. As the unnamed American anthropologist-narrator of "Bruns" remarks: "Sometimes I think anthropology should be considered a form of voyeurism rather than a science." The book's riskiest offering is "Thieving," in which Rush, anomalously, inhabits the voice of a young Botswana houseboy who has been "chopped from hope." All six tales in *Whites* are as feverish, dry, and bracing as the drought-stricken country they depict.

The award-winning *Mating* is more ambitious and challenging. The anthropologist-narrator of "Bruns" (still unnamed) is the heroine here, and the setting is Tsau, a feminist commune deep in the Kalahari Desert, founded by a man-hating white male sociologist, Nelson Denoon. Is Tsau a utopia or a benevolent dictatorship imposed on African women by a presumptuous outsider? Can it remain self-contained or does its proximity to pre-Mandela South Africa threaten it? Are its residents fated, by their gender, to part ways with Denoon? Could they, in fact, have engineered a romance for him with the book's narrator in order to get him out of their hair?

Mating seethes with wit, crankiness, hypotheses, and ambiguities, as well as Latinisms, Frenchisms, sociology jargon, and a dauntingly eccentric vocabulary not found in your average dictionary. The book's heroine is smart, sassy, and either shrewdly observant or worryingly paranoid. The more she is lured into Denoon's orbit, the more unreadable she becomes, even to herself—which may, paradoxically, be the key to her appeal. Or perhaps it's the wary idealism she brings to investigating a communal world of low-tech resourcefulness and innovative social custom that would have fascinated Gulliver.

The tour-de-force flourishes in *Mating* can feel like self-indulgence at times, and some readers prefer *Whites*. As for Rush's standing, the jury is still out. He's careful about what he publishes; a novel scheduled for publication in 1992 has yet to materialize. In interviews, he has also alluded to American-set stories written before *Whites* and *Mating*, but still in manuscript.

All we can do is wait—for Rush, despite his name, seems to be in no hurry.

See Also: Hilary Mantel's novel, A Change of Climate, *powerfully depicts British missionaries running amok in Botswana. Zimbabwean writer Tsitsi Dangarembga's novel,* Nervous Conditions, *explores African-Western culture collision, and much more, from an African point of view.*

—*Michael Upchurch*

Rushdie, Salman
1947–
b. Bombay, India

FICTION: Grimus (1975), **Midnight's Children** (1980), **Shame** (1983), The Satanic Verses (1988), Haroun and the Sea of Stories (1990), East, West (stories, 1994), ***The Moor's Last Sigh** (1995), The Ground Beneath Her Feet (1999)

SELECTED NONFICTION: The Jaguar Smile: A Nicaraguan Journey (1987), Imaginary Homelands: The Collected Essays (1991), The Wizard of Oz: BFI Film Classics (1992)

One side effect of the death sentence pronounced by the Ayatollah Ruhollah Khomeini of Iran upon the author Salman Rushdie in 1989 was the Solzhenitszyn-

330

ification of one of world literature's jolliest writers. There's nothing like political persecution to convince the public that an author is *serious*: that is, worthy of reverence but not much fun to read.

But it was precisely Rushdie's cheekiness, his refusal to take certain things too seriously, that offended conservative Muslims to begin with. He made the profane city of Bombay, where he grew up in a nonobservant Muslim family, his muse. "This great cosmopolis of ours," he wrote, "was and is the Central Junction of . . . the hottest tales, the juiciest-bitchiest yarns, the most garish and lurid not-penny-but-paisa-dreadfuls." Rushdie has also called the film *The Wizard of Oz* his first literary influence, and he wrote a story about the political divisions between two men who shared a boyhood passion for *Star Trek*. Like the best of India's new writers, he channels the energy of a former colonial culture seizing the English novel for its own. And he does it without succumbing to the inhibiting American conviction that to be entertaining is to be unliterary.

He has handled his role as a public figure so gracefully that few notice how well he's pulled it off. Under the *fatwa* (which was withdrawn in 1999), he behaved with dignity but not pomposity. He doesn't attempt to deny his flaws; he rubs shoulders with pop stars and film directors but gives generously of his time and energy to many political causes; and he knows how to participate in a good literary feud (most notably with John le Carré).

Midnight's Children (which followed *Grimus*, a book the author would prefer to forget) testifies to Rushdie's belief in the inextricability of the personal from the historical. It set the prototype for almost all his novels, which often feel like swaths cut from the same vast bolt of splendid brocade. Here are: the constitutionally peripheral narrator with his mysteriously metaphorical physical ailment; the teeming, fantastical family histories; imperious women seized by idées fixes; the political and religious intolerance that strangles the dream of a brash, secular, panoplied India; the ebullient combination of social observation and pop culture with myth and magic; the rude satires of various leaders; scandal, gossip, infidelity, and unrequited love. Saleem Sinai, born at the exact moment when India gains its independence, literally embodies the young nation: Its turmoils are reflected in his guts and extremities. Not only that, he's telepathically connected to one thousand other Indians born in that first hour, each with a different paranormal gift.

That number is no accident. Rushdie likens himself to Scheherazade, she who spun the myriad tales of the *Arabian Nights* to postpone her own death sentence. Like Scheherazade, he captivated his audience: *Midnight's Children* was named by the Booker Prize committee as the best novel to win the Booker in its twenty-five-year history. However, unlike Scheherazade, Rushdie showed a suspense-squelching tendency toward elaborate foreshadowing, his signature weakness and one that drains a considerable amount of pleasure from reading his fiction.

His next novel, *Shame*, pretends to pretend not to be about Pakistan, where

Rushdie's family moved in 1964. Exploring the distortions people inflict on themselves and others for the sake of honor, it relates the history of "a fellow who is not even the hero of his own life," and the author wanders in every so often to make assorted observations, including the oddly prescient speculation that if he'd written the book as "a realist novel" it would have been "banned, dumped in the rubbish bin, burned."

The extravagant surrealism of *The Satanic Verses*, however, offered it no shelter from such attacks. With its decidedly unsaga-like, fragmented structure, its metaphysical ambitions, its (mostly) London setting, and its profuse allusions to Eastern and Western mythology, the book represented a real departure. Apart from the furor it provoked, many readers find it his least satisfying novel. They usually blame this failure on the density of the book's mythic references, but it's probably due more to the confused theme—something about cultural self-hatred and the interpenetration of good and evil—and its dual "heroes," Indian actors who survive a thirty thousand-foot fall from an airliner with the result that one grows horns and the other a halo, though their behavior doesn't match these accessories (until it does). Definitely a head-scratcher, but *Verses* does contain some of Rushdie's loveliest writing.

Rushdie had expected the book's saucy parodies of Islamic parables to rile "the faithful," but he certainly didn't expect anything like the fatwa. He went into deep hiding, separated from his wife (the novelist Marianne Wiggins), briefly espoused Islam, then renounced it again, and eventually, very slowly, reemerged into public life. In 1990, he published *Haroun*, a charming if somewhat self-conscious fairy tale about an imaginary land whose evil ruler intends to destroy all stories.

Then, in 1996, Rushdie came roaring back with *The Moor's Last Sigh*, his best work (to those not stuck on the historical allegories of *Midnight's Children*). The novel is narrated by Moraes Zogoiby, half-Jewish, half-Coptic Christian, who ages at twice the normal rate, but it's commandeered by his mother, Aurora, the most divine of Rushdie's many divas. A brilliant painter, heart-breaker, and political gadfly who speaks Bombay's exuberant, improvised slang, she dismisses Hindus who ritually throw icons into the ocean as fools who "dumpofy their dollies in the drink." With 1999's *The Ground Beneath Her Feet*, Rushdie virtually recreates Aurora, with less success, as a rock singer who plays Eurydice to a reclusive, Bob Dylanesque Orpheus. The author claims to be finished with writing about India, particularly Bombay—although way back in *Shame* he professed to be penning "my last words on the East."

See Also: Gabriel García Márquez writes similarly imaginative epic family sagas about Colombia, and Thomas Pynchon plays lots of frisky, brainy word games. If you're truly adventurous, seek out The Manuscript Found in Saragossa, *an eighteenth-century proto-novel by the suicidal Polish nobleman Jan Potocki.*

—Laura Miller

Russo, Richard

1949–
b. Johnstown, New York

FICTION: Mohawk (1986), ***The Risk Pool** (1988), Nobody's Fool (1993), **The Straight Man** (1997)

To read Richard Russo is to understand why country music is such a commercial success. Passing through his depressed little upstate New York towns proves that the South has not cornered the misery market. These are country music towns populated by losers and scrimpers and hard-luck cases. The surprising thing about Russo's novels is that despite all the divorce and debt and car trouble, they're drop-dead funny, not to mention poetic, complex, and smart.

Russo's first novel, *Mohawk*, takes its name from the New York nowheresville that is its setting. In its review of the book, *The New York Times* said that the author "movingly dramatizes an older, innocent way of life." Which is true if by "innocent" you mean: the mistake of falling in love with your favorite cousin's husband, the grim fact of folks out of work when the tannery shuts down, a skyrocketing cancer rate thanks to said tannery, or the gnawing guilt one man takes to his grave.

While *Mohawk* offers a lovely, resonant, almost aerial view of the town—the place itself is the main character—Russo's second book, *The Risk Pool*, has everything you'd ever want from an American novel: humor, grace, intelligence, sociology, redemption. It tracks Mohawk native Ned Hall's coming of age as he shuffles between his unstable mother and ne'er-do-well father, finally lighting out of town, as he "join[s] the great multitude of wandering Americans, so many of whom have a Mohawk in their past, the memory of which propels us we know not precisely where, so long as it's away."

Nobody's Fool, like its main character, Donald "Sully" Sullivan, is sad and decent and funnier than it looks. It takes place in Bath, a resort town with a glorious past which has now sunk to Mohawk's level. Sully is a sexagenarian divorcè who confronts getting old and comes to the conclusion that he might have "misspent his life." Russo's prickliest book, its central theme is luck and the lack of it.

While the yuks in *Nobody's Fool* are of the grim, should-I-be-laughing variety, *The Straight Man* is outright hilarious. That it is an academic farce set in a small Pennsylvania college town might suggest a change of scene. But Russo's genius is that this sad song is sung in the key of Mohawk, describing the same job insecurities, money woes, marital

333

traumas, and all-around malaise. The protagonist, English professor William Henry Devereaux, Jr., ponders his stalled career (and stalled life) and admits that successfully moving up the ladder at "an institution like West Central Pennsylvania University was a little bit like being proclaimed the winner of a shit-eating contest." The prizes? Dead ducks, deranged undergrads, and male feminist theorists. *The Straight Man* is Russo's funniest work, not to mention the most comfortable one to read—because snickering at working-class decline isn't nearly as satisfying as howling at academics.

See Also: Fans of the melancholy humor and upstate setting of the Mohawk duet might enjoy T. Coraghessan Boyle's World's End, *which chronicles a Hudson Valley town from the colonial past to the post-war present. And if* The Straight Man's *Henry Devereaux ever bumped into Jack Gladney, the professor antihero of Don DeLillo's* White Noise, *at the MLA, they'd have a lot to talk about.*

—*Sarah Vowell*

Salter, James
1925–
b. New York, New York

FICTION: The Hunters (1956), The Arm of Flesh ([revised and republished as CAS-SADA, 2000] 1961), *A Sport and a Pastime (1967), **Light Years** (1975), **Solo Faces** (1979), Dusk and Other Stories (1988)

NONFICTION: Burning the Days (1997)

334

There may be no more important author in contemporary American literature with fewer books to his credit than James Salter, and his five novels, a memoir, and a collection of short stories have enjoyed little commercial success, although *A Sport and a Pastime* has been made a Modern Library selection. Instead, Salter remains something of a cult writer, with a small but fiercely appreciative readership. Perhaps that's because, even in Salter's more action-oriented novels, the writing is more poetic than plot-driven, and he is not easily categorized. His books range widely in subject matter, often following the events of his own adventurous life.

Critics and readers alike praised Salter, a West Point graduate and veteran, for his depiction of the Korean War in his first two novels, *The Hunters* and *The Arm of Flesh*, both about fighter pilots. He later renounced the books as imperfect efforts. It was not until *A Sport and A Pastime* that Salter wrote a novel that he thought "acceptable." Set in France, it tells the story of two young lovers, an American college student and a French shop girl, whose affair is both observed and imagined by an older man. The book is Salter at his most lyrically erotic and yearningly romantic, a masterwork of detail in which the countryside of France is as completely and authentically rendered as the passion of the lovers and the loneliness, "the overwhelming emptiness" of the man who watches them.

Light Years chronicles the dissolution of the seemingly perfect marriage of Nedra and Veri. It's set in the comfortable suburbs of New York's Hudson River Valley, where Salter himself lived for several years with his wife and children before the end of his own first marriage. The world Nedra and Viri inhabit seems charmed and effortless, full of art, music, handmade shirts, and bottles of fine Bordeaux. Yet there is devastation and loss at its heart. If *A Sport and a Pastime* is about the destructive force of passion, *Light Years* traces the kind of destruction that the lack of passion can cause. Salter describes Viri's desolation after Nedra leaves him: "A fatal space had opened, like that between a liner and dock which is suddenly too wide to leap; everything is still present, visible, but it cannot be regained."

The novel *Solo Faces* examines the forces that drive men to climb mountains. Originally written as a screenplay and star vehicle for Robert Redford (Salter was a film writer for a number of years before disavowing that too), it combines the best parts of all his works—half-taut adventure novel and half-tragedy, the story of a man living in self-imposed isolation from love and life yet somehow still heroically striving.

James Salter may never gain the larger audience he deserves. But his books will endure not only because they are beautifully written but because they are authentically felt. There is not a single false emotion, nor an unlikely scene in any of their pages.

See Also: Two other modern American masters: Ernest Hemingway, for his portraits of similarly wounded, heroic men; and William Maxwell, another "writer's writer" of a slightly earlier generation than Salter, an evocative short story writer and equally poignant, often semi-autobiographical novelist.

—*Lettie Teague*

Sanders, Dori

1934–
b. York County, South Carolina

FICTION: *Clover (1990), **Her Own Place** (1993)

NONFICTION: Dori Sanders' Country Cooking: Recipes and Stories from the Family Farm Stand (1995)

America's racial history has resulted in African-American literature that attempts to fulfill two aims: 1) to entertain a black audience that grows increasingly diverse; and 2) to prove to whites that blacks are, at the least, human and at best, just as good as them. Even the most accomplished black novelists must meet these demands without sacrificing the more conventional requirements of successful fiction.

Dori Sanders, who published her first novel, *Clover*, at fifty-four, showed immediately that she could surmount those difficulties. Story and character reign supreme in her bittersweet tale of a black girl left in the care of her white stepmother following the accidental death of her beloved father, and Sanders's masterful metaphors vividly paint Clover Hill's rural-yet-modern South Carolina world. A neighbor's lips "close like sunflowers at sundown" and open "like morning glories at dawn." Gravediggers' long strides remind Clover of "the gliding wings of buzzards flying down to feast on the dead." *Her Own Place*, Sanders's second novel, covers some fifty years of a Southern black matriarch's life. The story of Mae Lee Barnes's triumphs and trials is free of the bumpy historical exposition that occasionally slowed *Clover*'s momentum.

Sanders's white characters, though sympathetically drawn, are rarely as fully developed as her black ones. Yet, by insisting on recognizing whites' humanity, Sanders subtly exposes the folly of racial stereotyping. If her work has any message, it lies in Clover's observation: "It takes time to learn a person."

336

See Also: Convincing portraits of black Southern small-town life can be found in Alice Walker's early short fiction. Wronged woman heroines like Mae Lee populate the work of Walker, Zora Neale Hurston (especially Spunk*), and J. California Cooper's early collections.*

—*Jabari Asim*

Scott, Joanna

1960–
b. Greenwich, Connecticut

FICTION: Fading, My Parmacheene Belle (1987), The Closest Possible Union (1988), Arrogance (1990), *****Various Antidotes** (stories, 1994), **The Manikin** (1996), Make Believe (2000)

Can you pity a writer who's been awarded a MacArthur fellowship, the coveted "genius award"? You can if that means the writer will be forever shadowed by her oversized intellect. In Joanna Scott's case, you need only read one of her books to conclude that a fecund, acute, visionary imagination is the biggest thing about her.

In her first six books, each wildly different, Scott has shown herself to be a lapidary: Her fictions are multifaceted and precise, so detailed that whatever world she composes—a nineteenth-century slave ship (*The Closest Possible Union*), a rural estate in 1920s New York (*The Manikin*), artist Egon Schiele's fin-de-siecle Vienna (*Arrogance*), the capricious mindscape of a four-year-old orphan boy (*Make Believe*), a blind beekeeper's orchard (a story in the collection *Various Antidotes*)—rises up in the mind of the reader, powered by narrative force and dimensionality. But it isn't just her settings that become believable. Scott's deepest curiosity is clearly the excavation of human behavior with all its shadows and light.

The Manikin—a delicious, full-blown Gothic mystery set in a rich taxidermist's isolated mansion, where each of the characters is as trapped as the stuffed creatures that line the halls—is set apart from her earlier inventions by its sustained authorial voice. Here Scott allows us to experience her entire imagined vista through her own omniscient eyes—its dappled light and snowstorms, its owl thoughts and housekeeper's dreams and shaped loaves of bread—proving that her mind is, indeed, a wonderous place to explore.

See Also: Scott's fiction has the insoluble Americanism and allegorical weight and strangeness of Nathaniel Hawthorne and Eudora Welty.

—*Kate Moses*

337

Self, Will
1961–
b. London, England

FICTION: The Quantity Theory of Insanity (stories, 1991), **Cock & Bull** (two novellas, 1992), My Idea of Fun: A Cautionary Tale (1993), **Grey Area and Other Stories** (1994), The Sweet Smell of Psychosis (1996), ***Great Apes** (1997), Tough, Tough Toys for Tough, Tough Boys (stories, 1998)

NONFICTION: Junk Mail (essays, 1995)

In 1998, Will Self added religious book publishers to the lengthy list of people he's offended. A British publisher asked Self to write an introduction to Revelation for a series devoted to individual books of the Bible; in his essay, Self called it "a portentous horror film," and "a sick text," prompting calls for withdrawal of the books and a possible official blasphemy action.

Anybody familiar with Self's writing would know that he meant his statements as a compliment. His novels and short stories are caustic, irreverent, and satirical examinations of modern life, filled with characters whose grotesque obsessions and macabre activities make them symbols for a London society that's rotting from the inside out. Unsurprising, then, that he's working on a script for a modern-day version of *The Portrait of Dorian Gray*.

It's an ugly life that Self, a former heroin addict (he was found shooting up on Prime Minister John Major's press plane in 1997), knows about firsthand. His first collection of short stories, *The Quantity Theory of Insanity*, spun tales of madness and introduced a unique prose style that matched its topic, full of passionate emotional swings. The outrageousness deepened in *Cock & Bull*, a pair of novellas. In "Cock" a housewife finds herself possessing a penis, while the title character of "Bull" wakes up one morning to learn he has a vagina located, oddly enough, behind his knee. Self uses the concept to explore—sometimes hilariously, sometimes horrifyingly—the often arbitrary complexities of gender stereotypes.

His first novel, *My Idea of Fun: A Cautionary Tale*, is equally absurd, if less successful as an extended narrative. A satire of modern capitalist culture (embodied in the horrifically obese and psychologically manipulative figure The Fat Controller), the book suggests that Self brings more enthusiasm to crafting pungent turns of phrase about society, sexuality, and addiction than to tying together his myriad ideas into a long book. *Great Apes*, however, is a masterpiece. Focused on the high-living artist Simon Dykes and doctor Jack Busner (who both make cameo appearances in Self's 1994 short story collection *Grey Area*), the book is a riff on *Planet of the Apes*. Dykes wakes up one morning to discover that his girlfriend—and the rest of his world—have turned into chimpanzees, provoking an extended examination of the often surprisingly blurry line between man and ape. For Self, as a satirist and master of language, it's a tour de force. And further proof that whenever you hear somebody speak proudly about "humanity," "morality," or "man's better nature," Self is probably out there somewhere, laughing at the very concept in knowing disbelief and working on his next sick text.

See Also: Like Self, Martin Amis often pushes the envelope of literary propriety, and early on, Self was rumored to be merely a pseudonym of Amis's. Much of Self's writing also echoes the works of Doris Lessing and Salman Rushdie at their most unapologetically scandalous.

—*Mark Athitakis*

Seth, Vikram
1952–
b. Calcutta, India

FICTION: *The Golden Gate: A Novel in Verse** (1986), A Suitable Boy (1993), An Equal Music (1999)

NONFICTION: From Heaven Lake: Travels through Sinkiang and Tibet (1983)

SELECTED POETRY: The Humble Administrator's Garden (1985), Beastly Tales from Here and There (1991), The Poems, 1981–1994 (1995)

Vikram Seth, the irrepressible literary polymath, has always been unpredictable. While studying economics at Stanford in the early 1980s, the Indian-born author penned his first novel, *The Golden Gate*, which *The New York Times* called "one of the curiosities of the season" and Gore Vidal heralded as "the great California novel."

(Seth's award-winning travel diary of hitching home through China and Tibet, *From Heaven Lake*, as well as two books of poetry, had already established a sense of his restless and buoyant spirit.)

The Golden Gate not only captured the temporal and moral dilemmas of a group of Bay Area yuppies, it was also written as a long narrative poem comprising nearly six hundred sonnets in iambic tetrameter. Seth had blended his puckish erudition with a pop culture fluency. The result was a witty, sweetly profound, and entirely engaging rendering of the West Coast zeitgeist. Who woulda thunk it?

But if the critics were both awed and confounded by Seth's "novel in verse," there was even more of a hullabaloo seven years later, when he emerged from his working hibernation in Delhi with a novel so huge that it dwarfed its diminutive author. At nearly 1400 pages (two hundred more than *War and Peace*) and weighing in at four pounds, *A Suitable Boy* was clearly 1993's "big" book ("Buy me," Seth jokingly rhymes on the opening page, "before good sense insists / You'll strain your purse and sprain your wrists"). It earned Seth a gargantuan advance and was hyped as a return to the great *roman-fleuve* classics of Proust, Balzac, Tolstoy, and Dickens.

Yet this quintessentially Indian sprawl of a novel—a cacophonous, light-showered saga of four connected families in the years following independence—was also, according to one *Newsweek* critic, a case of "easy reading, heavy lifting." (Seth coyly shrugged off criticism of the book's "soap opera" qualities with the admission that he had once been a *Dynasty* junkie.) Assessments of the book have varied, but one thing is clear: The publication of *A Suitable Boy* was a watershed event for a generation of young Indian writers, just as the appearance of Salman Rushdie's *Midnight's Children* had been a decade earlier.

Seth has remained uncomfortable with any pigeonholing. Shrugging off the great expectations following *A Suitable Boy*, he had, until recently, put aside writing in favor of more challenging pursuits, including the classical piano. When his new novel, *An Equal Music*—a European love story about a string quartet—finally appeared in 1999, it came in, as promised, underweight and under four hundred pages. But who knows what to expect next from this phenomenally gifted and dexterous writer? "My main motivation is not to get bored," he says of his literary virtuosity. "I'm just hoping I get a vaguely maverick reputation."

See Also: For a sampling of fiction from India's "midnight's children" (the generation borne of independence), as well as the children's children, see the Rushdie-edited anthology, Mirrorworks *(which was published to coincide with the fiftieth anniversary of independence in 1997).*

—*Anderson Tepper*

Shields, Carol
1935–
b. Oak Park, Illinois

FICTION: Small Ceremonies (1976), The Box Garden (1977), Happenstance (1980), A Fairly Conventional Woman (1982), **Various Miracles** (stories, 1985), Swann: A Mystery (1987), The Orange Fish (stories, 1989), A Celibate Season (with Blanche Howard, 1991), **The Republic of Love** (1992), *The Stone Diaries (1994), **Larry's Party** (1997), Dressing up for the Carnival (2000)

When *The Stone Diaries* won the National Book Critics Circle Award and the Pulitzer Prize for fiction in 1995, it was high time. Carol Shields, Canadian expatriate from Chicago, has been publishing fiction (and poetry and plays) since 1972. She's always had good reviews, and built up a discerning readership. But the reviews condescend, without a clue to what's wrong with them and right with her. "Graceful" they call her, admiring her "gentle" satire and her wisdom about the "ordinary" lives she chronicles, as if wisdom was just another ladylike accomplishment.

Effete praise smudges Shields's rigorous style, her classical irony of smiling detachment, her shape-shifting ability to inhabit men and women. She's a great read, a witty good friend, sentence by sentence. At the same time, Carol Shields is a postmodernist's dream of a novelist. Without making a big fuss about it, she embeds big ideas in her conversational, ambling stories. A considerable esthetic intelligence is slyly interrogating, deconstructing (forgive me the word, but how else to make a claim for major literary respect?), and remaking the novel form.

All of Shields's fiction engages with the fundamental questions of narrative and meaning. What, in life as well as art, constitutes a story? Must there be a thematic arc, must there be a trajectory up a long slope of gathering clouds to a crisis, then a release into redemption or revelation or recognition? Must events be metaphors? Must life have a plot?

Shields gambles on a different, much older narrative strategy. Her characters are magnets, each the center of a dense little universe, the way we all experience ourselves in life. Things happen; people, experiences, impressions, and emotions accumulate and cling, and the accumulation is what you are and what it all means. They're "scenes" (in the wonderful collection *Various Miracles*) that "bloom out of nothing, out of the thin, uncolored air of defeats and pleasures . . . They're useless, attached to nothing, can't be . . . shaped into instruments to prise open the meaning of the universe."

In *The Republic of Love*, a smart and comically tender examination of True Love,

341

we follow Tom and Fay, through alternating chapters, before and after they meet. As in all her novels, Shields ends with the uniting rituals of Shakespearian comedy: marriage, reconciliation, reunion, or just a plain old party. The end is only a pause, she makes clear. More will happen, life goes on, nothing is finished. The characters, likeable, confused, well-meaning people, glow in Shields's prose like true heroes and heroines.

The Stone Diaries is Shields at her best. It is a "biography"—complete with photos, lists, timelines, secondary sources, eyewitness accounts, and interpretations—of the life and times of Daisy Goodwill, a woman so insignificant, she's anonymous even to herself. We're awash in "biographical debris . . . Biography is a thrifty housewife." Life stories are "raw data, no sorting machine, no briny episodes underlined in yellow pencil—it's all here, the sweepings and the leavings, the most trivial events encoded with history" (from "Collisions" in *The Orange Fish*). Shields's fictions eddy, stray off course, loop back and forth. Sometimes misery or happiness falls out of the blue. The more-or-less-examined normal life has never been rendered so thrillingly.

See Also: Like Jane Austen, Shields knows that gossip is news, and that the rituals and small talk of social gatherings aren't trivial, but a kind of relational cement. Phillip Lopate's essays and novels have a similar tone and an "unfooled," sophisticated, unsentimental but forgiving gaze at people's behavior. Georges Perec's fiction, especially Life, A User's Guide, *deals, like Shields's in minutiae and is chock-full of "biographical debris." Perec is considered a Major Novelist. Would he be so admired if his name were Georgette?*

—*Brigitte Frase*

Simpson, Mona
1957–
b. Green Bay, Wisconsin

FICTION: *Anywhere But Here (1986), The Lost Father (1992), **A Regular Guy** (1996)

For Mona Simpson's fictional families, the car is a peculiarly American vehicle of obsession, permitting the pursuit of restless, impossible dreams. *Anywhere But Here*, Simpson's bestselling first novel, opens with a drama-queen mother taking her daughter to California, then angrily banishing the girl from the car and driving off. In *A Regular*

Guy and *The Lost Father* (the sequel to *Anywhere But Here*), emotionally neglected daughters take to the road to track down the fathers who've abandoned them.

Because Simpson's novels sprawl, some praised her work as a welcome relief from the bare-bones realism of the 1980s. Simpson disputes this assessment and acknowledges a serious debt to Raymond Carver, the high priest of minimalism. The outsized preoccupations of Simpson's dysfunctional characters sometimes distract her readers from the fact that the basic unit of her work is, as she said in 1996, the individual line. Her sentences are sublime, her openings as seductive as inspired pick-up lines. "We fought," are the first two words of *Anywhere But Here*, and *A Regular Guy* begins this way: "He was a man too busy to flush toilets."

In *A Regular Guy*, Simpson's most original novel, the hero is an emotionally distant millionaire/entrepreneur who resembles Steve Jobs, the co-founder of Apple Computer and Simpson's real-life half-brother. Like Simpson's first two novels, *A Regular Guy* explores the drive to coax forth withheld love, but with more nuanced characters and language both poetic and unexpected. Simpson has proven she's a writer who can go absolutely anywhere she wants.

See Also: Fans who relish Simpson's portraits of generational conflict should try Jane Smiley's A Thousand Acres. *Thomas Bernhard, Vladimir Nabokov (*Lolita*), and Jeffrey Eugenides (*The Virgin Suicides*). All investigate misguided zealots and the desperate side of human relationships.*

—Elizabeth Judd

Smiley, Jane
1949–
b. Los Angeles, California

FICTION: Barn Blind (1980), At Paradise Gate (1981), Duplicate Keys (1984), *****The Age of Grief** (stories, 1987), The Greenlanders (1988), **Ordinary Love and Good Will** (novellas, 1989), **A Thousand Acres** (1991), Moo (1995), The All-True Travels and Adventures of Lidie Newton (1998)

There are those of us who struggle with writer's block—and then there's Jane Smiley. Her approach to fiction is singularly no nonsense; any idea is fair game. Smiley made her name by recasting King Lear, the most sorely mistreated of all literary fathers, as a dirty old man, sexually preying on his daughters. After pulling that off in *A Thousand Acres*, which won the Pulitzer Prize in 1992, she blindsided critics with her next novel, *Moo*, a send-up of academia with a vaudevillian sense of humor. Smiley is uniquely American in her can-do attitude toward all literary styles and genres. Who else would admit to an interviewer that she penned *Duplicate Keys*, a murder mystery, "for a craft purpose, because I wanted to write a plot"?

Smiley's first two novels, *Barn Blind* and *At Paradise Gate*, are arguably her most conventional, both finely wrought investigations of familial claustrophobia. With *A Thousand Acres*, parents and children confront the corrosive anger barely checked in Smiley's earlier works. When Larry Cook retires, handing over his multimillion-dollar farm to his daughters, he sets in motion a post-Freudian chain of wrongdoing and revenge. The novel opens with a naturalistic depiction of Midwestern family life ("Most issues on a farm return to the issue of keeping up appearances") before descending into increasing melodrama, which, while faithful to Lear's storm-addled state, sometimes veers uncomfortably close to an episode of *Hard Copy*.

In interviews, Smiley has said that *A Thousand Acres* and *Moo* share the same theme—the intersection of agriculture and technology—but the former is a tragedy and the latter, comedy. At cash-strapped Moo University, the faculty grapples with the commodification of higher education (students are dubbed "customers"). Smiley's satire has the unmistakable ring of firsthand experience; she was an English professor at Iowa State University. Smiley herself sparked an intellectual firestorm in 1996, when she assailed *The Adventures of Huckleberry Finn* in *Harper's*, questioning both its artistry and the legitimacy of its role as standard-bearer for the literary debate on slavery.

Although Smiley has ventured into historical fiction with two fat novels, *The Greenlanders* and *The All-True Travels and Adventures of Lidie Newton*, she seems most comfortable inside the heads of the confessional narrators of her shorter fiction. Her three novellas, *The Age of Grief*, *Ordinary Love*, and *Good Will*, are disarming in their simplicity and candor. The real masterpiece of the bunch, "The Age of Grief," is about nothing more than a husband desperately trying to prevent his wife from confiding her love for another man. As long as the narrator's fears go unconfirmed, he can revel in the joyful dailiness of marriage, the "ironic middle, where man and wife are at their best, good-humored and matter-of-fact." Herself a creature of the ironic middle, Smiley tackles murder, incest, obsessive jealousy, and other everyday hassles with irreverence and witty detachment.

See Also: Alison Lurie; she, too, has satirized academia, fretted over the mysteries of marriage, and played around with mock biography.

—*Elizabeth Judd*

Family Values: In Praise of Janes and Alices and Sues and Annes

By Caroline Knapp

When Alice McDermott won the National Book Award for fiction in 1998, I looked up from the morning paper, lifted my coffee cup, and silently cheered. McDermott's novel, *Charming Billy*, was up against two front-runners I'd already shelved in my mental library of novels I should read but probably won't: Robert Stone's *Damascus Gate*, which sounded far too dense and ponderous for my taste, and Tom Wolfe's *A Man in Full*, which I'd rather blithely relegated to the shelf labelled: Probably a great read/too bad it's 528 pages long.

As a reader, I have nothing against Stone or Wolfe, brilliant writers both. It's just that McDermott is my kind of novelist; hers are precisely the sorts of stories that beckon to me, that offer a particular, transporting promise. *Come; enter into this deeply resonant world with me; meet my family*.

There is nothing quite as compelling to me, as voyeuristically thrilling, as a good family drama. Marriages that sour, spouses who cheat and betray, children who rage and storm, whole lives stamped and irrevocably shaped by incest, alcoholism, divorce, skeletons in the dark family closet. This is *it* for me, the stuff I like to curl up with in bed at night and burrow into.

In part, this is a purely personal preference. I'm the child of a psychoanalyst. When I was growing up, almost everyone in my extended family over the age of twenty-five had been in either analysis or long-term therapy; the sense that families were complex and dark and mysterious was a given in my household, as though a certain awe about their power had been encoded in the Knapp DNA. So I'm instinctively drawn to the subject matter: how people are formed by their parents; how anger and guilt are expressed or not; how communication works and fails; how family dramas are enacted and reenacted through generations. I sometimes think that were it not for novels, which give me a way to study and explore what goes on within these complicated units, I would have taken the family path and become a psychiatrist myself, as two of my sisters and half a dozen cousins did.

Mercifully, I followed words instead of science. I first read Virginia Woolf's *To the Lighthouse* when I was sixteen, in an eleventh grade English class, and I remember the quiet astonishment I felt at her depiction of family disconnection.

There was the remote, larger-than-life Mr. Ramsey, the sense of individual family members hovering around each other in separate orbits. There were miscommunications, missed opportunities, and here and there a bright flash of intimacy that seemed to evaporate as quickly as it materialized. Woolf articulated family dynamics and feelings I'd been aware of in my own household since childhood but had never been able to define. I don't want to overstate the case, but *To the Lighthouse* went a long way toward keeping me out of medical school: It helped me not only to identify my own feeling of disconnection and my efforts, most of them unsuccessful, to alleviate it within my own family, but also showed me how powerful words could be, how they could generate insight, name the unnameable, provide solace.

Woolf is only the first in a long line of family dramatists that have kept me up at night, glued to their pages. The genre, ill-defined as it may be, has never exactly been out of vogue, and in many respects it's as old as literature itself (what is *King Lear* if not a family drama?), but as subject matter, families have been flourishing in recent years. Not long ago, I realized that almost every new novel I'd deeply enjoyed was written by a woman named Jane or Susan or Alice. Jane Smiley, Jane Hamilton. Sue Miller, Susan Minot. Alice Adams, Alice Munro, Alice McDermott, Alice Hoffman. Draw from the work of a few other authors— Mona Simpson, Gail Godwin, Rosellen Brown, Lorrie Moore, Anne Tyler—and you'll get a miniature library of family love and guilt, broken hearts and broken ties, nuclear *sturm und drang*.

You also get a very female library. True, not all family dramas are written by women—family themes are woven through the novels of writers like Philip Roth and Richard Ford and John Updike; it would be both simplistic and wrong to suggest that male writers categorically ignore spouses and parents and children. But there is something distinctly female about these books by Janes and Alices and Sues and Annes. *Intimate* is probably the better word: The lens in their works is trained squarely on the emotional world rather than the social one; relationships are their primary themes, rather than leitmotifs. Shedding light on the subtleties and subterranean nature of family feeling is the very point.

Given that women purchase most of the literary fiction sold in America, it makes sense that the family would move to center stage in today's novels: There's a market for it, driven by female readers and fostered by media forces like Oprah Winfrey. I'm gratified to see this more intimate subject matter welcomed, validated, even lauded. Family dramas are capturing major awards (I also cheered when Jane Smiley's *A Thousand Acres* won the Pulitzer Prize in 1992); they're occupying prime spots on the bestseller lists (Stephen King and John Grisham have had to make room for Anne Tyler and Gail Godwin); and they're materializing on celluloid (Anna Quindlen's *One True Thing*, Rosellen Brown's *Before and After*, Mona

Simpson's *Anywhere But Here*, to name a few). This is heaven to me. Bring them on, I say. Introduce us to ever more complicated families! The more angst the better!

Actually, I'm serious about that, in part for the sake of sheer entertainment. Family dramas appeal to my essentially nosy nature, which is why I tend to like them even when they're not particularly literary or ambitious. I wouldn't call Elinor Lipman a writer of the same caliber or depth as, say, Alice Munro, but I still read all of her books, still get sucked in by the notion that even if this isn't a beautifully wrought piece of literature, at least I'll get a peek at some twisted mother-daughter relationship. Even the cheesiest family dramas, like Barbara Taylor Bradford's, can have a soap opera appeal.

More importantly, in a culture that so often medicalizes ordinary human experience and describes family behavior in the flat, one-dimensional language of dysfunction, the family drama can illuminate some of the murkiest aspects of contemporary life. In *A Thousand Acres*, incest becomes not just a black-and-white pathological evil with obvious villains and victims, but a dark, complicated, multilayered force that reverberates across a family landscape in profound and subtle ways. In Susan Minot's *Monkeys*, which so gently and elegantly describes the effect on children of a father's alcoholism and a mother's death, the family emerges not as merely "dysfunctional" but as richly textured: vulnerable and resilient, malleable and intractible, healthy and hurt. A good family drama doesn't pathologize; it says, *This is life, this is what happens between people who love each other, rage at each other, live with and affect each other.*

There is something deeply reassuring to me about this. In both my professional and personal life, I tend to be preoccupied pretty much round the clock with themes of attachment and loss, connection and disconnection, intimacy and distance. I analyze and pick and prod and poke; I draw heavily on my own family experience and upbringing for material in my own work; I've spent a million years in therapy. So what a relief it is to journey periodically into someone else's living room; how satisfying to watch *other* families struggle and clash and change and fail to change; how gratifying to be a fly on the walls of strangers and find them not so strange at all.

There's much to recognize in these voyeuristic forays: the weird uncle in an Anne Tyler novel sums up your mother's brother in a way you never quite could; the depiction of a whacked-out, disconnected family Christmas in a Lorrie Moore short story reminds you why you, too, hate the holidays. Family dramas also offer literary yardsticks that restore perspective and proportion. Whew, you may think, my family was nuts, but at least my mother didn't nearly ruin her marriage by contemplating an affair with a murderer, like the protagonist of Sue Miller's *While I Was Gone*. At least my brother didn't hack his girlfriend to death, like the son in Rosellen Brown's *Before and After*. At least I didn't grow up in an Ann Beattie novel.

And sometimes—in the best cases—I find the stuff of compassion and insight. I loved and admired many things about Susan Minot's novel *Evening* which follows the memories and imaginings of a sixty-five-year-old woman as she lies on her deathbed, but mostly I loved that Minot made me think in new ways about my own mother's death at the same age, about the regrets she may have died with, the loves she might have lost, the fleeting nature of a human life, the randomness of choices.

Literature that not only engages and entertains but also moves you? That alters the way you look at the world, at loved ones, at your own family? You can't ask for much more than that.

Smith, Lee
1944–
b. Grundy, Virginia

FICTION: The Last Day the Dogbushes Bloomed (1968), Something in the Wind (1971), Fancy Strut (1973), **Black Mountain Breakdown** (1980), Cakewalk (stories, 1981), **Oral History** (1983), Family Linen (1985), **Fair and Tender Ladies** (1988), Me and My Baby View the Eclipse: Stories (1990), *The Devil's Dream (1992), **Saving Grace** (1995), The Christmas Letters: A Novella (1996), News of the Spirit (1997)

You never catch Lee Smith being poetic. Like the country music singers she loves, Smith is attuned to the lyricism of plain speech. Her characters can be frighteningly direct. Torn between clinging to the rural homes that confirm their identity and the gnawing desire that they are meant for more, Smith's heroines might take the old hymn "This World Is Not My Home" as their anthem. A delicate, mournful undertow beneath the celebration of deliverance on the surface reveals it as a song of exile, an expression of the fear that, having renounced this world, you won't be good enough to get into Heaven.

In her earlier books, *Fancy Strut* and *Black Mountain Breakdown* (which Roy Blount described as being like "reading *Madame Bovary* while listening to Loretta Lynn and watching *Guiding Light*"), Smith was inside her characters' heads but not inside their voices. Starting with *Oral History* and continuing with her most recent novels—*Fair and Tender Ladies*, *The Devil's Dream*, *Saving Grace*—Smith left the suburbia of the New South for the mountains of Virginia and Tennessee and North Carolina. Perhaps remembering the stories she heard and the people she met growing up as a shopkeeper's daughter in rural Virginia, Smith now draws on an oral tradition of storytelling. She filters out the barriers of culture or education that might distance us from her characters until we hear the beauty and emotion and rough-hewn eloquence in their untutored voices. Family chronicles stretching over many years, the books resist notions of the past as a simpler, more innocent place. Families are loving but precarious here, threatened by poverty as well as sickness, early death, incest, drunkenness, and madness. And still Smith's characters harbor a memory of community that never leaves them; the lives they go off to seek become a form of exile.

Smith's masterpiece, *The Devil's Dream*, is nothing less than a fictional history of one of America's great indigenous art forms—country music. Smith slips in and out of male and female voices, ranging over a hundred years. It's the perfect way to tell the history of a form of popular music, in which voices come and go, sometimes one making a single indelible mark before slipping off to God knows where. The voices of people very far away from us—in consciousness if not in time—seem as close as the voices of our family. *The Devil's Dream* is a major American novel still awaiting discovery.

See Also: Jill McCorkle's novels, like Carolina Moon, *offer generous-spirited comedy and genuine tenderness in the manner of Smith's. But it may be in country music where Smith's real soulmates can be found, particularly* The Bristol Sessions, *whose participants included the Carter Family. In modern country, the themes of exile and escape are played out indelibly in Martina McBride's great song "Independence Day," and those of fidelity and freedom throughout Bobby Cryner's album* Girl of Your Dreams.

—*Charles Taylor*

Southern, Terry
1924–1995
b. Alvarado, Texas

FICTION: Flash and Filigree (1958), **Candy** (with Mason Hoffenberg, under the pseudonym Maxwell Keaton, 1958), **The Magic Christian** (1960), **Red-Dirt Marijuana and Other Tastes** (stories, 1967), *Blue Movie (1970), Texas Summer (1991)

SELECTED NONFICTION: The Journal of the Loved One: The Production Log of a Motion Picture (1965), Virgin: A History of Virgin Records (with Richard Branson, Simon Draper, and Ken Berry, 1996)

Time: Near the beginning of the millennium. As *The X-Files* comes to the end of its highly successful run, Agents Mulder and Scully have met a great and powerful wizard who's promised to reveal the truth they've always known was out there. In exchange, the wizard has demanded a tribute. J. Edgar Hoover's stash of body-building mags in hand, the pair venture to the wizard's secret lair where they discover, behind a beaded curtain, an aging hipster toking furiously on a joint as he cackles and works a control panel. Our heroes, emboldened by the chance to see the man who has manipulated their movements, who has dreamt up every government insanity they've stumbled upon, approach the curtain, draw it back, and, with a shock, exclaim, "Good grief! It's Terry Southern!!"

Despite all the confirmed and rumored reasons that Terry Southern published almost nothing during the last years of his life, it's hard to shake the suspicion that he'd decided satire could no longer keep pace with the escalating excesses of American political and cultural life. The notion of a half-senile B-movie actor who becomes president is at least as wild as anything Southern invented for *Dr. Strangelove* (with *Easy Rider* and *Barbarella*, one of the screenplays he worked on). Toss in the "greed is good" era, and the parade of celebs storming the bestseller lists and talk shows with their heartbreaks and addictions and scandals, and it's easy to believe Southern dreamed them all up.

The closest thing to a credo in Southern's writing was a determination to laugh when most of us would cringe. That implies a willingness to be cruel, even, to a degree, to deaden the emotions. Southern aimed to incite a brawl in our heads in which disgust battles it out with helpless laughter, and loses. Like Guy Grand, the millionaire hero of *The Magic Christian* whose life's work is a series of malicious hoaxes, Southern wanted to "make it hot for people."

A master stylist, Southern wrote prose that was a curious mixture of both the sophisticated and the vernacular. Often, the outrageousness of his subject is heightened by a "My gosh!" Rotary Club tone. *Candy*—Candide rewritten as the tale of an American teen queen—and *Blue Movie* (Southern's funniest and most extreme work) use the single-mindedness of porn—how every situation is an excuse for sex—as the basis for verbal and physical slapstick.

But it's *Red-Dirt Marijuana and Other Tastes*, Southern's best book, that contains the most of him, the maniacal satirist testing himself against the master he referred to as "the Fab Faulk." In Southern's writing, the elation and isolation of hipsterism are inseparable. Reading him now, you can't help wondering if, as America lapsed into self-parody, the almost complete public silence that Southern maintained was, for him, the ultimate stance of hipster cool.

See Also: Henry Green, whose novels are dependent on the voices of his characters, was an acknowledged idol of Southern's, as was Faulkner. His more fantastic short stories suggest his love of Poe.

—*Charles Taylor*

Spackman, W. M.
1905–1990
b. Coatesville, Pennsylvania

FICTION: Heyday (1953), **An Armful of Warm Girl** (1978), **A Presence with Secrets** (1980), **A Difference of Design** (1983), A Little Decorum, for Once (1985), *****The Complete Fiction of W. M. Spackman** ([includes revised Heyday and a final novel, As I Sauntered Out, One Midcentury Morning], 1997)

NONFICTION: On the Decay of Humanism (essays, 1967)

Imagine an upper-class American equivalent of Ingmar Bergman's *Smiles of a Summer Night* scripted by Henry James and P. G. Wodehouse and you'll be close to the flavor of William Mode Spackman's slender comedies of infidelity and pursuit among the well-bred. Spackman's fiction (six short novels and two brief stories, all of it collected in *The Complete Fiction of W. M. Spackman*) constitute what may be the most graceful and sophisticated erotic comedy ever produced by an American writer. To read him is to enter a world of old money where pleasure springs continually anew. There is always a vintage to be sampled, a meal to be savored, a woman to be seduced.

Preoccupied with style, and fond of conflating third-person narrative with a character's voice (". . . the one thing she'd meant to say to him, too! it had just skidded out of her mind utterly, she urbanely informed him, and it had been almost her main reason for meeting him as she had, only fancy!"), Spackman's writing is self-consciously a performance. But—crucial to his vision of romance and sex as a game that all enter into fully

351

aware of the rules of pursuit and to his doting on sensual pleasure—the sweat never shows. Spackman marks us for seduction as surely as his characters are marked for luxurious seduction by each other.

See Also: Spackman expressed admiration for the likes of Ivy Compton-Burnett, Henry Green and Raymond Queneau. It's Henry James, however, with whom he shares a close and thorny relationship.

—Charles Taylor

Spark, Muriel
1918–
b. Edinburgh, Scotland

FICTION: The Comforters (1957), Robinson (1958), The Go-Away Bird and Other Stories (1958), **Memento Mori** (1959), The Ballad of Peckham Rye (1960), The Bachelors (1960), *The Prime of Miss Jean Brodie (1961), The Girls of Slender Means (1963), The Mandelbaum Gate (1965), Collected Stories 1 (1967), The Public Image (1968), The Driver's Seat (1970), Not to Disturb (1971), The Hothouse by the East River (1973), The Abbess of Crewe (1974), The Takeover (1976), Territorial Rights (1979), **Loitering with Intent** (1981), Bang-Bang You're Dead and Other Stories (1982), The Only Problem (1984), The Stories of Muriel Spark (1985), A Far Cry from Kensington (1988), Symposium (1990), The Novels of Muriel Spark (selections, 1995), Reality and Dreams (1996), Open to the Public: New and Collected Stories (1997)

SELECTED NONFICTION: Child of Light: A Reassessment of Mary Wollstonecraft Shelley ([republished in 1987 as Mary Shelley], 1951), The Essence of the Brontes (1993), Curriculum Vitae: Autobiography (1992)

SELECTED POETRY: Collected Poems 1 ([republished in 1982 as Going Up to Sotheby's and Other Poems], 1967)

.

When Muriel Spark was a young girl in Edinburgh in the 1920s—"destined for poetry," as she remarks in her autobiography, and already "beginning to practice memories"—she had a friend named Daphne, "an only child whose father had died 'out in India.' . . . Daphne had been told about sex," Spark writes, "and she gave me her elementary version of the affair in a matter-of-fact way: I well remember that she was concentrating on something else, like making a daisy-chain, while she informed me what 'the gentleman' did to 'the lady.' "

It's the original Sparkian twist: the juxtaposition of seemingly innocent and unrelated details with a matter of grave personal and moral importance. Spark is a writer of crisp economy and exquisite phrase: brisk, detached, skeptical, satiric, often screamingly funny, but never far in word or thought from momentous human concerns. Good and evil, joy and suffering, faith and the play of free will are her accustomed themes—*The Only Problem*, as she encapsulates them in her 1984 novel of that name. In a body of work that now includes twenty novels, short stories, poems, plays, essays, biographies, and literary criticism, Spark has been weaving daisy-chains for forty-five years, startling readers with her peremptory judgments and pondering the questions of mortal existence while picking out stains in the carpet.

From her first novel, *The Comforters*, Spark set her stamp on an elegant, pared-down, utterly distinctive narrative style and a view of the world that is simultaneously dispiriting and glorious, a place riven with deceit, self-delusion, infidelity, greed, violence, and all manner of human chicanery, but transfigured, somehow, if not redeemed, by unexpected bursts of the spirit. It's a world made up of fully realized and recognizable characters who've been stripped to their essentials, where ordinary issues of love, lust, and the desire to get ahead are routinely interrupted by supernatural—or, at any rate, inexplicable—events. Anonymous phone calls threaten the elderly in *Memento Mori*. The sound of a mysteriously clacking typewriter dictates the contents of a novel along with the events of the novelist's life in *The Comforters*. A woman plots her own murder in *The Driver's Seat*. Always, Spark is concerned with the larger picture—the nature of truth, of lies, of autonomy and its lack. Goodness is no protection in a Spark novel, and calamity rains on the just and unjust alike.

"I think that a lot of the world's problems should be ridiculed," Spark has said, "but ridiculed properly rather than, well, wailed over . . . I do believe in satire as a very, very potent art form." A well-known convert to Catholicism, a moral rather than a religious writer, Spark has been accused of coldness, "cruelty," and even complete indifference to the fate of her characters. She is critically undervalued (although she has won several of Britain's most prestigious literary awards), unclassifiable, and irritating to mournful souls. The illusive simplicity of her prose is partly to blame for this, along with her preference for comedy over gloom and her failure to get worked up over anything in the fashionable sense. "I found myself vigilant of every detail in Wally's lovemaking," says Fleur, the heroine of Spark's most overtly autobiographical novel, *Loitering With Intent*. "I was noticing, I was *counting*. I was single-mindedly conscious. In desperation I tried thinking of General de Gaulle, which made matters worse, far, far worse."

The bewitching combination of lightness and solemnity in Spark's work can be traced to her childhood in Edinburgh, and specifically to the influence of her teachers at the James Gillespie High School for Girls—among them, Christina Kay, the model for Miss Jean Brodie in her prime, whose dark eyes, olive skin, and "dazzling non sequiturs" were more than anything responsible for Spark's particular refinement. *The Prime of Miss Jean Brodie* is universally acknowledged as Spark's masterpiece, but it's only one in a long string of pearls, bright, purely formed, and all the more alluring for their fearless simplicity.

Since 1967, Spark has lived in Italy, first in Rome and more recently in a converted thirteenth-century Tuscan monastery. She was made a Dame of the Order of the British Empire in 1993, and is currently enjoying a much-publicized feud with her only son, Robin.

See Also: In her style, Muriel Spark is without peer in the exact sense: No one else writes like she does. It would appear that no one can. Critical assessment links her automatically to Iris Murdoch and, less frequently, to Barbara Pym.

—*Peter Kurth*

Spencer, Scott
1945–
b. Washington, D.C.

FICTION: Last Night at the Brain Thieves Ball (1973), Preservation Hall (1976), *Endless Love (1979), **Waking the Dead** (1986), Secret Anniversaries (1990), **Men in Black** (1995), The Rich Man's Table (1998)

Spencer is an old-fashioned novelist—a prototype of the fervent, steadily productive, unfailingly intelligent, middlebrow realist writer no longer rewarded by our fretful literary culture with its respectful attention and highest esteem. His first book, *Last Night at the Brain Thieves Ball*, is a forgettable (and uncharacteristic) jape in the Vonnegut mode, but with *Preservation Hall*, Spencer found his métier—post-1960s emotional disaster stories about the collision between the erotic and the Oedipal realms—and his unmistakable narrative voice—a prolix first-person narrator whose emotional fluency is matched only by his propensity to love, rage, blurt, and strike out impulsively.

354

But whereas *Preservation Hall* is the somewhat stagy melodrama of how a son's embarrassment over his loser father results in an accidental death and the disintegration of his own marriage, *Endless Love* is an astonishment and succeeds triumphantly as a sustained celebration and lamentation of sexual rapture. Chicago teenagers David Axelrod and Jade Butterfield fall in oceanic love (he almost as much with her alluring family as with her), but in the grip of his frustrated obsession with Jade, David burns down the Butterfields' house and eventually kills (by his mere infuriating presence) Jade's father. The novel remains unmatched in its explicit depiction of the heat and sopping actuality of first love's consummation.

The success of *Endless Love* (it was made into an abysmal film) led Spencer into a dalliance with Hollywood, and his next book appeared seven years later. Although it doesn't attain the near-perfection of its predecessor, *Waking the Dead* is a compelling attempt to marry another story of true love with the contemporary political saga of a freshman congressman haunted by the martyrdom of his activist lover and by the conviction that she isn't really dead.

Spencer's subsequent career has followed a zigzagging course as he has tried various modes, with mixed results. *Secret Anniversaries* was his venture into historical fiction. *Men in Black*, his best novel since *Waking the Dead*, explores the consequences of infidelity and the strange influence of pop culture on the lives of a novelist-turned-hackwriter and his miserable young son, who runs away from home and into the orbit of a fanatical would-be Manson. *The Rich Man's Table* is a *roman à clef* of uncertain import that centers on a young man's quest for the truth about his paternity. His mother was a famous beauty and muse to a folkie rock star clearly based on Bob Dylan, but the legendary superstar refuses to acknowledge he is the father. Unfortunately, the novel provides neither the postmodern critical frisson its premise seems to promise nor the deeper emotional explorations of Spencer's best work. Whether Spencer the traditionalist can again achieve the intensity of his earlier novels while addressing the complications of middle-aged life and the mimesis-defeating surrealism of media-saturated contemporary America will be a provocative question in the new millennium.

See Also: Nabokov's Lolita *is a close relative of* Endless Love, *with its amalgam of lyrical, guilt-shadowed eroticism and beautiful sorrow. Philip Roth's* Sabbath's Theater *provides an idea of what Spencer's visionary approach to sexuality might achieve if he could find a way to harness it to a plot about aging adults.*

—*Hal Espen*

Stegner, Wallace
1909–1993
b. Lake Mills, Iowa

FICTION: Remembering Laughter (1937), The Potter's House (1938), On a Darkling Plain (1940), Fire and Ice (1941), **The Big Rock Candy Mountain** (1943), Second Growth (1947), The Women on the Wall (stories, 1950), The Preacher and the Slave ([republished in 1969 as Joe Hill: A Biographical Novel], 1950), The City of the Living (stories, 1956), A Shooting Star (1961), All the Little Live Things (1967), *Angle of Repose (1971), **The Spectator Bird** (1976), Recapitulation (1979), **Crossing to Safety** (1987), **Collected Stories of Wallace Stegner** (1990)

NONFICTION: Mormon Country (1942), One Nation (with the editors of *Look*, 1945), Beyond the Hundredth Meridian: John Wesley Powell and the Second Opening of the West (1954), Wolf Willow: A History, a Story, and a Memory of the Last Plains Frontier (1962), The Gathering of Zion: The Story of the Mormon Trail (1964), The Sound of Mountain Water (essays, 1969), The Uneasy Chair: A Biography of Bernard DeVoto (1974), American Places (with Stuart Page Stegner and Eliot Porter, 1981), One Way to Spell Man (essays, 1982), The American West as Living Space (1987), Where the Bluebird Sings to the Lemonade Springs: Living and Writing in the West (stories and essays, 1992)

There are three principal reasons why Wallace Stegner is not widely understood to be one of the most important American novelists of the twentieth century, the equal of, say, John Cheever. First and foremost, Stegner was never part of the New York literary scene. Although his fictional settings ranged as far afield as Vermont, Denmark, and Egypt, his passion for the American West ("the native home of hope," in his immortal phrase), its landscape, and its troubled history got him labeled as an eccentric provincial talent. The antipathy some Manhattan mandarins felt toward Stegner's work sometimes reached ludicrous proportions—*Angle of Repose* and *The Spectator Bird*, novels which won the Pulitzer Prize and the National Book Award, respectively, were never reviewed in *The New York Times*.

Second, Stegner had almost no interest in literary innovation or formal experimentation. A self-described "nineteenth-century anachronism" who was born on a farm and first saw an indoor toilet when he was twelve, Stegner wrote realistic fiction grounded in history and geography, with a moral function never far beneath its surface. Third, he was an anti-Communist in his youth and an acerbic critic of the New Left and the counterculture in his later years, leading some to assume he was politically reactionary. Again, it was really a question of his moral temperament: "I fear immoderate zeal, Christian,

356

Moslem, Communist, or whatever," he wrote, "because it restricts the range of human understanding and the wise reconciliation of human differences, and creates an orthodoxy with a sword in its hand."

From the vantage point of posterity, Stegner is vindicated on all three counts. Few laugh at the idea of Western literature these days, and as both model and teacher (he spent twenty-six years directing the highly influential writing program at Stanford), he was instrumental in shaping its identity. Stegner is now remembered almost as much for his political advocacy as his fiction; *Beyond the Hundredth Meridian* and the essays in *The Sound of Mountain Water* are crucial early texts of the modern environmental movement. At times, Stegner's writing can feel stilted or old-fashioned, but his commitment to realism and to complex historical understanding are strikingly contemporary. He is justly famous for his lyrical yet precise descriptive prose, capable of flooding the reader's senses with the sights, sounds, and smells of the Pacific Coast Range or the Saskatchewan prairie. But his greater accomplishment is his remarkably mature, guardedly sympathetic consideration of human nature and its "struggle toward ambiguous ends."

After publishing a few minor novellas (the appealing rural gothic *Remembering Laughter* has hints of what is to come), Stegner launched his literary career in earnest with *The Big Rock Candy Mountain*, a sprawling, hard-luck family saga, often exquisite and heartbreaking in its details. Bo Mason, a classic American dream-seeker closely modeled on Stegner's peripatetic father, drags his long-suffering wife Elsa and their two sons all over the Great Plains and the Rocky Mountain West, buying and selling bars, hotels, diners, homesteads, and carloads of bootleg liquor in a futile chase after the big score. Although Stegner is not immune to the romantic allure of a rambler like Bo, his heart is closer to Elsa and her more modest, thwarted dreams of gentility and stability. He sees the Western myth of masculine self-reliance as false and destructive, poisonous to both the country and the human spirit. What was best about the European-American settlement of the West, he argues, arose from a bedrock of family and community responsibility—largely, that is, from the unpaid and little-acknowledged labor of women.

The Big Rock Candy Mountain might be the great epic novel of the West—up there with the best of Steinbeck and Willa Cather—if Stegner hadn't written an even better one almost three decades later. Discouraged by the commercial failures of *Second Growth* and *The Preacher and the Slave*, he mainly focused on teaching and short fiction through the 1950s and 1960s. His next major novel was the bleak, contemporary California satire *All the Little Live Things*, which introduced his crusty alter ego, retired New York literary agent Joe Allston. This marked the beginning of Stegner's golden age. In 1971 he published *Angle of Repose*, his undoubted masterpiece. Its narrator is crippled California historian Lyman Ward, trying to recreate and understand the story of his grandparents—a nineteenth-century mining engineer and his artist/writer wife, part of the elite group of educated migrants who "civilized" the West—while forgetting his own ruined life. To some extent, *Angle of Repose* echoes *Big Rock Candy Mountain*'s odyssey. But it's a subtler and richer narrative, weaving together Stegner's concerns with the devastation of the Western wilderness, the volatility of good intentions, and the difficulty of sustaining a mutually nurturing marriage.

Many of the same issues reappear in highly concentrated form in *The Spectator Bird*, the second Joe Allston novel. It's a near-perfect miniature, in which well-insulated misanthrope Joe must confront a powerful memory that challenges his sense of himself as "a wisecracking fellow traveler in the lives of other people, and a tourist in his own." Stegner's final two novels are almost equally good; perhaps it's no surprise that a writer so deeply interested in history, family, and community should thrive in old age. *Recapitulation* brings Bo and Elsa Mason's son Bruce back to a much-changed Salt Lake City to face the forgotten traces of his adolescence, while the best-selling *Crossing to Safety* traces the uneasy but loyal friendship of two couples from youth to twilight. *Collected Stories* contains the essential Saskatchewan novella "Genesis," the hilarious Joe Allston story "A Field Guide to the Western Birds," and the haunting, nearly religious "The City of the Living."

See Also: Stegner would be pleased to imagine a reader or two following him back to Western literary pioneers like Cather or Walter Van Tilburg Clark. His influence is everywhere in contemporary Western writing. His students included Raymond Carver, Ken Kesey, Larry McMurtry, N. Scott Momaday, Tillie Olsen, and Robert Stone, and he is also an obvious father figure to "Montana school" novelists like Richard Ford, Jim Harrison, and another of his students, Thomas McGuane.

—Andrew O'Hehir

Stephenson, Neal
1959–
b. Fort Meade, Maryland

FICTION: The Big U (1984), Zodiac: The Eco-thriller (1988), *****Snow Crash** (1992), **The Diamond Age, or A Young Lady's Illustrated Primer** (1995), **Cryptonomicon** (1999)

Science fiction fans have always had good reason to worship Neal Stephenson, but he has a growing readership among the mainstream literati as well. As would befit the scion of a family of engineers, Stephenson's detours through Sumerian culture, neurolinguistics, nanotechnology, and high-tech pizza delivery are authoritative. Less poetic, perhaps, than the technocultural visions that emanate from William Gibson, but eminently believable. Even when Stephenson is conjuring up a whacked-out future in which resurgent neo-Victorians—complete with top hats and snuff boxes—rule the twenty-first-century roost, as he does in *The Diamond Age*, his fiction hardly seems speculative. After all, the increasingly fragmented and yet intimately networked world envisioned in *Snow Crash*, Stephenson's breakthrough novel, has already arrived.

But neither his shrewd imagination nor his engineering acumen are what truly separates Neal Stephenson from his cyberpunk peers. Stephenson's broader appeal stems from other sources: his sure feel for Dickensian storytelling and his hilarious sense of humor. His most recent novel, the extraordinarily ambitious *Cryptonomicon*, displays both of these Stephensonian strong points in nearly every paragraph of its 928 pages.

Stephenson's novels are great sprawling affairs, packed with characters who leap off the page—monomaniacal Texas tycoons, "granola" James Bonds, kung fu fighting nymphettes. The narrative thrust is irresistible—like Dickens, Stephenson makes you care about his creations, makes you itch to turn the page and find out what happens next. If his endings sometimes fail to wrap everything up neatly, that's because the task is well nigh impossible—too much is going on for an immaculate resolution.

The reader is usually laughing too hard to notice, anyway. Readers who skim, without chortling, past the line in *Snow Crash* in which a pizza delivery car is described as a "black chariot of pepperoni fire" need to have their own neurolinguistic pathways re-hacked. *Snow Crash* stands alone in the cyberpunk canon not just because it nails the technological imperative hurling us all towards dystopia, but because it is a flat-out giggle-fest.

The same is not true for 1995's *The Diamond Age*, which takes on some knotty subjects—the role of culture in human society, the socioeconomic consequences of revolutionary technological change, and, most daringly for a science fiction writer, the relationship between a father and his young daughter. To longtime Stephenson fans, though, *The Diamond Age*'s lack of humor was a trifle distressing. If Stephenson was growing up, does that mean the rest of us had to, also?

Cryptonomicon assuaged any fears that Stephenson might be losing his risibility, however. In a mighty literary performance that is at once a riveting historical novel and a definitive exploration of the roots and psychology of computing culture, Stephenson not only shatters any sense that he is limited to a single genre, but also proves once and for all that he has one of the finest senses of humor of any contemporary novelist. Best of all, *Cryptonomicon*'s flair demonstrates the chops of a writer who is only getting better at his job.

See Also: William Gibson and Bruce Sterling are cyberpunk's two other leading lights, but admirers of Cryptonomicon *will probably enjoy Thomas Pynchon's work as well. If you're looking for the next Neal Stephenson, try Ken McCloud, the Scottish, Trotskyist, libertarian science fiction writer of the future.*

—Andrew Leonard

Stone, Robert
1937–
b. New York, New York

FICTION: A Hall of Mirrors (1967), *****Dog Soldiers** (1974), **A Flag for Sunrise** (1981), Children of Light (1986), **Outerbridge Reach** (1992), Bear and His Daughter (stories, 1997), Damascus Gate (1998)

When I think of Robert Stone I say a little prayer for his first novel, *A Hall of Mirrors*, a book too amazing to forget and too flawed to make it onto anyone's list of favorites. All the trademark characters from the later, more perfect novels make their debut here: the cynical, still questing male lead, once talented, now tarnished; the scarred woman who is too good for the men around her; the religious fanatic; the political fanatic; the con man; the addict/alcoholic. It's all grim and fascinating and chokingly sad.

A Hall of Mirrors plunges us into a world where happiness, love, beauty, and God's radiance are possible (or at least were possible), but misery and brutal violence are much more likely. It shakes you hard. What Stone's first novel fails to do, but what his next two, *Dog Soldiers* and *A Flag for Sunrise*, do brilliantly, is build suspense around a credible and compelling plot.

In *Dog Soldiers* a drug deal goes spectacularly bad. John Converse, a weasely American journalist in Saigon decides to send three kilos of heroin back to his wife Marge in the U.S.—next thing he knows, the courier, a very hard-case veteran named Ray Hicks, is on the lam with Marge, being chased by a crooked "regulatory agent." Heroin has never been so dangerous or so alluring; as Marge says, "it's just gross how nice it is."

ROCKETS' RED GLARE: WAR NOVELS *by Robert Stone*

Tiger the Lurp Dog by Kenn Miller
The kind of book that casually and effortlessly incorporates a deep understanding of war. Its authenticity makes its unpretentious whimsy and grim humor doubly effective. It is a memorable and touching novel almost in spite of itself.

One Very Hot Day by David Halberstam
A stylish, sardonic invocation of the early days of the Vietnam War, with a strong central character.

The Things They Carried by Tim O'Brien
Nothing casual here except perhaps for the sleight of hand of great art. This is the beautifully executed work of a major writer.

An Ice-Cream War by William Boyd
Boyd's complex characters, irony, and humor seem to combine properties of the traditional English novel with innovative psychological intimacy.

Horn of Africa by Philip Caputo
Terrific battle scenes, described with great verve and skill by a Vietnam veteran and war correspondent.

The violence (there's plenty of it) is unbearably real. The snapshot of drug-addled America, with its wicked Vietnam hangover, is appalling.

But there's worse: the crummy Central American nation on the brink of revolution in *A Flag for Sunrise*. An anthropologist, a nun, and a murderously paranoid speed freak, each hurtling towards an unhappy destiny, meet up on the coast of bedraggled, repressive, spy-infested Tecan (nearly Nicaragua). Almost everything about this novel astonishes, from the variety of the characters to the intricacy of their political and religious entanglements, but what stands out is the sheer muscle of Stone's prose—as impressive and alarming as the local volcanoes that "burst excrescences on Tecan's pocked dusty hide." Not for the fainthearted.

Hall of Mirrors and *Dog Soldiers* were made into movies (*WUSA* and *Who'll Stop the Rain*, respectively), and the experience, evidently less than pleasant, inspired *Children of Light*, Stone's densely allusive Hollywood novel, a bitter love story about a schizophrenic actress and a drunken, coke-fiend screenwriter. The danger here comes from

361

STRICTLY SOUTHERN *by William Styron*

The Moviegoer by Walker Percy
A witty and ironic novel in which melancholia and existential anomie are persistent themes. One of the reasons that Percy's work has achieved the status of a modern classic is that it helped redefine the modern South, marking off the boundary line between the traditional landscape of moonlight and magnolias and the new cosmos of shopping malls, country clubs, and the anxieties of urban society.

Airships by Barry Hannah
Barry Hannah is an original, and one of the most consistently exciting writers of the post-Faulkner generation. The stories in *Airships* are fiercely imagined fables in which hilarity and pain achieve a remarkable equipoise; sometimes funny, often terrifying, they are told in a captivating and unforgettable voice.

Kate Vaiden by Reynolds Price
Reynolds Price is a master of modern Southern fiction and has staked out for his territory the Piedmont region of North Carolina and southern Virginia. *Kate Vaiden* is a brilliant tour de force, one that plumbs the soul of a middle-aged woman at a moment of crisis as she begins to deal with the search for a son she abandoned while still in her teens. A Milton scholar at Duke, Price writes prose that can range from the sonorous and elegant to the breezily colloquial. *Kate Vaiden*'s high comic moments are adumbrated by a tragic sense of life that might be deemed Miltonian.

A Lesson Before Dying by Ernest J. Gaines
Ernest J. Gaines's rich talent has placed him in the forefront of contemporary American literature. Set in Louisiana of the 1940s, *A Lesson Before Dying* concerns a young black man named Jefferson who is about to die in the electric chair for murdering a white storekeeper. Another young black, Grant Wiggins, who is university-educated, finds it his mission to impart courage and pride to Jefferson before his execution. This is a painful story told with spare eloquence, and the resonance it creates long after one's reading gives it a classic dimension.

Dirty Work by Larry Brown
Like his fellow Mississippian Barry Hannah, Larry Brown comes to the reader with an arresting and unique voice. In *Dirty Work*, Brown tells of two Vietnam veterans—one black, one white, both horribly mutilated—who lie next to each other in a VA hospital two decades after the war. The stories they exchange wrenchingly reveal much about the war's agony but even more about its injustice, and the massive wrong inflicted on young men already disadvantaged in Southern (and American) society.

within, from madness and addiction, but somehow those are just as scary as vengeful narcs and tinpot dictators.

With *Outerbridge Reach*, Stone scales to new heights of lyric dazzle. He sends Owen

Browne, a dull and dreamy idealist, an upright Vietnam vet, a man of the '90s straining for a cause, on a 'round-the-world sailing race—solo. Out on the ocean Browne loses his moral bearings and cheats to try to win the race. He also thinks deep thoughts about religion and hallucinates. Back on land, a sly documentary filmmaker, an amoral creature whose function is to pare illusion from reality, seduces Owen's beautiful, tippling wife.

His most recent books are a solid but unremarkable collection of stories, *Bear and His Daughter*, and *Damascus Gate*, which wants to be a thriller but flops because the plot (fanatics, political and religious, conspire to blow up the Muslim shrines on Jerusalem's Temple Mount) is too weak to qualify. The conspiracy cranks up slowly, slowly, and loose ends flap dispiritedly through the final pages. This is Stone's most abstract, theologically knotty novel, and the action, except for a few white-knuckle riot scenes, lacks vigor. But Stone patiently, skillfully evokes the palimpsest feel of long, tortured Holy Land history.

Would you be surprised to hear that Stone was raised Catholic? That his mother was schizophrenic, his father absent? That as a young man he put in psychedelic time with the Merry Pranksters, did a journalist's tour in Vietnam, and scoped out Nicaragua and other nasty places where the United States has no proper business? Oh yeah: Stone also loves to sail. The surprise is that there's never more than the faintest whiff of autobiography in his writing. And what's that whiff? A weakness for risk and danger, a vigil for a God gone AWOL, and a fierce dedication to literature.

See Also: Recovered from Stone? Still looking for action and thought in the same bursting package? Check out Joan Didion, Don DeLillo, and Tom Wolfe (way over on the opposite end of the political spectrum). And visit the dead, too: Graham Greene and Joseph Conrad.
—Adam Begley

Styron, William
1925–
b. Newport News, Virginia

FICTION: Lie Down in Darkness (1951), The Long March (1952), Set This House on Fire (1960), **The Confessions of Nat Turner** (1967), *Sophie's Choice* (1979), **A Tidewater Morning: Three Tales from Youth** (1993)

NONFICTION: This Quiet Dust and Other Writings (1982), **Darkness Visible: A Memoir of Madness** (1990)

Born into a literary generation dominated by Northerners—John Updike, Philip Roth, Norman Mailer—William Styron may be the last great inheritor of the Southern tradition of William Faulkner and Thomas Wolfe. Even when he's writing about Brooklyn or Europe, Styron comes back again and again to his native Tidewater Virginia, a place whose somnolent, heat-infused landscape and ancient troubled history move through his work the way the James River flows through the heart of the region. And it's in the particular burdens of the South—slavery and the lingering guilt of it—that Styron finds his best and most universal material.

Faulkner casts a long shadow over Styron's first novel, *Lie Down in Darkness*, though Styron draws heavily on his own biography to furnish the scene. The novel takes place mostly in Port Warwick, Virginia, the fictional twin of the writer's hometown, Newport News. In the years before World War II, it was a sleepy place. Styron's father, an engineer, helped design ships for the Navy; his mother, a Pennsylvanian, died bitterly of cancer when her only son was thirteen. Both are recurring characters throughout Styron's fiction, as is the author himself, an only child who took early to books.

As *Lie Down in Darkness* opens, a train pulls into Port Warwick, bearing the coffin of Peyton Loftis, a beautiful wild-child-turned-suicide. How Peyton came to take a dive off a New York skyscraper—driven to the brink by her drunk, too-doting father, Milton, and her furiously icy mother, Helen—is the subject of the rest of the novel. Notable for its Southern Gothic overtones of cruelty, rage, and incest, its lyrical evocation of the Tidewater, and an interior monologue (the suicidal Peyton's) that would have done Faulkner proud, *Lie Down in Darkness* made its author a literary celebrity at the age of twenty-six.

Styron's novels aim high, and he takes years to write them; he didn't publish another book until the novella *The Long March* appeared. It follows a troop of Marine reservists as they undergo a thirty-six-mile forced march; their bodies suffer, but it's the spiritual ordeal, the tension of men unsure whether to resist or obey, that makes the tale compelling. In 1960, he published *Set This House on Fire*, probably his least-read novel.

Then, in 1967, came the ambitious and controversial *The Confessions of Nat Turner*. As a boy, Styron was fascinated by the story of Turner, a black man who in August 1831 provoked the antebellum South's most significant slave uprising a stone's throw from Styron's youthful haunts. Some fifty-five whites died before Turner's rebels were captured. When Styron began writing, little was known about Turner, except that he was a lay preacher, highly literate in a time when slaves were forbidden to read and write, and that for a man consumed by apocalyptic visions he was curiously unable to kill; only one person, eighteen-year-old Margaret Whitehead, died at his hands.

All these things caught Styron's imagination, and in the resulting novel, drawing on the lush landscapes and communal brutality of old rural Virginia, he imagined the story entirely from Nat's point of view. Especially interesting to Styron was Nat's relationship to and murder of Margaret. In his essay "Nat Turner Revisited," Styron writes, "from the first page I was drawn irresistibly to that final scene of horror in the August heat, knowing that, to my own satisfaction at least, I had discovered a dramatic image for slavery's annihilating power, which crushed black and white alike, and in the end a whole society."

Confessions earned Styron a Pulitzer Prize; it also landed him in a whole lot of hot water, perhaps not surprising given the turbulent racial climate of the late '60s and the audacity of the project. Many black critics took issue with the white writer's depiction of Nat, a character troubled by violent, lustful fantasies and often deeply disdainful of his fellow slaves as well as of their white masters. Other critics, white and black, came to his defense. (In muted form the controversy persists, continuing to spawn articles and books.)

Undaunted, Styron chose another equally audacious project: telling the story of an Auschwitz survivor, which he did in his bestselling (and most satisfying) novel Sophie's Choice. The book's narrator, Stingo, an unmistakable stand-in for Styron, is a young Southerner desperate to be a writer and living in New York in 1947. There, in a Brooklyn rooming house, Stingo meets beautiful Sophie, a Pole still consumed physically and mentally by the horrors of the concentration camp, and her Jewish lover, Nathan, brilliant and manic, who alternately bewitches Sophie and terrifies her.

Cruelty, guilt, love, and torment, the way the past slides down to crush the present: All the big Styron themes come together in Sophie's Choice. Through Stingo and his reconstruction of what Sophie suffered in Auschwitz, Styron connects the tragedy of the South with that of the Holocaust in a series of powerful, complex exchanges between attachment and guilt, oppressor and oppressed.

Since Sophie's Choice, Styron has published several smaller but notable books. They include This Quiet Dust and Other Writings, a collection of articles and essays; Darkness Visible: A Memoir of Madness, an exquisitely rendered account of the depression that almost overwhelmed him in the 1980s; and A Tidewater Morning: Three Tales from Youth, autobiographical fictions that return the author to the Virginia scenes of his childhood, that lovely, conflicted place where "the very trees seemed to hover on the edge of combustion."

See Also: Nobody approaches the South quite like Styron does, but his fellow Southerner and literary hero William Faulkner offers an earlier take on some of the same themes. Those interested in the brouhaha surrounding The Confessions of Nat Turner should see William Styron's Nat Turner: Ten Black Writers Respond, edited by John Henrik Clarke (1968), and Styron's essay "Nat Turner Revisited," reprinted as the introduction to the 1994 Modern Library edition of the novel.

—Jennifer Howard

Susann, Jacqueline
1918–1974
b. Philadelphia, Pennsylvania

FICTION: Every Night, Josephine! (1963), *Valley of the Dolls** (1966), The Love Machine (1969), Once is Not Enough (1973), Dolores (1976), Yargo (1978)

You can cite all sorts of precedents for Jacqueline Susann's novels: *Peyton Place*, Harold Robbins's *romans à clef* of the rich, beautiful, and tawdry. But there were no precedents for the success of *Valley of the Dolls*, or the two fat blockbusters that followed it right to the number one spot on the bestseller lists, *The Love Machine* and *Once is Not Enough*. She was the first author to orchestrate a full-scale media blitz around both her books and herself as a personality, and she was tireless in wooing not only the press but booksellers and even the truckers who shipped her titles to stores.

Susann's true forebears are writers like Fannie Hurst and Olive Higgins Prouty, who wrote "women's weepers," novels of heartbreak and romantic sacrifice. Susann updated that formula to suit an era when women were growing dissatisfied with their role but lacked the focus to voice that discontent. Her heroines—well-bred young women caught up in the glamorous worlds of movies, modelling, and television, the worlds Susann knew as an aspiring actress and television personality in the 1940s and 1950s—all yearn for rugged, unattainable men and are usually too polite to enjoy sex. Their coarser, less attractive friends have a great time in bed but can't hold onto men or careers. The tension between their desire for independence and their longing for romantic fidelity usually sends them to drugs and booze.

Overwrought and purple as they are, Susann's novels are also undeniably sincere. She condescended neither to her material nor her readers. She spawned dozens of imitators who made careers churning out fat, trashy reads. None has ever equaled her.

Swift, Graham
1949–
b. London, England

FICTION: **The Sweet-Shop Owner** (1980), Shuttlecock (1981), **Waterland** (1983), Learning to Swim and Other Stories (1982), Out of This World (1988), **Ever After** (1992), *Last **Orders** (1996)

It isn't his keen intelligence that makes Graham Swift one of the finest contemporary novelists, nor his skill at weaving together multiple narratives, nor his ability to tell a gripping story while exploring philosophical themes. No, what raises Swift to the top rank is his knowledge of the human heart—a profound empathy, at once compassionate and disillusioned, that can be felt on every page.

Generations, history, the bond between parents and children, the inescapable nature of the past—these are the universal themes the fifty-year-old London native has explored in six novels and a collection of short stories. To them he brings a quietly stunning sensitivity, a gift for withdrawal—Keats's "negative capability"—that allows his fictional tuning fork to vibrate unerringly to a life's deepest, truest note.

In a time suspicious of the idea that a life even has a single "truth," this formulation sounds unabashedly romantic and old-fashioned, like asserting the existence of the soul. And Swift is indeed a romantic, in the sense that he believes that pure elements—love, betrayal, lies—do exist and that our lives are ineluctably haunted by the way we deal with them. But Swift is also a modern, an existentialist romantic: His is a recognizably contingent world, filled with noise and error and the eternal weight of ordinariness, within which his characters must make themselves what they are. In the Swiftian universe, a soul is not something you are given: You have to make it, and more often than not you botch it. And it is the secret battles inside the human heart that his work so beautifully illuminates: Reading his books is like watching a psychoanalysis performed

367

by God. At its best, Swift's work recalls the piercing, heartbreaking vision of Joyce in great stories like "Clay" or "The Dead."

Swift has written two masterpieces: *Waterland* and *Last Orders*. *Waterland*, Swift's third novel, published in 1983, immediately established him as one of the leading British novelists of his generation. His longest and most ambitious book, it combines a vast historical canvas with a profound investigation of place—in this case, the Fens, the English waterland. At once a murder mystery, an exploration of family secrets, a portrait of the land itself (with a breathtaking excursus on, of all things, eels), and a meditation on the meaning of history, it is a full-course fictional meal, combining the sweep of Hardy, the intimacy of Joyce, the intelligence of Murdoch, and the craft of Fowles.

Swift's first novel, *The Sweet-Shop Owner*, is a Chekhovian tale of a good man whose simple life ends in utter loneliness—an extraordinary subject for a thirty-one-year-old novelist to engage. His second, *Shuttlecock*, is a diabolically clever story about a man's exploration of his father's supposedly heroic past. *Out of This World* and *Ever After* also have ruptured family relationships at their heart; both are subtle novelistic explorations of larger ideas—respectively, the ethics of photography (and of art itself) and the collision of science and religion. *Learning to Swim* is a fine collection of intense, enigmatic short stories in which Swift's vision of romantic relationships is at its bleakest.

Finally, there is Swift's latest and most moving book: *Last Orders*. The winner of the 1996 Booker Prize, this novel tells the story of four aging, working-class men from South London who gather in their local pub to carry out their friend Jack's last orders: to drive an urn containing his ashes to the sea. Their pilgrimage—related in a superbly muscular vernacular that captures the grain not just of voices but of personalities—strips away their secrets, exposes them to each other and to themselves, and forges an elegiac but ringing affirmation of friendship, honor, honesty, and love. *Last Orders* could only have been written by a man who not only has a profound understanding of his characters, but a profound respect for them. It is a simple and majestic achievement—required reading for those who may have forgotten that the human heart is more than an organ filled with blood.

368

See Also: Swift writes with a combination of psychological insight and fatalistic passion that recalls the James Joyce of Dubliners *and* Portrait of the Artist as A Young Man. *Thomas Hardy's deep feeling for landscape and region is echoed in* Waterland, *and Iris Murdoch's intelligence and range of interests are akin to Swift's.*

—Gary Kamiya

Tan, Amy

1952–
b. Oakland, California

FICTION: *The Joy Luck Club* (1989), **The Kitchen God's Wife** (1991), The Hundred Secret Senses (1995)

Just as her characters find their Chinese names fashionable after years of insisting on the American versions (June becomes Jing-mei again), Amy Tan seems happy being marketed as a Chinese-American writer—a bestselling one, of course. Her subject is the Catch-22 of immigrant families, where parents shelter their children only to see their own sorrowful pasts forgotten. In *The Joy Luck Club*, Tan's best novel, four daughters and four mothers—the four corners of a mahjong table—tell their stories in an attempt to bridge the divide. The endearing quirk at the heart of Tan's fiction is that all sympathy goes to the older generation. The Chinese mamas and aunties with their fractured English, culinary secrets, and bickering over family accomplishments steal every scene. Their well-coiffed, easily embarrassed daughters either fade into the wallpaper or are caricatures of materialism and ingratitude.

The Joy Luck Club was wildly successful (the paperback rights sold for a then-unprecedented $1.23 million). Although it also bagged the National Book Award, Tan's less a writer's writer than an entertainer with an unerring finger on the popular pulse. In the opening pages of *The Joy Luck Club*, Jing-mei is charged with explaining her recently deceased mother's life, the cue for sixteen carefully constructed stories about mother-and-daughter dyads. The novel works because its myriad characters create a mosaic-like complexity, partially concealing how schematic, even manipulative, the novel sometimes is.

Tan's straightforward literary style matches her up-front literary persona. She jokes about how far short she fell of her parents' aspirations; they imagined her "a neurosur-

369

geon by trade and a concert pianist by hobby." She's said that *The Kitchen God's Wife*, the tale of a female Chinese Job, is her mother's story. Tan is equally forthcoming about her own personal history: former workaholism (she was a freelance corporate writer), marriage outside the tribe (her husband is Italian-American), and bouts with depression (eased by Zoloft). She's a flamboyant regular in the Rock Bottom Remainders, along with other writer/bandmembers Stephen King and Dave Barry.

What was lucid in *The Joy Luck Club* and *The Kitchen God's Wife* becomes exaggerated and cartoonish in *The Hundred Secret Senses*, the loopy tale of Olivia, a woman whose marital breakdown brings her closer to her half-sister Kwan. Kwan is a Chinese transplant with no fashion sense and a knack for linguistic bungling. She acts heartbroken when she learns someone lives in Missouri ("Misery! Tst! Tst! . . . This too sad"), and freely corrects her husband's grammar ("Not stealed . . . stolened.") Though *The Hundred Secret Senses* is Tan's worst novel—it's hamstrung by improbable plot developments and a reincarnation subplot—it also has scenes so funny and lively that it suggests a second act for the celebrity author. If Tan tires of ethnic chic, perhaps she'll turn her hand to comedy.

See Also: Louise Erdrich, who uses her Native American heritage to wonderful fictional effect, has a sensibility similar to Tan's. For readers interested in China and Chinese-Americans, look for The Woman Warrior *by Maxine Hong Kingston and Gish Jen's* Typical American.

—*Elizabeth Judd*

Theroux, Paul
1941–
b. Medford, Massachusetts

FICTION: Waldo (1967), Fong and the Indians (1968), Girls at Play (1969), Murder in Mount Holly (1969), **Jungle Lovers** (1971), Sinning with Annie and Other Stories (1972), **Saint Jack** (1973), The Black House (1974), The Family Arsenal (1976), The Consul's File (stories, 1977), Picture Palace (1978), World's End and Other Stories (1980), ***The Mosquito Coast** (1981), The London Embassy (stories, 1983), Half Moon Street: Two Short Novels (Doctor Slaughter and Doctor DeMarr, 1984), O-Zone (1986), **My Secret History** (1989), Chicago Loop (1990), Millroy the Magician (1994), My Other Life (1996), Kowloon Tong (1997), The Collected

Stories (1997), The Collected Short Novels (1999, U.K. only, includes Murder in Mount Holly, The Greenest Island, Doctor Slaughter, Doctor DeMarr, Bottom Feeders and The Rat Room)

NONFICTION: V. S. Naipaul: An Introduction to His Works (1972), **The Great Railway Bazaar: By Train through Asia** (1975), The Old Patagonian Express: By Train through the Americas (1979), Sailing Through China (1983), The Kingdom by the Sea: A Journey around Great Britain (1985), The Imperial Way: By Rail from Peshawar to Chittagong (with Steve McCurry, 1985), Sunrise with Seamonsters: Travels and Discoveries, 1964–1984 (1985), Patagonia Revisited (with Bruce Chatwin, 1985), **Riding the Iron Rooster: By Train through China** (1988), To the Ends of the Earth ([published in U.K. as Travelling the World], selected travel writings, 1990), Nowhere Is a Place: Travels in Patagonia (with Bruce Chatwin, 1991), The Happy Isles of Oceania: Paddling the Pacific (1992), The Pillars of Hercules: A Grand Tour of the Mediterranean (1995), Sir Vidia's Shadow: A Friendship Across Five Continents (1998)

Paul Theroux is one of the most eclectic American writers of his generation—and, when read with the subtlety that he deserves, one of the best. His specialty is problem characters, and his books' teeming gallery of visionary charlatans, tyrannical bigots, victims and vamps, sexual malcontents and self-styled mavericks is impressive. So is the variety of tone in which he portrays them, for his novels range from satire to science fiction, from blue-collar bildungsroman to purest psychosexual fantasy (at least one hopes so). He's a smart aleck with a pungently lyrical prose style, a globe-hopper with an indelible Yankee sensibility. Chilled sensuality and violent hilarity collide in his pages, as overweening confidence and blighted self-esteem do in his characters.

Theroux is best known for his travel writing, which has gained him a reputation for being cranky. Still, his targets—obstructive bureaucrats, greedy developers, crusading missionaries—are often deserving of the flak he gives them, and for his every moment of chagrin, there are compensating moments of rapturous delight.

Theroux's fiction, too, has its moments of rapture, although they often serve as jump-off points into territory more sinister. The typical Theroux hero/villain (it can be difficult to tell which is which) frequently makes a fractured sort of sense at first, before getting entirely out of hand. The best-known of these is Allie Fox from *The Mosquito Coast*, a disgruntled New Englander who whisks his family off to Central America to escape the mind-numbing junk culture of the U.S. Needless to say, his Swiss Family Robinson-style experiment ends badly.

Theroux's early fiction follows the trail of his 1960s–1970s travels as a Peace Corps volunteer and a teacher (his first novels can safely be skipped). *Fong and the Indians.*

Girls at Play, and *Jungle Lovers* evoke a 1960s Africa of former colonies becoming independent nations. Of these, *Jungle Lovers* is particularly wicked as it tells how a white American insurance salesman's spoof of a black-power manifesto becomes the real thing. *Saint Jack*, inspired by Theroux's Singapore years, is a terrific yarn of a washed-up pimp who unexpectedly stumbles across his own integrity.

Theroux moved to England in 1971, and several of his subsequent novels are set there. *The Black House*, the first of these, is a weak venture into realms of sexual despair, with gothic overtones. Theroux's later excursions in this vein—the *Doctor Slaughter*, *Doctor DeMarr*, and *Chicago Loop*—are more unnerving and accomplished. (Note: The English version of *Doctor DeMarr* is an expanded, improved version of the story that appears in the U.S.-published *Half Moon Street*.) *The Family Arsenal*, a deft homage to Joseph Conrad's *The Secret Agent* about fumbling terrorists in 1970s London, charts the city in detail.

Vivid glimpses of 1970s London also appear in *My Secret History* and *My Other Life*, both symphonic books more varied in mood and setting than Theroux's earlier fiction. *My Secret History* feels as solid and expansive as a Victorian novel, but *My Other Life* turns the notion of autobiographical fiction on its head, attributing eyebrow-raising episodes—some blatantly fantastical, others less so—to a much-humiliated character named Paul Theroux. Readers unfamiliar with other Theroux works will be better off leaving this clever and disorienting masterpiece for later.

Since returning to the U.S. in 1990, Theroux has continued to roam in setting. *Chicago Loop* is a kinky morality tale about a murderer who, by way of atonement, does his best to *become* his female victim. *Millroy the Magician* takes a fabulist look at a fast-talking vegetarian guru whose magic tricks win him a Pied Piper-like following among troubled teens in inner-city Boston. *Kowloon Tong* acidly depicts the plight of Hong Kong Brits at the time of the colony's "handover" to China. *Bottom Feeders*, one of Theroux's finest recent tales (first titled "The Lawyer's Story," and available in *The Collected Short Novels*), deftly limns the fate of a Singapore-based American businessman-lawyer who, for tax evasion purposes, foolishly gives up his U.S. passport to become a citizen of Guinea-Bissau.

372

Theroux's recent *Sir Vidia's Shadow* is in a class all its own, a memoir about his ruptured thirty-year friendship with the writer V. S. Naipaul. Theroux has been roundly vilified for the book—but for the true Theroux devotee, *Sir Vidia* seems almost a skeleton key to his work. Thoroughgoing skeptics with no illusions about the glamour of the literary life may even want to start here.

See Also: *Henry James's* A London Life *and Doris Lessing's* In Pursuit of the English *usefully complement Theroux's take on outsiders entering English society. Christina Stead's*

The Man Who Loved Children serves up a dad every bit as motor-mouthed and manic as Theroux's Allie Fox.

—*Michael Upchurch*

Tóibín, Colm

1955–
b. Enniscorthy, County Wexford, Ireland

FICTION: **The South** (1990), *The Heather Blazing** (1992), The Story of the Night (1996), The Blackwater Lightship (1999)

NONFICTION: Martyrs and Metaphors (1987), **Walking Along the Border** (1987, republished in 1994 as Bad Blood: A Walk Along the Irish Border), Homage to Barcelona (1990), The Trial of the Generals: Selected Journalism, 1980–1990 (1990), The Sign of the Cross: Travels in Catholic Europe (1994)

Colm Tóibín (pronounced, roughly, toe-BEEN) may be the least stereotypically "Irish" of the new Irish writers. His powers of observation—honed in his exemplary work as a journalist—are remarkable, and his writing is lyrical, but spare, almost ascetic, completely devoid of gratuitous flourish or forced epiphany. He scarcely, if ever, calls upon conventional images of an agrarian island haunted by fairies, troubled by a traitorous history, and dominated by a repressive church and a self-destructive nationalism. Nor does his work resemble the ribald, exaggerated urban comedy of Roddy Doyle. But it would be a mistake to conclude that Tóibín is not interested in his country, its heritage, or its vexed relationship with the contemporary world.

His only novel set in Ireland, *The Heather Blazing*, is probably his finest, the story of a prominent Dublin judge who finds, in late middle age, that his family has slipped away from him. Tóibín's remarkable first novel, *The South*, follows an Irish Protestant woman's flight from a loveless marriage to a new, but hardly untroubled, life in 1950s Catalonia. Like the ambitious if flawed *The Story of the Night* (a sprawling emotional-cum-political saga of a gay man's coming of age in Argentina), *The South* explores the limits to freedom in tradition-bound societies where modernity arrives in a sudden rush while the specter of recent catastrophic violence still lingers in the air.

See Also: Tóibín's modern influences might include Iris Murdoch and Anita Brookner. Anyone interested in contemporary Ireland should also read Tóibín's journalism, especially Bad Blood, *his extraordinary account of walking the entire length of the Northern Ireland border.*

—*Andrew O'Hehir*

Tolkien, J. R. R.
1892–1973
b. Bloemfontein, South Africa

FICTION: The Hobbit (1937), Farmer Giles of Ham (1949), Tree and Leaf (1964), *THE LORD OF THE RINGS: The Fellowship of the Ring (1955), The Two Towers (1955), The Return of the King (1955),* Smith of Wooton Major (1967), The Silmarillion (1977), Unfinished Tales of Numenor and Middle-Earth (1980)

POETRY: The Road Goes Ever On: A Song Cycle (1967), The Adventures of Tom Bombadil and Other Verses from the Red Book (1962)

The Lord of the Rings is one of those works whose mere existence, whenever you happen to recall it, can make you smile. There is nothing like it in literature. An epic of unparalleled breadth, a fantasy of stunning originality, a magnificent celebration of language, John Ronald Reuel Tolkien's masterpiece is one of the great feats of the human imagination. Most authors write books; Tolkien created a world.

Tolkien's detractors—many of whose real complaint seems to be that his books are too easy to read—belittle him as a naive fantasy writer whose genre carries a declasse whiff of childish obsession. No doubt there is something childlike and escapist about fantasy. But even the loftiest, most self-consciously "literary" literature is in some measure a child's attempt to escape from the world. And the right kind of naivete—and obsession—is indistinguishable from genius.

Tolkien places himself utterly in the hands of his storytelling god—and what a story he tells! As a pure adventure, it is unparalleled. No quest in all of literature is more hopeless—and no epic with this weight of symbolic and archetypal significance is also related in such (almost unbearable) detail, step by weary step, past mazy rivers and parched canyons, as the Fellowship of the Ring marches the long, the impossible way to Mordor.

AN EDITOR'S PICK *by Michael Korda*

The Lord of the Rings by J. R. R. Tolkien

I can't help it. I have read it umpteen times. Gandalf the Wizard, the hobbits, the journey into a wonderful imaginary world that somehow parallels our own, the sense of wonder and mystery—this is English fantasy at its richest and best, a far deeper read than *The Sword and the Stone*, and truly a book to be read slowly, patiently, savoring every page. In the 1960s and 1970s kids adopted Tolkien, but he's better than that. Hardly anybody has ever created such a rich world and made it so believable, and few writers have ever sustained a cliff-hanger adventure story for so many pages. I cry every time I read the end. What more can you ask from fiction?

Brighton Rock by Graham Greene

Dark, spare, pessimistic, shocking, a novel that says everything about adolescent violence and angst, and about the limits of faith and love—still an overwhelming reading experience.

Brideshead Revisited by Evelyn Waugh

Forget the *Masterpiece Theatre* version, however good it was. The novel is the perfect distillation of English class-consciousness and storytelling; deeply romantic, a love story anchored in the profligate 1930s and highlighted by the experience of World War II; and filled with Waugh's particular blend of wit, savagery, and pure English rage. It is a major work of art, far beyond the fashionable gloss that has come to surround it.

After Many a Summer Dies the Swan by Aldous Huxley

California, the quest for eternal youth and sex, William Randolph Hearst and Marion Davies seeking nirvana via monkey gland shots: This is a biting, witty, nasty book about L.A. and America that makes *The Day of the Locusts* and *The Loved One* seem tame, and by a supremely intelligent writer. In this age of glamour and celebrity worship, this book is necessary reading, an antidote to the belief that youth, sexual vitality, beauty, and happiness are all that matters, the supreme anti-Calvin Klein ad manifesto, and hilarious—albeit disturbing—reading.

The Last Picture Show by Larry McMurtry

So you saw the movie, with Cybill Shepherd, so what? The book is much better, everything there is to say about sexuality, class, and the pain of growing up in a small West Texas town in the 1950s. It's told by a master storyteller, the Flaubert of the Plains when it comes to creating believable women characters, and still a book that you just can't put down until you reach the last page.

375

And how he tells it! The philologist Tolkien (that dusty discipline's greatest gift to literature since Nietzsche) employs a superbly flexible style, moving from the vernacular to majestic King James cadences without ever sounding inflated or quaint. Only a pedant could fail to thrill at the perfection of Tolkien's language, rising up in incantatory power when the Riders of Rohan thunder across the plains as Gondor makes its last desperate stand.

Tolkien creates a world of absolute good and absolute evil, and places into that desperately threatened world a frail everyman and his faithful squire, whose magnificent quest to destroy the all-corrupting Ring of Power is at once a Christian tale of salvation, a Homeric or medieval saga of dauntless courage, and, perhaps most movingly, an unredeemable tragedy. The triumph of Frodo and the Fellowship saves the world, but the world that is saved is a lesser world, a world from which the elves are departing, a world to which even Frodo, whose wounds are too deep to be healed, must bid farewell. In this great symphony, it is the grace notes of loss that sound deepest.

Who could forget Tom Bombadil, or the Ents, or Aragorn's long march, or the final departure to the Grey Havens? It is a universe; it is a gift.

You have to read all three books of the trilogy, and in order. *The Hobbit* is a much slighter work, and need not be read first. *The Silmarillion*, with its interminable genealogical lists and tiresome archaic diction, is strictly for Tolkien cultists.

See Also: C. S. Lewis's Chronicles of Narnia. *Tolkien's colleague's seven-volume children's tale has a much heavier-handed Christian moral than Tolkien's endlessly ambiguous tale, and the English schoolkid setup gets smarmy, but Lewis has a marvelous imagination.*

—*Gary Kamiya*

Tolkin, Michael
1950–
b. New York, New York

FICTION: **The Player** (1988), *****Among the Dead** (1993)

Michael Tolkin's first novel, the nasty Hollywood satire *The Player* (the basis for Robert Altman's film), earned him the reputation of a with-it hipster satirist, the sort of guy who can parody the ins and outs of studio deal-making *and* pinpoint the newest hot spot for a power lunch. But the novel that followed, 1993's *Among the Dead*, and Tolkin's two films as writer-director, *The Rapture* and *The New Age*, revealed a moralist incapable of being shocked at the most horrendous human behavior. The only certainty in Tolkin's work is that things will get far worse than you feared. One of the few contemporary writers who can be called religious (*The Rapture*, of all things, was a serious vision of Judgment Day), Tolkin casts himself as an Old Testament scourge for a self-absorbed age.

There are few characters in recent fiction as appallingly self-absorbed as Frank Gale, the protagonist of *Among the Dead*. Frank's wife and daughter die in a plane crash en route to a family vacation. Frank misses the flight because he's breaking things off with his mistress. He had planned the vacation as a way for the family to "heal themselves," and that mealymouthed phrase, from a letter of confession he had slipped into his wife's luggage, sums up his style. Frank has crafted the letter to make his wife take pity on *his* anguish. Only minutes after the crash Frank is toting up the privileges his role as bereaved survivor confers on him: "He had an erection, and the feeling that at this moment, if he gave in to all of his impulses, he could taste immortality, no one would punish him for anything, he had the king's right to take whomever he wanted." When Frank's letter is discovered among the plane's debris and is held up as an example of love that expects nothing in return, Frank imagines that his true calling might be writing. He is that peculiarly modern mixture of the determination to do whatever you please without regard for others, and the craving to be admired.

Tolkin uses the chic veneer of his characters' lives (the well-to-do L.A. couple of *The New Age* are like Americanized Antonioni characters) to disguise moral parable as ultrablack comedy. In *The Rapture*, and especially in *Among the Dead*, he comes as close as anyone has to Flannery O'Connor. The only thing resembling mercy that he allows Frank Gale are actually words of damnation: "This is more than you deserve." Tolkin makes it very clear that his characters deserve everything they get.

See Also: Bruce Wagner offers a crass, shallow version of the Hollywood satire of The Player. *The Hollywood fiction of John O'Hara (particularly the short story "Natica Jackson"), while not as venomous, shares with Tolkin an understanding of the industry's workings. Tolkin's novels also bear some relation to the psychosexual disturbances of Patricia Highsmith, though it's Flannery O'Connor that* Among the Dead *most recalls.*

—*Charles Taylor*

Tremain, Rose

1943–
b. London, England

FICTION: Sadler's Birthday (1976), Letter to Sister Benedicta (1978), The Cupboard (1981), The Colonel's Daughter and Other Stories (1984), The Swimming Pool Season (1985), The Garden of the Villa Mollini and Other Stories (1987), **Restoration: A Novel of Seventeenth-Century England** (1989), *Sacred Country (1992), Evangelista's Fan and Other Stories (1994), **The Way I Found Her** (1997), Music and Silence (1999)

Rose Tremain moves in a mysterious way, her wonders to perform. All right, that's actually the first line of an Anglican hymn, and it's supposed to describe God, not Tremain, but it aptly captures the haunting powers of this surprising and adventurous English novelist.

Unpredictability is a mark of Tremain's work. She had written a novel about a loyal, aging butler (*Sadler's Birthday*) and one about an eighty-seven-year-old writer interviewed by an American journalist (*The Cupboard*) when she attained prizes and prominence with her fifth novel, the bright and bawdy story of seventeenth-century England, *Restoration*. With its broad canvas, its layered comedy, and especially the complex portrayal of its flawed hero, Robert Merivel, *Restoration* helped reestablish the historical novel as a respectable endeavor for "literary" fiction writers.

Tremain is happiest, she has said, chronicling people who are "on the edge of the main event," whether outside their time, like Robert Merivel (who never feels entirely comfortable with the excesses of his age), or their gender, like *Sacred Country*'s troubled transsexual, Mary Ward, who spends most of her difficult life trying to become Martin. After the vibrant colors of *Restoration*, the painful greys of *Sacred Country* baffled some readers and critics. But this superbly sympathetic work shares much of the melancholy and humor of Tremain's other novels, and was a masterful study of gender dysphoria written before such material was fashionable. Tremain turned temper again with *The Way I Found Her*, a warmer story of a precocious English adolescent, Lewis, who spends a transformative summer in Paris, learning the interlocking ways of love and literature.

Tremain is of roughly the same literary generation as Ian McEwan or Julian Barnes (with whom she shares an interest in France), and like them she shuffled off the imperative of earlier English fiction to worry over people's social standing. Class interests her very little. Tremain and her characters care more about love, pain, and the rugged difficulty of emotional survival. Her characters generally suffer loss: Merivel loses the affection of the king, Lewis loses his Parisian love; and various characters, for shorter or longer spells, lose their sanity. Her generous writing is never small or quaint, and her failures, when they occur—most frequently in dialogue, where she can write lines that sound jarringly wrong—are forgivable. Tremain is also a gifted short story writer, so any of her collections are worth sampling to get a taste of her distinctive prose, her sly comedy, and the great range of subjects seized on by her busy, inventive mind.

See Also: "Quirky British women writers" seems to be a growing fiction genre—it might include anyone from Jane Gardam to Muriel Spark. Tremain's voracious intelligence brings to mind the work of other experimenters in historical fictions such as Penelope Fitzgerald, Jeanette Winterson, and Hilary Mantel—with whom Tremain shares a passion for both the broad social canvas and the small and vivid local detail.

—Sylvia Brownrigg

Trevor, William
1928–
b. William Trevor Cox in Mitchelstown, County Cork, Ireland

FICTION: A Standard of Behavior (1958), The Old Boys (1964), The Boarding-House (1965), The Love Department (1966), The Day We Got Drunk on Cake and Other Stories (1967), Mrs. Eckdorf in O'Neill's Hotel (1969), Miss Gomez and the Brethren (1971), The Ballroom of Romance and Other Stories (1972), Elizabeth Alone (1973), Angels at the Ritz and Other Stories (1975), The Children of Dynmouth (1976), Lovers of Their Time and Other Stories (1978), Other People's Worlds (1980), Beyond the Pale and Other Stories (1981), Fools of Fortune (1983), The Stories of William Trevor (1983), The News from Ireland and Other Stories (1986), Nights at the Alexandra (1987), **The Silence in the Garden** (1988), Family Sins and Other Stories (1990), Two Lives (comprises Reading Turgenev and My House in Umbria, 1991), *William Trevor: Collected Stories** (1992), **Felicia's Journey** (1994), **After Rain** (stories, 1996), Death in Summer (1998), Ireland: Selected Stories (1998)

SELECTED NONFICTION: A Writer's Ireland: Landscape in Literature (1984), Excursions in the Real World: Memoirs (1994)

"I'm very interested in the sadness of fate," William Trevor once explained. So interested, indeed, that hope and redemption rarely chip at the hard, sunstruck shale of his stories and novels. For him, "fate" is a synonym. It means burden, really, the immovable stone of circumstance. Writers who revere Trevor have grappled with this everseeping darkness. Reynolds Price believes the Irish author's works all contain "a core of defeat." John Fowles calls it a "malevolent, drifting determinism."

The beauty of Trevor's work, though, lies in this: he always writes about the disappointed, but his work is never disappointing. In fact, it is quietly masterful. Trevor is not an "innovator," per se, but a classicist. In his insinuating, painful body of work, one finds a Greek tragedian crossed with Turgenev, maybe Maupasant. Unavoidably, he is also often likened to his countryman, James Joyce. Alight on any Trevorian sentence, and it becomes obvious there is a lineage, though not from the language-intoxicated Joyce of *Ulysses*, but the leaner prose-smith of *Dubliners*.

One might attribute Trevor's fatalism to a heavy-hearted childhood; the author's parents were unhappily married, and the family moved often about rural Ireland. Or perhaps one can credit The Troubles themselves for Trevor's bleak brand of compassion; he's an Irish Protestant, and as a sculptor (his occupation before prose) once won the Irish Section prize for the "Unknown Political Prisoner" sculpture competition. In short, he's seen firsthand how stabbingly impossible peace seems between Republicans and Unionists.

This current resident of Dorset often sets his works in England, also sometimes in begrimed cities where the terra-cotta "has blackened to the insistent local sheen," to quote his most Hitchcockian novel, *Felicia's Journey*. Just as Hitchcock matched the tempo of his film's scores to the heartbeat of his audience, rising in suspense, so does Trevor expertly drop in hints and foreshadowings. He knows creepy. This technique works best in his unsettling conman-as-protagonist novels, such as the Whitbread Prize-winning *The Children of Dynmouth* or *Other People's Worlds*. Each work employs the scaffolding of a thriller, but they resonate, finally, because Trevor so meticulously builds the characters within. A too-used phrase, but: We feel their pain.

Trevor has written more than a dozen novels, but for the ages, his reputation will spring from his short stories. His *Collected Stories* belongs on any desert island reading list, so much does it keep on giving. A quick roster of the greats would include "The Ballroom of Romance," about the reluctant compromises of an Irish dance-hall frequenter; "The Grass Widows," about two married couples who unsettlingly reflect each other; "Raymond Bamber and Mrs. Fitch," in which Trevor even manages to make us ache for a total bore; and "The Original Sins of Edward Tripp," in which a guilt-ridden man reaches out, frantically, to a neighbor who cannot help him.

In 1996, nowhere near depleted, Trevor issued another astonishingly fine story collection, *After Rain*. What strikes you again and again, reading Trevor, is that he possesses such remarkable powers of seeing. In the title story, a young woman, recuperating from an ended love affair, has an epiphany after studying an Italian Renaissance depiction of the Annunciation. The landscape within is shown, she realizes, after rain, when the Italian countryside softens and clarifies before the heat returns. It's that kind of painterly, emotional illumination which flowers throughout Trevor's prose. But you have to let it work on you. Some critics (the late Anatole Broyard, for one) have found his prose precision, his economy, off-putting.

Just let them read "The Piano Tuner's Wives," the brilliant first story in *After Rain*. It's about a blind piano tuner whose first wife, Violet, described the world to him; when she dies, his new wife, Belle, not only pictures things differently, but becomes jealously bent on erasing Violet's perspective and therefore her place in his past. " 'A primrose isn't flamboyant,' Violet said. 'More like straw or country butter, with a spot of colour in the middle.' And he would nod, and know."

See Also: There's Joyce's Dubliners, *of course. As for other Irish writers, probably Sean O'Faolain is the best, in an understated Trevorian way. Otherwise, Trevor's work most resembles that of Chekhov and Turgenev.*

—**Katherine Whittemore**

Tuten, Frederic
1936–
b. New York, New York

FICTION: The Adventures of Mao on the Long March (1971), ***Tallien: A Brief Romance** (1988), Tintin in the New World (1993), Van Gogh's Bad Cafe (1997)

Tuten's most recent novel, *Van Gogh's Bad Cafe*, proved he was someone on intimate terms with contemporary painting and polished, visionary writing: Eric Fischl did the cover, Susan Sontag provided the laudatory notes. Tuten, a longtime East Village resident, treasured the late Roy Lichtenstein as a best friend and instructed both Oscar Hijuelos and Walter Mosley in creative writing at City College of New York. If he can be said to be any one thing, it's regenerative. The intense sensations of the art he loves magnify in his stories and rebound fiercely at the reader.

Tallien: A Brief Romance, his best book, mingles a frustrated love story from the French Revolution with a remarkable and vivid account of Tuten's own red diaper youth in the Bronx. The writing is visual, olfactory, sexual, and yet delicate, although Tuten

381

will chop his sentences down to a coarse word or two when it fits. In *Tintin in the New World*, the clarifying moment comes when the clean-cut European cartoon kid, on vacation at Macchu Picchu, loses his virginity to Mme. Chauchat, the female fatale of Thomas Mann's *The Magic Mountain*. That stunt is almost faced down, however, by a purely descriptive passage about a thunderstorm assailing a lonely tower, with the hero trapped inside. Tuten's audacious blending of pop and high culture may sound far-fetched, but the effect is always dead-on.

See Also: Flann O'Brien's The Third Policeman *may masquerade as a crime novel, but like much of Tuten's fiction, it's more illuminating when seen as a linguistic adventure— and it's funny. So is* A Void, *by the wildly experimental Georges Perec, written (and translated from the French) without a single letter "e."*

—*Sally Eckhoff*

FOUND IN TRANSLATION   *by Laura Miller and Brigitte Frase*

Although this book covers only authors who write in English, most avid readers don't limit themselves to fiction originally written in their native tongue. In fact, in the past forty years English-speaking readers' tastes have become even more global, with the work of authors from Latin America, Asia, Eastern Europe, and Africa commanding the kind of attention and book sales once reserved for the Germans and the French. Here is our list of writers whose translated works are well worth seeking out.

Isabel Allende (1942–)

Allende's accessible version of magic realism has earned her the reputation, not unjustified, of being a Gabriel García Márquez lite. Her novels swarm with colorful subplots, eccentric characters, and fabulist elements, but she foregrounds the experiences of those trampled in Latin America's wrenching political struggles and often brutal gender relations more overtly than García Márquez does. Such concerns befit a former journalist whose uncle, Chilean President Salvador Allende, was assassinated in 1973 when a military coup overthrew his socialist government. Recommended title: *The House of the Spirits.*

Ingeborg Bachmann (1926–1973)

An Austrian-born poet and short story writer, Bachmann is one of the best postwar women writers in German, and a true cosmopolite. She also wrote opera librettos (mostly for Hans Werner Henze) and radio plays. When the poet wunderkind turned to stories, her critical contemporaries were displeased with her philosophical interrogations and feminist questionings. Recommended title: *Malina.*

Jorge Luis Borges (1899–1986)

The key short fiction of this immensely erudite, Argentinian Europhile was for the most part written in the 1940s and translated and published in English in the 1960s. Borges's most influential stories are intellectual and metaphysical games or puzzles, featuring such marvels as infinite libraries, imaginary civilizations, and basements that contain the universe. He finds the human mind's attempt to transcend its own limitations, and to subject reality to reason, amusing but not very promising. Recommended title: *Ficciones*.

Italo Calvino (1923–1985)

Fable is the basis of Calvino's playful, imaginative fiction; he compiled a massive collection of Italian folktales in 1956. His stories and novels usually fuse the cosmic with the quotidian, as when a recurring character, Qfwfq (a protean, atom-like entity), explains that the universe, formerly contained in a single point, expanded into infinity when someone within the point decided to make pasta for everyone else. He can be earthy one moment, then take your breath away with his dazzling, kaleidoscopic visions the next. Recommended title: *Invisible Cities*.

Marguerite Duras (1914–1996)

Duras had been writing for forty years when her 1984 novel *The Lover* captured French awards and international attention. At eighteen, she moved from Saigon to France, became a Communist, then an ex-Communist. She was a young beauty, then an old ravaged one who lived with a young lover and massaged her Image. She wrote novels, plays, and the famous screenplay for Alain Resnais's 1959 film *Hiroshima Mon Amour*. Recommended title: *The Lover*.

Umberto Eco (1932–)

This jolly novelist-scholar is without a doubt the only semiotician to score a number one bestseller by writing a cerebral thriller about medieval monks. Eco's theme—and, it would appear, his passion—is the "seduction of knowledge." Readers of Eco's subsequent novels will encounter literary and philosophical greats (Shakespeare, Descartes) and figures from pop culture (Scarlett O'Hara, Sam Spade), along with heaping portions of history and linguistics. Recommended title: *The Name of the Rose*.

Gabriel García Márquez (1928–)

That rarest of creatures, a Nobel laureate with a large popular readership, Garciá Márquez has written one unqualified masterpiece, *One Hundred Years of Solitude*, and several qualified ones. Whether his setting is the invented Colombian town of Macondo or someplace that can be located on the map, his vision is lush, soulful, and epic, that quintessential mixture of saga and fabulism called "magic realism," and his preferred subjects are baroque family histories and the complicated, melancholy reflections of aging men. Recommended title: *One Hundred Years of Solitude*.

David Grossman (1954–)

Born and raised in a nation-proud Israel, Grossman doesn't like what he sees. He criticized Israeli politics directly in 1987's *The Yellow Wind*, for which he interviewed Palestinians and West Bank settlers. But his deepest indictment is in the keening, metaphorical, magical 1994 novel, *The Book of In-*

timate Grammar. It's about another one of those boys (see Grass for the model) who refuses to grow up: the Six Day War is on the yellow horizon. Recommended title: *The Book of Intimate Grammar.*

Guenter Grass (1927–)

Grass is the grand old man of postwar German letters and still a politically engaged writer. In his scorching magic-baroque novel *The Tin Drum*, a boy named Oscar refuses to grow up when he sees what Nazism is doing to his world. That book is already a classic tale of modern German literature. With *Cat And Mouse* and *Dog Years*, it forms a surreal trilogy about the emergence of the Third Reich. Recommended title: *Tin Drum.*

Milan Kundera (1929–)

This Czech-born French writer combines Eastern Europe's dark humor and disillusioned view of human nature (unwittingly nurtured by Communist regimes) with a subtle philosophical imagination. The latter has recently been in ascendance with *Slowness* and *Identity*. Impatient readers will have more fun in his earlier work. Recommended title: *The Unbearable Lightness of Being.*

Naguib Mahfouz (1912–)

People who wish that contemporary fiction were more like Balzac's or George Eliot's—observant, socially engaged, and meaty with human conflict—should sample the early realist work of Egyptian Nobel laureate Mahfouz. His novels portray family and street life (often in Cairo) as his characters grapple for purchase in a world made turbulent by the encounter between tradition and modernity. Mahfouz's later work became more allegorical, experimental, and, alas, less engrossing. Recommended title: *Palace Walk.*

Andrei Makine (1957–)

A Siberian-born novelist who sought asylum in France in 1987, Makine writes poetically in French about Siberia, the two big wars, and about harboring dreams of civilized life in the midst of barbarism and privation. His fiction is Proust via Pasternak. Recommended title: *Dreams of My Russian Summers.*

Yukio Mishima (1925–1979)

Mishima is now well-known for falling on his sword after launching an assault, with a small group of followers, on Japan's Self-Defense Ministry. He was a Romantic, besotted with Japan's lost manhood. Will he also be remembered and read for his lyrical death-haunted novels? Although three-times nominated for a Nobel, he's an adolescent's writer, like Hermann Hesse and Thomas Wolfe. Not that there's anything wrong with that . . . Recommended title: *The Sailor Who Fell from Grace with the Sea.*

Haruki Murakami (1949–)

The cool, hip, bemused tone of Murakami's slightly surreal but always entrancing fiction seems neither Japanese nor Western, just distinctly Murakami. His introverted, post-noir, outsider heroes are more likely to consume spaghetti and scotch than sushi or saki, and that's Miles Davis you hear on their stereos. They drift through life, get mixed up with mysterious women, chase down enigmatic leads, tangle with odd characters and usually wind up confronting some evocative but baffling existential conundrum. Recommended title: *A Wild Sheep's Chase.*

384

Ngugi Wa Thiong'O (1938–)

Although this Kenyan's novels are overtly and passionately political (some Western critics have called them too didactic), his characters and their dilemmas are nevertheless vivid and tragic. Ngugi's subject is not so much colonialism as its aftermath and the bitterness of revolutionary hopes betrayed. At his best, he brings an elemental, almost Shakespearean grandeur to the throes of an Africa struggling to become itself again. (In 1977, Ngugi renounced English prose and vowed to continue writing only in Gikuyu.) Recommended title: *Petals of Blood*.

Georges Perec (1936–1982)

Sociologist, essayist, translator, and novelist, Perec is the trickster of modern French literature. He reveled in lipograms: a form in which one or more letters of the alphabet are deliberately suppressed. *A Void* (a novel published in 1969 as *La disparition* and translated into English in 1996) managed without the letter E. He's more than just clever, although his novels always have a puzzle form. Recommended title: *Life: A User's Manual*.

Jose Saramago (1922–)

Unlikely things happen in this Nobel laureate's novels: Portugal breaks off from the Iberian peninsula, everyone in the world goes blind, a flying machine is powered by human minds. Yet if Saramago is a novelist of ideas, he is also political (his characters battle dictators and tyrannical bureaucrats) and psychological (as demonstrated in his sensitive depictions of human love), as well as fantastic—and he can tie this all together with a corker of a plot. Something for every reader, in short, can be found in the pages of his work. Recommended title: *Blindness*.

Georges Simenon (1903–1989)

Belgian-born and a Dostoevsky wanna-be, Simenon was deservedly beloved for his Inspector Maigret series, eighty-four books in all. The unassuming inspector never let crime interfere with a good lunch at home, cooked by the solid, stolid Mme. Maigret. Simenon is the leading candidate for most prolific twentieth-century novelist: four hundred books. Recommended titles: *The Patience of Maigret* and *Maigret Hesitates*.

Isaac Bashevis Singer (1904–1991)

Born in Poland, Singer became an American citizen and a New Yorker, but he wrote and thought in Yiddish. He won the Nobel Prize for writing lusty, passionate, often mystical fiction that plumbed ghetto and shetl culture in order to ask profound questions about morality, human nature, the destiny of the Jews, and the often occluded will of God. In Singer's stories and novels, the demons and angels of Jewish folklore make their presence felt (sometimes literally) among both villagers and their descendents: the shaken survivors of the Holocaust attempting to patch a life together in Manhattan. Recommended title: *Enemies, A Love Story*.

Christa Wolf (1929–)

She was the gadfly and conscience of Communist East Germany, a Brechtian socialist who didn't hesitate to criticize her country's shortcomings in plain, hard language. After reunification she was accused of being a Stasi informer. She explained and defended herself in *Was Bleibt*, translated as *What Remains*, an autobiographical novella. Conflicted idealists and ideologues are the most interesting kind. Recommended title: *The Quest For Christa T*.

FICTION: If Morning Ever Comes (1964), The Tin Can Tree (1965), A Slipping-Down Life (1970), The Clock Winder (1972), Celestial Navigation (1974), Searching for Caleb (1976), Earthly Possessions (1977), Morgan's Passing (1980), *Dinner at the Homesick Restaurant** (1982), **The Accidental Tourist** (1985), Breathing Lessons (1988), **Saint Maybe** (1991), Ladder of Years (1995), A Patchwork Planet (1998)

It's unattainable knowledge, of course, how much these two biographical details matter: 1) Anne Tyler was raised in various Quaker communes and, at age eleven, had never once used a phone; 2) Her late husband was a psychiatrist. Such twin forces imply a resistance to modernity but also a decidedly contemporary—it's quiet but fierce—intention to heed the subconscious of her characters. Even though they won't heed it themselves—or can't. As Macon Leary wonders in *The Accidental Tourist*, thinking of his wife who leaves him after their young son dies, "Maybe all these years, they'd been keeping each other on a reasonable track. Separated, demagnetized somehow, they wandered wildly off course."

Tyler's novels rarely wander "wildly off course," but a sort of writerly demagnetization seems to account for their flaws. Her least successful books fall into one polar trap or another. Sometimes they're too Fannie Flagg-cute; *Morgan's Passing* comes to mind, about a Walter Mitty sort who embarks on various tiresome antics. The book was nominated for a National Book Critics Circle Award, but it's too arch by half. Strained humor, likewise, defeats her two earliest novels, *If Morning Ever Comes* and *The Tin Can Tree*, both of which Tyler is said to dislike. And sometimes, her characters live lives so unexamined, we can't work up much heart for them. Take *Celestial Navigation*, which, admittedly, has moments of shrewd loveliness, but the protagonist, a dire agoraphobic, is hard to abide, no matter how humane our sympathy. Or note 1995's dissatisfying *Ladder of Years*, in which mom-and-wife Delia, nebulously feeling unseen and underappreciated, walks out—for a year and a half. And doesn't know why. And comes back, seemingly unchanged.

Still, Tyler's best books—*Dinner at the Homesick Restaurant*, *The Accidental Tourist*, and *Saint Maybe*—ache with beauty. She has a fine plainsong style (she credits Eudora Welty as her biggest influence) and an ear for the unobtrusive perfect word. In

The Accidental Tourist, for instance, "chips" of cloudy sky show through Sarah Leary's hair. In *Saint Maybe*, the trees on the Bedloe's street look "elderly."

"Elderly" Baltimore, by the way, belongs as much to Tyler as to film directors John Waters or Barry Levinson. All her books are set in or near the city where she herself lives. The place mirrors her characters: traditional, somewhat provincial, real—and family-riveted, for better or worse, too. Tyler's highest gift, in fact, is for banking through a cumulus of familial hope and longing and disappointment, especially in *Dinner at the Homesick Restaurant*. It's a great book, her best; there's an *Ah, Wilderness!* tone to the proceedings. Ezra, one of the three grown children of Pearl Tull, a wife abandoned in the 1940s, doesn't want to see *The Long Day's Journey Into Night* aspects of his childhood. But brother Cody, (Cain, to Ezra's Abel) and sister Jenny recall a pinched, love-deprived existence. Each time sweet Ezra tries to gather the clan for a homey family dinner, it shards into argument and sulking. Tyler's rendering of angry, fatigued Pearl, by the way, is heartbreakingly fine. Blind and dying, Pearl asks Ezra to search through her girlhood diaries. She's hunting for a passage that memorializes a moment of unerodable happiness. When Ezra hits upon it, the prose shimmers and cuts.

That bit, though, vies with the most compelling chapter Tyler has written yet, entitled "The Department of Reality," in *Saint Maybe*. Death is often a plot propellent in Tyler's slow-paced books (she majored in Russian studies); here, through two concentric tragedies, three small children are left fatherless and will soon be motherless. Agatha, seven, and Thomas, five, try to care for their baby sister, Daphne, who "had been crying so hard that her upper lip was glassed over. She blinked and stared at them and then gave a big, sloppy grin. 'Now what is this nonsense I'm hearing?' said Agatha sternly. She was trying to sound like Grandma Bedloe. Grownups had these voices they saved just for babies. If she'd wanted, she could have put on her mother's voice. 'Sweetheart!' Or Danny's. 'How's my princess?' he would ask. Used to ask. In the olden days asked."

Tyler's work is uneven, but uncanny, too, and at times deeply moving. Maybe the way to understand her is thus: She writes therapeutic books about people who would never, ever, get therapy.

See Also: The less Gothic strain of Southern women writers, past and present, such as Eudora Welty, Gail Godwin and Kaye Gibbons.

387

—*Katharine Whittemore*

Updike, John
1932–
b. Shillington, Pennsylvania

FICTION: The Poorhouse Fair (1959), The Same Door (stories, 1959), Rabbit, Run (1960), Pigeon Feathers and Other Stories (1962), The Centaur (1963), Olinger Stories: A Selection (1964), Of the Farm (1965), The Music School (stories, 1966), Couples (1968), Bech: A Book (stories, 1970), **Rabbit Redux** (1971), Museums and Women and Other Stories (1972), A Month of Sundays (1975), Marry Me (1976), **The Coup** (1978), Too Far to Go: The Maples Stories (1979), Problems and Other Stories (1979), *****Rabbit Is Rich** (1981), Bech Is Back (stories, 1982), The Witches of Eastwick (1984), **Roger's Version** (1986), Trust Me (stories, 1987), S. (1988), **Rabbit at Rest** (1990), Memories of the Ford Administration (1992), The Afterlife and Other Stories (1994), Brazil (1994), **In the Beauty of the Lilies** (1996), Toward the End of Time (1997), Bech at Bay: A Quasi-Novel (1998), Gertrude and Claudius (2000)

SELECTED NONFICTION: Assorted Prose (1965), Picked-Up Pieces (1975), **Hugging the Shore** (1983), Just Looking: Essays on Art (1989), **Self-Consciousness: A Memoir** (1989), Odd Jobs (1991), Golf Dreams: Writings on Golf (1996), More Matter: Essays and Criticism (1999)

SELECTED POETRY: Collected Poems 1953–1993 (1995)

Just reading the list of John Updike's titles can make a normal person—one of the billions of non-Updikes who populate the world—*winded*: Think what it took to write them. The fiction titles work together like a loose narrative: At first, you enter a festival space (*The Poorhouse Fair*; *Rabbit, Run*), moving past lots of exciting bird and animal imagery at a pretty good clip. Then the strong, solid domestic titles of the middle years (*Couples*, *A Month of Sundays*), filled with marriage and comfortable entanglements. Next the suave titles—a seasoned, been-around voice pouring out the whiskey and telling you where it's at: *Trust Me*, *Roger's Version*. In recent years, a post-game sigh of

TIMELESS NOVELS ABOUT LOVING *by John Updike*

Loving by Henry Green
   An English estate in Ireland during World War II lyrically houses amorous doings among both masters and servants.

Madame Bovary by Gustave Flaubert
   A young bourgeois wife seeks spiritual and sexual fulfillment away from the marital bed and runs grievously into debt.

La Princesse de Clèves by Madame de Lafayette
   A long extramarital attraction is consummated by the heroine's announcement that the way to keep love alive is not to marry.

Les Liaisons Dangereuses by Choderlos de Laclos
   Polymorphous seduction and betrayal among the terminally jaded eighteenth-century aristocracy: an epistolary novel.

The Scarlet Letter by Nathaniel Hawthorne
   Among the Puritan pioneers of Boston, a promising clergyman falls afoul of a dark-haired protofeminist and her wizardly older husband.

an imagination moving gratefully out to pasture, with an occasional snap of irritation: *The Afterlife*, *Bech at Bay*. Updike is so compulsively a writer that even his "Also by John Updike" pages tell an interesting story.

There's a discomfort about Updike. America is still new to its celebrity culture—we've never decided what to do with our veteran actors, athletes, and writers. (Do we go on applauding them? Do we slip them a pension and get them away from our population centers?) When Updike comes up, so does a kind of sub-auditory impatience: He's probably still the best word-by-word, thought-by-thought, sentence-by-sentence writer we have, *but isn't it time he moved on?*

By tacking so closely to his own experience, Updike has made this a character question—do we like the kind of man Updike appears, from his books, to be? He is without question the most successful literary writer of his era, but his career has also been a series of hairsbreadth escapes, of jumping out of the dirigible just before it crashes. Updike broke into print with light verse, just as the world decided that funny, rhyming poetry was something it could possibly do without. He rode the old *New Yorker* style (of dapper, frosty wit) from 1954 until that brave and reliable horse gave out in the mid-1990s.

There are moments in the recent novels, firing up the high style, when he sounds the way you do on a telephone call when you aren't sure whether you've been cut off; Updike is speaking to a literary audience that may or may not still be listening. (Since Updike is exquisitely sensitive to all things Updike, he's covered this material himself in a short story called "Learn a Trade" in which an artist argues his kids away from the business: "He was like a man who, having miraculously survived a shipwreck, wants to warn all others back at the edge of the sea.")

From the beginning Updike set himself the task of recording every input a fairly ordinary, ordinarily lucky middle-class person might be expected to log over a seventy-year life. In this, he's had no serious competition for four decades. (The Vietnam-era *Rabbit Redux* gives a better 3-D sense of what 1969 America felt like than any book—not to mention movies, TV shows, or straight history.) He's been aided by three qualities that, by themselves, would have guaranteed impressive careers in any writer: He's funny; he's able to express how anything feels (for example, there are a number of rapturous scenes where characters find longed-for toilets); and he writes beautiful sentences that bop around in your head after you read them like show tunes.

Updike's early books cover childhood, parental conflict, small towns, and adolescence. The voice is endlessly, mechanically receptive, as if a NASA robot lander had been outfitted with the "Talk of the Town" sensibility and set loose on Updike's bio. *Rabbit, Run* cemented his reputation as a writer willing to go the extra mile for data about sex, on which he could be ugly and comic, and then resolve the discomfort with a beautifully literary punch, like this bit from *A Month of Sundays*: "Head and heart, tongue and cunt, mouth and cock—what an astonishing variety of tunes were played on this scale of so few notes."

To avoid literary celebrity, Updike ditched New York in 1957 for the Boston suburbs. ("Celebrity," Updike writes in his memoir *Self-Consciousness*, "is a mask that eats into the face.") The sixties made him famous anyway, as a chronicler of the problems suburban husbands got into being faithful and unfaithful to suburban wives. These novels vary in quality from the over-staged adulteries of *Couples* to the truly heart-rending *Marry Me* and *Too Far To Go*.

In the mid-1970s, Updike divorced his first wife, remarried, and picked Vladimir Nabokov as his literary model. Jazzed up, he produced some of his strongest work. There was enough career behind Updike to leave him open to two charges: The first is misogyny. But the charge feels groundless. Updike writes about everything, and the capacity to dislike, desire, misjudge, and occasionally abhor the opposite sex is one of the many things both genders have in common.

The second charge was leveled by the younger writer David Foster Wallace in a giant-killing, hey-fogies-get-off-of-my-interstate 1997 essay called "Twilight of the Phallocrats." Updike was, according to Wallace, one of America's last "Great White

Narcissists." But to call Updike a narcissist (and this charge has gotten around) misses the point, since the impulse behind his self-examination is so basically generous: Our smallest encounters and realignments of feeling are worthy of inspection; if Updike's life is a story, everybody's is. What could be a less selfish notion than that?

Updike finished up high school as yearbook editor and class president; he learned the local standard of excellence, and he met it, and in certain ways he didn't look beyond it. That impulse may never have left him. In the closing semesters of his career, the author has slipped comfortably into serving as a kind of class president and yearbook editor for American writing. His 1970s and 1980s book reviews are taken as definitive, like an alumni magazine's "Class Notes" section. He's president of the American Academy of Arts and Letters. His most recent bestseller list appearance was as editor of the administrative-sounding *Best American Stories of the Century*. If Updike missed an opportunity, it was to play a different role, to be not the dependable class president, but the class goat who surprises everyone with a stunt they never knew they were longing for. But his forty books record his forty productive years with a fidelity unmatched by any competitor, or by any of the other media that have become a writer's scariest competition. It's an immense achievement.

See Also: For their loyalty to keeping every sentence as alive and crammed with information as possible, try Martin Amis and Vladimir Nabokov. There's also Philip Roth, with whom Updike has been engaged in a long generational footrace. Then there's Nicholson Baker's weird meditation U & I, *a gesture of near-homicidal love that's one of the few examples we have of the literary genre of stalking.*

—*David Lipsky*

Vidal, Gore
1925–
b. West Point, New York

FICTION: Williwa (1946), In a Yellow Wood (1947), The City and the Pillar (1948), The Season of Comfort (1949), A Search for the King: A Twelfth-Century Legend (1950), Dark Green, Bright Red (1950), **The Judgment of Paris** (1952), Messiah (1954), A Thirsty Evil: Seven Short Stories (1956), *Julian (1964), Washington, D.C. (1967), **Myra Breckinridge** (1968), Two Sisters: A Novel in the Form of a Memoir (1970), **Burr** (1973), Myron (1974), 1876 (1976), Kalki (1978), Creation (1981), Duluth (1983), Lincoln (1984), Empire (1987), Hollywood: A Novel of

America in the 1920s (1990), Live from Golgotha: The Gospel According to Gore Vidal (1992), The Smithsonian Institution (1998)

NONFICTION: Rocking the Boat (essays, 1962), Sex, Death and Money (1968), Reflections upon a Sinking Ship (essays, 1969), Homage to Daniel Shays: Collected Essays, 1952–1972 (1972), Matters of Fact and Fiction: Essays, 1973–1976 (1977), The Second American Revolution and Other Essays (1982), Armageddon? Essays, 1983–1987 (1987), At Home: Essays (1988), A View from the Diner's Club: Essays, 1987–1991 (1991), Screening History (essays, 1992), The Decline and Fall of the American Empire (essays, 1992), United States: Essays, 1952–1992 (1993), **Palimpsest: A Memoir** (1995), The American Presidency (1998), Gore Vidal Sexually Speaking (1999)

Visitors to the chamber of the United States Senate on a particular June afternoon in the mid-1930s were rewarded with an unusual sight: a skinny blond boy wandering among the lawmakers with perfect insouciance, stark naked except for a bathing suit. The boy, a congressional page, was the grandson of Oklahoma's distinguished Senator Thomas Pryor Gore, and already accustomed to taking liberties.

In some sense, Gore Vidal has always been a casual insider, a flash of Grecian nakedness among the suited Puritans, a troublemaker at large in American history. Most critics agree that he has written no masterpiece; a few even say that he has written no book of lasting importance. But everyone agrees that his greatest talent lies in making an impression.

To understand him, it is best to start with his life, brilliantly laid out in his 1995 memoir *Palimpsest*. A world-class seducer in every sense, Vidal counts among his conquests (some platonic, some not) everyone from Jack Kerouac to Jackie Kennedy, Eleanor Roosevelt to Anaïs Nin, George Santayana to Bob Guccione. *Palimpsest* also makes it clear that throughout Vidal's career he has reached aggressively for greatness, and often come up short.

His first three books were written, as the author himself has observed, in the "some-

FIVE USEFUL NOVELS *by Gore Vidal*

Doctor Faustus by Thomas Mann

This is one of those great world novels that Americans keep trying to write on the grounds that *Finnegan's Wake* is bound to wear out or, worse, be read. We have had no luck with this sort of book. But then, our national genius is for the short story and the novella. Mann dramatized the nature of the demonic in our affairs and how, like the spirochete, a disease like Nazism can permeate the body politic just as, in Mann's genius-protagonist, syphilis proves to be a malignant source to his genius as well as to his destruction. Powerful metaphor, great novel.

Good as Gold by Joseph Heller

I suppose it's because Heller is a superb comic novelist with an eye and ear for American idiocies that he's never included on lists of novelists to be venerated. (*Catch-22* went into the language before it got to the syllabus.) Here he is at his deadly best, illuminating a hustler on the make in politics. Can it possibly be Dr. Henry Kissinger?

Cosmicomics by Italo Calvino

Sorry, but the European product has, at its best, outdone us in my time. Fortunately, our English departments will be the last to know: Unfortunately, our readers will never have easy access to some wonderful books. Calvino presents us with a primordial atom that contains a Neapolitan family quarrelling about dinner—we hear only their voices. Eventually the atom bursts and there, all over space, is our universe jump-started. Total fireworks, as we follow Qfwfq through his various metamorphoses down the ages from dinosaur to mollusk to a "shell on a railroad embankment as a train passes by. A party of Dutch girls looks out the window," and he realizes, "The eyes that finally open to see us didn't belong to us but to others." But—triumph—Q realizes, "All those eyes were mine." To be seen is half of seeing.

The Golden Spur by Dawn Powell

Readers are now finding Powell's wonderfully tough novels, and in this late one (1962) she recreates the golden age of Manhattan, as a young man from the hinterlands comes to town to find the allegedly famous man who got his mother pregnant. This is probably *the* New York novel—Greenwich Village transfer, you might say—and wildly funny, funny with a true wit's wildness.

Creation by Gore Vidal

Mary McCarthy, another true wit, once observed that if you got nothing else out of *War and Peace*, there was always Tolstoy's gourmet recipe for strawberry jam. I sometimes write novels that tell things we ought to know about but don't. In the fifth century B.C., one man, had he lived to seventy-five, could have known Socrates, the Buddha, Confucius, and Zoroaster, not to mention Lao Tse, Mahavira, Democritus, et al. I invented such a character, and these admittedly unlikely confrontations take place as we encounter, at its root, every religious and political system that we know today. My recommendation here is entirely disinterested: One writes this sort of book to pass on knowledge of worlds we are encouraged to know nothing of—which explains why, when we were in Vietnam, we were amazed that Buddhists were setting themselves on fire. Our educational system and media have seen to it that we know nothing at all of other cultures and religions and next to nothing of our own. Worst of all, curiosity is carefully switched off in our schools.

what affected, plain-plywood style" popularized by Hemingway. His third effort won him (in the long term) a place in American literary history, as well as (in the short term) ostracism by the American literary establishment. *The City and the Pillar* was the first American novel to deal frankly and positively with homosexual love. With it, Vidal assumed a lifelong role: that of a Cold War-era Marquis de Sade, shocking bien-pensant America with his real and fictional enormities. (He resists the "gay" label—saying that there is no such thing as a homosexual person, only homosexual acts.) His shock tactics proved all too effective, and he spent much of the 1950s writing scripts for movies and television.

In the 1960s Vidal finally came into his own. He launched the first of several unsuccessful attempts at a political career. Then he published two vastly different, bestselling books. *Julian*, a fictional memoir, portrayed the fourth-century Roman emperor who made a doomed, last-ditch attempt to supplant Christianity with paganism. Impeccably researched, and yet contemporary in its use of language, it portrayed the past with deadly seriousness as a battle of the contending forces that created the present.

Myra Breckinridge, Vidal's best-known book, featured a very different pagan hero: Myra, formerly known as Myron, a recent recipient of sex-change surgery who runs amok in a Los Angeles acting school. The novel is a gleeful send-up of American culture, sexual politics, and literature. The sequel, *Myron*, and *Duluth, Kalki, Live from Golgotha*, and *The Smithsonian Institution* continue in the same vein. These are the most irritating of Vidal's works, in which his irony grows shrill and his protests inflated.

In the spirit of *Julian*, Vidal also wrote several historical novels spanning America's past from 1775 to 1952, beginning with *Burr*, which narrates the Revolution and the nation's founding from the viewpoint of a political outcast and accused traitor. Aaron Burr is Vidal's most fully rounded character, with equal parts wisdom and ambition, worldliness and self-delusion. With *Lincoln, 1876, Empire, Hollywood*, and *Washington, D.C.*, he made his grand subject the passing of the republic and the arrival of the empire, and in the process drew unforgettable portraits of such figures as Thomas Jefferson, Mary Todd Lincoln, Theodore Roosevelt, and William Randolph Hearst. His insights are more those of a historian than a novelist, though. There is penetrating intelligence on every page, but no flights of genius. (Indeed, many critics feel that Vidal's true gift is as an essayist.)

That Gore Vidal has so thoroughly succeeded at infiltrating American culture is strange, for he is one of the few truly aristocratic voices our democratic society has produced: ironic, cosmopolitan, erudite, a sexual nonconformist with a superbly honed sense of envy who needs to be both gate-crasher and guest of honor at every party and uses sentences as playing fields of blood sport. Certainly Vidal's blue-blooded self-confidence helps explain his huge, diverse output. Perhaps it explains some of his intellectual accomplishments, as well, and his literary shortcomings.

See Also: Comparisons to Vidal's contemporaries usually end up sounding far-fetched; his literary models are mostly long-dead: Jonathan Swift, Mark Twain, Suetonius, Henry Adams. But his ambition and his political/historical/religious interests invite comparison to his mortal rival Norman Mailer. Vidal's comic-satiric pastiches of American culture have affinities with the work of Don DeLillo and David Foster Wallace.

—*Adam Goodheart*

Vollmann, William T.
1959–
b. Santa Monica, California

FICTION: You Bright and Risen Angels: A Cartoon (1987), The Rainbow Stories (1989), The Ice Shirt (Volume One of Seven Dreams: A Book of North American Landscapes series, 1990), **Whores for Gloria** (1991), Fathers and Crows (Volume Two of Seven Dreams series, 1992), The Rifles (Volume Six of Seven Dreams series, 1993), **Thirteen Stories and Thirteen Epitaphs** (1991), **Butterfly Stories: A Novel** (1993), *The Atlas: People, Places, and Visions** (1996), **The Royal Family** (2000)

NONFICTION: An Afghanistan Picture Show: Or, How I Saved the World (1992)

B ecause he has plumbed the depths of the international underworld, William T. Vollmann is often tarred with the brush of "transgression." However, unlike the cool, discombobulating efforts of the Transgressive Lit pack (Dennis Cooper, Kathy Acker, and the granddaddy of them all, William S. Burroughs), Vollmann's work, swerving clear of irony and gratuitous gross-outs, swells with heart. That he examines the full range of bad human behavior voraciously and unsentimentally—yet refrains from treating it as a crude device or an end unto itself—makes him one of the more courageous storytellers of our time.

Vollmann's reputation is built largely on the physical and artistic daring displayed in his magazine journalism and short stories. He garnered national attention for a 1994 article in *Spin* that chronicled his mission to save a young female sex slave in Thailand, and again when a journalistic foray to the former Yugoslavia (Croatia) resulted in a car bombing that left his two travel companions dead.

Unlike stoic male writers venerated for their Hemingway-esque machismo, Vollmann manages to map exotic territory and go nose-to-nose with danger while maintaining a certain emotional accessibility. In his fact-meets-fiction story collections—*The Atlas, The Rainbow Stories, Butterfly Stories, Thirteen Stories and Thirteen Epitaphs*—and his early memoir, *An Afghanistan Picture Show*, he's a quivery, curious spirit cloaked in a he-man's hide. This is not to suggest that he's cute or boyish—in his clumsier moments, his fascination with prostitutes and miscellaneous thuggy types seems repellent, the obtuse ramblings of a tragedy tourist. Generally, however, he is keenly observant—especially of atmospheric details that support his overarching themes of loneliness, isolation, bungled good intentions, and the quest for personal and political dominance.

Less publicized, but no less worthy, are the novels in Vollman's "Seven Dreams: A Book of North American Landscapes" series—a damning look at the notion of "progress." The first volume, *The Ice Shirt*, recounts the Viking colonization of Greenland. The plot veers all over the place—Pynchon scrambled in a skillet—but the digressions, as well as the impressive historical and mythological references, create a powerful message about the cost of colonialism. *Fathers and Crows*, the second volume, is about the French settlement of eastern Canada, including the Jesuits' attempt to convert the indigenous population. The third novel, *The Rifles*, (intended as the sixth volume in the series) is every bit as ambitious as the other two, but Vollman's reach exceeds his grasp here, with the two major plot lines—the story of the doomed expedition of nineteenth-century British explorer Sir John Franklin in search of the Northwest Passage and the travels of one Captain Subzero, who, in his Arctic travels in the 1980s, ends up in a typically miserable Vollmanesque relationship with an Inuit woman—don't quite mesh.

The reason why Vollman's male characters seem saddled by a troublesome, and trouble-seeking, redeemer complex probably lies in a personal tragedy whose profound effect he freely—if painfully—acknowledges: When Vollmann was nine, his six-year-old sister accidentally drowned in a pond while he was supposed to be looking after her. He refers to the incident in several books, suggesting that it drives the attempts of his characters and himself to rescue imperiled or disadvantaged women. The short story, "Under the Grass," from *The Atlas*, is an agonizing, beautifully wrought allusion to the misfortune and Vollman's subsequent compulsion to both redeem and punish himself. The "Hanover, New Hampshire, USA, 1968" section of this story will wrench tears from the most hardened reader.

Astonishingly prolific, Vollmann might, in truth, be considered an even better writer if he published less—or didn't appear so hurried in some of his books. As it is, though, he remains a nervy, formidable talent whose work will captivate those with a passion for history, lyrical complexity, and finding the tender spots in a hard world.

See Also: Readers with an appetite for the taboo element in Vollman might enjoy the aforementioned transgressive writers (Burroughs, Cooper, Acker) and Mary Gaitskill. Stylistically, Vollman's adventurousness resembles that of David Foster Wallace, although Wallace covers entirely different territory and has a somewhat lighter touch. Finally, Vollmann has often been compared to Thomas Pynchon—fans of complex plot, dense sentences, and great leaps of imagination may find reading satisfaction there.

—Lily Burana

Vonnegut, Kurt, Jr.
1922–
b. Indianapolis, Indiana

FICTION: Player Piano (1952), The Sirens of Titan (1959), **Cat's Cradle** (1963), God Bless You, Mr. Rosewater; or, Pearls Before Swine (1965), Mother Night (1966), **Welcome to the Monkey House** (stories, 1968), *****Slaughterhouse Five; or the Children's Crusade: A Dance with Death** (1969), **Breakfast of Champions; or, Goodbye Blue Monday** (1973), Slapstick, or Lonesome No More (1976), Jailbird (1979), Deadeye Dick (1982), Galapágos (1985), **Bluebeard** (1987), Hocus Pocus (1990), Timequake (1997), Bagombo Snuff Box (stories, 1999)

397

Kurt Vonnegut is one of the few writers in this guide that I can be sure that everyone has already read (unless "everyone" includes people who cannot read, or do not read, or are very young, or speak a language into which his work has not been translated). So. Vonnegut is a science fiction afficionado, WWII vet, lover of women, pitier of the poor, cranky luddite, fun-loving doomsayer, sometime postmodernist. His books—very personal novels disguised as allegories disguised as science fiction—nearly always take the entire world (or more) as their canvas. Usually there is a world war, or some catastrophic event, or often genocide, or a scientific or political innovation that threatens to, or has succeeded in, destroying all that we hold dear.

Because of this, Vonnegut could be dismissed as a cranky pessimist. Because his prose is frank and uncomplicated and often very funny, he could be passed off as a "humorist." Gore Vidal once called him "America's worst writer." But despite Vidal (did you know he's related to Al Gore? *And* the Kennedys?) and other critics, for some inexplicable reason, Vonnegut is taken seriously (by many at least), and he is loved by millions—even by superintellectuals like yourself.

He has written many books. Following are inadequate plot summaries of each, sometimes accompanied by trenchant commentary. After each there are notations indicating:

WWII = indicates presence of WWII facts, imagery, themes
V = book touches on senselessness of violence
P = presence of prejudice, and its deleterious effects
A = presence of apocalypse (actual), or apocalyptic imagery
SF = heavy science fiction element
$ = emphasis on issues of economic disparity
-F = loss or threatened sense of family, heritage, community
T = complaints about pervasiveness/soullessness of technology
Ar = one or more of the characters is an artist
S = presence of sex scenes

Oh, and for readers who like a good joke now and again:

VF = book is very funny
F = book is funny
NSF = book is not so funny

Player Piano: What one man does to force change in an America lost in the wheels of progress. (Did I just write that?) A/SF/-F/T/$—VF

The Sirens of Titan: Establishes soon-familiar themes of the essential brutality of man and the futility of attempting change. A/V/SF/T—VF

Mother Night: A former Nazi radio propagandist and his life of depressed exile in New York's Greenwich Village. Perhaps Vonnegut's most straightforwardly told novel. P/S/-F—NSF

Cat's Cradle: One of his most successful and effectively apocalyptic books—not to give away the ending—about a substance that freezes, in a death-inducing sort of way, anything containing water. A/SF/T—F

God Bless You, Mr. Rosewater: About a man who gives millions to poor and pathetic people, this book is not that funny and disappointingly slight. Also contains a vicious portrayal of a gay man, for no discernible reason. A/$/-F—NSF

Welcome to the Monkey House: A collection of short stories. WWII/P/A/SF/-F/$/T/Ar/S—F, VF, NSF (depending on the story)

Slaughterhouse Five: Vonnegut's most famous book and usually the starting point for Vonnegut inductees, and rightfully so. It crystallizes the author's passions and fears and addresses the pivotal moment in his life: as a WWII POW in Dresden, he witnessed the merciless, earth-levelling Allied bombing of the city. The protagonist is also abducted by aliens and forced to breed with a gorgeous starlet. WWII/V/P/A/SF/S—VF

Breakfast of Champions: Vonnegut's version of a writer writing about writing, incorporating a number of his alter egos—Kilgore Trout, et al. Big fun for fans of Vonnegut-as-clown-faced deconstructionist. A/SF/$/T—VF

Slapstick: An homage to Vonnegut's late sister (whose three sons he raised) about two exceptional siblings. The book posits that Americans suffer from the erosion of the extended family. P/A/SF/-F/$/ T—F

Jailbird: In which the world's power and wealth resides with a old woman who chooses to be homeless. A/$/T/-F—F

Deadeye Dick: About a boy who inadvertently kills a pregnant woman while playing with a gun. A treatise on violence, heritage, prejudice. WWII/A/V/-F/P/ $/Ar—F

Galapagos: Speculates that if man were stranded on those islands, he might evolve in a way that would mean less pain for humanity and planet. As pessimistic as Vonnegut gets. V/A/SF—NSF

Bluebeard: Largely a complaint about the absurdity and impersonality of modern art—particularly targeting Abstract Expressionism. WWII/P/V/$/Ar—F

Hocus Pocus: A Biblical-scale apocalypse takes place in 2001: more realistic than most of his work and very dark. V/A/SF/T—NSF

Timequake: A rambling essay-cum-novel about not finishing a book, featuring familiar anecdotes, complaints, and visits from old characters like Kilgore Trout. Satisfying for fans, though unsettling, for in it, he claims that it will be his last book. WWII/V/P/A/SF/$/T—VF

So. Vonnegut is good. If you like books, and like to read them even if they are easy to read and frequently funny, you will like the work of Kurt Vonnegut, a writer. Also: He has a mustache.

See Also: George Saunders shares with Vonnegut a sense of humor and many themes—corporate-sponsored absurdity, prejudice, barbarism, the erosion of meaning, the coming Armageddon—but Saunders's writing is more fluid and lyrical.

—David Eggers

Wagner, Bruce
1954–
b. Madison, Wisconsin

FICTION: Force Majeure (1991), *****I'm Losing You** (1996)

Bruce Wagner's success as both serious novelist and screenwriter-for-hire gives him an edge in dissecting literature's least favorite city. In his as-yet-uncompleted Hollywood trilogy, Wagner plumbs the unsettling depths of the usual stereotypes (producers are not just sex addicts, but also fetishize handmade watches; massage therapist/prostitutes see themselves as spiritualists as much as budding starlets). Most impressively he avoids the common pitfall of mistaking High Art for salvation—his highbrows suffer from their ideals as much as from having sold out. Wagner's richly drawn grotesques justify the oft-invoked comparison to Nathanael West.

Wagner's first novel, *Force Majeure*, tracks screenwriter-turned-limo-driver Bud Wiggins through the plentiful disappointments of a city built on false promises. Wiggins's complex character—a loser amalgam of literary ambition, filial oppression, and deluded hopefulness—distinguishes this from the standard tinsel town tale. Wagner's second novel, *I'm Losing You*, leavens this unmediated bleakness with occasional glimpses of tenderness and decency. Taking its title from a phrase uttered thousands of times daily as cell phones break up on the L.A. freeways, the novel diagrams the banal perversities and failed emotional connections at every level of the epicenter of mass culture. The completion of the trilogy has been delayed by Wagner's own screen adaptation of *I'm Losing You*. But no worries—everything's material.

See Also: In The Player, *Michael Tolkin offers a more pat, plot-driven indictment of Hollywood amorality—call it* Crime and No Punishment. *A sexually confused Peter Lorre narrates Leslie Epstein's audacious* Pandaemonium, *a historical attack on the golden age of film that never was.*

—Hugh Garvey

Walker, Alice
1944–
b. Eatonton, Georgia

FICTION: The Third Life of Grange Copeland (1970), In Love and Trouble: Stories of Black Women (1973), Meridian (1976), You Can't Keep a Good Woman Down (stories, 1981), ***The Color Purple** (1982), The Temple of My Familiar (1989), Possessing the Secret of Joy (1992), By the Light of My Father's Smile (1998)

NONFICTION: In Search of Our Mother's Gardens: Womanist Prose (1983), Living by the Word: Selected Writings, 1973–1987 (1988), Warrior Marks: Female Genital Mutilation and the Sexual Blinding of Women (with Pratibha Parmar, 1993), The Same River Twice: Honoring the Difficult (1996), Anything We Love Can Be Saved: A Writer's Activism (1997)

SELECTED POETRY: Her Blue Body Everything We Know: Earthling Poems, 1965–1990 Complete (1991)

Alice Walker's books always make the best-seller lists; *The Color Purple* won critical praise and the Pulitzer Prize; and Walker's book tours and media appearances draw admiring crowds. Yet out of the nearly one hundred contributors to this book, it proved impossible to find one to write about her work; in fact, the request was usually greeted with a groan or a visible shudder. No other author demonstrates more emphatically how a merely adequate novelist can enjoy a thriving career by appealing to a readership almost entirely outside the core audience for literary fiction.

The oppression of black women and their capacity for eventual triumph is Walker's primary theme. In her early fiction, that oppression takes the form of physical, sexual, and psychological abuse dished out by black men who in turn have been humiliated and rendered powerless by whites. There's a stark, elemental drama to the family struggles Walker depicts in *The Third Life of Grange Copeland* (about a former sharecropper trying to defy this legacy) that can be compelling despite the clumsiness of her prose.

In *The Color Purple*, Walker felicitously chose to tell the story of Celie—a poor rural Southern girl who is raped by her stepfather and married off to a wife-beater—in the form of Celie's letters, written, at first, to God. The restraints imposed by Celie's naive world view and the declarative music of her dialect prevented Walker from lapsing into the smug didacticism and long passages of pat psychological summarizing that plague her other fiction. Ironically, by trying not to write like a writer, Walker produced her one truly writerly—and truly good—book.

Although Walker's fiction claims a superior warmth, sensuality, and humanity for women and people of color, her early short stories betray her as an ideologue; in one, the rape of a white civil rights worker by a black colleague is coldly treated as a political conundrum by the black narrator, who claims to be the victim's best friend. These stories date from the period when Walker was the darling of, and a contributing editor to, *Ms.* magazine, and the ones about gender relations sometimes consist of little more than one character lecturing another, or Walker lecturing us. Almost all the black women depicted in them are long-suffering saints.

The success of *The Color Purple* only encouraged Walker's worst inclinations. She reached a nadir with *The Temple of My Familiar*, an endless mass of New Age pieties and maunderings like this: "The bees contributed honey, but not really—it was taken from them . . . It was the flowers that contributed honey to both bees and people, the flowers that were always giving something: beauty, cheerfulness, pollen, and seeds. They did not care who saw them, whom they gave to. And on his feet, Suwelo also realized with disgust, he was wearing moccasins made of leather." *Possessing the Secret of Joy*, a condemnation of female genital mutilation in African tribal cultures, was better if only because the subject resists Walker's usual simplistic moralizing.

But if Walker's work lacks the complexity, the depth of character, the artful dramatization and questing intelligence most readers of literature seek, it nevertheless speaks to others. Hers is the fiction of empowerment, writing meant to shore up the reader's sense of grievance and righteousness. In that, it doesn't differ much from those sanctimonious Christian novels intended to instruct women readers, especially young ones, published in the early part of the twentieth century. For all her celebration of sex and (historically dubious) ancient, goddess-worshipping cultures, Walker is a Church Lady at heart.

Wallace, David Foster
1962–
b. Ithaca, New York

FICTION: The Broom of the System (1987), **Girl with Curious Hair** (stories, 1989), **Infinite Jest* (1996), Brief Interviews with Hideous Men (1999)

NONFICTION: Signifying Rappers: Rap and Race in the Urban Present (with Marie Costello, 1990), **A Supposedly Fun Thing I'll Never Do Again: Essays and Arguments** (1997)

Is David Foster Wallace, as some believe, the most important writer of his generation? He certainly has the necessary combination of intellect, talent, and ambition—in extravagant amounts. Wallace's journalism, perhaps more popular than his fiction, shows an omniverous appetite for detail—he's like a perpetual noticing machine—and a hunger for meaning that latches onto phenomena as mundane as a cruise ship brochure or a Midwestern state fair and ferverishly sucks out every last drop of cultural significance. He also understands the biggest challenge now facing any writer attempting what used to be called the Great American Novel: how to speak for a society saturated by mass media, especially TV and advertising, without seeming as ephemeral and vapid as the media itself. He's a compulsive yarn-spinner and frequently very, very funny.

Marshalled against Wallace is the reading public's general mistrust of hype and disdain for novelistic hubris in an age when most writers don't dare to speak for anyone very different from themselves. He may face a trickier obstacle, however, in his own self-consciousness. His first novel *The Broom of the System*, with its philosophical subtext

403

FIVE DIRELY UNDERAPPRECIATED U.S. NOVELS
PUBLISHED SINCE 1960 *by David Foster Wallace*

Omensetter's Luck by William H. Gass

Gass's first novel, his least avant-gardeish, and his best. Basically a religious book. Very sad. Contains the immortal line "The body of Our Saviour shat but Our Saviour shat not." Bleak but gorgeous, like light through ice.

Steps by Jerzy Kosinski

This won some big prize or other when it first came out, but today nobody seems to remember it. *Steps* gets called a novel but it is really a collection of unbelievably creepy little allegorical tableaux done in a terse elegant voice that's like nothing else anywhere ever. Only Kafka's fragments get anywhere close to where Kosinski goes in this book, which is better than everything else he ever did combined.

Angels by Denis Johnson

This was Johnson's first fiction after the horripilative lyric poetry of *Incognito Lounge*. Even cult-fans of *Jesus's Son* often haven't heard of *Angels*. It's sort of *Jesus Son*'s counterpoint, a novel-length odyssey of mopes and scrotes and their brutal redemptions. A totally *American* book, it's also got great prose, truly great, some of the eighties best; e.g., has lines like "All around them men drank alone, staring out of their faces."

Blood Meridian: Or the Evening Redness in the West by Cormac McCarthy

Don't even ask.

Wittgenstein's Mistress by David Markson

W's M is a dramatic rendering of what it would be like to live in the sort of universe described by logical atomism. A monologue, formally very odd, mostly one-sentence ¶s. Tied with *Omensetter's Luck* for the all-time best U.S. book about human loneliness. These wouldn't constitute ringing endorsements if they didn't all happen to be simultaneously true—i.e., that a novel this abstract and erudite and avant-garde could also be so moving makes *Wittgenstein's Mistress* pretty much the high point of experimental fiction in this country.

404

and references to Wittgenstein, suffered from a grad-studentish tendency to gratuitously show off his smarts. (He was only twenty-five when it was published.) From the silly names (Candy Mandible, Judith Prietht) to the hazy conspiracy driving its shaggy dog plot, *Broom* is thoroughly under the sway of Pynchon (a comparison the author resists), although Wallace was already displaying a deeper interest in character.

Girl with Curious Hair, a short story collection published two years later, better displayed Wallace's range. He slips with uncanny ease into a variety of voices: rural story-teller, aged urban Jew, emotionally stunted yuppie, closeted homosexual aide to Lyndon Johnson, neurotically self-preoccupied intellectual (a favorite), long-suffering girlfriend of the aforementioned intellectual, and a coolly omniscient third-person narrator. "Little Expressionless Animals" sets a tale of the fragile intimacy between two women, one cruelly abandoned by a roadside as a child, against the backstage intrigues of the TV game show *Jeopardy!*—and, astonishingly, pulls it off.

With 1996's *Infinite Jest*, a 1076-page novel set in the near future and centering on an elite tennis academy and a halfway house for former substance abusers, Wallace made a rather ambivalent bid for fame. Reviewers tended to focus on the book's flashier qualities—its length, Wallace's penchant for footnotes, and his many pointed jokes about commercialization (the years have been named after sponsors' products) and consumption (everyone is searching for a videotape of a movie so entertaining it turns its viewers into addicted zombies). But the halfway house passages are *Infinite Jest*'s biggest revelation. They have the hard-earned insight and compassion needed to win over the kind of reader alienated by writing that seems simply or superficially "clever." The 1999 short story collection *Brief Interviews with Hideous Men* includes some intriguing formal experiments and wince-inducing insights into gender relations but had less heart than its two fictional precedents.

Nevertheless, the girth of *Infinite Jest* (and, perhaps, the book's lavish publicity campaign) may have scared off potential fans. At present, Wallace has earned more admirers with his magazine articles, particularly two published in *Harper's*: "Getting Away from Already Being Pretty Much Away from It All" (1994, about a trip to the Illinois State Fair) and "A Supposedly Fun Thing I'll Never Do Again" (1996, relating Wallace's seven-day cruise on an ocean liner). These dazzling and hilarious *tours de force* are collected in a book titled after the cruise piece. In it, you'll also find "E Unibus Pluram: Television and U.S. Fiction," an impressive critical essay in which Wallace limns the perilous allure of irony and calls for writers who "treat of plain old untrendy human troubles and emotions in U.S. life" and "eschew self-consciousness and hip fatigue"—indicating, promisingly, that he knows the precise location of his own Achilles heel.

Along the way, Wallace has developed a distinctive and infectious style, an acrobatic cartwheeling between high intellectual discourse and vernacular insouciance, which makes him tremendously fun to read. This, combined with his formidable intelligence and the blossoming maturity evident in *Infinite Jest*, lead this critic to answer the question at the begining of this entry with a tentative—but decidely optimistic—yes.

See Also: Wallace often gets grouped with several friends, other writers of about the same age, "the white guys" as he puts it—Jonathan Franzen, William Vollman, Rick Moody, Richard Powers, Donald Antrim, and Jeffrey Eugenides. Of them, only Vollman shares much stylistic similarity with Wallace, and the two men favor entirely different subject matter. Although Wallace clearly has tremendous respect for Don DeLillo, it is Thomas Pynchon's fiction that remains the most obvious influence on his writing and an excellent choice for readers seeking similar work.

—Laura Miller

Weldon, Fay
1931–
b. Alvechurch, Worcestershire, England

FICTION: **The Fat Woman's Joke** (1967), Down Among the Women (1971), Female Friends (1974), Remember Me (1976), Words of Advice (published in England as Little Sisters, 1977), Praxis (1978), Puffball (1979), Watching Me, Watching You (stories, 1981), The President's Child (1982), ***The Life and Loves of a She-Devil** (1983), Polaris and Other Stories (1985), The Shrapnel Academy (1986), The Hearts and Lives of Men (1987), Leader of the Band (1988), The Heart of the Country (1987), **The Cloning of Joanna May** (1989), Darcy's Utopia (1990), Moon Over Minneapolis: or, Why She Couldn't Stay (stories, 1991), Life Force (1992), Trouble (1993, published in Britain as Affliction), Splitting (1995), **Wicked Women: A Collection of Short Stories** (1995), Worst Fears (1996), Big Girls Don't Cry (1997), A Hard Time to Be a Father (1999)

NONFICTION: Letters to Alice: On First Reading Jane Austen (1984)

The characters in Fay Weldon's books exist in a post-feminism world—they only burn their bras to torch their houses. Her women are far from the spunky-yet-appealing heroines who populate what is flippantly referred to as "women's literature." They're more Charles Bronson than Diane Keaton—ordinary folks who, when pushed too far, go extraordinarily, satisfyingly ballistic.

From her blistering first novel, *The Fat Woman's Joke*, and through over thirty years of writing and more than twenty novels and short story collections, Weldon has savaged marriage, family, and the female condition with a most unladylike and famously brutal wit. The prototypical Weldon character is Ruth, the ugly, mole-marked, and grossly underappreciated protagonist of *The Life and Loves of a She-Devil*. Sexually betrayed and publicly humiliated by her husband, Ruth decides that nice girls finish last. She commits arson, kills the family gerbil, abandons the kids, and then she *really* gets vengeful. Ultimately, she becomes rich and beautiful, and it is at this point that Weldon distinguishes her heroine and herself as women to be reckoned with. Any other funnygal author would let the now-desirable Ruth fall in love, reunite with her children, and live happily ever after. Weldon's ending, on the other hand, involves the mistress's death, the husband's financial and spiritual ruin, and the kids long gone. Winning, in her world, means making absolutely sure everybody in your path loses in the biggest possible way.

Unsurprisingly, Weldon's unflinching, caustic style has earned her sharp criticism from all sides of the war of the sexes. Conservatives are quick to brand her as a man-hating harpy; feminists chide her for her unsympathetic depictions of careerist bitches and codependent housewives. But if her egalitarian fury at the foibles of men and women exasperates at times, it's also what makes her so provocative. Weldon has the audacity to

WHO'S SCREWING WHOM *by Fay Weldon*

Lolita by Vladimir Nabokov
The best of all novels. Humbert Humbert, European academic, pursues his all-too-successful love of the nymphet Lolita across America. Exquisitely written, twice-filmed, regarded sometimes as a metaphor for Europe's relationship with the U.S., sometimes as a tale of abuse fit to be banned.

The Quiet American by Graham Greene
Written in 1956 by the English writer who should have won the Nobel Prize but didn't, this is a work of literature masquerading as a thriller, the prophetic tale of America's first tentative venture into Vietnam and of the sought-after Third Way, which ends not in reconciliation but bombs and death.

The Three Stigmata of Palmer Eldritch by Philip K. Dick
In the not-too-distant future corporate psychics wage a battle for the human soul. This great prophetic writer, the William Blake of Marin County, lurks at the dangerous edge where science fiction and literature meet.

The Handmaid's Tale by Margaret Atwood
Food for the flagging feminist. Stop socializing men, and they revert at once to womb exploitation. Margaret Atwood looks forward to a future compared to which today's Taliban are nothing.

The Roaches Have No King by Daniel Evan Weiss
This brilliantly comic novel is not for the squeamish. The cockroaches view the disgusting behavior of humans and wage war on Ira Fishplatt, legal-aid lawyer, when they feel he betrays them. Love it or hate it.

suggest that both sexes are capable of cruelty and spite, that children can be unlovable, ungrateful bastards, and that virtue won't get you half as far in life as good looks and piles of money.

Taken en masse, Weldon's work can seem repetitive, self-absorbed, and outright bitter. Newcomers to her work are often astonished to discover that her acrimonious divorce occurred *after* she wrote several of her most scathing works. (Weldon did, nevertheless, vent ample spleen with her first post-breakup novel—1993's *Trouble* may be her angriest book to date.)

Yet Weldon's remarkable talent for dark comedy (she is one of the few truly funny women writing contemporary fiction) is undeniable, and her no-brakes outrageousness is exhilaratingly original. She might be spinning tales of neat suburban families, but within them she sticks characters who dabble in DNA splicing (*The Cloning of Joanna May*), mysticism (*Puffball*), multiple personality (*Splitting*), channeling (*Remember Me*), and rebuilding society from scratch (*Darcy's Utopia*). Nature, she seems to say, is capable of any miracle you can dream of—it's humanity that's the bothersome, untamable enigma.

See Also: Helen Fielding's Bridget Jones' Diary *reads like Weldon Lite, but if Fay Weldon has any counterpart in British fiction, it may well be Martin Amis, whose novels share both her gleeful misanthropy and bordering-on-science-fiction appreciation of the bizarre.*
—*Mary Elizabeth Williams*

Welsh, Irvine
1960–
b. Edinburgh, Scotland

FICTION: *Trainspotting (stories, 1993), The Acid House (stories, 1994), Marabou Stork Nightmares (1995), Ecstasy: Three Tales of Chemical Romance (1996), Filth (1998)

For a generation of ecstasy-popping rave kids, Irvine Welsh's first book, *Trainspotting*, was their *Catcher in the Rye*. The Bible, some called it, and this loosely knotted, dislocated string of stories about Edinburgh's junkies, psychos, and bad boys put Irvine Welsh on the map as a distinctive, imaginative writer. An antidote to what he considered inaccessible—i.e., boring—English novelists, Welsh gave the people what they wanted: real, unsentimental stories penned in Scotland's indigenous brogue. Welsh wrote about drugs, AIDS, the dole, and life in and around the Edinburgh schemes (Scotland's equivalent to housing projects) and bestowed compassion and humanity on what many considered a brand of thugs. Although American readers might need a glossary to decipher the Scottish slang, Welsh more than proved that he was a master of voice with a first-rate ear.

Published in Britain in 1993 but not in the States until 1996, when the Danny Hodge-directed film was released, *Trainspotting* is arguably Welsh's most popular and best book. In the wake of an enormous amount of press, Welsh issued three more in rapid-fire succession: *The Acid House*, a collection of short fiction; *Marabou Stork Nightmares*, his first attempt at a more traditional novel; and *Ecstasy: Three Tales of Chemical Romance*, a book that the author himself recognizes as his worst and which he apologized to his readers for writing.

Of the three, *The Acid House* contains some of Welsh's funniest and most pungent prose, while *Marabou Stork Nightmares* proved he could tackle a single, continuous narrative (albeit one laced with a fantasy sequence involving a hunt for a mythical African stork). *Marabou Stork Nightmares* presents Roy Strang, a football hooligan lying comatose in an Edinburgh hospital, and relates how he got there. Welsh indicates flashbacks, character shifts, and changes in his narrator's states of consciousness by using graphics and varying typefaces. *Filth* uses the same technique to introduce Detective Sergeant Bruce Robertson, Welsh's coarsest and most callous character, and the tapeworm living in Robertson's gut.

Welsh's work proves that black, pungent humor can coexist with the conundrums of morality and redemption, loyalty and betrayal. His characters struggle with themselves and with their lot, but for all the sordid details, Welsh seems to harbor a soft spot for them. Despite their raunchy words and deeds, Welsh always provides them with excuses for their inexcusable behavior. In *Filth*, for example, the tapeworm (which plays superego to Robertson's id) soliloquizes on the reasons for its host's scabrous inclinations. Welsh might, though, have invented a more interesting explanation than an unsubtle story of childhood abuse.

In the five works of fiction Welsh has delivered in only five years, the Scotsman has more than perfected his distinctive voice. It remains to be seen whether his talent and unquestionable imaginative powers will help him make the transition from cult scribe to top-quality writer.

See Also: Check out fellow Scots Alan Warner, Janice Galloway, Duncan McLean, William Boyd, and the grandfather of the bunch, James Kelman, many of whom have been conveniently anthologized in Acid Plaid: New Scottish Writing, *edited by Harry Ritchie (Arcade, 1997).*

—*Jenifer Berman*

The **Salon.com** Reader's Guide to Contemporary Authors

Welty, Eudora

1909–
b. Jackson, Mississippi

FICTION: *A Curtain of Green and Other Stories** (1941), The Robber Bridegroom (1942), The Wide Net and Other Stories (1943), **Delta Wedding** (1946), **The Golden Apples** (stories, 1949), The Ponder Heart (1954), The Bride of Innisfallen and Other Stories (1955), Losing Battles (1970), ***The Optimist's Daughter** (1972)

SELECTED NONFICTION: The Eye of the Story: Selected Essays and Reviews (1978), **One Writer's Beginnings** (1984), A Writer's Eye: Collected Book Reviews (1994)

It's too bad that Eudora Welty—who has published no new stories or novels since 1972—has been so thoroughly canonized. Which is not to say that the praise Welty has enjoyed ("America's greatest living short story writer," "one of the most admired Southern writers ever") is unmerited, just that such laurels sound unalluringly academic, when, in fact, Welty's work remains utterly fresh and vibrantly readable.

The attributes that earned Welty her standing in American fiction—her perfect pitch for Southern dialect and culture; her comic, satirical extravagance; her range of tone and form; her experimentation with folklore and myth—are less compelling now than her career-long questioning of what shapes our inner lives, what Welty has herself termed the "human mystery." Welty herself admits to having led "a sheltered life"—never married, now in her nineties, and still living in the home of her parents—but not even her modesty can mask the rare wisdom she possesses.

Welty's powers of observation are legendary, no doubt honed during her brief stint as a reporter for the WPA during the Depression, but literary witnesses of Welty's caliber are born, not made. She has proven herself a virtuoso of metaphor and description: a stiff old collie rises off a quilt on the floor "like a table walking"; the flames of birthday candles on a carried cake appear "laid back like ears"; a bit of ham is a "little red rag" on a Ritz cracker; and the bayou "had a warm breath, like a person."

Welty laid virtually all of her stylistic and thematic cards on the table with *A Curtain of Green*: her knife-edged ability to render place, her fascination with journeys, and her characteristic plot, a meandering story that resolves itself (or doesn't) in ways wholly impossible to anticipate. It's like entering an elevator in which a conversation is already taking place—one that will unmistakably alter lives—with no choice but to get out, an unsettled voyeur, at your own floor. Most of Welty's best-known stories, including "Why

410

I Live at the P.O.," "A Worn Path," "Petrified Man," and "The Hitch-Hikers" come from this book.

The Robber Bridegroom, Welty's first novel, is a slim but muscular alloy of lyrical, ironic storytelling and folk heroism. *The Wide Net and Other Stories* deepened Welty's use of overt myth and symbol by applying them to the lives of ordinary people. In *Delta Wedding*, she illuminates the sticky intricacies of families, balancing a vast cast of characters focused on a single event while submerging her use of a cross-cultural handful of fertility myths. Welty's personal favorite of her books, *The Golden Apples*, takes these themes a step further in a story cycle recording the small-town legends and communal memories of a Mississippi hamlet.

The Bride of Innisfallen and Other Stories, the last of Welty's story collections, lacks the full vigor of her earlier books: The European locales where half the stories take place seem truly exotic and unbroachable. *Bride* also pales in comparison to the audacious *The Ponder Heart*, the wackiest of Welty's many *tour de force* novels, which unfolds into a spring-wound, satiric comedy of manners about the trial for a scandalous murder in which the victim was tickled to death.

Although Welty has said that the epic novel *Losing Battles* was her greatest challenge, its success as a lasting achievement is dubious. Written during the decade when Welty was caring for her dying mother, *Losing Battles* is a literary exercise that eschews interior character exposition in favor of plot movement and dialogue. By contrast, *The Optimist's Daughter* is a quiet, introspective gem of a book. Welty's memoir, *One Writer's Beginnings*, makes it clear that her life has seeped into many of her stories and novels, but only in *Optimist's Daughter* does autobiography overtly steer her fiction. Welty's protagonist is a woman nursing a long-buried grief, just as Welty was herself affected by the deaths of her parents. As the story unfolds, Laurel Hand remarks that "some things don't bear going into"; by book's end, Laurel has removed herself from the category of "those who never know the meaning of what has happened to them." Throughout her career Welty has never presumed to force that meaning upon her characters or her readers. It remains enough for her to keep asking the question.

See Also: There are flickers of Welty in the stories of Alice Munro and Mavis Gallant. Welty herself has spoken of the inspiration of Virginia Woolf. But in their melding of redemptive introspection, unpredictable plotting, and reverence for the ordinary—and extraordinary—strangeness of life, both Denis Johnson and Raymond Carver are particularly complementary.

411

—*Kate Moses*

West, Paul

1930–
b. Eckington, Derbyshire, England

FICTION: A Quality of Mercy (1961), Tenement of Clay (1965), Alley Jaggers (1966), I'm Expecting to Live Quite Soon (1970), **Caliban's Filibuster** (1971), Bela Lugosi's White Christmas (1972), Colonel Mint (1972), *Gala (1976), The Very Rich Hours of Count von Stauffenberg (1980), Rat Man of Paris (1986), The Place in Flowers Where the Pollen Rests (1988), The Universe and Other Fictions (stories, 1988), Lord Byron's Doctor (1989), The Women of Whitechapel and Jack the Ripper (1991), **Love's Mansion** (1992), The Tent of Orange Mist (1995), Sporting with Amaryllis (1996), Terrestrials (1997), Life with Swan (1999)

SELECTED NONFICTION: Byron and the Spoiler's Art (1960), The Modern Novel (two volumes, 1963), Words for a Deaf Daughter (biography, 1969), **Out of My Depths: A Swimmer in the Universe** (memoir, 1983), Sheer Fiction (essays, 1987), Portable People (1990), A Stroke of Genius: Illness and Self-Discovery (memoir, 1995), My Mother's Music (memoir, 1996)

SELECTED POETRY: The Spellbound Horses (1960), The Snow Leopard (1964)

Paul West writes "purple prose." That's not meant as a knock against his style; indeed, he proudly claims the description for his work. He winds his sentences into overdrive so as to catch what he calls "the impetuous abundance of Creation." West deepens his purple by setting many of his novels within the minds of assassins, madmen, and poets. This lush flood of brainwaves is channeled into language both precise and feverish. The effect can be likened to inhaling pure oxygen: The rich intake lights up the senses but—and this is the chief complaint about West—such intensity when unabated can eventually grow wearying.

The prolific West has written seventeen novels and another eighteen books of poetry, memoir, and criticism. His fiction runs a wide gamut from gritty realism to the fantastical, from historical to philosophical, and the memoirs—one is devoted to learning to swim, another to the experience of having a stroke—testify to a sensibility incapable of anything less than rigorous enthrallment. Creation may be abundant but West does his best to keep up. A good place to begin might be the 1976 autobiographical novel, *Gala*, in which West followed up a memoir about his autistic child—*Words for a Deaf Daughter*—with an attempt to jimmy the lock on his daughter's closed world. He imagines them building a basement model of the Milky Way and from there explores the rarified precincts of brain biochemistry, astrophysics, and linguistics. The tale is anything but dry meditation; his prose burns with the incandescent passion only a parent (and one in love with words) could muster.

In *Rat Man of Paris*, West digs further into unfamiliar mental states. He tells the story of a Parisian eccentric who carries on a one-man crusade against a Nazi war criminal. With an unmemorable plot, *Rat Man* nonetheless captivates by sheer force of its meditative intricacy and language. "Whatever else it did," the Rat Man muses to himself, "the soul should be eloquent." This might be an epigraph for all of West's writing. Whether in his historical craniotomies of Jack the Ripper (*The Women of Whitechapel*) and Hitler's would-be assassin (*The Very Rich Hours of Count von Stauffenberg*), or his habitations of landscapes as diverse as Navajo myth (*The Place in the Flower Where the Pollen Rests*) or the rape of Nanking (*The Tent of Orange Mist*), he is always alert to the music of what Wallace Stevens called "mental things." For beautiful sentences fed on brainpower, there is perhaps no other contemporary writer who can match him.

See Also: A primer for big-think purple prose can be found in almost anything by Vladimir Nabokov, especially Speak Memory, Pnin, *or* Ada. *For high style and profligate invention in a Westian mode, look to the ripe fabulists of Spain and Latin America like Juan Goytisolo, Julio Cortázar, and Josè Donoso. The French* nouveau roman—*particularly Nathalie Sarraute, Alain Robbbe-Grillet, and Maurice Blanchot—anticipates West's tactic of microscopic attention to ordinary things as a way of rendering them extraordinary.*

—Albert Mobilio

White, Edmund
1940–
b. Cincinnati, Ohio

413

FICTION: Forgetting Elena (1973), Nocturnes for the King of Naples (1978), *****A Boy's Own Story** (1982), **Caracole** (1985), The Beautiful Room Is Empty (1988), Skinned Alive: Stories (1995), The Farewell Symphony (1997)

SELECTED NONFICTION: The Joy of Gay Sex: An Intimate Guide for Gay Men to the Pleasures of a Gay Lifestyle (with Charles Silverstein, 1977), **States of Desire:**

Travels in Gay America (1980), **Genet: A Biography** (1993), The Burning Library: Essays (1994), Our Paris: Sketches from Memory (1995), Marcel Proust (1999)

No contemporary author has so prolifically, imaginatively, and skillfully limned a gay sensibility as Edmund White, and if the term "gay writer" carries with it the taint of the ghetto, White has rarely let it distract him from his own literary aspirations. At its best—as with his 1982 classic, *A Boy's Own Story*—his writing has spoken deeply to readers both gay and straight. That novel has become a touchstone—following in the tradition of great novels about adolescence by such writers as J. D. Salinger and James Baldwin—at the same time that it addressed a protean gay readership hungry for self-representation.

Today, in an age of myopic, self-absorbed memoirs, the "coming out" narrative can seem a tired subgenre. But White's semi-autobiographical fictions—starting with *A Boy's Own Story*, and continuing with *The Beautiful Room Is Empty* and *The Farewell Symphony*—form a transcendent modern bildungsroman. They chronicle one young man's intellectual, social, and sexual history, carrying him from the American Midwest of 1950s to New York in the 1970s and 1980s and Paris and Venice in the early 1990s—precisely the author's own trajectory. White's voluble narrator both charms and seduces, a witty raconteur full of delicious gossip and leisurely digressions, cultured (snobbish even) yet highly sympathetic and sometimes wise.

The Edmund White who made a literary name for himself in 1973—impressing no less an authority than Nabokov—debuted with a very different sort of novel. *Forgetting Elena* is a strange, precisely written fantasy narrated by a (self-willed?) amnesiac attempting to make his way among a highly refined and ritualized island society. White says he'd been struck by similarities between Fire Island—a favored summer resort for New York gays—and the eleventh-century Japanese court. In an equally baroque vein are *Nocturnes for the King of Naples*, in which a young man composes a series of apostrophes to an older lover he has rejected and now misses, and *Caracole*. The latter, underappreciated by many critics, is a clever pastiche of the nineteenth-century French novel, in which a young boy and girl from the provinces, both heterosexual, receive a decidedly unsentimental education in "the city," a mysterious cross between Paris and Venice. All White's fiction is characterized by a rich, sensuous prose style approaching but rarely descending into preciosity. The reader is rafted along a stream of epigrams and elegant, unexpected metaphors.

Also of note is White's nonfiction, especially *Genet: A Biography*, which won a National Book Critics Circle Award. His *States of Desire: Travels in Gay America* is a compelling travelogue and portrait of gay society on the eve of the AIDS epidemic. Throughout his career, White has walked the tightrope between acceptance by the literary establishment and his vanguard status as a "gay writer." One imagines he will be remembered above all as an author of the first order: intelligent, gifted, and humane.

See Also: Though White's style and sensibility are distinctive, readers might explore the novels of Andrew Holleran which chronicle New York gay life in the 1970s and its aftermath; Neil Bartlett is a kindred spirit in his preoccupation with the nature of homosexual desire.

—*Tom Beer*

Wideman, John Edgar
1941–
b. Washington, DC

FICTION: A Glance Away (1967), Hurry Home (1970), The Lynchers (1973), Damballah (stories, 1981), Hiding Place (1981), Sent for You Yesterday (1983), Reuben (1987), Fever (stories, 1989), *Philadelphia Fire (1990), All Stories Are True (1992), The Stories of John Edgar Wideman (1992), Identities: Three Novels (1994), The Cattle Killing (1996), Two Cities (1998)

NONFICTION: Brothers and Keepers (1984), Fatheralong: A Meditation on Fathers and Sons, Race and Society (1994)

In the spring of 1999, in the Mayan shadows of Chichen Itza, among writers on a week-long boondoggle to consider "The American Mosaic," John Edgar Wideman allowed as how maybe his fifteenth book would be about basketball. Whatever. It's not as if basketball hasn't shown up before in Wideman's fiction and memoirs. In *Philadelphia Fire*, for instance, it was combined with an all-black children's production of *The Tempest*, a play by "Earl the Pearl" Shakespeare. In *Two Cities*, the violence that erupts on a Pittsburgh basketball court almost destroys the love affair between two adults so wounded by the past that the whole idea of a future seems problematic. And Wideman himself in high school was the captain of the basketball team, as well as valedictorian, which is what propelled him out of Pittsburgh's Homewood ghetto in 1959 to the University of Pennsylvania, where he would lead the Quakers to an undefeated Ivy League season and end up in the Big 5 Hall of Fame. But instead of turning pro, he went to Ox-

415

ford, on a Rhodes scholarship, and then on to the Iowa Writers Workshop, and finally to a teaching career at Penn, the University of Wyoming at Laramie, and the University of Massachusetts at Amherst.

Yet for Wideman every elsewhere that isn't Homewood might as well be exile. Homewood—founded, he told us in *Damballah*, by a runaway slave—is, if not his Yoknapatawpha, then his Mississippi River, a stream of race consciousness in which he hooks history. In *Damballah* we also meet a plantation boy who knew that "in his village across the sea were men who hunted and fished with their voices. Men could talk the fish up from their shadowy dwellings and into the woven baskets slung over the fishermen's shoulders." Wideman talks up everything—kinship and ancestry, politics and deracination, voodoo and servitude, Moors and Xhosas, Europe, Africa, America—in monologues both interior and cosmicomic; in first persons and thirds; in flashback and flashforward; in dreams, sermons, epiphanies, and puns. He uses a prose as often exquisite as it is suspicious of its own sweet tooth for the lyrical, as if what he knows and needs to say ought not to be beautiful but nevertheless insists on surprising us with gravity and grace.

On this mean-streets Mississippi, Wideman is a Jim no longer infantilized by Huck—come back, like Cecil in *Hurry Home*, from dreaming of black kings in ancient Spain to race war and self-hate at home; come back, like Cudjoe in *Philadelphia Fire*, from an Aegean island to the bombing of Osage Avenue; come back, like Wideman the Rhodes scholar, from *Ulysses* and *The Waste Land* to an extraliterary violence, always such violence, visited upon his abducted people. That violence is handed on by those people to each other and themselves, like the brother he puzzles over in the memoir *Brothers and Keepers* and the lost son he mourns in *Fatheralong*, both of whom are serving life terms in prison. Who survives, at what cost, and why?

To see how Homewood writ large will come to signify the whole history of urban African-America, begin with the omnibus *Stories of John Edgar Wideman*, which includes the best of *Damballah*. Don't miss *The Cattle Killing*, his passionate careening from eighteenth-century Philadelphia, where freed slaves were blamed for the plague, to nineteenth-century South Africa, where a false prophecy led the Xhosas to slaughter their herds and murder their own identity, to a twentieth-century author, writing this book and reading it to his father. But memorize *Philadelphia Fire*, part fiction, part memoir, part deconstruction of a text of black American manhood, an encyclopedia of failed marriages and exile, of politics, history, and Indian ghosts with flame-colored bodies, of Calibans who will never sleep with Miranda, of warpainted children lost to drugs and rage, shot, burned, blown up, drowned, or hanged from the rims on the basketball courts. If, indeed, his next book dribbles and shoots, it can be counted on to be about basketball in the way that Balzac was about boardinghouses or Dickens about dust heaps or Dostoevsky about droshkies. Anyway, his daughter is already playing pro ball in the WNBA.

See Also: Toni Morrison and Ralph Ellison, *naturally, and Toni Cade Bambara in* The Salt Eaters *and Charles Johnson's* Middle Passage. *And also, of course, Faulkner, Hemingway, and Flannery O'Connor.*

—John Leonard

Winterson, Jeanette
1959–
b. Manchester, England

FICTION: **Oranges Are Not the Only Fruit* (1985), **The Passion** (1987), **Sexing the Cherry** (1989), Written on the Body (1992), Art & Lies: A Piece for Three Voices and a Bawd (1994), Gut Symmetries (1997), World and Other Places (1998)

NONFICTION: Fit for the Future (1986), Art Objects (1995)

Contemporary women writers are so prone to Little Me self-deprecation that Jeanette Winterson deserves credit for the freshness of her egomania. Her early work won praise from such critics as Salman Rushdie and Gore Vidal, but by 1992, when a newspaper asked her to name the best book of the year and she famously picked *Written on the Body*, she'd become her own most ardent admirer. Her bravado wouldn't have struck such a sour note if *Written on the Body* had been even pretty good, but it wasn't. In fact, it marked a severe decline from the imaginative, impassioned braininess of her first three novels.

Winterson (who was adopted) used her childhood among an evangelical Pentecostal sect in working-class Northern England as the basis for *Oranges Are Not the Only Fruit.* Although her lesbianism ultimately led to her ejection from the church, she paints her early years among the fanatical congregation with a droll, humane fondness. Taught that she had been singled out for a remarkable destiny as a missionary and that the world was an arena for momentous struggles between good and evil, Winterson has brought a similar zeal and drama to her writing. Deciding what to embroider on a sampler, the ambitious young Jeanette depicted in *Oranges* prefers "a sort of artist's impression of the terrified damned" to the saccharine homilies of her classmates; fire and brimstone strike her as more "interesting."

Winterson eventually went to London, where she is reputed to have been a dashing "serial Lothario" in her twenties. Tempestuous affairs with married women were a theme in both her novels and her life until she settled into relative seclusion with her current lover. In *The Passion*—a luscious historical fantasia—Napoleon's cook falls for the web-footed, cross-dressing daughter of a Venetian boatman who in turn pines for the wife of a nobleman. The much less readable *Written on the Body* is a long paean to a woman the narrator has abandoned to the husband who can afford to pay for her cancer treatments.

In the best of her books after *Oranges* (*The Passion* and *Sexing the Cherry*), Winterson combines fairy tale, memory, history, psychology, science, and philosophy into dreamy, fierce, sensual allegories about romantic love and the quest for a transcendant identity. At her worst (*Written on the Body*, the turgid *Art & Lies*, and *Gut Symmetries*), she noodles on, spinning out lofty poetical abstractions with the confidence that even her idlest metaphysical thought must be worth recording. That Winterson's belief in her own genius is not without grounds only makes her self-indulgence more infuriating: Her intelligence would be unquestionably first rate were it not for the fact that it never questions itself. Alas, she now seems firmly mired in solipsism.

See Also: Winterson compares herself to Virginia Woolf, but extravagant fantasists like Angela Carter and Gabriel García Márquez, and romantics like Milan Kundera are better matches. Those who relish Oranges' *deadpan depiction of religious fundamentalism should investigate the work of Flannery O'Connor.*

—*Laura Miller*

Wolfe, Tom
1931–
b. Richmond, Virginia

418

FICTION: *The Bonfire of the Vanities (1987), A Man in Full (1998)

NONFICTION: The Kandy-Kolored Tangerine-Flake Streamline Baby (1965), The Pump House Gang (1968), The Electric Kool-Aid Acid Test (1968), **Radical Chic & Mau-Mauing the Flak Catchers** (1970), The Painted Word (1975), Mauve Gloves & Madmen, Clutter & Vine, and Other Stories, Sketches and Essays (1976), The Right Stuff (1979), In Our Time (essays, 1980), From Bauhaus to Our House (1981), The Purple Decades (1982)

Just how important a writer is Tom Wolfe? In spite of being at the forefront of American journalism for over three decades and producing two major works of fiction he has yet to receive his full complement of literary honors. Can this be put down to envy over his huge advances and colossal sales, as he seems to think, or is he in essence little more than a showman, a writer of diverting entertainments?

Part of the reason the literary establishment has been so reluctant to embrace him is that he's spent a lifetime attacking it. "Tiny Mummies! The True Story of The Ruler of 43d Street's Land of the Walking Dead!", his 1965 broadside against *The New Yorker*, was so well-aimed it provoked a volley of responses from the praetorian guard of American letters, including J. D. Salinger. In 1972 he wrote a series of articles extolling the virtues of "The New Journalism" which stopped just short of announcing the death of the novel, and in 1989 he published "Stalking the Billion-Footed Beast," a literary manifesto in which he called for a return to nineteenth-century social realism and proclaimed that the only contemporary novelist on a par with Balzac, Zola, Dickens and, Thackeray was . . . Tom Wolfe.

Indeed, it's Wolfe's impudence, his relish for a fight, that makes him such an entertaining writer. His liveliest nonfiction books—*Radical Chic & Mau-Mauing the Flak Catchers, The Painted Word, From Bauhaus to Our House*—take aim at the Northeastern intellectual elite and its absurd notions of what's good for the rest of America. He's not so much a satirist as a *provocateur,* peppering his targets with wit, sarcasm, bile, and spleen. Even *The Right Stuff*, his only work to receive a National Book Award, thumbs its nose at liberals. Its unabashedly patriotic celebration of the American space program anticipated the chest-beating jingoism of the Reagan era.

As a prose stylist, Wolfe is without equal. According to legend, the Wolfe style was born in 1963 when he was up against a deadline for *Esquire* on a story about custom cars. Without enough time to write the story properly, he pulled an all-nighter and typed

419

up his notes in the form of a forty-nine-page memo addressed to Byron Dobell, the managing editor. *Esquire* decided to simply strike the words "Dear Byron" from the top and run the rest as written. That story became *The Kandy-Kolored Tangerine-Flake Streamline Baby*, a landmark of American journalism. Tom Wolfe had found his voice.

When it comes to fiction, though, Wolfe's critics are not easily dismissed. *The Bonfire of the Vanities* possesses all the strengths of his nonfiction—breathtakingly well-informed, polemically on-target, uproariously funny—but doesn't quite succeed as a serious novel. The characters are cartoonish, lacking any real interior life, and the plot is sprawling and unwieldy. Above all, the book lacks the moral compass that a great work of fiction requires. Wolfe's cynicism and mean-spiritedness, the very qualities which make his nonfiction so readable, handicap him as a novelist. In the hands of Zola and Dickens, social realism was a tool for illuminating the plight of the poor and dispossessed. For Wolfe, it's a slick device for making everyone else look like an idiot.

A Man in Full is a more mature work in which Wolfe clearly tries to address some of these problems. The characters, particularly the black characters, are more subtly drawn and there is one fully realized, sympathetic figure in the form of Conrad Hensley, a twenty-three-year-old laborer. The novel contains some beautifully rendered comic set pieces and there is even a stab at intellectual depth. Yet, strangely, it is a much less satisfying read than *Bonfire*. The central character, the Atlanta real estate developer Charlie Croker, dwindles away to almost nothing by the end of the book and the conclusion feels rushed and inadequate. In spite of being eleven years in the making, you get the impression that *A Man in Full* isn't quite ready for publication, that Wolfe should have taken another year to finish it.

See Also: The writer that Wolfe the novelist is most frequently compared to is Richard Price. Price's two novels which most closely meet the requirements set out in "Stalking the Billion-Footed Beast" are Clockers *and* Freedomland.

—*Toby Young*

420 | **Wolff, Tobias**
1945–
b. Birmingham, Alabama

FICTION: Ugly Rumours (1975), *In the Garden of the North American Martyrs (stories, 1981), The Barracks Thief and Other Stories (1984), Back in the World (stories, 1985), The Stories of Tobias Wolff (1988), The Night in Question: Stories (1996)

NONFICTION: This Boy's Life: A Memoir (1989), In Pharaoh's Army: Memories of the Lost War (1994)

Tobias Wolff has always been a damn good liar. Growing up in Washington state, he forged checks, cooked up papers for high school classmates, even faked recommendations to wiggle his way into a New England prep school. Now, as a short story writer and professor at Syracuse, Wolff still fraternizes with charlatans by putting them into his fictions. This con-artistry—both real and imagined—runs in the family. His elusive father was a car thief, swindler, and lovable deadbeat.

But it'd be a mistake to say that Wolff isn't honest. In fact, Wolff's strongest work comes out of his unflinching examinations of his past. His most well-known and wrenching book, *This Boy's Life*, describes his itinerant childhood and seething relationship with his stepfather. The memoir begins with an unforgettable example of Wolff's signature tonal control. On their way to Salt Lake City, Tobias (then ten) and his mother wait on the side of a steep mountain road for their overheated car to cool. Moments later, a truck that has lost its brakes hurtles around the corner and plunges off the edge. "Nobody spoke," Wolff writes. "My mother put her arms around my shoulder. For the rest of the day she kept looking over at me . . . I saw that the time was right to make a play for souvenirs."

While his two memoirs (the second, *In Pharaoh's Army: Memories of the Lost War*, was about his time as a translator and self-effacing Army officer in Vietnam) have garnered him the most renown, Wolff's muted but gripping short stories are surely the wine of his work. Wolff, along with his pals Raymond Carver and Richard Ford, were labeled "Dirty Realists" for their portraits of the incidental lives of the American middle class. It's a label that never really stuck, mostly because Wolff's best tales, from *In the Garden of the North American Martyrs*, *Back in the World*, and *The Night in Question*, aren't particularly hard-hitting or gritty. He's a remarkably consistent writer. When he's great (like "Say Yes," "The Liar," or the crystalline "Mortals," wherein an older man writes his own obituary), Wolff nails the moral grapplings of regular folk. When he's simply good, he just leaves you hanging. If he could be faulted for anything, it's that he has no real failures. He doesn't always take big gambles in his work, but the hands he's got are expertly played.

421

See Also: Wolff's buddies Raymond Carver (Will You Please Be Quiet, Please) *and Pulitzer Prize-winner Richard Ford* (The Sportswriter) *have both secured more prominent literary reputations, but they're all working remarkably similar ground. Fans of Wolff's Vietnam stories might enjoy the far more explicit* Dispatches *by Michael Herr or* The Things They Carried *by Tim O'Brien.*

—Austin Bunn

Wright, Stephen
1946–
b. Warren, Pennsylvania

FICTION: Meditations in Green (1983), *__M31: A Family Romance__ (1988), **Going Native** (1994)

Certain passages in Stephen Wright's novels have such a hair-raising vividness, such a lyric certainty, that reading them is like watching an arrow strike the dead center of a bullseye; you almost don't care what he's writing *about*. And unlike that other, more revered exerciser of sheer literary talent, Don DeLillo, Wright isn't so intent on convincing his readers that they're holding a Great American Novel in their trembling hands. It's ironic then that he should have created just that with his second book, *M31: A Family Romance*, the story of a family of UFO believers shacked up in an abandoned Midwestern church.

Wright's first novel, *Meditations in Green*, laces the chaotic, horrific, and absurd story of a compound of soldiers stationed in Vietnam with scenes from the ramshackle urban life of one of the group's few survivors. James Griffin, who scrutinizes aerial photos of the jungle looking for signs of the enemy, comes to see the war as a deluded struggle against the unthinking, ruthless fecundity of the vegetable kingdom, and he identifies heroin (a drug he refuses to name) as the best route to reconciliation with the plants. Like all of Wright's novels, this one ends in madness and carnage.

M31 offers an image of average American life that's virtually as "stupid and cruel" as the theater of war, this time seen from the viewpoint of a schizophrenic contactee/drifter named Gwen. She falls in with the financially marginal clan of Dash and Dot (based on Bo and Peep, who in 1997 would lead the Heaven's Gate cult to mass suicide), a husband-and-wife team of ufologists who claim to be descended from aliens hailing from the M31 galaxy. This threadbare mythos bestows meaning and purpose on the arbitrary tragedies of their lives, from Gwen's creeping dementia to the autism of Dash and Dot's daughter, whose fits they see as communications from "the Occupants." Meanwhile the family simmers with more commonplace menaces—a hormone-steeped teenage son on the verge of Oedipal violence, the inane chatter of the television, the telephone incessantly ringing with unanswered calls from collection agencies.

The enthusiasm that *M31* kindled was somewhat stifled six years later by *Going Native*. A collection of stories masquerading as a novel, Wright's third book boasts some of his best writing yet, including an uncanny depiction of a drug binge and a grueling trek through Borneo. But the strand that connects these often dazzling set pieces—a runaway suburban husband who becomes increasingly criminal—feels thin. If Wright has a weakness, it's for a cool punk solipsism that relies too heavily on drugs and violence as a semaphore for truth or authenticity. *M31* had seemed to transcend that. Still, *Going Native* further testifies to Wright's ferocious power to conjure both drama and character, and so there are few books as ardently awaited among the congnoscenti as Wright's next one.

See Also: Don DeLillo, obviously, for a similarly glorious exercise of style, but also William Vollman, who favors the same bad-boy subject matter. David Foster Wallace grapples with some of the American uneasiness Wright portrays in M31, *and Joseph Heller's* Catch-22 *is clearly an ancestor of the savage cosmic nonsense in* Meditations in Green.

—*Laura Miller*

ABOUT THE CONTRIBUTORS

Jabari Asim is a poet, playwright, and fiction writer. He works as a senior editor at *Washington Post Book World*.

Mark Athitakis is music editor of *SF Weekly*.

Bruce Barcott is a contributing editor at *Outside* magazine.

Tom Beer is editor-in-chief of *OUT* magazine.

Adam Begley is the books editor of *The New York Observer*. He lives in England.

Jennifer Berman is a writer and editor living in New York. Her work has appeared in *The New York Times Book Review*, *Bookforum*, *Newsday*, and *BOMB*, where she is Editor at Large.

Jesse Berrett teaches high school in San Francisco. He is presently finishing his own book and likes Philip Roth even if he is a pig.

Brian Blanchfield is a poet living in Brooklyn, and has written book reviews for Salon.com and *American Book Review*.

Will Blythe is a contributing editor for *Mirabella* and *Harper's* magazine and the editor of the anthology *Why I Write* (Little, Brown).

Brian Bouldrey's latest novel is *Love, the Magician*. He is the editor of *Travelling Souls* and *Writing Home*, and Associate Editor for *Lit.*, the *San Francisco Bay Guardian*'s literary supplement. He is a frequent contributor to that paper.

David Bowman writes cultural criticism for Salon.com, *The New York Times*, and other publications. He is the author of two novels, *Let The Dog Drive* and *Bunny Modern*, as well as *fa fa fa fa fa fa: A History of the Talking Heads*.

Susie Bright is the author of *Full Exposure*, *The Sexual State of the Union*, and is the editor of *The Best American Erotica* series. She can be reached at http://www.susiebright.com.

Sylvia Brownrigg is the author of a novel, *The Metaphysical Touch*, and a book of short stories, *Ten Women Who Shook the World*; her reviews have appeared in a wide range of papers including the *TLS* and *The New York Times*, and she is a contributor to *The Cambridge Guide to Women's Writing*. She grew up in Northern California, and now lives in London.

Austin Bunn writes for *The Village Voice* and other publications.

Lily Burana lives in Wyoming. She is a frequent contributor to Salon.com.

Alexander Chee is the recipient of a Michner/Copernicus Fellowship for distinguished fiction and teaches literary nonfiction writing at the New School University. He lives in Brooklyn.

John Clute is the editor of *The Encyclopedia of Science Fiction* and *The Encyclopedia of Fantasy*, and the author of *The Book of End Times*.

Dan Cryer is a book critic at *Newsday*. He has been a finalist for the Pulitzer Prize in criticism, a juror for the Pulitzer Prize in general nonfiction, and a vice president of the National Book Critics Circle.

Ray Davis is a multimedia consultant and writer. He lives in the San Francisco Bay area and his Web site is at www.kokonino.com.

Stacey D'Erasmo is the author of the novel *Tea*. Her nonfiction work has appeared in *Out*, *The Nation*, *The New York Times Book Review*, and *The Village Voice*.

Dennis Drabelle, a Washington, D.C., writer, won the National Book Critics Circle Award for excellence in reviewing in 1996. He is a contributing editor at *The Washington Post Book World*.

Sally Eckhoff is a painter and critic who lives in upstate New York. Formerly a *Village Voice* columnist, she now specializes in the study of large animals in public places.

Dave Eggers edits *McSweeney's*, a quarterly, and its internet companion, mcsweeneys.net. His books include *Shiny Adidas Tracksuits and the Death of Camp and Other Essays* from *Might* magazine, and a memoir, *A Heartbreaking Work of Staggering Genius*.

Hal Espen is the editor of *Outside* magazine.

Andrew Essex is a writer who lives in New York. His work has appeared in *The New Yorker*, *The New York Times*, *Entertainment Weekly*, *Rolling Stone*, and *Details*.

Karen Joy Fowler is the author of *Sarah Canary*, *The Sweetheart Season*, and the short story collection *Black Glass*. She lives in Davis, California.

Brigitte Frase is Critic at Large for *The Ruminator Review*, and an editor at Milkweed Editions. She is working on a family history-memoir about immigration and culture clash.

David Futrelle is a writer living in Chicago. His writing has appeared in Salon.com, *Newsday* and *New York* magazine.

Jon Garelick is associate arts editor at *The Boston Phoenix*.

Dwight Garner is an editor at *The New York Times Book Review* and the former book editor of Salon.com.

Hugh Garvey was an editor at *The Voice Literary Supplement*. His journalism has appeared in *Vibe*, *Details*, *GQ*, *Travel & Leisure*, *Food Arts*, *The Utne Reader*, *Newsday*, and *The Washington Post*.

David Gates is the author of the novels *Jernigan* and *Preston Falls* and a collection of stories, *The Wonders of the Invisible World*. He writes about books and music for *Newsweek*.

Roger Gathman lives in Austin, Texas. He writes for *Green* magazine, the *Austin Chronicle*, Salon.com, and *Publishers Weekly*, and edits the webmagazine *Calumny and Art*.

Adam Goodheart is a columnist for *Civilization* magazine and a member of the editorial board of *The American Scholar*. He reviews books for *The New York Times*, *The Washington Post*, and other publications. He lives in Washington, D.C.

Emily Gordon is the assistant book editor at *Newsday*.

Laura Morgan Green teaches in the Department of English and the Program in Women's and Gender Studies at Yale University. She has written for Salon.com and *The New York Times Book Review*.

Hal Hinson is a former film critic for *The Washington Post*. He lives in Los Angeles.

Jennifer Howard, a contributing editor at *The Washington Post Book World*, has just completed her first novel. Her fiction has appeared in *Virginia Quarterly Review* and online in the *Blue Moon Review*.

Maya Jaggi is an award-winning British journalist and critic who works for *The Guardian* newspaper in London and was formerly literary editor of the journal *Third World Quarterly*.

Greg Johnson's nine books include *Distant Friends*, a collection of stories, and *Invisible Writer: A Biography of Joyce Carol Oates*. He lives in Atlanta and teaches in the graduate writing program at Kennesaw State University.

Cynthia Joyce is a writer living in New York and a former editor at Salon.com.

Elizabeth Judd is a freelance writer and reviewer, living in Washington, D.C. Her work has appeared in *The Village Voice*, *The Philadelphia Inquirer*, and *The New York Times Book Review*.

Pauline Kael was film critic for *The New Yorker* and is the author of *For Keeps* and many other books about the movies.

Gary Kamiya is the executive editor of Salon.com.

Jonathon Keats, Senior Editor at *San Francisco Magazine*, is the author of *The Pathology of Lies: A Novel*.

Deborah Kirk is a freelance writer and editor who lives in New York.

Michael Korda was editor-in-chief at Simon & Schuster for many years. He is the author of *Another Life: A Memoir of Other People* and other books.

Caroline Knapp is the author of *Drinking: A Love Story* and *Pack of Two: The Intricate Bond Between People and Dogs*.

David Kurnick is studying English literature at Columbia University. He lives in Brooklyn.

Peter Kurth is a freelance writer and critic in Burlington, Vermont. His biography of Isadora Duncan will be published in Fall 2001.

Andrew Leonard is the senior technology writer for Salon.com. He is also the author of *Bots: The Origin of New Species* and is working on a book about the history of the free software movement.

John Leonard is the Culture Watch columnist for *The Nation*, media critic for *CBS Sunday Morning*, and television critic for *New York* magazine.

Wendy Lesser is the editor of *The Threepenny Review* and the author of six books, including *The Amateur: An Independent Life in Letters*.

Jonathan Lethem is the author of *Motherless Brooklyn* and four other novels. He lives in New York City.

David Lipsky is a contributing editor at *Rolling Stone*. He is the author of the novels *The Art Fair* and *The Pallbearer* and the short story collection *Three Thousand Dollars*. His work has appeared in *The New Yorker*, *The New York Times*, and *Harper's*.

D. T. Max is a contributing editor for *The Paris Review*.

Daniel Mendelsohn writes frequently about books and the arts. His memoir, *The Elusive Embrace: Desire and the Riddle of Identity*, was published by Knopf in 1999.

Lisa Michaels is the author of *Split: A Counterculture Childhood*, a *New York Times* Notable Book of the Year. Her work has appeared in *Glamour*, *The New York Times Magazine*, and *The Wall Street Journal*. Her novel will be published in 2001.

Sia Michel is the executive editor of *Spin* magazine. Her criticism has also appeared in *The New York Times* and *The Village Voice*.

Jonathan Miles is a contributing editor to *Sports Afield*, and his work has appeared in *The New York Times Book Review*, *Food & Wine*, *GQ*, and *The Best American Sports Writing 1999*. He is at work on a novel.

Laura Miller is the New York Editorial Director of Salon.com.

Albert Mobilio has received the National Book Critics Circle Nona Balakian citation for excellence in reviewing. His last book of poetry, *The Geographics*, was published by Hard Press.

Michael Scott Moore writes for *San Francisco Weekly*. He just finished a novel.

Kate Moses is a staff writer for Salon.com, a founding editor of Salon.com's Mothers Who Think site, and coeditor of *Mothers Who Think: Tales of Real-Life Parenthood*.

Laurie Muchnick is the book editor of *Newsday*. She has written about books for *The Village Voice*, *The Wall Street Journal*, *The Washington Post*, and many other publications.

Edward Neuert lives and writes in northern Vermont. He has been a contributor to Salon.com since 1995.

430   **Richard Nicholls** is the literary editor of *The American Scholar*.

Andrew O'Hehir is a native of Northern California who now lives in New York. He has been a reporter, critic, and editor for numerous publications and is the author of two produced plays.

Alan Michael Parker is the author of two collections of poems, *Days Like Prose* and *The Vandals*, and reviews books for various journals including *The New Yorker* and the *Charlotte Observer*. He teaches at Davidson College in North Carolina.

Vince Passaro is a contributing editor for Harper's magazine and is finishing a novel.

Todd James Pierce's fiction has appeared in many magazines and journals, including *The Missouri Review* and *American Short Fiction*.

Alison Powell is a writer living in New York and a former senior editor of *Interview* magazine.

Ann Powers is rock critic for *The New York Times* and the author of *Weird Like Us: My Bohemian America*.

Scott Rosenberg is Salon.com's managing editor and vice president for site development. Before helping found Salon.com in 1995, he was theater critic, movie critic, and digital culture columnist for *The San Francisco Examiner*—where his theater reviews won the George Jean Nathan Prize in 1989.

Ray Sawhill works as an arts reporter at *Newsweek* magazine and lives in New York City.

Carter Scholz was born in New York City and lives now in California. He is the author of *Palimpsests* (with Glenn Harcourt) and *Kafka Americana* (with Jonathan Lethem).

A. O. Scott is a film critic for *The New York Times*. His work has appeared in *The New York Times Book Review*, *The New York Review of Books*, *Newsday*, *Slate*, and other publications.

Craig Seligman is a senior editor at Salon.com.

Elaine Showalter is a professor of English at Princeton University and the author of *Hystories: Hysterical Epidemics and Modern Media*.

For ten years **Michael Silverblatt** has hosted *Bookworm*, a literary program heard on National Public Radio since 1988. He lives in Los Angeles.

Rob Spillman is the coeditor of the literary magazine *Tin House*.

Alexander Star is the editor of *Lingua Franca: The Review of Academic Life*. His writing has appeared in *The New Republic*, *The New Yorker*, *The London Review of Books*, and other publications.

Lorin Stein's work has appeared in *Might*, Salon.com, *The Threepenny Review*, and the *Yale Review*. He lives in New York.

Charles Taylor is critic-at-large for Salon.com. His work has also appeared in *Sight and Sound*, *The New Yorker*, *The New York Times*, *Details*, and *Spin*.

Lettie Teague is the Wine Editor of *Food & Wine* magazine.

Anderson Tepper works for *Vanity Fair* magazine and has contributed reviews to *The New York Times Book Review*, *Time Out New York*, *PAPER*, and Salon.com.

Calvin Trillin is a regular contributor to *Time*, *The Nation*, and *Brill's Content* and the author of several books.

David L. Ulin writes for *The Chicago Tribune*, *The New York Times Book Review*, *The Village Voice*, *Newsday*, *LA Weekly*, and the *Los Angeles Times*. He is editing an anthology of Southern California literature for City Lights Books and writing a book about earthquakes for Viking Penguin.

Michael Upchurch's novels include *Passive Intruder*, *The Flame Forest*, and *Air*. He is the book critic for *The Seattle Times*, and also writes for *The New York Times Book Review*, *The Chicago Tribune*, and other publications.

Maryanne Vollers is the author of *Ghosts of Mississippi*, which was a nonfiction finalist for the National Book Award in 1995. She lives in Montana.

Sarah Vowell is a Salon.com columnist, a "This American Life" contributing editor, and author of the books *Take the Cannoli* and *Radio On*.

432

Katharine Whittemore lives in Cambridge, Massachusetts, and is the editor of *American Movie Classics Magazine*. Her work has appeared in many publications, including *The New York Times*, *New England Monthly Magazine*, Salon.com, *Lingua Franca*, and *Smithsonian*.

Mary Elizabeth Williams is the host of Table Talk, Salon.com's reader community. She has also written for *The New York Times*, *The Nation*, and other publications.

Mark Winegardner, director of the Creative Writing Program at Florida State University, is the author of several books, including the novels *The Veracruz Blues* and *Crooked River Burning*.

Toby Young is a columnist for *The New York Press* and *The Spectator*.

Stephanie Zacharek is a staff writer for Salon.com. Her work has also appeared in *The New Yorker*, *The New York Times Book Review*, *Rolling Stone*, *Spin*, *Entertainment Weekly*, and *Newsday*.

INDEX

435

437

439

Index

445

Index

447

448

Index

451

Index

Index

453

FOR THE BEST IN PAPERBACKS, LOOK FOR THE

In every corner of the world, on every subject under the sun, Penguin represents quality and variety—the very best in publishing today.

For complete information about books available from Penguin—including Puffins, Penguin Classics, and Arkana—and how to order them, write to us at the appropriate address below. Please note that for copyright reasons the selection of books varies from country to country.

In the United Kingdom: Please write to *Dept. EP, Penguin Books Ltd, Bath Road, Harmondsworth, West Drayton, Middlesex UB7 0DA.*

In the United States: Please write to *Penguin Putnam Inc., P.O. Box 12289 Dept. B, Newark, New Jersey 07101-5289* or call 1-800-788-6262.

In Canada: Please write to *Penguin Books Canada Ltd, 10 Alcorn Avenue, Suite 300, Toronto, Ontario M4V 3B2.*

In Australia: Please write to *Penguin Books Australia Ltd, P.O. Box 257, Ringwood, Victoria 3134.*

In New Zealand: Please write to *Penguin Books (NZ) Ltd, Private Bag 102902, North Shore Mail Centre, Auckland 10.*

In India: Please write to *Penguin Books India Pvt Ltd, 11 Panchsheel Shopping Centre, Panchsheel Park, New Delhi 110 017.*

In the Netherlands: Please write to *Penguin Books Netherlands bv, Postbus 3507, NL-1001 AH Amsterdam.*

In Germany: Please write to *Penguin Books Deutschland GmbH, Metzlerstrasse 26, 60594 Frankfurt am Main.*

In Spain: Please write to *Penguin Books S. A., Bravo Murillo 19, 1° B, 28015 Madrid.*

In Italy: Please write to *Penguin Italia s.r.l., Via Benedetto Croce 2, 20094 Corsico, Milano.*

In France: Please write to *Penguin France, Le Carré Wilson, 62 rue Benjamin Baillaud, 31500 Toulouse.*

In Japan: Please write to *Penguin Books Japan Ltd, Kaneko Building, 2-3-25 Koraku, Bunkyo-Ku, Tokyo 112.*

In South Africa: Please write to *Penguin Books South Africa (Pty) Ltd, Private Bag X14, Parkview, 2122 Johannesburg.*